Information Systems Essentials

THIRD EDITION

Information Systems Essentials

THIRD EDITION

Stephen Haag

DANIELS COLLEGE OF BUSINESS

UNIVERSITY OF DENVER

Maeve Cummings

COLLEGE OF BUSINESS

PITTSBURG STATE UNIVERSITY

McGraw-Hill Irwin

Boston   Burr Ridge, IL   Dubuque, IA   New York   San Francisco   St. Louis
Bangkok   Bogotá   Caracas   Kuala Lumpur   Lisbon   London   Madrid   Mexico City
Milan   Montreal   New Delhi   Santiago   Seoul   Singapore   Sydney   Taipei   Toronto

INFORMATION SYSTEMS ESSENTIALS

Published by McGraw-Hill/Irwin, a business unit of The McGraw-Hill Companies, Inc., 1221 Avenue of the Americas, New York, NY, 10020. Copyright © 2009, 2008, 2006 by The McGraw-Hill Companies, Inc. All rights reserved. No part of this publication may be reproduced or distributed in any form or by any means, or stored in a database or retrieval system, without the prior written consent of The McGraw-Hill Companies, Inc., including, but not limited to, in any network or other electronic storage or transmission, or broadcast for distance learning.

Some ancillaries, including electronic and print components, may not be available to customers outside the United States.

This book is printed on acid-free paper.

1 2 3 4 5 6 7 8 9 0 CCI/CCI 0 9 8

ISBN 978-0-07-337675-2
MHID 0-07-337675-2

Publisher: *Paul Ducham*
Development editor II: *Trina Hauger*
Markting manager: *Natalie Zook*
Manager of photo, design & publishing tools: *Mary Conzachi*
Lead production supervisor: *Micahel R. McCormick*
Senior photo research coordinator: *Jeremy Cheshareck*
Photo researcher: *Jennifer Blankenship*
Media project manager: *Suresh Babu, Hurix Systems Pvt. Ltd*
Cover and interior design: *Cara Hawthorne*
Type face: *11/13 Bulmer MT*
Compositor: *Laserwords Private Limited*
Printer: *Courier Kendallville*

Library of Congress Cataloging-in-Publication Data

Haag, Stephen.
    Information systems essentials / Stephen Haag, Maeve Cummings. — 3rd ed.
      p. cm.
    Includes index.
    ISBN-13: 978-0-07-337675-2 (alk. paper)
    ISBN-10: 0-07-337675-2 (alk. paper)
    1. Management information systems. 2. Information technology. I. Cummings,
Maeve. II. Title.
    T58.6.H17 2009
    658.4′038—dc22

                                                                2008035199

www.mhhe.com

For Darian and Trevor: You are my children, my youth, and my smile.

Stephen Haag

To the memory of my late husband, Slim: When I saw myself through his eyes I saw the woman I would like to be—and could be. That made everything possible.

Maeve Cummings

BRIEF CONTENTS

TABLE OF CONTENTS

FEATURES

GROUP PROJECTS

ELECTRONIC COMMERCE PROJECTS

PREFACE

The business world hires only the best knowledge workers—equipped with a well-balanced repository of IT skills and business knowledge. *Information Systems Essentials*, *3e,* provides your students with tools to help them prepare for a seamless transition to that professional world.

Nine chapters cover the essential business and managerial applications of MIS and IT, from strategic and competitive technology opportunities to the organization and management of information using databases and data warehouses. The first two appendixes—Appendix A Computer Hardware and Software and Appendix B Network Basics—provide your students a technical glimpse into the world of IT. Appendix C Careers in Business identifies why MIS is important in each business profession and encourages your students to explore how MIS will impact their future careers.

The text contains a variety of real-life examples from both industry and global perspectives, applications exercises requiring Web exploration and Excel/Access/PowerPoint skill development, individual and group projects, an extensive end-of-chapter assortment, and three case studies per chapter, aimed at transforming your undergraduates into technology- and information-literate knowledge workers.

Changes for The Third Edition

Throughout the text, you'll find new or updated opening and closing case studies, Industry Perspectives, Global Perspectives, and Electronic Commerce and Group Projects, as well as new or expanded coverage of such topics as:

- Call center success metrics
- Ad-supported e-commerce model
- Blogs
- Web-centric success metrics
- Botnets
- Business continuity planning
- Component- based development (CBD)
- Crowdsourcing
- Porter's three generic strategies
- Digital immigrants
- Digital natives
- Drones
- GIGO
- Infrastructure-centric metrics
- Intrusion prevention systems
- Invisible backlog
- IT culture
- Location mashups

- The *Long Tail*
- Mashups
- Microsoft Windows Vista
- Nanotechnology
- Near Field Communication
- Open-source information
- Path-to-profitability (P2P)
- Pharming
- Podcasting
- Predictive analytics
- Requirement recovery document
- RSS feeds
- Screenagers
- Service level agreements
- Service-oriented architecture
- Technology innovation failure
- Web 2.0
- Wiki
- Zombie

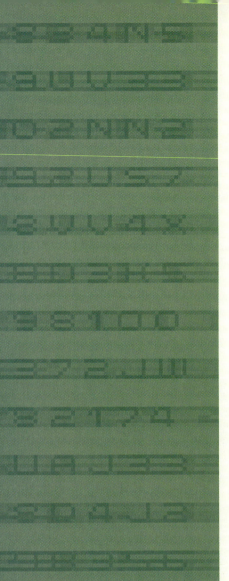

Assurance of Learning Ready

All educational institutions today are focused on the notion of assurance of learning, the demonstration that students are indeed learning in the classroom. Assurance of learning is key in accreditation and in assuring all constituents (employers, prospective students, the parents of prospective students, institutional administration, and so on) that the value of the educational dollar is very high.

Information Systems Essentials, 3e, is designed specifically to support your assurance of learning initiatives. It does so in simple, yet powerful, fashion . . .

Information Systems Essentials, 3e, maps each test bank question to a learning outcome for the chapter or appendix. The instructor can use the test bank software to easily query for learning outcome questions that relate directly to the learning objectives for the course. The instructor can then use the reporting features of the software to aggregate results in similar fashion, making the collection and presentation of assurance of learning information simple and easy.

If you're just starting your assurance of learning initiatives, take a close look at the diagram on the opposite page.

1. **School Mission**—start here to clearly define and understand the focus of your educational institution in delivering its undergraduate degree.

2. **Program Learning Goals**—from your school's mission, derive a list of program learning goals. Each of these usually maps to a specific business functional area. For example, a program learning goal for MIS might be: "Understand the use of information technology in business (and other types of organizations, i.e., not-for-profit, etc.) (1) to create and sustain a competitive advantage, (2) to be more efficient in operations, (3) to make more effective decisions, and (4) to transform the organization to remain viable in the marketplace."

3. **Courses**—map each program learning goal to one or more courses delivered in your undergraduate degree business core curriculum. This will tell you in which courses you need to provide assurance of learning for each program learning goal.

4. **Course Objectives**—for each course, develop a list of course objectives. You probably already have these and include them in your syllabus to inform students of what they will be learning.

5. **Learning Outcomes by Chapter/Appendix**—map your course objectives to the learning outcomes for each chapter and appendix in *Information Systems Essentials, 3e.* Some of your course objectives may cross more than one chapter or appendix or they may be inclusive of just one chapter or appendix.

6. **Testing Software**—use the testing software provided with the text to query for questions by the learning outcomes you identified in the previous step. Choose the questions most appropriate to you. Use the reporting features of the testing software to aggregate results by learning outcome.

AACSB Statement

The McGraw-Hill Companies is a proud corporate member of AACSB International. Understanding the importance and value of AACSB accreditation, *Information Systems Essentials, 3e,* has sought to recognize the curricula guidelines detailed in the AACSB standards for business accreditation by connecting selected questions in the test bank to the general knowledge and skill guidelines found in the AACSB standards.

The statements contained in *Information Systems Essentials, 3e,* are provided only as a guide for the users of this text. The AACSB leaves content coverage and assessment

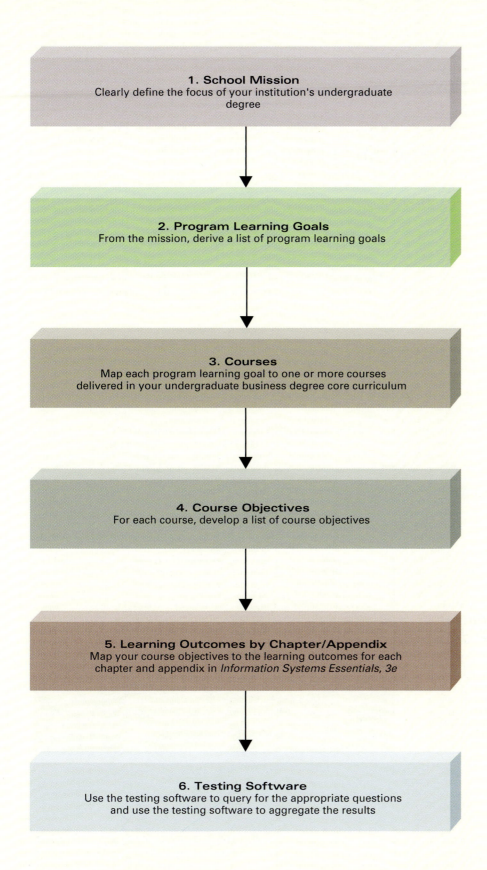

1. School Mission
Clearly define the focus of your institution's undergraduate degree

2. Program Learning Goals
From the mission, derive a list of program learning goals

3. Courses
Map each program learning goal to one or more courses delivered in your undergraduate business degree core curriculum

4. Course Objectives
For each course, develop a list of course objectives

5. Learning Outcomes by Chapter/Appendix
Map your course objectives to the learning outcomes for each chapter and appendix in *Information Systems Essentials, 3e*

6. Testing Software
Use the testing software to query for the appropriate questions and use the testing software to aggregate the results

within the purview of individual schools, the mission of the school, and the faculty. While *Infomation Systems Essentials, 3e,* and the teaching package make no claim of any specific AACSB qualification or evaluation, we have, within *Infomation Systems Essentials, 3e,* labeled selected questions according to the six general and skills area.

Guided Tour

Student Engagement and Enrichment Support

Learners exhibit three different learning styles:

1. Auditory (hearing)
2. Visual (seeing)
3. Tactile (doing and experiencing)

To be at your best in the classroom, you need engagement and enrichment support that fosters learning within each of the three different styles. *Information Systems Essentials, 3e*, provides you with a vast array of engagement and enrichment support for all learning styles, including:

- High-quality, relevant videos
- An opening case study and two closing case studies per chapter
- 24 electronic commerce projects
- 22 Group Projects requiring your students to use technology to solve a problem or take advantage of an opportunity
- Concept reinforcement boxes with software exercises (these appear in the Instructor's Manual)

Use high-quality videos covering such topics as Hurricane Katrina, Motley Fool, Spawn.com, and Digital Domain to challenge your students to define the role of IT and MIS in real-life situations.

ETHICAL COMPUTING GUIDELINES

Ethical computing encompasses many topics: privacy, intellectual property, abuse of resources, character defamation, to name just a few. Unethical behavior can be as mild as rudeness in an e-mail or as lethal as stalking and death threats. Some unethical behavior is illegal, but not all of it is.

The Computer Ethics Institute Web site at www.brook.edu/its/cei/cei_hp.htm has a list of 10 commandments to guide the use of information technology and the Association for Computer Machinery (ACM) specifies a code of ethical behavior as do many other organizations.

Find answers to the following questions on the Web:

A. Find a code of ethics from an organization of your choosing. What do you think are the best five guiding principles from all the tips that you found?

B. Are chain letters good or bad? Are they illegal? Summarize the opposing arguments you find.

C. How does anonymous e-mail work and why would you use it?

D. What are five ways that e-mail use can be unethical?

E. Why is the deliberate spreading of viruses unethical? Name at least five reasons.

EXPLORING GOOGLE EARTH

Google Earth is a free virtual globe program that uses satellite and aerial images combined with a geographic information system. It allows you to pick a place on the globe and zoom in to see all sorts of features like the locations of schools, sports venues, coffee shops, shopping malls, movie/DVD rental stores, etc. The list is very long.

You can even layer multiple searches and save your results. The site also hosts a large Google Earth Community that shares information and annotations.

The image resolution varies across regions, but most large cities a[...]
in high-resolution detail showing buildings and streets and trees an[...]
Download the Google Earth application from http://earth.googl[...]
ing questions:

A. In the area where you live, how is the resolution compared t[...] Washington, D.C.?

B. Can you see your own street? How about individual houses[...]

C. Zoom in to your home county and mark elementary schools[...] than 10? More than 10? More than 50?

D. Choose a university location and zoom in. How clearly can y[...] about the cars in the parking lots?

E. Can you find the Eiffel Tower in Paris, France; the Brandenl[...] Tor) in Berlin, Germany; and Buckingham Palace in London[...]

Have your students apply their knowledge with 24 electronic commerce projects and 22 software-focused group projects.

PROJECTS

Group Projects

CASE 1:
ASSESSING THE VALUE OF CUSTOMER RELATIONSHIP MANAGEMENT

TREVOR TOY AUTO MECHANICS

Trevor Toy Auto Mechanics is an automobile repair shop in Phoenix, Arizona. Over the past few years, Trevor has seen his business grow from a two-bay car repair shop with only one other employee to a 15-bay car repair shop with 21 employees.

Trevor wants to improve service and add a level of personalization to his customers. However, Trevor has no idea who his best customers are, the work that is being performed, or which mechanic is responsible for the repairs. Trevor is asking for your help. He has provided you with a spreadsheet file, **TREVOR.xls**, that contains a list of all the repairs his shop has completed over the past year including each client's name along with a unique identifier. The spreadsheet file contains the fields provided in the table below.

Column	Name	Description
A	CUSTOMER #	A unique number assigned to each customer.
B	CUSTOMER NAME	The name of the customer.
C	MECHANIC #	A unique number assigned to the mechanic who completed the work.
D	CAR TYPE	The type of car on which the work was completed.
E	WORK COMPLETED	What type of repair was performed on the car.
F	NUM HOURS	How long in hours it took to complete the work.
G	COST OF PARTS	The cost of the parts associated with completing the repair.
H	TOTAL CHARGE	The amount charged to the customer for the repair.

Your analysis should include (1) Trevor's best customers (top 10 in terms of volume and revenue); (2) Trevor's worst customers (bottom 10 in terms of lowest volume and lost revenue); and (3) the mechanics that perform the repairs for each customer.

SOME PARTICULARS YOU SHOULD KNOW

1. As you consider the information provided to you, think in terms of what information is important. You might need to use the existing information to create new information.

2. In your analysis, provide examples of the types of marketing campaigns Trevor should offer his most valuable customers.

3. Upon completing your analysis, please provide concise yet detailed and thorough documentation (in narrative, numeric, and graphic forms) that justifies your recommendations.

4. File: **TREVOR.xls** (Excel file).

Projects—Electronic Commerce

These projects each have a singular focus and can be applied to many different chapters and appendixes. They are located at the end of the text after *Appendix C*. Each chapter and appendix includes a closing box that denotes which electronic projects are most appropriate to use. As a quick reference, please refer to the table below.

	CHAPTER/APPENDIX											
	1	2	3	4	5	6	7	8	9	A	B	C
1. Best in Computer Statistics and Resources	X		X	X		X	X				X	
2. Consumer Information		X	X	X								
3. Interviewing and Negotiating Tips	X								X			X
4. Meta Data		X	X	X		X	X				X	
5. Bureau of Labor and Statistics		X	X	X		X						X
6. Demographics		X	X	X								
7. Free and Rentable Storage Space					X				X	X		
8. Gathering Competitive Intelligence		X			X							
9. Ethical Computing Guidelines	X									X	X	X
10. Exploring Google Earth			X	X	X							
11. Financial Aid Resources	X		X						X			X
12. Finding Hosting Services					X	X	X		X	X	X	
13. Global Statistics & Resources	X	X	X		X	X			X	X		
14. Gold, Silver, Interest Rates, and Money		X		X	X							
15. Privacy Laws & Legislation								X			X	
16. Protecting Your Computer	X							X		X	X	
17. Learning About Investing				X	X							X
18. Locating Internships												X
19. Small Business Administration		X			X							X
20. Stock Quotes				X								
21. Researching Storefront Software					X	X		X		X		X
22. Searching for Shareware and Freeware						X	X	X		X	X	
23. Searching Job Databases	X		X				X	X	X	X		X
24. Searching for MBA Programs									X			X

Projects—Group Projects

After Appendix C in the text, you'll find 22 Group Projects. These require your students to use technology to solve a problem or take advantage of an opportunity. A quick warning to instructors: Some of these take an entire weekend to solve. Be careful not to assign too many at one time. These projects can be applied to many different chapters and appendices. As a quick reference, please refer to the table below.

	CHAPTER/APPENDIX										
	1	2	3	4	5	6	7	8	9	A	B
1. Assessing the Value of Information	X			X				X			
2. Analyzing the Value of Information	X							X			
3. Executive Information System Reporting		X		X		X					
4. Building Value Chains			X		X						
5. Using Relational Technology to Track Projects			X								
6. Building a Decision Support System				X							
7. Advertising with Banners Ads				X	X						
8. Assessing the Value of Outsourcing Information Technology				X		X	X				X
9. Demonstrating How to Build Web Sites											
10. Making the Case with Presentation Software	X										X
11. Building a Web Database System			X		X						
12. Creating a Decision Support System				X		X	X				
13. Developing an Enterprise Resource Planning System				X			X	X	X		
14. Assessing a Wireless Future		X									
15. Evaluating the Next Generation					X				X	X	X
16. Analyzing Strategic and Competitive Advantage	X			X							
17. Building a Decision Support System				X							
18. Creating a Financial Analysis				X							
19. Building a Scheduling Decision Support System		X		X							
20. Creating a Database Management System			X								
21. Evaluating the Security of Information								X	X	X	X
22. Assessing the Value of Supply Chain Management		X		X			X				

xxi

The Support Package

We realize that no text is complete without a well-rounded and value-added support package. Our support package is designed to ease your teaching burden by providing you with a Web site full of valuable information, a test bank with more than 1,000 questions and easy-to-use test generating software, an Instructor's Manual that walks you through each chapter and appendix and provides value-added teaching notes and suggestions, and PowerPoint presentations.

ONLINE LEARNING CENTER AT WWW.MHHE.COM/HAAG

The Web site for *Information Systems Essentials, 3e,* contains information and all supplements for both the instructor and the student.

INSTRUCTOR'S MANUAL

The Instructor's Manual is provided to you in an effort to help you prepare for your class presentations. In its new format, you will find a separate box for each PowerPoint slide. In that box, you will find an overview of the slide and a list of key points to cover. This enables you to prepare your class presentation by working solely with the Instructor's Manual because you also see the PowerPoint slide presentations. We've also provided embedded links within each Instructor's Manual document to the various in-text pedagogical elements including:

- **The Global and Industry Perspectives boxes**—how to introduce them, key points to address, possible discussion questions to ask, etc.

At the beginning of each Instructor's Manual document you'll find other useful information including the appropriate author to contact if you have questions or comments, a list of the Group Projects that you can cover, and a list of any associated data files.

POWERPOINT PRESENTATIONS

The PowerPoint presentations are ready for you to use in class. In preparing to use these, you simply work through the Instructor's Manual which includes thumbnails of each slide and important points to cover. Of course, we realize that you'll probably want to customize some of the presentations. So, we've made available to you most of the images and photos in the text.

TEST BANK

For each chapter, there are approximately 125 multiple-choice, true/false, and fill-in-the-blank questions aimed at challenging the minds of your students. McGraw-Hill's EZ Test is a flexible and easy-to-use electronic testing program. The program allows instructors to create tests from book-specific items. It accommodates a wide range of question types and instructors may add their own questions. Multiple versions of the test can be created and any test can be exported for use with course management systems such as WebCT, BlackBoard, or PageOut. EZ Test Online is a new service and gives you a place to easily administer your EZ Test–created exams and quizzes online. The program is available for Windows and Macintosh environments.

VIDEOS

New videos will be downloadable from the instructor side of the OLC. Selections from our archive of videos from previous years will be delivered upon request.

MBA MIS CASES

Developed by Richard Perle of Loyola Marymount University, these 14 comprehensive cases allow you to add MBA-level analysis to your course. Visit our Web site to review a sample case.

ONLINE COURSES

Content for the Third Edition is available in WebCT, Blackboard, and PageOut formats to accommodate virtually any online delivery platform.

USE OUR EZ TEST ONLINE TO HELP YOUR STUDENTS PREPARE TO SUCCEED WITH APPLE IPOD® IQUIZ.

Using our EZ Test Online you can make test and quiz content available for a student's Apple iPod®.

Students must purchase the iQuiz game application from Apple for 99¢ in order to use the iQuiz content. It works on the iPod fifth generation iPods and better.

Instructors only need EZ Test Online to produce iQuiz ready content. Instructors take their existing tests and quizzes and export them to a file that can then be made available to the student to take as a self-quiz on their iPods. It's as simple as that.

Empowered Instruction

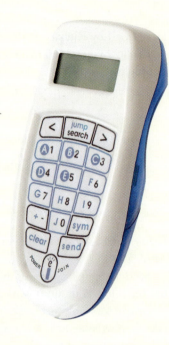

Classroom Performance System

Engage students and assess real-time lecture retention with this simple yet powerful wireless application. You can even deliver tests that instantly grade themselves.

PORTER'S THREE GENERIC STRATEGIES

- Porter identified 3 generic business strategies for beating the competition
  1. Overall cost leadership
  2. Differentiation
  3. Focus

PowerPoint Presentation

Robust, detailed, and designed to keep students engaged.

Software Skills & Computer Concepts

MISource provides animated tutorials and simulated practice of the core skills in Microsoft Office 2007 Excel, Access, and PowerPoint.

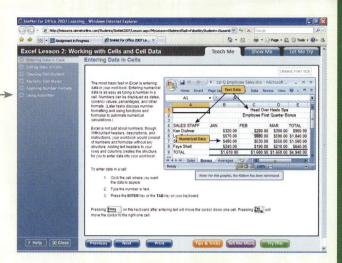

Spend less time reviewing software skills and computer literacy.

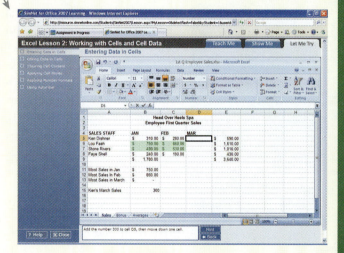

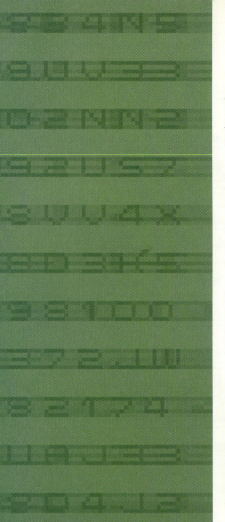

ACKNOWLEDGMENTS

At McGraw-Hill/Irwin, there are several groups of people who have made this project successful. They are strategic management, EDP, and editorial.

McGraw-Hill/Irwin's strategic management is simply second to none. We gratefully acknowledge the dedicated work of Ed Stanford, Kevin Kane, and David Littlehale. Their guidance is invaluable.

EDP includes all those people who take our thoughts on paper and bring them to life in the form of an exciting and dynamic book. This wonderful group of people includes Mary Conzachi (the book's project manager), Jeremy Cheshareck (photo research coordinator), and Cara Hawthorne (cover and interior designer).

Editorial comprises those people who determine which projects to publish, and they have guided us every step of the way with a wealth of market intelligence. Brent Gordon (editor-in-chief) leads the editorial group that includes Paul Ducham (our publisher) and Trina Hanger (the book's developmental editor). We are indebted to them for leading the way.

We would also like to acknowledge the dedicated work of the following people at McGraw-Hill/Irwin: Suresh Babu (media producer), and Natalie Zook (marketing manager). Without Suresh, our text would be just a text, with no supplements or great supporting Web site. Without Natalie, you might never know we created this text.

We wish to acknowledge the wonderful efforts of our contributor team: Dan Connolly, David Cox, Laura Nee, Jeff Engelstad, and Syl Houston. Each has brought to the table unique talents and knowledge indispensable to the success of this text. As authors, we have come to realize that it's an impossible task to single-handedly keep up with technology—its advancements and how it's being used in the business world.

Last, but certainly not least, we offer our gratitude to our reviewers, who took on a thankless job that paid only a fraction of its true worth. We had the best. They include

Lawrence L. Andrew
Western Illinois University

Noushin Ashrafi
University of Massachusetts—Boston

Emill Boasson
Ithaca College

James Carson
Porterville College

Jerry Carvalho
University of Utah—Salt Lake City

Kuan Chen
Purdue University—Calumet

Edward Cherian
George Washington University

Yong S. Choi, PhD.
California State University—Bakersfield

Joobin Choobineh, PhD.
Texas A&M University

Tony Coulson
California State University—San Bernardino

Dai Cui
University of Utah—Salt Lake City

Dawna Dewire
Babson College

Charles Finkbeiner
Washtenaw Community College

Frederick Fisher
Florida State University—Tallahassee

Mark Goudreau
Johnson & Wales University

Dale Gust
Central Michigan University

A. T. Jarmoszko
Central Connecticut State University

Beata Jones, PhD.
Texas Christian University

Chang E. Koh
University of North Texas

Brett J. L. Landry, PhD.
University of New Orleans

FROM THE AUTHORS

FROM STEPHEN HAAG To the entire author team—coauthors and contributors alike—I commend you for all your efforts. I am also grateful to the many people who helped me along the career path of writing books. They include Peter Keen, Dr. L. L. Schkade, JD Ice, Rick Williamson, Paul Ducham, and a host of people at McGraw-Hill.

My colleagues in the Daniels College of Business at the University of Denver also provide support. I wish I could name all of you, but there isn't enough room. To James Griesemer (Dean Emeritus), Karen Newman, and Glyn Hanbery (Senior Associate Dean), I thank you all.

And my writing efforts would not be successful nor would my life be complete without my family. My mother and father live just a few minutes away from me and give me unending support. My two sons—Darian and Trevor—make me smile after long nights of working. My four-legged son—Zippy—doesn't really care that I write books; he offers me unconditional love. And I have a new daughter, Alexis, who we adopted in the summer of 2007 from the Ukraine. I cannot put into words how much happiness she has brought into our lives. Finally, my wife, Pam, should be listed as a coauthor on many of my books. Her work is never done, and she loves every minute of it.

FROM MAEVE CUMMINGS My sincere thanks to the many people who helped directly and indirectly with this edition and the previous ones. Thanks to Steve, who is every bit as good a friend as he is a lead author. Thanks to all the people at McGraw-Hill who put in long hours and a lot of work to bring this book to completion.

A special thanks to Keith Neufeld, who is an expert on networks and generous with his knowledge, and to Lanny Morrow, who keeps me in touch with the fascinating world of computer forensics. Felix Dreher and Barbara Clutter were, and always have been, unwaveringly supportive and helpful.

Thanks to the Holy Faith and Loreto nuns who gave me an excellent early education, which served as a solid foundation on which I was able to build. These were exceptionally dedicated teachers and I learned much more from them than the basics of reading, writing, and arithmetic. Much credit goes to Jan Guynes Clark, who helped me through several exhilarating and terrifying years at the University of Texas at Arlington.

As always, I want to thank my great family: my parents (Dolores and Steve), sisters (Grainne, Fiona, and Clodagh), and brother (Colin).

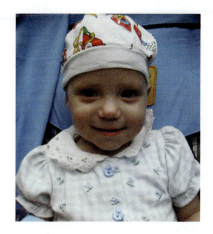

STEPHEN HAAG is a professor of Information Technology and Electronic Commerce in the Daniels College of Business at the University of Denver. Previously, Stephen has served as Chair of the Department of Information Technology and Electronic Commerce, Director of the Master of Science in Information Technology program. Director of the MBA program, and Associate Dean of Graduate Programs. Stephen holds a B.B.A. and M.B.A. from West Texas State University and a Ph.D. from the University of Texas at Arlington.

Stephen is the author/coauthor of numerous books including *Computing Concepts in Action* (a K-12 textbook), *Interactions: Teaching English as a Second Language* (with his mother and father), *Information Technology: Tomorrow's Advantage Today* (with Peter Keen), *Excelling in Finance, Business Driven Technology,* and more than 40 books within the *I-Series.* He has also written numerous articles appearing in such journals as *Communications of the ACM, Socio-Economic Planning Sciences,* the *International Journal of Systems Science, Managerial and Decision Economics, Applied Economics,* and the *Australian Journal of Management.* Stephen lives with his family in Highlands Ranch, Colorado.

MAEVE CUMMINGS is a professor of Information Systems at Pittsburg State University. She holds a B.S. in Mathematics and Computer Science and an M.B.A. from Pittsburg State and a Ph.D. in Information Systems from the University of Texas at Arlington. She has published in various journals including the *Journal of Global Information Management* and the *Journal of Computer Information Systems.* She serves on various editorial boards and is a coauthor of *Case Studies in Information Technology,* the concepts books of the *I-Series,* entitled *Computing Concepts* and *Information Systems Essentials,* now in its second edition. Maeve has been teaching for 25 years and lives in Pittsburg, Kansas.

Information Systems Essentials

THIRD EDITION

CHAPTER ONE OUTLINE

STUDENT LEARNING OUTCOMES

1. Define management information systems (MIS) and describe the three important organizational resources within it—people, information, and information technology.

2. Describe how to use Porter's Five Forces Model to evaluate the relative attractiveness of and competitive pressures in an industry.

3. Compare and contrast Porter's three generic strategies; top line versus bottom line; and the run-grow-transform framework as approaches to the development of business strategy.

4. Describe the role of value-chain analysis in identifying value-added and value-reducing processes.

PERSPECTIVES

WEB SUPPORT

www.mhhe.com/haag

- Searching job databases
- Interviewing and negotiating tips
- Financial aid resources
- Protecting your computer
- Ethical computing guidelines
- Global statistics and resources

The Information Age in Which You Live
Changing the Face of Business

OPENING CASE STUDY:
IS YOUR SOCIAL SECURITY NUMBER WORTH $98?

The answer for many people is yes. But they're not referring to the worth of their own social security numbers; they're referring to how much they are willing to pay for *your* Social Security number. And they're willing to pay for other data such as:

- $490—credit number and PIN.
- $78–$294—billing data including account number, address, birth date, etc.
- $147—driver's license number.
- $147—birth certificate.
- $6–$24—credit card number with security code and expiration date.
- $6—PayPal logon and password.

On the Internet, you can find sites such as CardingWorld.cc, Dumps International, and TalkCash.net that sell such information and much more including malware, software that can be used to infiltrate the identity management systems of organizations and steal personal information. These sites typically stay in existence only for about six months or so before having to change their names to elude law enforcement officials.

From a personal point of view, identity theft should be high on your priority list. From an organizational point of view, identity management and the protection of identity information are usually at the top of the priority list. Unfortunately, hackers have found ways to steal identity information; they may spoof or phish you into giving away your personal information and they may unleash malware (the generalized term for malicious software such as viruses, worms, and Trojan horses) on organizational identity management systems to steal millions of identities. In late 2006, TJX Holdings—the parent company for retail outlets including T. J. Maxx, Marshalls, and HomeGoods—reported the infiltration of its identity management systems, which may eventually affect over 40 million customers.

By some accounts, the black market for identity information is now a billion-dollar-a-year industry. Transactions occur daily with the buying and selling of identities, credit card information, and even brokerage accounts. One man stole numerous online brokerage accounts and used them to employ the old "pump-and-dump" stock scam. With his legitimate personal account he bought many shares of a penny stock. He then used the accounts he'd stolen to buy more shares of the same stock, which raised the price significantly. He then sold the shares in his legitimate personal account for a tidy profit of $82,000. We can tell you this story because he got caught.

In today's digital world, computers can be used for all sorts of nefarious scams; they can also be used in many wonderful and legal ways—to increase profit, to reduce costs, to increase product and service quality, to reach suppliers and customers all over the world, and to benefit society in general. This book focuses on helping you learn to use technology for the sustained competitive advantage of your organization and for your personal productivity. Along the way, however, we will talk about the bad uses of technology and inform you of steps you can take to avoid being a victim of cyber crimes.[1]

Questions

1. Have you, a friend, or a family member been a victim of identity theft? If so, tell the story to your class.

2. How often do you buy your credit report? Did you know you get one for free annually?

3. Is technology good or bad?

Introduction

You live in the "digital age." You live, work, learn, play, drive, network, eat, and shop in a digital world. The influence of technology permeates everything you do. The average American relies daily on more than 250 computers. Every part of your life depends on technology. Your TV, iPod, DVD player, car, and cell phone are all technology enabled and—more important—not "able" without technology. Technology is so pervasive in your life it is often considered "invasive." Here's a wild statistic: According to a worldwide survey conducted by *Time* magazine in 2005, 14 percent of cell phone users stated they had stopped having sex to take a phone call.[2] Hmmm . . .

Your generation, specifically, the group of people born in the mid-to-late 1980s and very early 1990s, was born into the digital age unlike older people. In the early 1990s, few people as yet had ever heard of the Internet, "surfing" was a term identified only as a water sport, and Microsoft was not the dominant software publisher for word processing, spreadsheet, presentation, or DBMS applications. Viruses were seen only under a microscope, worms were used for fishing, and "spam" was just a canned meat. But all this changed in your first years on earth.

As you moved through your early teens, e-commerce exploded and then quickly imploded, transforming overnight Internet millionaires into overnight Internet paupers. You are probably more than familiar with unique and interesting IT terms such as podcasting, wiki, avatars, emoticons, spoofing, acorns, and phishing (now with a completely different kind of bait). Technology has been so much a part of your life that you may consider it more of a necessity than a convenience.

Generations of people before you witnessed the evolution and revolution of many other technologies, automobiles, airplanes, radios, televisions, telephones. Your generation has been at the center of the digital revolution. Perhaps more than any technology before, digital technologies such as computers and the Internet have radically transformed the very fabric of how people live their lives.

The reach of digital technologies is vast and wide. Technology touches your personal life every day. Equally so, digital technologies have dramatically altered the competitive landscape of business. Fifty of the *Fortune* top 500 companies in 2006 (that's one in every 10) were digital technology companies such as Cisco Systems, Hewlett-Packard, and Dell. Dell was formed in 1984 (about the time you were born); now it has over 65,000 employees worldwide. Its famous sell-source-ship model of delivering custom personal computers directly to consumers is the envy of the industry. Amazon.com ranked 272 on the *Fortune* list and eBay ranked 458—both of these companies have been around for only about 10 years.[3]

Technology companies are by no means the only ones interested in using technology effectively in the workplace. Every business you can name wrestles with management information systems on a daily basis. Broadly, *management information systems* is both a business discipline that deals with the use of information technology (IT)—or computers, computer technology, or simply technology—and an academic field of study. Technology is so important to businesses because we are in the information age, a time when knowledge is power. Today, more than ever, businesses need information, information technology, and the overarching MIS function to massage, assimilate, and distribute information and knowledge to create and sustain a competitive advantage.

As businesses approach the acquisition and use of technology, they do so very differently from you in your personal life. You find a cool piece of technology and quickly calculate in your head if you have enough money to purchase it. You may not get everything you want, such as a large hard disk or a really fast processor, but you can usually buy the personal technology you need. Businesses are different; they carefully scrutinize their technology purchases, seeking to find and justify a competitive advantage and a return on a big investment. Businesses ask such questions as

1. Can this technology help streamline and lower the cost of our business processes while not sacrificing the quality we deliver to our customers?
2. Can this technology enable us to reach larger markets of customers, understand our customers better so we can deliver more tailored products and services to them, and/or help us design and develop products that are better than the competition's?
3. Can this technology enable us to innovate our business operations and move into completely new markets?

This book's goal is to introduce you to the fast-paced and ever-changing dynamics of information technology, focusing specifically on how organizations can use technology to increase profit, expand market share, serve the needs of society, eliminate time and location boundaries, and engage in a host of other worthy activities. We'll start in this very first chapter by stating that *business strategy drives technology decisions, not the reverse*. To decide what technology to use and then build strategy around it is like putting the cart before the horse.

What you need to always keep in mind is that technology is simply a set of tools, assets, and resources that businesses use to support strategy development and execution. No business would decide to spend money just because it had a large reserve of cash on hand. No business would ever decide to hire more people just because there was an abundant workforce. No business would ever decide to buy more land just because property was inexpensive in the immediate vicinity. Likewise, businesses don't use a particular set of technologies just because they are available.

Rather, businesses start by understanding the complete competitive landscape (both current and projected), then developing strategy and processes to compete effectively, and finally choosing supporting technologies (see Figure 1.1). This is a

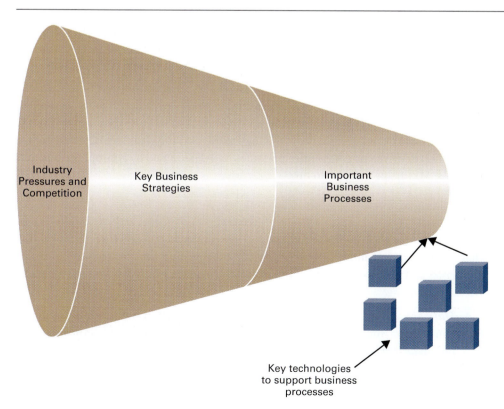

Figure 1.1

How Businesses Decide
What Technology to Use

Industry Pressures and Competition

Key Business Strategies

Important Business Processes

Key technologies to support business processes

"refinement approach" that moves from the big picture (the industry in which your business operates) to the details (the technologies you should choose). So, you start with the bigger view of your industry and continually refine your analysis unit until you arrive at the technology or technologies you should use (see Figure 1.1).

The steps are as follows:

1. Assess the state of competition and industry pressures affecting your organization.
2. Determine business strategies critical to successfully address those competitive and industry pressures.
3. Identify important business processes that support your chosen business strategies.
4. Finally, align technology tools with those important business processes.

So, you first need to understand the industry in which your business operates and the competitive forces affecting that industry. Decisions regarding business strategies, business processes, and finally technology follow. Your organization must perform these steps in this order. If you don't understand the competitive nature of your industry, you can't determine business strategies that ensure success. If you don't then identify the most important business processes to support those business strategies, you will undoubtedly implement the wrong technologies and doom your organization to failure. It is our goal in this first chapter to help you through the first two steps above. The remaining chapters focus on further refinement of business strategies and the identification of important business processes—and the technology tools that support them.

Management Information Systems

Just like finance, accounting, marketing, and many others, *management information systems* is a business function vitally important to the success of your organization. Formally, we define management information systems as follows:

LEARNING OUTCOME 1

- *Management information systems (MIS)* deals with the planning for, development, management, and use of information technology tools to help people perform all tasks related to information processing and management.

So, MIS deals with the coordination and use of three very important organizational resources—information, people, and information technology. Stated another way, *people* use *information technology* to work with *information.* And to do so they are involved in MIS. Ideally, of course, people use technology to support the goals and objectives of the organization as driven by competitive pressures and determined by appropriate business strategies. MIS helps them to do this.

INFORMATION AS A KEY RESOURCE

As the truism goes, we are in the information age, a time when knowledge is power. But what *are* information and knowledge? Let's first define *data, information,* and *business intelligence* and give an example to understand them better. Finally, we'll discuss the elusive term *knowledge.*

- *Data* are raw facts that describe a particular phenomenon such as the current temperature, the price of a movie rental, or your age. (Actually, the term *data* is plural; *datum* is singular.)

- **_Information_** is data that have a particular meaning within a specific context. The current temperature becomes information if you're deciding what to wear; in deciding what to wear, the data describing the price of a movie rental are not pertinent information.

- **_Business intelligence (BI)_**—collective information – about your customers, your competitors, your business partners, your competitive environment, and your own internal operations that gives you the ability to make effective, important, and often strategic business decisions.

Consider Figure 1.2. In the left is a single Excel cell containing the number 21; let's assume that's your age. That is a piece of data, some sort of fact that describes the amount of time you have been alive. Now let's create a list of customers for a business that contains the age of each customer (the right portion of Figure 1.2). This is potential _information_ since your business can use it. Notice that you can create an average, find the ages of the youngest and oldest customers, and build a frequency distribution of customers by age.

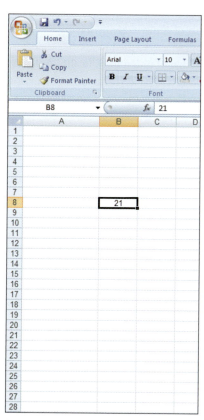

In an Excel cell, you can store a single piece of data. Here, the cell contains the number 21, which we're assuming to be your age.

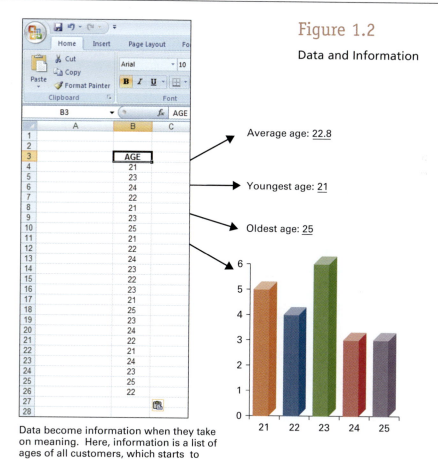

Data become information when they take on meaning. Here, information is a list of ages of all customers, which starts to provide insight into your customers.

Figure 1.2

Data and Information

Now, look at Figure 1.3. There you'll see an Excel workbook containing many pieces of information for each customer. This is *business intelligence*. What does this mean? Take a careful look at some of the columns of information. For each customer, we know the preferred salesperson. We can also see the number of coupons each customer has used. Now we can start to derive more meaningful information—business intelligence. We can compare how men and women use coupons. We can derive the customer average age by preferred salesperson.

Notice how data, information, and business intelligence all build on each other. Information is a more complete picture of multiple data points; in our example, an age was a single piece of data while information was the collective ages of all customers. Business intelligence extends that information to include gender behavior, the use of coupons, preferred salespersons, and total purchases. And *knowledge* builds upon all of those. You acquire knowledge in a business or field through practice over time using information and intelligence. You will understand better what we mean by knowledge as we go along.

Knowledge is a broad term that can describe many things: (1) it can provide contextual explanation for business intelligence; (2) it can point toward actions to take to affect business intelligence; (3) it can include intellectual assets such as patents and trademarks; and (4) it includes organizational know-how for things such as best practices.

Consider our example in Figures 1.2 and 1.3. Knowledge can provide context by explaining the reason that more women than men use coupons is that the majority of coupons are placed in women's magazines. You would derive this sort of knowledge by having the business intelligence in Figure 1.3 and at the same time having access to the marketing strategies. Given the business intelligence in the figure, the knowledge of individuals in the organization would help them make use of it. Knowledge would address what marketing strategy, for instance, should be undertaken to get more customers on Plan B to increase total purchases.

Figure 1.3

Business Intelligence

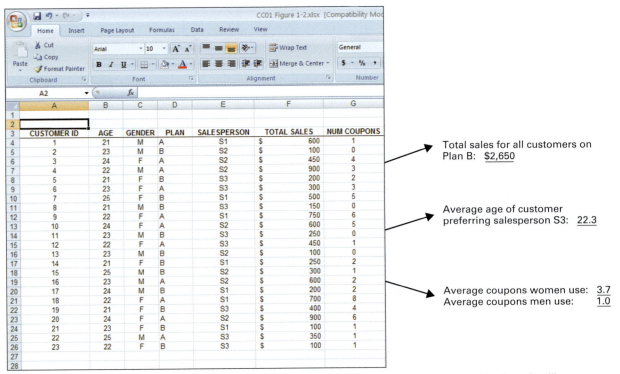

CUSTOMER ID	AGE	GENDER	PLAN	SALESPERSON	TOTAL SALES	NUM COUPONS
1	21	M	A	S1	$ 600	1
2	23	M	B	S2	$ 100	0
3	24	F	A	S2	$ 450	4
4	22	M	A	S2	$ 900	3
5	21	F	B	S3	$ 200	2
6	23	F	A	S3	$ 300	3
7	25	F	B	S1	$ 500	5
8	21	M	B	S3	$ 150	0
9	22	F	A	S1	$ 750	6
10	24	F	A	S2	$ 600	5
11	23	M	B	S3	$ 250	0
12	22	F	A	S3	$ 450	1
13	23	M	B	S2	$ 100	0
14	21	F	B	S1	$ 250	2
15	25	M	B	S2	$ 300	1
16	23	M	A	S2	$ 600	2
17	24	M	B	S1	$ 200	2
18	22	F	A	S1	$ 700	8
19	21	F	B	S3	$ 400	4
20	24	F	A	S2	$ 900	6
21	23	F	B	S1	$ 100	1
22	25	M	A	S3	$ 350	1
23	22	F	B	S3	$ 100	1

Total sales for all customers on Plan B: $2,650

Average age of customer preferring salesperson S3: 22.3

Average coupons women use: 3.7
Average coupons men use: 1.0

When you start to combine multiple sets of information, you can generate a considerable amount of business intelligence. Business intelligence helps you make effective strategic business decisions.

The *quality* of intelligence and knowledge is obviously critical. We'll talk next about the quality of these assets. Quality has different meanings in different contexts. Then we'll discuss some other characteristics of information. (In the following discussion, we'll be using the term *information* generically to refer to all intellectual assets—data, information, business intelligence, and knowledge. We don't mean to be confusing, but the fact is that the term *information* is also used by business people and academics alike in a shorthand fashion in this way.)

DEFINING INFORMATION QUALITY   Information exhibits high quality only if it is pertinent, relevant, and useful to you. Unfortunately, in today's information age, information is not exactly at a premium; you are bombarded daily with information, much of which is not really important to you in any way. Below are some information attributes that help define its quality.

- **Timeliness**—There are two aspects here. Do you have access to information *when you need it?* If you're preparing to make a stock trade, for example, you need access to the price of the stock right now. Second, does the information describe the time period or periods you're considering? A snapshot of sales today may be what is relevant. Or for some important decisions, you really need other information as well—sales yesterday, sales for the week, today's sales compared to the same day last week, today's sales compared to the same day last year, and so on.

- **Location**—Information is of no value to you if you can't access it. Ideally, your location or the information's location should not matter. IT can definitely create information quality here with technologies that support telecommuting, workplace virtualization, mobile e-commerce, and so on, so you can access information at or from any location.

- **Form**—There are two aspects here also. Is the information in a form that is most useful to or usable by you—audio, text, video, animation, graphical, or other? Depending on the situation, the quality of information is defined by its form and your ability to make use of it. Second, is the information free of errors? Think of information as you would a physical product. If you have a defective product, it lacks quality in that you cannot use it. Information is the same. This is the concept of **garbage-in garbage-out (GIGO).** If the information coming into your decision-making process is in bad form (i.e., garbage-in), you'll more than likely make a poor decision (i.e., garbage-out).

- **Validity**—Validity is closely related to the second aspect of form above. Validity addresses the credibility of information. Information is all over the Internet, but does it come from a credible source? Much of the information on the Internet has not gone through any sort of quality control or verification process before being published, so you have to question its validity.

CONSIDERING INFORMATION FROM AN ORGANIZATIONAL PERSPECTIVE
Organizations must treat information as any other resource or asset. It must be organized, managed, and disseminated effectively for the information to exhibit quality. Within an organization, information flows in four basic directions (see Figure 1.4 on the next page):

1. **Upward.** Upward information flows describe the current state of the organization based on its daily transactions. When a sale occurs, for example, that information originates at the lowest level of the organization and is passed upward through the various levels. Along the way, the information takes on a finer level of *granularity*. **Information granularity** refers to the extent of detail within the information. At lower organizational levels, information exhibits fine granularity because people need to work with information in great detail. At the upper

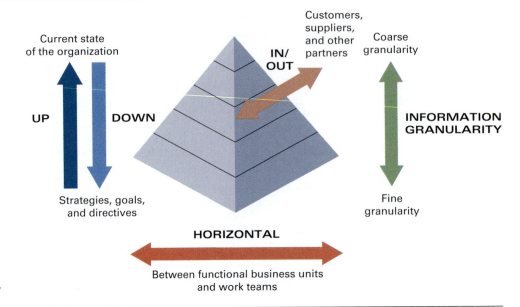

Figure 1.4

An Organization, Its Information Flows, and Information Granularity

organizational levels, information becomes coarser because it is summarized or aggregated in some way. That is, strategic managers need sales by year, for example, as opposed to knowing the detail of every single transaction.

2. **Downward.** Strategies, goals, and directives that originate at a higher level are passed to lower levels in downward information flows. The upper level of an organization develops strategies; the middle levels of an organization convert those strategies into tactics; and the lower levels of an organization deal with the operational details.

3. **Horizontal.** Information flows horizontally between functional business units and work teams. The goal here is to eliminate the old dilemma of "the right hand not knowing what the left hand is doing." All units of your organization need to inform other units of their processes and be informed by the other units regarding their processes. In general, everyone in a company needs to know everything relevant in a business sense (personal, sensitive data not included).

4. **Outward/inward.** Information is communicated from and to customers, suppliers, distributors, and other partners for the purpose of doing business. These flows of information are really what electronic commerce is all about. Today, no organization is an island, and outward/inward flows can yield a competitive advantage.

Another organizational perspective on information regards what information describes. Information is internal or external, objective or subjective, and various combinations of these.

- *Internal information* describes specific operational aspects of an organization.
- *External information* describes the environment surrounding the organization.
- *Objective information* quantifiably describes something that is known.
- *Subjective information* attempts to describe something that is unknown.

Consider a bank that faces the decision about what interest rate to offer on a CD. That bank will use internal information (how many customers it has who can afford to buy a CD), external information (what rate other banks are offering), objective information (what is today's prime interest rate), and subjective information (what the prime interest rate is expected to be in the future). Actually, the rate other banks are offering is not only external

OVERCOMING LANGUAGE BARRIERS ON THE INTERNET

The Internet is certainly a disruptive technology that has eliminated geographical and location barriers. With almost one-sixth of the world's population having access to the Internet, "location, location, location" in the physical world is becoming less and less and less important.

However, we now have new issues to deal with, notably a language barrier. What happens if you connect to a site that offers information in a language you don't understand? How can you send an e-mail to someone in Japan who doesn't speak English?

One solution is language translation software, and one company leading the way in the development of language translation software is SYSTRAN. SYSTRAN offers a suite of software tools that enables you, among other things, to translate about 3,700 words per minute, translate e-mail, Web page, and pdf content, and display Asian fonts. Most of SYSTRAN's software products are also available as plug-ins for Microsoft Outlook, Word, Excel, and PowerPoint.

Is it perfect? Not according to SYSTRAN's disclaimer. It states specifics about what its products will do, then encourages you to carefully review any translation before making it a part of your business communications.

Indeed, when Kentucky Fried Chicken wanted to translate its slogan "finger-lickin good" into Chinese, it came out as "eat your fingers off." Product names are another example. When General Motors tried to sell the Chevy Nova in South America, people didn't buy it because *No va* means "it won't go" in Spanish. (Neither of those two companies were using language translation software provided by SYSTRAN.)

Experiment with this. Connect to SYSTRAN's Web site at www.systransoft.com. Type in a phrase and choose the language into which you would like it translated.[4]

---

information (it describes the environment surrounding the organization) but objective information (it is quantifiably known). Information usually has more than one aspect to it.

PEOPLE AS A KEY RESOURCE IN MIS

The single most important resource in any organization is its people. People set goals, carry out tasks, make decisions, serve customers, and, in the case of IT specialists, provide a stable and reliable technology environment so the organization can run smoothly and gain a competitive advantage in the marketplace. So, this discussion is all about *you*.

In business, your most valuable asset is *not* technology but rather your *mind*. IT is simply a set of tools that help you work with and process information. It's really a mind support tool set. Technology such as spreadsheet software can help you quickly create a high-quality and revealing graph. But it can't tell you whether you should build a bar or a pie graph, and it can't help you determine whether you should show sales by territory or sales by salesperson. Those are *your* tasks, and that's why your business curriculum includes classes in human resource management, accounting, finance, marketing, and perhaps production and operations management.

Nonetheless, technology is an important set of tools for you. Technology can help you be more efficient and can help you dissect and better understand problems and opportunities. So, it's as important for you to learn how to use your technology tool set as it's important that you understand the information to which you're applying your technology tools.

TECHNOLOGY LITERACY   A *technology-literate knowledge worker* knows how and when to apply technology. The "how" aspect includes knowing which technology to purchase, how to exploit the many benefits of application software, and what technology infrastructure is required to get businesses connected to each other, just to name a few.

We encourage you to read all the appendices, especially *Appendix C (Careers in Business)*. That appendix covers career opportunities in a variety of business disciplines including finance, marketing, accounting, management, and many others. Reading *Appendix C* will help prepare you for whatever career you choose. You'll find a discussion there of key technologies for each business discipline that will help you succeed in your career.

A technology-literate knowledge worker also knows "when" to apply technology. Unfortunately, in many cases, people and organizations blindly decide to use technology in a desperate effort to solve a business problem. What you need to understand is that technology is not a panacea. You can't simply apply technology to any given process and expect that process instantly to become more efficient and effective. Look at it this way—if you apply technology to a process that doesn't work correctly, then you'll only be doing things wrong millions of times faster. There are cases when technology is not the solution. Being a technology-literate knowledge worker will help you determine when and when not to apply technology.

INFORMATION LITERACY   An *information-literate knowledge worker*

- Can define what information is needed.
- Knows how and where to obtain information.
- Understands the information once it is received (i.e., can transform the information into business intelligence).
- Can act appropriately based on the information to help the organization achieve the greatest advantage.

Consider a unique and real-life example of an information-literate knowledge worker. Several years ago, a manager of a retail store on the East Coast received some interesting information: diaper sales on Friday evenings accounted for a large percentage of total sales of that item for the week. Most people learning this would have immediately jumped to the decision to ensure that diapers were always well stocked on Friday evenings or to run a special on diapers Friday evenings to increase sales even further, but not our information-literate knowledge worker. She first looked at the information and decided that she needed more information in order to create business intelligence. She simply needed to know more before she could act.

She decided the business intelligence she needed was *why* a rash of diaper sales (pardon the pun) occurred on Friday evenings and *who* was buying the diapers. That intelligence was not stored within the computer system, so she stationed an employee in the diaper aisle on Friday evening to record any information pertinent to the situation (i.e., she knew how and where to obtain the information). The store manager learned that young businessmen purchased the most diapers on Friday evenings. Apparently, they had been instructed to buy the weekend supply on their way home from work. The manager's response was to stock premium domestic and imported beer near the diapers. Since then, Friday evening has been a big salestime not only for diapers but also for premium domestic and imported beer.

There are a couple of important lessons you can learn from this story. First, as we've stated, technology is not a panacea. Although a computer system generated the initial report detailing the sales of diapers on Friday evenings, our retail store manager did not make any further use of technology to design and implement her innovative and highly effective solution. Second, this story can help you distinguish between information and business intelligence. In this case, the information was the sales of diapers on Friday evening. The business intelligence, however, included

- *Who* was making diaper purchases on Friday evening.
- *Why* those people were purchasing diapers on Friday evening.
- *What* complementary product(s) those people might also want or need. (This last point might also illustrate the manager's special *knowledge*.)

As a good rule of thumb, when you receive information and need to make a decision based on it, ask yourself questions that start with who, what, when, why, where, and how. Answers to those questions will help you create business intelligence and make better decisions.

YOUR ETHICAL RESPONSIBILITIES   Your roles as a technology-literate and information-literate knowledge worker extend far beyond using technology and business intelligence to gain a competitive advantage in the marketplace for your organization. You must also consider your social responsibilities: This is where ethics become important. *Ethics* are the principles and standards that guide our behavior toward other people. Your ethics have consequences for you just as laws do. But ethics are different from laws. Laws either clearly require or prohibit an action. Ethics are more subjective, more a matter of personal or cultural interpretation. Thus, ethical decision making can be complex. A decision or an action in some cases might have—or be expected to have—an outcome that is actually right or wrong according to different people's ethics. Consider the following examples of actions:

1. Copying software you purchase, making copies for your friends, and charging them for the copies.
2. Making an extra backup of your software just in case both the copy you are using and the primary backup fail for some reason.
3. Giving out the phone numbers of your friends and family, without their permission, to a telecom provider of some sort of calling plan so you can receive a discount.

Each of these examples is either ethically (according to you or some people) or legally (according to the government) incorrect or both. In the second example, you might be ethically okay in making an extra backup copy (because you didn't share it with anyone), but according to some software licenses you're prohibited by law from making more than one backup copy. What do you think about the first and third examples? Illegal? Unethical? Both?

To help you better understand the relationship between ethical acts and legal acts, consider Figure 1.5. The graph is composed of four quadrants, and the complexity of ethical decisions about behavior is suggested by quadrant III (legal but unethical). Do any of the three examples above fall in quadrant III? Perhaps you can think of some other actions that although legal might still be unethical (how about gossiping?). You always want your actions to remain in quadrant I. If all your actions fall into that quadrant, you'll always be acting both legally and ethically and thus in a socially responsible way. Clearly, technology has further increased the complexity of ethics in our society because of the speed and casual ease with which people can access, distribute, and use information.

Being socially and ethically responsible in the information age involves not only the actions you initiate yourself but also what you do to protect yourself and your organization against the actions of others— that is, protecting yourself and your organization against cyber crimes.

Figure 1.5

Acting Ethically and Legally[5]

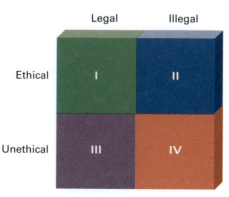

E-LEARNING: NOT JUST FOR SCHOOL

To become effective in your use of information, you can use technology to learn—not only about what information means, but more basically how to perform your work responsibilities better. Brink's Home Security recently implemented an e-learning management system to help (1) train its 2,600 employees, (2) increase customer retention, (3) improve profits, and (4) reduce employee turnover.

Many of Brink's field personnel work nights and weekends, installing home security systems. For them, instructor-led classes in a central location (Brink's has a nationwide field workforce) created problems and simply didn't work.

The new e-learning management system helps managers develop customized online training modules and allows field personnel to access those modules 24 hours per day, seven days per week. The system even provides skills assessment and other forms of evaluation.

The total investment in the system for Brink's was $300,000. It expects to save $500,000 in the first three years as a result of replacing instructor-led classes with the e-learning modules. Brink's has already noticed that its better-trained field personnel have improved profit margins and increased customer retention.[6]

There are many types of cyber crimes—such as promulgating viruses or worms, committing identity theft, and engaging in Web defacing—performed by a variety of hackers such as black-hat hackers and cyberterrorists, and it is your responsibility to guard against them. It might even be considered an ethical lapse not to do so. We cannot stress enough how important it is for you to protect yourself and your organization's assets in cyberspace. We'll talk more about these issues in Chapter 8 (Protecting People and Information).

INFORMATION TECHNOLOGY AS A KEY RESOURCE IN MIS

The third key resource for management information systems (MIS) is *information technology (IT),* any computer-based tool that people use to work with information and support the information and information-processing needs of an organization. IT includes a cell phone or PDA that you use to obtain stock quotes, your home computer that you use to write term papers, large networks that businesses use to connect to one another, and the Internet that almost one in every six people in the world currently uses.

KEY TECHNOLOGY CATEGORIES One simple—yet effective—way to categorize technology is as either *hardware* or *software* (see Figure 1.6). *Hardware* is the physical devices that make up a computer. *Software* is the set of instructions that your hardware executes to carry out a specific task for you. So, your PDA is the actual hardware; and it contains software that you use to maintain your calendar, update your address book, check your e-mail, watch videos, obtain stock market quotes, and so on.

All hardware technology falls into one of the following six basic categories:

1. An *input device* is a tool you use to enter information and commands. Input devices include such tools as keyboard, mouse, touch screen, game controller, and bar code reader.

2. An *output device* is a tool you use to see, hear, or otherwise recognize the results of your information-processing requests. Output devices include such tools as printer, monitor, and speakers.

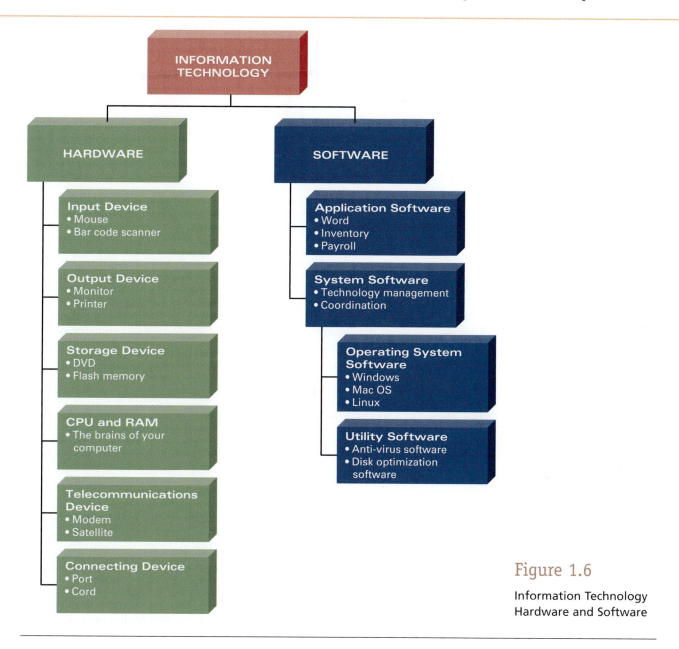

Figure 1.6

Information Technology
Hardware and Software

---

3. A ***storage device*** is a tool you use to store information for use at a later time.
   Storage devices include such tools as thumb drive, flash memory card, and DVD.

4. The ***central processing unit (CPU)*** is the hardware that interprets and executes
   the system and application software instructions and coordinates the operation of
   all the hardware. ***RAM,*** or ***random access memory,*** is a temporary holding area
   for the information you're working with as well as the system and application
   software instructions that the CPU currently needs.

5. A ***telecommunications device*** is a tool you use to send information to and
   receive it from another person or computer in a network. If you connect to the
   Internet using a modem, the modem is a telecommunications device.

6. *Connecting devices* include such things as a USB port into which you would
   connect a printer, connector cables to connect your printer to the USB port, and
   internal connecting devices on the motherboard.

There are two main types of software.: *application* and *system.* ***Application software*** is the software that enables you to solve specific problems and perform specific tasks. Microsoft Word, for example, can help you write term papers. From an organizational point of view, payroll software, collaborative software, and inventory management software are all examples of application software.

System software handles tasks specific to technology management and coordinates the interaction of all technology devices. System software includes network operating system software, drivers for your printer and scanner, operating system software such as Windows XP and Mac OS, and utility software such as anti-virus software, uninstaller software, and file security software.

If this is your first exposure to technology hardware and software, we suggest you explore *Appendix A (Computer Hardware and Software).*

As we have seen, *management information systems* really is all about three key organizational resources—the people involved, the information they need, and the information technology that helps them. MIS is about getting the right technology and the right information into the hands of the right people at the right time. To meet the technology and information needs of your organization, you must understand the industry in which you operate, build the appropriate business strategies, and then identify the important business processes that support the strategies. Finally, you select the right technologies.

Porter's Five Forces Model: Assessing the State of the Competition

LEARNING OUTCOME 2

Businesses should never "throw technology" at a problem, or use technology just for the sake of technology. To the contrary, businesses engage in discussion and strategic decision making to determine how technology can best support their efforts, which are quite different for each business. As you learn about the field of management information systems and the use of information technology, your foremost question should be: How do businesses decide which technologies to use and when? As we stated earlier, organizations determine which technology to use and when to use it by following a process similar to the following:

1. Assess the state of competition and industry pressures affecting your organization.
2. Determine business strategies critical to success in meeting those competitive and industry pressures.
3. Identify important business processes that support your chosen business strategies.
4. Align technology tools with the important business processes.

In this section we'll examine the first step—understanding the competitive forces within an industry. We'll do so by exploring the use of Porter's Five Forces Model. In the remaining two sections of the chapter, we'll cover several useful models for developing business strategy, the second step above, and then finally we'll cover value-chain analysis as a tool for identifying important business processes. Throughout the entire book, we'll introduce you to technology and discuss its importance for supporting business processes.

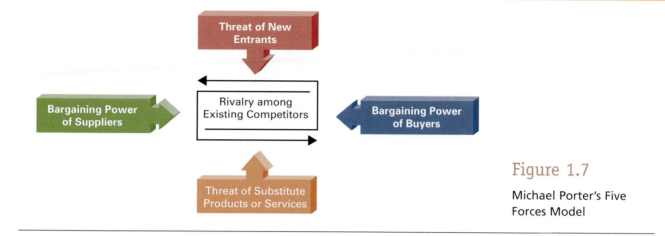

Figure 1.7

Michael Porter's Five Forces Model

Michael Porter's framework—called the Five Forces Model—has long been accepted as a useful tool for business people to use when thinking about business strategy and the impact of IT.[7] The *Five Forces Model* helps business people understand the relative attractiveness of an industry and the industry's competitive pressures in terms of the following five forces (see Figure 1.7):

1. Buyer power
2. Supplier power
3. Threat of substitute products or services
4. Threat of new entrants
5. Rivalry among existing competitors

BUYER POWER

Buyer power in the Five Forces Model is high when buyers have many choices from whom to buy, and low when their choices are few. Providers of products and services in a particular industry wish to reduce buyer power. They create a competitive advantage by making it more attractive for customers to buy from them than from their competition. Below are a few of the many companies using IT-enabled processes to reduce buyer power.

- NetFlix.—Set up your movie list. After you watch a movie and return it, NetFlix will send you the next movie on your list.
- United Airlines.—Enroll in the *Mileage Plus* program. As you travel using United (or perhaps make purchases using your United credit card), you accumulate miles for free air travel, upgrades, and hotel stays. Programs like this one, which reward customers based on the amount of business they do with a particular organization, are called *loyalty programs.*
- Apple iTunes.—Create an iTunes account and buy and download whatever music you want. Then, you can organize and manage your music, move it to your iPod, and burn CDs.
- Dell Computer.—Completely customize your computer purchase. It will be delivered to your doorstep within a few business days.

What's interesting about each of these examples (as well as all the others you can think of) is that the competitors in those industries have responded by creating similar programs. This simply means that no competitive advantage is ever permanent. A *competitive advantage* is providing a product or service in a way that customers value more than what the competition is able to do. NetFlix was the first to offer movie rentals (with a profitable business model) using the Internet as the primary platform. Therefore, it had *first-mover advantage,* a significant impact on gaining market share by being the first to market with a competitive advantage. However, Blockbuster and others soon followed with similar offerings, thus nullifying that competitive advantage. Every major airline has a loyalty program similar to that of United Airlines. There are many places on the Internet where you can buy and download music. Almost every major computer vendor allows you to customize your computer purchase. The lesson learned here—and for all strategies that result in a competitive advantage—is that a competitive advantage is only temporary and your organization must constantly innovate to find new competitive advantages.

SUPPLIER POWER

Supplier power in the Five Forces Model is high when buyers have few choices from whom to buy, and low when their choices are many. Supplier power is the opposite of buyer power: As a supplier organization in an industry, you want buyer power to be low and your supplier power to be high.

In a typical supply chain (see Figure 1.8), your organization will probably be both a supplier (to customer organizations) and a buyer, or customer (of other supplier organizations). As a customer of other supplier organizations, you want to increase your buyer power. As a supplier to other organizations, you want to increase your supplier power, thus reducing your customer's buyer power.

In the quest for increasing supplier power, organizations use many tools at their disposal, not just IT. Companies obtain patents and trademarks to minimize the extent to which products and services can be duplicated and offered by other organizations. The De Beers Group for many years has fought fiercely to tightly control the supply and distribution of diamonds. OPEC (the Organization of the Petroleum Exporting Countries) has organized 11 oil-producing nations to better control the distribution of the world's most popular energy resource (supposedly to ensure the stabilization of oil prices).

THREAT OF SUBSTITUTE PRODUCTS OR SERVICES

The *threat of substitute products or services* in the Five Forces Model is high when there are many alternatives to a product or service, and low when there are few alternatives from which to choose. Ideally, your organization would like to be a supplier organization in a market in which there are few substitutes for the products and services you offer. Of course, that's seldom possible in any market today, but you can still create a competitive advantage by increasing *switching costs.* *Switching costs* are costs that make customers reluctant to switch to another product or service supplier. What you need to realize is that a switching cost does not necessarily have to be an actual monetary cost.

Figure 1.8

Evaluating Buyer and Supplier Power for Your Organization

As you buy products at Amazon.com over time, for example, Amazon develops a unique profile of your shopping and purchasing habits through such techniques as collaborative filtering. When you visit Amazon, products are offered to you that have been tailored to your profile. This is only possible through the use of sophisticated technologies. If you choose to do your shopping elsewhere, there is a switching cost of sorts because the new site you visit will not have a profile of you or a record of your past purchases. (This is an effective variant of a loyalty program.) So, Amazon has reduced the threat of substitute products and services, in a market in which there are many substitutes, by tailoring offerings to you, by creating a "cost" to you to switch to another online retailer.

Switching costs can of course be real monetary costs too. You've probably been introduced to a switching cost when you signed up for the services of a cell phone provider. All the options and plans sound really great. But there is a serious switching cost in that most cell phone providers require you to sign a long-term contract (as long as two years) in order to receive a free phone or unlimited night and weekend calling minutes. The very successful substitute to this is disposable cell phones that you buy and which contain a certain number of minutes for your use.

THREAT OF NEW ENTRANTS

The ***threat of new entrants*** in the Five Forces Model is high when it is easy for new competitors to enter a market, and low when there are significant entry barriers to entering a market. An ***entry barrier*** is a product or service feature that customers have come to expect from organizations in a particular industry and that must be offered by an entering organization to compete and survive. Such barriers are erected, and overcome, and then new ones are created again. This is that vicious business cycle of build a competitive advantage, enjoy first-mover advantage, and then watch your competition develop similar initiatives thereby nullifying your competitive advantage.

For example, if you're thinking of starting a bank, you must offer your customers an array of IT-enabled services, including ATM use, online bill paying and account monitoring, and the like. These are significant IT-based entry barriers to entering the banking market because you must offer them for free (or a very small fee). If you consider our previous example of cell phone providers, a significant entry barrier in the past had to do with your phone number. Previously, if you wanted to change cell phone providers, you couldn't take your telephone number with you (i.e., you had to get a new cell phone number). This created a significant entry barrier because new cell phone providers entering the industry were mainly limited to obtaining new customers who did not currently have a cell phone. But that has all changed with *LNP, Local Number Portability,* your ability to take your cell phone number with you to a new provider.

RIVALRY AMONG EXISTING COMPETITORS

The ***rivalry among existing competitors*** in the Five Forces Model is high when competition is fierce in a market, and low when competition is more complacent. Simply put, competition is more intense in some industries than in others, although the overall trend is toward increased competition in just about every industry. Rarely can you identify an industry that exhibits complacent competition. (One example might be mortician and burial services. Solely because of the nature of the services offered, you don't see mortician and burial service organizations actively advertising on TV, offering reduced rates, and so on.)

The retail grocery industry is intensely competitive. While Kroger, Safeway, and Albertson's in the United States compete in many different ways, essentially they try to beat

COMPARING THE E-COMMERCE ACTIVITIES OF DIFFERENT GOVERNMENTS—A NEW KIND OF COMPETITION

Most people don't think that the government has any competitors but it does in many ways. Think about Social Security, MediCare, and other types of programs that compete with for-profit companies offering retirement programs, health care insurance, prescription medication policies, and so on. Governments even compete with each other, after a fashion, to see who's doing the best job of serving its citizenry.

For example, according to a report presented by the United Nations, the U.S. government ranks first overall in the aggregated categories of number of computers per 100 citizens, number of Internet hosts per 1,000 citizens, percentage of population online, number of telephone lines per 100 citizens, and an information access index (the ease with which government information can be found). That's pretty impressive.

However, according to a second report released by Accenture, the government of Canada ranked first in overall citizen satisfaction with the provision of e-government services. Categories in that report included e-government customer relationship management activities, maturity level of delivering services electronically, number of multichannel service delivery options, and extent to which the government shares information with its citizens. So, while the United States has the best infrastructure in place for e-government activities, Canada seems to be the best at determining what its citizens want and need. By the way, the United States ranked third in the Accenture study.

E-government is a major force and player on the Internet. According to Nielsen Net Ratings, the U.S. government ranked sixth among the most popularly visited sites, behind Microsoft, Time Warner (AOL), Yahoo!, Google, and eBay but ahead of the likes of Lycos, Walt Disney, RealNetworks, Amazon, and Ask.[8, 9, 10]

or match the competition on price. For example, most of them have loyalty programs that give shoppers special discounts. Customers get lower prices while the store gathers valuable business intelligence on their buying habits that helps them craft pricing, advertising, and coupon strategies.

Since margins are quite low in the grocery retail market, grocers build efficiencies into their supply chains, connecting with their suppliers in IT-enabled information partnerships. Communicating with suppliers over telecommunications networks rather than using paper-based systems makes the procurement process much faster, cheaper, and more accurate. That equates to lower prices for customers—and increased rivalry among existing competitors.

As you can see, Porter's Five Forces Model is extremely useful in helping you better understand the positioning of your organization within its industry and in helping you better understand the competitive forces affecting your organization. With this knowledge in mind, your organization's second task is to develop specific business strategies to remain competitive and profitable.

Porter's Three Generic Strategies: Building Business Strategy

LEARNING OUTCOME 3

The development of business strategies is a vast and wide discipline. There are literally hundreds of methodologies and approaches to the development of business strategy. There are even more books on the subject. (One such book with a particularly

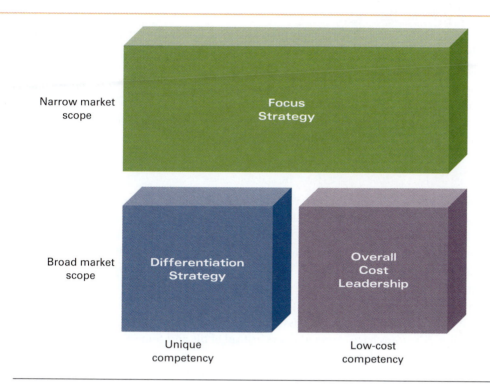

Narrow market scope — **Focus Strategy**

Broad market scope — **Differentiation Strategy** / **Overall Cost Leadership**

Unique competency   Low-cost competency

Figure 1.9

Michael Porter's Three Generic Strategies

innovative approach is *Blue Ocean Strategy* by Kim and Mauborgne. Be sure to put it on your wish list of business books to read.) Here, we'll focus on Michael Porter's three generic strategies and two other approaches.

Michael Porter identified three approaches or strategies to beating the competition in any industry (see Figure 1.9). They are

1. Overall cost leadership
2. Differentiation
3. Focus

OVERALL COST LEADERSHIP

Overall cost leadership is defined by Porter as offering the same or better quality product or service at a price that is less than what any of the competition is able to do. Examples of organizations focusing on overall cost leadership are numerous and change almost daily, with the most well-known example being Wal-Mart. Wal-Mart's slogans of "Always Low Prices!" and "Every Day Low Prices" accurately describe the strategy of overall cost leadership. For everything from women's lingerie to car batteries, Wal-Mart's focus is on offering the same products as the competition but at a lower price. Wal-Mart relies on an IT-enabled tight supply chain management system to squeeze every penny possible out of the procurement, distribution, and warehousing of its products. It uses sophisticated business intelligence systems to predict what customers will want and when.

Dell Computer works in similar fashion. Its famous sell-source-ship model of customizing computer purchases is the envy of the industry. Automobile makers Hyundai and Kia similarly attempt to sell reliable low-cost vehicles to a wide audience, in contrast to Hummer and Mercedes-Benz which have no overall cost leadership strategy. The large grocery retail chains we identified earlier such as Kroger, Safeway, and Albertson's essentially compete on price, often offering loss leaders just to get customers in the store. A *loss leader* is a product sold at or below cost to entice customers into a store in the hope that they will also buy more profitable products. Loss leaders are often placed in the back of the store so customers will have to walk by products with higher profit margins.

IT can be a particularly effective tool if your organization chooses an overall cost leadership strategy. IT can tighten supply chain systems, help you capture and assimilate customer information to better understand buying patterns in an effort to better predict product inventory and shelf placement, and make it easy (efficient) for customers to order your products through Web-enabled e-commerce systems.

DIFFERENTIATION

Differentiation is defined by Porter as offering a product or service that is perceived as being "unique" in the marketplace. Hummer is an excellent example. Its differentiation strategy is reinforced by the unique design and eye-appeal of its H1, H2, and H3 vehicle lines. Even its slogan—"Like Nothing Else"—clearly attempts to differentiate Hummer vehicles from anything on the road. Another example is Lunds & Byerly's (usually just referred to as Byerly's) in the grocery retail industry. While other competitors compete mainly on price, Byerly's focuses on the shopping experience for differentiation. All of the Byerly's stores offer cooking classes and in-store restaurants for lunch and dinner. Many Byerly's stores have carpeted floors instead of tile and some even have chandeliers instead of fluorescent lighting.

Apple Computer also focuses on differentiation as a business strategy. Not only do Apple computers look different, they have a different screen interface and focus more on nontextual information processing such as photos, music, and videos than any of the competition. Both Audi and Michelin have successfully created a differentiation strategy based on safety. To be sure, differentiation is not about being different based on lower price—that's the strategy of overall cost leadership—but the two are interrelated. While many people are willing to pay extra for grocery products at Byerly's, they are not willing to pay too much extra. Organizations focusing on differentiation must still be concerned about price in relation to the competition.

FOCUS

Focus as a strategy is usually defined as focusing on offering products and services (1) to a particular market segment or buyer group, (2) within a segment of a product line, and/or (3) to a specific geographic market. Focus is the opposite of attempting to be "all things to all people." Many restaurants focus on only a certain type of food—Mediterranean, Mexican, Chinese, and so forth. Stores such as the Vitamin Cottage Natural Foods Market sell only natural and organic food and nutrition supplements (one form of focus on products within a product line) to a specific buyer group (another form of focus on a particular market segment). Many doctors focus on only a particular type of medical help—oncology, pediatrics, and so on; similarly, many law offices focus on a particular legal venue—workman's compensation, living trusts, patents and trademarks.

As with the other generic strategies defined by Porter, focus cannot be practiced in isolation. If your organization chooses a particular buyer group on which to focus, you can bet that other competitors will do so as well, so you'll also have to compete on price (overall cost leadership) and/or differentiation too.

TWO INTERESTING AND COMPLEMENTARY STRATEGY FRAMEWORKS

Besides Porter's three generic strategies, there are numerous other strategy frameworks. Most people tend to use more than one as each provides another perspective from which

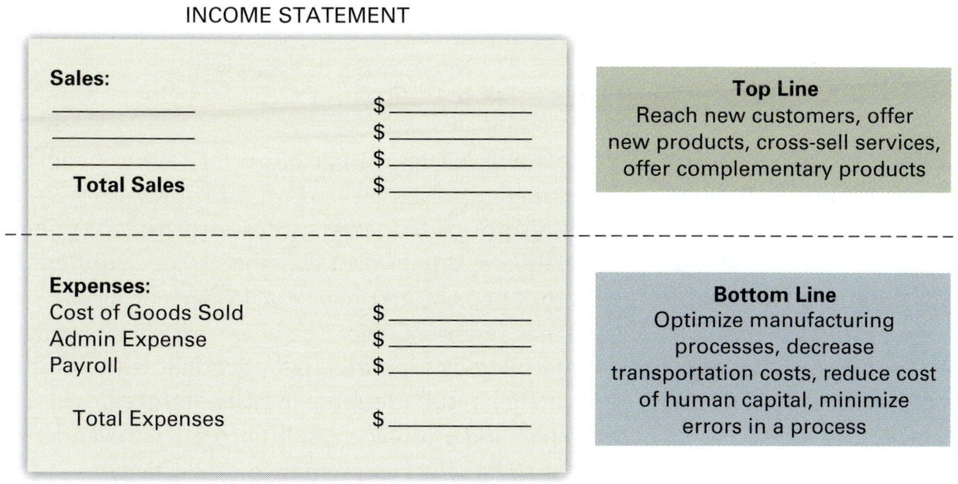

INCOME STATEMENT

Sales:

_____ $ _____
_____ $ _____
_____ $ _____
Total Sales $ _____

- -

Expenses:
Cost of Goods Sold $ _____
Admin Expense $ _____
Payroll $ _____

Total Expenses $ _____

Top Line
Reach new customers, offer new products, cross-sell services, offer complementary products

Bottom Line
Optimize manufacturing processes, decrease transportation costs, reduce cost of human capital, minimize errors in a process

Figure 1.10

Business Strategy: Top Line versus Bottom Line

to make decisions regarding the best business strategy given the competitive pressures of the industry. Here, we'll briefly look at two other frameworks; you'll easily see they are both different from and similar to Porter's three generic strategies (and each other).

TOP LINE VERSUS BOTTOM LINE   A typical income statement for a business has two main parts: (1) revenues and (2) expenses (see Figure 1.10). Revenues are monies your organization receives from selling its products and services while expenses are the costs it incurs providing those products and services. From a strategy point of view, you can focus on the "top line" (revenues) or the "bottom line" (expenses).

When focusing on the top line, your strategy is to *increase revenues,* which can be achieved any number of ways—reaching new customer segments, offering new products, cross-selling related services, offering complementary products, just to name a few. Conversely, when focusing on the bottom line, your strategy is to *minimize your expenses* in making your products or providing your services, which can be achieved in a number of ways as well—optimizing manufacturing processes, decreasing transportation costs, reducing the costs of human capital, minimizing errors in a process, again to name just a few. A bottom-line strategy is similar to Porter's strategy of overall cost leadership. And a top-line strategy is analogous to either or both differentiation and focus as defined by Porter. You will never focus solely on one to the neglect of the other; rather, you will focus on some combination of the two, since they are means to the same end (greater profitability).

From an IT point of view, you must form a business strategy that addresses the role of IT in affecting both the top line and bottom line, though not necessarily equally. For example, you could use technology to implement a customer self-service system on the Web. A *customer self-service system* is an extension of a transaction processing system that places technology in the hands of an organization's customers and allows them to process their own transactions. (A *transaction processing system* or *TPS* is a system that processes transactions within an organization.) Online banking and ATMs are examples of self-service systems. With these, bank customers have the ability to do their banking anywhere at anytime.

Online banking and ATMs have allowed banks to reduce the costs associated with the delivery of many types of services. Thus, they support a bottom-line strategy. Financial institutions also use these IT-enabled systems to attract new customers. Many financial institutions now also offer various products such as stamps for sale through ATMs.

CREATING SYNERGY AMONG TOP LINE AND BOTTOM LINE

Top-line and bottom-line initiatives are different means to the same end: increased net profit. Top-line initiatives achieve that end by focusing on increasing revenue while bottom-line initiatives achieve that end by focusing on decreasing costs. What you really hope to find is a technology-supported initiative that will allow you to do both—simultaneously increase revenues and decrease costs. That's what UrbanFlorist was able to.

A Canadian retailer serving all of Canada and most of the United States, UrbanFlorist previously processed all orders manually, which required each and every order to pass through the hands of at least 11 people. According to Alif Somani, CEO of UrbanFlorist, "We used to have a very heavy paper trail and our staff handled almost 10,000 printed pages per day." The manual process also led to a 6 percent error rate in handling the orders.

Using order management software provided by CommercialWare, UrbanFlorist was able to cut error rates in half to 3 percent and realize a 15 percent increase in sales per representative. This is an excellent example of a technology-supported initiative that led to both a bottom-line result (decrease in costs—error rates in this example) and a top-line result (increase in revenues as measured by sales representative productivity).

Alif sums it up best in these statements: "We have invested in a technology that supports our customer service department so that they can do their jobs more effectively . . . After all, our concern is not putting out orders but taking care of customers' needs, and having the right technology in place is essential to do that."[11]

Again, this is an example of using IT to focus on the top line, increasing revenues, by selling new products.

As you learn about various technologies in this book, ask yourself

1. How can I apply these technologies in a business environment to help my organization implement a top-line strategy (i.e., increase revenues)?

2. How can I apply these technologies in a business environment to help my organization implement a bottom-line strategy (i.e., minimize expenses)?

RUN-GROW-TRANSFORM FRAMEWORK A helpful conceptual framework for viewing the bigger organizational picture and determining the use of IT in it is the *run-grow-transform (RGT) framework,* an approach in which you allocate in terms of percentages how you will spend your IT dollars on various types of business strategies. For example, if you're only interested in "business-as-usual" but cheaper and faster than the competition, you would focus a great percentage of your IT dollars on a "run" strategy. If you wanted to transform your business in some way, you would allocate a certain percentage of your IT dollars to a "transformation" strategy. The following are the aspects of the RGT framework:

- *Run*—optimize the execution of activities and processes already in place. Seek organizational growth through offering products and services faster and cheaper than the competition.

- *Grow*—increase market reach, product and service offerings, expand market share, and so on. Seek organizational growth by taking market share from the competition (i.e., get a bigger piece of the pie).

- *Transform*—innovate business processes and/or products and services in a completely new way, move into seemingly different markets, and so on. Seek organizational growth through new and different means.

As you can see, the RGT framework is similar in many ways to both Porter's three generic strategies and a top-line versus bottom-line approach as follows:

- Run = overall cost leadership = bottom line
- Grow = focus and differentiation = top line
- Transform = (new) differentiation = top line (when the focus is innovation)

The application of the RGT framework is often best considered with an eye to the maturity of the organization and the maturity of the industry (see Figure 1.11). A new venture start-up, for example, will often focus more of its efforts on the grow aspect, while a mature organization—with a well-defined and successful line of products and services—in a mature industry will often focus more of its efforts on the run aspect. In the latter instance, the organization may already be a market leader and want to ensure and sustain its competitive advantage through price and cost optimization.

Regardless of maturity, however, all organizations must focus on the *transformation* aspect. In the business world, as is often said, if you're standing still, you're falling behind. It's a simple fact—your competition is always trying to do something better than you are. Therefore, your organization must constantly seek to evolve and, in most cases, to transform itself. Many times, your organization can take a proactive approach to using technology to transform itself. Below are just a few of the many examples of organizations that have focused on transformation.

- eBay.—The world's most popular online auction site, a few years ago, eBay acquired PayPal and began offering payment services to its buyers and sellers. In

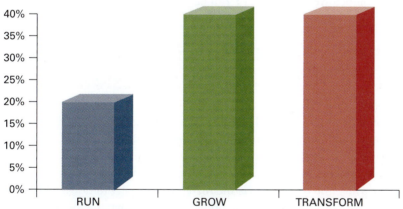

A new venture start-up focusing less on running the organization and more on growing and transforming the organization.

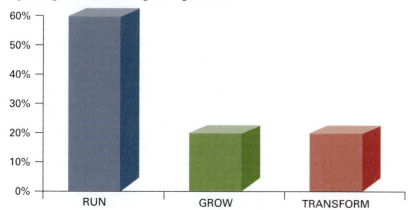

A mature organization within a mature industry focusing mainly on efficiently running the organization.

Figure 1.11

Illustrations of the Run-Grow-Transform (RGT) Framework

2003, it began offering its own credit card (a great example of transformation), with its "Anything Points" program offering eBay members the ability to buy products and pay for seller services with points accumulated from using a credit card.

- General Motors (GM).—Many people believe that GM's core competency is the production of automobiles. While that may be true, a major portion of its revenue comes from the financing of automobiles (and other big-ticket items such as homes). Its financing business segment (GMAC) is now more profitable than the actual manufacturing and selling of automobiles. GM doesn't want you to pay cash for a car—it wants you to finance the purchase or lease the car through GMAC.

- AOL.—In March 2004, America Online (AOL) launched a streamlined new service for online bill payments. Although it doesn't yet provide you with the capability of paying online bills directly through AOL, the initiative (called *AOL Bill Pay*) does seem to indicate that AOL is positioning itself to potentially transform from a pure Internet service provider (ISP) to an online bank in the future.

- Disney.—Known for its famous characters like Mickey, Disney now offers cell phone service targeted at families with children. Ring tones can be character voices, parents can set minute limits for children, and all subscribers can access Disney content year round.

Like these examples, your organization too must constantly seek to transform itself. The highly competitive business environment necessitates this focus on evolving toward ever greater competitive advantage. IT can help.

Identifying Important Business Processes: Value-Chain Analysis

LEARNING OUTCOME 4

Thus far, you've learned how to (1) understand your organization within the context of its industry and competitive pressures and (2) define your organization's major strategy for effectively competing using three approaches—Porter's three generic strategies, top line versus bottom line, and the run-grow-transform framework. Now, your organization is at a point "where the rubber meets the road" with respect to how technology will be used in a positive way to affect various processes in support of your strategy. A helpful tool is *value-chain analysis*. **Value-chain analysis** is a systematic approach to assessing and improving the value of business processes within your organization to further increase its competitive strengths.

A **value chain** is the chain or series of business processes, each of which adds value to your organization's products or services for customers. A **business process** is a standardized set of activities that accomplishes a specific task, for instance, processing a customer's order, delivering the customer order, service after the sale, and so on. Overall, value-chain analysis helps your organization identify valuable business processes.

Figure 1.12 depicts the typical components of a value chain. The chain of **primary value processes** along the bottom half takes in the raw materials and makes, delivers, markets and sells, and services your organization's products or services.

- *Inbound logistics*—receiving and warehousing raw materials and distributing those raw materials to manufacturing as needed.
- *Operations*—processing raw materials into finished products and services.

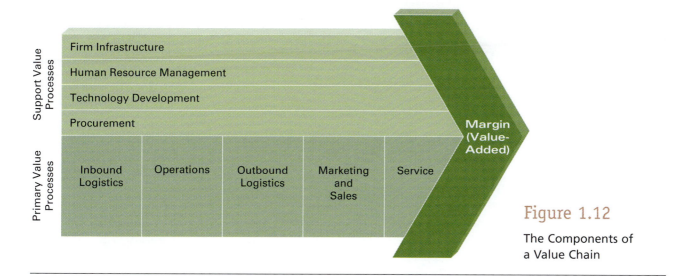

Figure 1.12

The Components of a Value Chain

- *Outbound logistics*—warehousing and distributing finished products and services.
- *Marketing and sales*—identifying customer needs and generating sales.
- *Service*—supporting customers after the sale of products and services.

Support value processes along the top half of the chain—firm infrastructure (culture, structure, control systems, accounting, legal, and so on), human resource management, technology development, and procurement (purchasing of raw materials)—support the primary value processes. Your organization requires these support value processes to ensure the smooth operations of the primary value processes.

Your organization's margin or profit depends on how well you perform both the primary value processes and support value processes. That is, the amount that your customers are willing to pay (defining the value your customers place on your products and services) must exceed the cost of the processes in the value chain. This concept is similar to top-line and bottom-line strategies in that your success (profit) depends on the revenue from customers (top line) exceeding the costs of your operations (bottom line).

If you've ever purchased a necktie, you may have heard of the Robert Talbott Company of Carmel Valley, California.[12] Talbott is a premier necktie manufacturer in the United States. Talbott traditionally shunned the use of technology; for example, all of its tie orders were written on paper forms. That used to work fine, because Talbott always ensured value-added by utilizing high-quality workmanship, unique designs, and fine fabrics. However, in today's fast-changing consumer market customers want constantly updated styles and more of them. Talbott now creates four neckwear lines for Nordstrom each year with up to 300 designs per line.

How might a value-chain analysis help Talbott in its operations? It could do so by identifying both value-added and value-reducing processes within its value chain. Let's look at the identification of value-added processes first.

IDENTIFYING PROCESSES THAT ADD VALUE

Talbott should first construct a survey instrument for its customers and ask which of the processes (both primary and support) within the value chain add the most value. This type of survey is often in a format in which a customer must assign a total of 100 points

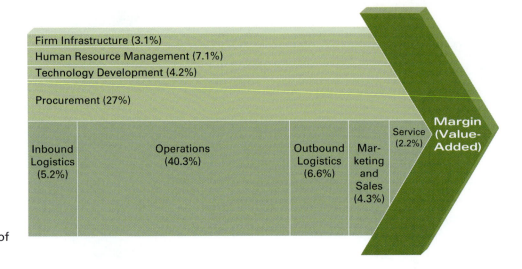

Figure 1.13

The Value-Added View of
a Necktie Manufacturer

across all the processes. Then, by summing all the responses and creating a percentage of total for each process, Talbott can determine which processes add the most value. Figure 1.13 depicts one possible customer survey result. Notice how the processes in the figure are sized to depict the value that customers attribute to each process. The largest value-added source is the high-quality manufacturing process. Still, a close second is the purchasing procurement process that provides access to high-quality silks and other fabrics. As these processes are the ones that are most visible to customers, they will quickly add even more value when supported by IT. Therefore, Talbott has created a computer-aided design system to reduce the time it takes to create and manufacture new ties. It could also further strengthen its quality control systems to ensure that the procurement of raw materials results in the highest quality of silks and other fabrics.

IDENTIFYING PROCESSES THAT REDUCE VALUE

After identifying value-added processes, it's important to identify those processes that reduce value for the customers. To do this, Talbott creates a second part to its survey instrument. In this part, Talbott asks customers to assign 100 points across all processes according to which processes reduce value. Then, by once again summing all the responses and creating a percentage of total for each process, Talbott can determine which processes reduce value the most.

Talbott identified the marketing and sales process as the process that reduced value the most, as shown in Figure 1.14. It found that sales were lost because salespeople were promising neckties that were out of stock. Customers were beginning to lose faith in Talbott's ability to deliver high-quality ties. They saw this process failure as one that reduced Talbott's value to them as customers.

To correct its marketing and sales process deficiencies, Talbott implemented a new IT system to get timely product information to the sales force. Using laptop computers, the sales force now carries product line information on the road with them. They place orders over their computers from their hotel rooms and receive inventory updates at the same time. As a result, neckties that customers want are on the shelves on a timely basis and customers have new faith in an old friend who now adds more value than ever.

Evaluating value chains is particularly effective because it forces your organization to gather and analyze quantifiable information from your customers. It eliminates much of the "flying by the seat of your pants" in making decisions. And as you begin to quantify important

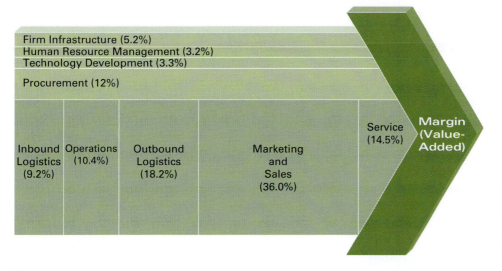

Figure 1.14

The Value-Reduced View of a Necktie Manufacturer

---

information, you can build a better return-on-investment case for the acquisition, development, and use of IT to further add value to your processes and reduce ineffectiveness.

To briefly summarize our main points in this chapter, management information systems (MIS) is all about people using technology to work with information as they support the organization in its quest for a competitive advantage. You can't blindly apply technology; you must carefully select technology within the context of the competitive pressures of your industry, the business strategies that you choose, and the important business processes you identify.

Summary: Student Learning Outcomes Revisited

1. **Define management information systems (MIS) and describe the three important organizational resources within it— people, information, and information technology.** *Management information systems (MIS)* deal with the planning for, development, management, and use of information technology tools to help people perform all tasks related to information processing and management. People, as an organizational resource within MIS, are the most important of the three. To be successful in their use of technology, people must be both *information-literate* and *technology-literate.* Information in various forms goes by many names such as *data, business intelligence*, and *knowledge.* All are intellectual assets but exhibit subtle differences. *Information* is data that has

meaning within a specific context. *Information technology (IT)* is any computer-based tool that people use to work with information and support the information and information-processing needs of an organization.

2. **Describe how to use Porter's Five Forces Model to evaluate the relative attractiveness of and competitive pressures in an industry.** Porter's *Five Forces Model* focuses on industry analysis according to five forces: (1) *buyer power*—high when buyers have many choices and low when choices are few; (2) *supplier power*—high when buyers have few choices and high when choices are many; (3) *threat of substitute products and services*—high when many alternative are available and low when alternatives are few; (4) *threat of new entrants*—high when it is easy to get into a market and low when it is difficult to

get into a market; and (5) *rivalry among existing competitors*—high when competition is fierce and low when competition is more complacent.

3. **Compare and contrast Porter's three generic strategies; top line versus bottom line; and the run-grow-transform framework as approaches to the development of business strategy.** Porter's *three generic strategies* are: (1) *overall cost leadership*—the same or better quality products at a price less than that of the competition; (2) *differentiation*—a product or service that is perceived as being "unique;" and (3) *focus*—products or services for a particular buyer group, within a segment of a product line, and/or a specific geographic market. A *top-line* strategy focuses on increasing revenues by increasing market share, cross-selling complementary products, etc. A *bottom-line* strategy focuses on decreasing costs by optimizing processes, reducing errors, etc. Finally, the *RGT framework* requires that you allocate in terms of percentages how you will spend your IT dollars among running the organization, growing the organization, and transforming the organization.

4. **Describe the role of value-chain analysis in identifying value-added and value-reducing processes.** *Value-chain analysis* is a systematic approach to assessing and improving the value of business processes within your organization to further increase its competitive strengths. Value-chain analysis allows you to gather customer data and quantifiably assess the extent to which different processes add value and reduce value, thus identifying those processes that would benefit from IT support.

CLOSING CASE STUDY ONE

EXPLORING YOUR SPACE AT MYSPACE.COM

While being interviewed by *The Hollywood Reporter* concerning MySpace, Rupert Murdoch stated, "In a sense, we say we've got 30 million portals." In November 2005, MySpace.com boasted having 37 million registered users, growing at an unbelievable pace of 4 million new members per month. According to comScore, it ranked third in page views among all domains.

Social networking sites are an interesting phenomenon on the Web. In a sense, eBay (www.ebay.com) is a social networking site that supports the gathering of consumer buyers and sellers. Epinions.com (www.epinions.com) is a social networking site enabling consumers to share product reviews. Wikipedia (www.wikipedia.org) is a social networking site focusing on the development of free open-source information and content.

In MySpace.com, you create and maintain your own "portal," a sort of personal Web site. In that portal, you create a personal page about yourself, sharing just about any information you care to. You can include photos, create a blog about a topic of interest, and establish relationships with other people in chat rooms.

Beyond just personal social networking, MySpace is becoming the space for many types of businesses. Most notably, musicians and bands are using MySpace to post and sell music. Over 660,000 musicians and bands maintain user profiles on MySpace. And those musicians aren't just limited to fledgling "wannabes." Madonna pursued an aggressive campaign at MySpace for her new album *Confessions on a Dance Floor.* Madonna even posted her own confessions on MySpace, describing how she loves to go through people's bags while they're not looking (and other questionable acts). Other MySpace users can watch Madonna's videos and even copy and paste them into their own profile sections.

Television shows and movies are also jumping into MySpace. TV shows like *Family Guy, The Man Show,* and *Kitchen Confidential* have a MySpace presence. Popular movies like *Walk the Line* and *Saw II* have their own space.

Book publishers spend extensive time reading and reviewing self-print books written on MySpace. Many people have found MySpace to be an excellent venue for self-publishing a book, getting people to read it, and getting publishers to take a look at their manuscripts. Many book publishers have profiles on MySpace and encourage authors to submit books and manuscripts there.

Of course, there is also a dark side to MySpace. Recently, a man created a MySpace portal and used it to attract underage girls for the purpose to committing sexual acts with them. He was caught but not before making contact with several young girls.[13, 14]

Questions

1. Visit MySpace (www.myspace.com). What process do you go through to create your own personal portal? Do you have to pay a fee? What information do you have to provide MySpace to create a personal portal?

2. Search for a "friend" on MySpace. How do you do this? What are the search criteria you can use?

3. Peruse the various blogs on MySpace. What seem to be the dominant blog topics? Did you find any blogs that are of questionable social value (according to your own ethics)? If so, what were the topics?

4. Search for your favorite garage band or perhaps a popular well-known band. What content were you able to find? Could you view a music video? If so, could you view the entire video or just a segment of it?

5. In your opinion, why have social networking sites grown in popularity? Do you have a MySpace profile? If so, why did you create it?

6. According to one account, MySpace is designed to be "unedited and democratic." But as you read above, MySpace has been used by pedophiles to attract young children. Should MySpace be completely uncontrolled and unedited? Does MySpace have a societal obligation to censor questionable content? In your view, what does "questionable content" mean?

7. A growing and significant competitor to MySpace is Cyworld (www.cyworld.com). Visit Cyworld and compare it to MySpace. If you don't have an account at either and had to choose one, which would you choose and why? If you have a MySpace account, what features does Cyworld offer that are not present at MySpace? If you have a Cyworld account, what features does MySpace offer that are not present at Cyworld? Do you have an account at both? If so, why?

CLOSING CASE STUDY TWO

IS THE WORLD DUMPING DATA ON YOU?

It goes by many terms—information overload, analysis paralysis, data dumping, and so on. You know what we're talking about. It is indeed great to live in the information age with a plethora of digital technologies at your fingertips giving you access almost instantly to massive amounts of information. But is all of that information really useful? Do you find yourself spending hours on end searching through that vast amount of information to find exactly what you need? Are search engines really good at helping you quickly locate the exact information you need?

Those are very important questions in the business world. Time is money, and time spent looking for the right information is wasted time and therefore an increased cost which results in a decrease in profits. An Accenture study of 1,009 managers at U.S. and U.K. companies with annual revenues exceeding $500 million in revenues revealed the following startling facts:

- IT managers spend 30 percent of their time trying to find information relevant to their jobs.
- 42 percent say they are bombarded by too much information.
- 44 percent complain that other departments don't share data.
- 39 percent can't figure out which information is current.
- 38 percent often receive duplicate data.
- 21 percent don't understand the value of the information once they receive it.
- 84 percent say they store information on hard drives or e-mail and don't share data that might be relevant to others.
- Only 16 percent state that they use collaborative tools, essentials tools for sharing information.

Information is a critical and valuable resource to any organization. It can easily be shared and used by many people, unlike other resources such as money. Knowing the right information about your competitors, your own internal operations, and your customers can yield a significant competitive advantage in the marketplace.

From a personal point of view, having the right information is essential as well. It will help you pick the right classes to take and when. It can make you more efficient and effective in writing term papers. It can help you with your taxes, plan your retirement, and determine which car best fits within your budget and meets your needs.[15]

Questions

1. Critically evaluate the bulleted list of information-related items in this case study. How are each contradictory to the notion of being an information-literate knowledge worker?

2. Consider again Figure 1.1 on page 5 and the steps we presented in the chapter for determining which technologies are most appropriate in an organization. Why is this process so important? During *each* of the four steps in that the decision process, what information should be derived and used in the next step?

3. Again, considering the four steps in determining which technologies are most appropriate in an organization, for the information you identified as crucial to be derived during each step in Question 2, which of that information is internal, external, objective, or subjective information? Which information is some combination of internal, external, objective, or subjective?

4. Is it ethical for people in an organization to withhold information and not share it with other employees? Under what circumstances would it be acceptable not to share certain types of information with other employees? What can organizations do to encourage their employees to share information?

5. What about your personal life at your school? How easy is it to find the following information on your school's Web site?
   - The course description for the classes you are currently taking.
   - A list of classes you need to take to complete your degree.
   - The requirements you must meet to qualify for various types of government-supported loan programs.
   - The process you go through to apply for graduation.

6. Overall, how would you rate your school's Web site in terms of providing the information you need? How would you rate your school's Web site in terms of allowing you to process your own transactions, such as signing up for a class, scheduling time with an advisor, and so on?

Key Terms and Concepts

Application software, 16
Business intelligence (BI), 7
Business process, 26
Buyer power, 17
Central processing unit (CPU), 15
Competitive advantage, 17
Customer-self service system, 23
Data, 6
Differentiation, 22
Entry barrier, 19
Ethics, 13
External information, 10
First-mover advantage, 18
Five Forces Model, 17
Focus, 22

Garbage-in garbage-out (GIGO), 9
Hardware, 14
Information, 7
Information granularity, 9
Information-literate knowledge worker, 12
Information technology (IT), 14
Input device, 14
Internal information, 10
Knowledge, 8
Loss leader, 21
Loyalty program, 17
Management information systems (MIS), 6
Objective information, 10

Output device, 14
Overall cost leadership, 21
Primary value processes, 26
RAM (random access memory), 15
Rivalry among existing competitors, 19
Run-grow-transform (RGT) framework, 24
Software, 14
Storage device, 15
Subjective information, 10
Supplier power, 18
Support value processes, 27
Switching cost, 18
System software, 16

Short-Answer Questions

1. What is the relationship between management information systems (MIS) and information technology (IT)?
2. What four steps should an organization follow in determining which technologies to use?
3. What are some relationships among data, information, business intelligence (BI), and knowledge?
4. How does the granularity of information change as it moves from lower to upper organizational levels?
5. What is the difference between a technology-literate knowledge worker and an information-literate knowledge worker?
6. How do ethics differ from laws?
7. What role does the Five Forces Model play in decision making?
8. Why are competitive advantages never permanent?
9. What are the three generic strategies according to Michael Porter?
10. How are Porter's three generic strategies, a top-line versus bottom-line approach, and the RGT framework similar?
11. Why is value-chain analysis so useful to companies?

Assignments and Exercises

1. **USING PORTER TO EVALUATE THE MOVIE RENTAL INDUSTRY** One hotly contested and highly competitive industry is the movie rental business. You can rent videos from local video rental stores, you can order pay-per-view from the comfort of your own home, and you can rent videos from the Web at such sites as NetFlix. Using Porter's Five Forces Model, evaluate the relative attractiveness of entering the movie rental business. Is buyer power low or high? Is supplier power low or high? Which substitute products and services are perceived as threats? Can new entrants easily enter the market? What are the barriers to entry? What is the level of rivalry among existing competitors? What is your overall view of the movie rental industry? Is it a good or bad industry to enter?

2. **REVIEWING THE 100 BEST COMPANIES TO WORK FOR** Each year *Fortune* magazine devotes an issue to the top 100 best companies to work for. Find the most recent issue of *Fortune* that does this. First, develop a numerical summary that describes the 100 companies in terms of their respective industries. Which industries are the most dominant? Pick one of the more dominant industries (preferably one in which you would like to work) and choose a specific highlighted company. Prepare a short class presentation on why that company is among the 100 best to work for.

3. **YOUR SCHOOL'S VALUE CHAIN** Develop a value chain for your school. You don't have to gather information to construct the value chain, but you do have to determine which processes are support value processes and which processes are primary value processes. Draw your value chain according to Figure 1.12 on page 27. Finally, list the three most important processes to you as a student and provide a short explanation of why they are the most important to you.

4. **BUSINESS STRATEGY FOR ENTERING THE CELL PHONE SERVICE INDUSTRY** Assume that you run a start-up and have decided to enter the cell phone service industry. Which of the three generic strategies would you choose as your primary business strategy—overall cost leadership, differentiation, or focus? Explain your choice by elaborating on the product and service features you would offer to lure customers from the competition.

5. **RESEARCHING YOUR CAREER AND INFORMATION TECHNOLOGY** To position yourself in the best possible way to succeed in the business world, you need to start researching your career right now. Here, we would like you to focus on the IT skills your career requires. First, consider what career you want to have. Second, visit Monster.com (www.monster.com) and search for jobs that relate to your career. Read through several of the job postings and determine what IT skills you need to acquire.

Discussion Questions

1. The three key resources in management information systems (MIS) are information, information technology, and people. Which of these three resources is the most important? Why? The least important? Why?

2. We often say that hardware is the *physical* interface to a technology system while software is the *intellectual* interface. How is your hardware your physical interface to your computer? How is your software your intellectual interface to your computer? Do you see technology progressing to the point that we may no longer distinguish between hardware and software and thus no longer perceive differing physical and intellectual interfaces?

3. In a group of three to four students, consider eBay in the context of Porter's Five Forces Model. How does eBay reduce the threat of new entrants? If necessary, you may want to explore eBay's site (www.ebay.com) and determine the role of buyer and seller ratings, its integration with PayPal, and how it helps buyers and sellers resolve disputes.

4. In this chapter, we discussed the use of loyalty programs in the travel industry as a mechanism for reducing buyer power. What is another industry that also uses loyalty programs to reduce buyer power? How does that industry use loyalty programs to do so?

5. As an information-literate knowledge worker for a local distributor of imported foods and spices, you've been asked to prepare a customer mailing list that will be sold to international cuisine restaurants in your area. If you do so, will you be acting ethically? Suppose you don't consider the proposal ethical. What will you do if your boss threatens to fire you if you don't prepare the list? Do you believe you would have any legal recourse if you didn't prepare the list and were subsequently fired?

CHAPTER PROJECTS

Group Projects

- Assessing the Value of Customer Relationship Management: Trevor Toy Auto Mechanics (p. 364)
- Analyzing the Value of Information: Affordable Homes Real Estate (p. 365)
- Making the Case with Presentation Software: Information Technology Ethics (p. 374)
- Analyzing Strategic and Competitive Advantage: Determining Operating Leverage (p. 381)

e-Commerce Projects

- Searching Job Databases (p. 399)
- Interviewing and Negotiating Tips (p. 389)
- Financial Aid Resources (p. 393)
- Protecting Your Computer (p. 395)
- Ethical Computing Guidelines (p. 392)
- Global Statistics & Resources (p. 394)

CHAPTER TWO OUTLINE

STUDENT LEARNING OUTCOMES

1. Define supply chain management (SCM) systems and describe their strategic and competitive opportunities.

2. Define customer relationship management (CRM) systems and describe their strategic and competitive opportunities.

3. Define e-collaboration and describe its strategic and competitive opportunities.

4. Discuss the impact IT culture has on technology choices and their implementations within an organization.

5. Explain the significance of enterprise resource planning (ERP) software as the integration of functional software systems.

PERSPECTIVES

WEB SUPPORT

www.mhhe.com/haag

- Consumer information
- Demographics
- Bureau of Labor and Statistics
- Gathering competitive intelligence
- Meta data
- Gold, silver, interest rates, and money
- Small Business Administration
- Global statistics and resources

Major Business Initiatives
Gaining Competitive Advantage with IT

A *smack* is actually both. It is the term for a group of jellyfish (just like a group of crows is called a *murder*), and it's also the term Mark McGuire uses to describe how customers shop on his social commerce site, that is, *smack shopping*. Mark is the CEO of Jellyfish.com (www.jellyfish .com), a Web site that provides for collaborative shopping by groups of customers to get the best deals.

Jellyfish is actually a reverse auction site. A seller of a given product—say 100 Apple iPods—posts those items for sale on Jellyfish with a zero percent discount at the beginning of the auction. As the auction continues, the discount begins to go up. As a buyer, you can choose to buy at any time at a given discount percentage. The longer you wait, the higher the percentage discount you receive. But be careful, because none of the buyers ever knows how many of the iPods the seller has. So, if you wait until the percentage discount rises to 75, the seller may have already sold his or her lot for a discount rate of 50 percent or less.

And 50 percent isn't that unreasonable. Smack shoppers have purchased Apple iPods for 41 percent off, Microsoft Xboxes for 46 percent off, and TiVo DVRs for a 23 percent discount.

Jellyfish supports other collaborative and social networking tools that also benefit buyers. A live chat board lets buyers interact with each other. Smacks (groups) of buyers on the chat board will attempt to persuade other buyers from buying too early, letting everyone profit from rising discounts. As you might guess, many of these buyers then resell the items on other traditional auction sites such as eBay.

The whole concept of *social commerce shopping* seems to be catching on. Jellyfish has more than 100,000 participants (both buyers and sellers) on a monthly basis. In the first five months of operation, the users of Jellyfish rose by a factor of five. As Mark describes it, smacking is turning marketing into entertainment. "We call it the Internet's first live shopping game show," says Mark.

Social commerce shopping certainly doesn't represent any new advance in technology, but rather a new and innovative way of *using* technology to reach customers. Customers in this case are both sellers (wanting to unload a lot of product) and buyers (seeking the best deals). In this chapter, we'll look at how organizations can use technology in support of major business initiatives such as supply chain management (for companies providing products and services), customer relationship management (for companies wanting to know everything about their customers), and e-collaboration.[1]

Questions

1. Do you use a live auction site like eBay? How does it differ from Jellyfish?

2. Visit Jellyfish.com. What is the process of becoming a participant?

3. What sort of products would be best suited for a reverse auction format?

Introduction

In almost any study you care to read, research shows that as competition intensifies in an industry, companies must develop innovative products, services, and business processes to compete and survive. Further, most of these studies point to the use of information technology as a way to help companies separate from the competition and develop a significant competitive advantage. In Chapter 1, we explored how a company can use tools such as Porter's Five Forces Model and Porter's three generic strategies, top-line versus bottom-line initiatives, and the run-grow-transform framework to develop business strategy to address the ever-intensifying competitive environment. In this chapter, we focus on three of the most important IT implementations of business processes to support those business strategies:

- Supply chain management
- Customer relationship management
- E-collaboration

As a company implements one of more of these IT-based systems, it must carefully consider its own internal IT culture and, just as important, how it will integrate these systems throughout the company using *enterprise resource planning* software. After examining the three IT implementations above, we'll also explore IT culture and enterprise resource planning software.

Supply Chain Management

LEARNING OUTCOME 1

Dell Computer's supply chain management system is the envy of the industry. Its direct model gives the company a huge advantage over any competitor still using a traditional model of selling through retailers. Traditional computer manufacturers build computers and ship them to wholesalers, distributors, or directly to retailers. The computers sit in a warehouse or on the retailers' shelves until somebody comes in and buys them. If you took a look at a typical distribution chain, you would see that there are too many computers in inventory. A **distribution chain** is simply the path a product or service follows from the originator of the product or service to the end consumer. Holding onto inventory in a distribution chain costs money, because whoever owns the inventory has to pay for the operation of a warehouse or stores while waiting for someone to buy it. In the retailing of computers, not only does excess inventory cost money to hold, but the computers themselves can become obsolete, requiring retailers to slash prices in an effort to sell older models before the newer ones arrive. Many such retailers use sites like Jellyfish.com (from the opening case study) to dump old and obsolete inventory.

Dell's model is different. Dell sells computers directly from its Web site so there is no inventory in its distribution chain. Dell has enhanced its *supply chain* as well. It uses i2 supply chain management software to send orders for parts to suppliers every two hours, enabling it to manufacture and deliver exactly what its customers want with little or no inventory in its supply chain.[2] The differences between Dell's "sell, source, and ship" model and the traditional "buy, hold, and sell" model are illustrated in Figure 2.1.

For a company the size of General Motors, with operations all over the world and tens of thousands of suppliers, supply chain management and IT-based supply chain management systems are critical necessities to ensure the smooth flow of parts to GM factories. **Supply chain management (SCM)** tracks inventory and information among business

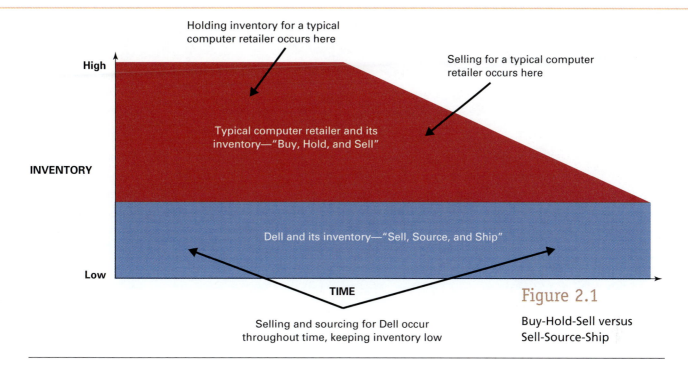

Figure 2.1

Buy-Hold-Sell versus
Sell-Source-Ship

processes and across companies. A **supply chain management (SCM) system** is an IT system that supports supply chain management activities by automating the tracking of inventory and information among business processes and across companies.

Most large manufacturing companies use *just-in-time* manufacturing processes, which ensure that the right parts are available as products in process move down the assembly line. **Just-in-time (JIT)** is a method for producing or delivering a product or service just at the time the customer wants it. For retailers, such as Target, this means that products customers want to buy are on the shelves when the customers walk by. Supply chain management systems also focus on making sure that the right number of parts or products are available, not too many and not too few. Too many products on hand means that too much money is tied up in inventory and also increases the risk of obsolescence. Too few products on hand is not a good thing either, because it could force an assembly line to shut down or, in the case of retailers, lose sales because an item is not in stock when a customer is ready to buy.

Consider snow blowers in Michigan around the month of November. If a store like Home Depot has too many, it may not be able to sell them all early in the snowy season when most customers buy them. Snow blowers are large and bulky and also cost a considerable sum of money. Having too many is an expensive proposition for Home Depot. Likewise, if Home Depot has too few snow blowers on hand and runs out early in the snowy season, a customer looking for a snow blower won't wait for new Home Depot inventory; instead, the customer will go to another store.

Companies with suppliers around the globe often employ inter-modal transportation. **Inter-modal transportation** is the use of multiple channels of transportation—railway, truck, boat, and so on—to move products from origin to destination (see Figure 2.2 on the next page). This further complicates the logistics of SCM because companies are required to carefully schedule, monitor, and track parts and supplies as they move among different modes of transportation. Consider that a given train may be carrying 50 or more truck trailers that will each eventually be connected to different trucks. Even purely domestic supply chains often employ inter-modal transportation such as railway lines and carrier trucks.

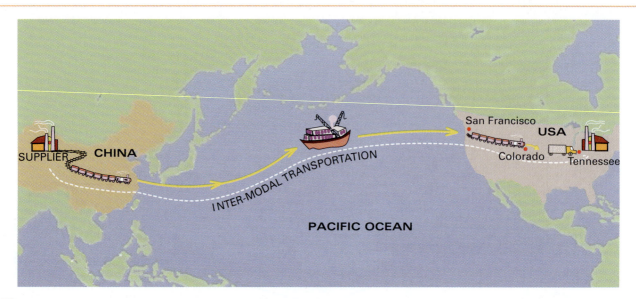

Figure 2.2

Inter-Modal Transportation

STRATEGIC AND COMPETITIVE OPPORTUNITIES WITH SCM

Overall, a tight supply chain management system focuses on squeezing every penny possible out of the supply chain process. Thus, the primary focus of supply chain management may be described in terms of our discussion in Chapter 1 as

- Overall cost leadership (from Porter's three generic strategies)
- Bottom-line initiative (cost reduction)
- Running the organization (run-grow-transform framework)

Of course, lower costs in the supply chain lead to lower prices to consumers, which in turn can increase market share and top-line revenue. A well-designed supply chain management system helps your organization by optimizing the following specific supply chain activities:

- *Fulfillment*—ensuring that the right quantity of parts for production or products for sale arrive at the right time.
- *Logistics*—keeping the cost of transporting materials as low as possible consistent with safe and reliable delivery.
- *Production*—ensuring production lines function smoothly because high-quality parts are available when needed.
- *Revenue and profit*—ensuring no sales are lost because shelves are empty.
- *Cost and price*—keeping the cost of purchased parts and prices of products at acceptable levels.

Cooperation among supply chain partners for mutual success is another hallmark of modern supply chain management systems. For example, many manufacturing companies share product concepts with suppliers early in the product development cycle. This lets suppliers contribute their ideas about how to make high-quality parts at a lower cost. Such an arrangement is enabled through IT and is usually referred to as an ***information partnership***—two or more companies cooperating by integrating their IT systems, thereby providing customers with the best of what each can offer.

STAPLES MAKES A BET ON ITS SUPPLY CHAIN MANAGEMENT SYSTEM

If you were running a highly successful retail operation, would you guarantee the availability of your fastest moving inventory or play it safe and guarantee only the availability of your slowest moving inventory that is seldom purchased? If you chose the latter, you'd be like many retailers, who play it safe, but you would be beaten by some of the competition such as Staples. Staples makes an in-stock guarantee to its customers for its fast-selling lines of ink-jet and toner cartridges, both of which Staples relies on heavily for revenue. If you find a cartridge is not in stock, Staples will ship it to your home with no delivery fee the next business day. It will also include a $10 coupon you can use the next time you purchase the same toner cartridge. Now that's an ambitious guarantee—Staples will deliver an out-of-stock item the next business day *and* give you $10 off your next purchase of the same item!

Staples's computer systems are linked with those of shipping companies such as UPS, a form of an *information*

partnership. If an item is out of stock, the Staples systems find the item at another store and immediately send UPS a request for package pickup and delivery. That's the way Staples can guarantee the next-day delivery.

Staples can make the guarantee because of its tight supply chain management system. Through its inventory monitoring function, Staples's SCM system carefully tracks the daily sales of its hottest items. When inventory starts to run low, the Staples SCM system sends an electronic order for more toner and/or ink-jet cartridges to the likes of HP. The product arrives in a timely manner to ensure shelf placement in light of forecasted demand.

While most retailers will offer you a rain-check and perhaps even help you find the out-of-stock product at another nearby store, Staples simply asks you to go home and wait for the next business day arrival of your product (and a $10 coupon). That's a tall bet on Staples's IT-based supply chain management system.[3]

IT SUPPORT FOR SUPPLY CHAIN MANAGEMENT

While the SCM market was pioneered by specialist companies such as i2 and Manugistics, it is now dominated by ERP software providers such as SAP, Oracle/PeopleSoft, SSA Global, and Microsoft (more on ERP later in this chapter). If your career choice takes you into industries that focus on the manufacturing of products and/or the distribution and use of those products (such as hospitality, resort, and tourism management), you will have a great deal to do with SCM software. To learn more about this area, we encourage you to visit the following resources:

- Supply Chain Knowledge Base—http://supplychain.ittoolbox.com/
- Supply Chain Management Review—http://www.scmr.com/
- i2 Technologies—www.i2.com
- *CIO Magazine*—www.cio.com
- About Inc. (Logistics/Supply Chain)—http://logistics.about.com/
- Oracle/PeopleSoft Supply Chain—http://www.oracle.com/applications/scm/index.html

Customer Relationship Management

LEARNING OUTCOME 2

Wells Fargo Bank's customer relationship management system tracks and analyzes every transaction made by its 10 million retail customers at its branches, at its ATMs, and through its Web-based online banking systems. Wells Fargo has become so good at predicting customer behavior that it knows what customers need even before many of them realize they need it. Wells Fargo's CRM system collects every customer transaction and combines it with personal information provided by the customer. The system is able to provide tailored offerings that will appeal to individual customers (a money-saving second mortgage, for example) at just the right time. As a result, Wells Fargo sells four more banking products or services per customer than the industry average of 2.2.[4]

Acquiring customers and then retaining them are the basic objectives of any organization, and thus, *customer relationship management* systems have become one of the hottest IT systems in business today. A ***customer relationship management (CRM) system*** uses information about customers to gain insights into their needs, wants, and behaviors in order to serve them better. Customers interact with companies in many ways, and each interaction should be easy, enjoyable, and error free. ***Multi-channel service delivery*** is the term that describes a company's offering multiple ways in which customers can interact with it. E-mail, fax, phone, and the Web are all ways in which most companies interact with their customers. A fundamental goal of a CRM system, then, is the management and tracking of all these interactions. The communications within the various channels must be organized and carefully recorded for each customer. If that doesn't happen, then your experience with the company may be less than optimal and you may choose to change companies or perhaps return the product for a refund. It's not uncommon for a customer to change companies after having a negative experience. Thus, the overriding goal of CRM is to limit such negative interactions and provide customers with positive experiences (even delightful ones).

CRM systems (see Figure 2.3) typically include such functions as

- Sales force automation
- Customer service and support
- Marketing campaign management and analysis

It's important to note that CRM is not just the software. It is a total business objective which encompasses many different aspects of a business including software, hardware,

Figure 2.3

Customer Relationship Management (CRM) System

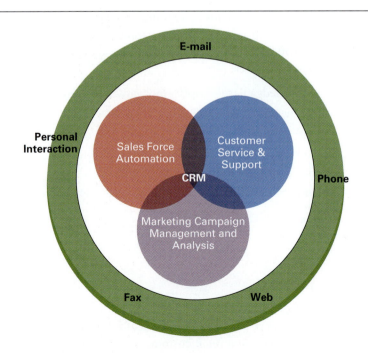

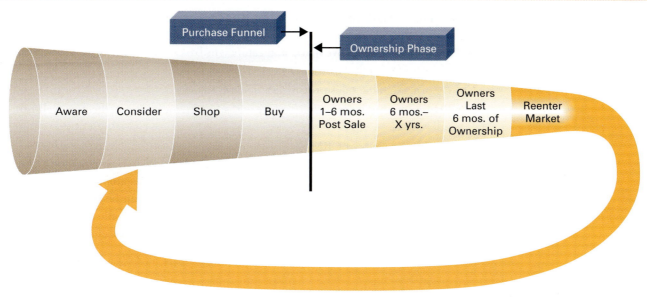

Figure 2.4

General Motors
Purchase Funnel[5]

services, support, and strategic business goals. The CRM system you adopt should support all these functions and should also be designed to provide the organization with detailed customer information. In many cases, companies begin with a sales force automation application and then progress to the other two functions. ***Sales force automation (SFA) systems*** automatically track all the steps in the sales process. The sales process contains many steps, including contact management, sales lead tracking, sales forecasting and order management, and product knowledge.

Some basic SFA systems perform sales lead tracking, or listing potential customers for the sales team to contact. They also perform contact management, which tracks all the times a salesperson contacts a potential customer, what they discussed, and the next steps. More sophisticated SFA systems perform detailed analysis of the market and customers and can even offer product configuration tools enabling customers to configure their own products. Some of the more robust CRM systems and methodologies, such as at General Motors (see Figure 2.4), focus on creating repeat customers. It is far more expensive to acquire a new customer than it is to retain an existing customer, especially in the automotive retail industry.

STRATEGIC AND COMPETITIVE OPPORTUNITIES WITH CRM

Overall, a well-designed customer relationship management system focuses on increasing revenue by providing delightful experiences for the customer in a variety of ways—tailored product and service offerings, seamless interaction, product knowledge, and so on. Thus, the primary focus of customer relationship management is

- Differentiation and focus (Porter's three generic strategies)
- Top-line initiative (revenue enhancement)
- Growing the organization (run-grow-transform framework)

Of course, customers are willing to pay only so much for these "delightful" interactions and product selections, so your organization must have a tight supply chain management system in place to ensure an acceptable price.

One of the rewards of CRM is competitive advantage through superior performance in CRM functions, in particular:

- Devising more effective marketing campaigns based on more precise knowledge of customer needs and wants.

- Assuring that the sales process is efficiently managed.

- Providing superior after-sale service and support, for example, through well-run call centers.

All the classic goals of CRM—treating customers better, understanding their needs and wants, tailoring offerings in response—are likely to result in buyers choosing your product or service instead of the competition's. Predicting the amount by which the CRM-enabled organization will gain market share, however, can be difficult. But certainly, it is something that can be measured after the fact, thus allowing your organization to understand the true results of better CRM in terms of customers' buying decisions.

IT SUPPORT FOR CUSTOMER RELATIONSHIP MANAGEMENT

Figure 2.5 shows a sample CRM system infrastructure. The ***front office systems*** are the primary interface to customers and sales channels; they send all the customer information they collect to the database. The ***back office systems*** are used to fulfill and support customer orders and they also send all their customer information to the database. The CRM system analyzes and distributes the customer information and provides the organization with a complete view of each customer's experience with the business. A typical back office function such as order fulfillment would have direct ties to the supply chain management system, creating synergy between the customer relationship management system and the supply chain management system.

There are many systems available today that a company can purchase that offer CRM functionality. Some of the bigger providers of these packages are Clarify,

Figure 2.5

A Sample CRM System Infrastructure

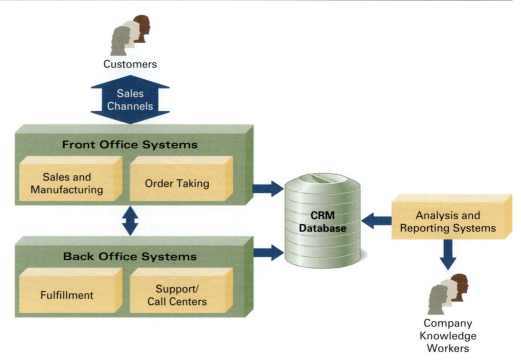

APC CREATES A WORLDWIDE PROTECTION PRESENCE WITH CUSTOMER RELATIONSHIP MANAGEMENT

"We want to know as much information about customers as we can possibly get . . . It's not only about being a supplier but a trusted business partner and advisor for customers to solve real business problems," explains Brian Belliveau, CIO of American Power Conversion (APC). APC's customers include consumers who purchase surge protection for high-end items such as home PCs and plasma TVs and also other businesses wanting to protect expensive computers and data centers from frying during thunderstorms.

APC's operational presence is already worldwide. With its corporate offices in Rhode Island, APC has sales offices all over the world and manufacturing facilities in the United States, Brazil, India, China, Ireland, Switzerland, the Philippines, and Denmark; it ships products around the world to over 160 countries. In 2005, 52 percent of APC's revenues were in the United States and Central America, 30 percent in Europe, the Middle East, and Africa, and 18 percent in Asia.

APC established a CRM initiative called the *Customer Loyalty Framework*. Using CRM technology provided by such companies as Siebel, APC identifies each and every touch point with customers, failed transactions, and what is needed to elevate customer satisfaction. APC has developed an automated credit approval process and expects the new function to yield $8 million in benefits over a three-year period.

Now, all employee bonuses are tied to customer satisfaction. As Brian Belliveau explains it, "All employee bonuses are tied back to customer satisfaction. If customers aren't happy and the satisfaction numbers are going down, everybody gets a piece of that. And if the numbers are doing better, we get a piece of that, too."[6, 7]

Oracle/PeopleSoft, SAP, and Siebel Systems (now a part of Oracle/PeopleSoft). Clarify and Siebel are also two of the most prominent SFA software providers; others are Salesforce.com and Vantive. Salesforce.com was the first company to offer CRM using an ASP (application service provider, which hosts its software on a Web server and allows customer organizations to use the software via the Internet) model, and others have since followed suit. For additional CRM resources, we encourage you to visit the following:

- Siebel Systems—http://www.oracle.com/siebel/index.html
- Salesforce.com—http://www.salesforce.com/
- *CIO Magazine*—www.cio.com
- MyCustomer.com—http://www.mycustomer.com/
- CRMToday—http://www.crm2day.com/
- CRM Knowledge Base—http://crm.ittoolbox.com/
- destinationCRM.com—http://www.destinationcrm.com/

E-Collaboration

LEARNING OUTCOME 3

Almost everything you do in an organization will be performed in a team environment. So, improving team collaboration greatly increases your organization's productivity and competitive advantage. Broadly defined, *e-collaboration* is the use of technology to support

1. Work activities with integrated collaboration environments.
2. Knowledge management with knowledge management systems.

3. Social networking with social networking systems.
4. Learning with e-learning tools.
5. Informal collaboration to support open-source information.

WORK ACTIVITIES WITH INTEGRATED COLLABORATION ENVIRONMENTS

For support of work activities you'll find *integrated collaboration environments (ICEs),* environments in which virtual teams do their work. *Virtual teams* are teams whose members are located in varied geographical locations and whose work is supported by specialized ICE software or by more basic collaboration systems. A collaboration system is software that is designed specifically to improve the performance of teams by supporting the sharing and flow of information. More and more, virtual teams are composed of people from your company's information partnerships as well, as we discussed earlier in the context of supply chain management systems.

Many companies first use e-mail and then move on to ICEs incorporating more advanced features such as giving employees access to each other's calendars, group scheduling software, imaging software, and the following.

- *Workflow systems* facilitate the automation and management of business processes. A *workflow* defines all the steps or business rules, from beginning to end, required for a business process. For example, all the steps to process a loan application in a bank could be enabled by a workflow system with the necessary documents updated and passed from employee to employee as electronic documents (complete with electronic signatures).
- *Document management system* manages a document through all the stages of its processing. It is similar to a workflow system except that the focus is more on document storage and retrieval.

KNOWLEDGE MANAGEMENT WITH KNOWLEDGE MANAGEMENT SYSTEMS

We introduced you to the notion of *knowledge* in Chapter 1. A *knowledge management (KM) system* is an IT system that supports the capturing, organizing, and dissemination of knowledge (i.e., know-how) throughout the organization. The objective of KM systems is to be sure that a company's knowledge of facts, sources of information, solutions, patents, trademarks, and best-practice processes are available to all of its employees whenever needed. For example, consulting firms make very effective use of KM systems by ensuring that consultants, working on a new project, can see and read what other consultants have done on similar types of projects. The idea is that there is both efficiency and effectiveness on an organizationwide basis if consultants don't have to continually "reinvent the wheel" when faced with a challenge similar to a challenge faced on another project.

SOCIAL NETWORKING WITH SOCIAL NETWORKING SYSTEMS

Most likely, you're familiar with some very popular social networking sites such as Myspace and Facebook. A *social networking site* is a site on which you post information about yourself, create a network of friends, read about other people, share content such as photos and videos, and communicate with other people. In the business world, social networks take on a different meaning and are referred to by the term *social networking system.* A *social networking system* is an IT system that links you to people you know and, from there, to people your contacts know. For example, if a salesperson at your company wants an introduction to an influential executive at another company, a social networking system could find out if someone in your company has good enough connections to arrange an introduction. This is exactly the kind of question that could get a quick reply from the right kind of social networking system.

Business-focused social networking systems, such as LinkedIn (www.linked.in.com), have been slower in subscriber growth than general-population sites such as Myspace and Google's Orkut. Nonetheless, business-focused social networking systems are gaining in acceptance, use, and profitability.

LEARNING WITH E-LEARNING TOOLS

Also in the area of e-collaboration we find *e-learning tools*. E-learning tools are IT-enabled systems that facilitate learning. You've probably worked with an e-learning tool such as WebCT, Blackboard, or e-College. These tools primarily focus on educational environments such as your school. But an important part of your career is ongoing learning and you will find numerous organizations that provide e-learning tools so their employees can learn on the job, in virtual classrooms, or in self-study environments $24 \times 7 \times 365$ days a year.

INFORMAL COLLABORATION TO SUPPORT OPEN-SOURCE INFORMATION

Integrated collaboration environments (ICEs), knowledge management systems, and e-learning tools are vitally important organizational resources. We say "organizational" here in reference to an actual organization such as a company or your school. There are also many informal organizations, such as a network of friends on Myspace, supported by social networking systems. Even more informally, groups of people may want to share information on specific ideas and topics. While you can do this with a blog or within a social networking system, many people are now gathering around *wikis*.

A *wiki* is a Web site that allows you—as a visitor—to create, edit, change, and often eliminate content—or *open-source information*. **Open-source information** is content that is publicly available (in a broad sense), free of charge, and most often updateable by anyone. The most popular and well-known wiki is Wikipedia (www.wikipedia.org). Millions of people use Wikipedia as a reference site and a large percentage of those people then participate in no predefined manner in the development, editing, and review of the content (hence, *open-source* information). Thus, wikis support very informal collaboration as opposed to the more formal collaboration that would take place in an organization when a team is working on a project.

STRATEGIC AND COMPETITIVE OPPORTUNITIES WITH E-COLLABORATION

The payoffs from collaboration can be huge. For example, while oil and gas exploration companies usually form joint ventures on large projects, they often do not collaborate on purchases of high-dollar-value commodities for the project. A recent survey estimated that the industry could realize up to $7 billion in annual savings by using collaborative technologies and seeking more collaborative preferred provider relationships.[8]

There are many examples of knowledge management systems successfully adding value. For example, in making the case for a knowledge system at Hewlett-Packard (HP), John Doyle, the former head of HP Labs, is credited with saying, "If only HP knew what HP knows."[9] What he meant by this was that there was a huge amount of valuable

Figure 2.6

A Few E-Collaboration Systems

Type	Basic Functions	Example	Web Site
Collaboration	Real-time collaboration and conferencing	LiveMeeting	www.microsoft.com
Workflow	Business process management	Metastorm	www.metastorm.com
Document management	Enterprise content management	FileNet	www.filenet.com
Peer to peer	Desktop and mobile collaboration	Groove	www.groove.net
Knowledge management	Knowledge capture, organization, location, and reuse	IBM Knowledge Discovery	www-306.ibm .com/software/lotus/ knowledge/
Social network	Leveraging your personal and professional network	Linkedin	www.linkedin.com

knowledge in the brains and files (both paper and computer) of HP employees. If HP knew what knowledge was there, and it was shared and accessible to others, it could be useful in solving critical problems, or could lead to ideas for new products and services. Finally, social networking systems and e-learning tools promise to forever change the face of business with respect to finding and making new contacts and facilitating learning. These types of e-collaboration tools are relatively new to business, but they already offer great efficiencies and effectiveness.

IT SUPPORT FOR E-COLLABORATION

There are literally scores of different e-collaboration software vendors and tools on the market today. Figure 2.6 provides a list of just a very few. The broad integrated collaboration environment market is dominated by the likes of IBM/Lotus, Microsoft, and Novell. There are many knowledge management systems available today with no clear-cut market leader. Social networking systems that are business focused are still relatively new but include LinkedIn, Spoke, and Tribe.net. A quick search of Google yielded over 300,000 valuable Web sites for exploring e-collaboration and supporting IT-based e-collaboration tools.

IT Culture—An Organizational Perspective

How your organization chooses its technologies and their implementation to support major business initiatives (and, for that matter, simple and mundane day-to-day processing activities) depends greatly on its IT culture. *IT culture* refers to how the IT function is placed structurally within an organization and the organization's philosophical

LEARNING OUTCOME 4

CONSTELLATION ENERGY: CONNECT. INTERACT. TRANSFORM.

When Beth Perlman joined Constellation Energy as its CIO in 2002, she noticed that employees didn't seem to communicate with each other—not necessarily around the water cooler or at lunch, but rather concerning vitally important documents, information, and knowledge. She immediately acquired and implemented a suite of standardized collaboration tools for everyone to use. The suite includes Microsoft Live Meeting for information sharing, SharePoint for document collaboration, and Windows Messenger for instant messaging. Just a year later the results were astounding.

Through Live Meeting, for example, the company held more than 10,000 hours of meetings, saving the company $41 per attendee and gaining an average of 98 minutes in productivity per employee. Constellation's "Connect. Interact. Transform." initiative has literally been enabled through the use of technology. And although initially Beth didn't think many employees would take advantage of document collaboration through SharePoint, she now believes that just about everyone is doing so. Take Kevin Hadlock, Constellation Energy's director of investor relations, for example. Because of SharePoint's deployment, Kevin can now spend more time analyzing data for earnings releases because he spends hundreds of fewer hours collecting the documents that go into the releases. For his analyst presentations, Kevin now claims to spend at least one week less in preparation because of SharePoint.

Collaboration tools can yield great benefits in the business environment. They don't have to be fancy or hard to use—they simply need to support people in their sharing of information.[10]

approach to the development, deployment, and use of IT. As you can see, IT culture has two primary aspects:

1. The structuring of the IT function.
2. The organization's philosophy as to the use of IT.

IT CULTURE—STRUCTURING THE IT FUNCTION

Structurally, your organization can place the IT function in any number of ways, with these three being the most common (see Figure 2.7 on the next page):

1. Top-down silo
2. Matrix
3. Fully integrated throughout the organization

In a *top-down silo* approach (the structure in the upper left of Figure 2.7), your organization would create a department or IT function devoted exclusively to everything related to technology—budgeting, project management, capacity, processing, and so on. Such an approach exhibits a strong "command and control" management style. All other functions (e.g., marketing, finance, etc.) must go through the IT department for approval of new projects, the generation of ad hoc reports, support functions, and the like.

In a *matrix* approach (the structure in the upper right of Figure 2.7), you will still find a separate IT department or function, but the goal here is to maintain IT personnel within the IT department but matrix them across the other functions. In this instance, IT considerations such as budgeting, project management, processing, and the like are done in concert with significant input from the other functions. While control still rests with the IT function or branch, everything becomes more collaborative across the organization.

In a *fully integrated* approach (the structure in the bottom of Figure 2.7), many IT personnel are now located within the other functional units, although there is still

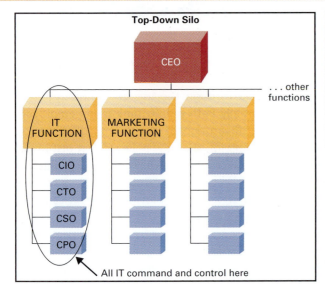

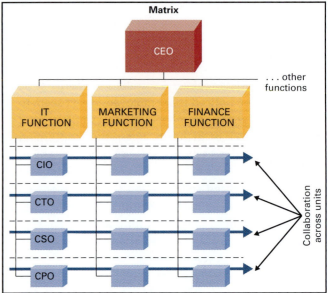

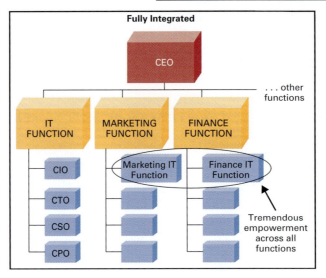

Figure 2.7

IT Culture—Structuring
the IT Function

usually a separate IT department or function. Moreover, these integrated IT people have their own budget, can approve department projects, and can initiate the end-user development of smaller projects, ad hoc reports, and so on.

In Figure 2.7, you'll notice a number of acronyms that may be new to you; these are significant and important strategic IT functions within an organization. They include

- *CIO (chief information officer)*—responsible for overseeing every aspect of an organization's information resource.
- *CTO (chief technology officer)*—responsible for overseeing both the underlying IT infrastructure within an organization and the user-facing technologies (such as CRM systems).
- *CSO (chief security officer)*—responsible for the technical aspects of ensuring the security of information such as the development and use of firewalls, intranets, extranets, and anti-virus software.

- *CPO (chief privacy officer)*—responsible for ensuring that information is used in an ethical way and that only the right people have access to certain types of information such as financial records, payroll, and health care.

All of these functions have in recent years joined the ranks of strategic management such as CFO (chief financial officer) and CEO (chief executive officer).

IT CULTURE—PHILOSOPHICAL APPROACH TO IT

The placement of the IT function within an organization is greatly influenced by the organization's philosophy as to the development, deployment, and use of IT. In Figure 2.8, you can see two axes. The horizontal axis provides a spectrum of philosophy ranging from organizations that are early adopters of IT to organizations that "wait and see" whether emerging technologies prove themselves before adopting them. Along the vertical axis structural placement of the IT function ranges from greatly decentralized ("fully integrated" in our previous discussion) to greatly centralized ("top-down silo" in our previous discussion).

Decentralized, early adopters of technology (top right quadrant in Figure 2.8) empower employees throughout the organization to try new and emerging technologies in the hope of finding a few that can provide significant competitive advantage. These organizations support and encourage *technology innovation failure,* a reward system for trying new technologies even if they prove to be unsuccessful. At the opposite extreme are centralized, wait-and-see organizations (bottom left quadrant in Figure 2.8) that require the demonstration of significant ROI (return on investment) before first adopting a new technology within the IT function and then deploying that technology to the rest of the organization.

Is any particular IT structure or philosophical approach better than another? The answer is definitely yes, depending on a number of factors. Companies looking for significant growth in an emerging industry would probably emphasize being a decentralized early adopter, while companies in a mature industry with little possibility for increasing market share would not. Overall, the IT culture within your organization should match its overall culture and be developed keeping in mind the industry in which your organization competes.

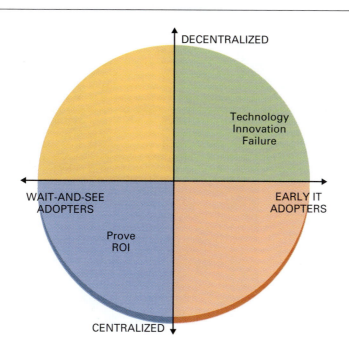

Figure 2.8

IT Culture—Philosophical Approach to IT

Enterprise Resource Planning— Bringing IT All Together

To this point, we've considered major business initiatives such as supply chain management, customer relationship management, and e-collaboration individually, focusing on the key strengths and advantages of each. But in the business world, you will deal with the issue of integrating them and making them work together. Consider supply chain and customer relationship management. They must work together, sharing information. To create tight supply chains that provide the right products and services at exactly the right time, you must know what customers want and when they want it (the province of customer relationship management). That brings us to enterprise resource planning systems, also known as enterprise software. An *enterprise resource planning (ERP) system* is a collection of integrated software for business management, accounting, finance, human resources management, project management, inventory management, service and maintenance, transportation, e-business, and—yes—supply chain management, customer relationship management, and e-collaboration. It may sound like a long list (and it is), but the central notion behind an ERP system is that it includes all technology systems and software in your organization.

In Figure 2.9, an ERP system allows transparent integration of functions, providing flows of information among all areas within the enterprise in a consistently visible manner. ERPs allow companies to implement a single integrated system replacing their *legacy* information systems. A *legacy information system (LIS)* represents a massive,

Figure 2.9

Overview of ERP System

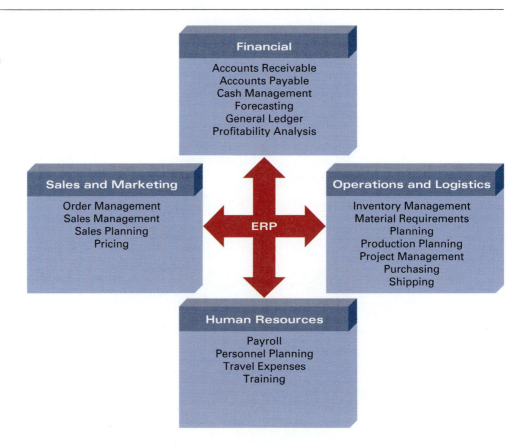

long-term business investment in a software system with a single focus; such systems are often brittle, slow, and nonextensible. ERP systems are configurable information systems packages that seamlessly integrate all the information processes in the company within and across all functional areas—financial, accounting, human resources, supply chain, and customer information. The result is (1) integrated information across the board (data, information, and business intelligence), (2) one suite of applications, and (3) a unified interface across the entire enterprise. An ERP system is required to have the following characteristics:

- Modular design comprising many distinct business functions such as financial, manufacturing, and distribution.
- A centralized database that organizes and manages information.
- Integrated functions that provide seamless information flow among them.
- Flexible best practices.
- Functions that work in real time.
- Internet-enabled.[11]

Different ERP vendors provide ERP systems with some degree of specialty, but the core functions are almost the same for all of them (see Figure 2.10). Some of the core ERP functions found in the successful ERP systems are the following:

- Accounting
- Financials
- Manufacturing
- Production
- Transportation
- Sales and distribution

Vendor/Web Address	ERP Specialties/Characteristics	Target Market
SAP www.sap.com	Customer relationship management, financial management, human resource management, and supply chain management	Large business
Oracle/PeopleSoft www.oracle.com	Financial management, human resource management, and supply chain management	Large business
SSA Global (Baan) www.ssaglobal.com	Customer relationship management, financial management, human resource management, and supply chain management	Large business
Microsoft (Great Plains) www.microsoft.com	Financial management, distribution, manufacturing, project accounting, human resource management, and business analytics	Small-to-medium business

Figure 2.10

ERP Vendors

- Human resources
- Supply chain
- Customer relationship
- E-business

You need to realize that ERP systems will not improve organizations' functionalities overnight. The high expectation of achieving cost savings (bottom-line initiative) and service improvements (leading to top-line revenue increases) is very much dependent on how good the chosen ERP system fits the organizational functionalities and how well the tailoring and configuration process of the system matches with the business culture, the IT culture, the strategy, and the structure of the organization. Overall, an ERP system is expected to improve both back-office and front-office functions simultaneously. Organizations choose and deploy ERP systems for many different benefits and reasons. In many cases the calculation of return on investment (ROI) is weighted against the many benefits expected.

It may be a challenge for you to wrap your brain around the concept of an ERP system without first-hand experience in using one. Consider your school for example, which to a greater or lesser degree, has some form of an ERP system. When you register for classes, for instance, you may not be able to do so because of outstanding parking tickets, overdue library books, an unpaid tuition balance, or a host of other reasons. And if you can register for classes, when you receive your tuition bill, it already includes allowances for government loans, scholarships, and the like. This is all possible because your school's individual IT systems—that each handle a different function such as registration, parking, tuition financials, and loans and scholarships—are tied together in the form of an ERP system. Businesses in the private sector (and some public sector ones as well) attempt to do the same thing on a grander scale (see Figure 2.11). These organizations integrate predictions of customer demands (customer relationship management) into an ERP system to drive other functions such as finance, manufacturing, inventory, transportation, and distribution (with the latter four being an integral part of supply chain management). Organizations even attempt to predict the acquisition of human resource talent in light of existing human resource attrition and the need for increased human resource capacity based on predicted customer demands.

Figure 2.11

The Integration within an ERP System

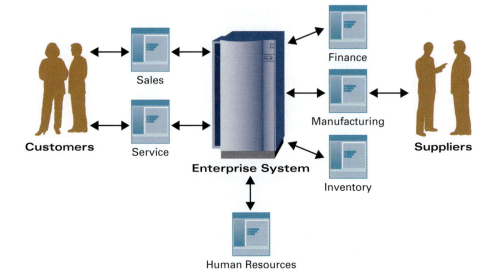

Customers — Sales — Service — Enterprise System — Finance — Manufacturing — Inventory — Human Resources — Suppliers

INVITE FEDEX INTO YOUR ERP

As you know from Chapter 1, competitive advantages can be fleeting and are at best only temporary. A few years ago, FedEx rolled out a customer-integrated Web package tracking system that gave it a substantial competitive advantage for about a year. The other package carriers then followed with similar systems and FedEx's competitive advantage was nullified.

FedEx's latest innovation through IT promises to be even better. Its new offering is called *Ship Manager,* a complete computer system that FedEx will install on your organization's site. Ship Manager allows you to easily weigh packages, calculate shipping, and print shipping labels. Of course, it will also automatically notify FedEx that you have a package ready to ship.

But it doesn't stop there. Ship Manager can then tie seamlessly into your ERP back-office systems, providing data to your customer billing, inventory, and warehouse operations functions. For example, the FedEx shipping number and expected arrival date for a specific package can flow directly into a customer purchase record. If that customer calls, your organization can quickly provide the shipping number and also the expected arrival date.

What FedEx really hopes to create with Ship Manager is a sustainable competitive advantage. Because Ship Manager integrates with your ERP system to provide the automated flow of information, why would you consider ever switching carriers? We'll have to see how the likes of UPS respond to FedEx's latest IT-based innovation.[12]

To say the least, everything in business is related to everything else in business. An effective customer relationship management system that accurately predicts product and service demand is of no use to your organization if that information is not seamlessly electronically flowed to a supply chain management system. Further, that CRM system is of no value if the SCM system doesn't effectively monitor the quality and shipping timeliness of suppliers to identify any weaknesses. Conversely, the best SCM system is no value to your organization if you don't have a CRM system that tracks the right information about your customers. Everything in business is related to everything else in business.

Summary: Student Learning Outcomes Revisited

1. **Define supply chain management (SCM) systems and describe their strategic and competitive opportunities.** A *supply chain management (SCM) system* is an IT system that supports supply chain management by automating the tracking of inventory and information among business processes and across companies. Strategic and competitive opportunities for SCM systems include:

   - Overall cost leadership (Porter), bottom-line initiative (cost reduction), running the organization (RGT framework)

   - Fulfillment—right quantity of parts or products at the right time
   - Logistics—low cost of transporting materials
   - Production—ensuring production lines run smoothly
   - Revenue and profit—no sales are lost
   - Cost and price—keeping part costs down and product prices at acceptable levels

2. **Define customer relationship management (CRM) systems and describe their strategic and competitive opportunities.** A *customer*

relationship management (CRM) system uses information about customers to gain insights into their needs, wants, and behaviors in order to serve them better. Strategic and competitive opportunities for CRM systems include:

- Differentiation and focus (Porter), top-line initiative (revenue enhancement), and growing the organization (RGT framework)
- Devising more effective marketing campaigns
- Assuring the sales process is efficiently managed
- Providing superior after-sale service and support

3. **Define e-collaboration and describe its strategic and competitive opportunities.** *E-collaboration* is the use of technology to support

- Work activities with **integrated collaboration environments (ICEs),** also with **workflow systems** and **document management systems**
- Knowledge management with **knowledge management systems**
- Social networking with **social networking systems**
- Learning with e-learning tools
- Informal collaboration to support **open-source information**

4. **Discuss the impact IT culture has on technology choices and their implementations**

within an organization. *IT culture* has two aspects. First is the structural placement of the IT function within the organization: *top-down silo* for a command-and-control approach to technology choices and their implementations; *matrix* for a more collaborative approach; and *fully integrated* for truly empowering employees to make technology choices and implementations. The second aspect of IT culture is the philosophy of an organization toward IT ranging from early adopters, who aggressively pursue emerging technologies hoping to find some good ones, to wait-and-see cultures that demand proven ROI before adopting a technology.

5. **Explain the significance of enterprise resource planning (ERP) software as the integration of functional software systems.** An *enterprise resource planning (ERP) system* is a collection of integrated software for business management, accounting, finance, project management, SCM, e-collaboration, and a host of other business functions. The basic goal of an ERP system is to provide (1) integrated information (data, information, and business intelligence), (2) one suite of applications, and (3) a unified interface across the enterprise. An ERP system replaces legacy systems and seamlessly integrates all functional software systems within an organization.

CLOSING CASE STUDY ONE

IS ERP THE ANSWER FOR A COMPANY THAT HASN'T MADE A PROFIT IN SIX YEARS?

Sun Microsystems lived and operated in a dream world throughout most of the 1990s, realizing significant revenue mainly from its line of server computers. Then, along came the dot-com implosion around 2000 and a new entrant into the market, Dell Computer. Dell had previously focused most of its efforts on providing customized personal computers. Its growth strategy was to take its famous and world-renowned sell-source-ship model into the server market. And that hurt Sun probably more so than the dot-com implosion. In fact, Sun hasn't earned an annual profit since fiscal year 2001.

When its fiscal year 2006 ended on June 30, it posted a loss of $864 million.

Previously, Sun did what many computer vendors did. It received unfinished products from manufacturers, stored them in warehouses, and configured them according to customer needs once a customer placed an order. As Eugene McCabe, executive VP of worldwide operations for Sun, explained it, "We knew we had to make some changes." And Sun did, with the rollout of the One Touch Supply Chain effort in 2004, in which products are sent directly from manufacturers to customers. This alone has cut in half the time between when you order a computer from Sun and when you receive it. As Eugene summarized it, "What we wanted to do is take that step out of the supply chain." "That step" was Sun itself—now when you order a computer from Sun, it never sees, handles, or warehouses it. Sun's logistics expenses have been reduced by more than $20 million annually, which helps alleviate the financial losses the company has been experiencing.

According to Robert Worrall, Sun's CIO, who has been with the company for 16 years, "We live and die by the supply chain and the demand cycle." So much so, that Robert estimated that 20 percent of the company's IT staff spends part of its time devoted to demand planning and supply chain systems. Those staff are now focused on One Touch Supply Chain. The infrastructure of that initiative is ERP applications from Oracle, supply chain management software from Manugistics, and demand planning software from i2 Technologies.

When you order a Sun server, One Touch Supply Chain determines which manufacturer can best fulfill your order and electronically transmits your order information to the manufacturer. The manufacturer assembles, configures, and tests your system before sending it directly to you. This increased efficiency in the supply chain has enabled Sun to deliver products to customers within the promised time 95 percent of the time, up from 85 percent. The manufacturers even tap into Sun's order-processing system and generate a customer invoice and shipping order for you.

Equally important, Sun has been able to close distribution centers in Asia, Europe, and the United States, creating valuable cost savings. It has also significantly cut inventory costs.[13]

Questions

1. In reference to Porter's Five Forces Model from Chapter 1, how was Sun affected by Dell Computer? Do you think Dell had a similar impact on other computer vendors in the same server market? Why or why not?

2. How closely does Sun's supply chain now mirror that of Dell Computer? Is it wise to "mimic" a competitor so closely? What about Blockbuster following the model of Netflix? How are they similar? What has Blockbuster added to its video rental model that appeals to people?

3. In this case study, we explained that Sun is now using software from multiple vendors—ERP from Oracle, supply chain management from Manugistics, and demand planning from i2 Technologies. Can this collection of software truly be an integrated, seamless, unified-interface, all-encompassing ERP system? How do you believe organizations get different pieces of software from different vendors to talk to each other?

4. What's on the customer relationship management side for Sun? How can it use the information it gathers on customers and their ordering habits to create a competitive advantage?

5. How has Sun created an information partnership with its supplier manufacturers? How has this information partnership created efficiencies in the supply chain?

CLOSING CASE STUDY TWO

IT'S ALL ABOUT CUSTOMER RELATIONS IN THE FINANCIAL SERVICES MARKET

Recently, the Principal Financial Group was honored as holding the number one ranking in *InformationWeek*'s annual survey of U.S. companies making the best of use of information technology. Principal's best use of technology centers around customer relationship management

as a strategy to fuel current and future growth. Principal manages $206 billion in retirement savings, investments, and insurance for more than 15 million employees working in over 100,000 small and medium-sized businesses.

Principal has a strong presence in the United States and also abroad. Principal's international business in 2006 grew to $604 million, up nearly 17 percent from the previous year. Principal operates in such countries as India, Hong Kong, Brazil, Chile, and Mexico. All told, it managed $6.7 billion in retirement assets outside the United States in 2006. Total revenues worldwide grew 8.5 percent in 2006, to $9 billion, while profits were up 9 percent, to just slightly over $900 million.

Principal's integrated approach to portfolio development and knowing each and every customer intimately has led it to engage its over 1,000 benefits counselors and 15 million customers in a Web-based and easy-to-use system that offers investment advice and gives each customer a personalized monthly snapshot (on paper as well) of their retirement outlook.

What's the role of information technology in all of this? As CIO Gary Scholten explains the big picture, "Our main purpose for IT is helping Principal grow, but the mantra we have is to help it grow responsibly." Nonetheless, the nitty-gritty of IT is where the real money is made.

Principal collects and analyzes huge amounts of information on each customer. Using that information, Principal can then sell them retirement plans, adding additional financial service products such as mutual funds and insurance. In the realm of insurance, for example, Principal can determine which of its customers would benefit most from fast-growing add-ons like vision, dental, disability, and life. The company even has a series of "milestone" financial service products. These allow Principal to offer advice to customers about moving money among funds and financial products as they near retirement or perhaps have children going off to college. To support this, Principal has gathered extensive information on each customer such as age, marital and family status, salary, and benefits.

Within the IT infrastructure, Principal has invested heavily in technologies that support fast turnaround times for transactions. Gary estimates that Principal processes almost 1 million online transactions per day (that's only 1 for every 15 customers). These transactions are processed and posted in record time, giving customers the satisfaction of real-time financial transactions.[14]

Questions

1. How are Principal's efforts an excellent example of the implementation of customer relationship management? In what ways has Principal developed significant knowledge and insight into the wants and needs of its customers?

2. With respect to the use of information technology, is Principal focusing on a top-line or bottom-line initiative? Perhaps a combination of both? Justify your answer. Within the context of the RGT framework (described in Chapter 1), what is Principal's focus?

3. Within the context of Porter's three generic strategies, is Principal mainly focusing on overall cost leadership, differentiation, or focus? Pick only one and justify your answer.

4. Principal really offers only services to customers; that is, it has no physical products to sell. How would Principal make effective use of an ERP system, while not needing modules such as manufacturing, transportation, and logistics? As more and more companies focus on only service offerings, do you see a need for a *service* ERP that targets companies like Principal?

5. If you were to consider the financial services needs of a customer over his or her entire lifetime (after college), what specific information would you want to know about a customer? We identified information such as age, marital and family status, salary, and benefits. What five other information "milestones" would you want to track?

Key Terms and Concepts

Back office system, 44
Chief information officer
  (CIO), 50
Chief privacy officer (CPO), 51

Chief security officer (CSO), 50
Chief technology officer (CTO), 50
Customer relationship
  management (CRM) system, 42

Distribution chain, 38
Document management
  system, 46
E-collaboration, 45

Short-Answer Questions

1. Why is the traditional buy-hold-sell inventory model an expensive and potentially risky one?
2. What is the role of a supply chain management (SCM) system?
3. How does SCM fit into Porter's three generic strategies?
4. What are the typical functions in a CRM system?
5. How does CRM fit into the RGT framework?
6. What is the difference between front-office and back-office systems?
7. For what five things does e-collaboration provide support?
8. What is the difference between a social network site and a social networking system?
9. What is open-source information?
10. What are the three most common ways in which the IT function can be placed within an organization?
11. How are the structuring of the IT function and the philosophical approach to IT interrelated?
12. What is an enterprise resource planning (ERP) system?

Assignments and Exercises

1. **COLLABORATION WORK** In a group of three or more students, collaborate on a project to make a list of your group's most popular music CDs. Then, classify the CDs into musical genres such as pop, classical, and so on. All communication about your project must be electronic (but not by voice or video phone). You can use e-mail, set up a Web site, use a chat room, use instant messaging, or use a collaboration e-room, if your school has that facility. Print out a copy of all correspondence on the project and put the correspondence together in a folder in chronological order. Was this task very different from collaborating face to face with your partners? In which ways was it better? In which ways was it worse? What additional problems or advantages would you expect if people you were working with were in a different hemisphere?

2. **WAL-MART'S SCM SYSTEM** Wal-Mart is famous for its low prices, and you may have experienced its low prices first-hand. At least, you have probably seen its motto, "Always Low Prices—Always." One of the biggest reasons Wal-Mart is able to sell at prices lower than almost everyone else is that it has a superefficient supply chain. Its IT-enabled supply chain management system is the envy of the industry because it drives excess time and unnecessary costs out of the supply chain. So, because Wal-Mart can buy low, it sells low. As a matter of fact, if your company wants to sell items to Wal-Mart for it to sell in its stores, you will have to do business with it electronically. If your company can't do that, Wal-Mart won't buy anything from you. Log on to Wal-Mart's Web site (www.walmart.com), search for supplier information, and find out what Wal-Mart's requirements are for its suppliers to do business with it electronically. Prepare a brief summary of its requirements for presentation in class.

3. **REAL WORLD APPLICATIONS** In the chapter we mentioned that many CRM installations have been less than successful. On the other hand, there are many satisfied users of CRM applications. Log on to the Internet and find at least three examples of companies that are getting real business benefits from their CRM systems. Prepare a report on the results they are getting and the ways they achieved them. One place to start your search is at www.searchcrm.com. Another good source is the Web sites of CRM application software vendors Siebel and Salesforce.com (www.siebel.com and www.salesforce.com). At least one of your examples must be from a site other than the three mentioned.

4. **ERP FOR THE SMALL BUSINESS** Most major ERP vendors have been focusing on selling multimillion dollar installations of their software to very large organizations. That is shifting in focus somewhat as ERP vendors realize that the small-to-medium-size business market is probably just as large. Search the Internet for ERP vendors that focus on small-to-medium size businesses. Also, search for open-source ERP software. Prepare a short report for class presentation and offer the vendors that you found and their Web site addresses.

5. **IT CULTURE** Interview someone working in the business world, a friend, a family member, or simply someone you know. Explain to him or her the three most common ways of structurally placing the IT function within an organization. Also, explain to him or her the range of philosophical approaches to the development, deployment, and use of IT in an organization. Finally, show the person Figure 2.8 on page 51. Ask him or her to point out on that figure where his or her organization would be located. Understand the justification for the decision. Make a short presentation to class. If necessary, you can omit the company name but do provide its characteristics.

Discussion Questions

1. Do you think your school would benefit from installing a customer relationship management (CRM) system? How might it benefit you as a student? How could it benefit your school?

2. Spoke is e-collaboration software that examines all employees' e-mail contact lists searching for people at potential customer sites who may be known to employees. Do you think a company has an ethical obligation to notify employees it is going to use Spoke, or (because it will search only computer files on company-owned computers) is it none of the employees' business?

3. In the run-grow-transform (RGT) framework, the third component is transformation, or enabling your organization to operate in entirely new ways. Of the three major business IT applications we discussed in this chapter (supply chain management, customer relationship management, and e-collaboration), which one(s) do you believe most support organizational transformation? Justify your answer.

4. Think about IT culture and its two main aspects—(1) the structural placement of the IT function within an organization and (2) the philosophical approach to the development, deployment, and use of IT. In terms of changing and transforming an organization, which of these two would present the greatest challenge? Justify your answer. Of the three types of structural placement of the IT function within an organization that we described, which do you believe is most common? Justify your answer.

5. We noted that it is extremely difficult to measure the success of a CRM system prior to its implementation and use. Why do you believe this is so? What can organizations do to develop measures of success before implementing a CRM system?

CHAPTER PROJECTS

Group Projects

- Executive Information System Reporting: Political Campaign Finance (p. 366)
- Developing an Enterprise Resource Planning System: Planning, Reporting, and Data Processing (p. 377)
- Evaluating the Next Generation: Dot-Com ASPs (p. 379)
- Building a Scheduling Decision Support System: Airline Crew Scheduling (p. 384)
- Assessing the Value of Supply Chain Management: Optimizing Shipments (p. 387)

e-Commerce Projects

- Consumer Information (p. 388)
- Demographics (p. 390)
- Bureau of Labor and Statistics (p. 390)
- Gathering competitive intelligence (p. 391)
- Meta data (p. 389)
- Gold, silver, interest rates, and money (p. 394)
- Small Business Administration (p. 396)
- Global statistics and resources (p. 394)

CHAPTER THREE OUTLINE

STUDENT LEARNING OUTCOMES

1. List and describe the key characteristics of a relational database.

2. Define the five software components of a database management system.

3. List and describe the key characteristics of a data warehouse.

4. Define the four major types of data-mining tools in a data warehouse environment.

5. Describe business intelligence and its role in an organization.

6. List key considerations in information ownership in an organization.

PERSPECTIVES

WEB SUPPORT

www.mhhe.com/haag

- Searching job databases
- Exploring Google Earth
- Financial aid resources
- Consumer information
- Demographics
- Bureau of Labor and Statistics
- Best of computer resources and statistics
- Global statistics and resources

CHAPTER THREE

Databases and Data Warehouses
Building Business Intelligence

OPENING CASE STUDY:
CAN COMPANIES KEEP YOUR PERSONAL INFORMATION PRIVATE AND SECURE?

Without a doubt, databases are one of the most important IT tools that organizations use today. Databases are large repositories of very detailed information. When a transaction occurs, a sale, for example, a database stores every detail of the transaction including your credit card number and other personal information, which products you purchased, what discount you received, the shipping schedule for your products, and so on.

Organizations must carefully manage their databases. This management function includes properly organizing the information in these information repositories in the most efficient way, ensuring that no erroneous information ever enters the databases, and—most important— protecting the information from theft and loss.

Information is a valuable commodity, and, sadly, there are bad people who want to steal valuable information. Much of that information is personal information. When someone steals your personal information (not necessarily by taking it from you but rather stealing it from a company you do business with), you can become a victim of identity theft. Identity theft is not some isolated event, something that happens to everyone else but you. Consider this short list of organizations that have lost information and the huge numbers of customers affected.

- CardSystems (40 million customers)
- Citigroup (3.9 million customers)
- DSW Shoe Warehouse (1.4 million customers)
- Bank of America (1.2 million customers)
- Wachovia (676,000 customers)

All those incidents of information loss occurred in 2005, and they represent only some of the worst losses in terms of numbers of customers. If each customer in the above list is unique, almost 47 million people had their personal information either stolen or lost. An even more staggering information loss was reported by TJX Companies—information on 45.6 million credit cards stolen between July 2005 and January 2007.

All organizations rely on a variety of technologies to analyze, manage, and securely store information. At the very heart of every organization are databases that store vast amounts of transaction information. This information is often very personal to large numbers of individuals, and all organizations have the responsibility to keep that information secure from predators. This chapter focuses on those large repositories of information (both databases and data warehouses) and the tools organizations use to manage and secure that information.[1,2]

Questions

1. Have you been a victim of identity theft? If so, what happened?

2. What can you do to protect yourself from identity theft?

3. How many organizations have your credit card number?

Introduction

As we've discussed in the first two chapters, you and your organization need more than just data and information. You need **business intelligence (BI)**—collective information about your customers, your competitors, your business partners, your competitive environment, and your own internal operations—that gives you the ability to make effective, important, and often strategic business decisions. Business intelligence enables your organization to extract the true meaning of information so that you can take creative and powerful steps to ensure a competitive advantage. Many such actions by your organization support some or all the initiatives we discussed in Chapter 2—customer relationship management, supply chain management, and collaboration, to name just a few.

Of course, to create business intelligence you need both data and *information* (we'll commonly refer to both as *information* in this chapter). Business intelligence doesn't just magically appear. You must first gather and organize all your information. Then, you have to have the right IT tools to define and analyze various relationships within the information. In short, knowledge workers such as you use IT tools to create business intelligence from information. The technology, by itself, won't do it for you. However, technology such as databases, database management systems, data warehouses, and data-mining tools can definitely help you build and use business intelligence.

As you begin working with these IT tools (which we'll discuss in great detail throughout this chapter), you'll be performing the two types of information processing: online transaction processing and online analytical processing. **Online transaction processing (OLTP)** is the gathering of input information, processing that information, and updating existing information to reflect the gathered and processed information. Databases and DBMSs are the technology tools that directly support OLTP. Databases that support OLTP are most often referred to as **operational databases.** Inside these operational databases is valuable information that forms the basis for business intelligence.

As you can see in Figure 3.1, you can also query operational databases to gather basic forms of business intelligence, such as how many products individually sold over $10,000 last month and how much money was spent last month on radio advertising. While the results of these queries may be helpful, you really need to combine product and advertising information (with several other types of information including customer demographics) to perform online analytical processing.

Online analytical processing (OLAP) is the manipulation of information to support decision making. At Australian P&C Direct, OLAP within a data warehouse is a must. P&C has created a data warehouse that supports its customer relationship management activities, cross-selling strategies, and marketing campaigns. By creating a data warehouse with customer information (including census data and lifestyle codes), its wide array of insurance and financial products, and its marketing campaign information, P&C agents can view all the products a given customer has purchased and more accurately determine cross-selling opportunities and what marketing campaigns a given customer is likely to respond to.[3]

A data warehouse is, in fact, a special form of a database that contains information gathered from operational databases for the purpose of supporting decision-making tasks. When you build a data warehouse and use data-mining tools to manipulate the data warehouse's information, your single goal is to create business intelligence. So, data warehouses support only OLAP; they do not at all support OLTP. As you can see

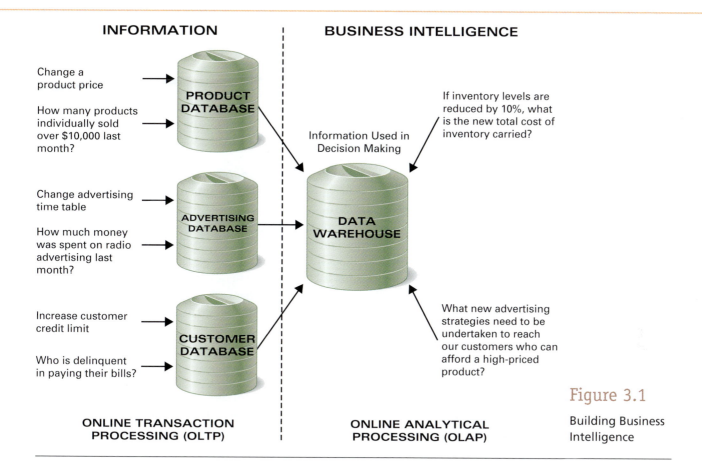

INFORMATION   **BUSINESS INTELLIGENCE**

Change a product price → **PRODUCT DATABASE**

How many products individually sold over $10,000 last month? →

Information Used in Decision Making

If inventory levels are reduced by 10%, what is the new total cost of inventory carried? →

Change advertising time table → **ADVERTISING DATABASE**

How much money was spent on radio advertising last month? →

DATA WAREHOUSE

Increase customer credit limit → **CUSTOMER DATABASE**

Who is delinquent in paying their bills? →

What new advertising strategies need to be undertaken to reach our customers who can afford a high-priced product?

ONLINE TRANSACTION PROCESSING (OLTP)

ONLINE ANALYTICAL PROCESSING (OLAP)

Figure 3.1

Building Business Intelligence

in Figure 3.1, you can perform more in-depth queries to gather business intelligence from a data warehouse than you can with a single database. For example, "What new advertising strategies need to be undertaken to reach our customers who can afford a high-priced product?" is a query that would require information from multiple databases. Data warehouses better support creating that type of business intelligence than do databases.

As this chapter unfolds, we'll look specifically at (1) databases and database management systems, (2) data warehouses and data-mining tools, and (3) the whole notion of business intelligence. Databases today are the foundation for organizing and managing information, and database management systems provide the tools you use to work with a database. To say the least, databases are the "heart and soul" of any organization because they organize and manage all of the organization's information resources. Data warehouses are relatively new technologies that help you organize and manage business intelligence, and data-mining tools help you extract that vitally important business intelligence.

As we first look at databases and database management systems in this chapter, we'll be exploring their use by Solomon Enterprises in support of customer relationship management and order processing. Solomon Enterprises specializes in providing concrete to commercial builders and individual homeowners in the greater Chicago area. Solomon tracks detailed information on its concrete types, customers, raw materials, raw materials' suppliers, trucks, and employees. It uses a database to organize and manage all this information. As we discuss Solomon Enterprises and its use of a database, we'll focus mostly on CRM and ordering processing.

The Relational Database Model

For organizing and storing basic and transaction-oriented information (that is eventually used to create business intelligence), businesses today use databases. There are actually four primary models for creating a database. The object-oriented database model is the newest and holds great promise. Right now, let's focus on the most popular database model: the relational database model.

As a generic definition, we would say that any **database** is a collection of information that you organize and access according to the logical structure of that information. In reference to a **relational database,** we say that it uses a series of logically related two-dimensional tables or files to store information in the form of a database. The term **relation** often describes each two-dimensional table or file in the relational model (hence its name **relational** database model). A relational database is actually composed of two distinct parts: (1) the information itself, stored in a series of two-dimensional tables, files, or relations (people use these three terms interchangeably) and (2) the logical structure of that information. Let's look at a portion of Solomon's database to further explore the characteristics of the relational database model.

COLLECTIONS OF INFORMATION

In Figure 3.2, we've created a view of a portion of Solomon's database. Notice that it contains five files (also, again, called tables or relations): *Order, Customer, Concrete Type, Employee,* and *Truck.* These files are all related for numerous reasons—customers make orders, employees drive trucks, an order has a concrete type, and so on. And you need all these files to manage your customer relationships and process orders.

Within each file, you can see specific pieces of information (or *attributes*). For example, the *Order* file contains *Order Number, Order Date, Customer Number, Delivery Address, Concrete Type, Amount* (this is given in cubic yards), *Truck Number,* and *Driver ID.* In the *Customer* file, you can see specific information including *Customer Number, Customer Name, Customer Phone,* and *Customer Primary Contact.* These are all important pieces of information that Solomon's database should contain. Moreover, Solomon needs all this information (and probably much more) to effectively process orders and manage customer relationships.

CREATED WITH LOGICAL STRUCTURES

Using the relational database model, you organize and access information according to its logical structure, not its physical position. So, you don't really care in which row of the *Employee* file Allison Smithson appears. You really need to know only that Allison's *Employee ID* is 984568756 or, for that matter, that her name is Allison Smithson. In the relational database model, a **data dictionary** contains the logical structure for the information in a database. When you create a database, you first create its data dictionary. The data dictionary contains important information (or logical properties) about your information. For example, the data dictionary for *Customer Phone* in the *Customer* file would require 10 digits. The data dictionary for *Date of Hire* in the *Employee* file would require a month, day, and year, as well.

This is quite different from other ways of organizing information. For example, if you want to access information in a certain cell in most spreadsheet applications, you must

ORDER FILE

Order Number	Order Date	Customer Number	Delivery Address	Concrete Type	Amount	Truck Number	Driver ID
100000	9/1/2004	1234	55 Smith Lane	1	8	111	123456789
100001	9/1/2004	3456	2122 E. Biscayne	1	3	222	785934444
100002	9/2/2004	1234	55 Smith Lane	5	6	222	435296657
100003	9/3/2004	4567	1333 Burr Ridge	2	4	333	435296657
100004	9/4/2004	4567	1333 Burr Ridge	2	8	222	785934444
100005	9/4/2004	5678	1222 Westminster	1	4	222	785934444
100006	9/5/2004	1234	222 East Hampton	1	4	111	123456789
100007	9/6/2004	2345	9 W. Palm Beach	2	5	333	785934444
100008	9/6/2004	6789	4532 Lane Circle	1	8	222	785934444
100009	9/7/2004	1234	987 Furlong	3	8	111	123456789
100010	9/9/2004	6789	4532 Lance Circle	2	7	222	435296657
100011	9/9/2004	4567	3500 Tomahawk	5	6	222	785934444

CUSTOMER FILE

Customer Number	Customer Name	Customer Phone	Customer Primary Contact
1234	Smelding Homes	3333333333	Bill Johnson
2345	Home Builders Superior	3334444444	Marcus Connolly
3456	Mark Akey	3335555555	Mark Akey
4567	Triple A Homes	3336666666	Janielle Smith
5678	Sheryl Williamson	3337777777	Sheryl Williamson
6789	Home Makers	3338888888	John Yu

CONCRETE TYPE FILE

Concrete Type	Type Description
1	Home foundation and walkways
2	Commercial foundation and infrastructure
3	Premier speckled (concrete with pea-size smooth gravel aggregate)
4	Premier marble (concrete with crushed marble aggregate)
5	Premier shell (concrete with shell aggregate)

EMPLOYEE FILE

Employee ID	Employee Last Name	Employee First Name	Date of Hire
123456789	Johnson	Emilio	2/1/1985
435296657	Evaraz	Antonio	3/3/1992
785934444	Robertson	John	6/1/1999
984568756	Smithson	Allison	4/1/1997

TRUCK FILE

Truck Number	Truck Type	Date of Purchase
111	Ford	6/17/1999
222	Ford	12/24/2001
333	Chevy	1/1/2002

Figure 3.2

A Portion of Solomon Enterprises' Database for Customer Relationship Management and Ordering Processing

know its physical location—row number and column character. With a relational database, however, you need only know the field name of the column of information (for example, *Amount*) and its logical row, not its physical row. As a result, in Solomon's database example, you could easily change the amount for an order, without having to know where that information is physically stored (by row or column).

And with spreadsheet software, you can immediately begin typing in information, creating column headings, and providing formatting. You can't do that with a database. Using a database, you must clearly define the characteristics of each field by creating a data dictionary. So, you must carefully plan the design of your database before you can start adding information.

WITH LOGICAL TIES WITHIN THE INFORMATION

In a relational database, you must create ties or relationships in the information that show how the files relate to each other. Before you can create these relationships among files, you must first specify the primary key of each file. A ***primary key*** is a field (or group of fields in some cases) that uniquely describes each record. In Solomon's database, *Order Number* is the primary key for the *Order* file and *Customer Number* is the primary key for the *Customer* file. That is to say, every order in the *Order* file must have a unique *Order Number* and every customer in the *Customer* file must have a unique *Customer Number*.

When you define that a specific field in a file is the primary key, you're also stating as well that the field cannot be blank. That is, you cannot enter the information for a new employee in the *Employee* file and leave the *Employee ID* field blank. If that were possible, you could potentially have two employees with identical primary keys (blank), which is not possible in a database environment.

Again, this is quite different from working with spreadsheets. Using a spreadsheet, it would be almost impossible to ensure that each field in a given column is unique. This reinforces the notion that, while spreadsheets work with information according to physical location, databases work with information logically.

If you look back at Figure 3.2, you can see that *Customer Number* appears in both the *Customer* and *Order* files. This creates a logical relationship between the two files and is an example of a foreign key. A ***foreign key*** is a primary key of one file that appears in another file. Now look at Figure 3.3. In it, we've provided the logical relationships among all five files. Notice, for example, that *Truck Number* is the primary key for the *Truck* file.

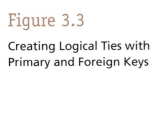

Figure 3.3

Creating Logical Ties with Primary and Foreign Keys

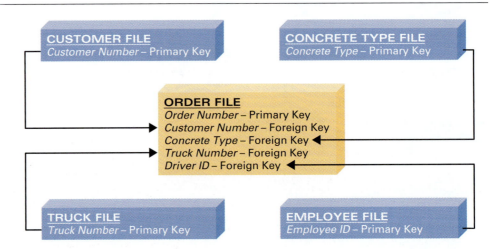

CUSTOMER FILE
Customer Number – Primary Key

CONCRETE TYPE FILE
Concrete Type – Primary Key

ORDER FILE
Order Number – Primary Key
Customer Number – Foreign Key
Concrete Type – Foreign Key
Truck Number – Foreign Key
Driver ID – Foreign Key

TRUCK FILE
Truck Number – Primary Key

EMPLOYEE FILE
Employee ID – Primary Key

BRITANNIA AIRWAYS FLIES HIGH WITH A CONTENT MANAGEMENT DATABASE

Airlines fly millions of passengers around the globe each year. That creates a lot of paperwork, too much, in fact. According to John Gough, Britannia Airways' E-Business Program Manager, "Britannia had over 120 forms related to the flight. We urgently needed to rationalize the amount of paperwork we were generating and the efficiency of our databases processes around the paperwork."

To create a competitive advantage and reduce the paperwork involved, Britannia implemented a content management database (a special kind of database) solution provided by Open Text Corporation (www .opentext.com). The content management database tracks and organizes information such as:

- Departure and destination times and locations of flight crews and passengers
- Capacity utilization information for flight crews and baggage handlers

- Customer relationship management information to flight attendants

The new system goes far beyond just an operational database that manages and organizes transaction information. It provides each crew member with a single log-in and point of access through a Web portal. The new system provides automated workflow capabilities to ensure that the right employees receive and process the necessary information in the least amount of time. It even provides forums in which all employees can record and discuss ideas for making flights better and more comfortable for passengers.

So, the new system supports both bottom-line efforts (i.e., optimizing information processing to reduce costs) and top-line initiatives (such as customer relationship management), giving Britannia the ability to grow and nurture relationships with its most frequent flyers.[4]

It also appears in the *Order* file. This enables Solomon to track which trucks were used to deliver the various orders. So, *Truck Number* is the primary key in the *Truck* file and is also a foreign key that appears in the *Order* file. There are other examples of foreign keys as well in Figure 3.3.

Foreign keys are essential in the relational database model. Without them, you have no way of creating logical ties among the various files. As you might guess, we use these relationships extensively to create business intelligence because they enable us to track the logical relationships within many types of information.

WITH BUILT-IN INTEGRITY CONSTRAINTS

By defining the logical structure of information in a relational database, you're also developing *integrity constraints*—rules that help ensure the quality of the information. For example, by stating that *Customer Number* is the primary key of the *Customer* file and a foreign key in the *Order* file, you're saying (1) that no two customers can have the same *Customer Number* and (2) that a *Customer Number* that is entered into the *Order* file must have a matching *Customer Number* in the *Customer* file. So, as Solomon creates a new order and enters a *Customer Number* in the *Order* file, the database management system must find a corresponding and identical *Customer Number* in the *Customer* file. This makes perfect sense. You cannot create an order for a customer who does not exist.

Consumer Reports magazine has rated the Ritz-Carlton first among luxury hotels.[5] Why? It's simple: Ritz-Carlton has created a powerful guest preference database to provide customized, personal, and high-level service to guests of any of its hotels. For example, if you leave a message at a Ritz-Carlton front desk that you want the bed turned down at 9 P.M., prefer no chocolate mints on your pillow, and want to participate in the 7 A.M. aerobics class, that information is passed along to the floor maid (and others) and is also stored in the guest preference database. By assigning to you a unique customer ID that creates logical ties to your various preferences, the Ritz-Carlton transfers your information to all of its other hotels. The next time you stay in a Ritz-Carlton hotel, in Palm Beach for example, your information is already there, and the hotel staff immediately knows of your preferences.

For the management at Ritz-Carlton, achieving customer loyalty starts first with knowing each customer individually (the concept of customer relationship management). That includes your exercise habits, what you most commonly consume from the snack bar in your room, how many towels you use daily, and whether you like a chocolate on your pillow. To store and organize all this information, Ritz-Carlton uses a relational database, and employees use it to meet your needs (or whims).

Database Management System Tools

LEARNING OUTCOME 2

When working with word processing software, you create and edit a document. When working with spreadsheet software, you create and edit a workbook. The same is true in a database environment. A database is equivalent to a document or a workbook because they all contain information. And while word processing and spreadsheet are the software tools you use to work with documents and workbooks, you use database management system software to work with databases. A ***database management system (DBMS)*** helps you specify the logical organization for a database and access and use the information within a database. A DBMS contains five important software components (see Figure 3.4):

1. DBMS engine
2. Data definition subsystem
3. Data manipulation subsystem
4. Application generation subsystem
5. Data administration subsystem

The DBMS engine is perhaps the most important, yet seldom recognized, component of a DBMS. The ***DBMS engine*** accepts logical requests from the various other DBMS subsystems, converts them into their physical equivalent, and actually accesses the database and data dictionary as they exist on a storage device. Again, the distinction between logical and physical is important in a database environment. The ***physical view*** of information deals with how information is physically arranged, stored, and accessed on some type of storage device such as a hard disk. The ***logical view*** of information, on the other hand, focuses on how you as a knowledge worker need to arrange and access information to meet your particular business needs.

Databases and DBMSs provide two really great advantages in separating the logical from the physical view of information. First, the DBMS engine handles the physical tasks. So you, as a database user, can concentrate solely on your logical information needs.

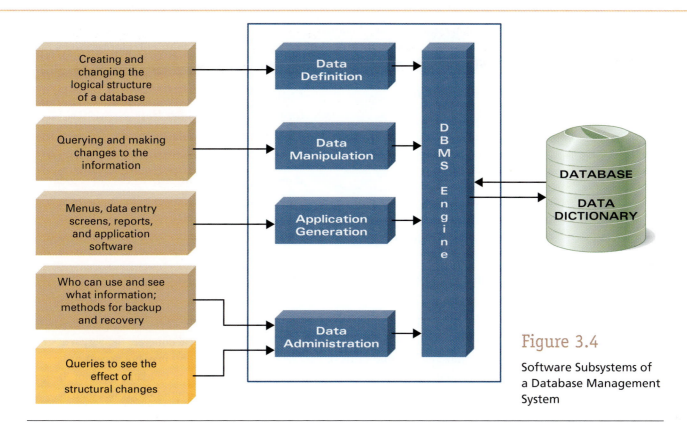

Figure 3.4

Software Subsystems of a Database Management System

Second, although there is only one physical view of information, there may be numerous knowledge workers who have different logical views of the information in a database. That is, according to what business tasks they need to perform, different knowledge workers logically view information in different ways. The DBMS engine can process virtually any logical information view or request into its physical equivalent.

DATA DEFINITION SUBSYSTEM

The *data definition subsystem* of a DBMS helps you create and maintain the data dictionary and define the structure of the files in a database.

When you create a database, you must first use the data definition subsystem to create the data dictionary and define the structure of the files. This is very different from using something like spreadsheet software. When you create a workbook, you can immediately begin typing in information and creating formulas and functions. You can't do that with a database. You must define its logical structure before you can begin typing in any information. Typing in the information is the easy part: Defining the logical structure is more difficult.

If you ever find that a certain file needs another piece of information, you have to use the data definition subsystem to add a new field in the data dictionary. Likewise, if you want to delete a given field for all the records in a file, you must use the data definition subsystem to do so.

As you create the data dictionary, you're essentially defining the logical properties of the information that the database will contain. Logical structures of information include the following:

Logical Properties	Examples
Field name	*Customer Number, Order Date*
Type	Alphabetic, numeric, date, time, etc.
Form	Is an area code required for a phone number?
Default value	If no *Order Date* is entered, the default is today's date.
Validation rule	Can *Amount* exceed 8?
Is an entry required?	Must you enter *Delivery Address* for an order or can it be blank?
Can there be duplicates?	Primary keys cannot be duplicates; but what about amounts?

These are all important logical properties to a lesser or greater extent depending on the type of information you're describing. For example, a typical concrete delivery truck can hold at most eight cubic yards of concrete. Further, Solomon may not accept orders for less than four cubic yards of concrete. Therefore, an important validation rule for *Amount* in the *Order* file is "must be greater than or equal to 4 and cannot be greater than 8."

DATA MANIPULATION SUBSYSTEM

The *data manipulation subsystem* of a DBMS helps you add, change, and delete information in a database and query it for valuable information. Software tools within the data manipulation subsystem are most often the primary interface between you as a user and the information contained in a database. So, while the DBMS engine handles your information requests from a physical point of view, it is the data manipulation tools within a DBMS that allow you to specify your logical information requirements. Those logical information requirements are then used by the DBMS engine to access the information you need from a physical point of view.

In most DBMSs, you'll find a variety of data manipulation tools, including views, report generators, query-by-example tools, and structured query language.

Figure 3.5

A View in Microsoft Access

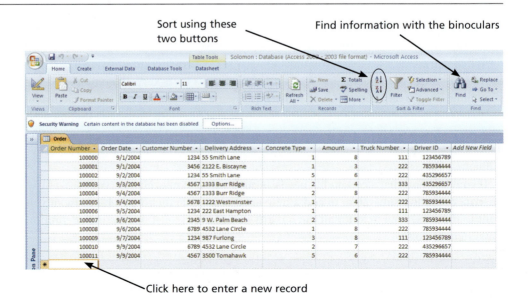

Sort using these two buttons

Find information with the binoculars

Click here to enter a new record

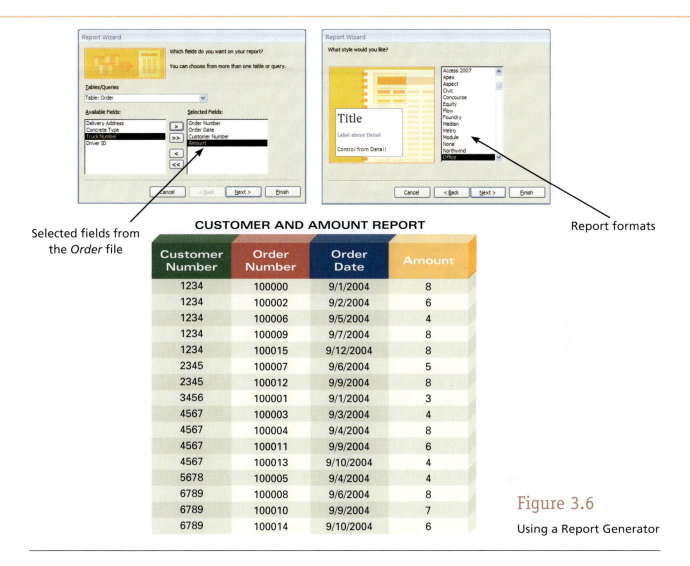

Selected fields from
the *Order* file

Report formats

CUSTOMER AND AMOUNT REPORT

Customer Number	Order Number	Order Date	Amount
1234	100000	9/1/2004	8
1234	100002	9/2/2004	6
1234	100006	9/5/2004	4
1234	100009	9/7/2004	8
1234	100015	9/12/2004	8
2345	100007	9/6/2004	5
2345	100012	9/9/2004	8
3456	100001	9/1/2004	3
4567	100003	9/3/2004	4
4567	100004	9/4/2004	8
4567	100011	9/9/2004	6
4567	100013	9/10/2004	4
5678	100005	9/4/2004	4
6789	100008	9/6/2004	8
6789	100010	9/9/2004	7
6789	100014	9/10/2004	6

Figure 3.6

Using a Report Generator

VIEWS   A *view* allows you to see the contents of a database file, make whatever changes you want, perform simple sorting, and query to find the location of specific information. Views essentially provide each file in the form of a spreadsheet workbook. The screen in Figure 3.5 shows a view in Microsoft Access for the *Order* file in Solomon's database. At this point, you can click on any specific field and change its contents. You could also point at an entire record and click on the Cut icon (the scissors) to remove a record. If you want to add a record, simply click in the *Order Number* field of the first blank record and begin typing. You can also perform a variety of other functions such as sorting, searching, spell checking, and hiding columns.

REPORT GENERATORS   *Report generators* help you quickly define formats of reports and what information you want to see in a report. Once you define a report, you can view it on the screen or print it. Figure 3.6 shows two intermediate screens in Microsoft Access. The first allows you to specify which fields of information are to appear in a report. We have chosen to include *Customer Number, Order Number, Order Date,* and *Amount* from the *Order* file. The second allows you to choose from a set of predefined report formats. Following a simple and easy-to-use set of screens (including the two in Figure 3.6), we went on to specify that sorting should take place by *Customer Number* and that the name of the report should be "Customer and Amount Report." The completed report is also shown in Figure 3.6. Notice that it displays only those fields we requested, that it's sorted by *Customer Number,* and that the title is "Customer and Amount Report."

A nice feature about report generators is that you can save a report format that you use frequently. For example, if you think you'll use the report in Figure 3.6 often, you can save it by giving it a unique name. Later, you can request that report and your DBMS will generate it, using the most up-to-date information in the database. You can also choose from a variety of report formats (we chose a simple one for our illustration). And you can choose report formats that create intermediate subtotals and grand totals, which can include counts, sums, averages, and the like.

QUERY-BY-EXAMPLE TOOLS   *Query-by-example (QBE) tools* help you graphically design the answer to a question. Suppose for example that Janielle Smith from Triple A Homes (*Customer Number* 4567) has called and ordered a delivery of concrete. Although she can't remember the name of the driver, she would like to have the driver that comes out the most often to deliver concrete to Triple A Homes. Solomon's task, from a customer relationship management point of view, is to go through all the orders and determine which employee most often delivers concrete to Triple A Homes. The task may seem simple considering that Solomon currently has very few orders in its database. However, can you imagine trying to answer that question if there were thousands of orders in Solomon's database? It would not be fun.

Fortunately, QBE tools can help you answer this question and perform many other queries in a matter of seconds. In Figure 3.7, you can see a QBE screen that formulates the answer to the question. When you perform a QBE, you (1) identify the files in which the needed information is located, (2) drag any necessary fields from the identified files to the QBE grid, and (3) specify selection criteria.

Figure 3.7

Using a Query-by-Example to Find Information

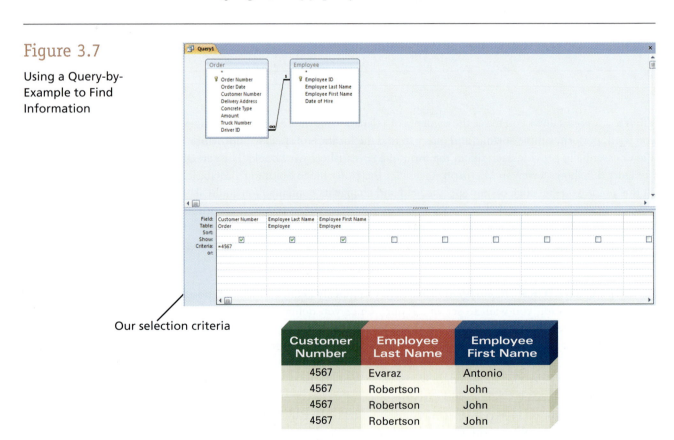

Our selection criteria

For the names of employees who have delivered concrete to Triple A Homes, we identified the two files of *Order* and *Employee*. Second, we dragged *Customer Number* from the *Order* file to the QBE grid and dragged *Employee Last Name* and *Employee First Name* from the *Employee* file to the QBE grid. Finally, we specified in the Criteria box that we wanted to view only the orders for *Customer Number* 4567 (Triple A Homes). Access did the rest and provided the information in Figure 3.7.

QBEs rely heavily on the logical relationships within a database to find information. For example, *Order Number* 100004 has the *Customer Number* of 4567 (Triple A Homes). So, the QBE tool took the *Driver ID* from the *Order* file for that order and found a match in the *Employee* file. When it found a match, it presented the *Employee Last Name* and *Employee First Name* (John Robertson). Without the logical relationships being correctly defined, this QBE query would not have worked properly.

STRUCTURED QUERY LANGUAGE   *Structured query language (SQL)* is a standardized fourth-generation query language found in most DBMSs. SQL performs the same function as QBE, except that you perform the query by creating a statement instead of pointing, clicking, and dragging. The basic form of an SQL statement is

SELECT . . . FROM . . . WHERE . . .

After the SELECT, you list the fields of information you want; after the FROM, you specify what logical relationships to use; and after the WHERE, you specify any selection criteria. Thoroughly introducing you to the syntax of building SQL statements is outside the scope of this text and would easily require almost 100 pages of material. But you should be aware that SQL does exist. If you're majoring in IT or MIS, you'll undoubtedly take a course in SQL.

APPLICATION GENERATION SUBSYSTEM

The *application generation subsystem* of a DBMS contains facilities to help you develop transaction-intensive applications. These types of applications usually require that you perform a detailed series of tasks to process a transaction. Application generation subsystem facilities include tools for creating visually appealing and easy-to-use data entry screens, programming languages specific to a particular DBMS, and interfaces to commonly used programming languages that are independent of any DBMS.

As with SQL, application generation facilities are most often used by IT specialists. As a knowledge worker, we recommend that you leave application generation to IT specialists as much as you can. You need to focus on views, report generators, and QBE tools. These will help you find information in a database and perform queries so you can start to build and use business intelligence.

DATA ADMINISTRATION SUBSYSTEM

The *data administration subsystem* of a DBMS helps you manage the overall database environment by providing facilities for backup and recovery, security management, query optimization, concurrency control, and change management. The data administration subsystem is most often used by a data administrator or database administrator—someone responsible for assuring that the database (and data warehouse) environment meets the entire information needs of an organization:

- *Backup and recovery facilities*—provide a way for you to (1) periodically back up information and (2) restart or recover a database and its information in case of a failure. A *backup* is simply a copy of the information stored on a computer.

SERVING CITIZENS AND GOVERNMENT AGENCIES WITH A GIS DATABASE

Databases on the Web typically serve a variety of users. In the case of Pierce County, Washington, its Web-based geographic information system database serves both its citizenry and county agencies. In a geographic information system (GIS) format, users of all types can query information according to geographical location. The county expects to save almost $3 million in maintenance costs by implementing its new Web-based GIS database.

The county citizens will use the database, via a simple Web interface, to query such information as neighborhood crime statistics, property-tax information, property-survey reports, and voting information like polling information and locations. The GIS database serves the citizens of Pierce County by providing easy access to these types of vitally important information.

Government agencies such as law enforcement, natural resource management, land development, and utilities will also have access to the GIS information. They will use the database to access and analyze such information as crime patterns, maps of public facilities, and information on terrains and contours. Law-enforcement and emergency-services personnel can even use wireless handheld devices to access the GIS database while in the field.

All told, Pierce County's databases will serve its citizenry and government agencies with almost 10 terabytes of GIS information.[6]

Recovery is the process of reinstalling the backup information in the event the information was lost. In Chapter 7, we talk specifically about how to develop plans and strategies in the event of some sort of failure. We call this business continuity planning or disaster recovery planning.

- *Security management facilities*—allow you to control who has access to what information and what type of access those people have. Always remember **CRUD**—**C**reate, **R**ead, **U**pdate, and **D**elete. Identifying who can perform those functions on various database information is vitally important.

- *Query optimization facilities*—often take queries from users (in the form of SQL statements of QBEs) and restructure them to minimize response times. Basically, these facilities find the "shortest route" to the information you want so you don't have to.

- *Reorganization facilities*—continually maintain statistics concerning how the DBMS engine physically accesses information and reorganizes how information is physically stored. For example, if you frequently access a file by a specific order, the reorganization facilities may maintain the file in that presorted order by creating an index that maintains the sorted order in that file.

- *Concurrency control facilities*—ensure the validity of database updates when multiple users attempt to access and change the same information. Consider your school's online registration system. What if you and another student try to register for a class with only one seat remaining at exactly the same time? Who gets enrolled in the class? What happens to the person who does not get his or her desired class schedule?

- *Change management facilities*—allow you to assess the impact of proposed structural changes to a database. For example, if you decide to add a character identifier to a numeric truck number, you can use the change management facilities to see how many files would be affected.

All these—backup and recovery, security management, query optimization, reorganization, concurrency control, and change management—are vitally important facilities in any DBMS and thus any database environment. As a user and knowledge worker, you probably won't deal with these facilities specifically as far as setting them up and maintaining them is concerned. But how they're set up and maintained will affect what you can do. So knowing that they exist and understanding their purpose are important.

Data Warehouses and Data Mining

Suppose as a manager at Victoria's Secret, you wanted to know the total revenues generated from the sale of shoes last month. That's a simple query, which you could easily implement using either SQL or a QBE tool. But what if you wanted to know, "By actual versus budgeted, how many size 8 shoes in black did we sell last month in the southeast and southwest regions, compared with the same month over the last five years?" That task seems almost impossible, even with the aid of technology. If you were actually able to build a QBE query for it, you would probably bring the organization's operational database environment to its knees.

This example illustrates the two primary reasons so many organizations are opting to build data warehouses. First, while operational databases may have the needed information, the information is not organized in a way that lends itself to building business intelligence within the database or using various data manipulation tools. Second, if you could build such a query, your operational databases, which are probably already supporting the processing of hundreds of transactions per second, would seriously suffer in performance when you hit the Start button to perform the query.

To support such intriguing, necessary, and complex queries to create business intelligence, many organizations are building data warehouses and providing data-mining tools. A data warehouse is simply the next step (beyond databases) in the progression of building business intelligence. And data-mining tools are the tools you use to mine a data warehouse and extrapolate the business intelligence you need to make a decision, solve a problem, or capitalize on an opportunity to create a competitive advantage.

WHAT IS A DATA WAREHOUSE?

LEARNING OUTCOME 3

A *data warehouse* is a logical collection of information—gathered from many different operational databases—used to create business intelligence that supports business analysis activities and decision-making tasks. Sounds simple enough on the surface, but data warehouses represent a fundamentally different way of thinking about organizing and managing information in an organization. Consider these key features of a data warehouse, detailed in the sections that follow.

DATA WAREHOUSES ARE MULTIDIMENSIONAL   In the relational database model, information is represented in a series of two-dimensional files or tables. Not so in a data warehouse—most data warehouses are multidimensional, meaning that they contain layers of columns and rows. For this reason, most data warehouses are really *multidimensional databases*. The layers in a data warehouse represent information according to different dimensions. This multidimensional representation of information is referred to as a *hypercube*.

In Figure 3.8 on the next page, you can see a hypercube that represents product information by product line and region (columns and rows), by year (the first layer), by customer segment (the second layer), and by the timing of advertising media (the third layer). Using this hypercube, you can easily ask, According to customer segment A, what

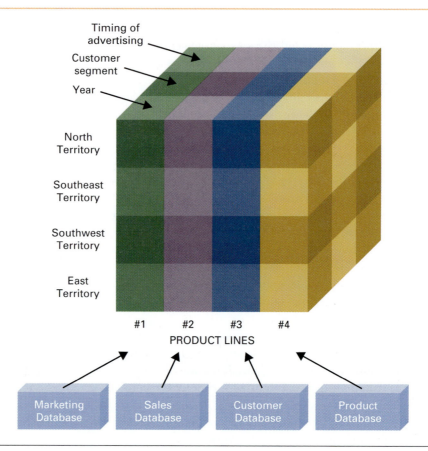

Figure 3.8

A Multidimensional
Data Warehouse with
Information from
Multiple Operational
Databases

percentage of total sales for product line 1 in the southwest territory occurred immediately after a radio advertising blitz? The information you would receive from that query constitutes business intelligence.

Any specific subcube within the larger hypercube can contain a variety of summarized information gathered from the various operational databases. For example, the forwardmost and top-left subcube contains information for the North territory, by year, for product line 1. So, it could contain totals, average, counts, and distributions summarizing in some way that information. Of course, what it contains is really up to you and your needs.

DATA WAREHOUSES SUPPORT DECISION MAKING, NOT TRANSACTION PROCESSING   In an organization, most databases are transaction-oriented. That is, most databases support online transaction processing (OLTP) and, therefore, are operational databases. Data warehouses are not transaction-oriented: They exist to support decision-making tasks in your organization. Therefore, data warehouses support only online analytical processing (OLAP).

As we just stated, the subcubes within a data warehouse contain summarized information. So, while a data warehouse may contain the total sales for a year by product line, it does not contain a list of each individual sale to each individual customer for a given product line. Therefore, you simply cannot process transactions with a data warehouse. Instead, you process transactions with your operational databases and then use the information contained within the operational databases to build the summary information in a data warehouse.

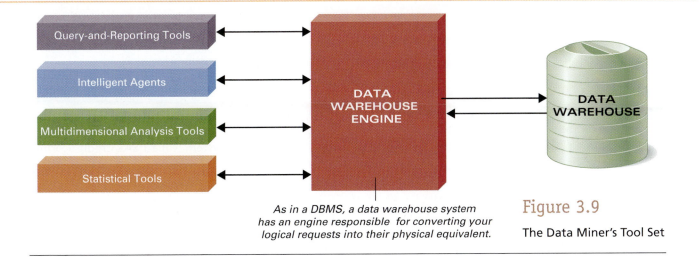

As in a DBMS, a data warehouse system
has an engine responsible for converting your
logical requests into their physical equivalent.

Figure 3.9

The Data Miner's Tool Set

WHAT ARE DATA-MINING TOOLS?

Data-mining tools are the software tools you use to query information in a data warehouse. These data-mining tools support the concept of OLAP—the manipulation of information to support decision-making tasks. Data-mining tools include query-and-reporting tools, intelligent agents, multidimensional analysis tools, and statistical tools (see Figure 3.9). Essentially, data-mining tools are to data warehouse users what data manipulation subsystem tools are to database users.

QUERY-AND-REPORTING TOOLS   *Query-and-reporting tools* are similar to QBE tools, SQL, and report generators in the typical database environment. In fact, most data warehousing environments support simple and easy-to-use data manipulation subsystem tools such as QBE, SQL, and report generators. Most often, data warehouse users use these types of tools to generate simple queries and reports.

INTELLIGENT AGENTS   Intelligent agents utilize various artificial intelligence tools such as neural networks and fuzzy logic to form the basis of "information discovery" and building business intelligence in OLAP. For example, Wall Street analyst Murray Riggiero uses OLAP software called Data/Logic, which incorporates neural networks to generate rules for his highly successful stock and bond trading system.[7] Other OLAP tools, such as Data Engine, incorporate fuzzy logic to analyze real-time technical processes.

Intelligent agents represent the growing convergence of various IT tools for working with information. Previously, intelligent agents were considered only within the context of artificial intelligence and were seldom thought to be a part of the data organizing and managing functions in an organization. Today, you can find intelligent agents being used not only for OLAP in a data warehouse environment but also for searching for information on the Web. In Chapter 4, we'll explore artificial intelligence techniques such as intelligent agents.

MULTIDIMENSIONAL ANALYSIS TOOLS   *Multidimensional analysis (MDA) tools* are slice-and-dice techniques that allow you to view multidimensional information from different perspectives. For example, if you completed any of the recommended group projects for Chapter 1, you were using spreadsheet software to literally slice and dice the

CREDIT SCORING WITH SAS AT CANADA'S LAURENTIAN BANK

Data mining has an untold number of applications that can help all types of businesses make better decisions. In the financial services industry, Canada's Laurentian Bank has turned to SAS (www.sas.com), the leading provider of statistical tools, to create a credit scoring model to approve loans for snowmobiles, ATVs, boats, RVs, and motorcycles.

According to Sylvain Fortier, senior manager for Retail Risk Management at Laurentian Bank, "Our objective was to improve our use of the technological tools available for data exploitation and analysis

that we needed to develop a scorecard internally. We wanted to develop a flexible system that would help us learn about our customers and business through the loan process." The system, called SAS Credit Scoring, develops a credit risk scorecard for each loan applicant based on a variety of information including socioeconomic data and determines the risk level of the applicant in the form of a score.

In just a few shorts months, the bank realized a 33 percent return on investment and expects to reduce losses on automotive loans by 8 percent.[8]

provided information. Within the context of a data warehouse, we refer to this process as "turning the cube." That is, you're essentially turning the cube to view information from different perspectives.

This turning of the cube allows you to quickly see information in different subcubes. If you refer back to the data warehouse in Figure 3.8, you'll notice that information by customer segment and timing of advertising is actually hidden. Using MDA tools, you can easily bring this to the front of the data warehouse for viewing. What you've essentially done is to slice the cube vertically by layer and bring some of the background layers to the front. As you do this, the values of the information are not affected.

STATISTICAL TOOLS   Statistical tools help you apply various mathematical models to the information stored in a data warehouse to discover new information. For example, you can perform a time-series analysis to project future trends. You can also perform a regression analysis to determine the effect of one variable on another.

Sega of America, one of the largest publishers of video games, uses a data warehouse and statistical tools to effectively distribute its advertising budget of more than $50 million a year.[9,10] With its data warehouse, product line specialists and marketing strategists "drill" into trends of each retail store chain. Their goal is to find buying trends that will help them better determine which advertising strategies are working best (and at what time of the year) and how to reallocate advertising resources by media, territory, and time. Sega definitely benefits from its data warehouse, and so do retailers such as Toys "Я" Us, Wal-Mart, and Sears—all good examples of customer relationship management through technology.

To learn more about today's best data warehousing and data-mining tools, visit the Web site that supports this text at www.mhhe.com/haag.

DATA MARTS: SMALLER DATA WAREHOUSES

Data warehouses are often perceived as organizationwide, containing summaries of all the information that an organization tracks. However, some people need access to only a portion of that data warehouse information as opposed to all of it. In this case, an organization can create one or more data marts. A *data mart* is a subset of a data

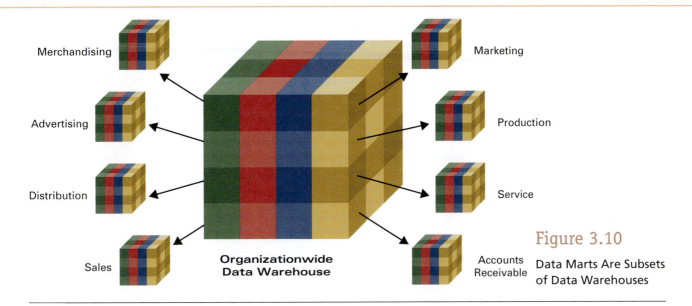

Figure 3.10

Data Marts Are Subsets of Data Warehouses

Merchandising

Advertising

Distribution

Sales

Organizationwide Data Warehouse

Marketing

Production

Service

Accounts Receivable

warehouse in which only a focused portion of the data warehouse information is kept (see Figure 3.10).

Lands' End first created an organizationwide data warehouse for everyone to use, but soon found out that there can be "too much of a good thing."[11] In fact, many Lands' End employees wouldn't use the data warehouse because it was simply too big, too complicated, and included information they didn't need access to. So, Lands' End created several smaller data marts. For example, Lands' End created a data mart just for the merchandising department. That data mart contains only merchandising-specific information and not any information, for instance, that would be unique to the finance department.

Because of the smaller, more manageable data marts, knowledge workers at Lands' End are making better use of information. If some of your employees don't need access to organizationwide data warehouse information, consider building a smaller data mart for their particular needs.

If you do choose to build smaller data marts for your employees, the data-mining tools are the same. That is, data marts support the use of query-and-reporting tools, intelligent agents, multidimensional analysis tools, and statistical tools. This yields efficiency in an organization with respect to training. Once you've trained your employees to use any or all data-mining tools, they can apply them to an organizationwide data warehouse or smaller data marts.

DATA MINING AS A CAREER OPPORTUNITY

Data mining represents a substantial career opportunity for you, no matter what your career choice. In the business world, you'll face numerous situations in which you need business intelligence to make the right and most effective decisions.

Fortunately, you don't have to be an IT expert to perform data mining. You can actually use a spreadsheet tool such as Microsoft Excel to build a three-dimensional cube similar to the one in Figure 3.8. You can then use Excel's other decision support features to build a graph, perform a regression analysis, and "turn the cube" by bringing new layers of information forward. You can do the same with Microsoft Access, by building a three-dimensional cube (i.e., data warehouse) of information stored in a database.

We definitely recommend that you learn to use these tools and then note your proficiency in your e-portfolio under "Technology Skills."

Beyond personal productivity tools, you should consider learning how to use some data-mining tools specific to the data warehouse environment. Some of the more popular ones include:

- Query and Analysis and Enterprise Analytic tools in Business Objects (www.businessobjects.com)
- Business Intelligence and Information Access tools in SAS (www.sas.com)
- ReportNet, PowerPlay, Visualizer, NoticeCast, and DecisionStream tools in Cognos (www.cognos.com)
- PowerAnalyzer tools in Informatica (www.informatica.com)

There are many, many others. You should have a look at your school's catalog of courses in data mining—you may find them offered in the technology department, statistics department, and other departments. We recommend that at the very least you become acquainted with the following: SAS (the leading vendor in statistical software), Cognos (the leading vendor in data warehousing and data-mining tools), and Informatica (the second-leading vendor in data warehousing and data-mining tools).

IMPORTANT CONSIDERATIONS IN USING A DATA WAREHOUSE

As is true with all types of technology, you can't simply implement a data warehouse and use data-mining tools just because they're a "hot" set of technologies and expect automatically to increase your efficiency and effectiveness. Always let your business needs drive your technology decisions. You have to need the technology and the technology has to fit your needs. With respect to data warehouse and data-mining tools, consider your answers to the following questions.

1. **Do you need a data warehouse?** Although great IT tools, they are not necessarily the best technologies for all businesses because (1) they are expensive, (2) they may not be necessary since some businesses can easily extract all the business intelligence they need from databases, and (3) they require extensive and often expensive support.

2. **Do all your employees need an entire data warehouse?** If not, consider building data marts.

3. **How up-to-date must the information be?** To create a data warehouse, you take "snapshots" of database information and load it into a data warehouse. If crucial information changes every second, this may not be possible.

4. **What data-mining tools do you need?** User needs should always drive the answer to this question. Whichever you choose, training will be key. If your users can fully exploit all the features of their chosen data-mining tools, your entire organization will reap the benefits.

Business Intelligence Revisited

LEARNING OUTCOME 5

Business intelligence is one of the hottest topics and markets today. The entire BI market (both hardware and software) is in the range of $50 billion annually with double-digit growth expected for the next several years. When *InformationWeek* asked 300 business technology managers about their immediate project plans, 44 percent identified data warehouses and 43 percent identified data-mining tools.[12]

"We were desperate to get good information quickly," explained Joel Taylor, director of IS for FiberMark North America, a manufacturer of specialty packaging and paper, which could not easily retrieve business intelligence from its expensive transaction processing systems. To address this problem, Taylor spent less than $75,000 on QlikView—BI software from QlikTech (www.qliktech.com). FiberMark's 29 salespeople, who previously printed 1,000-page monthly sales reports, now print on the average only four pages and it's exactly the four pages of business intelligence they need. The $75,000 investment paid for itself in nine months in saved paper and related costs alone. Of course, the real benefit is that salespeople and executives can get the specific, up-to-date BI they want anytime they want it.[13]

FiberMark is one of thousands of success stories related to business intelligence. (Of course, an equal number have probably not met with as much success, sometimes because they did not adequately identify which technology they needed.) The objective of BI is to improve the timeliness and quality of the input for decision making by helping knowledge workers to understand the

- Capabilities available in the organization.
- State of the art, trends, and future directions in the markets.
- Technological, demographic, economic, political, social, and regulatory environments in which the organization competes (remember Porter's Five Forces Model).
- Actions of competitors and the implications of these actions.[14]

As illustrated in Figure 3.11, BI encompasses both internal and external information. Some business people treat *competitive intelligence* as a specialized branch of business intelligence. **Competitive intelligence (CI)** is business intelligence focused on the external competitive environment. There is even an organization for people who specialize in competitive intelligence called the Society for Competitive Intelligence Professionals (SCIP, at www.scip.org).

A survey of the strategic uses of business intelligence by the Gartner Group found that such uses were ranked by firms in the following order of importance:

1. Corporate performance management.
2. Optimizing customer relations, monitoring business activity, and traditional decision support.
3. Packaged stand-alone BI applications for specific operations or strategies.
4. Management reporting of business intelligence.[15]

As we have stressed, one of the primary purposes of BI is to improve the timeliness and quality of input to the decision process. Companies with well-designed BI systems available to their managers find that their managers make better decisions on a variety of business issues. Higher quality managerial decision making lets companies gain an advantage over their competitors who operate without the benefit of BI systems for their managers to use. BI systems provide managers with actionable information and knowledge:

- at the right time
- in the right location
- in the right form[16]

One particularly interesting feature of many BI software packages is a *digital dashboard*. A **digital dashboard** displays key information

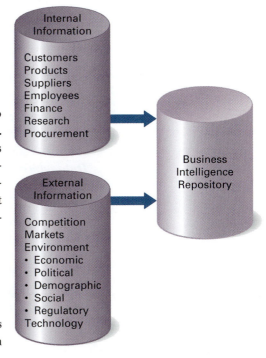

Figure 3.11

Building Business Intelligence

Internal Information

Customers
Products
Suppliers
Employees
Finance
Research
Procurement

External Information

Competition
Markets
Environment
- Economic
- Political
- Demographic
- Social
- Regulatory
Technology

Business Intelligence Repository

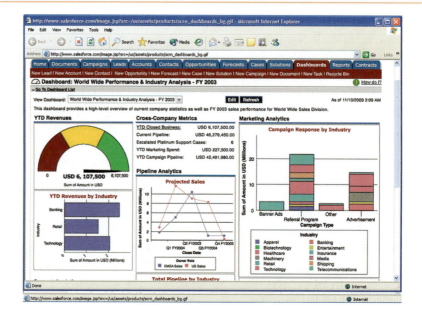

Figure 3.12

Sample Digital Dashboard

gathered from several sources on a computer screen in a format tailored to the needs and wants of an individual knowledge worker (see Figure 3.12). Digital dashboards can provide up-to-the-minute snapshots of any type of information and can often help you identify trends that may represent opportunities or that may be problems.

Information Ownership

LEARNING OUTCOME 6

Your organization will be successful, in part, because of your ability to organize and manage information in a way that best moves the organization toward its goals. As we close this chapter, let's look at the notion of *information ownership* and what it means.

STRATEGIC MANAGEMENT SUPPORT

As we discussed in Chapter 2, an organization's *IT culture* defines how the organization structures and views both the IT department and information responsibilities within it. Starting with vitally important roles such as CPO (chief privacy officer), CSO (chief security officer), CIO (chief information officer), and CTO (chief technology officer), organizations work down through the organization defining additional positions of responsibility with respect to the management of information and IT. Two of those positions are data administration and database administration.

Data administration is the function in an organization that plans for, oversees the development of, and monitors the information resource. This function must be completely in tune with the strategic direction of the organization to assure that all information requirements can be and are being met. *Database administration* is the function in an organization that is responsible for the more technical and operational aspects of managing the information contained in organizational information repositories (databases, data warehouses, and data marts). Database administration functions include defining and organizing database structures and contents, developing security procedures (in concert with the CSO), and approving and monitoring the development of database and database applications.

SUPPORTING HEALTH CARE WITH ELECTRONIC MEDICAL RECORDS

In 2008, employers are estimated to pay 58 percent and employees 81 percent more for health care than they did in 2002. Those are percentage increases we would like to have in our investment portfolios, not in an expense category such as health care. In 2007, Intel spent approximately $1 billion on employee health care.

To be sure, health care costs are rising. In spite of low-cost generic prescription medications and the like, it's simply becoming more and more expensive to provide quality health care. But there is another factor weighing on rising health care costs and it's technology related. The costs associated with storing, organizing, and managing health care information are skyrocketing at an astronomical pace. Even more so, there are no well-defined standards for what an electronic medical record should look like. As a result, almost every health care provider and insurer stores medical records in different formats, making it almost impossible to share information from company to company.

This has everyone scared—so much so, that the federal government has created a panel, the Health Information Technology Standards Panel, and charged it with selecting a single standard for the health care industry to adopt. But therein lies another problem. To select the electronic standard being used by only one or a few health care companies would mean that all others have to change their systems, and that would be expensive.

Nonetheless, the standardized electronic medical record is an imperative. With it in place, health care costs can go down because of the ease, speed, and efficiency with which organizations will be able to organize and manage information in a database.[17]

In large organizations, both of these administrative functions are usually handled by steering committees rather than by a single individual. These steering committees are responsible for their respective functions and for reporting to the CIO.

SHARING INFORMATION WITH RESPONSIBILITY

Information sharing in your organization means that anyone—regardless of title or department—can access and use whatever information he or she needs. But information sharing brings to light an important question: Does anyone in your organization *own* the information? In other words, if everyone shares the information, who is ultimately responsible for providing the information and assuring the quality of the information? Information ownership is a key consideration in today's information-based business environment. Someone must accept full responsibility for providing specific pieces of information and ensuring the quality of that information. If you find the wrong information is stored in the organization's data warehouse, you must be able to determine the source of the problem and whose responsibility it is.

INFORMATION CLEANLINESS

Information "cleanliness" (an aspect of information ownership) is an important topic today and will be for many years. Have you ever received the same piece of advertising mail (snail mail, that is) multiple times from the same company on the same day? Many people have, and it's an example of "unclean" information. The reason may be your name may appear twice in a database, once with your middle initial and once without it. Or your name may appear twice in a database with two different spellings of your last name.

In all popular business-oriented DBMSs, such as Oracle, you can find utilities to help you "clean" your information. In the case of having your information twice in a database with two different spellings of your last name, the utility would probably determine that the two records actually belong to the same person (you) because of the identical nature of other associated information such as your address and phone number. Always remember GIGO—garbage in, garbage out (from Chapter 1). If bad information—such as duplicate records for the same customer—goes into the decision-making process, you can rest assured that the decision outcome will not be optimal.

Summary: Student Learning Outcomes Revisited

1. **List and describe the key characteristics of a relational database.** The *relational database* model uses a series of logically related two-dimensional tables or files to store information in the form of a database. Key characteristics include

   - A collection of information—Composed of many files or tables of information that are related to each other
   - Contain logical structures—You care only about the logical information and not about how it's physically stored or where it's physically located
   - Have logical ties among the information—All the files in a database are related in that some *primary keys* of certain files appear as *foreign keys* in others
   - Possess built-in *integrity constraints*—When creating the data dictionary for a database, you can specify rules by which the information must be entered (e.g., not blank, etc.)

2. **Define the five software components of a database management system.** The five software components of a database management system include

   - *DBMS engine*—Accepts logical requests from the various other DBMS subsystems, converts them into their physical equivalent, and actually accesses the database and data dictionary as they exist on a storage device
   - *Data definition subsystem*—Helps you create and maintain the data dictionary and define the structure of the files in a database

   - *Data manipulation subsystem*—Helps you add, change, and delete information in a database and query it for valuable information
   - *Application generation subsystem*—Contains facilities to help you develop transaction-intensive applications
   - *Data administration subsystem*—Helps you manage the overall database environment by providing facilities for backup and recovery, security management, query optimization, concurrency control, and change management

3. **List and describe the key characteristics of a data warehouse.** The key characteristics of a data warehouse include

   - Multidimensional—While databases store information in two-dimensional tables, data warehouses include layers to represent information according to different dimensions
   - Support decision making—Data warehouses, because they contain summarized information, support business activities and decision-making tasks, not transaction processing

4. **Define the four major types of data-mining tools in a data warehouse environment.** The four major types of data-mining tools in a data warehouse environment include

   - *Query-and-reporting tools*—Similar to QBE tools, SQL, and report generators in the typical database environment
   - *Intelligent agents*—Utilize various artificial intelligence tools such as neural networks and fuzzy logic to form the basis of "information

discovery" and building business intelligence in OLAP

- *Multidimensional analysis (MDA) tools*— Slice-and-dice techniques that allow you to view multidimensional information from different perspectives
- **Statistical tools**—Help you apply various mathematical models to the information stored in a data warehouse to discover new information

5. **Describe business intelligence and its role in an organization.** *Business intelligence* is collective information—about your customers, your competitors, your partners, your competitive environment, and your own internal operations— that gives you the ability to make effective, important, and often strategic business decisions. Business intelligence is much more than just a list of your products or to whom you've sold them. It might combine your product information with your advertising strategy information and customer demographics, for instance, to help you determine the effectiveness of various advertising media on demographic groups segmented by location.

6. **List key considerations in information ownership in an organization.** Key considerations in information ownership in an organization include:

- Strategic management support
- The sharing of information with responsibility
- Information cleanliness

BEN & JERRY'S, BIGELOW TEAS, AND BUSINESS INTELLIGENCE

Organizations want information. Organizations need information. However, information must be in an organized format that supports the creation of business intelligence. Otherwise, according to Rebecca Wettemann, vice president of Research at Nucleus Research, "It's like having a bank account with millions of dollars in it but no ATM card. If you can't get it [business intelligence] and can't make it work for you, then it is not really useful."

In support of creating and using business intelligence, companies have focused much of their spending efforts on business intelligence software and data-mining tools. According to a Merrill Lynch survey in 2003, business intelligence software and data-mining tools were at the top of the technology spending list of CIOs. And according to A. G. Edwards, the market for that type of software is expected to grow from $4.7 billion in 2003 to $7.5 billion in 2006.

Consider two companies—Ben & Jerry's and Bigelow Teas—and their approach to creating and using business intelligence.

BEN & JERRY'S

Ben & Jerry's, located in Waterbury, Vermont, produces 190,000 pints of ice cream and frozen yogurt daily and ships to over 50,000 grocery stores in the United States and 12 other countries. Every single pint is meticulously tracked, first by being entered into an Oracle database. With that information carefully organized, Ben & Jerry's uses a sophisticated data-mining tool set from a company called Business Objects.

For example, the sales people can easily monitor sales to determine how much ground Cherry Garcia Frozen Yogurt is gaining on Cherry Garcia Ice Cream, its number one selling product. The consumer affairs staff can even correlate each of the several hundred calls and e-mails received each week to the exact pint of ice cream. If complaints are consistent concerning a specific batch, the consumer affairs staff can drill down to the supplier who provided the ingredients such as milk or eggs.

In one particular instance, Ben & Jerry's received a large number of complaints that its Cherry Garcia Ice Cream didn't have enough cherries. The complaints were coming in from all over the country, so it wasn't a regional problem. Employees continued drilling through business intelligence with Business Objects and determined that the manufacturing process (from the supplies of raw materials to the mixing) was satisfactory and had no anomalies. Eventually the problem was determined to be that the ice cream box for Cherry Garcia Ice Cream had on it a photo of frozen yogurt, a product with more cherries than the ice cream. Simply changing the photo on the box solved the problem.

BIGELOW TEAS

Bigelow Teas provides over 50 varieties of flavored, traditional, iced, decaffeinated, and herbal teas. Over the past 50 years, Bigelow Teas has relied on business intelligence to determine the success of each individual tea, and today is no different.

Although it may not seem like it, bringing a new tea to the market is a risky endeavor. It could fail in every way or it could simply cannibalize the sales of an existing tea, neither of which makes business sense. Employees at Bigelow Teas pore over consumer, sales, marketing, and finance business intelligence to ensure that they are making the right decisions in all aspects of the business.

To help facilitate the creation and use of business intelligence, Bigelow Teas turned to the Andrews Consulting Group and BusinessObjects. Prior to using BusinessObjects, Bigelow employees had a difficult time finding and using the right information. As Melanie Dower, project leader at Bigelow Teas, describes it, "Our existing end-user reporting tool wasn't user-friendly, so users simply weren't using it. Most users were unable to create their own reports, so we looked for a solution that offered self-serve business intelligence (BI) to free up IT resources." BusinessObjects is both easy to learn and easy to use because it looks like Microsoft Excel. Explains Dower, "Enterprise 6 [of BusinessObjects] looks and feels like Microsoft Excel, which speeds up the learning curve for our end users."

With BusinessObjects, Bigelow employees can access and view business intelligence in real time, more accurately predict sales forecasts based on shipment levels, identify where to increase sales efforts before it's too late, and even compare current consumer, sales, and marketing information with similar types of information up to five years old.

Gourmet coffees exploded onto the consumer market about seven years ago and gourmet teas quickly followed. Bigelow Teas is riding this wave of success with success of its own because of its use of business intelligence.[18,19,20]

Questions

1. Ben & Jerry's tracks a wealth of information on each pint of ice cream and frozen yogurt. If you were to design Ben & Jerry's data warehouse, what dimensions of information would you include? As you develop your list of dimensions, consider every facet of Ben & Jerry's business operations, from supply chain management to retail store monitoring.

2. Databases are the underlying technology that allows Ben & Jerry's to track ice cream and frozen yogurt information. Based on your knowledge of databases, what sort of tables or files of information would Ben & Jerry's need in its database? What would be the primary keys for each of those? What would be the foreign keys among those to create the necessary relationships?

3. According to the discussion of Bigelow Teas, part of the success of BusinessObjects comes from its look and feel being similar to Microsoft Excel. Why do you believe this is true? When introducing employees to enterprisewide BI tools such as BusinessObjects, why is it an advantage to have the BI tool look like and work like personal productivity software tools? Why was a similar look and feel to spreadsheet software more important than word processing or presentation software?

4. How could Bigelow Teas open up its business intelligence information to its suppliers and resellers? What benefits would Bigelow Teas gain by keeping its suppliers and resellers more informed with business intelligence? What types of business intelligence would Bigelow Teas want to exclude its suppliers and resellers from seeing? Why?

5. Neil Hastie, CIO at TruServe Corporation, once described most decision making in all types of businesses as "a lot of by-guess and by-golly, a lot of by-gut, and a whole lot of paper reports." That statement is not kind to managers in general or to IT specialists charged with providing the right people with the right technology to make the right decisions. What's the key to turning Neil's statement into a positive one? Is it training? It is providing timely information access? Is it providing everyone with a wide assortment of data-mining tools? Other solutions? Perhaps it's a combination of several answers?

MINING DINING DATA

Restaurants and fast-food chains rely heavily on business intelligence to make important decisions. Casinos do as well. Some of the leading restaurants, fast-food chains, and casinos using data warehouses include AFC Enterprises (operator and franchiser of more than 3,300 Church's Chicken, Popeye's Chicken and Biscuits, Seattle Coffee Company, Cinnabon, and Torrefazione outlets worldwide); Red Robin International (a 170-unit casual-dining chain); Harrah's Entertainment (owner of 26 U.U. casinos); Pizzeria Uno; and Einstein/Noah Bagel (operator of 428 Einstein's and 111 Noah's New York Bagel stores).

AFC ENTERPRISES

AFC Enterprises cultivates a loyal clientele by slicing and dicing its data warehouse to strategically configure promotions and tailor menus to suit local preferences. AFC's data warehouse helps it better understand its core customers and maximize its overall profitability. AFC tracks customer-specific information from name and address to order history and frequency of visits. This enables AFC to determine exactly which customers are likely to respond to a given promotion on a given day of the week.

AFC also uses its data warehouse to anticipate and manipulate customer behavior. For example, AFC can use its data warehouse to determine that coffee is added to the tab 65 percent of the time when a particular dessert is ordered and 85 percent of the time when that dessert is offered as a promotional item. Knowing that, AFC can run more promotions for certain desserts figuring that customers will respond by ordering more desserts and especially more coffee (coffee is a high-margin item in the restaurant business).

RED ROBIN INTERNATIONAL

Red Robin's terabyte-size data warehouse tracks hundreds of thousands of point-of-sale (POS) transactions, involving millions of menu items and more than 1.5 million invoices. As Howard Jenkins, Red Robin's vice president of Information Systems, explains it, "With data mining in place, we can ask ourselves, 'If we put the items with high margins in the middle of the menu, do we sell more versus putting it at the top or bottom, [and if so], to whom and where?' We can also tell if something cannibalizes the sale of other items and can give the marketing department an almost instant picture of how promotions are being sold and used."

The placement of items on a menu is strategic business, just as the placement of promotional items in a grocery store can mean increased sales for one item and reduced sales for another. The job of finding the right mix is definitely suited to mining a data warehouse.

Using Cognos Business Intelligence, Red Robin now has measurable results of promotion and menu changes, makes better and more timely decisions, and has realized seven-figure savings in operational costs.

HARRAH'S ENTERTAINMENT

Harrah's Entertainment uses its data warehouse to make decisions for its highly successful Total Gold customer recognition program. Depending on their spending records, Total Gold members can receive free vouchers for dining, entertainment, and sleeping accommodations. Knowing which rewards to give to which customers is key.

John Boushy, senior vice president of Entertainment and Technology for Harrah's, says, "We can determine what adds value to each customer and provide that value at the right time." Dining vouchers or free tickets for shows are awarded to day visitors, not sleeping accommodations. Customers who consistently visit a particular restaurant and order higher-end foods receive free dinners and cocktails, not vouchers for free (and cheaper) breakfasts.

PIZZERIA UNO

Pizzeria Uno uses its data warehouse to apply the 80/20 rule. That is, it can determine which 20 percent of its customers contribute to 80 percent of its sales and adjust menus and promotions to suit top patron preferences. These changes can often lead to converting some of the other 80 percent of Pizzeria Uno's customers to the more profitable 20 percent.

EINSTEIN/NOAH BAGEL

Einstein/Noah Bagel uses its data warehouse in real time to maximize cross-selling opportunities. For example, if data warehouse information reveals that a manager in a given store might be missing a cross-selling opportunity on a particular day, an e-mail is automatically sent out to alert managers to the opportunity. Salespeople can then respond by offering the cross-selling opportunity ("How about a cup of hot chocolate with that bagel since it's so cold outside?") to the next customer.[21, 22, 23, 24]

Questions

1. Consider the issue of timely information with respect to the businesses discussed in the case. Which of the businesses must have the most up-to-date information in its data warehouse? Which business can have the most out-of-date information in its data warehouse and still be effective? Rank the five businesses discussed with a 1 for the one that needs the most up-to-date information and a 5 for the one that is least sensitive to timeliness of information. Be prepared to justify your rankings.

2. Harrah's Entertainment tracks a wealth of information concerning customer spending habits. If you were to design Harrah's Entertainment's data warehouse, what dimensions of information would you include? As you develop your list of dimensions, consider every facet of Harrah's business operations, including hotels, restaurants, and gaming casinos.

3. AFC Enterprises includes information in its data warehouse such as customer name and address. Where does it (or could it) gather such information? Think carefully about this, because customers seldom provide their names and addresses when ordering fast food at a Church's or Popeye's. Is AFC gathering information in an ethical fashion? Why or why not?

4. Visit a local grocery store and walk down the breakfast cereal aisle. You should notice something very specific about the positioning of the various breakfast cereals. What is it? On the basis of what information do you think grocery stores determine cereal placement? Could they have determined that information from a data warehouse or from some other source? If another source, what might that source be?

5. Suppose you're opening a pizza parlor in the town where you live. It will be a "take and bake" pizza parlor in which you make pizzas for customers but do not cook them. Customers buy the pizzas uncooked and take them home for baking. You will have no predefined pizza types but will make each pizza to the customer's specifications. What sort of data warehouse would you need to predict the use of toppings by time of day and by day of the week? What would your dimensions of information be? If you wanted to increase the requests for a new topping (such as mandarin oranges), what information would you hope to find in your data warehouse that would enable you to do so?

Key Terms and Concepts

Application generation subsystem, 75
Backup, 75
Business intelligence (BI), 64
Competitive intelligence (CI), 83
Data administration, 84
Data administration subsystem, 75
Database, 66
Database administration, 84
Database management system (DBMS), 70
Data definition subsystem, 71
Data dictionary, 66

Data manipulation subsystem, 72
Data mart, 80
Data-mining tool, 79
Data warehouse, 77
DBMS engine, 70
Digital dashboard, 83
Foreign key, 68
Integrity constraint, 69
Logical view, 70
Multidimensional analysis (MDA) tool, 79
Online analytical processing (OLAP), 64

Online transaction processing (OLTP), 64
Operational database, 64
Physical view, 70
Primary key, 68
Query-and-reporting tool, 79
Query-by-example (QBE) tool, 74
Recovery, 76
Relation, 66
Relational database, 66
Report generator, 73
Structured query language (SQL), 75
View, 73

Short-Answer Questions

1. What is business intelligence? Why is it more than just information?
2. What is online transaction processing (OLTP)?
3. What is online analytical processing (OLAP)?
4. What is the most popular database model?
5. How are primary and foreign keys different?
6. What are the five important software components of a database management system?
7. How are QBE tools and SQL similar? How are they different?
8. What is a data warehouse? How does it differ from a database?
9. What are the four major types of data-mining tools?
10. What is a data mart? How is it similar to a data warehouse?

Assignments and Exercises

1. **FINDING "HACKED" DATABASES** The Happy Hacker (www.happyhacker.org/news/newsfeed .shtml) is a Web site devoted to "hacking"—breaking into computer systems. When people hack into a system, they often go after information in databases. There, they can find credit card information and other private and sensitive information. Sometimes, they can even find designs of yet-to-be-released products and other strategic information about a company. Connect to The Happy Hacker Web site and find an article that discusses a database that was hacked. Prepare a short report for your class detailing the incident.

2. **DEFINING QUERIES FOR A VIDEO RENTAL STORE** Consider your local video rental store. It certainly has an operational database to support its online transaction processing (OLTP). The operational database supports such things as adding new customers, renting videos (obviously), ordering videos, and a host of other activities. Now, assume that the video rental store also uses that same database for online analytical processing (OLAP) in the form of creating queries to extract meaningful information. If you were the manager of the video rental store, what kinds of queries would you build? What answers are you hoping to find?

3. **CREATING A QUERY** On the Web site that supports this text (www.mhhe.com/haag, choose Chapter 3 and then Solomon Enterprises), we've provided the database (in Microsoft Access) we illustrated in this chapter. Connect to the text's Web site and download that database. Now, create three queries using the QBE tool. The first one should extract information from only one file (your choice). The second one should extract information found in at least two files. The third should include some sort of selection criteria. How easy or difficult was it to perform these three queries? Would you say that a DBMS is just as easy to use as something like word processing or spreadsheet software? Why or why not?

4. **CAREER OPPORTUNITIES IN YOUR MAJOR** Knowledge workers throughout the business world are building their own desktop databases (often called end-user databases or knowledge worker databases). To do so, they must understand both how to design a database and how to use a desktop DBMS such as Microsoft Access or FileMaker (made by FileMaker). The ability to design a database and use a desktop DBMS offers you a great career advantage. Research your chosen major by looking at job postings (the Web is the best place to start). How many of those jobs want you to have some database knowledge? Do they list a specific DBMS package? What's your take—should you expand your education and learn more about databases and DBMSs? Why or why not?

5. **SALARIES FOR DATABASE ADMINISTRATORS** Database administrators (DBAs) are among the highest paid professionals in the information technology field. Many people work for 10 to 20 years to get a promotion to DBA. Connect to Monster.com (www.monster.com) or another job database of your choice and search for DBA job openings. As you do, select all locations and job categories and then use "dba" as the keyword search criteria. How many DBA job postings did you find? In what industries were some of the DBA job openings? Read through a couple of the job postings. What was the listed salary range (if any)? What sort of qualifications were listed?

6. **HOW UP-TO-DATE SHOULD DATA WAREHOUSE INFORMATION BE?** Information timeliness is a must in a data warehouse—old and obsolete information leads to poor decision making. Below is a list of decision-making processes that people go through for different business environments. For each, specify whether the information in the data warehouse should be updated monthly, weekly, daily, or by the minute. Be prepared to justify your decision.

   a. To adjust classes sizes in a university registration environment.

   b. To alert people to changes in weather conditions.

   c. To predict scores of professional football games.

   d. To adjust radio advertisements in light of demographic changes.

   e. To monitor the success of a new product line in the clothing retail industry.

   f. To adjust production levels of food in a cafeteria.

   g. To switch jobs to various printers in a network.

   h. To adjust CD rates in a bank.

   i. To adjust forecasted demands of tires in an auto parts store.

Discussion Questions

1. Databases and data warehouses clearly make it easier for people to access all kinds of information. This will lead to great debates in the area of privacy. Should organizations be left to police themselves with respect to providing access to information or should the government impose privacy legislation? Answer this question with respect to (1) customer information shared by organizations, (2) employee information shared within a specific organization, and (3) business information available to customers.

2. Business intelligence sounds like a fancy term with a lot of competitive advantage potentially rolled into it. What sort of business intelligence does your school need? Specifically, what business intelligence would it need to predict enrollments in the coming years? What business intelligence would it need to determine what curriculums to offer? Do you think your school gathers and uses this kind of business intelligence? Why or why not?

3. Consider your school's registration database that enforces the following integrity constraint: to enroll in a given class, the student must have completed or currently be enrolled in the listed prerequisite (if any). Your school, in fact, probably does have that integrity constraint in place. How can you get around that integrity constraint and enroll in a class for which you are not taking nor have completed the prerequisite? Is this an instance of when you should be able to override an integrity constraint? What are the downsides to being able to do so?

4. In this chapter, we listed the five important software components of a DBMS: the DBMS engine, the data definition, data manipulation, application generation, and data administration subsystems. Which of those are most and least important to users of a database? Which of those are most and least important to technology specialists who develop data applications? Which of those are most and least important to the chief information officer (CIO)? For each of your responses, provide justification.

5. Some people used to believe that data warehouses would quickly replace databases for both online transaction processing (OLTP) and online analytical processing (OLAP). Of course, they were wrong. Why can data warehouses not replace databases and become "operational data warehouses"? How radically would data warehouses (and their data-mining tools) have to change to become a viable replacement for databases? Would they then essentially become databases that simply supported OLAP? Why or why not?

6. Consider that you work in the human resources management department of a local business and that many of your friends work there. Although you don't personally generate payroll checks, you still have the ability to look up anyone's pay. Would you

check on your friends to see if they're earning more money than you? For that matter, would you look up their pay just out of simple curiosity, knowing that you would never do anything with the information or share it with anyone else? Why or why not? People working at the Internal Revenue Service (IRS) were caught just curiously looking up the reported incomes of movie stars and other high-profile public figures. Is this acceptable? Why or why not?

7. In spite of the need for "clean" information, many organizations have databases with duplicate records for you. You've probably experienced the consequences of this by receiving two identical pieces of junk mail from the same company. One record in the database may have your middle initial while the other doesn't, or there is some other type of minor discrepancy. Why would some organizations intentionally *not* go through a process of cleaning their database information?

CHAPTER PROJECTS

Group Projects

- Building Value Chains: Helping Customers Define Value (p. 367)
- Using Relational Technology to Track Projects: Foothills Construction (p. 369)
- Building a Web Database System: Web-Based Classified System (p. 375)
- Creating a Database Management System: Mountain Bike Rentals (p. 384)

e-Commerce Projects

- Searching Job Databases (p. 399)
- Exploring Google Earth (p. 392)
- Financial Aid Resources (p. 393)
- Consumer Information (p. 388)
- Demographics (p. 390)
- Bureau of Labor and Statistics (p. 390)
- Best of Computer Resources and Statistics (p. 388)
- Global Statistics and Resources (p. 394)

CHAPTER FOUR OUTLINE

STUDENT LEARNING OUTCOMES

1. Compare and contrast decision support systems and geographic information systems.

2. Define expert systems and describe the types of problems to which they are applicable.

3. Define neural networks and fuzzy logic and the use of these AI tools.

4. Define genetic algorithms and list the concepts on which they are based and the types of problems they solve.

5. Describe the four types of agent-based technologies.

PERSPECTIVES

WEB SUPPORT

www.mhhe.com/haag

- Best in computer statistics and resources
- Consumer information
- Metadata
- Bureau of Labor and Statistics
- Demographics
- Exploring Google Earth
- Gold, silver, interest rates, and money
- Learning about investing
- Stock quotes

3. **Choice** (pick a fix): Examine and weigh the merits of each solution, estimate the consequences of each, and choose the best one (which may be to do nothing at all). The "best" solution may depend on such factors as cost, ease of implementation, staffing requirements, and timing. This is the prescriptive phase of decision making—it's the stage at which a course of action is prescribed.

4. **Implementation** (apply the fix): Carry out the chosen solution, monitor the results, and make adjustments as necessary. Simply implementing a solution is seldom enough. Your chosen solution will always need fine-tuning, especially for complex problems or changing environments.

This four-phase process is not necessarily linear: You'll often find it useful or necessary to cycle back to an earlier phase. When choosing an alternative in the choice phase, for example, you might become aware of another possible solution. Then you would go back to the design phase, include the newly found solution, return to the choice phase, and compare the new solution to the others you generated.

A second model of decision making, also proposed by Simon, is *satisficing*, which differs from the four-phase process. **Satisficing** is making a choice that meets your needs and is satisfactory without necessarily being the best possible choice available. The term is a combination of the words "satisfied" and "sufficient."

Organizations in the private and public sectors are "satisficing" all the time in setting goals such as "fair price" or "reasonable profit." There's a fundamental difference between setting a goal of "high growth" and one of "maximum growth." "Maximum growth" is an optimizing strategy while "high growth" is a satisficing strategy. Usually a term like "high growth" is precisely defined. It may be 3 percent or 30 percent, but the idea is that when you reach that level, you can declare success.

In both business and your personal life, you'll face decisions that are some combination of four main types of decisions (see Figure 4.2): The first type is a **structured decision**, which involves processing a certain kind of information in a specified way so that you will always get the right answer. No "feel" or intuition is necessary. These are the kinds of decisions you can program—if you use a certain set of inputs and process them in a precise way, you'll arrive at the correct result. Calculating gross pay for hourly workers is an example. You can easily automate these types of structured decisions with IT.

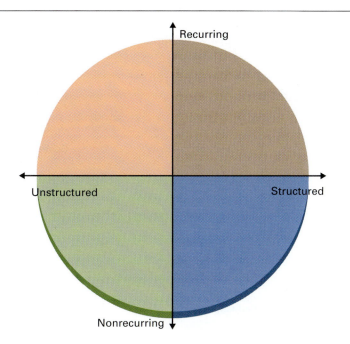

Figure 4.2

Categorizing Decisions by Type

On the other hand, a **nonstructured decision** is one for which there may be several "right" answers, and there is no precise way to get a right answer. No rules or criteria exist that guarantee you a good solution. Deciding whether to introduce a new product line, employ a new marketing campaign, or change the corporate image are all examples of decisions with nonstructured elements. In reality, most decisions fall somewhere between structured and unstructured, for example, choosing a job. Structured elements of choosing a job include consideration of such things as salary and signing bonus. Unstructured elements of such a decision include things like the potential for advancement.

Another type of decision regards frequency with which the decision is made. A **recurring decision** is one that happens repeatedly, and often periodically, whether weekly, monthly, quarterly, or yearly. Deciding how much inventory to carry and deciding at what price to sell the inventory are recurring decisions. A **nonrecurring**, or **ad hoc, decision** is one that you make infrequently (perhaps only once), and you may even have different criteria for determining the best solution each time. Deciding where to build a distribution center or company mergers are examples of nonrecurring or ad hoc decisions (although, the general trend in business today is for companies to consider mergers on a more consistent basis).

Decision Support Systems

LEARNING OUTCOME 1

In Chapter 3, you saw how data mining can help you make business decisions by giving you the ability to slice and dice your way through massive amounts of information. Actually, a data warehouse with data-mining tools is a form of decision support. A **decision support system (DSS)** is a highly flexible and interactive IT system that is designed to support decision making when the problem is not structured. A DSS is an alliance between you, the decision maker, and specialized support provided by IT (see Figure 4.3). IT brings speed, vast amounts of information, and sophisticated processing capabilities to help you create information useful in making a decision. You bring know-how in the form of your experience, intuition, judgment, and knowledge of the relevant factors. IT provides great power, but you—as the decision maker—must know what kinds of questions to ask of the information and how to process the information to get those questions answered. In fact, the primary objective of a DSS is to improve your effectiveness as a decision maker by providing you with assistance that will complement your insights. This union of your

Figure 4.3

The Alliance between You and a Decision Support System

What You Bring	Advantages of a DSS	What IT Brings
Experience	Increased productivity	Speed
Intuition	Increased understanding	Information
Judgment	Increased speed	Processing capabilities
Knowledge	Increased flexibility	
	Reduced problem complexity	
	Reduced cost	

know-how and IT power helps you generate business intelligence so that you can quickly respond to changes in the marketplace and manage resources in the most effective and efficient ways possible. Following are some examples of the varied applications of DSSs:

- A national insurance company uses a DSS to analyze its risk exposure when insuring drivers with histories of driving under the influence. The DSS revealed that married male homeowners in their forties with one DUI conviction were rarely repeat offenders. By lowering its rates to this group the company increased it market share without increasing its risk exposure.[7]

- Burlington Northern and Santa Fe (BNSF) railroad regularly tests the rails its trains ride on to prevent accidents. Wornout or defective rails result in hundreds of derailments every year, so it's important to address the problem. Using a decision support system to schedule rail testing, BNSF decreased its rail-caused derailments by 33 percent in 2000, while the other three large railroad companies had a 16 percent rise in such accidents.[8]

- Customer relationship management (CRM), as you saw in Chapter 2, is an important part of any successful company's strategy. Decision support is an important part of CRM. On Wall Street, retail brokerage companies analyze customers' behaviors and goals with decision support, which highlights opportunities and alerts brokers to beginning problems.[9]

COMPONENTS OF A DECISION SUPPORT SYSTEM

DSSs vary greatly in application and complexity, but they all share specific features. A typical DSS has three components (see below and Figure 4.4 on the next page): model management, data management, and user interface management.

Before we look at these three components individually, let's get a quick overview of how they work together: When you begin your analysis, you tell the DSS, using the user interface management component, which model (in the model management component) to use on what information (in the data management component). The model requests the information from the data management component, analyzes that information, and sends the result to the user interface management component, which in turn passes the results back to you. Here's an example of a decision support system at Lands' End clothing business.

- *Model management:* The DSS at Lands' End has to have models to analyze information. The models create new information that decision makers need to plan product lines and inventory levels. For example, Lands' End uses a statistical model called regression analysis to determine trends in customer buying patterns and forecasting models to predict sales levels.

- *Data management:* The DSS's data management component stores Lands' End's customer and product information. In addition to this organizational information, the company also needs external information, such as demographic information and industry and style trend information.

- *User interface management:* A user interface enables Lands' End decision makers to access information and specify the models they want to use to create the information they need.

Now we'll examine the three DSS components in more general terms.

MODEL MANAGEMENT COMPONENT The *model management* component consists of both the DSS models and the DSS model management system. A model is a representation of some event, fact, or situation. Businesses use models to represent

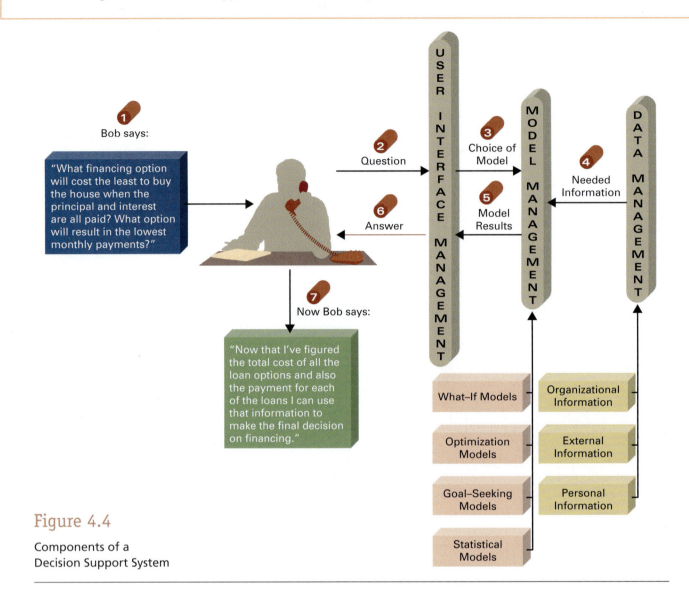

Figure 4.4

Components of a
Decision Support System

variables and their relationships. For example, you would use a statistical model called analysis of variance to determine whether newspaper, television, and billboard advertising are equally effective in increasing sales. DSSs help in various decision-making situations by using models that allow you to analyze information in many different ways. The models you use in a DSS depend on the decision you're making and, consequently, the kind of analysis you require. For example, you would use what-if analysis to see what effect the change of one or more variables will have on other variables, or optimization to find the most profitable solution given operating restrictions and limited resources. You can use spreadsheet software such as Excel to create a simple DSS for what-if analysis.

The model management system stores and maintains the DSS's models. Its function of managing models is similar to that of a database management system. The model management component can't select the best model for you to use for a particular problem—that requires your expertise—but it can help you create and manipulate models quickly and easily.

DATA MANAGEMENT COMPONENT   The *data management* component performs the function of storing and maintaining the information that you want your DSS to use.

GOT MILK? THEY DO IN BRITISH COLUMBIA

The British Columbia Milk Marketing Board has the responsibility of collecting raw milk from farmers and transporting it to the processing plants. The Marketing Board transfers payments from the processors to the farmers—to the tune of $17 million every two weeks. Milk is picked up from 350 farms per day by a fleet of 70 trucks, so that all 700 farms in the system see collection every other day. The milk goes to 26 processors across the vast province.

The paper-based system of record keeping was collapsing under its own weight. Upon pumping a farmer's milk into his truck, a driver recorded the number of liters collected on a four-part paper form and gave the farmer one copy. To fill a two-trailer truck, a driver collected milk from five farms and kept track, on paper, of how much milk came from each one. When the trailers were full of milk, the driver headed for the processing plant where a receipt for the quantity of milk was filled out. The truck then proceeded to the next farm and repeated the process.

Each day's work generated 350 producer slips from the farms and about 70 truck slips used to keep track of payments to the truck companies. To enter and process all this information, even using a computer, took many hours each day, especially with the problems of slips that truck drivers lost or forgot to turn over and mistakes made entering data onto forms that had to be investigated. The cost of the paper system was about $100,000 per year. The basic accounting of incoming milk and outgoing payments took so much time that there wasn't much left for the in-depth analysis necessary for the type of decision making that would have led to more effective use of resources.

The new decision support system handles data entry in real time. Each driver uses a handheld wireless scanning unit to send information to the central system. Each farm and processing plant has a unique bar code that the driver just has to scan. All that's left is to enter the volume of milk and add any comments like the temperature of the milk and so on. A wireless printer in the truck's cab can produce a printed copy of the transaction for the farmer or processing plant. The data is then sent over the cellular data network to the Marketing Board's Internet access point, and from there to the main computer for processing.

Quite apart from collecting data faster and more accurately, enabling more efficient decision making, the IT system allows the British Columbia Milk Marketing Board to quickly identify any farm that was the source of a substandard shipment so that corrective action can be taken immediately. And it's not just management that benefits from the decision support aspect of the new system. IT also supplies drivers with useful information, such as how much space is left in each trailer and how a load should be divided between trailers. The new decision support system not only brings costs down; it increases profits too.[10]

The data management component, therefore, consists of both the DSS information and the DSS database management system. The information you use in your DSS comes from one or more of three sources:

1. *Organizational information:* You may want to use virtually any information available in the organization for your DSS. You can design your DSS to access this information directly from your company's databases and data warehouses.

2. *External information:* Some decisions require input from external sources of information. Various branches of the federal government, Dow Jones, and the Internet, to mention just a few, can provide additional information for use with a DSS.

3. *Personal information:* You can incorporate your own insights and experience— your personal information—into your DSS.

USER INTERFACE MANAGEMENT COMPONENT The *user interface management* component allows you to communicate with the DSS. It consists of the user interface and the user interface management system. This is the component that allows you to combine your know-how with the storage and processing capabilities of the computer. The user interface is the part of the system you see; through it you enter information, commands, and models. If you have a DSS with a poorly designed user interface—if it's too rigid or too cumbersome to use—you simply won't use it no matter what its capabilities. The best user interface uses your terminology and methods and is flexible, consistent, simple, and adaptable.

Geographic Information Systems

In 1992, Hurricane Andrew attacked the east coast of the United States leaving devastation throughout several states in its wake. One of the places hardest hit was Miami, Florida, where the hurricane came on land smashing businesses and private buildings and causing billions of dollars in damage. Reporters at the *Miami Herald* believed that not all the damage was due to Andrew. They hypothesized that at least some of the harm was a result of shoddy construction of homes built after 1980.

Four months after Hurricane Andrew, the paper ran a series of reports and used geographic information system maps to make its point. A ***geographic information system (GIS)*** is a decision support system designed specifically to analyze spatial information. Spatial information is any information that can be shown in map form, such as roads, the distribution of the bald eagle population, sewer systems, or the path of a hurricane.

The *Miami Herald* plotted the arrival point of the hurricane where winds were strongest and charted the progress of Andrew inland, where it lost some of its initial punch. Then the reporters plotted the damaged houses with one dot representing 10 homes. These dots were color-coded to show level of damage—blue showed 10 repairable homes and orange dots represented 10 destroyed homes. When the two maps were laid over each other, it was clear that the wind strength did not match up with damage as it should have. That is, the reporters showed that Hurricane Andrew alone was not responsible for all the devastation. The net result was that building codes in Dade County were tightened so that contractors had to use more nails and install stronger windows, doors, and shutters on homes. The *Miami Herald* received the Pulitzer Prize for its investigative work.

Businesses use GIS software too to analyze information, generate business intelligence, and make decisions. GIS is a powerful combination of database and graphics technology. There is virtually no limit to the sort of information you can plot with a GIS, including the placement of roads, the course of rivers, income levels, health conditions, areas of high or low crime, and so on. Of course, you can do this with paper maps too. The strength of an electronic GIS is in the ability you get to layer information with a mouse click.

Figure 4.5 is a map of the Denver area shown using the real estate search function in Zillow (www.zillow.com). On the left-hand side you can see the layers (or types of information) that can be shown on the map—homes for sale, homes recently sold, and so on. The map itself is color-coded to show the estimated dollars per square foot for residential areas. Color shadings of red through maroon are in the $500 to $700 per square foot range and variations of blue are in the $0 to $200 per square foot range.

This is an example of the feature of GIS software that represents information thematically (i.e., in map or theme form). With themes, you can show the layers in combination as the *Miami Herald* reporters did for Hurricane Andrew. You can represent either statistical information, for instance, the average salary of homeowners, or point information, such as the location of a bank's customers.

When businesses use GIS software to generate maps showing information of interest to them, we call it *business geography*. You can find a wealth of information to incorporate

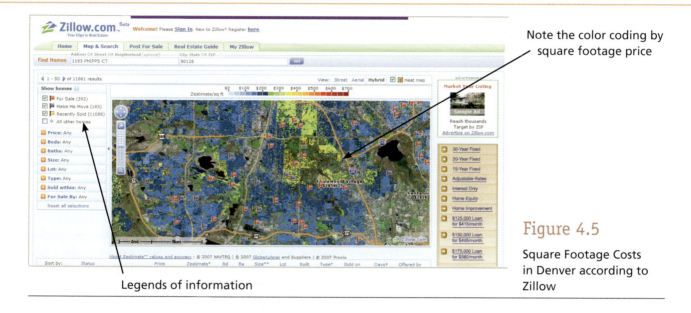

Note the color coding by square footage price

Legends of information

Figure 4.5

Square Footage Costs in Denver according to Zillow

into your GIS from various sources. For example, the U.S. Census Bureau has a vast database of demographic information and the Bureau of Labor Statistics has employment information. Both of these would be statistical information. In the private sector, many research companies would be happy to sell you consumer habit information.

Studies show that how information is presented significantly impacts the effectiveness and efficiency of the decision-making process. Here are other examples of GISs in use:

- The city of Chicago has 40 departments and a fleet of 7,300 vehicles, ranging from snowplows to sanitation trucks to construction vehicles. The city implemented a system that improved the accountability of the departments and the efficiency of the use of its diverse vehicles. Combining GIS technology with GPS and a wireless network, the city has a system that allows supervisors to use the city's intranet to view the location of any vehicle. The system keeps information on where each truck, van, or earth mover goes, its speed, and the path it took to get to its current location. This allows the city to reassign vehicles for greater effectiveness and to tell where each one is or was at any particular time.[11]

- During the bovine spongiform encephalopathy (BSE, or more commonly, mad cow disease) outbreak in 2003 it became clear that a national tracking system of cattle, from birth on, was needed to help keep the beef supply—and the people who consume it—safe. During 2003, only 87 cattle and 15 calves were at risk of being susceptible to BSE, but over 400 were slaughtered because officials did not have complete enough records on the movement of these animals. To correct that problem, the Kansas Animal Health Department (KAHD) has developed a tracking system to log every producer, sales barn, feed yard, and processing facility through which each animal passes. This is a gargantuan task since every year millions of cattle come through the state on their way from one part of the country to the other. KAHD's tracking system combines RFID (radio frequency identification, see Chapter 9) tags on the ears of cattle, GPS, GIS, and a wireless network to track each animal's movements and transmit the information to a national database.[12]

DSSs and GISs are IT systems that augment business brainpower. IT can further expand business brainpower by means of **artificial intelligence (AI)**—the science of making machines imitate human thinking and behavior. Financial analysts use a variety of artificial intelligence systems to manage assets, invest in the stock market, and perform other financial operations. Hospitals use artificial intelligence in many capacities, from

LOCATION MASHUP = GIS + THE INFORMATION YOU WANT

Broadly defined, a *mashup* is a combination of content from more than one source. Due in large part to the technologies of Web 2.0, people produce and post mashups of all kinds—music mashups (a single song using parts of numerous other songs), video mashups (just like a music mashup but using video), and even location mashups. A *location mashup* is a geographic information system (GIS) that displays a particular geographic area and then overlays content according to the user's desires. For example, at www.gawker.com/stalker, you can view a mashup showing the latest travels and locations of celebrities like Madonna.

Location mashups are actually quite easy to create using many new and emerging tools. Pipes (by Yahoo!), GeoCommons (by FortiusOne), and GeoIQ (also by FortiusOne) are among the many tools you can use to create your own location mashup. Many of them come with

location data that you can instantly add to a GIS map to create a location mashup. GeoIQ, for example, includes a wealth of data such as the location of spammers by street address and incidents of the West Nile virus.

Location mashups are not limited to the personal space. Many businesses are using them too. British Petroleum, UPS, Best Buy, Century 21, DaimlerChrysler, FedEx's Kinko's, Ford, General Motors, H&R Block, Starbucks, and Target are among the many businesses taking advantage of the capabilities of location mashups. Some are using them for internal efficiency and decision-making efforts (e.g., BP uses them to provide updated weather patterns to employees in the Gulf of Mexico), while others are using them in the form of a customer-facing technology (e.g., Starbucks' location mashup helps customers find their next caffeine fix).[13]

---

scheduling staff, to assigning beds to patients, to diagnosing and treating illness. Many government agencies, including the IRS and the armed forces, use artificial intelligence. Credit card companies use artificial intelligence to detect credit card fraud, and insurance companies use artificial intelligence to spot fraudulent claims. Artificial intelligence lends itself to tasks as diverse as airline ticket pricing, food preparation, oil exploration, and child protection. It is widely used in the insurance, meteorology, engineering, and aerospace industries. The AI systems that businesses use most can be classified into the following major categories:

1. Expert systems
2. Neural networks (and fuzzy logic)
3. Genetic algorithms
4. Intelligent agents (or agent-based technologies)

Expert Systems

LEARNING OUTCOME 2

In business, people are valuable because they perform important business tasks. Many business tasks require expertise, and people often carry this expertise in their heads—often that's the only place it can be found in the organization. AI can provide you with an expert system that can capture expertise, thus making it available to those who are not experts so that they can use it, either to solve a problem or to learn how to solve a problem.

An *expert system,* also called a *knowledge-based system,* is an artificial intelligence system that applies reasoning capabilities to reach a conclusion. Expert systems are excellent for diagnostic and prescriptive problems. Diagnostic problems are those requiring an answer to the question, "What's wrong?" and correspond to the intelligence phase of decision making. Prescriptive problems are those that require an answer to the question, "What to do?" and correspond to the choice phase of decision making.

An expert system is usually built for a specific application area called a *domain.* You can find expert systems in the following domains, among others:

- *Accounting*—for auditing, tax planning, management consulting, and training.
- *Medicine*—to prescribe antibiotics where many considerations must be taken into account (such as the patient's medical history, the source of the infection, and the price of available drugs).
- *Process control*—to control offset lithographic printing, for example.
- *Human resource management*—to help personnel managers determine whether they are in compliance with an array of federal employment laws.
- *Financial management*—to identify delinquency-prone accounts in the loan departments of banks.
- *Production*—to guide the manufacture of all sorts of products, such as aircraft parts.
- *Forestry management*—to help with harvesting timber on forest lands.

A DSS sometimes incorporates expert systems, but an expert system is fundamentally different from a DSS. To use a DSS, you must have considerable knowledge or expertise about the situation with which you're dealing. As you saw earlier in this chapter, a DSS *assists* you in making decisions. That means that you must know how to reason through the problem. You must know which questions to ask, how to get the answers, and how to proceed to the next step. When you use an expert system, however, the know-how is in the system—you need only provide the expert system with the facts and symptoms of the problem for which you need an answer. The know-how, or expertise, that actually solves the problem came from someone else—an expert in the field. What does it mean to have expertise? When someone has expertise in a given subject, that person not only knows a lot of facts about the topic but also can apply that knowledge to analyze and make judgments about related topics. It's this human expertise that an expert system captures.

Let's look at a very simple expert system that would tell a driver what to do when approaching a traffic light. Dealing with traffic lights is an example of the type of problem to which an expert system is well-suited. It is a recurring problem, and to solve it you follow a well-defined set of steps. You've probably gone through the following mental question-and-answer session hundreds of times without even realizing it (see Figure 4.6 on the next page).

When you approach a green traffic light, you proceed on through. If the light is red, you need to stop. If you're unable to stop, and if traffic is approaching from either side, you'll surely be in trouble. Similarly, if the light is yellow, you may be able to make it through the intersection before the light turns red. If not, you will again be faced with the problem of approaching traffic.

WHAT EXPERT SYSTEMS CAN AND CAN'T DO

An expert system uses IT to capture and apply human expertise. For problems with clear rules and procedures, expert systems work very well and can provide your company with great advantages. An expert system can

- Handle massive amounts of information
- Reduce errors
- Aggregate information from various sources
- Improve customer service

Rule	Symptom or Fact	Yes	No	Explanation
1	Is the light green?	Go through the intersection.	Go to Rule 2.	Should be safe if light is green. If not, need more information.
2	Is the light red?	Go to Rule 4.	Go to Rule 3.	Should stop, may not be able to.
3	Is the light likely to change to red before you get through the intersection?	Go to Rule 4.	Go through the intersection.	Will only reach this point if light is yellow, then you'll have two choices.
4	Can you stop before entering the intersection?	Stop.	Go to Rule 5.	Should stop, but there may be a problem if you can't.
5	Is traffic approaching from either side?	Prepare to crash.	Go through the intersection.	Unless the intersection is clear of traffic, you're likely to crash.

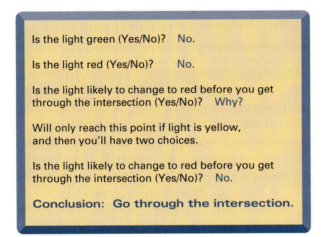

Is the light green (Yes/No)?   No.

Is the light red (Yes/No)?   No.

Is the light likely to change to red before you get through the intersection (Yes/No)?   Why?

Will only reach this point if light is yellow, and then you'll have two choices.

Is the light likely to change to red before you get through the intersection (Yes/No)?   No.

Conclusion: Go through the intersection.

Figure 4.6

Traffic Light Expert System Rules

- Provide consistency in decision making
- Provide new information
- Decrease personnel time spent on tasks
- Reduce cost

You can run into trouble, however, in building and using an expert system. Difficulties can include the following:

1. Transferring domain expertise to the expert system is sometimes difficult because domain experts cannot always explain how they know what they know. Often experts are not aware of their complete reasoning processes. Experience has given them a feel for the problem, and they just "know."

2. Even if the domain expert can explain the whole reasoning process, automating that process may be impossible. The process may be too complex, requiring an excessive number of rules, or it may be too vague or imprecise. In using an expert system, keep in mind that it can solve only the problems for which it was designed. It cannot deal with inconsistency or a newly encountered problem situation. An expert system can't learn from previous experience and can't apply previously acquired expertise to new problems the way humans can.

3. An expert system has no common sense or judgment. One of the early expert systems built into an F-16 fighter plane allowed the pilot to retract the landing gear while the plane was still on the ground and to jettison bombs while the plane was flying upside down.

Neural Networks and Fuzzy Logic

LEARNING OUTCOME 3

Suppose you see a breed of dog you've never encountered before. Would you know it's a dog? For that matter, would you know it's an animal? Probably so. You know, because you've learned by example. You've seen lots of living things, have learned to classify them, and so can recognize a dog when you see one. A neural network simulates this human ability to classify things without taking prescribed steps leading to the solution. A *neural network* (often called an *artificial neural network* or *ANN*) is an artificial intelligence system that is capable of finding and differentiating patterns. Your brain has learned to consider many factors in combination to recognize and differentiate objects. This is also the case with a neural network. A neural network can learn by example and can adapt to new concepts and knowledge. Neural networks are widely used for visual pattern and speech recognition systems. If you've used a PDA that deciphered your handwriting, it was probably a neural network that analyzed the characters you wrote.[14]

Neural networks are useful in a variety of situations. For example, bomb detection systems in U.S. airports use neural networks that sense trace elements in the air that may indicate the presence of explosives. The Chicago Police Department uses neural networks to identify corruption within its ranks.[15] In medicine, neural networks check 50 million electrocardiograms per year, check for drug interactions, and detect anomalies in tissue samples that may signify the onset of cancer and other diseases. Neural networks can detect heart attacks and even differentiate between the subtly different symptoms of heart attacks in men and women.[16,17,18] In business, neural networks are very popular for securities trading, fraud detection, real estate appraisal, evaluating loan applications, and target marketing, to mention a few. Neural networks are used to control machinery, adjust temperature settings, and identify malfunctioning machinery.

Neural networks are most useful for identification, classification, and prediction when a vast amount of information is available. By examining hundreds, or even thousands of examples, a neural network detects important relationships and patterns in the information. For example, if you provide a neural network with the details of numerous credit card transactions and tell it which ones are fraudulent, eventually it will learn to identify suspicious transaction patterns.

Here are some examples of the uses of neural networks:

- Many banks and financial institutions use neural networks. Citibank uses neural networks to find opportunities in financial markets.[19] By carefully examining historical stock market data with neural network software, Citibank financial managers learn of interesting coincidences or small anomalies (called market inefficiencies). For example, it could be that whenever IBM stock goes up, so does Unisys stock. Or it might be that a U.S. Treasury note is selling for 1 cent less in Japan than it is in the United States. These snippets of information can make a big difference to Citibank's bottom line in a very competitive financial market.

- In Westminster, California, a community of 87,000 people, police use neural network software to fight crime. With crime reports as input, the system detects and maps local crime patterns. Police say that with this system they can better predict crime trends, improve patrol assignments, and develop better crime-prevention programs.[20]

- Fingerhut, the mail order company based in Minnesota, has 6 million people on its customer list. To determine which customers were and were not likely to order from its catalog, Fingerhut recently switched to neural network software. The company finds that the new software is more effective and expects to generate millions of dollars by fine-tuning its mailing lists.[21]

- Fraud detection is one of the areas in which neural networks are used the most. Visa, MasterCard, and many other credit card companies use a neural network to spot peculiarities in individual accounts. MasterCard estimates neural networks save them $50 million annually.[22]

- Many insurance companies (Cigna, AIG, Travelers, Liberty Mutual, Hartford) along with state compensation funds and other carriers use neural network software to identify fraud. The system searches for patterns in billing charges, laboratory tests, and frequency of office visits. A claim for which the diagnosis was a sprained ankle and which included an electrocardiogram would be flagged for the account manager.[23]

- FleetBoston Financial Corporation uses a neural network to watch transactions with customers. The neural network can detect patterns that may indicate a customer's growing dissatisfaction with the company. The neural network looks for signs like decreases in the number of transactions or in the account balance of one of Fleet's high-value customers.[24]

All of the above situations have pattern recognition in common. They all require identification and/or classification, which may then be used to predict a finding or outcome. Neural networks are often called predictive systems since they can see patterns in huge volumes of information.

Neural networks have many advantages. For example, neural networks can

- Learn and adjust to new circumstances on their own.
- Lend themselves to massive parallel processing.
- Function without complete or well-structured information.
- Cope with huge volumes of information with many dependent variables.
- Analyze nonlinear relationships in information (they've been called fancy regression analysis systems).

The biggest problem with neural networks to date has been the fact that the hidden layers are "hidden." That is, you can't see how the neural network is learning and how the neurons are interacting. Newer neural networks no longer hide the middle layers. With these systems you can manually adjust the weights or connections giving you more flexibility and control.

FUZZY LOGIC

Fuzzy logic is a way of reaching conclusions based on ambiguous or vague information. Humans tend to make decisions based on approximate information, since not every type of information can be separated into mutually exclusive categories. For example, you might consider 20 degrees Fahrenheit to be very cold, 40 degrees to be cold, 60 degrees to be warm, 90 degrees to be hot, and 105 to be very hot, but you can't really specify exact degree values that would separate these categories of warmth (or lack of it). Compounding the problem is the fact that somebody else might experience it differently;

HOW PROFITABLE WOULD A NEURAL NETWORK SAY YOU ARE?

Would your banker give you an A, B, or C? What about your supermarket? You know you're being graded in your classes, but did you know that you're also being graded by businesses?

Special treatment for certain customers is not new. Airline customers who fly first class have always received preferential treatment, even when flights were cancelled or delayed. You won't find them napping on a stone floor with their backpacks as pillows. This makes business sense to the airlines, since these are the customers who are most profitable.

Although companies have always offered preferential treatment to their more profitable customers, the speed and capacity of computers today are making the segmenting of customers possible to a degree unheard of just a few years ago. Part of the reason for this is neural networks. Using neural network software,

businesses now have the ability to look for patterns in their customer information and classify customers according to how they affect the company's bottom line and thus to gauge whether it's worth the trouble of making them happy.

The First Union Bank uses software that categorizes people into red, green, and yellow classes depending on the customer's history and value to the bank. Customers who are green might get better credit card rates than customers who are red and are judged to add less to the bank's bottom line.

Say you called the bank that issued you your credit card and said that you didn't want to pay the annual fee anymore. The bank could look at your credit card activity and decide whether it's more profitable to the bank to waive your fee rather than risk your not using the credit card anymore.[25,26]

subjectively, a temperature some people consider warm others would judge to be hot—or cool. Thus, you need a way to translate an approximate or vague judgment into something that a computer, requiring a precise assignment of numbers to all events, can handle. This is the type of situation in which fuzzy logic is very effective.

Fuzzy logic is a mathematical method of handling imprecise or subjective information. The basic approach is to assign values between 0 and 1 to vague or ambiguous information. The higher the value, the closer it is to 1. For example, you might assign the value of 0.8 to the value "hot." Then you would construct rules and processes, called *algorithms*, to describe the interdependence among variables. A fuzzy logic algorithm is a set of steps that relate variables representing inexact information or personal perceptions.

Fuzzy logic and neural networks are often combined to express complicated and subjective concepts in a form that makes it possible to simplify the problem and to apply rules. The rules are executed with a level of certainty. This is similar to, but not the same as, confidence levels in statistics. In statistics, probability is used to estimate the likelihood of an outcome, whereas fuzzy logic describes the data point itself while incorporating subjective perception.

In the business world, fuzzy logic has been applied to financial analysis, the pharmaceutical industry, the wood processing and metal cutting industries, the manufacture of antilock brakes, and washing machines that determine by themselves how much water to use or how long to wash. (They wash until the water is "clean.") In accounting and finance, for example, fuzzy logic allows you to analyze information with subjective financial values (say, on an important intangible resource like goodwill) that are very important considerations in economic analyses.

Fuzzy logic is used by Google to find answers to your search terms, which makes sense, since your perception of a topic often influences how you phrase your query, hence determining the relevance of the Web pages that Google delivers.

Genetic Algorithms

Have you ever wondered how chefs around the world create recipes for great-tasting foods? For example, how did the Chinese discover that cashew nuts and chicken taste good when combined? How did Mexican chefs arrive at combining tomatoes, onions, cilantro, and other spices to create pica de gallo? All those great recipes came about through *evolutionary processes*. Someone decided to put together a few ingredients and taste the result. Undoubtedly, many of those combinations resulted in unpalatable concoctions that were quickly discarded. Others were tasty enough to warrant further experimentation of combinations.

Today significant research in AI is devoted to creating software capable of following a similar trial-and-error process, leading to the evolution of a good result. Such a software system is called a genetic algorithm. A *genetic algorithm* is an artificial intelligence system that mimics the evolutionary, survival-of-the-fittest process to generate increasingly better solutions to a problem. In other words, a genetic algorithm is an optimizing system: It finds the combination of inputs that give the best outputs.

Here's an example. Suppose you were trying to decide what to put into your stock portfolio. You have countless stocks to choose from but a limited amount of money to invest. You might decide that you'd like to start with 20 stocks and you want a portfolio growth rate of 7.5 percent.

Probably you'd start by examining historic information on the stocks. You would take some number of stocks and combine them, 20 at a time, to see what happens with each grouping. If you wanted to choose from a pool of 30 stocks, you would have to examine 30,045,015 different combinations. For a 40-stock pool, the number of combinations rises to 137,846,500,000. It would be an impossibly time-consuming, not to mention numbingly tedious, task to look at this many combinations and evaluate your overall return for each one. This is just the sort of repetitive number-crunching task at which computers excel, however.

So, instead of a pencil, paper, and calculator, you might use a genetic algorithm. You could input the appropriate information on the stocks, including the number of years the company has been in business, the performance of the stock over the last five years, price to earnings ratios, and other information.

You would also have to tell the genetic algorithm your exact "success" criteria. For example, you might use a growth rate in the company over the last year of at least 10 percent, a presence in the marketplace going back at least three years, a connection to the computer industry, and so forth. The genetic algorithm would simply combine and recombine stocks eliminating any combinations that don't fit your criteria and continuing to the next iteration with the acceptable combinations—those that give an aggregate growth rate of at least 7.5 percent while aiming for as high a growth rate as possible.

Genetic algorithms use three concepts of evolution:

1. *Selection*—or survival of the fittest. The key to selection is to give preference to better outcomes.

2. *Crossover*—or combining portions of good outcomes in the hope of creating an even better outcome.

3. *Mutation*—or randomly trying combinations and evaluating the success (or failure) of the outcome.

Genetic algorithms are best suited to decision-making environments in which thousands, or perhaps millions, of solutions are possible. Genetic algorithms can find and evaluate solutions intelligently and can get through many more possibilities more thoroughly and faster than a human can. As you might imagine, businesses face decision-making environments for all sorts of problems like engineering design, computer graphics, strategies for game playing, anything, in fact, that requires optimization techniques. Here are some other examples.

- Genetic algorithms are used by business executives to help them decide which combination of projects a firm should invest in, taking complicated tax considerations into account.[27]

- They're used by investment companies to help in trading choices and decisions.[28]

- In any garment that you buy, the fabric alone accounts for between 35 percent and 40 percent of the selling price. So, when cutting out the fabric to make the garment, it's important that there be as little waste as possible. Genetic algorithms are used to solve this problem of laying out the pieces of the garment and cutting fabric in a way that leaves as little waste as possible.[29]

- US West uses a genetic algorithm to determine the optimal configuration of fiber-optic cable in a network that may include as many as 100,000 connection points. By using selection, crossover, and mutation, the genetic algorithm can generate and evaluate millions of cable configurations and select the one that uses the least amount of cable. At US West, this process used to take an experienced design engineer almost two months. US West's genetic algorithm can solve the problem in two days and saves the company $1 million to $10 million each time it's used.[30]

Genetic algorithms are good for these types of problems because they use selection, crossover, and mutation as methods of exploring countless solutions and the respective worth of each.

You have to tell the genetic algorithm what constitutes a "good" solution. That could be low cost, high return, among other factors, since many potential solutions are useless or absurd. If you created a genetic algorithm to make bread, for example, it might try to boil flour to create moistness. That obviously won't work, so the genetic algorithm would simply throw away that solution and try something else. Other solutions would eventually be good, and some of them would even be wonderful. According to David Goldbert, a genetic algorithm pioneer at the University of Illinois at Urbana–Champaign, evolution is the oldest and most powerful algorithm there is, and "three billion years of evolution can't be wrong!"[31]

Intelligent Agents

LEARNING OUTCOME 5

Do you have a favorite restaurant? Is there someone there who knows you and remembers that you like Italian dressing, but not croutons, on your salad; and ice cream and a slice of cheddar cheese with your apple pie? Does this person familiar with your tastes put a glass of diet cola on your favorite table when you come in the door? If so, he or she has the qualities that artificial intelligence scientists are working on incorporating into intelligent agents. An ***intelligent agent*** is software that assists you, or acts on your behalf, in performing repetitive computer-related tasks. Future intelligent agents will most likely be autonomous, acting independently, and will learn and adapt to changing circumstances.

You may not realize it, but you're probably already familiar with a primitive type of intelligent agent—the shifty-eyed paper clip that pops up in some versions of Word. For example, if your document looks as if it is going to be a business letter—that is, you type in a date, name, and address—the animated paper clip will offer helpful suggestions on how to proceed.

You can find hundreds of intelligent agents, or bots, for a wide variety of tasks. The BotSpot and SmartBot Web sites at www.botspot.com and www.smartbots.com are good places to get an idea of the many different types of agents that are available.

Essentially there are four types of intelligent agents:

- Information agents (including buyer agents or shopping bots)
- Monitoring-and-surveillance agents
- Data-mining agents
- User or personal agents

INFORMATION AGENTS

Information agents are intelligent agents that search for information of some kind and bring it back. The best known information agents are buyer agents. A *buyer agent,* also known as a *shopping bot,* is an intelligent agent on a Web site that helps you, the customer, find products and services that you need. They work very efficiently for commodity products such as CDs, books, electronic components, and other one-size-fits-all products. Amazon.com uses intelligent technology to show you a list of books or other products that you might like. The Web site classifies you into a category of people with similar tastes and, based on that category, presents you with a list of products that Amazon hopes you will find appealing enough to buy.

Shopping bots make money by selling advertising space, from special promotions in cooperation with merchants, or by charging click-through fees, which are payments to the site that provided the link to the merchant site. Some shopping bots give preference to certain sites for a financial consideration. The people who run shopping bot sites have two, sometimes competing, objectives. They want to present as many listings as possible to the consumer in the most useful way, but they also want to make money doing it.

Both the Google and Ask Jeeves Web sites use information agents to find information—and not just when you request it. The URL server at Google sends thousands of Googlebots out to surf the Web sites of all the sites in Google's index. They copy individual pages, at the rate of more than 100 per second, to Google's repository, where the Google software indexes them. This means that when you perform a Google search, the search engine builds a list of all the pages that have the keywords you specify and presents them to you in PageRank order. Google's PageRanking process sorts the pages in order of links pointing to each page. That is, the more links on the Web that point to a Web site, the higher that Web site will be in the list.[32]

Government sites have information agents you can use to get the information you need. FERRET (Federal Electronic Research and Review Extraction Tool) was developed jointly by the Census Bureau and the Bureau of Labor Statistics. With FERRET you can find information on employment, health care, education, race and ethnicity, health insurance, housing, income and poverty, aging, and marriage and family. Other types of information agents include intelligent agents that scan Web pages and highlight relevant text for you, and still others can assemble customized news reports. There are several versions of these. A CNN Custom News bot will gather news from CNN on the topics you want to read about—and only those.

MONITORING-AND-SURVEILLANCE AGENTS

Monitoring-and-surveillance agents (also called *predictive agents*) are intelligent agents that constantly observe and report on some entity of interest, a network, or manufacturing equipment, for example. NASA's Jet Propulsion Laboratory has an agent that monitors inventory, planning, and the ordering of scheduled equipment to keep costs

INTELLIGENT AGENTS RUN EXPERIMENTS ABOARD SPACECRAFT

We all know that NASA sends various types of craft into space for a variety of purposes. We've heard of the Hubble telescope that has been sending back terrific pictures for years. A lesser known but similarly spectacular observation craft—although in this case its mission is to observe the earth—is the Earth Observing-1 (or simply EO1) satellite.

During 2004, NASA uploaded intelligent agent software to EO1 to run experiments and even the spacecraft itself. One of EO1's tasks was to avoid wasting fuel without disrupting the onboard experiments or otherwise compromising the mission. This was a job that used to be handled by ground control, but now the people at mission headquarters are free to concentrate on tasks other than routine maintenance while the agents do the job in space.

EO1 was launched in 2001 on a one-year mission to observe the earth from space. It was part of NASA's New Millennium Program mission and was originally intended as a pilot project to test new space technologies. Now, several years later it's still going strong collecting and sending back to us valuable information about our earth with about 20 times more detail than any previous Earth-observing satellites. The information that EO1 sends back encompasses all manner of happenings on earth, like the spread of forest and bush fires, the impact of cattle grazing in South America, the state of the rain forest, and the spread of harmful plant species.

The beauty of incorporating intelligent agents into the spacecraft is that they can learn and adapt to changing and unexpected conditions. NASA's software engineers have designed these agents to achieve certain goals rather than to react to prespecified situations, making them able to handle complex interactions. Since the software can "learn" and function autonomously, it can react to unexpected situations, allowing scientists to conduct more complex and interesting research on board.[33]

down.[34] Other monitoring-and-surveillance agents work on the manufacturing shop floor, finding equipment problems and locating other machinery that can perform the same job.

Monitoring-and-surveillance agents are often used to monitor complex computer networks. Allstate Insurance has a network with 2,000 computers. The company uses a network monitoring agent from Computer Associates International called Neugent that watches its huge networks 24 hours a day. Every five seconds, the agent measures 1,200 data points and can predict a system crash 45 minutes before it happens. Neugent combines intelligent agent technology with neural network technology to look for patterns of activity or problems. The neural network part can learn what conditions predict a downturn in network efficiency or a slowing in network traffic. Neugent also watches for electronic attacks and can detect them early so that they can be stopped.

Another type of monitoring-and-surveillance agent is one that works on computer networks keeping track of the configuration of each computer connected to the network. It tracks and updates the central configuration database when anything on any computer changes, like the number or type of disk drives. An important task in managing networks is prioritizing traffic and shaping bandwidth. That means sending enough network capacity or bandwidth to the most important tasks versus those that are secondary. At a university, for example, processing end-of-semester grades might take precedence.

Some other types of monitoring-and-surveillance agents include

- Agents that watch your competition and bring back price changes and special offer information.
- Agents that monitor Internet sites, discussion groups, mailing lists, and so on, for stock manipulation, insider training, and rumors that might affect stock prices.

- Agents that monitor sites for updated information on the topic of your choice.
- Agents that watch particular products and bring back price or terms changes.
- Agents that monitor auction sites for products or prices that you want.

DATA-MINING AGENTS

A *data-mining agent* operates in a data warehouse discovering information. A data warehouse brings together information from lots of different sources. Data mining is the process of looking through the data warehouse to find information that you can use to take action—like ways to increase sales or to keep customers who are considering defecting. Data mining is so called because you have to sift through a lot of information for the gold nuggets that will affect the bottom line (or top line). This sort of nugget spotting is similar to what the FBI and CIA do when they bring together little bits of information from diverse sources and use the overall pattern to spot trouble brewing.

As you learned in Chapter 3, database queries answer questions like "How much did we spend on transportation in March of this year?" Multidimensional analysis is the next step in complexity and answers questions like "How much did we spend on transportation in the southeast during March of the last five years?" Data mining goes deeper and may suggest questions you may not even have thought to ask like the retail manager we mentioned in Chapter 1 who thought "What else do young men buy on Friday afternoons when they come in to buy diapers?"[35]

One of the most common types of data mining is classification, which finds patterns in information and categorizes items into those classes. You may remember that this is just what neural networks do best. So, not surprisingly, neural networks are part of many data-mining tools. And data-mining agents are another integral part, since these intelligent agents search for information in a data warehouse.

A data-mining agent may detect a major shift in a trend or a key indicator. It can also detect the presence of new information and alert you. Volkswagen uses an intelligent agent system that acts as an early-warning system about market conditions. If conditions become such that the assumptions underlying the company's strategy are no longer true, the intelligent agent alerts managers.[36] For example, the intelligent agent might see a problem in some part of the country that is about to or will shortly cause payments to slow down. Having that information early lets managers formulate a plan to protect themselves.

USER AGENTS

User agents (sometimes called *personal agents*) are intelligent agents that take action on your behalf. In this category belong those intelligent agents that already perform, or will shortly perform, the following tasks:

- Check your e-mail, sort it according to priority (your priority), and alert you when good stuff comes through—like college acceptance letters.
- Play computer games as your opponent or patrol game areas for you.
- Fill out forms on the Web automatically for you. They even store your information for future reference.
- "Discuss" topics with you from your deepest fears to your favorite sports.

One expanding application of intelligent agent technology is in automating business functions. For example, Mission Hockey, a company that manufacturers and distributes in-line and ice hockey skates and other gear, uses software from Sweden called Movex that has a user-agent component. Movex will search the Internet or a company intranet or extranet to negotiate and make deals with suppliers and distributors. In this case, the intelligent agent is incorporated into an enterprise resource planning system. Enterprise resource planning (or ERP) is a very important concept in today's business world. The term refers to a method of getting and keeping an overview on every part of the business (a bird's-eye view, so to speak), so that production, development, selling, and servicing of goods and services will all be coordinated to contribute to the company's goals and objectives. We discussed ERPs in Chapter 2 and will explore them further in Chapter 7.

Multi-Agent Systems and Agent-Based Modeling

What do cargo transport systems, book distribution centers, the video game market, a flu epidemic, and an ant colony have in common? They are all complex adaptive systems and thus share some common characteristics. By observing parts of the ecosystem, like ant or bee colonies, artificial intelligence scientists can use hardware and software models that incorporate insect characteristics and behavior to (1) learn how people-based systems behave; (2) predict how they will behave under a given set of circumstances; and (3) improve human systems to make them more efficient and effective. This concept of learning from ecosystems and adapting their characteristics to human and organizational situations is called *biomimicry.*

In the last few years, AI research has made much progress in modeling complex organizations as a whole with the help of multi-agent systems. In a *multi-agent system* groups of intelligent agents have the ability to work independently and to interact with each other. The simulation of a human organization using a multi-agent system is called agent-based modeling. *Agent-based modeling* is a way of simulating human organizations using multiple intelligent agents, each of which follows a set of simple rules and can adapt to changing conditions.

Agent-based modeling systems are being used to model stock market fluctuations, predict the escape routes that people seek in a burning building, estimate the effects of interest rates on consumers with different types of debt, and anticipate how changes in conditions will affect the supply chain, to name just a few. See Figure 4.7 for examples of companies that have used agent-based modeling to their advantage.

- Southwest Airlines—to optimize cargo routing.

- Procter & Gamble—to overhaul its handling of what the company calls its "supply network" of 5 billion consumers in 140 countries.

- Air Liquide America—to reduce production and distribution costs of liquefied industrial gases.

- Merck & Co.—to find more efficient ways of distributing anti-AIDS drugs in Africa.

- Ford Motor Co.—to build a model of consumer preferences and find the best balance between production costs and customers' demands.

- Edison Chouest Offshore LLC—to find the best way to deploy its service and supply vessels in the Gulf of Mexico.

Figure 4.7

Companies That Use Agent-Based Modeling[37]

ANT COLONIES AND SWARM INTELLIGENCE

The ant ecosystem is one of the most widely used types of simulations in business problems. If you've ever tried to remove ants from your home, you know how determined and effective ant colonies are. Individual ants are autonomous, acting and reacting independently. (If you drop a crumb into the middle of a group of ants, they'll all scatter in different directions.) However, ants are unusual insects in that they are social. (Less than 2 percent of insects are social, with termites being the only other entirely social species, although some types of bees and wasps are, too.) The term "social" implies that all the members of a colony work together to establish and maintain a global system that's efficient and stable. So, even though the ants are autonomous, each ant contributes to the system as a whole. Ants have been on Earth for 40 million years, compared to the relatively short human occupation of 100 thousand years, and their extraordinary evolutionary success is the result of ants' collective behavior, known as swarm intelligence.

Swarm (collective) intelligence is the collective behavior of groups of simple agents that are capable of devising solutions to problems as they arise, eventually leading to coherent global patterns.[38] That is to say, complex collective behavior can result from the individuals in the system consistently following a small number of simple rules. Swarm intelligence allows the creation and maintenance of systems that have the following four characteristics:

1. *Flexibility,* so that the system can respond to changes, both large and small, in the environment around it. In an ant colony, for example, if you move the food, the ants will find it again very quickly.

2. *Robustness,* so that even if some individual members of the system don't succeed, the work gets done. For example, if you remove some of the ants, others will step in and continue the work.

3. *Decentralization,* in that each individual has a relatively simple job to do and performs that job without supervision. In the ant colony there are forager ants, soldier ants who protect the nest, queens who produce the new generations, ants who take care of and feed the cocoons, and so on.

4. *Self-organization,* in that the methods of problem solving are not prescribed from a central authority, but rather are developed as problem-solving strategies by the individuals in the group who are responsible for the completion of the work. For example, if an ant finds a food morsel that's too large for one ant to carry, others come to help and they run around changing positions until they have the morsel balanced well enough that they can carry it off. See the Web site at www.scottcamazine.com/personal/research/index.htm for other examples of self-organization in nature.[39]

So, how are the workings of ant colonies related to information technology in modern business? Swarm intelligence gives us a way to examine collective systems where groups of individuals have certain goals, solve problems, and make decisions without centralized control or a common plan.

A comparison of the activities of forager ants and those of the cargo-handling arm of Southwest Airlines affords a striking example of the similarities between ecosystems and human organizations, which we will consider shortly. There are some uncanny parallels that surprised Southwest's management. First, though, let's ponder the ants.

Forager ants have the sole responsibility of providing food to the colony. They don't form committees and discuss strategies or look to a central authority for direction; they just find food and bring it back to the nest, and in doing so they follow a simple procedure.

Say two ants (A and B) leave the same point to search for food. Ant A finds food first because ant B has to traverse around several rocks before finding food (i.e., Ant A found a shorter route to the food). Having found a food source, Ant A returns to the nest by the same route, leaving behind a trail of pheromones (a biological breadcrumb trail) so that it will know what path to take next time and so will the other ants. The first ant that returns "lays the trail" first so that's the one that other ants take. Then the other ants strengthen the pheromone trail on their return journey by leaving their own pheromone tracks along the path Ant A found.

Meanwhile, Ant B arrives back at the nest after the shorter path has already been established. The other ants that are already on the move don't change their route. The pheromone trail on the unused path (that left by ant B) evaporates after a certain length of time so that it's effectively deleted from the system as a desirable route to food. The approach is straightforward but effective, and can be expressed in the following rules:

- Rule 1: Follow the trail if one exists, otherwise create one.
- Rule 2: Find food.
- Rule 3: Return to the nest, making a pheromone trail.

If changes occur (say, for example, that the food source is removed), the ants cease returning to the place where the food used to be, and the trail disappears. Then the process begins again, and proceeds relentlessly, with forager ants finding a new food source and creating pheromone corridors that lead the way.

The problem that the ants have just solved is one of the oldest problems that humans (as well as ants) have faced. It's known as "the shortest path problem" or the "traveling salesman problem." Anyone who schedules drop-off and pick-up routes for delivery trucks, or schedules jobs on the factory floor, or even colors maps, making sure that no two adjacent components have the same color, has had to find a solution to the same type of problem.

Taking their cue from nature, AI researchers built sets of small robots and incorporated software that allowed the robots to follow rules and interact with each other in the same basic ways as the ants. They also dispensed with the physical forms altogether, creating virtual ants in the form of small autonomous blocks of code that we call intelligent agents. And each code block could follow certain rules, interact, and adapt. These virtual ants were then arranged into multi-agent systems that were further refined into agent-based models. Enter Southwest Airlines as a case in point.

Even though cargo is a small part of Southwest's business, it was causing management headaches and bottlenecks at busy airports. Southwest consulted with swarm intelligence experts, who used a virtual model of foraging ants to simulate the cargo-handling process. And that was how Southwest managers discovered, to their surprise, that there were actually better ways to handle cargo than to put it on the first plane flying in the right direction. Surprisingly, the computer's swarm intelligence model showed that it might actually be better to leave cargo on a plane heading in the wrong direction. For example, cargo headed from Chicago to Boston would be better left on a plane going from Chicago to Atlanta and then reloaded onto a flight to Boston, requiring less unloading and reloading. Following the ant model, Southwest decreased its cargo transfer rates by 80 percent, reduced the workload of cargo employees by 20 percent, and also found that there was spare cargo space on flights that were previously full, enabling the company to accept more business. The overall gain to Southwest was in excess of $10 million per year.[40]

The future will see many more uses of intelligent agents. It's a pretty safe bet that these applications will include swarm intelligence and agent-based modeling. Already, swarm intelligence is being implemented widely for scheduling, resource allocation, and routing. Other applications in the early stages include networks that have self-organizing components and robots that assemble themselves. There must be many, many more that have not yet been dreamt of. Some people believe that intelligent agents will replace many of the other types of simulations in the future since swarm intelligence supports individuality, flexibility, and entities that can adapt quickly and effectively in a fast-changing business environment.

Summary: Student Learning Outcomes Revisited

1. **Compare and contrast decision support systems and geographic information systems.** A *decision support system (DSS)* is a highly flexible and interactive IT system that is designed to support decision making when the problem is not structured. A *geographic information system (GIS)* is a decision support system designed specifically to analyze spatial information. So, they both are designed to support decision-making efforts. While traditional DSSs mainly use text and numeric data, GISs represent many types of information in spatial or map form.

2. **Define expert systems and describe the types of problems to which they are applicable.** An *expert system* (or *knowledge-based system*) is an artificial intelligence system that applies reasoning capabilities to reach a conclusion. A rule-based expert system asks the user questions and, based on the answers, asks other questions until it has enough information to make a decision or a recommendation. Expert systems are good for diagnostic (what's wrong) and prescriptive problems (what to do). For example, you could use an expert system to diagnose illness or to figure out why a machine is malfunctioning. And you could use an expert system to determine what to do about the problem.

3. **Define neural networks and fuzzy logic and the uses of these AI tools.** A *neural network* (also called an *artificial neural network* or *ANN*) is an artificial intelligence system that is capable of finding and differentiating patterns. Neural networks are good for finding commonalities in situations that have many variables. *Fuzzy logic* is a mathematical method of handling imprecise or subjective information. It is used to represent relative terms such as "hot" and "cold" so that a computer can use them in processing.

4. **Define genetic algorithms and list the concepts on which they are based and the types of** problems they solve. A *genetic algorithm* is an artificial intelligence system that mimics the evolutionary, survival-of-the-fittest process to generate increasingly better solutions to a problem. Genetic algorithms use the principles of *selection, crossover,* and *mutation* from evolution theory. These systems are best suited to problems where hundreds or thousands of solutions are possible and you need an optimum solution.

5. **Describe the four types of agent-based technologies.** An *intelligent agent* is software that assists you, or acts on your behalf, in performing repetitive computer-related tasks. The four types are

   - *Information agents*—the most common are *buyer agents* (or *shopping bots*) that search the Web for products and services

   - *Monitoring-and-surveillance agents* (or *predictive agents*) track conditions, perhaps on a network, and signal changes or troublesome conditions

   - *Data-mining agents* search data warehouses to discover information

   - *User agents* (or *personal agents*) take action for you, particularly in repetitive tasks like sorting e-mail

   - Two emerging variants within agent-based technologies are (1) *multi-agent systems,* groups of intelligent agents that have the ability to work independently and to interact with each other, and (2) *agent-based modeling,* a way of simulating human organizations using multiple intelligent agents, each of which follows a set of simple rules and can adapt to changing conditions. Both are based on *biomimicry,* learning from ecosystems and adapting their characteristics to human and organizational situations.

CLOSING CASE STUDY ONE

CRYSTAL BALL, CLAIRVOYANT, FORTUNE TELLING. . . CAN PREDICTIVE ANALYTICS DELIVER THE FUTURE?

In the Tom Cruise movie *Minority Report,* police were able to accurately predict a crime, its location, and the criminal in advance of the event in time to send police to prevent the crime from occurring. Science fiction at its best, huh? Actually, that's somewhat of a reality now through predictive analytics.

Predictive analytics uses a variety of decision tools and techniques—such as neural networks, data mining, decision trees, and Bayesian networks—to analyze current and historical data and make predictions about the likelihood of the occurrence of future events. Along the lines of *Minority Report,* police in Richmond, Virginia, are using predictive analytics to determine the likelihood (probability) that a particular type of crime will occur in a specific neighborhood at a specific time.

Using the system, the mobile task force of 30 officers is deployed to the areas with the greatest likelihood of crimes occurring. According to Richmond Police Chief, Rodney Moore, "Based on the predictive models, we deploy them [the mobile task force] almost every three or four hours." Sixteen fugitives have been arrested directly as a result of the system's prediction of the next time and location of a crime. Moreover, in the first week of May in 2006, no homicides occurred, compared to three in the same week of the previous year.

The predictive analytics system uses large databases that contain information on past calls to police, arrests, crime logs, current weather data, and local festivals and sporting and other events. From an IT point of view, the system is a combination of software—SPSS's Clementine predictive analysis software and reporting and visualization tools from Information Builder—and decision support and predictive models developed by RTI International.

The Richmond police afford just one of many examples of the use predictive analytics. Some others include the following:

- *Blue Cross Blue Shield of Tennessee*—uses a neural network predictive model to predict which health care resources will be needed by which postoperative patients months and even years into the future. According to Soyal

Momin, manager of research and development at Blue Cross Blue Shield, "If we're seeing a pattern that predicts heart failure, kidney failure, or diabetes, we want to know that as soon as possible."

- *FedEx*—uses a predictive analytics system that is delivering real and true results 65 to 90 percent of the time. The system predicts how customers will respond to new services and price changes. It also predicts which customers will no longer use FedEx as a result of a price increase and how much additional revenue the company will generate from proposed drop-box locations.
- *University of Utah*—uses a predictive analytics system to generate alumni donations. The system determines which of its 300,000 alumni are most likely to respond to an annual donation appeal. This is particularly appealing to most higher-education institutions as they have limited resources to devote to the all-important task of fund raising. Donations increased 73 percent in 2005 for the University of Utah's David Eccles School of Business as a result of the system.

The future of predictive analytics is very bright. Sales of predictive analytics software exceeded $3 billion in 2008. Moreover, businesses are beginning to build predictive analytics into mainstream, operational applications—such as CRM, SCM, and inventory management—which will further increase their use. According to Scott Burk, senior statistician and technical lead for marketing analytics at Overstock.com, "Predictive analytics is going to become more operational. We're definitely doing things a lot smarter than we were six months ago." Overstock.com uses its predictive analytics system to predict demand levels for products at various price points.[41]

Questions

1. Many predictive analytic models are based on neural network technologies. What is the role of neural networks in predictive analytics? How

can neural networks help predict the likelihood of future events? In answering these questions, specifically reference Blue Cross Blue Shield of Tennessee.

2. What if the Richmond police began to add demographic data to its predictive analytics system to further attempt to determine the type of person (by demographic) who would in all likelihood commit a crime? Is predicting the type of person who would commit a crime by demographic data (ethnicity, gender, income level, and so on) good or bad?

3. In the movie *Gattaca,* predictive analytics were used to determine the most successful career for a person. Based on DNA information, the system determined whether or not an individual was able to advance through an educational track to become something like an engineer or if the person should complete only a lower level of education and become a janitor. The government then acted on the system's recommendations and placed people in various career tracks. Is this a good or bad

use of technology? How is this different from the variety of personal tests you can take that inform you of your aptitude for different careers?

4. What role can geographic information systems (GISs) play in the use of predictive analytics? As you answer this question, specifically reference FedEx's use of predictive analytics to (1) determine which customers will not respond positively to a price increase and (2) project additional revenues from proposed drop-box locations.

5. The Department of Defense (DoD) and the Pacific Northwest National Laboratory are combining predictive analytics with visualization technologies to predict the probability that a terrorist attack will occur. For example, suspected terrorists caught on security cameras who loiter too long in a given place might signal their intent to carry out a terrorist attack. How can this type of predictive analytics be used in an airport? At what other buildings and structures might this be used?

CLOSING THE GREAT HEALTH CARE DIVIDE WITH PATTERN RECOGNITION AND DATA-MINING TECHNOLOGIES

In today's world, people, cultures, and nations are distinguished by which side of the "*great divides*" they are on. There are the financial and economic divides, which differentiate between the haves and have-nots with respect to wealth, income, and prosperity. There are the educational divides that distinguish among people on the basis of their access to education and according to whether a college degree is achieved. There is a "great digital divide," on either side of which are those who have or do not have access to technology.

Worldwide—and certainly in the United States—is a health care divide between those who can and cannot afford good health care. With health care costs spiraling out of control, the health care divide is widening and the population with access to affordable health care is shrinking. Therefore, many health care providers and technology providers such as IBM, the Mayo Clinic, and the Cleveland Clinic are collaborating on IT-enabled strategies to reduce the cost of health care while providing better health care than ever before.

IBM and the Mayo Clinic are collaborating on cost-efficient ways to provide customized medical treatments to individual patients, such as choosing the right chemotherapy treatment for a specific patient given his or her unique genetic makeup, by applying pattern recognition and data-mining technologies to the electronic medical records of some 4.4 million patients.

In the first phase of the project, IBM and the Mayo Clinic worked together to consolidate into one database all patients' medical records from numerous separate systems—including digitized (electronic) patient files, lab results, X-rays, and electrocardiograms—and from all of Mayo's hospitals in Arizona, Florida, and Minnesota. In the current, second, phase, IBM and the Mayo Clinic are applying pattern recognition, data-mining technologies, and other decision support tools to help health care providers determine the best therapies for each patient. The goal of the decision support system is to find patterns relating to how well different types of patients respond to certain types of therapies. The system sifts through patient information concerning age, medical history, and genetics to find patterns that suggest the best treatments.

For example, the Mayo Clinic recently began using a new chemotherapy treatment for lung cancer that produced disappointing results, despite all the positive research findings. The decision support system, however, was able to determine that a small percentage of patients, all with the same genetic pattern, did respond positively to the therapy, which is now targeted for only those individuals matching that genetic profile.

Similarly, IBM and the Cleveland Clinic are working on a decision support system to identify patients most susceptible to abdominal aortic aneurysms. The presence of aneurysms often shows no symptoms until the aneurysm is about to rupture, and the survival rate of the rupture is less than 50 percent.

According to Dr. Kenneth Ouriel, chairman of the Division of Surgery and the Department of Vascular Surgery at the Cleveland Clinic, "If we can predict what patients are at risk for these ruptures, we can identify the patients who need surgery or other treatments." To identify such patients, the system evaluates a wealth of information including lab, genetic, imaging, and drug history and how different factors contribute to risks as well as to treatment outcomes.[42,43,44]

Questions

1. In the case study, we referred to the systems being developed and used as *decision support systems.* However, we also identified various artificial intelligence (AI) technologies. How can a decision support system incorporate and use AI technologies such as pattern recognition?

2. At the Mayo Clinic, patients are given opt-in and opt-out rights concerning whether or not their information is used in the system that determines the most appropriate therapies given the specific patient profile. So far, 95 percent of the patients have opted to have their information included in the system. (This is the notion of *opting in.*) Why do you believe that 5 percent of the patients have opted out? Would you opt in or opt out in this case? Please provide your reasoning.

3. In this case, demographic information such as ethnicity, gender, and age greatly impacts the quality of the decision support and analysis. The same could be argued for the predictive analytics system used by the Richmond police in this chapter's first closing case study. Why would some people find it acceptable to use such demographic data in this case (for medical purposes) and not in the first case (for predicting crime, its location, and its timing)?

4. One of the most popular and widely used application areas for expert systems is medicine. What role could an expert system play in helping the Cleveland Clinic identify patients susceptible to abdominal aortic aneurysms? What sort of rules would the expert system include?

5. How might a monitoring-and-surveillance agent be used for patients in a medical environment? How can health care providers take advantage of the capabilities of an information agent to stay abreast of the latest medical trends and treatments?

Key Terms and Concepts

Agent-based modeling, 115
Artificial intelligence (AI), 103
Biomimicry, 115
Buyer agent (shopping bot), 112
Choice, 97
Crossover, 110
Data management, 100
Data-mining agent, 114
Decision support system (DSS), 98
Design, 96
Expert system (knowledge-based system), 104
Fuzzy logic, 109
Genetic algorithm, 110

Geographic information system (GIS), 102
Implementation, 97
Information agent, 112
Intelligence, 96
Intelligent agent, 111
Location mashup, 104
Mashup, 104
Model management, 99
Monitoring-and-surveillance agent (predictive agent), 112
Multi-agent system, 115
Mutation, 110

Neural network (artificial neural network, ANN), 107
Nonrecurring (ad hoc) decision, 98
Nonstructured decision, 98
Predictive analytics, 119
Recurring decision, 98
Satisficing, 97
Selection, 110
Structured decision, 97
Swarm (collective) intelligence, 116
User agent (personal agent), 114
User interface management, 101

Short-Answer Questions

1. What are the four types of decisions discussed in this chapter? Give an example of each.
2. What are the four steps in making a decision?
3. What is a DSS? Describe its components.
4. What is a geographic information system used for?
5. How is information represented in a geographic information system?
6. What is artificial intelligence? Name the artificial intelligence systems used widely in business.
7. What are the advantages of an expert system?
8. What sort of problems is an expert system used for?
9. How does a neural network work?
10. What three concepts of evolution are used by the genetic algorithm?
11. What are intelligent agents? What tasks can they perform?
12. What is a multi-agent system?
13. What do monitoring-and-surveillance agents do?

Assignments and Exercises

1. **MAKE A GIS** Make a GIS-type map using transparencies. Draw a map of your campus on one plastic transparency sheet. You can use software or felt-tip pens to do the actual drawing of the map. Next, use a second sheet as an overlay and mark on it what classes you have taken in what buildings. Take a third sheet and enter the type of classroom you had the course in (i.e., auditorium, lab, small, medium, large room). Make a fourth layer with special facilities, like a computer lab or a biology lab, and so on. What problems did you encounter while designing your GIS? What other information would you like to see in a real GIS of this type? Would this handmade GIS be helpful for new students? What layers would you keep for general use? What layers would you keep for sentimental value when your college days are over?

2. **CHOOSE A FINANCING OPTION** Using a spreadsheet (like Excel, for example) evaluate your options for a $12,000 car. Compare the payments (use the =pmt function in Excel), the total amount of interest, and the total you'll pay for the car under the following four options:

   a. 3 years at 0 percent interest
   b. 2 years at 1.99 percent annual percent rate (APR)
   c. 4 years at 5 percent APR
   d. 6 years at 6 percent APR

What other considerations would you take into account if you were going to buy a new car? Are there considerations other than the interest rate and the other parts that can be calculated? What are they? How is a car different from other purchases, such as CDs or TV sets or computers?

3. **WHICH SOFTWARE WOULD YOU USE?** Which type or types of computer-aided decision support software would you use for each of the situations in the table below? Note why you think each of your choices is appropriate. The decision support alternatives are

- Decision support system
- Geographic information system
- Expert system
- Neural network
- Genetic algorithm
- Intelligent agent

Problem	Type of Decision Support
You and another marketing executive on a different continent want to develop a new pricing structure for products	
You want to predict when customers are about to take their business elsewhere	
You want to fill out a short tax form	
You want to determine the fastest route for package delivery to 23 different addresses in a city	
You want to decide where to spend advertising dollars (TV, radio, newspaper, direct mail, e-mail)	
You want to keep track of competitors' prices for comparable goods and services	

4. **WHAT SHOULD THE MUSIC STORE OWNER DO?** A music store owner wants to have enough of the hottest CDs in stock so that people who come in to buy a particular CD won't be disappointed—and the store won't lose the profit. CDs that are not sold within a certain length of time go onto the sale table where they may have to be sold at cost, if they sell at all.

The owner wants to design a decision support system to predict how many copies she should purchase and what information she will need. List some of the considerations that would go into such a system. Here are a couple to start you off: (1) the population of the target market; (2) sales for particular types of music in similar markets.

Discussion Questions

1. Some experts claim that if a business gets 52 percent of its decisions right, it will be successful. Would using a decision support system guarantee better results? Why or why not? What does the quality of any decision depend on? Do you think it matters what type of decisions are included in this 52 percent? For example, would getting the right type of paper clips be as influential a decision as deciding where to locate the business? Can you think of a situation where the type of paper clip matters a great deal?

2. Consider the topic of data warehouses in Chapter 3. In the future, AI systems will be increasingly applied to data warehouse processing. Which AI systems do you think might be helpful? For which tasks, or situations, might they best be applied? Do you think that AI systems will someday play a greater role in the design of databases and data warehouses? Why or why not?

3. Consider the differences and similarities among the four AI techniques discussed in this chapter.

Name some problems that might be amenable to more than one type of AI system. Say you sell baseballs from your Web site. What types of AI systems could you use to generate information that would be useful to you in deciding what direction to take your company in the future? If you were pretty successful at selling baseballs, would you expect to have the amount of information on customers that, say, Wal-Mart has? Why or why not?

4. AI systems are relatively new approaches to solving business problems. What are the difficulties with new IT approaches in general? For each of the systems we discussed, identify some advantages and disadvantages of AI systems over traditional business processes. Say you were selling specialty teas and had both brick and click stores. Would you use the same type of AI systems for each part of your business? In what way would you use them or why would you not? Is there a place for decision support and artificial intelligence techniques in small specialty businesses? In what way would decision support add value? Can you think of how a DSS or an AI system would be value reducing (in terms of the value chain concept we discussed in Chapter 1)? What do you see as the major differences between running a mammoth concern and a small specialty business?

5. Neural networks recognize and categorize patterns. If someone were to have a neural network that could scan information on all aspects of your life, where would that neural network potentially be able to find information about you? Consider confidential (doctor's office) as well as publicly available (department of motor vehicles) information.

6. What type of AI systems could your school use to help with registration? Intelligent agents find vast amounts of information very quickly. Neural networks can classify patterns instantaneously. What sorts of information might your school administration be able to generate using these (or other AI systems) with all of its student data?

7. For which activities that are part of college life could you use agent-based modeling to simulate what happens? Describe three such scenarios. ▪

CHAPTER PROJECTS

Group Projects

- Assessing the Value of Customer Relationship Management: Trevor Toy Auto Mechanics (p. 364)
- Analyzing the Value of Information: Affordable Homes Real Estate (p. 365)
- Executive Information System Reporting Political Campaign Finance (p. 366)
- Building a Decision Support System: Creating an Investment Portfolio (p. 370)
- Creating a Decision Support System: Buy versus Lease (p. 376)
- Building a Decision Support System: Break-Even Analysis (p. 382)
- Building a Scheduling Decision Support System: Airline Crew Scheduling (p. 384)

e-Commerce Projects

- Best in Computer Statistics and Resources (p. 388)
- Consumer Information (p. 388)
- Metadata (p. 389)
- Bureau of Labor and Statistics (p. 390)
- Demographics (p. 390)
- Exploring Google Earth (p. 392)
- Gold, Silver, Interest Rates, and Money (p. 394)
- Learning about Investing (p. 396)
- Stock Quotes (p. 397)

CHAPTER FIVE OUTLINE

STUDENT LEARNING OUTCOMES

1. Define and describe the nine major e-commerce business models.

2. Identify the differences and similarities among customers and their perceived value of products and services in the B2B and B2C e-commerce business models.

3. Compare and contrast the development of a marketing mix for customers in the B2B and B2C e-commerce business models.

4. Summarize the ways of moving money in the world of e-commerce and related issues.

5. Discuss some major trends that are impacting both the e-commerce business world and society in general.

PERSPECTIVES

WEB SUPPORT

www.mhhe.com/haag

- Exploring Google Earth
- Learning about investing
- Gathering competitive intelligence
- Researching storefront software
- Finding hosting services
- Gold, silver, interest rates, and money
- Free and rentable storage space
- Small Business Administration
- Global statistics and resources

CHAPTER FIVE

Electronic Commerce
Strategies for the New Economy

OPENING CASE STUDY:
WHAT'S REPLACING THE DAY AFTER THANKSGIVING FOR SHOPPING SALES?

You've heard that the most profitable retail shopping day before Christmas is the Friday after Thanksgiving. It's often called Black Friday, because it's the day retailers move out of the *red* and into the *black* on their income statements. But not anymore . . . Cyber Monday is quickly replacing Black Friday as the big shopping day.

Cyber Monday occurs on the Monday after Black Friday weekend. Cyber Monday is the day when consumers go back to work and shop on the Internet for products they found on Black Friday on retail shelves. Almost 80 percent of online retailers state that sales significantly increased on Cyber Monday last year. And, yes, we are talking about people being at work and shopping for Christmas gifts. According to a BIGresearch/shop.org survey of 7,200 consumers, 37 percent stated that they have used or will use the Internet at work to shop for gifts online. While that creates a problem for productivity in the workplace, online retailers are redefining their business models to take advantage of Cyber Monday.

Ice.com, an online jewelry retailer, sees this as a new business dimension, so much so that it's offering free shipping and a gift-with-purchase promotion for everyone ordering products on Cyber Monday. According to Pinny Ginwisch, Ice.com founder and executive vice president of marketing, "The results are unbelievable." Ice.com expects 400,000 to 600,000 visitors on Cyber Monday, almost double the usual traffic.

Like all online businesses, Ice.com recognizes that danger lies within any opportunity. For example, increased Web traffic means potential processing delays. So, Ice.com is adding five backup servers just to handle the additional traffic and take over in event of a site crash. Ice.com has hired an additional 10 customer service representatives to handle ordering processing, and has prepared 4,000 packages of its most popular items ready to ship the day after Cyber Monday.

Just like in the traditional brick-and-mortar business environment, in the world of e-commerce you must constantly strive to stay ahead of the competition. You have to determine innovative ways in which to offer products and services that your customers will perceive add value. And you must constantly reevaluate traditional business models such as Black Friday. Black Friday still has its place in the brick-and-mortar world, but Cyber Monday is now the big shopping day in the virtual world. If your organization doesn't act on this information, you may be out business.

In this chapter, we'll explore the world of e-commerce, and we'll continue to introduce you to many special considerations that you must take into account to be successful in e-commerce. Commerce will always be commerce—the buying and selling of products and services. But the "e" in e-commerce presents new challenges and opportunities.[1,2]

Questions

1. Do you shop for gifts online? If so, at what sites and for what occasions?

2. What's your take on people spending time at work to shop for personal items?

3. How can brick-and-mortar retailers take advantage of Cyber Monday?

Introduction

The past 10 years of the new economy introduced by the World Wide Web have certainly been interesting. There has been an entrepreneurial frenzy unlike anything the world has ever seen. Fortunes have been made and lost. Dot-com millionaires and billionaires were literally created overnight—many became dot-bomb paupers in about the same amount of time.

What fueled this frenzy and is still doing so today? It's electronic commerce enabled by information technology. ***Electronic commerce (e-commerce)*** is commerce, but it is commerce accelerated and enhanced by IT, in particular the Internet. E-commerce enables customers, consumers, and companies to form powerful new relationships that would not be possible without the enabling technologies. E-commerce breaks down business barriers such as time, geography, language, currency, and culture. In a few short hours, you can set up shop on the Internet and be instantly accessible to millions of consumers worldwide.

Is there a catch? The answer is both no and yes. It's "no" because it doesn't take much effort to create your own e-commerce Web site. It's "yes" because you still have to follow sound business fundamentals and principles to be successful. Let's not forget that fundamentally it's still all about commerce, businesses and people buying and selling products and services. E-commerce is no "silver bullet," as some entrepreneurs have found out to their chagrin.

In short, you must have a clear path-to-profitability. A ***path-to-profitability (P2P)*** is a formal business plan that outlines key business issues such as customer targets (by demographic, industry, etc.), marketing strategies, operations strategies (e.g., production, transportation, and logistics), and projected targets for income statement and balance sheet items. That is to say, running an e-commerce operation is no different from running a traditional brick-and-mortar business. You must identify your customers, determine how to reach them with a compelling story, and so on. The major error that most dot-com businesses made in the late 1990s—and they are no longer in existence today—is that they never developed a clear *path-to-profitability*.

Figure 5.1

Nine Major E-Commerce Business Models

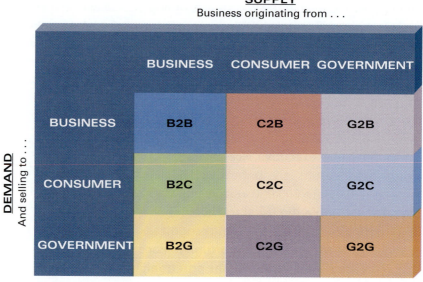

E-Commerce Business Models

As illustrated in Figure 5.1, there are nine major e-commerce business models. While we focus the majority of this chapter on Business to Business (B2B) e-commerce and Business to Consumer (B2C) e-commerce (both in the e-commerce private sector), let's start by exploring each e-commerce business model.

BUSINESS TO BUSINESS (B2B) E-COMMERCE

Business to Business (B2B) e-commerce occurs when a business sells products and services to customers who are primarily other businesses. So, for example, when Gates Rubber Company sells belts, hoses, and other rubber and synthetic products to General Motors or any other manufacturer that needs those parts, this is B2B e-commerce. B2B e-commerce is where all the money is right now in the e-commerce world. It's not the flashy consumer-oriented businesses you read about and see everyday such as eBay, Myspace, and so on. It's the many behind-the-scenes interactions that businesses engage in ultimately to support interacting with you as a customer, such as Gates selling a hose to General Motors for a car that you eventually buy. Another example is First Data Corporation. First Data Corporation is a payments infrastructure provider that many businesses use. When you pay with a credit card at most major stores, your credit card authorization and verification is handled by First Data for the store. You may not have even heard of First Data, but it is one of America's top-250 largest corporations.

As you can see in Figure 5.2, businesses are taking full advantage of e-commerce by creating and using B2B e-marketplaces. *B2B e-marketplaces* are virtual marketplaces in which businesses buy from and sell products to each other, share information (as in information partnerships from Chapter 2), and perform other important activities. B2B e-marketplaces represent one of the fastest growing trends in the B2B e-commerce model.

Figure 5.2

Business to Business and Business to Consumer E-Commerce Business Models

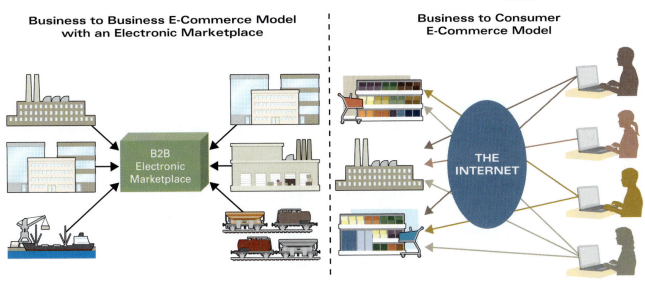

Business to Business E-Commerce Model with an Electronic Marketplace

B2B Electronic Marketplace

Business to Consumer E-Commerce Model

THE INTERNET

Businesses are increasingly aware that they must create supply chain management systems, drive out costs, create information partnerships with other businesses, and even collaborate with other businesses on new product and service offerings. B2B e-marketplaces offer tremendous efficiencies to businesses for performing all of these tasks.

BUSINESS TO CONSUMER (B2C) E-COMMERCE

Business to Consumer (B2C) e-commerce occurs when a business sell products and services to customers who are primarily individuals. You are no doubt familiar with this model of e-commerce. If you've ever ordered a book on Amazon (www.amazon.com), purchased a CD from Circuit City online (www.circuitcity.com), or ordered a movie from Netflix (www.netflix.com), you've participated in B2C e-commerce.

B2C e-commerce garners most of the attention these days in the popular media. B2C e-commerce is the model that fueled the early growth of e-commerce in the 1990s. B2C e-commerce is very much a cut-throat environment, no matter what the product and service. Amazon, one of the most well-known B2C businesses, daily faces stiff competition from hundreds of other e-commerce businesses selling books, movies, music, clothing, computers, consumer electronics, health and beauty products, and home and garden products.

As you can see in Figure 5.2, the B2C e-commerce business model is very different from the B2B e-commerce business model. Consumers interact directly with businesses via the Web. Consumers surf around the Web evaluating products and services at numerous separate e-commerce sites until they eventually choose one site from which to make a purchase. And while businesses prefer to enter into long-term partnerships with other businesses in B2B e-commerce, consumers are fickle and purchase the same types of products and services from many different sites.

CONSUMER TO BUSINESS (C2B) E-COMMERCE

Consumer to Business (C2B) e-commerce occurs when an individual sells products and services to a business. The C2B e-commerce business model is a true inversion of the B2C e-commerce business model. In the B2C e-commerce business model, demand is driven by the consumer and supply is driven by the business. In C2B it is inverted; the consumer drives supply and the business drives demand.[3] Many people have mistakenly lumped such sites as Priceline.com (www.priceline.com) into the C2B category. At Priceline.com you, as a consumer, can set your price for items such as airlines tickets and hotel rooms, but you (as a consumer) still provide the demand and the airline or hotel still provides the supply.

A good example of a true C2B e-commerce business model is offered by Fotolia (www.fotolia.com). There, as an individual, you can post your photos and videos for sale to businesses. Businesses search through the photo and video archives, and, if they choose yours, will pay you a royalty fee to use the photo or video.

Affiliate programs are another good example of the C2B e-commerce business model. Through an affiliate program relationship with Amazon, for example, you can post links on your personal Web site to Amazon for products and services it sells. If a visitor to your site clicks on one of those links and eventually buys the product or service from Amazon, Amazon will pay you a commission fee, which is usually some small percentage of the sale. With this arrangement, you are selling advertising space to Amazon on your Web site; hence, it is an example of the C2B e-commerce business model.

Currently, the C2B e-commerce business model represents only a fraction of the total revenues in the e-commerce space, but it is expected to grow as businesses realize that individuals are more than just consumers of products and services. Blogging, for example, can easily become a C2B e-commerce business model, if you know what you're doing.

CONSUMER TO CONSUMER (C2C) E-COMMERCE

Consumer to Consumer (C2C) e-commerce occurs when an individual sells products and services to another individual. C2C e-commerce usually takes place through an intermediary organization, such as eBay. eBay is a hybrid of both a B2C e-commerce site and a C2C e-commerce site. It is a B2C e-commerce site because it sells a service to you, that of giving you the ability to interact in the auctioning of items. (You pay eBay only if you're the seller, not the buyer.) And it is really an intermediary supporting your engagement in a C2C e-commerce business model. That is, you use eBay to sell products and services to other consumers, and you use eBay to buy products and services from other consumers.

Many C2C Web sites don't really support any sort of e-commerce (i.e., money exchanging hands for products and services). Rather, they facilitate the gathering of people with common interests and something to share. Kazaa (www.kazaa.com) is an example of such a site because it brings together people who want to share mainly MP3 music files. Blogs might also fall into the category of C2C, as they support people sharing and discussing common interests. Many of these types of sites are **ad-supported,** meaning that they derive their revenue by selling advertising space, much like the concept of an affiliate program.

BUSINESS TO GOVERNMENT (B2G) E-COMMERCE

Business to Government (B2G) e-commerce occurs when a business sells products and services to a government entity. Lockheed Martin, for example, generates almost 80 percent of its revenue by providing products and services to the U.S. Department of Defense (DoD).[4] Lockheed Martin sells tactical aircraft, aeronautical research equipment, commercial satellites, government satellites, strategic missiles, naval systems, and IT equipment and services to the U.S. federal government.

Lockheed Martin does this through e-commerce. A major initiative of the U.S. federal government—found in the President's Management Agenda (PMA)[5]—over the past 10 years has been to automate the solicitation and procurement of products and services through e-commerce. According to the PMA, **electronic government (e-government)** is the use of digital technologies to transform government operations in order to improve efficiency, effectiveness, and service delivery. Government entities such as the DoD electronically submit a request for proposal (RFP) or request for quote (RFQ) to vendors for products and services. Those vendors—including Lockheed Martin—provide the RFPs and RFQs electronically back to the government. In fact, in most instances, if you can't perform these types of functions electronically, the U.S. government (and many U.S. state governments) won't do business with your organization.

CONSUMER TO GOVERNMENT (C2G) E-COMMERCE

Consumer to Government (C2G) e-commerce occurs when an individual sells products and services to a government entity. This is very similar to the C2B e-commerce business model, except that the buying partner is a government entity, not a business. The C2G market is quite small, and, to say the least, unremarkable. While you could receive royalties from a government entity for the photos and videos you post on Fotolia, most government entities do not engage in buying products and services from individuals. For example, to sell products and services to the U.S. federal government, you must register yourself as a formal business within the Central Contractor Registration (CCR) system at www.ccr.gov. So, you're not really an individual anymore, but, at a minimum, an individual "doing business as" (DBA) some organization or business.

GOVERNMENT TO BUSINESS (G2B) E-COMMERCE

Government to Business (G2B) e-commerce occurs when a government entity sells products and services to businesses. There are several good examples within this e-commerce business model. The first is the Small Business Administration (SBA, at www.sba.gov). In addition to providing small business loans (which do have an interest accruing), the SBA offers services in many areas such as surety guarantees, disaster assistance, ombudsman, and so on. Most of these services are free, to be sure, but some that involve financial backing and guarantees carry with them various fees and commissions.

Another example is government surplus auctions. At all levels of government—local, district, state, and federal—many entities sell off government surplus, often to individuals but sometimes only to registered businesses. For example, the Transportation Security Administration (TSA) holds frequent auctions to sell off confiscated items at airport security installations, such as small knives, fingernail clippers, and the like, and also items left at those installations by passengers who forgot to gather all their personal belongings.

Some branches of government also sell information to businesses wanting to perform research. While most of the information gathered by the U.S. Geological Survey (Department of Interior) is freely and publicly available, a business can buy more detailed information (none of it being sensitive, of course).

GOVERNMENT TO CONSUMER (G2C) E-COMMERCE

Government to Consumer (G2C) e-commerce refers to the electronic commerce activities performed between a government and its citizens or consumers including paying taxes, registering vehicles, providing information and services, and so on. This particular model of e-commerce does not often fit well within the supply-and-demand notion. Again, supply is the first partner and demand is the second partner. In the B2C model for example, Amazon has the supply of books, movies, and other products, and you—as a consumer—provide the demand. In the G2C model, a government often provides citizens with the ability to interact with it electronically to achieve efficiencies. Paying your taxes is an example. You can file your taxes electronically and receive your refund (or pay additional taxes) electronically. The notion of supply and demand isn't particularly applicable in this case.

In many instances, you can expect the U.S. government (and state governments) to do this to such an extent that it is no longer a click-and-mortar enterprise but rather a click-and-order enterprise. *Click-and-mortar* refers to an organization that has a presence in the physical world such as a building you can visit and also a presence in the virtual world of the Internet, while *click-and-order* (also known as *pure play*) refers to an organization that has a presence in the virtual world but no presence in the physical world. One such example is buying, holding, and redeeming savings bonds. At TreasuryDirect (www.treasurydirect.gov), you can set up an account, buy savings bonds with a credit card, check the maturation status and redeemable value of the bonds, and even redeem the bonds, all electronically. The federal government is aggressively moving in the direction of this being the only way you can buy, sell, and redeem savings bonds.

GOVERNMENT TO GOVERNMENT (G2G) E-COMMERCE

Government to Government (G2G) e-commerce refers to the electronic commerce activities performed within a nation's government. (It might also refer to the electronic commerce activities performed between two or more nations' governments including providing foreign aid.)

Vertical government integration refers to electronic integration of agencies, activities, and processes up and down federal, state, and local government levels. For example, if a manufacturing operation will be creating landfills of waste and pumping sanitized fluids into rivers and streams, it must meet EPA (Environmental Protection Agency) guidelines at local, state, and federal levels. Thus, those levels requiring EPA standards would integrate their IT systems to share information about that manufacturing operation. Another example here falls in the education arena. At all levels of government, there must be information sharing concerning K-12 education standards, test results, and the like.

Horizontal government integration refers to the electronic integration of agencies, activities, and processes across a specific level of government. For example, at the federal level, the EPA may work with the FDA (Food and Drug Administration) to develop standards for food processing plants that emit gases into the atmosphere as a result of their operations. The EPA and FDA share this information horizontally to ensure that each food processing plant is meeting both sets of guidelines (i.e., EPA guidelines and FDA guidelines). Another good example here is that of the armed forces and the Department of Veterans Affairs (VA). As a member of the armed forces moves from active service to the VA (through retirement, injury, etc.), a large amount of information must be communicated to the VA including vitally important medical information.

That ends our overview of the nine e-commerce business models. Although conceptually distinct, in practice each overlaps with one or more of the other models. The question for you now is how to execute on the e-commerce model in which your business operates. We'll focus specifically on B2B and B2C e-commerce, since that is where you'll most likely be working. We will explore three e-commerce *critical success factors:* (1) Understand your business and your customers; (2) Find and establish relationships with customers; (3) Move money easily and securely.

Understand Your Business, Products, Services, and Customers

LEARNING OUTCOME 2

To gain a competitive advantage and be successful in any business, you must clearly define the nature of your products and services, know who your target customers are, and understand how your customers perceive the use of your products and services in their business activities (for the B2B model) or in their personal lives (for the B2C model). To create sound business strategies you have to understand the value that your customers place on your products and services.

There are many worthwhile business activities. But as important as writing a mission statement and producing glitzy marketing brochures may be, what must come first is an objective, very down-to-earth understanding of what your business does. The reality is you can't be all things to all customers. You must answer two questions: (1) Who are your target customers? and (2) What is the value of your products and services as perceived by your customers? Let's look at each in turn.

WHO ARE YOUR CUSTOMERS?

Just as in a brick-and-mortar business, in the e-commerce world you focus your efforts on selling to other businesses, to individual end consumers, or to some combination of the two. If you were in a business like Gates Rubber Company, which produces mostly rubber and synthetic products primarily for sale to the automotive industry and manufacturers of such products as boats and bicycles, you would focus almost exclusively on the B2B e-commerce model, with other businesses as your target customers. If, however, you were selling resumé writing and job placement services to individuals looking for careers, your customers would be B2C individual end consumers. Finally, you might be like Monster.com (www.monster.com), which provides an electronic marketplace catering to both individuals looking for careers and businesses looking for employees. If you were in a business like Monster's, your customer mix would include both end consumers and businesses and you'd need to carefully consider both groups of customers, their needs, and the value to them of the products and services you sell.

Many businesses in the travel industry, American Express, for example, cater to both businesses and end consumers. As an individual consumer, you might work with American Express to plan and pay for a vacation. At the same time, many businesses use the services of American Express to handle all their business travel needs.

Whatever the nature of your business, you must know who your customers are. In the world of e-commerce, that means clearly distinguishing between end consumers (B2C) and other businesses (B2B), even if you target both. As you will see throughout this chapter, individual end consumers and other businesses have dramatically different needs.

WHAT IS THE VALUE OF YOUR PRODUCTS AND SERVICES AS PERCEIVED BY YOUR CUSTOMERS?

If a customer orders a product or service from your organization, it is because that customer perceives some value in what you provide—the customer either *wants* or *needs* your product or service. When we examine wants and needs, the distinctions between end consumers and businesses as customers become increasingly important and clearly evident. Let's look at product/service categories needed by each customer group in turn.

B2C: CONVENIENCE VERSUS SPECIALTY   In many respects, you can differentiate between convenience and specialty merchandise (or services) on the basis of price and consumers' frequency of purchase. To end consumers, *convenience* merchandise is typically lower priced but something they often need, usually frequently. Nonperishable

Figure 5.3

B2C and B2B Products and Services

Business to Consumer (B2C)	Business to Business (B2B)
• **Convenience**—low-priced but something needed on a frequent basis	• **Maintenance, repair, and operations (MRO) materials**—necessary items that do not relate directly to the company's primary business activities
• **Specialty**—higher-priced, ordered on a less frequent basis, and often requiring customization	• **Direct materials**—materials used in production in a manufacturing company or placed on the shelf for sale in a retail environment
• **Commoditylike**—the same no matter where you buy it	
• **Digital**—the best of all because of low cost of inventory and shipping	

food items such as breakfast cereals are a good example. From organizations such as Peapod (www.peapod.com), you can easily order food items and have them delivered to your home within 24 hours of making the order or at predetermined time intervals such as weekly. Consumers might pay more for these low-priced items in order to have them "conveniently."

Specialty merchandise might be such things as home stereo systems, computers, name-brand clothing, furniture, and the like. For consumers, these are higher-priced (than convenience merchandise) items, are typically ordered on a less-frequent basis, and often require some sort of customization or feature specification. For specialty merchandise, consumers will spend more time "shopping around," not only to find the best deal in terms of price but also because value for these items is perceived in terms of customization, warranty, service, and other after-sales features.

B2C: COMMODITYLIKE AND DIGITAL   In B2C e-commerce, as a general rule, the best merchandise to sell is either commoditylike, digital, or a combination of the two. This enables you to minimize your internal costs, but requires that you be innovative in how you offer your merchandise and attract consumers to your site.

Commoditylike merchandise, to your customers, is the same regardless of where they purchase it, and it is similar to convenience items in that respect. Books are a good example. No matter where you buy a particular book, it is the same. As a business, you compete in a commoditylike environment on the basis of:

- Price
- Ease and speed of delivery
- Ease of ordering
- Your return policy

Of course, commoditylike business environments are typically easy to enter (i.e., they have low barriers to entry) and thus buyer power is high (from Porter's Five Forces Model in Chapter 1). Your organization's goals in this type of environment would have to include (1) minimizing price to the end consumer and (2) minimizing your internal costs by creating a tight supply chain management system (from Chapter 2). You also want to create a "sticky" Web site that not only attracts consumers but also encourages them to return to your site again and again.

Digital merchandise offerings are also important in the B2C e-commerce model. The goal here is to eliminate shipping costs by delivering the digital product over the Internet once a consumer has made a purchase. Music is a good example. Apple's iTunes Web site (www.apple.com/itunes/store/) allows you to select exactly the song you want, pay for it, and then download it from the Internet. Apple can offer each song for just 99 cents because it has no physical delivery costs and no physical inventory. As this example illustrates, digital products are also advantageous (to the business and to the consumer) because they are customizable. That is, customers don't have to purchase an entire music CD—they can pick only the song or songs they want.

B2C: MASS CUSTOMIZATION   End consumers are often interested in customizing their purchases. In the B2C e-commerce model this need gives rise to the concept of *mass customization*—the ability of an organization to give its customers the opportunity to tailor its product or service to the customer's specifications. Customization can be appropriate and is a key competitive advantage regardless of other customer value perceptions. For example, Dell Computer (www.dell.com) is well regarded in its market especially for being the best at allowing consumers to customize a computer purchase. Music sites, such as Apple, now allow you to pick the songs you want instead of an entire CD. Clothing sites allow you to select from among various styles, colors, and sizes of clothing to fit your needs.

In a B2C environment, you're potentially dealing with millions of different consumers, each with unique tastes and needs. You must support the concept of mass customization.

B2B: MRO VERSUS DIRECT   *Maintenance, repair, and operations (MRO) materials* (also called *indirect materials*) are materials that are necessary for running a modern corporation, but do not relate to the company's primary business activities. MRO materials include everything from ballpoint pens to three-ring binders, repair parts for equipment, and lubricating oils. Thus, B2B MRO materials are similar to convenience and commoditylike items in the B2C e-commerce model.

In their purchases of these materials, however, business customers (B2B) are very different from end consumers (B2C) in many ways. For example, a business because of its volume of MRO materials purchases can bargain with suppliers for a discount (end consumers in the B2C e-commerce model usually don't have this ability). Many businesses may band together to create even more volume and thus demand an even higher discount from a supplier. This practice is known as *demand aggregation*—the combining of purchase requests from multiple buyers into a single large order, which justifies a discount from the business. If your organization is a supplier of MRO materials in the B2B e-commerce model, you will compete mostly on price (including discounts), delivery, and ease of ordering.

Direct materials are materials that are used in production in a manufacturing company or are placed on the shelf for sale in a retail environment. So, as opposed to MRO materials, direct materials relate to a company's primary business activities. It is critically important that the customer business receives exactly what is needed in terms of quality, quantity, and the timing of delivery of direct materials.

For direct materials acquisition, some businesses participate in a reverse auction (through an electronic marketplace). A *reverse auction* is the process in which a buyer posts its interest in buying a certain quantity of items with notations concerning quality, specification, and delivery timing, and sellers compete for the business by submitting successively lower bids until there is only one seller left. Reverse auctions create tremendous "power" for the buyer because multiple sellers are competing for the same business.

B2B: HORIZONTAL VERSUS VERTICAL   As a supplier to other businesses, you also need to understand whether you are selling in a horizontal or vertical e-marketplace (see Figure 5.4). An *electronic marketplace (e-marketplace)* is an interactive business providing a central market space where multiple buyers and suppliers can engage in e-commerce and/or other e-commerce business activities. E-marketplaces feature a variety of implementations including value-added network providers (which we'll discuss later in the chapter), horizontal e-marketplaces, and vertical e-marketplaces. A *horizontal e-marketplace* is an electronic marketplace that connects buyers and sellers across many industries, primarily for MRO materials commerce. Again, MRO materials include a broad of range of both products and services including office supplies, travel, shipping, and some financial services. Because horizontal e-marketplaces support MRO materials commerce, much of our previous discussion on B2B e-commerce for MRO materials holds true here.

A *vertical e-marketplace* is an electronic marketplace that connects buyers and sellers in a given industry (e.g., oil and gas, textiles, and retail). Covisint (www.covisint.com) is a good example. Covisint provides a B2B e-marketplace in the automotive industry where buyers and sellers specific to that industry conduct commerce in products and services, share mission-critical information for the development of products and parts,

A GLOBAL PARTNERSHIP TO CREATE GLOBAL PARTNERING OPPORTUNITIES

In March 2004, Business Commerce Limited, the Hong Kong subsidiary of Global eXchange Services (GXS), and ChinaECNet announced a new business partnership to establish a B2B electronic marketplace named "e-Hub." E-Hub connects China-based electronics manufacturers with other China-based manufacturers and international customers and suppliers as well.

ChinaECNet is China's leading digital media and e-commerce network, focused mainly on the electronic manufacturing industry. It represents a joint venture between the China Centre for Industry Information Development, Avnet Inc., and Global Techmart.

Global eXchange Services provides one of the largest B2B e-commerce business networks in the world, supporting over 1 billion transactions annually among over 100,000 trading partners.

E-Hub provides buyers and sellers with a standards-based transaction environment that supports more efficient and effective sourcing, purchasing, and tracking of inventory. According to Gou Zhongwen, vice minister of China's Ministry of Information Industry,

"Strengthening the electronics supply chain and material information management is an important step toward utilizing advanced information technology to reform and improve the manufacturing supply and distribution of electronics enterprises." As Wayne Chao, chairman and CEO of ChinaECNET, further explains, "We anticipate that the e-Hub will be China's premier procurement and logistic data exchange platform to connect Chinese electronics OEMs with other Chinese manufacturers of all sizes, and as importantly, with international customers and suppliers. This will greatly help the Chinese OEM market improve material management efficiency and overcome the challenges caused by the rapid globalization of the Chinese electronics industry."

Sometimes, you build partnerships with other businesses specifically so you can support e-commerce activities among other businesses that also want to build partnerships. In the case of Global eXchange Services and ChinaECNET, their partnership will enable other businesses to create partnerships.[6,7]

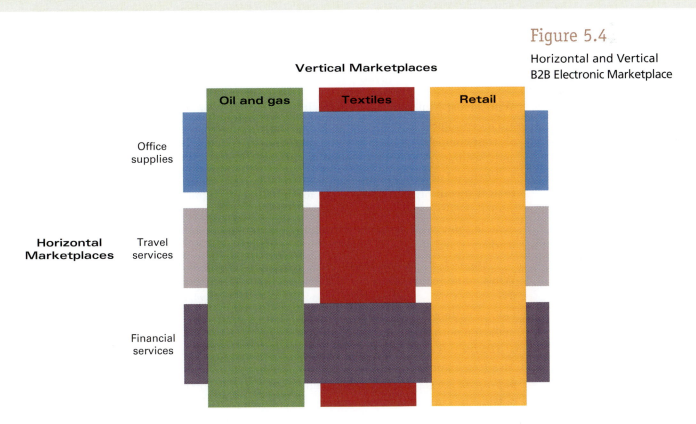

Figure 5.4

Horizontal and Vertical B2B Electronic Marketplace

collaborate on new ideas, and deploy infrastructure applications that enable the seamless communication of each other's proprietary IT systems.

To summarize, we have offered you some ideas to think about regarding the following aspects of e-commerce that will help you in understanding the nature of your business, products, services, and customers.

- **Business to Consumer**
  - Greatly varying customer demographics, lifestyles, wants, and needs
  - Distinctions of products and services by convenience versus specialty
  - E-commerce works best for commoditylike and digital products and services
  - Mass customization adds value in some instances
- **Business to Business**
  - Distinctions of products and services by maintenance, repair, and operations (MRO) materials versus direct materials
  - Demand aggregation and negotiation capabilities enhanced for businesses as customers (buyer power)
  - E-marketplaces connect buyers and sellers—horizontal e-marketplaces (primarily for MRO materials) and vertical e-marketplaces (specific to a given industry)

LEARNING OUTCOME 3

Find Customers and Establish Relationships

You can't make a sale until you find and reach customers and establish a relationship with them. This is *marketing*. There are special features of and technical considerations about marketing and creating customer relationships in e-commerce to keep in mind that can create a competitive advantage for you.

BUSINESS TO CONSUMER

With almost 1 billion people on the Internet, you'd think it would be easy to find and attract customers to your B2C e-commerce site. But that's not necessarily true because all your competition is trying to do the same thing—drive customers to their Web site and encourage them to make a purchase.

First, you need to determine your appropriate ***marketing mix***—the set of marketing tools that your organization will use to pursue its marketing objectives in reaching and attracting potential customers. In B2C e-commerce, your marketing mix will probably include some or all of the following: registering with search engines, online ads, viral marketing, and affiliate programs.

Many Web surfers use *search engines* to find information and products and services. While some search engines will include your site for free (FreeSearch.com at www. freesearch.com is an example), almost all the popular search engines such as Yahoo! and Google require you to pay a fee. Most of these sites will guarantee that your site appears in the top portion of a search list for an additional fee.

Online ads (often called ***banner ads***) are small advertisements that appear on other sites (see Figure 5.5). Variations of online ads include pop-up and pop-under ads. A ***pop-up ad*** is a small Web page containing an advertisement that appears on your screen outside the current Web site loaded into your browser. A ***pop-under ad*** is a form of a pop-up ad that you do not see until you close your current browser window. A word of

Banner ad for Vonage

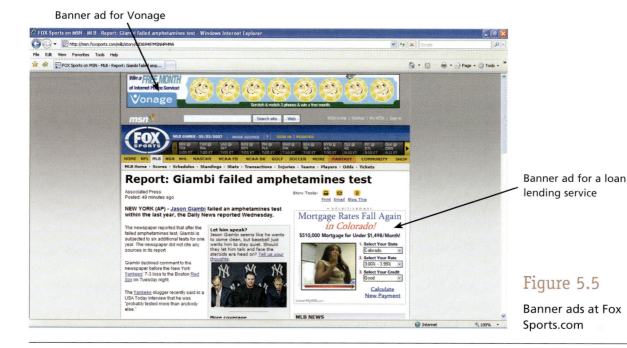

Banner ad for a loan lending service

Figure 5.5

Banner ads at Fox Sports.com

caution here: Most people don't mind banner ads because they appear as a part of the site they're visiting. However, most people consider pop-up and pop-under ads to be very annoying.

Viral marketing encourages users of a product or service supplied by a B2C e-commerce business to encourage friends to join in as well. Blue Mountain Arts (www. bluemountain.com) is a good example. When you use Blue Mountain to send an e-birthday card (or some other type of card), the intended recipient will receive an e-mail directing him or her to Blue Mountain's site. Once the recipient views the card, Blue Mountain provides a link so that person can send you a card in return. Of course, Blue Mountain charges for each card sent, so it makes money both ways.

An *affiliate program* is an arrangement made between two e-commerce sites that directs viewers from one site to the other. Amazon.com is the most well-known creator of an affiliate program. If you become an Amazon associate, your e-commerce Web site directs viewers to Amazon's site for certain purchases. If a sale results, Amazon pays you a fee, which is usually a percentage of the sale (see Figure 5.6 on the next page). Likewise, you can pay another site to direct traffic to yours, which may be through an online ad. In some instances, affiliate programs create relationships such that a payment is made for each click-through. A *click-through* is a count of the number of people who visit one site, click on an ad, and are taken to the site of the advertiser.

In general, you want your marketing mix to drive as many potential customers as possible to have a look at your B2C e-commerce offerings. From there, however, you need to focus on your conversion rate. A *conversion rate* is the percentage of potential customers who visit your site who actually buy something. So, while total views or "hits" to your e-commerce Web site are important, obviously even more so is your conversion rate.

BUSINESS TO BUSINESS

Finding and attracting customers to your B2B e-commerce site is much different. Businesses—customers in the B2B model—don't usually find products and services by surfing the Web or using search engines. Instead, business customers prefer to actively participate in e-marketplaces to find suppliers. Within an e-marketplace, an organization can participate in a reverse auction to find a supplier, as we discussed earlier.

Moreover, an organization can search an e-marketplace for suitable suppliers and then enter into negotiations outside the e-marketplace. This happens for organizations needing to purchase millions of dollars in inventory, parts, or raw materials, and it occurs for organizations wanting to establish a long-term relationship with just one supplier.

Relationships among businesses in B2B are very important. These relationships, characterized by trust and continuity, extend into the IT realm. In the B2B e-commerce business model, you must provide a level of integration of your IT systems with those of your business partners. Once a formal business relationship has been established, the goal is to use IT to streamline the ordering and procurement processes to create tight supply chain management systems and drive out cost, so your IT systems have to work closely together.

To summarize, some ideas about marketing, or finding customers and creating relationships with them, in e-commerce are:

- **Business to Consumer**
  - Design marketing mix to drive potential customers to a Web site
  - Register with a search engine; use online ads, viral marketing, and affiliate programs
  - Conversion rates measure success
- **Business to Business**
  - Businesses participate in e-marketplaces—business customers don't surf the Web, so e-marketplaces need your attention, not a broad and generic marketing mix
  - Formal establishment of business relationships based on trust and continuity required
  - Some level of IT system integration between you and your customer required
  - Online negotiations for pricing, quality, specifications, and delivery timing

Figure 5.6

Amazon.com's Affiliate Program Is Called *Associates*

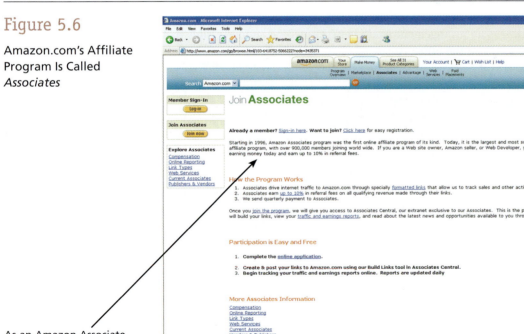

As an Amazon Associate, you can earn up to 10% for referrals.

TOTING THE E-COMMERCE LINE WITH eBAGS

For a true e-commerce success story you don't have to look any further than eBags (www.ebags.com). While many pure-play e-commerce Web sites have fallen by the wayside, eBags is not only surviving, it is thriving. It is the world's leading online provider of bags and accessories for all lifestyles. With 180 brands and over 8,000 products, eBags has sold more than 4 million bags since its launch in March 1999. It carries a complete line of premium and popular brands, including Samsonite, JanSport, The North Face, Liz Claiborne, and Adidas. You can buy anything from backpacks and carry-ons to computer cases and handbags at extremely competitive prices from its Web site.

eBags has received several awards for excellence in online retailing, among them:

- Circle of Excellence Platinum Award, Bizrate.com
- Web Site of the Year, *Catalog Age Magazine* (several years)
- Email Marketer of the Year, ClickZ.MessageMedia
- Marketer of the Year, Colorado AMA
- Rocky Mountain Portal Award

- Gold Peak Catalog, Colorado AMA
- Entrepreneur of the Year—Rocky Mountain Region, Ernst and Young
- E-Commerce Initiative Award of Merit, Colorado Software and Internet Association
- Best of Show, eTravel World Awards
- 50 Essential Web Sites, Conde Naste Traveler
- Internet Retailer's Best of the Web

A good part of the reason for eBags's success is its commitment to providing each customer with superior service, 24 hours a day, 365 days a year. eBags provides customers with the ability to contact customer service representatives for personal assistance by telephone or e-mail and also provides convenient, real-time UPS order tracking.

According to Jon Nordmark, CEO of eBags.com, "From a customer perspective, we've spent a great deal of time developing pioneering ways to guide our shoppers to the bags and accessories that enhance their lifestyles through function and fashion."[8,9]

Move Money Easily and Securely

LEARNING OUTCOME 4

In the world of e-commerce, you must create IT systems that enable your customers (other businesses or end consumers) to pay electronically, easily, and securely for their purchases. Of course, you can still accept credit cards as the form of payment just like in the brick-and-mortar world, but credit card payments are really an electronic form of payment.

BUSINESS TO CONSUMER PAYMENT SYSTEMS

Your customers in the Business to Consumer e-commerce model will most often pay for products and services using credit cards, financial cybermediaries, electronic checks, Electronic Bill Presentment and Payment (EBPP), or smart cards.

- *Financial cybermediary*—an Internet-based company that makes it easy for one person to pay another person or organization over the Internet. PayPal (www.paypal.com) is the best-known example of a financial cybermediary (see Figure 5.7 on the next page). You create a PayPal account by logging on to the PayPal Web site and providing it with personal, credit card, and banking information. When you want to send money, you go to the PayPal site and enter the amount of money you want to send and provide information for either the person or organization you want to send the money to. You can also accumulate money in your personal PayPal account by accepting money from other people.

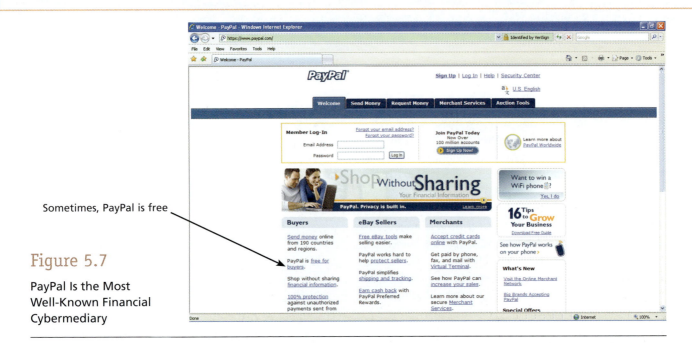

Sometimes, PayPal is free

Figure 5.7

PayPal Is the Most Well-Known Financial Cybermediary

You can transfer the money to one of your banking accounts, use it for other purposes, send the funds to someone else, or just leave it there for awhile.

- *Electronic check*—a mechanism for sending money from your checking or savings account to another person or organization. There are many implementations of electronic checks, with the most prominent being online banking.

- *Electronic Bill Presentment and Payment (EBPP)*—a system that sends bills (usually to end consumers) over the Internet and provides an easy-to-use mechanism (such as clicking on a button) to pay for them if the amount looks correct. EBPP systems are available through local banks or online services such as Checkfree (www.checkfree.com) and Quicken (www.quicken.com/banking_and_credit/).

- *Smart card*—plastic card the size of a credit card that contains an embedded chip on which digital information can be stored and updated. The chip, in this case, can contain information about how much money you have. When you swipe your card to pay for a purchase, the swiping device deducts the purchase amount from the amount you have stored on the chip. Some debit cards are implementations of the smart card concept.

The entire payment process encompasses more than accepting a form of payment. It also includes determining the shipping address for your customer. You can create a competitive advantage by having a way of asking each customer only once for his or her delivery information and storing it, thus creating a switching cost because when your customer makes another purchase, you can simply ask him or her to verify the delivery information and not have to provide it all over again. One implementation of this is called a digital wallet. A *digital wallet* is both software and information—the software provides security for the transaction and the information includes payment information (for example, the credit card number and expiration date) and delivery information. Digital wallets can be stored either on the client side or the server side. A *client-side digital wallet* is one that you create and keep on your computer; you can then use it at a variety of e-commerce Web sites. Most browsers such as Internet Explorer support your ability to create this type of digital wallet. A *server-side digital wallet* (sometimes referred

IS AMERICA ONLINE (AOL) INCHING TOWARD BECOMING AN INTERNET BANK?

In March 2004, America Online (AOL) launched a streamlined new service for online bill payment. No, it doesn't yet provide the capability to pay online bills directly through AOL, but it does seem to be a step by AOL toward making that a reality.

The service—called *AOL Bill Pay*—is free to all AOL members and is provided through an alliance with Yodlee.com, Inc. (www.yodlee.com), a company that provides a variety of online personal financial services. After AOL members sign up for the service, they will receive summaries of their online bills via AOL e-mail messages. The messages will include links directly to the business e-commerce Web sites where members can make their payments.

A nice feature of AOL Bill Pay is that it creates a single portal (the AOL account) with only one user ID and one password. Once inside his or her AOL account, an AOL member does not have to enter a new ID and password at any of the e-commerce Web sites.

AOL members can configure AOL Bill Pay to provide alerts in several different forms (multichannel service delivery): e-mail, instant messaging, or a text-based message to a cell phone. The system can also trigger an alert that is more of a warning message when, for example, an AOL member's bank account balance drops below a certain limit or a credit card transaction exceeds a prespecified amount. It is AOL's hope that its members will see these types of alerts and warnings as value-added services.

AOL Bill Pay connects directly to over 2,500 Web sites that offer bill paying over the Internet. If a certain AOL member makes payments to a Web site not on AOL Bill Pay's list, AOL can easily add the Web site to the list.[10,11]

---

to as a *thin wallet*) is one that an organization creates for and about you and maintains on its server. Many credit card issuers use this type of digital wallet to verify your credit card transactions.

All of this is significant because your customers in the B2C e-commerce model exhibit some common characteristics when paying for your products and services.

- They tend to make numerous purchases for small amounts.
- They pay for each transaction individually.
- You must validate each transaction.

BUSINESS TO BUSINESS PAYMENT SYSTEMS

Payments for products and services in the Business to Business e-commerce model are usually much different from those in the Business to Consumer e-commerce model. In B2B e-commerce, your customers tend to make very large purchases and will not pay using a credit card or a financial cybermediary such as PayPal. Instead, other businesses will want to pay (1) through financial EDI and (2) often in large, aggregated amounts encompassing many purchases.

ELECTRONIC DATA INTERCHANGE   In the B2B model, another business wants to order products and services from your organization via electronic data interchange. *Electronic data interchange (EDI)* is the direct computer-to-computer transfer of transaction information contained in standard business documents, such as invoices and purchase orders, in a standard format. Your organization can implement EDI-facilitated transactions in many ways; one of the more prominent is a B2B e-marketplace that supports EDI through a value-added network. Global eXchange Services (GXS at www. gsx.com) is one such B2B e-marketplace. (We introduced you to GXS in the Global Perspective on page 137.)

GXS, formerly known as General Electric (GE) Information Services, supports one of the largest B2B e-marketplaces in the world with more than 100,000 trading businesses processing 1 billion transactions annually and accounting for over $1 trillion in products and services. GXS focuses on providing value-added network capabilities primarily to supply chain management activities. Figure 5.8 illustrates how General Motors, Ford, and Gates Rubber Company might use GXS's services to support electronic data interchange. In this case, General Motors and Ford would submit orders to Gates through

Figure 5.8

How Value-Added
Network Providers
Support EDI

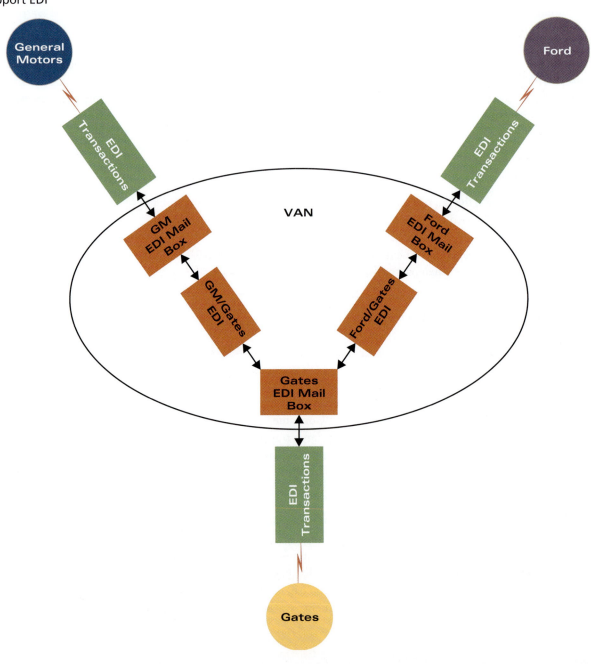

GXS's value-added network (VAN). The VAN supports electronic catalogs (from which orders are placed), EDI-based transactions (the actual orders), security measures such as encryption (which we'll discuss in a moment), and EDI mail boxes (similar to your personal e-mail box). When GM sends an order, for example, to Gates, the order waits in Gates's EDI mail box for processing. Once the order is processed, Gates sends an order confirmation back through the VAN to GM's mail box.

FINANCIAL ELECTRONIC DATA INTERCHANGE   Thereafter, at some predetermined time, Gates would create an invoice totaling many of the orders and purchases from GM. That invoice would be sent through the VAN much like the orders themselves. When the invoice was accepted and approved by GM, GM would make a financial EDI payment to Gates. *Financial EDI (financial electronic data interchange)* is an electronic process used primarily within the Business to Business e-commerce model for the payment of purchases. The actual reconciliation of the funds may occur through a bank or an automated clearing house (ACH) support site such as National Cash Management System (www.ach-eft-ncms.com/index.asp).

As you can see, B2B transactions among businesses are much more involved and complex than B2C transactions between a business and an end consumer such as yourself. Most notably, Business to Business transactions require a level of system integration between the businesses. Considering our previous example in Figure 5.8, Gates's order fulfillment and processing systems would have to be integrated with similar systems at GM and Ford. That is to say, Gates's order fulfillment and processing systems would have to be able to accept and process EDI-based and standardized electronic order records. GM and Ford would have to have similar systems to create EDI-based and standardized electronic order records. In doing so, costs for order processing among all businesses are minimized as the orders can be handled electronically, without paper and without much human intervention.

SECURITY: THE PERVADING CONCERN

Regardless of whether your customers are other businesses or end consumers, they are all greatly concerned about the security of their transactions. This includes all aspects of electronic information, but focuses mainly on the information associated with payments (e.g., a credit card number) and the payments themselves, that is, the "electronic money." Here, you need to consider such issues as encryption, Secure Sockets Layers, and Secure Electronic Transactions. This is by no means an exhaustive list but rather representative of the broad field of security relating to electronic commerce.

ENCRYPTION   *Encryption* scrambles the contents of a file so that you can't read it without having the right decryption key. Encryption can be achieved in many ways: by scrambling letters in a known way, replacing letters with other letters or perhaps numbers, and other ways.

Some encryption technologies use multiple keys. In this instance, you would be using *public key encryption (PKE)*—an encryption system that uses two keys: a public key that everyone can have and a private key for only the recipient (see Figure 5.9 on the next page). When implementing security using multiple keys, your organization provides the public key to all its customers (end consumers and other businesses). The customers use the public key to encrypt their information and send it along the Internet. When it arrives at its destination, your organization would use the private key to unscramble the encrypted information.

SECURE SOCKETS LAYERS   A *Secure Sockets Layer (SSL)* (1) creates a secure and private connection between a Web client computer and a Web server computer, (2) encrypts the information, and (3) then sends the information over the Internet.

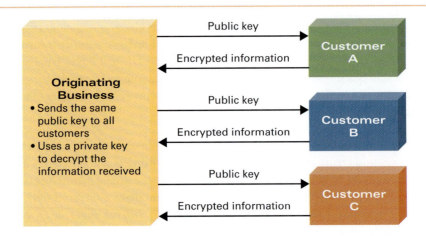

Figure 5.9

Public Key Encryption
(PKE) System

SSLs do provide good security for transferring information and are used widely by B2C e-commerce Web sites. As an end consumer, you can tell your information is being transferred via SSL if you see either (1) the Web site address starts with https:// (notice the inclusion of the "s") as opposed to just http:// or (2) the presence of a lock icon in the bottom portion of your Web browser window (see Figure 5.10).

SECURE ELECTRONIC TRANSACTIONS   A *Secure Electronic Transaction (SET)* is a transmission security method that ensures transactions are *legitimate* as well as secure. Much like an SSL, an SET encrypts information before sending it over the Internet. Taking it one step further, a SET enables you, as a merchant, to verify a customer's identity by securely transmitting credit card information to the business that issued the credit card for verification. SETs are endorsed by major e-commerce players including MasterCard, American Express, Visa, Netscape, and Microsoft.

To summarize:

- **Business to Consumer**

  - Methods include credit cards, financial cybermediaries, electronic checks, Electronic Bill Presentment and Payment (EBPP), smart cards, and digital wallets.
  - Consumers make numerous individual purchases for small amounts that must each be validated.

- **Business to Business**

  - The use of electronic data interchange (EDI) facilitates the ordering process.
  - Value-added network providers used for EDI and financial EDI.
  - Financial EDI used for payment of purchases.

- **Both Business to Consumer and Business to Business**

  - Security is an overriding concern.
  - Security is provided by the use of encryption, Secure Sockets Layers (SSLs), and Secure Electronic Transactions (SETs).

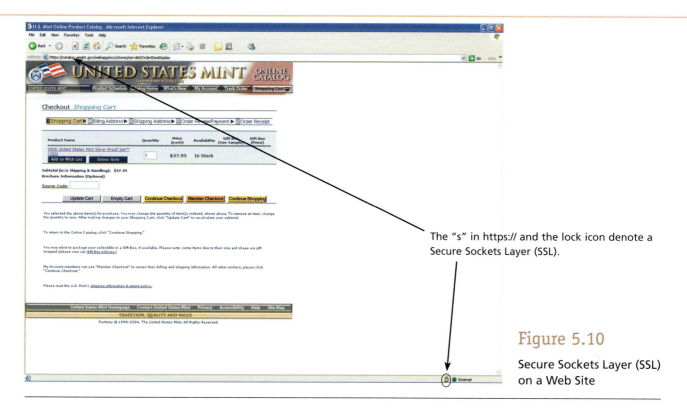

The "s" in https:// and the lock icon denote a Secure Sockets Layer (SSL).

Figure 5.10

Secure Sockets Layer (SSL) on a Web Site

E-Business Trends

LEARNING OUTCOME 5

If you look out over the e-business horizon, you can see many trends. In fact, we could write an entire book on e-business trends, but three seem particularly interesting right now.

YOUTH

Never before has the business world seen such an influence as that brought on by today's young people, and—yes—we are talking about you. Young people ages 6 to 24 are eagerly and aggressively adopting almost every new technology and new implementations of technology that hit the marketplaces. Your generation is now appropriately called *screenagers,* because you spend so much time in front of a screen—TV, computer, cell phone, iPod, etc. Now, you may be a 20-something, but you fall into the category of screenager. You are also called *digital natives,* a group of people ushered into this world alongside the digital revolution. Our generation (this book's authors'), the generation before you, is called *digital immigrants* because we were born and raised in a time prior to the digital society in which we now live. Here are some interesting statistics about *you.* You should take a poll to see how representative your class is of these statistics.

- 93 percent of all Americans ages 12 to 17 years old use the Internet (up from 87 percent in 2004 and 73 percent in 2000).
- 89 percent of online teenagers (i.e., screenagers) use the Internet at least once a week.
- 34 percent use the Internet more than once a day.
- 75 percent of you live in households with broadband connections. The average broadband user belongs to four online communities (i.e., social network sites).
- 49 percent of you believe that when you go online at home your parents don't check to see what Web sites you go to. However, two-thirds of parents of screenagers say they do check up on their children.

- 58 percent of girls ages 12 to 17 have created online profiles at social network sites. For boys of the same age, it's only 51 percent.
- 14 percent of teen online profiles include both a first and last name. (That, by the way, is a bad idea.)
- 63 percent of teenagers have cell phones. 55 percent of you have and daily use a digital camera.[12]

Of course, many of these statistics may seem unremarkable to you. After all, technology has been an important part of your entire life. But to the business world, those statistics tell an interesting story.

You have become the target audience for much of today's advertising either about technology or through the use of technology. Marketers are flocking to sites like Myspace to catch your attention. Every cell phone provider is developing features that are screenager-centric—circles of friends (calling minutes don't accrue against these), improved instant messaging capabilities, video, etc. Yours is a generation that has embraced technology and is the future of any technology revolution. You are also one of the fastest growing demographic groups being targeted for identity theft.

M-COMMERCE

Mobile computing is a broad general term describing your ability to use technology to wirelessly connect to and use centrally located information and/or application software. Mobile computing is all about wireless connectivity. For example, **m-commerce (wireless e-commerce)** describes electronic commerce conducted over a wireless device such as a cell phone, PDA, or notebook giving you the ability to purchase and download music, buy and sell stocks, check weather forecasts, read your e-mail, and a host of other functions.

The future is definitely wireless, no matter what the technology application. And e-commerce businesses are quickly pursuing the recasting of their Web site e-commerce capabilities to fit on the small screen of a cell phone or digital media player. Just as many businesses are implementing **push technologies,** an environment in which businesses and organizations come to you via technology with information, services, and product offerings based on your profile. Right now, for the most part, the Web is *pull*—you go to a Web site and request information, services, and products. In a *push* environment, cell phone providers may use the GPS chip in your cell phone to determine where you are and push advertising to your cell phone for businesses in the same vicinity.

According to the latest statistics, 34 percent of Internet users have accessed the Internet wirelessly, and 25 percent of Internet users have a cell phone with wireless capabilities.[13] Also, of the total Internet user population, 34.6 million use purely mobile devices (cell phones and the like) to access the Internet.[14] Already, you can begin to see the trend toward mobile computing, the precursor to m-commerce. And although m-commerce is still in its infancy, the research firm Strategy Analytics predicted that the global m-commerce market would reach more than $200 billion by the end of 2005. Revenues from game downloads to mobile phones alone are estimated to reach $1.5 billion worldwide by 2008.[15]

THE LONG TAIL

Finally, let's talk about the Long Tail. Think about Amazon, Netflix, and Rhapsody (a competitor to iTunes). In purely financial terms, how would you describe their paths-to-profitability? For Rhapsody, you might say that it has no physical store, no unsold inventory that must be eventually dumped at a loss, and so on. You would, in fact, be partially correct. And you might similarly describe Amazon and Netflix . . . no stores to manage, fewer employees, etc. Again, you would be partially correct. But the real key to their success lies in the Long Tail.

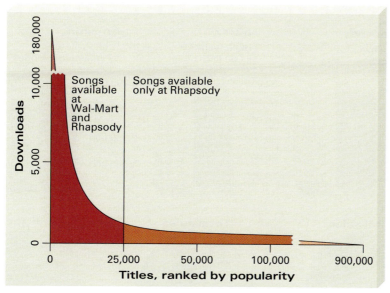

Figure 5.11

The Long Tail

Source: Chris Anderson, *The Long Tail* (New York: Hyperion, 2006), p. 25.

The ***Long Tail***—first offered by Chris Anderson, Editor-in-Chief of *Wired* Magazine, as a way of explaining e-commerce profitability—actually refers to the tail of a sales curve (see Figure 5.11).[16,17] Figure 5.11 shows music song titles, ranked by popularity, for Wal-Mart and Rhapsody (www.rhapsody.com). What you see is that a typical Wal-Mart store stocks about 25,000 songs. Because of the cost of shelf placement in a retailing environment, that's about all Wal-Mart can carry and make a profit. Rhapsody, however, because everything is digital and retail shelf placement costs are irrelevant, carries 1.5 million tracks. Moreover, a full 40 percent of Rhapsody's total sales come from songs in the Long Tail of the sales distribution. Hence, the notion of the Long Tail.

E-commerce businesses that can reach the audience in the Long Tail can do so without the typical brick-and-mortar retail costs and expenses. This is real *mass customization,* of which we spoke earlier, and also goes by the terms *slivercasting* (as opposed to *broadcasting*) and *massclusivity* (a combination of *mass production* and *exclusivity*). In Figure 5.12 on the next page, we've provided inventory and sales data for Rhapsody, Netflix, and Amazon. Notice that Netflix generates 21 percent of its total sales from the Long Tail, and Amazon generates 25 percent of its total sales from the Long Tail.

Long Tail represents an entirely new business model and requires new business thinking. Traditional business thinking looks at sales in terms of economies of scale, seeking to sell as many of one item as possible to offset fixed costs (such as shelf placement costs). The Long Tail model is quite different. Because fixed costs are so minimal, Rhapsody and iTunes can afford to sell only one or two downloads of a given song and still make a profit. Wal-Mart can't do that. In fact, Wal-Mart will only carry music CDs for which it believes sales will be at least four or five. So, it doesn't carry niche products, whereas Rhapsody and iTunes do. The same is true for Netflix. While a typical Blockbuster rental store carries only 3,000 movie DVDs, Netflix carries over 55,000. Likewise, while a typical Borders bookstore carries only 100,000 books, Amazon has over 3.7 million book titles in inventory.

This is a significant trend in the world of e-business. Some older, more traditional brick-and-mortar financial and inventory models no longer apply. It requires a new way of thinking. It is this sort of thinking that a younger generation like you can embrace and act on.

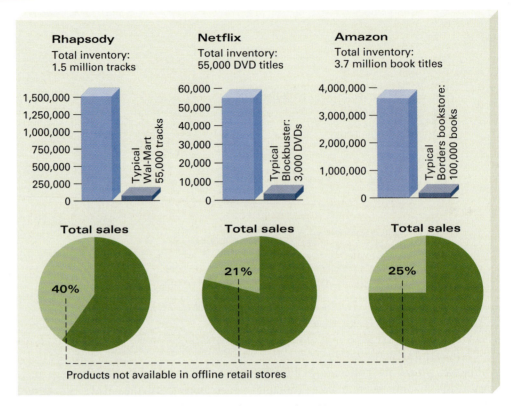

Figure 5.12

The Long Tail Economics for Rhapsody, Netflix, and Amazon

Source: Anderson, Chris, *The Long Tail,* 2006, Hyperion, New York, p. 23.

Summary: Student Learning Outcomes Revisited

1. **Define and describe the nine major e-commerce business models. The nine major e-commerce business models are:**

   - *Business to Business (B2B) e-commerce*—businesses selling products and services to other businesses.

   - *Business to Consumer (B2C) e-commerce*—businesses selling products and services to individual consumers.

   - *Consumer to Business (C2B) e-commerce*—individuals selling products and services to businesses.

   - *Consumer to Consumer (C2C) e-commerce*—individuals selling products and services to other individuals.

   - *Business to Government (B2G) e-commerce*—businesses selling products and services to a government entity.

   - *Consumer to Government (C2G) e-commerce*—individuals selling products and services to a government entity.

   - *Government to Business (G2B) e-commerce*—the government selling products and services to businesses.

   - *Government to Consumer (G2C) e-commerce*—the government selling products and services to individuals.

   - *Government to Government (G2G) e-commerce*—e-commerce activities within a single government or among two or more governments.

2. **Identify the differences and similarities among customers and their perceived value of products and services in the B2B and B2C e-commerce business models.** Customers in the B2C e-commerce business model are end consumers.

They (1) exhibit greatly varying demographics, lifestyles, wants, and needs, (2) distinguish products and services by convenience versus specialty, (3) often shop for commoditylike and digital products, and (4) sometimes require a level of *mass customization* to get exactly what they want. Customers in the B2B e-commerce business model are other businesses. They (1) distinguish products and services by *maintenance, repair, and operations (MRO) materials* versus *direct materials,* (2) aggregate demand to create negotiations for volume discounts on large purchases, and (3) most often perform e-commerce activities within an e-marketplace.

3. **Compare and contrast the development of a marketing mix for customers in the B2B and B2C e-commerce business models.** A *marketing mix* is the set of marketing tools that your organization will use to pursue its marketing objectives in reaching and attracting potential customers. In B2B e-commerce, marketing mixes do not usually include broad and generic strategies that reach all potential businesses. Instead, marketing often occurs in the context of an e-marketplace. Once a contact has been made between businesses, the development of the relationship is still formal and often includes negotiations for pricing, quality, specifications, and delivery timing.

In B2C e-commerce, a marketing mix will include some or all of the following:

- Registering your site with a search engine.
- *Online ads* (small advertisements that appear on other sites), including *pop-up ads* (small Web pages containing an advertisement that appears on your screen outside the current Web site loaded into your browser) and *pop-under ads* (a form of a pop-up ad that you do not see until you close your current browser session).
- *Viral marketing*—encourages users of a product or service supplied by a B2C e-commerce business to encourage friends to join in as well.
- *Affiliate program*—arrangement made between two e-commerce sites that directs viewers from one site to the other.

4. **Summarize the various ways of moving money in the world of e-commerce and related issues.** B2C e-commerce payment systems most commonly include credit cards, *financial cybermediaries* (such as PayPal), *electronic checks* (with online banking being an implementation), *Electronic Bill Presentment and Payment (EBPP), smart cards* (credit card with an embedded computer chip on which

digital information can be stored and updated), and *digital wallets* (software and instructions for completing a transaction). In the B2B e-commerce business model, financial EDI is the norm. *Financial EDI* is an electronic process used primarily in the Business to Business e-commerce business model for the payment of purchases. Security for the electronic transfer of funds is an overriding concern. Techniques such as *encryption, public key encryption (PKE), Secure Sockets Layers (SSLs),* and *Secure Electronic Transactions (SETs)* all address this issue of security.

5. **Discuss some major trends that are impacting both the e-commerce business world and society in general.** Major trends include: Youth—younger people (*digital natives* or *screenagers*) quickly embracing new technology developments and new innovative uses of technology; *M-commerce*—electronic commerce conducted over a wireless device such as a cell phone, PDA, or notebook computer; the *Long Tail model*—the tail of a sales curve which traditional businesses ignore but e-commerce businesses profit from.

CLOSING CASE STUDY ONE

WHEN YOU'RE BIG, YOU CAN BE YOUR OWN B2B E-MARKETPLACE

Business to Business (B2B) e-marketplaces are the growing trend in the B2B e-commerce business model. Businesses from all industries and countries can gather, perform commerce functions, share mission-critical information, and deploy infrastructure applications that allow those organizations to tie their internal systems to each other.

But some companies—the largest ones—don't have to play in the generic B2B e-marketplaces. Instead, they can build their own and literally require that their suppliers participate. One such company is Volkswagen AG. Its B2B e-marketplace is called VWgroupsupply.com (www.vwgroupsupply.com).

Volkswagen AG offers eight brands of automobiles—Volkswagen (passenger), Volkswagen Commercial Vehicles, Audi, Bentley, Bugatti, Lamborghini, Seat, and Skoda. In 2003, Volkswagen spent almost 60 billion euros, or approximately $77 billion, on components, automotive parts, and MRO materials for its manufacturing operations. When you spend that much money with your suppliers, you can open and run your own B2B e-marketplace.

VWgroupsupply.com handles 90 percent of Volkswagen global purchases. Almost all requests for quotes, contract negotiations, catalog updating and buying, purchase-order management, vehicle program management, and payments are handled electronically and online through VWgroupsupply.com.

Gains in efficiency and productivity coupled with material costs reductions have been tremendous. The cost savings alone generated over the last three years were more than 100 million euros, or approximately $127 million.

Volkswagen requires that each of its 5,500 suppliers use VWgroupsupply.com for any interactions. Suppliers place product and pricing catalogs on the system, respond to requests for quotes, and collaborate with Volkswagen engineers on new product designs, all in the safe and secure environment of Volkswagen's proprietary B2B e-marketplace.

By requiring its suppliers to interact with Volkswagen in the e-marketplace, purchasing agents no longer have to spend valuable time searching for information and pricing. Volkswagen has, in essence, created a system that brings the necessary information to the purchasing agents. This new system within VWgroupsupply.com is called iPAD, or Internal Purchasing Agent Desk.

Prior to the implementation of iPAD, purchasing agents entering a purchase order for a vehicle front module had to use numerous separate systems to complete the process. They had to retrieve information from a supplier system and its database, query information in Volkswagen's internal parts information system, obtain information from a request-for-quotes database, enter information into a contract-negotiation transcript system, and interact with several other systems and databases. In all, the purchasing agent had to log into and use seven separate systems. Analysis revealed that Volkswagen purchasing agents were spending 70 percent of their time finding, retrieving, analyzing, validating, and moving information. This took away valuable time from such tasks as negotiating better prices with suppliers.

Using a form of an integrated collaboration environment, or ICE, which we discussed in Chapter 2, purchasing agents now participate in a simple three-step process. First, iPAD captures and sends a business event to the purchasing agent, such as the need to order vehicle front modules. Second, iPAD attaches to that communication other necessary information such as information about potential suppliers, their costs, and other forms of analysis and descriptive information. Finally, iPAD sends the corresponding business processes and work flows to be completed electronically.

It works much like a digital dashboard, which we also introduced you to in Chapter 2. When purchasing agents log onto the iPAD portal in the morning, they receive a customized Web page with announcements, business alerts, analyses, and digital workflows to be completed. The purchasing agents can set out immediately to complete the tasks for the day, without having to spend 70 percent of their time finding, retrieving, and analyzing information. iPAD even customizes the Web page according to the purchasing agent's native language, something very necessary for a global manufacturer of automobiles with more than 2,000 purchasing agents worldwide.[19,20]

Questions

1. Volkswagen operates its own proprietary B2B e-marketplace in which its suppliers participate. What are the disadvantages to Volkswagen of not using a generic B2B e-marketplace with even more suppliers? What are the advantages to Volkswagen of developing and using its own proprietary B2B e-marketplace?

2. When Volkswagen needs a new part design, it uses VWsupplygroup.com to get its suppliers involved in the design process early. This creates a tremendous amount of interorganizational collaboration. What are the advantages to the suppliers and to Volkswagen in doing so?

3. How is Volkswagen's VWgroupsupply.com B2B e-marketplace an example of a vertical e-marketplace implementation? How is it an example of a horizontal e-marketplace implementation? Why is it necessary that Volkswagen combine both of these e-marketplaces into one e-marketplace? What would be the drawbacks to creating two different e-marketplaces—one for suppliers of direct materials and one for suppliers of MRO materials?

4. To make effective purchasing decisions, Volkswagen's purchasing agents need business intelligence. What kind of business intelligence does iPAD provide to purchasing agents for carrying out their tasks? What additional kinds of business intelligence not discussed in this case could Volkswagen's purchasing agents take advantage of to make more effective decisions?

5. IPAD manages the workflow for purchasing agents. Describe how iPAD manages this process including information provided, steps to be executed, and the presentation of information.

CLOSING CASE STUDY TWO

E-BUSINESS TREND: FAR-EAST E-COMMERCE EXPLOSION

Although most parts of the world lag behind the United States in terms of technology penetration (to the public at large), some parts more readily embrace new technology advances. For example, only 22.6 percent of U.S. citizens describe using a cell phone to access the Internet as important or very important. Compare that to Western Europe (30.4 percent), Eastern Europe (53.9 percent), Asia (56.4 percent), and Latin America

(63.5 percent). That should concern some of the U.S.-based e-commerce leaders.

Take, for example, Myspace. Myspace has 92 million registered users but only 23 percent of the U.S. 20-something group are among those 92 million. On the other hand, Cyworld, the South Korean version of Myspace, boasts only 18 million users but 90 percent of the South Korean 20-something use Cyworld.

Cyworld ("cy" is Korean for "relationship") is an interesting blend of a social networking site, blogging site, Flickr (a photo sharing Web site at www.flickr.com), and videogamelike avatars. Unlike the text-heavy bulky sites like Myspace, Facebook, Friendster, and Yahoo 360, Cyworld lets a user create an avatar called a mini-me. You can dress up the mini-me according to your mood on any particular day and even change hair styles. From your personal space, called a mini-room (which you can also decorate to your tastes), you can send out your mini-me to visit other people.

Cyworld is free to use, just like most other social networking sites, but it generates revenue by having users pay for virtual furniture and wall art for their mini-rooms and also to accessorize themselves in their virtual mini-mes. This may seem like an odd way to generate revenue, but Cyworld generates $7.78 annually per user while Myspace generates only $2.17 annually per user.

The creators of Cyworld are not content with owning the South Korean social networking market. Recently, Cyworld launched in Japan and China (where it already has 1.5 million users). Moreover, Cyworld spent almost a year "Americanizing" its site and launched it in the United States, going head-to-head with Myspace and the other popular social networking sites aimed at the 20-something group ("digital natives" and "screenagers").

Another Asian entrant into the hotly contested e-commerce space is TaoBao (www.taobao.com), China's main competitor to eBay. If you visit Taobao's Web site, it's in Chinese, but the look and feel are similar to eBay. But don't get the idea that Taobao is copying everything that eBay is doing. On a recent trip to China, eBay CEO Meg Whitman learned that Taobao was allowing buyers and sellers to instant message through the Taobao auction system. Meg came home and declared that eBay needed to do the same.

In the Chinese Consumer to Consumer auction space, eBay China holds a 29.1 percent market share. Taobao owns a remarkable 67.3 percent. If Taobao ever comes to the United States, it will give eBay a run for its money until the final gavel falls.[21,22,23]

Questions

1. According to Porter's Five Forces Model (from Chapter 1), how would you characterize the competitive space in which Cyworld and Myspace operate according to buyer power, supplier power, threat of substitute products or services, threat of new entrants, and rivalry among existing competitors? Pick one of Porter's Five Forces and describe what Cyworld has undertaken to shift that force in a positive way in its direction.

2. In our discussions of customers and their perceptions of value, we noted that customers tend to categorize products and services as either convenience or specialty. How would you characterize the products and services on Consumer to Consumer e-commerce auction sites such as Taobao and eBay—convenience, specialty, or perhaps a combination of the two? Justify your answer.

3. What sort of payment options does eBay provide? You may have to visit eBay's site to learn this information. If Taobao were to enter the U.S. market, would it have to offer similar payment options? That is, are these payment options entry barriers? Is there room for innovation in the payments space? If so (and the answer is yes), describe it.

4. Privacy is an overriding concern today on the Internet. At sites like Cyworld and Myspace, some people often divulge too much information such as a full name, an address, and even a phone number. From an ethical point of view, do you believe that social networking sites have an obligation to protect users from cyber stalkers? If you believe the answer is no, justify your answer. If you believe the answer is yes, describe what steps can be undertaken to protect users.

5. One key to consumer retention is creating a "sticky" Web site. Review the virtual environments for both Cyworld and Myspace. Which do you think is more "sticky" and better retains consumers? What is your definition of "sticky"?

Key Terms and Concepts

Ad-supported, 131
Affiliate program, 139
Business to Business (B2B)
  e-commerce, 129
Business to Consumer (B2C)
  e-commerce, 130
Business to Government (B2G)
  e-commerce, 131
Click-and-mortar, 132
Click-and-order (pure play), 132
Click-through, 139
Consumer to Business (C2B)
  e-commerce, 130
Consumer to Consumer (C2C)
  e-commerce, 131
Consumer to Government (C2G)
  e-commerce, 131
Conversion rate, 139
Demand aggregation, 136
Digital immigrant, 147
Digital native, 147
Digital wallet, 142
Direct materials, 136
Electronic Bill Presentment and
  Payment (EBPP), 142

Electronic check, 142
Electronic commerce
  (e-commerce), 128
Electronic data interchange
  (EDI), 143
Electronic government
  (e-government), 131
Electronic marketplace
  (e-marketplace), 136
Encryption, 145
Financial cybermediary, 141
Financial EDI (financial electronic
  data interchange), 145
Government to Business (G2B)
  e-commerce, 132
Government to Consumer, (G2C)
  e-commerce, 132
Government to Government (G2G)
  e-commerce, 132
Horizontal e-marketplace, 136
Horizontal government
  integration, 133
Long Tail, 149
M-commerce (wireless
  e-commerce), 148

Maintenance, repair, and
  operations (MRO) materials
  (indirect materials), 136
Marketing mix, 138
Mass customization, 135
Mobile computing, 148
Online ad (banner ad), 138
Path-to-profitability (P2P), 128
Pop-under ad, 138
Pop-up ad, 138
Public key encryption (PKE), 145
Push technology, 148
Reverse auction, 136
Screenager, 147
Secure Electronic Transaction
  (SET), 146
Secure Sockets Layer (SSL), 145
Smart card, 142
Vertical e-marketplace, 136
Vertical government integration,
  133
Viral marketing, 139

Short-Answer Questions

1. What is electronic commerce?
2. How can you use a B2B e-marketplace to reduce your dependence on a particular supplier?
3. How do convenience and specialty items differ in the B2C e-commerce business model?
4. Why do commoditylike and digital items sell well in the B2C e-commerce business model?
5. What is mass customization?
6. How does a reverse auction work?
7. How are vertical and horizontal e-marketplaces different?

8. What can a marketing mix include for a B2C e-commerce business?
9. What are the major types of B2C e-commerce payment systems?
10. What is the difference between a client-side digital wallet and a server-side digital wallet?
11. How are Secure Sockets Layers (SSLs) and Secure Electronic Transactions (SETs) different? How are they the same?

Assignments and Exercises

1. **YOUR STATE AND LOCAL GOVERNMENT E-COMMERCE ACTIVITIES** Visit the Web sites for your state and local governments. Do some looking around and make a list of what services, information deliveries, and transaction processing they offer that you previously could handle only by visiting a physical building. How are these different from and similar to comparable e-government activities now offered by the U.S. federal government?

2. **DEALING WITH THE GREAT DIGITAL DIVIDE** The "great digital divide" is a term coined to address the concerns of many people that the world is becoming one marked by "have's" and "have not's" with respect to technology—that is, the traditional notion of a "third world" is now also being defined by the extent to which a country has access to and uses technology. Find out what, if anything, the United Nations is doing about this issue and express an opinion on whether or not you believe its efforts will be successful. Determine if there are organizations such as private companies or foundations that have the digital divide high on their agendas. For any such organizations you find, evaluate their efforts and express an opinion as to whether or not they will be successful. Finally, search for a less developed country that is making significant local efforts to deal with the digital divide. If you can't find one, prepare a list of the countries you reviewed and briefly describe the conditions in one of them with respect to technology.

3. **RESEARCHING A BUSINESS TO BUSINESS E-MARKETPLACE** Biz2Biz (www.biz2biz.com/Marketplace/) is a B2B e-marketplace. Connect to its site and do some looking around. What sort of marketing services does it provide through its Biz2BizCommunication program? What sort of services does it provide for creating and maintaining an electronic catalog? If you owned a business and wanted to join, what process would you have to go through? How much does it cost your organization to join Biz2Biz? What buyer tools does Biz2Biz provide its membership?

4. **DEVELOPING M-COMMERCE SCENARIOS FOR GPS CELL PHONES** Soon, cell phones will be equipped with GPS chips that enable users to be located to within a geographical location about the size of a tennis court. The primary purpose for installing GPS chips in phones is to enable emergency services to locate a cell phone user. For example, if you dial an emergency assistance number (911 in the United States) from your home now, it is possible for a computer system to use your home telephone number to access a database and obtain your address. This could be very useful in situations in which you were unable to give address information to the emergency operator for some reason. The problem with trying to do the same thing with present-day cell phones is that you could be calling from anywhere and that is the problem GPS-enabled cell phones are intended to overcome.

   As you might imagine, marketers have been monitoring this development with great interest because GPS-phones will support m-commerce. When the new cell phones become available, marketers visualize scenarios where they will know who you are (by your telephone number) and where you are (by the GPS chip). One possible way they could use this information, for example, is to give you a call when you are walking past their shop in the mall to let you know of a special sale on items they know you would be interested in buying. Of course, retailers would have to possess IT systems that would permit them to craft such personalized offers, and you would have had to give them permission to call you.

   Find out what at least three e-commerce marketers are saying about personalized marketing using GPS-equipped cell phones and prepare an analysis of how the phones will be likely to be used when the technology is widely available.

5. **FINDING THE MOST POPULAR B2C E-COMMERCE SITES** Connect to the Web and do some research to find the most popular B2C e-commerce Web sites in terms of number of hits or views per month. What are the sites? Which of the sites in some way or another support the concept of an e-marketplace where end consumers can gather?

Discussion Questions

1. In what ways can shopping over the Internet be more convenient for consumers? In what ways can it be less convenient? List at least five products you would have no hesitation buying over the Internet, five products you might want to think about a bit before buying, and five products you would never consider buying over the Internet. Justify your reasons in each case.

2. In your opinion, according to Porter's Five Forces Model (refer to Chapter 1), has competition increased or decreased overall as a result of the Internet and e-commerce? Specifically address each of the five forces in Porter's model.

3. Under what circumstances would it be appropriate to consider using viral marketing? See if you can think of an organization with an online presence that could benefit from viral marketing but is not currently using it. It could be your school, for example, or it could be an organization you are involved with. How would you suggest the organization go about using viral marketing in order for it to achieve the desired results? What are some of the other marketing techniques available for an e-commerce Web site to use? Why is it important to consider a mix of techniques rather than just relying on a single one?

4. Describe the services provided by value-added networks that make it easier for companies to exchange EDI transactions with each other. What are the pros and cons of using value-added networks for B2B e-commerce? Why don't more companies use the Internet for EDI since it is much cheaper than using a value-added network? Assume that you work for a telecommunications company that operates a value-added network (AT&T or GXS). What sort of strategies would you encourage your company to explore to deal with the possibility of losing considerable amounts of revenues as your customers leave you in favor of using other Internet-based services?

5. In this chapter, we've identified differences between end consumers and businesses as customers. Review those differences and then write down the three you consider most significant. Discuss those three. For the differences that you did not choose as the three most important, be prepared to justify your decision.

6. In this chapter, we discussed using such technologies as B2B e-marketplaces to create tighter supply chain managements, thereby driving out costs. If you refer back to Chapter 2, you'll recall that another major business initiative is customer relationship management (CRM). How can B2C e-commerce businesses use the Internet to further enhance their CRM initiatives? How can B2B e-commerce businesses use the Internet to further enhance their CRM initiatives? Does it become easier or harder to maintain relationships with customers as businesses move toward more electronic commerce? Why?

CHAPTER PROJECTS

Group Projects

- Building Value Chains: Helping Customers Define Value (p. 367)
- Advertising with Banner Ads: HighwaysAndByways.com (p. 371)
- Building a Web Database System: Web-Based Classified System (p. 375)
- Assessing a Wireless Future: Emerging Trends and Technology (p. 378)
- Evaluating the Next Generation: Dot-Com ASPs (p. 380)

e-Commerce Projects

- Exploring Google Earth (p. 392)
- Learning about Investing (p. 396)
- Gathering Competitive Intelligence (p. 391)
- Researching Storefront Software (p. 398)
- Finding Hosting Services (p. 393)
- Gold, Silver, Interest Rates, and Money (p. 394)
- Free and Rentable Storage Space (p. 391)
- Small Business Administration (p. 397)
- Global Statistics and Resources (p. 394)

CHAPTER SIX OUTLINE

STUDENT LEARNING OUTCOMES

1. Define the traditional systems development life cycle (SDLC) and describe the seven major phases within it.

2. Compare and contrast the various component-based development methodologies.

3. Describe the selfsourcing process as an alternative to the traditional systems development life cycle.

4. Discuss the importance of prototypes and prototyping within any systems development methodology.

5. Describe the outsourcing environment and how outsourcing works.

PERSPECTIVES

WEB SUPPORT

www.mhhe.com/haag

- Best in computer resources and statistics
- Meta data
- Finding hosting services
- Searching for freeware and shareware
- Researching storefront software

CHAPTER SIX

Systems Development
Phases, Tools, and Techniques

**OPENING CASE STUDY:
SAVING LIVES THROUGH SYSTEMS
DEVELOPMENT AND INTEGRATION**

The Centers for Disease Control and Prevention (CDC) in Atlanta, Georgia, tracks a wealth of information on everything from antimicrobial-resistant infections in hospitals to influenza outbreaks to terrorist biochemical attacks. Unfortunately, not all of that information is kept in an accessible manner for everyone who needs it and for every application software environment that needs to draw from it.

With offices all over the country, interacting with literally hundreds of state and local agencies, the CDC has volumes of information siloed on disparate servers and application software incapable of easily communicating with other application software. The CDC's IT initiative is to bring all this information together within a service-oriented architecture (SoA). An SoA is a holistic perspective of information and application software that focuses on ease of integration across all information repositories, application software, and hardware platforms.

While most businesses in the private sector use IT metrics such as ROI (return on investment), conversion rates, and click-throughs to measure the worth of a system, the CDC does so in terms of human life. For example, the CDC's BioSense initiative could provide early warning and critical information during an influenza pandemic. And that system needs to be integrated with those of pharmacies dispensing medications. In the early stages of an influenza outbreak, sales of acetaminophen might alert government officials to the threat even before people start showing up at hospitals.

The scope of the CDC's integration initiative is almost incomprehensible. The interrelationships and interactions in the natural, living world are complicated and astronomical in number. Foodborne illnesses, adverse drug reactions, hospital infections, and even EPA estimates of bacteria in rivers and stagnant ponds all relate to each other in some way. Most of these have their own dedicated IT systems for data gathering and analysis that must be integrated for the CDC so that its Public Health Information Network initiative can provide the right information to researchers and health care professionals across the country.

Systems development and the integration of all systems throughout an organization are of paramount importance in today's business world. It doesn't matter if you're trying to thwart an influenza pandemic or selling clothing on the Internet. You need integrated systems and accessible information to make the best decisions possible. Systems development is the focus of this chapter—how organizations go about the process of systems development, various methodologies for systems development, and how you, as an end user, can (and must) participate in the systems development process, and often, build systems for yourself. We live in a digital economy, and IT systems don't just magically appear. They must be thoughtfully and rigorously developed.[1]

Questions

1. All computers use a common binary base language. That being true, why is it so difficult to get computer systems to easily communicate with each other?

2. In systems development, prototyping is used to build a model of a proposed system. How have you used prototyping in your personal life to build something?

3. Outsourcing—going to another country for systems development—is big business. Why would the CDC *not* want to pursue outsourcing?

Introduction

Billions of dollars are spent each year on the acquisition, design, development, implementation, and maintenance of information systems. The ongoing need for safe, secure, and reliable systems solutions is a consequence of companies' increasing dependence on information technology to provide services and develop products, administer daily activities, and perform short- and long-term management functions.

Systems developers must ensure that all the business's needs and requirements are met when developing information systems, establish uniform privacy and security practices for system users, and develop acceptable implementation strategies for the new systems. This chapter focuses on the many factors that must come together to develop a successful information system.

You have three primary choices as to who will build your system (see Figure 6.1). First, you can choose *insourcing*, which involves in-house IT specialists within your organization to develop the system. Second, you can choose *selfsourcing* (also called *end-user development*), which is the development and support of IT systems by end users (knowledge workers) with little or no help from IT specialists. Third, you can choose *outsourcing*, which is the delegation of specific work to a third party for a specified length of time, at a specified cost, and at a specified level of service.

As we introduce you to the systems development life cycle in the next section, we'll focus on insourcing and how the overall process works, key activities within each phase, roles you may play as an end user or knowledge worker, and opportunities you can capitalize on to ensure that your systems development effort is a success.

Insourcing and the Systems Development Life Cycle

LEARNING OUTCOME 1

The *systems development life cycle (SDLC)* is a structured step-by-step approach for developing information systems. It includes seven key phases and numerous activities within each (see Figure 6.2). This version of the SDLC is also referred to as a *waterfall methodology*—a sequential, activity-based process in which one phase of the SDLC is followed by another, from planning through implementation (see Figure 6.2).

There are literally hundreds of different activities associated with each phase of the SDLC. Typical activities include determining budgets, gathering business requirements,

Figure 6.1

Insourcing, Selfsourcing, and Outsourcing

Insourcing

IT Specialists Within
Your Organization

Selfsourcing

Knowledge Workers

Outsourcing

Another Organization

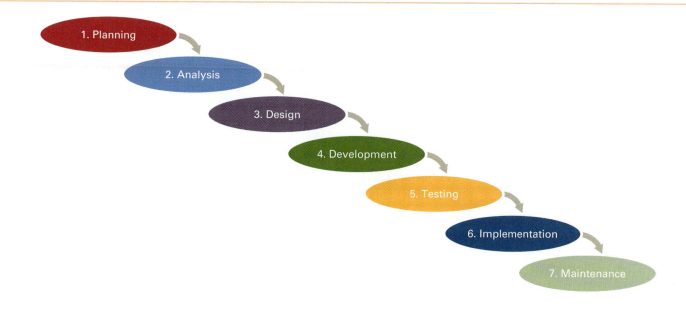

SDLC Phase	Activities
1. Planning	• Define the system to be developed • Set the project scope • Develop the project plan including tasks, resources, and timeframes
2. Analysis	• Gather the business requirements for the system
3. Design	• Design the technical architecture required to support the system • Design system models
4. Development	• Build the technical architecture • Build the database and programs
5. Testing	• Write the test conditions • Perform the testing of the system
6. Implementation	• Write detailed user documentation • Provide training for the system users
7. Maintenance	• Build a help desk to support the system users • Provide an environment to support system changes

Figure 6.2

The Systems Development Life Cycle (SDLC), Phases and Activities, and the Waterfall Methodology

designing models, writing detailed user documentation, and project management. The activities you, as an end user, perform during each systems development project will vary depending on the type of system you're building and the tools you use to build it. Since we can't possibly cover them all in this brief introduction, we have chosen a few of the more important SDLC activities that you might perform on a systems development project as an end user.

PHASE 1: PLANNING

During the ***planning phase*** of the SDLC you create a solid plan for developing your information system. The following are the three primary activities performed during the planning phase.

1. *Define the system to be developed:* You must identify and select the system for development or determine which system is required to support the strategic goals of your organization. Organizations typically track all the proposed systems and prioritize them based on business impact or critical success factors. A ***critical success factor (CSF)*** is simply a factor critical to your organization's success. This process allows your organization to strategically decide which systems to build.

2. *Set the project scope:* You must define the project's scope and create a project scope document for your systems development effort. The project scope clearly defines the high-level requirements. Scope is often referred to as the 10,000-foot view of the system or the most basic definition of the system. A ***project scope document*** is a written document of the project scope and is usually no longer than a paragraph. Project scoping is important for many reasons; most important it helps you avoid *scope creep* and *feature creep*. ***Scope creep*** occurs when the scope of the project increases beyond its original intentions. ***Feature creep*** occurs when developers (and end users) add extra features that were not part of the initial requirements.

3. *Develop the project plan:* You must develop a detailed project plan for your entire systems development effort. The ***project plan*** defines the *what, when,* and *who* questions of systems development including all activities to be performed, the individuals, or resources, who will perform the activities, and the time required to complete each activity. The project plan is the guiding force behind ensuring the on-time delivery of a complete and successful information system. Figure 6.3 provides a sample project plan. A ***project manager*** is an individual who is an expert in project planning and management, defines and develops the project plan, and tracks the plan to ensure that all key project milestones are completed on time. ***Project milestones*** represent key dates by which you need a certain group of activities performed. Either of the two *creeps* alluded to above can throw off a project plan.

Figure 6.3

A Sample Project Plan

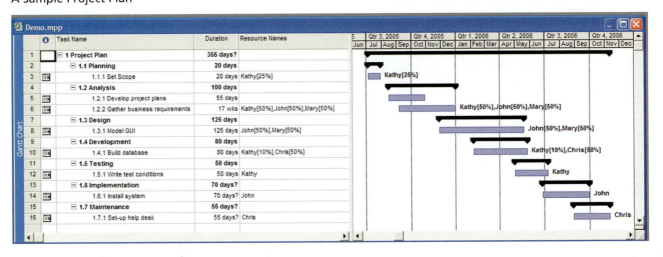

PHASE 2: ANALYSIS

Once your organization has decided which system to develop, you can move into the analysis phase. The ***analysis phase*** of the SDLC involves end users and IT specialists working together to gather, understand, and document the business requirements for the proposed system. The following are the two primary activities you'll perform during the analysis phase.

1. *Gathering the business requirements:* ***Business requirements*** are the detailed set of end-user requests that the system must meet to be successful. The business requirements drive the entire system. A sample business requirement might state, "The CRM system must track all customer inquiries by product, region, and sales representative." The business requirement states what the system must do from the business perspective. Gathering business requirements is similar to performing an investigation. You must talk to everyone who has a claim in using the new system to find out what is required. An extremely useful way to gather business requirements is to perform a joint application development session. During a ***joint application development (JAD)*** session users and IT specialists meet, sometimes for several days, to define and review the business requirements for the system.

2. *Prioritize the requirements:* Once you define all the business requirements, you prioritize them in order of business importance and place them in a formal comprehensive document, the ***requirements definition document.*** The users receive the requirements definition document for their sign-off. ***Sign-off*** is the users' actual signatures indicating they approve all the business requirements. Typically, one of the first major milestones in the project plan is the users' sign-off on business requirements.

One of the key things to think about when you are reviewing business requirements is the cost to the company of fixing errors if the business requirements are unclear or inaccurate. An error found during the analysis phase is relatively inexpensive to fix; all you typically have to do is change a Word document. An error found during later phases, however, is incredibly expensive to fix because you have to change the actual system. Figure 6.4 displays how the cost to fix an error grows exponentially the later the error is found in the SDLC.

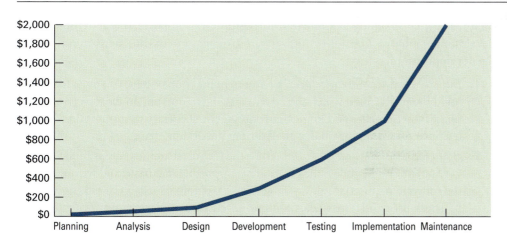

Figure 6.4

The Cost of Finding Errors

PHASE 3: DESIGN

The primary goal of the *design phase* of the SDLC is to build a technical blueprint of how the proposed system will work. During the analysis phase, end users and IT specialists work together to develop the business requirements for the proposed system from a logical point of view. That is, during analysis you document business requirements without respect to technology or the technical infrastructure that will support the system. As you move into design, the project team turns its attention to the system from a physical or technical point of view. You take the business requirements generated during the analysis phase and define the supporting technical architecture in the design phase. The following are the primary activities you'll perform during the design phase.

1. *Design the technical architecture:* The ***technical architecture*** defines the hardware, software, and telecommunications equipment required to run the system. Most systems run on a computer network with each employee having a workstation and the application software running on a server. The telecommunications requirements encompass access to the Internet and the ability for end users to connect remotely to the server. You typically explore several different technical architectures before choosing the final technical architecture.

2. *Design the system model:* Modeling is the activity of drawing a graphical representation of a design. You model everything you build including screens, reports, software, and databases. There are many different types of modeling activities performed during the design phase including a graphical user interface screen design.

It is at the point of the design phase in the SDLC that you, as an end user, begin to take a less active role in performing the various activities and divert your attention to "quality control." That is, IT specialists perform most of the functions in the design through maintenance phases. It is your responsibility to review their work, for example, verifying that the models of the screens, reports, software, and databases encapsulate all of the business requirements.

PHASE 4: DEVELOPMENT

During the *development phase* of the SDLC, you take all your detailed design documents from the design phase and transform them into an actual system. This phase marks the point at which you go from physical design to physical implementation. Again, IT specialists are responsible for completing most of the activities in the development phase. The following are the two main activities performed during the development phase.

1. *Build the technical architecture:* For you to build your system, you must first build the platform on which the system is going to operate. In the development phase, you purchase and implement equipment necessary to support the technical architecture you designed during the design phase.

2. *Build the database and programs:* Once the technical architecture is built, you initiate and complete the creation of supporting databases and writing the software required for the system. These tasks are usually undertaken by IT specialists, and it may take months or even years to design and create the databases and write all the software.

PHASE 5: TESTING

The *testing phase* of the SDLC verifies that the system works and meets all the business requirements defined in the analysis phase. Testing is critical. The following are the primary activities you'll perform during the testing phase.

1. *Write the test conditions:* You must have detailed test conditions to perform an exhaustive test. *Test conditions* are the detailed steps the system must perform along with the expected results of each step. The tester will execute each test condition and compare the expected results with the actual results to verify that the system functions correctly. Each time the actual result is different from the expected result, a "bug" is generated, and the system goes back to development for a "bug fix." A typical systems development effort has hundreds or thousands of test conditions. You must execute and verify all of these test conditions to ensure the entire system functions correctly.

2. *Perform the testing of the system:* You must perform many different types of tests when you begin testing your new system. A few of the more common tests include:
   - *Unit testing*—tests individual units or pieces of code for a system.
   - *System testing*—verifies that the units or pieces of code written for a system function correctly when integrated into the total system.
   - *Integration testing*—verifies that separate systems can work together.
   - *User acceptance testing (UAT)*—determines if the system satisfies the business requirements and enables users to perform their jobs correctly.

PHASE 6: IMPLEMENTATION

During the *implementation phase* of the SDLC you distribute the system to all the users and they begin using the system to perform their everyday jobs. The following are the two primary activities you'll perform during the implementation phase.

1. *Write detailed user documentation:* When you install the system, you must also provide employees with *user documentation* that highlights how to use the system. Users find it extremely frustrating to have a new system without documentation.

2. *Provide training for the system users:* You must also provide training for the users who are going to use the new system. You can provide several different types of training, and two of the most popular are online training and workshop training. *Online training* runs over the Internet or off a CD or DVD. Employees perform the training at any time, on their own computers, at their own pace. This type of training is convenient because they can set their own schedule to undergo the training. *Workshop training* is held in a classroom environment and is led by an instructor. Workshop training is most suitable for difficult systems for which employees need one-on-one time with an individual instructor.

You also need to choose the implementation method that best suits your organization, project, and employees to ensure a successful implementation. When you implement the new system, you have four implementation methods you can choose from:

1. *Parallel implementation* uses both the old and new systems until you're sure that the new system performs correctly.

2. *Plunge implementation* discards the old system completely and immediately uses the new system.

FEDEX BELIEVES TESTING DOESN'T DELIVER

Testing is a critical step in any systems development effort. Just ask the people at FedEx. FedEx believes so strongly in testing, and that current testing methodologies are antiquated and don't work, it has commissioned the University of Memphis to research and study software testing and develop a new methodology that will deliver real results.

Called Systems Testing Excellence Program, the University of Memphis faculty and students in the FedEx Institute of Technology program at the university will attempt to develop testing methodologies that ensure that applications are of the highest quality while doing so in a shorter period of time than current testing methodologies. Using current methodologies, software code is written and turned over to a testing group; testers look for bugs and send those back to the development team. The development team must then assess the bug and determine if in fact it is a bug or if it results from an incorrect business requirement specification. Whatever the case, FedEx doesn't believe current testing methodologies work. According to Dave Miller, vice president of IT at FedEx, "We sort of believe that testing as a discipline has probably not kept up pace."

University students who stand out during the project may potentially be hired by FedEx to continue their work in the testing field.[2]

3. **Pilot implementation** has only a small group of people using the new system until you know it works correctly and then the remaining people are added to the system.
4. **Phased implementation** installs the new system in phases (e.g., accounts receivable, then accounts payable) until you're sure it works correctly and then the remaining phases of the new system are implemented.

PHASE 7: MAINTENANCE

Maintaining the system is the final phase of any systems development effort. During the **maintenance phase** of the SDLC, you monitor and support the new system to ensure it continues to meet the business goals. Once a system is in place, it must change as your business changes. Constantly monitoring and supporting the new system involves making minor changes (for example, new reports or information retrieval) and reviewing the system to be sure that it continues to move your organization toward its strategic goals. The following are the two primary activities you'll perform during the maintenance phase.

1. *Build a help desk to support the system users:* One of the best ways to support users is to create a help desk. A **help desk** is a group of people who respond to users' questions. Typically, users have a phone number for the help desk they call whenever they have issues or questions about the system. Providing a help desk that answers user questions is a terrific way to provide comprehensive support for users using new systems.
2. *Provide an environment to support system changes:* As changes arise in the business environment, you must react to those changes by assessing their impact on the system. It might well be that the system needs to be adapted or updated to meet the ever-changing needs of the business environment. If so, you must modify the system to support the new business environment.

Component-Based Development

The systems development life cycle you just read about is one of the oldest software development methodologies. In design and development (as well as the other phases), the SDLC takes a very singular view of the system under consideration and focuses solely on its development. That is, the SDLC does not really allow the development team to look around a software library and find existing code that can be reused for the new system under consideration. This has some tremendous disadvantages. Most notably, all software is written from scratch each time it is needed for each application. For example, there are probably many applications in the typical organization that have some sort of customer view screen and the ability to update a customer's information. However, within the traditional SDLC, the software that supports the customer view screen and the ability to update the information would be written each time for each application.

This has given rise to the notion of component-based development. ***Component-based development (CBD)*** is a general approach to systems development that focuses on building small self-contained blocks of code (components) that can be reused across a variety of applications within an organization. The goal here, for example, is to write the customer view screen and updating software only once, place it in a library of software components, and then allow software development teams to plug in that component (rather like the notion of *plug-and-play*) into whatever system needs to be developed.

Component-based development dramatically changes the systems development life cycle. It requires teams to (1) look through the software library for reusable code that already exists and (2) build new software in the form of components that can be reused later in other software development projects. In this approach, you can find new systems development methodologies being used including *rapid application development, extreme programming,* and *agile.*

RAPID APPLICATION DEVELOPMENT METHODOLOGY

The ***rapid application development (RAD)*** (also called ***rapid prototyping) methodology*** emphasizes extensive user involvement in the rapid and evolutionary construction of working prototypes of a system to accelerate the systems development process (see Figure 6.5).

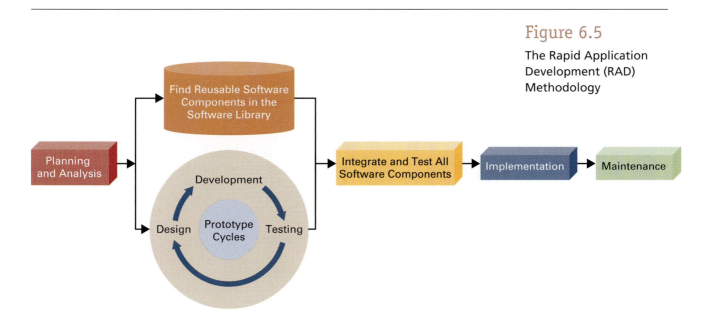

Figure 6.5

The Rapid Application Development (RAD) Methodology

The fundamentals of RAD include:

1. Perform the planning and analysis phases in a similar manner as if you were using the traditional systems development life cycle.

2. Review the software library to determine if components already exist that can be used as part of the new system.

3. Create prototypes (i.e., working models of software components) that look and act like aspects of the desired system. Design, develop, and test the prototypes until they become fully functional software components.

4. Integrate the software components from the previous two steps and test them as a complete system.

5. Implement the new system, following many of the guidelines found in the traditional SDLC.

6. Provide ongoing support and maintenance.

Overall, you want to actively involve end users in the analysis phase and in the iterative approach to the design, development, and testing of new software components. This end-user involvement and the use of prototyping tend to greatly accelerate the collecting of business requirements and the development of the software (i.e., software components). Moreover, if you can find reusable software components in the software library, the acceleration of the overall process is even greater. Prototyping is an essential part of the RAD methodology and we'll discuss it in more detail in a later section.

EXTREME PROGRAMMING METHODOLOGY

The *extreme programming (XP) methodology* breaks a project into tiny phases and developers cannot continue on to the next phase until the current phase is complete. XP is a lot like a jigsaw puzzle; there are many small pieces (i.e., software components). Individually, the pieces make no sense, but when they are combined together an organization can gain visibility into the entire system. The primary difference between the traditional SDLC and XP methodologies is that XP divides its phases into iterations. For example, the traditional SDLC approach develops the entire system, whereas XP develops the system in iterations (see Figure 6.6). Although not shown in Figure 6.6, the XP methodology, much like the RAD methodology, does rely heavily on reusing existing software components contained in a software library.

Figure 6.6

The Extreme Programming Methodology

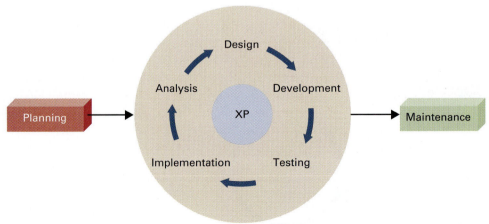

MERCEDES-BENZ: BUILT-TO-ORDER TRUCKS FROM BUILT-TO-ORDER SOFTWARE

"Which driver's cabs and radios are available for a 24-ton rig?" In the past, such a question would have cost Mercedes-Benz dealers a lot of time leafing through big manuals. Today, the Mercedes-Benz Web site offers orientation to the multitude of equipment variations with the Mercedes-Benz customer advisory system (MBKS), developed by CAS Software AG.

The online program, called Truck Online Configurator (TOC), required much more development time than simply displaying the finished online systems for the automobile and transporter divisions with other data and image material. The TOC was given a completely new user guide that orients itself on the different demands of the Web site visitors in three ways: through technical features, trade solution, and transport task. For example, interested customers are able to compile their own vehicle preference by entering the required technical details, such as the type of drive, wheelbase, or engine performance needed. Or an interested customer can select by trade solution or transport task (where he or she simply tells the TOC that a truck is required for the transportation of frozen foods, for example) and a list of suitable models is offered.

CAS had only five months in which to realize this complex and extensive application, from the definition of the specialist requirements, to the technical specifications, right up to the development, testing, and installation of the software. This tight deadline required a risk-driven project management, which meant that individual phases of the project would overlap. While a few developers, together with the project managers of Mercedes-Benz, were clarifying the technical requirements of the individual functions, other parts of the TOC were already being implemented.

The CAS solution was virtually tailor-made for this project. The finished programs run in an extremely fast and stable manner. These were the central, technical requirements of Mercedes-Benz for the TOC: The company wanted an application which boasts maximum availability but with minimum response times.

Thanks to using the rapid application development (RAD) process, CAS was capable of creating very fast a high-quality application.[3]

Microsoft Corporation developed Internet Explorer and Netscape Communications Corporation developed Communicator using extreme programming. Both companies did a nightly compilation (called a *build*) of the entire project, bringing together all the current components. They established release dates and expended considerable effort to involve customers in each release. The extreme programming approach allowed both Microsoft and Netscape to manage millions of lines of code as specifications changed and evolved over time. Most important, both companies frequently held user design reviews and strategy sessions to solicit and incorporate user feedback.[4]

XP is a significant departure from traditional software development methodologies, and many organizations in different industries have developed successful software using it. One of the reasons for XP's success is that it stresses customer satisfaction. XP empowers developers to respond to changing customer and business requirements, even late in the systems development life cycle, and emphasizes teamwork. Managers, customers, and developers are all part of a team dedicated to delivering quality software. XP implements a simple, yet effective, way to enable group style development. The XP methodology supports quickly being able to respond to changing requirements and technology.

AGILE METHODOLOGY

The *agile methodology,* a form of XP, aims for customer satisfaction through early and continuous delivery of useful software components. Agile is similar to XP but with less focus on team coding and more on limiting project scope. An agile project sets a minimum number of requirements and turns them into a deliverable product. Agile means what it sounds like: fast and efficient; small and nimble; lower cost; fewer features; shorter projects.

The Agile Alliance, a group of software developers, has made its mission to improve software development processes. Its manifesto includes the following tenets:

- Satisfy the customer through early and continuous delivery of valuable software.
- Welcome changing requirements, even late in development.
- Business people and developers must work together daily throughout the project.
- Build projects around motivated individuals. Give them the environment and support they need, and trust them to get the job done.
- The best architectures, requirements, and designs emerge from self-organizing teams.
- At regular intervals, the team reflects on how to become more effective, then tunes and adjusts its behavior accordingly.[5]

SERVICE-ORIENTED ARCHITECTURE—AN ARCHITECTURE PERSPECTIVE

Regardless of which component-based methodology your organization chooses to use as its software development approach, it will most likely be employing a software architecture perspective called a *service-oriented architecture.* A *service-oriented architecture (SOA or SoA)* is a software architecture perspective that focuses on the development, use, and reuse of small self-contained blocks of code (called *services*) to meet all the application software needs of an organization. These *services* within the SoA architecture perspective are exactly the same as *components* in any of the component-based development methodologies.

An SoA is a high-level, holistic organizational approach to how your organization views and acts on all its software needs. If adopted, your organization would, in essence, be saying that all software will be developed and managed as a series of reusable services (blocks of code). From within your SoA perspective, you would then choose from among the different component-based development methodologies that support the concept of reusable services (i.e., components) for the development of specific systems. Those development methodologies would not include the traditional SDLC, but rather the approaches we just covered—RAD, XP, and agile.

SoA is growing rapidly in business importance and we'll cover this topic further in Chapter 7.

LEARNING OUTCOME 3

Selfsourcing (End-User Development)

What we want to look at now is how you, as a knowledge worker and end user, can go about developing your own systems, which we call *selfsourcing* or *end-user development.* Recall that *selfsourcing (end-user development)* is the development and support of IT systems by end users (knowledge workers) with little or no help from IT specialists. End users are individuals who will use a system, who, although skilled in their own domain, are not IT or computer experts, and yet they know very well what they want from a system and are capable of developing such systems. Applications developed by end users support a wide range of decision-making activities and contribute to business processing in a wide range of tasks. Although certainly not on the level of enterprisewide enterprise resource planning systems, applications developed by end users are an important source for the organization's portfolio of information systems. The major tools for selfsourcing have been, and still continue to be, spreadsheets and database management systems and Web development.

Rapidly gaining in acceptance is the idea that selfsourcing can be a potent source of stress *relief* rather than a cause of stress. Rather than combating the trend toward end-user application development, IT staff should leverage it to offload solution building to end users. IT then frees its own scarce resources for complex, visible, infrastructure management tasks. A successful strategy for selfsourcing relies on two keys: (1) knowing which applications are good candidates and (2) providing end users with the right tools. After working through the selfsourcing process, we'll revisit the two keys.

THE SELFSOURCING PROCESS

You can probably create many of the small end-user computing systems in a matter of hours, such as customizing reports, creating macros, building queries, and interfacing a letter in a word processing package with a customer database to create individualized mailings. More complicated systems, such as a student registration system or an employee payroll system, require that you follow the formal SDLC process during development.

In Figure 6.7, we've illustrated the selfsourcing process. As you can see, the self-sourcing process is similar to the phases in the SDLC. However, you should notice that the selfsourcing process encompasses prototyping (model building, steps 3 through 6), which we'll cover thoroughly in the next section. This is key—when you develop a system for yourself, you will most often go through the process of prototyping, continually building on and refining your model or prototype until the system is

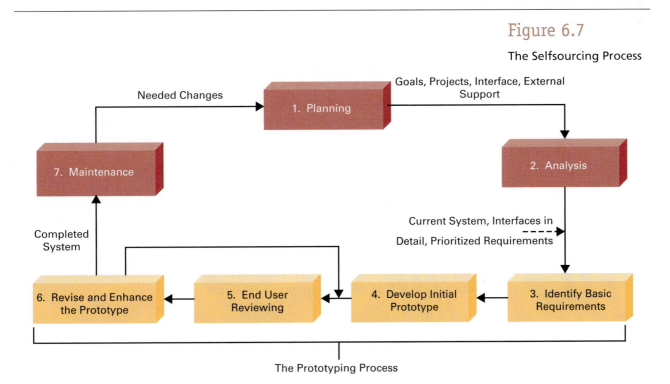

Figure 6.7

The Selfsourcing Process

The Prototyping Process

KEY TASKS IN SELFSOURCING	
Planning	**Analysis**
• Define system goals in light of organizational goals	• Study and model the current system
• Create a project plan	• Understand the interfaces in detail
• Identify any systems that require an interface	• Define and prioritize your requirements
• Determine what type of external support you will require	**Support**
	• Completely document the system
	• Provide ongoing support

Figure 6.8

Key Tasks in Selfsourcing

complete. As you consider the key tasks in selfsourcing in Figure 6.8, we would alert you to several important issues.

ALIGNING YOUR SELFSOURCING EFFORTS WITH ORGANIZATIONAL GOALS
When you first begin planning a system that you want to develop, you must consider it in light of your organization's goals. If you're considering developing a system for yourself that is counterintuitive to your organization's goals, then you should abandon it immediately. You also have to consider how you spend your time building systems carefully, since you are busy and your time is extremely valuable. It's important to remember that building a system takes time—your time.

DETERMINING WHAT EXTERNAL SUPPORT YOU WILL REQUIRE Some selfsourcing projects may involve support from IT specialists within your organization. These may be located within the IT department, as is the case when the IT function is located within its own area (i.e., top-down silo or matrix structure). They may also be located within your department, as is the case when the IT function is fully integrated across all units. Your in-house IT specialists are a valuable resource during the selfsourcing process. Don't forget about them and be sure to include them in the planning phase. The chances of building a successful system increase greatly when you have both end users and IT specialists working together.

DOCUMENTING THE SYSTEM ONCE COMPLETE Even if you're developing a system just for yourself, you still need to document how it works. When you get promoted, other people will come in behind you and probably use the system you developed and might even make changes to it. For this reason, you must document how your system works from a technical point of view as well as create an easy-to-read user's manual.

PROVIDE ONGOING SUPPORT When you develop a system through selfsourcing, you must be prepared to provide your own support and maintenance. Since you are the primary owner and developer of the system, you're solely responsible for ensuring the system continues to function properly and continues to meet all the changing business requirements. You must also be prepared to support other end users who use your system, as they will be counting on you to help them learn and understand the system you developed. The systems development process doesn't end with implementation: It continues on a daily basis with support and maintenance.

THE ADVANTAGES OF SELFSOURCING

- *Improves requirements determination*—During insourcing, end users tell IT specialists what they want. In selfsourcing, end users essentially tell themselves what they want. Potentially, this greatly improves the chances of thoroughly understanding and capturing all the business requirements and thus the prospect of success for the new system.

- *Increases end user participation and sense of ownership*—No matter what you do, if you do it yourself, you always take more pride in the result. The same is true when developing an IT system through selfsourcing. If end users know that they own the system because they developed it and now support it, they are more apt to participate actively in its development and have a greater sense of ownership.

- *Increases speed of systems development*—Many small systems do not lend themselves well to insourcing and the traditional SDLC. These smaller systems may suffer from "analysis paralysis" because they don't require a structured step-by-step approach to their development. In fact, insourcing may be slower than selfsourcing for smaller projects.

- *Reduces the invisible backlog*—Literally no organization has all the resources to develop every system that end users need. If end users can take on the development of some of the smaller systems, the end result is the reduction of the backlog of systems that the organization needs to develop. The ***invisible backlog*** is the list of all systems that an organization needs to develop but—because of the prioritization of systems development needs—never get funded because of the lack of organizational resources.

POTENTIAL PITFALLS AND RISKS OF SELFSOURCING

- *Inadequate end user expertise leads to inadequately developed systems*—Many selfsourcing systems are never completed because end users lack the real expertise with IT tools to develop a complete and fully working system. This seems like no big deal, since the system couldn't have been that important if the people who needed it never finished developing it. But that's not true. If end users devote time to the selfsourcing process and never complete the system, that time is wasted time.

- *Lack of organizational focus creates "privatized" IT systems*—Many selfsourcing projects are done outside the IT systems' plan for an organization, meaning there may be many private IT systems that do not interface with other systems and that contained uncontrolled and duplicated information. Such systems serve no meaningful purpose in an organization and can only lead to more problems.

- *Insufficient analysis of design alternatives leads to subpar IT systems*—Some end users jump to immediate conclusions about the hardware and software they should use without carefully analyzing all the possible alternatives. If this happens, end users may develop systems whose components are inefficient.

- *Lack of documentation and external support leads to short-lived systems*—When end users develop a system, they often forgo documentation of how the system works and fail to realize that they can expect little or no support from IT specialists. All systems—no matter who develops them—must change over time. End users must realize that anticipating those changes is their responsibility and making those changes will be easier if they document their system well.

WHICH APPLICATIONS FOR IT TO OFFLOAD

The following checklist helps IT staff to determine which applications are in IT's domain and which are good candidates for selfsourcing. IT delivers maximum value to the enterprise by focusing on high-cost, high-return applications with the following characteristics:

- Infrastructure-related
- Mission-critical ERP, CRM, SCM, business intelligence and e-business
- Support large numbers of concurrent users, for example, call center applications

Other applications may be good candidates for selfsourcing.

THE RIGHT TOOL FOR THE JOB

Requirements for selfsourcing tools and enterprise development tools (for IT specialists) are quite different. Ease of use is paramount for selfsourcing development tools. That's because end users are not skilled programmers and might use the development tools so infrequently that they can forget commands that aren't intuitive. Therefore, end users must have development tools that:

- *Are easy to use:* This is essential for rapid, low-cost development. For application programs, specific characteristics of ease-of-use include: simple data entry, error checking for values in lists and ranges, easy report generation (e.g., drag and drop), and ease of Web publishing.
- *Support multiple platforms:* To minimize support requirements, end users should select one or two development tools that run on the range of hardware platforms and operating systems within the organization.
- *Offer low cost of ownership:* Cost factors include not only the tool's purchase price, but also training time, speed of application development, and required skill level.
- *Support a wide range of data types:* By its very nature, data is dynamic. Therefore, the toolset should support all the features normally found in database management system products.

LEARNING OUTCOME 4

Prototyping

Prototyping is the process of building a model that demonstrates the features of a proposed product, service, or system. A ***prototype,*** then, is simply a model of a proposed product, service, or system. If you think about it, people prototype all the time. Automobile manufacturers build prototypes of cars to demonstrate and test safety features, aerodynamics, and comfort. Building contractors construct models of homes and other structures to show layouts and fire exits.

In systems development, prototyping can be an invaluable tool for you. Prototyping is an iterative process in which you build a model from basic business requirements, have users review the prototype and suggest changes, and further refine and enhance the prototype to include suggestions. Especially, prototyping is a dynamic process that allows end users to see, work with, and evaluate a model and suggest changes to that model to increase the likelihood of success of the proposed system. Prototyping is an invaluable tool in the component-based development methodologies (RAD, XP, and agile), selfsourcing, and insourcing.

You can use prototyping to perform a variety of functions in the systems development process:

- *Gathering requirements:* Prototyping is a great requirements gathering tool. You start by simply prototyping the basic system requirements. Then you allow end users to add more requirements (information and processes) as you revise the prototype.

- *Helping determine requirements:* In many systems development projects, end users aren't sure what they really want. They simply know that the current system doesn't meet their needs. In this instance, you can use prototyping to help end users determine their exact requirements.

- *Proving that a system is technically feasible:* Let's face it, there are some things to which you cannot apply technology. And knowing whether you can is often unclear when defining the scope of the proposed system. If you're uncertain about whether something can be done, prototype it first. A prototype you use to prove the technical feasibility of a proposed system is a ***proof-of-concept prototype.***

- *Selling the idea of a proposed system:* Many people resist changes in IT. The current system seems to work fine, and they see no reason to go through the process of developing and learning to use a new system. In this case, you have to convince them that the proposed system will be better than the current one. Because prototyping is relatively fast, you won't have to invest a lot of time to develop a prototype that can convince people of the worth of the proposed system. A prototype you use to convince people of the worth of a proposed system is a ***selling prototype.***

THE PROTOTYPING PROCESS

Prototyping is an excellent tool in systems development. Most often, IT specialists (insourcing) use prototyping in the SDLC to form a technical system blueprint. In self-sourcing, however, you can often continue to refine the prototype until it becomes the final system. The prototyping process for either case is almost the same up to a point; only the result differs. Figure 6.9 (on the next page) illustrates the difference between insourcing and selfsourcing prototyping. Regardless of who does the prototyping, the prototyping process involves four steps:

1. *Identify basic requirements:* During the first step, you gather the basic requirements for a proposed system. These basic requirements include input and output information desired and, perhaps, some simple processes. At this point, you're typically unconcerned with editing rules, security issues, or end-of-period processing (for example, producing W-2s for a payroll system at the end of the year).

2. *Develop initial prototype:* Having identified the basic requirements, you then set out to develop an initial prototype. Most often, your initial prototype will include only user interfaces, such as data entry screens and reports.

3. *End user reviewing:* Step 3 starts the truly iterative process of prototyping. When end users first initiate this step, they evaluate the prototype and suggest changes or additions. In subsequent returns to step 3 (after step 4), they evaluate new versions of the prototype. It's important to involve as many end users as possible during this iterative process. This will help resolve any discrepancies in such areas as terminology and operational processes.

4. *Revise and enhance the prototype:* The final sequential step in the prototyping process is to revise and enhance the prototype according to any end-user suggestions. In this step, you make changes to the current prototype and add any new requirements. Next, you return to step 3 and have the end users review the new prototype; then step 4 again, and so on.

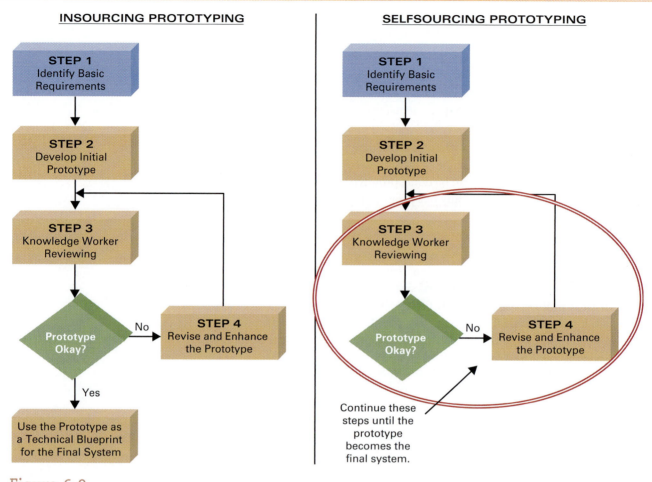

Figure 6.9

Prototyping Steps for
Insourcing and Selfsourcing

For either insourcing or selfsourcing, you continue the iterative processes of steps 3 and 4 until end users are happy with the prototype. What happens to the prototype after that, however, differs.

During selfsourcing, you're most likely to use the targeted application software package or application development tool to develop the prototype. This simply means that you can continually refine the prototype until it becomes the final working system. For example, if you choose to develop a simple CRM application using Microsoft Access, you can prototype many of the operational features using Microsoft Access development tools. Because you develop these prototypes using the targeted application development environment, your prototype can eventually become the final system. This also holds true for component-based development methodologies.

That process is not necessarily the same when insourcing and using the traditional SDLC. Most often, IT specialists develop prototypes using special prototyping development tools. Many of these tools don't support the creation of a final system—you simply use them to build prototypes. Therefore, the finished prototype becomes a blueprint or technical design for the final system. In the appropriate stages of the SDLC, IT specialists will implement the prototype in another application development environment better suited to the development of production systems.

THE ADVANTAGES OF PROTOTYPING

- *Encourages active end user participation*—First and foremost, prototyping encourages end users to actively participate in the development process. As opposed to interviewing and reviewing documentation, prototyping allows end users to see and work with models of a proposed system.

- *Helps resolve discrepancies among end users*—During the prototyping process, many end users participate in defining the requirements for and reviewing the prototype. The word *many* is key. If several end users participate in prototyping, you'll find it's much easier to resolve any discrepancies the end users may encounter.

- *Gives end users a feel for the final system*—Prototyping, especially for user interfaces, provides a feel for how the final system will look and work. When end users understand the look and feel of the final system, they are more likely to see its potential for success.

- *Helps determine technical feasibility*—Proof-of-concept prototypes are great for determining the technical feasibility of a proposed system.

- *Helps sell the idea of a proposed system*—Finally, selling prototypes can help break down resistance barriers. Many people don't want new systems because the old ones seem to work just fine, and they're afraid the new system won't meet their expectations and work properly. If you provide them with a working prototype that proves the new system will be successful, they will be more inclined to buy into it.

THE DISADVANTAGES OF PROTOTYPING

- *Leads people to believe the final system will follow shortly*—When a prototype is complete, many people believe that the final system will follow shortly. After all, they've seen the system at work in the form of a prototype—how long can it take to bring the system into production? Unfortunately, it may take months or even years. You need to understand that the prototype is only a model, not the final system missing only a few simple bells and whistles.

- *Gives no indication of performance under operational conditions*—Prototypes seldom take all operational conditions into consideration. This problem surfaced at the Department of Motor Vehicles in a state on the East Coast. During prototyping, the system, which handled motor vehicle and driver registration for the entire state, worked fine for 20 workstations at two locations. When the system was finally installed for all locations (which included more than 1,200 workstations), the system spent all its time just managing communication traffic; it had absolutely no time to complete any transaction. This is potentially the most significant drawback to prototyping. You must prototype operational conditions as well as interfaces and processes.

- *Leads the project team to forgo proper testing and documentation*—You must thoroughly test and document all new systems. Unfortunately, many people believe they can forgo testing and documentation when using prototyping. After all, they've tested the prototype; why not use the prototype as the documentation for the system? Don't make that mistake.

THE KEY TO PROTOTYPING MAY BE IN VISUALIZATION

Using high-fidelity prototyping and simulation, software developers are now able to greatly accelerate the already fast and efficient process of prototyping. These sorts of visual definition capabilities can be found in prototyping products published by the likes of Compuware, Borland, and Serena. According to Forrester analyst Carey Schwaber, these tools "let you construct upfront a fairly accurate simulation of what the application's going to look like down the road. Instead of describing what you want, you work with a business analyst or usability engineer to construct it. It serves as a visual contract between business and development."

According to Ron Beck, director of software development at Bally Technologies, his company has had great success using Serena's Composer, a definition modeling and prototyping tool. Bally offers many IT-related products to the casino and gaming industry. One such product is Bally's latest enterprise accounting product. According to Ron, Composer has greatly reduced the time it takes to map casino-specific processes to the accounting software. In a short amount of time, it gives users an understanding of how the accounting software will handle functions unique to the gaming industry.

As Ron explains it, "We used to waste so much time on mapping requirements due to lack of communication. Now we're able to model the interface and interactions between systems and users to see what works."[6]

LEARNING OUTCOME 5

Outsourcing

The third choice as to who will build your IT systems—beyond insourcing (in-house IT specialists) and selfsourcing (end users)—is outsourcing. *Outsourcing* is the delegation of specific work to a third party for a specified length of time, at a specified cost, and at a specified level of service. With competitive pressures to cut costs and reduce time-to-market, many organizations are looking to outsource their IT systems development (not to mention ongoing operation, maintenance, and support). The Outsourcing Research Council recently completed a study indicating that human resources (HR) is the top outsourcing area for many companies. Fifty percent of the companies surveyed said they were already outsourcing some or all of their payroll processing and another 38 percent said they were considering it.[7]

Energizer, the world's largest manufacturer of batteries and flashlights, outsourced its HR operations to ADP, one of the top HR outsourcing companies. Energizer currently has more than 3,500 employees and 2,000 retired employees who all require multiple HR IT-related services. ADP provides Energizer with centralized call centers, transaction-processing services, and Web-based employee self-service systems. Energizer's vice president of Human Resources, Peter Conrad, stated, "ADP was clearly the most capable, and offered the kind of one-stop shopping our company was looking for." For several of the systems provided by ADP employee usage topped over 80 percent in the first six months the systems were active.[8]

The main reasons behind the rapid growth of the outsourcing industry include the following:

- **Globalization:** As markets open worldwide, competition heats up. Companies may engage outsourcing service providers to deliver international services. And outsourcing service providers may be located throughout the globe.

- **The Internet:** Barriers to entry, such as the lack of capital, are dramatically reduced in the world of e-business. New competitors enter the market daily.
- **Growing economy and low unemployment rate:** Building a competitive workforce domestically is much harder and more expensive.
- **Technology:** Technology is advancing at such an accelerated rate that companies often lack the resources, workforce, or expertise to keep up.
- **Deregulation:** As private industries such as telecommunications and energy deregulate, markets open and competition increases.

IT outsourcing today represents a significant opportunity for your organization to capitalize on the intellectual resources of other organizations by having them take over and perform certain business functions in which they have more expertise than IT specialists in your company. Information technology outsourcing enables organizations to keep up with market and technology advances with less strain on human and financial resources and more assurance that the IT infrastructure will keep pace with evolving business practices. IT outsourcing for software development can take one of four forms (see Figure 6.10):

1. Purchasing existing software.
2. Purchasing existing software and paying the publisher to make certain modifications.
3. Purchasing existing software and paying the publisher for the right to make modifications yourself.
4. Outsourcing the development of an entirely new and unique system for which no software exists.

In these instances, we're not talking about personal productivity software you can buy at a local computer store. We're talking about large software packages that may cost millions of dollars. For example, every organization has to track financial information, and there are several different systems they can purchase that help them perform this activity. Have you ever heard of Oracle Financials? This is a great system your organization can buy that tracks all the organizational financial information. If Oracle Financials is exactly what you need (i.e., it meets all your business requirements), then you act on option 1.

1. Purchase existing software.

2. Purchase existing software and pay publisher to make certain modifications.

3. Purchase software and pay publisher for the right to make changes yourself.

4. Outsource the development of an entirely new and unique system for which no software exists.

Figure 6.10

Major Forms of Outsourcing Systems Development

If it meets most of your needs, you can act on either option 2 or 3. However, if you have a need for a unique suite of software that doesn't exist in the commercial market, you need to act on option 4. Let's explore that process.

THE OUTSOURCING PROCESS

The outsourcing process is both similar to and quite different from the systems development life cycle. It's different in that you turn over much of the design, development, testing, implementation, and maintenance steps to another organization. It's similar in that your organization begins with planning and defining the project scope (see Figure 6.11). It's during one of these first two phases of the process that your organization may come to understand that it needs a particular system but cannot develop it in-house. If so, that proposed system can be outsourced. That is step 3, of the process, in Figure 6.10, the selection of a target system for outsourcing. Below, we briefly describe the remaining steps in the outsourcing process, starting with step 4.

ESTABLISH LOGICAL REQUIREMENTS   Regardless of your choice of insourcing or outsourcing, you must still perform the analysis phase—especially the primary activity of gathering the business requirements for the proposed system. Remember that identification of the business requirements drives the entire systems development effort; if the business requirements are not accurate or complete, there is no way the system will be successful. If you choose to outsource, part of gathering the business requirements becomes step 5, your *request for proposal*.

DEVELOP A REQUEST FOR PROPOSAL (RFP)   Outsourcing involves telling another organization what you want. What you want is essentially the logical requirements for a proposed system, and you convey that information by developing a request for proposal. A *request for proposal (RFP)* is a formal document that describes in excruciating detail your logical requirements for a proposed system and invites outsourcing organizations (which we'll refer to as *vendors*) to submit bids for its development. An RFP is one of

Figure 6.11

The Outsourcing process

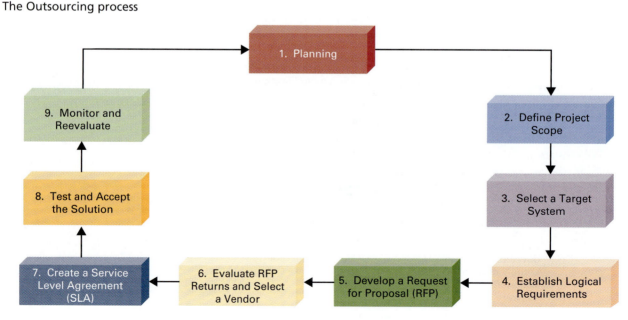

the two most important documents in the outsourcing process. (The other is a service level agreement and we'll not debate which is the most important.) For systems of great size, your organization may create an RFP that's hundreds of pages long and requires months of work to complete.

It's vitally important that you take all the time you need to create a complete and thorough RFP. Eventually, your RFP will become the foundation for a legal and binding contract into which your organization and the vendor will enter. At a minimum, an RFP includes key information such as an overview of your organization, underlying business processes that the proposed system will support, a request for a detailed development time frame, and a request for a statement of detailed outsourcing costs.

All this information is vitally important to both your organization and the vendors. For your organization, the ability to develop a complete and thorough RFP means that you completely understand what you have and what you want. For the vendors, a complete and thorough RFP makes it easier to propose a system that will meet most, if not all, your needs.

EVALUATE RFP RETURNS AND SELECT A VENDOR Your next activity in outsourcing (step 6 in Figure 6.11) is to evaluate the RFP returns and choose a vendor. You perform this evaluation of the RFP returns according to a scoring mechanism you identified in the RFP. This is not a simple process. No two vendors will ever provide RFP returns in the same format, and the RFP returns you receive are usually longer than the RFP itself.

CREATE A SERVICE LEVEL AGREEMENT (SLA) Once you've chosen a vendor, a lengthy legal process follows. Outsourcing is serious business, and serious business between two organizations almost always requires a lot of negotiating and the use of lawyers. Eventually, your organization has to enter into a legal and binding contract that very explicitly states the features of the proposed system, the exact system costs, the time frame for development, acceptance criteria, criteria for breaking the contract for nonperformance or noncompliance, and postdevelopment metrics for activities such as maintenance, support, operational performances, and so on. This legal and binding contract is often called a *service level agreement,* which we'll discuss in more detail after explaining the remaining steps in the outsourcing process.

TEST AND ACCEPT THE SOLUTION As with all systems, testing and accepting the solution are crucial. Once a vendor installs the new system, it's up to you and your organization to test the entire system before accepting it. You'll need to develop detailed test plans and test conditions that test the entire system. This alone may involve months of running and testing the new system while continuing to operate the old one (the parallel method).

When you "accept" a solution, you're saying that the system performs to your expectations and that the vendor has met its contractual obligations thus far according to the service level agreement. Accepting a solution involves granting your sign-off on the system, which releases the vendor from any further development efforts or modifications to the system.

MONITOR AND REEVALUATE Just like the systems you develop using the SDLC, systems you obtain through outsourcing need constant monitoring and reevaluation. In outsourcing, you also have to reassess your working relationship with the vendor. Is the vendor providing maintenance when you need it and according to the service level agreement? Does the system really perform the stated functions? Do month-end and year-end processes work according to your desires? Does the vendor provide acceptable support if something goes wrong? These are all important questions that affect the ultimate success of your outsourcing efforts.

THE SERVICE LEVEL AGREEMENT

When you contract the services of an outsourcing organization (i.e., vendor), you will most likely do so using a service level agreement. Broadly, a ***service level agreement (SLA)*** is a formal contractually obligated agreement between two parties. Within different environments, an SLA takes on different meanings. In the context of systems development, an SLA defines the work to be done, the time frame, the metrics that will be used to measure the success of the systems development effort, and the costs. Most SLAs are business oriented and void of detailed technical specifications. Technical specifications are included in a supporting document (similar to a contract addendum) called a ***service level specification (SLS)*** or ***service level objective (SLO).***

If the vendor further agrees to provide postdevelopment maintenance and support, then the SLA would outline in detail the terms of the maintenance and support activities, their costs, and—again—key metrics by which the success of those activities will be measured. The metrics you include in an SLA are the real key, and we'll describe and define such metrics in Chapter 7 when discussing how to create quantifiable measures of the value of an IT system.

GEOPOLITICAL OUTSOURCING OPTIONS

In a geopolitical sense, furthermore, there are three types of outsourcing:

1. ***Onshore outsourcing*** is the process of engaging another company in the same country for services. Much of the current jargon relating to outsourcing is based on the United States as the reference point. Thus, "onshore" outsourcing typically means contracting a U.S. company to provide business services.

2. ***Nearshore outsourcing*** is contracting an outsourcing arrangement with a company in a nearby country. Often, this country will share a border with the native country. Again, this term is often used with the United States as the frame of reference. In this case, nearshore outsourcing will take place in either Canada or in Mexico, usually.

3. ***Offshore outsourcing*** is contracting with a company that is geographically far away. For many companies, certain IT services, such as application development, maintenance, and help desk support, fall within the category of functions that are ideal for offshore outsourcing.

Although onshore and nearshore outsourcing are important forms in the outsourcing industry, when outsourcing is spoken about nowadays, it is usually *offshore* outsourcing that is being referenced.

OFFSHORE OUTSOURCING   From a humble beginning as a mere cost-cutting concept, offshore outsourcing has gradually moved ahead and established itself as a successful business model by rendering not only cost-effective but also sophisticated and highly efficient quality services. According to International Data Corporation (IDC), U.S.-based companies tripled their offshore outsourcing spending from $5.5 billion in 2000 to more than $17.6 billion in 2005. The offshore outsourcing trend has overcome all barriers of political turmoil, language problems, and culture differences, and has proved that no matter in which part of the world your outsourcer resides, what really matters is industry-standard, high-quality service together with decisive cost advantage.[9]

THE BANKING INDUSTRY BANKS ON OFFSHORE OUTSOURCING

According to a recent study by the consulting firm Deloitte, banks throughout the world, especially the United States, will dramatically increase their IT budgets over the next three years devoted to acquiring technology services abroad in the form of offshore outsourcing. Currently, banks' offshore outsourcing expenditures represent 6 percent of the banking industry's $44 billion total annual IT budget. That percentage is expected to rise to 30 percent by 2010.

According to the study, "Among larger institutions in particular, offshoring is not one available cost-cutting strategy, it's become a necessity." Banks are offshoring a variety of IT-related services ranging from low-level application maintenance to more sophisticated enterprisewide infrastructure and application development.

Offshoring IT-related services and application development can produce significant savings. For example, in India programmers are paid anywhere from 40 to 80 percent less than their U.S. counterparts. Indeed, many outsourcers in India are reaping the rewards from the banking industry. Wipro reported that banking industry offshoring accounted for 21 percent of its total annual revenue of $2.39 billion. TCS, a Wipro rival in India, reported that banking industry offshoring accounted for 38 percent of its $2.97 billion total revenue in 2006.[10]

Since the mid-1990s, major U.S. companies have been sending significant portions of their software development work offshore—primarily to vendors in India, but also to vendors in China, Eastern Europe (including Russia), Ireland, Israel, and the Philippines. The big selling point for offshore outsourcing to these countries is "good work done cheap." A programmer who earns $63,000 per year in the United States is paid as little as $5,000 per year overseas (see Figure 6.12). Companies can easily realize cost savings of 30 to 50 percent through offshore outsourcing and still get the same, if not better, quality of service.

Stories about U.S. companies outsourcing work offshore to India have been reported for years; however, it is becoming increasingly apparent that Romania, Bulgaria, Russia, China, Ghana, the Philippines, and dozens of other countries are also clamoring for and getting business from the United States. The reality is that offshore outsourcing is a growing trend. According to a recent study from Meta Group, the worldwide offshore outsourcing market will grow 20 percent annually through 2008. Meta also claims that offshoring growth will outpace outsourcing in general and predicts that the average enterprise will offshore 60 percent of application development by 2008 or 2009.[11]

Country	Salary Range per Year
China	$5,000–9,000
India	$6,000–10,000
Philippines	$6,500–11,000
Russia	$7,000–13,000
Ireland	$21,000–28,000
Canada	$25,000–50,000
United States	$60,000–90,000

Figure 6.12

Typical Salary Ranges for Computer Programmers

What types of functions or projects make good candidates for offshore outsourcing? Data conversions and system migrations with well-defined requirements and specifications and minimal end-user interaction with the development team are typical projects taken offshore. Naturally, the company must be willing to allow its application code to be located offsite during development. Application development projects are also good offshore candidates. From a SDLC perspective, offshore work is most beneficial in the development and testing phases where end-user interaction is limited, and the task is well defined. For stable applications, most maintenance activities can be performed remotely so application maintenance is also a good candidate for offshore outsourcing. With the right communication infrastructure and a clear understanding of your company's business language requirements, call center or help desk functions can also be moved offshore.

THE ADVANTAGES AND DISADVANTAGES OF OUTSOURCING

Making the decision to outsource may be critical one way or the other to your organization's success. Thus far in our discussion of outsourcing, we've alluded to some advantages and disadvantages of outsourcing. Following is a summary of the major advantages and disadvantages of outsourcing the systems development process, in order to help you make the important outsourcing decision.

ADVANTAGES   Your organization may benefit from outsourcing because outsourcing allows you to:

- *Focus on unique core competencies:* By outsourcing systems development efforts that support noncritical business functions, your organization can focus on developing systems that support important, unique core competencies.
- *Exploit the intellect of another organization:* Outsourcing allows your organization to obtain intellectual capital by purchasing it from another organization. Often you won't be able to find individuals with all the expertise required to develop a system. Outsourcing allows you to find those individuals with the expertise you need to get your system developed and implemented.
- *Better predict future costs:* When you outsource a function, whether systems development or some other business function, you know the exact costs.
- *Acquire leading-edge technology:* Outsourcing allows your organization to acquire leading-edge technology without having to acquire technical expertise and bear the inherent risks of choosing the wrong technology.
- *Reduce costs:* Outsourcing is often seen as a money saver for organizations. Reducing costs is one of the important reasons organizations outsource.
- *Improve performance accountability:* Outsourcing involves delegating work to another organization at a specified level of service. Your organization can use this specified level of service to guarantee that it gets exactly what it wants from the vendor.

DISADVANTAGES   Outsourcing may *not* be a beneficial option for you because it:

- *Reduces technical know-how for future innovation:* Outsourcing is a way of exploiting the intellect of another organization, so it can also mean that your organization will no longer possess that expertise internally. If you outsource because you don't have the necessary technical expertise today, you'll probably have to outsource for the same reason tomorrow.

- *Reduces degree of control:* Outsourcing means giving up control. No matter what you choose to outsource, you are in some way giving up control over that function.
- *Increases vulnerability of your strategic information:* Outsourcing systems development involves telling another organization what information you use and how you use that information. In doing so, you could be giving away strategic information and secrets.
- *Increases dependency on other organizations:* As soon as you start outsourcing, you immediately begin depending on another organization to perform many of your business functions.

Summary: Student Learning Outcomes Revisited

1. **Define the traditional systems development life cycle (SDLC) and describe the seven major phases within it.** The *systems development life cycle (SDLC)* is a structured step-by-step approach for developing information systems. The seven major phases within it include:

   - *Planning*—creating a solid plan for developing your information system
   - *Analysis*—gathering, understanding, and documenting the business requirements
   - *Design*—building a technical blueprint of how the proposed system will work
   - *Development*—taking all the design documents and transforming them into an actual system
   - *Testing*—verifying that the system works and meets all the business requirements
   - *Implementation*—distributing and using the new system
   - *Maintenance*—monitoring and supporting the new system

2. **Compare and contrast the various component-based development methodologies.** Component-based methodologies (CBD) include:

   - *Rapid application development (RAD or rapid prototyping)*—extensive user involvement in the rapid and evolutionary construction of working prototypes of a system to accelerate the systems development process
   - *Extreme programming (XP)*—breaks a project into tiny phases, with each phase focusing on a small aspect of the system that eventually becomes a component or small software module

   - *Agile*—aims for customer satisfaction through early and continuous delivery of useful software components

3. **Describe the selfsourcing process as an alternative to the traditional systems development life cycle.** *Selfsourcing (end-user development)* is the development and support of IT systems by end users with little or no help from IT specialists. While the traditional SDLC uses in-house IT specialists to develop a system, selfsourcing has the user developing his or her own system. The user typically prototypes the system using the targeted application software environment and can thus continually refine and enhance the prototype until it becomes the final working system.

4. **Discuss the importance of prototypes and prototyping within any systems development methodology.** *Prototyping* is the process of building a model (i.e., *prototype*) that demonstrates the features of a proposed product, service, or system. Prototyping can be used effectively to gather requirements, help determine requirements when they are unknown, prove that a system is technically feasible (*proof-of-concept prototype*), and sell the idea of a proposed system (*selling prototype*).

5. **Describe the outsourcing environment and how outsourcing works.** *Outsourcing* is the delegation of specific work to a third party for a specified length of time, at a specified cost, and at a specified level of service. Outsourcing is growing today because of globalization, the Internet, a growing economy and low unemployment rate,

technology, and deregulation. Everything from food service to payroll services to call centers is being outsourced. In the outsourcing process, you target a system for outsourcing and build a **request for proposal (RFP)** that invites vendors to bid for its development. You choose a vendor and enter into an agreement called a **service level agreement (SLA)** that states exactly what the vendor is going to do. In the end, you test and accept the solution from the vendor and begin using the system.

GETTING ON THE RIGHT TRACK AT GENERAL MOTORS

"Our data tells us that the vehicle owners that don't have a satisfactory dealership repair experience are only half as likely to buy that model car again." Think about the ramifications of that statement. If a vehicle owner has a poor experience with something as simple as an oil change, that person is only half as likely to spend $30,000 or more on that model of car again. That is quite the return on investment (ROI) for providing a good experience for an oil change that costs about $50.

Bryan Burkhardt, global director of retail inventory management for General Motors (GM) service and parts operations, made the above statement. Bryan very clearly understands the relationship between after-sales and service and retaining the loyalty of a customer. Unfortunately, left to their own devices, most parts managers at any of GM's 7,000 North American dealerships overstock too many of the more commonly sold parts and seldom have those on hand that are infrequently purchased. As Bryan explains, there is "not enough breadth of parts, but way too much depth on the ones they do have."

That "not enough breadth of parts" means that GM repair shops have been providing customers with a satisfactory repair experience only 67 percent of the time. Bryan and his team set out to change that and implemented a new inventory management system, upping the satisfactory repair experience to 96 percent of the time. The new inventory management system is a centralized, Web-based system that tracks inventory levels in real time. If the quantity-on-hand for any part ever falls below 5, the system notifies the parts manager and automatically routes an order for parts replenishment to one of 16 national parts distribution centers. The system can even accommodate regional differences and keep more of certain parts on hand for dealerships in a given region of the United States, such as more windshield wipers for dealerships in the northwest during the spring. All told, the system tracks over 500,000 GM parts from 4,000 different suppliers.

One of the biggest challenges facing Bryan and his team is that each of the dealerships is allowed to choose its own dealership management system, resulting in the use of 28 different systems. So far, the new centralized inventory management system has been certified to work with only 6 of those systems. Because of the increase in productivity and inventory efficiencies, GM is working with the new inventory management system to provide certification for more of the dealership-centric systems in the hope that all systems will be certified and all dealerships converted to the new inventory management system by the end of 2007. As the new inventory management system is certified to work with another dealership management system, GM pilots the system with a few of the dealerships interested in making the conversion. When the system is determined to work correctly, the remaining dealerships are encouraged to make the conversion.

The new inventory management system is yielding both efficiency and effectiveness. From an efficiency point of view, the new system improves inventory turnover by about 11 percent. It also reduces the time parts managers spend on reviewing inventory and ordering parts from 90 minutes per day to just 10 to 15 minutes per day.

But the most important results are being realized in the area of effectiveness, that is, customer-centric measures such as satisfaction. As Bryan explains it, "At heart, it's about enhancing the ownership experience." After all, providing a satisfactory repair experience doubles the chances that the automobile owner will buy that same model again. In short, customer retention is key.[12]

Questions

1. In implementing the new inventory management system and converting existing users (dealerships) to it, what sort of implementation method is GM using? In your opinion, why is this the most appropriate method? If you had to choose a different implementation method, what would it be and why?

2. Why do you believe that General Motors has allowed its 7,000 North American dealerships to choose different dealership management systems? What are the advantages to allowing this freedom of choice? What are the disadvantages to such an approach?

3. The new inventory management system provides a satisfactory repair experience 96 percent of the time, up from 67 percent. While that increase is both strong and good, is 96 percent really that good? Why or why not? What quantitative approach would you use to justify system enhancements to improve the 96 percent to 98 percent? To 100 percent?

4. If you refer back to Chapter 4 and decision support systems, how would you characterize the decision-making process of determining how many parts to keep on hand? Is that mainly a recurring decision or a nonrecurring decision? Is that mainly a structured decision or a nonstructured decision? For both the latter questions, justify your answers.

5. The new inventory management system reduces the overall costs of parts inventory and, at the same time, increases customer satisfaction. How is this an example of a bottom-line initiative? How is this an example of a top-line initiative? If necessary, refer back to Chapter 1.

CLOSING CASE STUDY TWO

SHOULD AN ORGANIZATION OUTSOURCE SECURITY?

It may seem like an odd question, one that gets an immediate "no," but think again. Many businesses realize that they do not possess the expertise, time, or money to detect, identify, isolate, and stop the hundreds of hackers, viruses, worms, and other malcontents that daily bombard most IT systems. Moreover, most organizations wouldn't identify "security" as a unique core competency, so there is some argument for outsourcing it. The following statistics come from a survey performed by InformationWeek/Accenture Global Information Security. They identify the percentage of respondents who use an outsourcer for some form of security.

- Firewall management—29 percent
- Intrusion detection management—25 percent
- Messaging protection—18 percent
- Security strategy development—15 percent
- Security governance—11 percent
- End device security—11 percent

The numbers show that many companies are willing to outsource IT-related security.

BOILING SPRINGS SAVINGS BANK

Most likely, the number one reason why companies outsource security functions is because they lack the resources and expertise to handle it themselves. According to Ken Emerson, director of strategic planning and CIO at Boiling Springs Savings Bank in New Jersey, "In the security world, it's a game of catch-up. I couldn't possibly throw enough resources at it internally." Ken contracted Perimeter Internetworking to provide security for e-mail and handle the function of intrusion detection and prevention. As Ken explained it further, "I didn't feel like I had the necessary knowledge on my staff, especially with the rapidly growing volume of spam."

But before hiring Perimeter, Ken thought about his customers who rely on Boiling Springs to keep their money safe. So, he did a background check on Perimeter and learned that it had passed the Statement of Auditing Standards No. 70, an in-depth audit of a service provider's control activities. He also found that none of the other security firms he was evaluating had received that sort of certification.

Perimeter electronically linked to Boiling Springs's systems and monitored all e-mail traffic and intrusion attempts. It even found a worm on a specific Boiling Springs PC and notified the bank so it could shut down the infected computer.

KETTERING MEDICAL CENTER NETWORK

Kettering Medical Center Network, a group of 50 health care facilities in the Dayton, Ohio, area, turned over some of its IT security to Symantec. Specifically, Kettering contracted Symantec to analyze all of its data collected by Check Point Technologies and Cisco Systems firewalls. The focus here was to protect remote physicians' offices that are on the network. These types of remote access areas are prime targets for infiltrating a much larger network. As Bob Burritt, IS network and technology manager at Kettering, explained it, "We need to be concerned if someone is trying to do a port scan against our systems or if our network contains ad bots or spy bots trying to communicate out."

If someone did succeed in penetrating Kettering's network and shutting down the system, the results would be catastrophic. Not only could doctors and other health care professionals not communicate with each other and share information, Kettering would lose approximately $1 million a day if it couldn't bill patients or its health care partners or collect fees.

Boiling Springs Savings Bank and Kettering Medical Center Network are just two examples of the many companies that are effectively outsourcing some portion of IT security. Overall among U.S. companies, 25 percent are now outsourcing some aspect of IT security.[13,14]

Questions

1. If you were developing a new system using the traditional systems development life cycle (SDLC), at what point would you need to identify that you needed to outsource some aspect of IT security?

2. In reference to the first question, how would you continue with the in-house systems development effort and, at the same time, carry on the process of outsourcing IT security with another company?

3. Boiling Springs Savings Bank did a background check on Perimeter before hiring it. Search the Web for resources than can help an organization do background checks on IT security firms. What did you find? Did you find a couple of Web sites or certification organizations that offer some guarantee of IT security firms? If so, whom did you find?

4. Turning over IT security to an outside organization is tantamount to giving another organization complete access to all your systems and information. What stipulations would you include in a service level agreement with an IT security outsourcer to ensure that it didn't exploit the openness of your systems and steal strategic and sensitive information?

5. Do some research on the Web for companies that specialize in IT security outsourcing besides Perimeter and Symantec. Whom did you find? Do they seem to be reputable? Do they include a list of clients you can contact for references?

Key Terms and Concepts

Short-Answer Questions

1. What are the three primary groups of people who undertake the systems development process?
2. What is the systems development life cycle?
3. What are scope creep and feature creep?
4. How do the four implementation methods differ?
5. What is component-based development?
6. How are component-based development and a service-oriented architecture related?
7. Why do organizations prototype?
8. What are the advantages of selfsourcing?
9. What is the difference between a selling prototype and a proof-of-concept prototype?
10. What is the role of a service level agreement (SLA) in outsourcing?
11. What are the three geopolitical forms of outsourcing?

Assignments and Exercises

1. **REQUEST FOR PROPOSAL** A request for proposal (RFP) is a formal document that describes in detail your logical requirements for a proposed system and invites outsourcing organizations to submit bids for its development. Research the Web and find three RFP examples. Briefly explain in a one-page document what each RFP has in common and how each RFP is different.
2. **MAKING THE WHO DECISION** Complete the table below by answering yes, no, or maybe in the columns of insource, selfsource, and outsource for each systems development condition listed on the left.

	INSOURCE	SELFSOURCE	OUTSOURCE
The system will support a unique core competency			
Cost is an overriding consideration			
Time-to-market is critical			
You possess the necessary expertise			
Organizational control of the system is critical			
The system will support a common business function			
Gaining and having technical expertise is part of your strategic plan			
The system will support only a very few users			

3. **YOUR RESPONSIBILITIES DURING EACH STEP IN THE SDLC** During insourcing, you have many responsibilities because you're a business process expert, liaison to the customer, quality control analyst, and manager of other people. According to which step of the SDLC you're in, your responsibilities may increase or decrease. In the table below, determine the extent to which you participate in each SDLC step according to your four responsibilities. For each row you should number the SDLC steps 1 through 7, with a 1 identifying the step in which your responsibility is the greatest and a 7 identifying the step in which your responsibility is the least.

	SDLC STEP						
	PLANNING	ANALYSIS	DESIGN	DEVELOPMENT	TESTING	IMPLEMENTATION	MAINTENANCE
Business process expert							
Liaison to the customer							
Quality control analyst							
Manager of other people							

4. **CONSTRUCTION AND THE SDLC** The systems development life cycle is often compared to the activities in the construction industry. Fill in the following chart listing some of the activities performed in building a house and how they relate to the different SDLC steps.

SDLC	Activities for Building a Home
Planning	
Analysis	
Design	
Development	
Testing	
Implementation	
Maintenance	

Discussion Questions

1. Why is it important to develop a logical model of a proposed system before generating a technical architecture? What potential problems would arise if you didn't develop a logical model and went straight to developing the technical design?

2. If you view systems development as a question-and-answer session, another question you could ask is, "Why do organizations develop IT systems?" Consider what you believe to be the five most important reasons organizations develop IT systems. How do these reasons

relate to topics in the first five chapters of this book?

3. Your company has just decided to implement a new financial system. Your company's financial needs are almost the same as those of all the other companies in your industry. Would you recommend that your company purchase an existing system or build a custom system? Would you recommend your company use end-user development or outsource the new system?

4. There are seven phases in the systems development life cycle. Which one do you think is the hardest? Which one do you think is the easiest? Which one do you think is the most important? Which one do you think is the least important? If you had to skip one of the phases, which one would it be and why?

5. You are talking with another student who is complaining about having to learn about the systems development life cycle, because he is not going to work in an IT department. Would you agree with this student? What would you say to him to convince him that learning about the systems development life cycle is important no matter where he works?

6. A company typically has many systems it wants to build, but unfortunately it usually doesn't have the resources to build all the systems. How does a company decide which systems to build?

7. People often think that a system is complete once it is implemented. Is this true? What happens after a system is implemented? What can you do to ensure the system continues to meet the knowledge workers' needs?

CHAPTER PROJECTS

Group Projects

- Executive Information System Reporting: Political Campaign Finance Consultants (p. 366)
- Using Relational Technology to Track Projects: Foothills Construction (p. 369)
- Assessing the Value of Outsourcing Information Technology: Creating Forecasts (p. 372)
- Creating a Decision Support System: Buy versus Lease (p. 376)

e-Commerce Projects

- Best in Computer Resources and Statistics (p. 388)
- Meta Data (p. 389)
- Finding Hosting Services (p. 393)
- Searching for Shareware and Freeware (p. 398)
- Researching Storefront Software (p. 398)

CHAPTER SEVEN OUTLINE

STUDENT LEARNING OUTCOMES

1. Describe how a service-oriented architecture can be used as a philosophical approach to help the organization of the future meet all its IT-related needs.

2. Define and describe the various hardware and software infrastructure considerations in an organization.

3. Compare and contrast commonly used metrics for assessing the success of IT systems and IT-related initiatives.

4. Describe business continuity planning (BCP) and its phases.

PERSPECTIVES

WEB SUPPORT

www.mhhe.com/haag

- Best in computer statistics and resources
- Meta data
- Finding hosting services
- Searching for shareware and freeware

CHAPTER SEVEN

Enterprise Infrastructure, Metrics, and Business Continuity Planning
Building and Sustaining the Dynamic Enterprise

**OPENING CASE STUDY:
NEITHER RAIN NOR SNOW NOR DARK OF NIGHT . . . IT'S NOT THE POST OFFICE—IT'S THE IRS**

In June 2006, a three-foot high wall of water rushed down Constitution Avenue and crashed into the Internal Revenue Service (IRS) building. A moat approximately six feet deep formed around the building. The basement windows gave way to the force and weight of the water, which poured into the building with such force that furniture and equipment were thrown through doors and windows. With more than a foot of rain falling in a short period of time, the IRS found its building useless and 2,400 employees without an office.

It almost sounds like a Hollywood disaster action movie but it's real life and it has happened to more than just the IRS. Almost daily, a business somewhere suffers from some sort of disaster. It may be fire or flood, or it may be the loss of electricity for an extended period of time.

Whatever the case, all organizations need *business continuity plans* in place they can execute to continue doing business. Especially for their information technology and related assets, backup plans for doing business are essential. Most businesses can survive only a few days without IT systems, application software, and an underlying and supporting IT infrastructure.

The IRS, fortunately, did have a business continuity plan. Its main data centers are located outside the District of Columbia and were therefore unaffected by the water. Information is a key resource in any business, and the IRS was fortunate to have its people and technology working in one location and its information secured in another.

Several years ago, the IRS created a remote network access infrastructure, called Enterprise Remote Access Project Virtual Private Network and designed by AT&T, which allows employees to work from home and other locations while still having access to IRS data centers. Part of the IRS's business continuity plan calls for even more employees working via telecommuting. And that's what many employees did. They worked from home and they even came in to other federal buildings and used temporary workstations set up in every inch of available space, even conference rooms.

The lesson all businesses can learn from the IRS flood disaster is that it is vitally important to plan for disasters and to have a business continuity plan in place that can be executed to ensure that downtime is as minimal as possible.

Business continuity planning is just as important as the technological infrastructure it seeks to support in the event of a disaster. In this chapter, we'll explore IT infrastructures and associated considerations as well as how to build a solid business continuity plan.[1]

Questions

1. What sort of "personal continuity plan" do you have for your car, apartment, and other important parts of your life?

2. Are brick-and-mortar businesses or click-and-order businesses more susceptible to disasters and other interruptions? Justify your answer.

3. When was the last time you were dealing with a company and someone said, "I'm sorry but our computer systems are down right now, so I can't help you"? How did that make you feel? How did you react?

LEARNING OUTCOME 1

Introduction

In Chapter 6, we introduced you to the concept of a service-oriented architecture within the context of systems development. A *service-oriented architecture (SOA or SoA)* is a software architecture perspective that focuses on the development, use, and reuse of small self-contained blocks of code (called *services*) to meet all the application software needs of an organization. Thus new applications build on past solutions organically using established building blocks. If SoA is adopted, the organization is saying that instead of bringing in brand new systems all its software will be developed from reusable units of code. SoA is a high-level, holistic organizational approach to how an organization views and acts on all its software needs.

By way of illustration, let's move away from software development—and IT in general—for just a moment and consider the concept of your organization adopting a service-oriented architecture perspective for *everything* it does, such that those self-contained building-blocks of code (services) apply not just to software but also to people, processes, departments and units, operations, and best practices. What would that look like? Your organization with a service-oriented architecture philosophy would:

- Be a lean, agile organization that takes advantage of every resource in the most efficient and effective way.
- React quickly in a proactive way to perceived changes in the market, competition, and customer demographics, wants, and desires.
- Respond quickly to and adapt to new advances in technology.
- Transform its processes, structure, and HR initiatives to match a changing and dynamic workforce.

In short, SoA would enable your organization to become the organization of the future . . . bound by very few structural constraints, able to change on a moment's notice, always looking for and capitalizing on the next great competitive advantage.

Of course this is a book about how organizations use technology, so exploring a service-oriented architecture approach to things like HR or changing customer demographics is beyond our scope. So, let's refocus on IT referring to Figure 7.1, which outlines how an SoA perspective enables your organization to respond more adeptly to customers, end users, software development, information needs, and hardware requirements.

CUSTOMERS

An IT-enabled SoA philosophy allows your organization to provide customers with multichannel service delivery options and customizable products and services. Customers should be able to *plug-and-play* into any communications channel with your organization, such as fax, the Web, face-to-face contact, phone call, and so on. Regardless of the communications channel, the experience should be the same—a consistent and high-quality interaction with your organization.

Customers should also be able to interact with IT systems that allow them to customize and personalize products and services. By simply "plugging in" their desires and wants, your organization should respond with unique and individually tailored offerings that satisfy and delight the customer. We spoke about the concept of mass customization (*slivercasting* and *exclusivity*) in Chapter 5.

THE FOCUS	NOTES
CUSTOMERS	• Multi-channel service delivery • Consistent, high-quality interactions regardless of the venue • Customizable product and service capabilities
END USERS	• Fully integrated ERP system • Interoperability among vendors • Interoperability of modules by the same vendor • Mobile computing (access to information and software regardless of location and device)
SOFTWARE DEVELOPMENT	• SoA as a framework • RAD, XP, and agile as development methodologies • Exciting new deployments like Web 2.0
INFORMATION NEEDS	• End users with access to all types of information • Integrated information, business intelligence, and knowledge • Data warehouses • Standard information formats • Integrity controls • No duplicate information
HARDWARE REQUIREMENTS	• Integration of different technologies and technology platforms • Large storage capacity • Your focus on logical, not physical • Safe and secure telecommunications platform

Figure 7.1

A Service-Oriented Architecture (SoA) Philosophy

END USERS

An SoA philosophy requires that your organization view its end users of IT (i.e., employees within the organization) just as it does external customers. This is mainly achieved through a fully integrated enterprise resource planning (ERP) system that meets every application software and information need of each and every employee. The ERP system should support transparent interoperability across multiple vendors and within ERP modules provided by the same vendor. Because ERP systems are so vitally important to today's integrated and agile organization, we'll further discuss them in this chapter in an upcoming section.

End users should as well be able to take advantage of multi-channel service delivery. In this case, end users (employees) should be able to access computing and information resources regardless of where they are (the notion of *mobile computing* from Chapter 5). And regardless of the IT device in hand (laptop, desktop, PDA, Web-enabled cell phone), employees should enjoy access to a full range of application software services and information.

SOFTWARE DEVELOPMENT

Organizations today can choose among numerous software development methodologies that focus on the production and reuse of blocks of code to speed the process of software development—rapid application development (RAD), extreme programming (XP), and agile methodology are among them.

If you delve into the nitty-gritty of software development, you'll find infrastructure platforms that support a service-oriented architecture approach. Some of these include Ajax (**A**synchronous **J**avaScript **a**nd **X**ML), SOAP (**S**ervice **O**riented **A**rchitecture **P**rotocol), WSDL (**W**eb **S**ervices **D**escription **L**anguage), UDDI (**U**niversal **D**escription, **D**iscovery, and **I**ntegration), and CORBA (**C**ommon **O**bject **R**equest **B**roker **A**rchitecture).

INFORMATION NEEDS

A service-oriented architecture philosophy leverages the most vitally important organizational resource—information. End users need access to all types of information on a moment's notice, regardless of where that information is located (or where the end user is located). People throughout your organization need access to information, business intelligence, and knowledge that supports their decision-making efforts. Recall from Chapter 3 that data warehouses are built by combining information from multiple sources. These data warehouses are of paramount importance to good decision making.

For those reasons and many more, an SoA approach to information requires that:

- Information be in a standard format no matter where it exists.
- Strict and rigorous integrity control mechanisms are in place to ensure the completeness, accuracy, and validity of the information.
- No duplicate information exists in disparate silos anywhere in your organization.
- Any kind of information from any source (even external) can be quickly and easily coupled with other information.

HARDWARE REQUIREMENTS

Finally, a service-oriented architecture philosophy must pervade all choices in the realm of hardware. Organizations should be free to choose different technologies and different technology platforms and integrate them seamlessly (i.e., plug-and-play). Powerful storage area networks should have the capacity to store all your information needs. And you should not have to care where within these networks information is stored; your access to the information should be simple and easy.

Your telecommunications platform should be safe and secure and, at the same time, enable you to access a network either wired or wirelessly using the same steps or procedures. You should never have to look at the back of your computer to determine if you need to log on using a wired protocol or a wireless protocol.

That is what a service-oriented architecture philosophy is all about. Of course, the question now becomes how you implement such a philosophy. That's what the remainder of this chapter is about, specifically:

1. Hardware and software infrastructure
2. Metrics for determining success
3. Measures to ensure consistent, uninterrupted success

Hardware and Software Infrastructure

Generally, *infrastructure* is a relative term meaning "the structure beneath a structure." This definition implies different layers of structure, which provide support or services. An IT infrastructure is the implementation of an architecture—in our discussion here a service-oriented architecture. In a city, the infrastructure includes its streets and street lighting, hospitals, schools, utility lines running above and below the ground, and so on. We all depend on this public infrastructure to make lives of communities, cities, and people safe and prosperous. In a corporation, the IT infrastructure includes the hardware, software (such as ERP software), and information that (1) ensure the components work together and (2) enable people, business processes, and customers to interact and perform their tasks (see Figure 7.2).

ENTERPRISE RESOURCE PLANNING (ERP) REVISITED

ERP systems are big business. At the top of the IT spending list is the ERP market. For instance, the U.S. federal government will spend $7.7 billion on ERP products and services in fiscal year 2009, up 37 percent from 2004 spending of $5.6 billion. More than 60 percent of the Fortune 1000 companies have installed or are in the process of implementing ERP systems to support their business activities. These packages implemented by the Fortune 1000 companies run well over the IT budgets for most small-to-medium-size enterprises, and ERP vendors are targeting this untapped market with scaled-back sys-

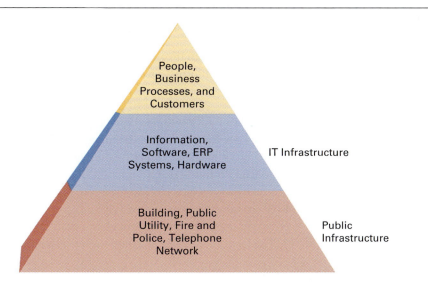

Figure 7.2

Infrastructure

Figure 7.3

Additional ERP Vendors and Their Web Addresses

Invensys www.invensys.com	Cincom www.cincom.com
Visibility www.visibility.com	Verticent www.verticent.com
i2 www.i2.com	Extensity www.extensity.com
QAD www.qad.com	Epicor www.epicor.com
IFS www.ifsab.com	Ceecom www.ceecom.com
Exact www.exactamerica.com	Ramco www.ramco.com

tems suitable for smaller firms by offering simple, cheaper, preconfigured solutions easy to install within budget and time constraints. For instance, Microsoft now offers an ERP solution (called *Microsoft Great Plains*) geared toward the small-to-medium-size company.[2,3]

The dominating ERP software suppliers are SAP, Oracle/PeopleSoft, SSA Global, and Microsoft (see Figure 2.10 in Chapter 2 on page 53). Together they control more than 70 percent of the multibillion-dollar global market. Each vendor, for historical reasons, has a specialty in one particular module area such as SAP in logistics, Oracle/PeopleSoft in financials, SSA Global in manufacturing, and Microsoft in retail management.

There are also about 50 established and a few more newly emerging smaller and mid-size ERP vendors including third-party developers competing for the very lucrative ERP market. Figure 7.3 displays a list of some other top ERP companies with links to their Web sites. There is stiff competition and overlapping products difficult to differentiate. The vendors are continuously updating their products and adding new technology-based features. Long-term vision, commitment to service and support, specialty features, experience, and financial strength for research and development are considered the major vendor qualities for product selection and implementation.

The ERP market has been growing at a rate of more than 30 percent per year and most forecasts predict more of the same. The growth of the ERP market has been boosted by both business and technical factors. With respect to business, the most cited reason is globalization, which has fostered mergers and stimulated the creation of big corporations with high information requirements that the former individual information systems were not able to fulfill. Another factor is general market maturity in developed countries, which has fostered competition among all companies and increased the power of consumers, thus forcing enterprises to upgrade the efficiency of their business processes. Finally, advances in information and communication technologies have made the development of ERP systems possible by allowing the database centralization to integrate with a distributed ERP environment.

A technical reason for ERP growth has been the introduction of the European Union (EU) currency, the euro, since most of the information systems in the EU zone were not able to handle multiple currencies.

THE EVOLUTION OF ERP SYSTEMS   ERP systems replace "islands of information and processes" with a single, packaged software solution that integrates all the traditional enterprise management functions such as financials, human resources, and manufacturing and logistics. Knowing the history and evolution of ERP is essential to understanding its current application and its future developments. To help give you a better perspective, let's review the evolution of ERP systems (also see Figure 7.4).

The early stage of ERP was carried out in the 1970s through a system called *Materials Requirement Planning (MRP)*. The focus of the MRP software was on internal production

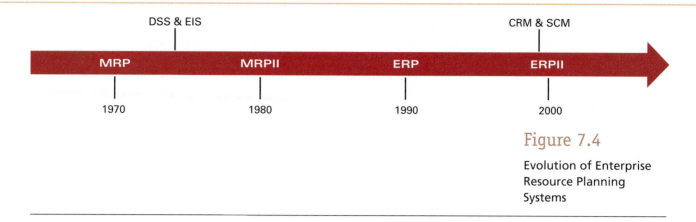

Figure 7.4

Evolution of Enterprise Resource Planning Systems

planning, calculating time requirements components, procurement, and materials planning. The MRP software did not focus on any type of service orientation, but rather was developed to provide the right materials at the right time.

MRP, or "little MRP," represented a huge step forward in the planning process. For the first time, based on a schedule of what was going to be produced, which was supported by a list of materials that were needed for that finished item, the computer could calculate the total needed and compare it to what was already on hand or committed to arrive. This comparison could suggest an activity—to place an order, cancel orders that were already placed, or simply move the timing of these existing orders. The real significance of MRP was that, for the first time, management was able to answer the question "when?"

The next generation of these systems was introduced by the early 1980s under the name *Manufacturing Resources Planning* or *MRPII*. MRPII did not mean that MRP was done incorrectly the first time, but rather that it had evolved. MRPII closed the loop with the accounting and financial management systems. MRPII systems crossed the boundaries of the production functionality and started serving as decision support systems (DSS) as well as executive information systems (EIS—in the modern day many people refer to implementations of these as *digital dashboards*).

For the first time, a company could have an integrated business system that provided visibility for the requirements of material and capacity. Good information leads to good decisions, and therefore these integrated IT systems provided a competitive advantage.

By the time each functional area of a company had developed its own software program, the need for tightly integrating them became obvious. The next major shift during the late 1980s and early 1990s was that "time to market" was becoming increasingly short. Lead times expected by the market continued to shorten and customers were no longer satisfied with the service level that was considered world class only a few years earlier.

The need to develop a tightly integrated system that would use data stored in common databases and would be used enterprisewide became the highest priority for IT professionals. No longer was it tolerable to submit a request to the IT department and wait several months to obtain this critical information. This common-database, companywide integrated system appeared at the beginning of the 1990s and was named *enterprise resource planning (ERP)*.

ERP encompasses all the resource planning for the enterprise including product design, warehousing, material planning, capacity planning, and communication systems. ERP systems help companies become leaner and more agile by integrating the basic transaction programs for all departments, allowing quick access to timely information.

ERP systems have evolved into what is now commonly referred to as *ERPII*. During the last few years, the functional perimeter of *ERPII* systems has begun an expansion into its adjacent markets, such as supply chain management (SCM), customer relationship management (CRM), data warehousing/business intelligence (DWBI), and e-business. The major ERP vendors have been busy developing, acquiring, and/or bundling new functionality so that their packages go beyond the traditional realms of finance, materials planning, and human resources.

ERP AND A SERVICE-ORIENTED ARCHITECTURE   Two of the primary goals of an ERP system within a service-oriented architecture are:

1. Provide interoperability within an ERP vendor and for modules among different ERP vendors.
2. Hide the underlying IT infrastructure of information and hardware from end users and customers.

In the first instance, ***interoperability*** refers to the capability of two or more computing components to share information and other resources, even if they are made by different manufacturers. In the top layer of Figure 7.5, you can see the software infrastructure of an ERP system. Let's assume it's provided by SSA Global, a leading publisher of ERP software. Notice that you see all the typical software modules present—accounting, distribution, supply chain, and the like.

However, two modules have been replaced in Figure 7.5—the HR component by in-house developed software and data analytics by BI and reporting software from Cognos. This is the concept of interoperability. Your organization chooses the best ERP solution on that market that meets most of its needs. Within the chosen ERP suite, you can replace software modules with in-house developed software and software modules from other vendors (and software developed through outsourcing for that matter). Long after implementation, you can add other modules and plug them directly into your ERP solution, as well. This is the concept of *sustainable interoperability*.

In the lower portion of Figure 7.5, you can see the implementation of the second goal of an ERP system, that is, hide the underlying IT infrastructure of information and hardware from end users and customers. The ERP system—specifically screens, reports, and the like—are the *customer-facing* aspect of the system. The physical structure and location of information should not be of concern to you, nor should the physical hardware infrastructure matter.

ERP ADVANTAGES AND DISADVANTAGES   Finally, although the benefits that an effective and SoA-enabled ERP system can provide are huge, and we have focused on many of those advantages throughout our discussions of ERP, unfortunately, your organization will need to overcome certain problems and disadvantages associated with ERP systems. While we expect these disadvantages to lessen in the coming years, they are important factors to consider when investing in ERP. The advantages and disadvantages of ERP are listed on the bottom of the next page. You'll notice that many of the advantages have a corresponding disadvantage. This simply means that overall the reaction is mixed to the perceived success of ERP implementations.

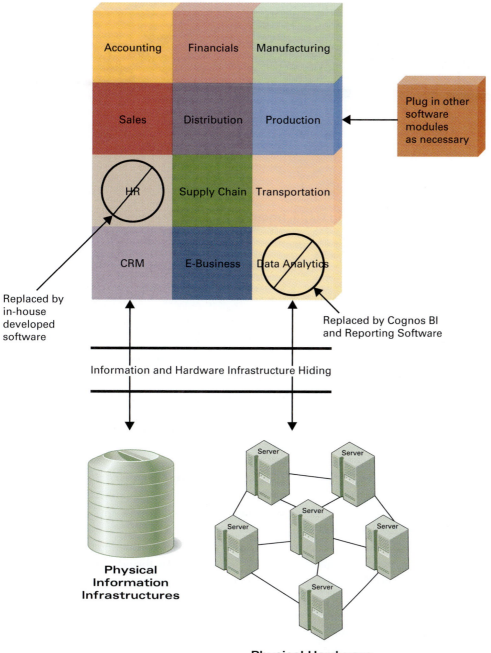

Figure 7.5

An ERP Infrastructure

Advantages	Disadvantages
• Reliable information access	• Time-consuming
• Avoid data and operations redundancy	• Expensive
• Delivery and cycle time reduction	• Lack of conformity of modules
• Cost reduction	• Vendor dependence
• Easy adaptability	• Too many features, too much complexity
• Improved scalability	• Questionable scalability and global outreach
• Global outreach	• Not enough extended ERP capability
• E-business support	

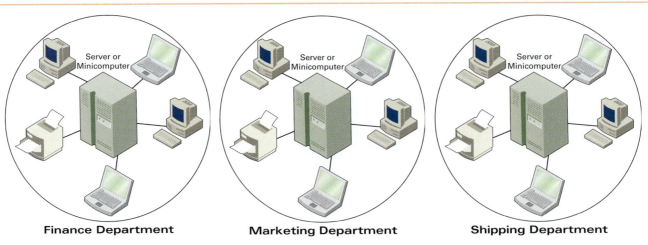

Finance Department   **Marketing Department**   **Shipping Department**

Figure 7.6

Decentralized
Infrastructure

SUPPORTING NETWORK INFRASTRUCTURES

The fundamental underlying infrastructure for any IT environment is a network, two or more computers sharing information, software, peripheral devices, and processing power. Network infrastructure is such a wide and vast field that volumes have been written on the subject and many schools (primarily within the computer science department) offer entire programs and majors in IT networks. Our discussion here focuses on only the five major types of network infrastructures.

DECENTRALIZED INFRASTRUCTURE   A *decentralized infrastructure* involves little or no sharing of IT and other resources such as information. Generally, this infrastructure arises from users or departments developing their own systems or applications, without any central control (see Figure 7.6).

The decentralized infrastructure gives users the liberty to develop applications that meet their needs and maintain control over the applications they develop. However, this infrastructure generally prevents users from easily combining processing power or even comparing information between various information systems. It also encourages data duplication, frequently leading to inconsistencies. For example, Figure 7.6 illustrates a finance, a marketing, and a shipping department, each technologically isolated from the other.

Figure 7.7

Centralized Infrastructure

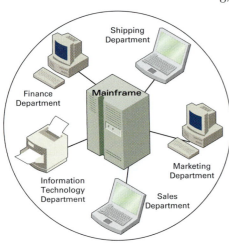

Decentralized infrastructures often arise in companies having a decentralized management approach and typically in companies built through acquisition. Decentralized infrastructures are almost a thing of the past.

CENTRALIZED INFRASTRUCTURE   A *centralized infrastructure* involves sharing information systems in one central area or on one central mainframe. For a long time, mainframes were the only computers available for business. By their nature, they dictated that information systems infrastructures be centralized because typically all applications and information were stored on a company's single mainframe. As an example, Figure 7.7 shows a typical layout of a centralized infrastructure. With the introduction of inexpensive desktop computers and reliable data communications technology, almost all organizations have moved away from the centralized infrastructure.

The great advantage of a centralized infrastructure is that it allows a high degree of control, making it easy to (1) maintain standards of hardware, software, procedures, and operations and (2) control access to information. The main disadvantage of a centralized infrastructure is its inflexibility. A centralized infrastructure is run so that it can be used by everyone, but that does not mean that the system is optimal for everyone. Different departments and remote sites have different information needs. As with the decentralized infrastructure, centralized infrastructures are dinosaurs from a different time.

DISTRIBUTED INFRASTRUCTURE   A *distributed infrastructure* involves distributing the information and processing power of IT systems via a network. (This is the first true *network* infrastructure.) By connecting all the information systems via a distributed infrastructure, all locations can share information and applications (see Figure 7.8). The major benefit of this is that processing activity can be allocated to the locations(s) where it can most efficiently be done. To improve performance and reduce network traffic, a distributed infrastructure will often store the same application and/or information in two or more locations.

Distributed infrastructures are more complex than centralized infrastructures for several reasons. First, the distributed infrastructure must be able to determine the location of specific applications and information. Second, it must be more sophisticated in determining the optimal way to request the application and information. The order in which the system processes a request can make a significant difference in the amount of data transmitted over the network.

CLIENT/SERVER INFRASTRUCTURE (CLIENT/SERVER NETWORK)   A *client/server infrastructure* (or *client/server network*) has one or more computers that are *servers* which provide services to other computers, called *clients*. The client/server infrastructure is a form of distributed infrastructure. The basic notion of a client/server infrastructure is that application processing is divided between the client and the server. The functions of an information system are divided among connected computers (or clients) on a network while centralizing processing and storage for all information on a server. For instance, when you are surfing on the Internet, this is an example of a client/server infrastructure.

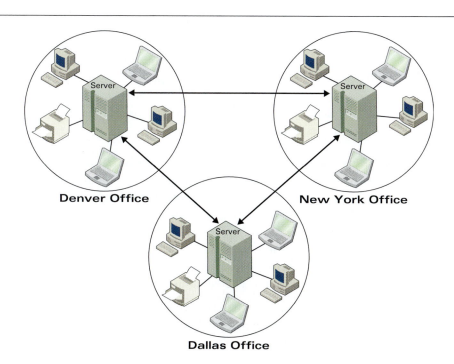

Denver Office

New York Office

Dallas Office

Figure 7.8

Distributed Infrastructure

ONE VIEW FOR DEL MONTE FOODS

From its roots in the California Gold Rush era, San Francisco–headquartered Del Monte Foods has grown to become the nation's largest producer and distributor of premium quality processed fruits, vegetables, and tomato products. With annual sales of over $3 billion, Del Monte is also one of the country's largest producers, distributors, and marketers of private-label food and pet products with a powerful portfolio of brands including Del Monte, StarKist, Nature's Goodness, 9Lives, and Kibbles 'n Bits.

Del Monte's acquisition of certain businesses (such as StarKist, Nature's Goodness, 9Lives, and Kibbles 'n Bits) from the H. J. Heinz Company required an integration between Del Monte's and H. J. Heinz's business processes. Del Monte needed to overhaul its IT infrastructure, migrating from multiple platforms including UNIX and mainframe systems and consolidating applications centrally on a single system. The work required integration of business processes across manufacturing, financial, supply chain, decision support, and transactional reporting areas.

The revamp of Del Monte's architecture stemmed from a strategic decision. Del Monte decided to implement an ERP system to support its entire U.S. operations, headquarters in San Francisco, operations in Pittsburgh, and distribution centers and manufacturing facilities across the country. The company concluded that the only way it could unite its global operations and open its system to its customers, which are mainly large retailers, was through the use of an ERP system.

Among other key factors was the need to embrace an e-business strategy. The challenge facing Del Monte was to select an ERP system to merge multiple systems quickly and cost effectively. If financial and customer service targets were to be achieved, Del Monte needed to integrate new businesses that more than doubled the size of the company. Since implementing the ERP system, customers and trading partners are now provided with a single, consistent, and integrated view of the company.[4,5]

Figure 7.9

Client/Server Infrastructure

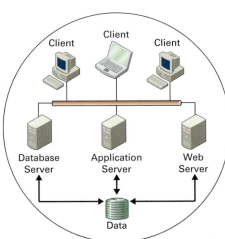

Typical components of this type of infrastructure include an Internet browser, a personal computer (e.g., the client), and a Web server.

The primary advantage of the client/server infrastructure is that it offloads the application programs and information from the server. However, because processing occurs at many client locations, and the client and server interact frequently and extensively, information must flow rapidly between server and clients for adequate performance (see Figure 7.9). The client/server infrastructure thereby places a heavy load on the network capacity, which can sometimes be a disadvantage.

TIERED INFRASTRUCTURE Most enterprise applications are now developed using a tiered infrastructure. In a *tiered infrastructure* (sometimes referred to as a *layer infrastructure*), the IT system is partitioned into tiers (or layers) where each tier (or layer) performs a specific type of functionality. The concept of a tiered infrastructure has evolved from 1-tier to n-tiers. A "tier" can be defined as "one of two or more rows, levels, or ranks arranged one above another." Figure 7.10 illustrates the concept of a tiered infrastructure.

- A *1-tier infrastructure* is the most basic setup because it involves a single tier on a single machine. Think of an application that runs on your PC—everything you need to run the application (data storage, business logic, user interface, and

SOA + SAP: COCA-COLA'S NEW SECRET RECIPE

Coca-Cola's business model is a common one among well-known, almost market dominant, franchisers. Coca-Cola gets the majority of its $18 billion in annual revenue from franchise fees it earns from bottlers all over the world. Bottlers, along with the franchise, license Coke's secret recipe and many others including recipes for Odwalla, Nestea, Minute Maid, and Sprite. What Coca-Cola is now hoping is that bottlers will also buy into adopting common business practices using a service-oriented architecture ERP system.

The target platform chosen by Coca-Cola is mySAP enterprise resource planning (ERP) by SAP. If it works, Coca-Cola and its bottlers stand to make and save a lot of money, and SAP will be able to position itself as one of the dominant players in SoA-enabled ERP.

Already, Coca-Cola and many of its bottlers use versions of SAP for finance, manufacturing, and a number of administrative functions. But Coca-Cola wants everyone to move to a "services" architecture environment. Coca-Cola hopes that this services standardization will make its supply chain more efficient and reduce costs.

In explaining why a services approach is so vitally important, Jean-Michel Ares, CIO of Coca-Cola, stated, "That will allow bottlers to converge one step at a time, one process area at a time, one module at a time, at a time that's right for the bottler. We can march across the bottling world incrementally."[6]

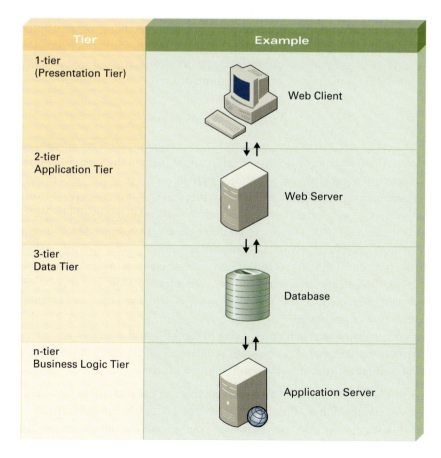

Figure 7.10

n-Tier Infrastructure Model

Tier	Example
1-tier (Presentation Tier)	Web Client
2-tier Application Tier	Web Server
3-tier Data Tier	Database
n-tier Business Logic Tier	Application Server

so forth) is wrapped up together. An example of a 1-tiered application is a basic word processor or a desktop file utility program.

- A **2-tier infrastructure** is the basic client/server relationship. In essence, the client handles the display, the server handles the request (e.g., database query), and the application tier is contained on one or both of the two tiers.

- A **3-tier infrastructure** is the most common approach used for Web applications today. A typical example of this model is the Web browser that acts as the client, an application server that handles the business logic, and a separate tier (such as a DBMS) that handles database functions.

- An **n-tier infrastructure** balances the work of the network over several different servers. The letter "n" stands for any number of tiers. Traditionally, an n-tier infrastructure starts with a basic 3-tier model and expands on it to allow for greater performance, scalability, and a host of other benefits.

IT Success Metrics

LEARNING OUTCOME 3

As with any organizational initiative, you must build a case for the acquisition, development, and use of technology. Technology costs money, not only for the hardware, software, and other IT-related components but also for the people involved, the changes to business processes, and the foregone opportunity to pursue other initiatives.

To justify the costs of technology, you need to be able to measure the success of technology. **Benchmarking** is the process of continuously measuring system results and comparing those results to **benchmarks**—baseline values a system seeks to attain. Benchmarks are most often industry-specific, process-specific, generated internal to your organization, or some combination of the three. With these metrics in hand you can make a cost/benefit judgment about technology. Benchmarking can lead to identifying steps and procedures to improve system performance.

EFFICIENCY AND EFFECTIVENESS METRICS

One way to categorize *metrics* (or ways to measure something) is by *efficiency* versus *effectiveness*. **Efficiency** means doing something right (e.g., in the least time, at the lowest cost, with the fewest errors, etc.), while **effectiveness** is doing the right thing. While the difference may seem subtle or purely semantic, it is not—the concepts are quite distinct. Let's consider a Web development project. A success metric would be Web traffic, perhaps as measured by the number of unique visitors. We refer to that as an *efficiency* metric because it simply means your organization is really good at driving customers to its Web site (i.e., creating traffic volume). But if those customers don't buy anything, it doesn't matter how many customers come to your site. So, while you may be very efficient in driving customers to your Web site, your Web site is not *effective* at getting those customers to make a purchase.

Most infrastructure-centric metrics today in the IT world are *efficiency metrics*. An **infrastructure-centric metric** is typically a measure of the efficiency, speed, and/or capacity of technology. Infrastructure-centric metrics include:

- **Throughput**—the amount of information that can pass through a system in a given amount of time. This is often associated with telecommunications capabilities (bandwidth) such as transmission speeds (kilobits per second, Kbps, and megabits per second, Mbps).

- **Transaction speed**—the speed at which a system can process a transaction.

- *System availability*—usually measured inversely as *downtime,* or the average amount of time a system is down and unavailable to end users and customers. This does not include regularly scheduled maintenance.
- *Accuracy*—also usually measured inversely as *error rate,* or the number of errors per thousand (or million) that a system generates. This is analogous to defects per thousand or million in manufacturing.
- *Response time*—average time to respond to a user-generated event, such as a request for a report, a mouse click, and so on.
- *Scalability*—how well a system can adapt to increased demands. This is more of a conceptual metric that assesses your ability to upgrade the implemented infrastructure at minimal cost and service interruption.

Effectiveness metrics, on the other hand, measure results of the technology or application in some environment. For example, call centers have numerous effectiveness (success) metrics as do Web e-business applications. We'll explore several metrics for both of those in a moment. Customer relationship management and supply chain management systems have numerous associated metrics, as well, including (but certainly not limited to):

- Customer relationship management (CRM)
  - Number of cross-selling successes
  - Cost-per-thousand (CPM)—sales dollars generated per dollar of advertising
  - Number of new customers generated
  - Average length of time a customer stays active (i.e., continues to buy products and services from you)
- Supply chain management (SCM)
  - Number of stockouts
  - Excess inventory
  - Distribution and warehousing costs

It's interesting to note in the above lists that you want to increase the value of all of the CRM metrics (e.g., the more cross-selling successes you have the better). This is a common characteristics of metrics that measure top-line initiatives. Conversely, you want to reduce the value of all the SCM metrics (e.g., have as little excess inventory as possible). This is a common characteristic of metrics that measure bottom-line initiatives.

If you consider the graph in Figure 7.11, you can begin to understand the relationship between efficiency and effectiveness metrics. Bottom-line initiatives, such as supply chain management, seek to optimize efficiency metrics while not negatively affecting

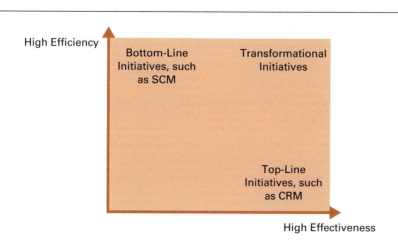

High Efficiency

Bottom-Line Initiatives, such as SCM

Transformational Initiatives

Top-Line Initiatives, such as CRM

High Effectiveness

Figure 7.11

Efficiency and Effectiveness Metrics

effectiveness metrics, and top-line initiatives, such as customer relationship management, seek to optimize effectiveness metrics while not negatively affecting efficiency metrics. (It might appear in Figure 7.11 that the optimal area of operation is the upper-right area, but that's simply not true and seldom achievable except when undertaking extraordinary transformational activities. An excellent example here is that of Apple iTunes, which created both tremendous efficiency and effectiveness.)

WEB-CENTRIC METRICS

A *Web-centric metric* is a measure of the success of your Web and e-business initiatives. There are literally hundreds of Web-centric metrics you can use, with some being general to almost any Web or e-business initiative and others being very dependent on the particular initiative. Common Web-centric metrics include:

- *Unique visitors*—the number of unique visitors to your sites in a given time. This is commonly used by Nielsen/Net ratings to rank the most popular Web sites.
- *Total hits*—number of visits to your Web site, many of which may be by the same visitor.
- *Page exposures*—average number of page exposures to an individual visitor.
- *Conversion rate*—percentage of potential customers who visit your site who actually buy something.
- *Click-through*—count of the number of people who visit a site, click on an ad, and are taken to the site of the advertiser.
- *Cost-per-thousand (CPM)*—sales dollars generated per dollar of advertising. This is commonly used to make the case for spending money to appear on a search engine.
- *Abandoned registrations*—number of visitors who start the process of completing a registration page and then abandon the activity.
- *Abandoned shopping carts*—the number of visitors who create a shopping cart and start shopping and then abandon the activity before paying for the merchandise.

CALL CENTER METRICS

Call center metrics measure the success of call center efforts. Typical call center metrics include:

- *Abandon rate*—the percentage number of callers who hang up while waiting for their call to be answered.
- *Average speed to answer (ASA)*—the average time, usually in seconds, that it takes for a call to be answered by an actual person.
- *Time service factor (TSF)*—the percentage of calls answered within a specific time frame, such as 30 or 90 seconds.
- *First call resolution (FCR)*—the percentage of calls that can be resolved without having to call back.

If your call center operations are partly automated in the hope of helping people with common questions, then you have additional metrics such as the percentage of people who use the automated system and then request also to speak to a service representative.

FINANCIAL METRICS

Ultimately, you must make sense of all your other metrics by comparing them to or incorporating them into financial metrics, or what is more commonly referred to as *capital analysis financial models*. Organizations must be able to express the success of their IT initiatives in terms of dollars and cents. How to compute and interpret all the various financial metrics is certainly beyond the scope of this book. You will, however, explore and work with these types of metrics in your finance, accounting, and business strategies. Here, we simply define each. Figure 7.12 provides more detail.

- *Payback method*—number of years to recoup the cost of an initiative based on projected annual net cash flow.
- *Cost-benefit ratio*—a ratio comparing the benefits to the costs.
- *Return on investment (ROI)*—the overall value of an initiative (total benefits minus total costs and depreciation) as compared to the useful life of the initiative, expressed as a percentage.
- *Net present value (NPV)*—the total net present value of all cash flows over the life of an initiative.
- *Internal rate of return (IRR)*—the net present value (from above) expressed as a percentage return.

Figure 7.12

Capital Analysis
Financial Models

Financial Model	Formula	Type of Result
Payback method (in years)	$\dfrac{\text{Original investment}}{\text{Annual net cash flow}}$	= time to pay back
Cost-benefit ratio (as a factor)	$\dfrac{\text{Benefits}}{\text{Costs}}$	= cost-benefit ratio
Return on investment (ROI, as a percent)	$\dfrac{(\text{Benefits} - \text{cost} - \text{depreciation})}{\text{useful system life}}$	= net benefit
Net present value (NPV, in $)	Total net present value of all cash flows*	= value today of return in future
Internal rate of return (IRR, as a percent)	The NPV represented as a percentage return*	= expected return

*The net present value and internal rate of return calculation are too complex to summarize above. So both are defined completely below:

Net present value   = sum of the present value of all future payments less the initial cost
$$= -CF_0 + \Sigma[CF_t/(1 + r)^t] \quad \text{where } CF_0 = \text{the initial cost}$$
$$CF_t = \text{each future payment}$$
$$r = \text{the discount rate}$$
$$t = \text{the number of the time payment}$$

Internal rate of return = the rate that completes the following summation equation
Cost $= \Sigma[CF_t/(1 + IRR)^t] \quad \text{where } CF_t = \text{the future payments}$
$$IRR = \text{the internal rate of return}$$
$$t = \text{the number of the payment}$$

THE LONDON BRIDGE MAY FALL DOWN BUT THE EXCHANGE WON'T

The London Stock Exchange is among the most admired equity exchanges in the world, not only for its long-standing position in the financial community but also for its technology deployment and infrastructure. And when you process 15 million real-time messages per day (with peaks of 2,000 messages per second), your infrastructure had better be good.

In choosing a new technology infrastructure on which to ride into the future, the London Stock Exchange focused a great deal of its efforts on requiring vendors to meet benchmarks across a broad range of metrics. Below are just a few.

- *Guaranteed performance*—in financial trading, information is valuable only if it reaches traders within the first second.

- *Development costs*—reduced development costs and development cycle times means more productivity. Ian Homan, head of Technology for the London Exchange, estimates that implementation of the new infrastructure occurred in one-fifth to one-third the time it would have taken to implement other vendor infrastructures.

- *Scalability*—according to David Lester, CIO for the London Stock Exchange, "We want to be able to extend it and make it richer. Investment decisions of this kind aren't made carelessly and the ability to scale to our future needs was a critical factor."[7,8]

SERVICE LEVEL AGREEMENTS REVISITED

To close our discussion of metrics, let's revisit the service level agreement. As we defined it in Chapter 6, a *service level agreement (SLA)* is a formal, contractually obligated agreement between two parties. We further described an SLA by saying that, within different environments, it takes on different meanings.

An important aspect of any SLA is a definition of the metrics that will be used to measure the success of the interactions between the two parties. Suppose, for example, that your organization decided to outsource its call center operations. The SLA would cover in great detail the financial agreement, such as how much money your organization will pay the call center outsourcing organization. It would also include key metrics and benchmarks that the outsourcing organization must meet to stay in compliance with the SLA. These metrics would include many of those we listed above including average speed to answer, abandon rate, and time service factor.

Many organizations today also outsource their Web development and e-business activities. In that case, your SLA would include key metrics and benchmarks around such areas as those we discussed within the context of Web-centric metrics. The definitions of these metrics and benchmarks are usually not present in the SLA, which is more business oriented and void of detailed technical specifications. They would, instead, appear in a supporting document (similar to a contract addendum) called a *service level specification (SLS)* or *service level objective (SLO).*

Another important business relationship in which you find the use of a service level agreement is that between an organization and an application service provider. An *application service provider (ASP)* supplies software applications (and often related services such as maintenance, technical support, information storage, and the like) over the Internet that would otherwise reside on customers' computers. The ASP model is very popular with businesses. For example, many businesses use CRM software provided by

Salesforce.com, which hosts its CRM software on its Internet servers. Businesses subscribing to Salesforce.com's CRM software access it over the Internet, thus eliminating the need to buy, store, and maintain the software on their own computers. A service level agreement is vitally important and includes application-specific metrics (such as those associated with CRM software if you use Salesforce.com's CRM software) and infrastructure-centric metrics such as system availability, transaction speed, response time, and throughput.

Business Continuity Planning

Business continuity planning (BCP) is a rigorous and well-informed organizational methodology for developing a *business continuity plan,* a step-by-step guideline defining how the organization will recover from a disaster or extended disruption of its business processes. In past years, with respect to IT systems and information, the business continuity plan went by other names, *disaster recovery plan* and *contingency plan.* Given the number of natural disasters and terrorist attacks worldwide, along with businesses' increasing dependency on all their processes and resources (not just IT and information), however, the general trend has been to develop a more all-encompassing *business continuity plan* that includes all aspects of the organization.

The BCP methodology looks very similar to the systems development life cycle (see Figure 7.13). It starts with the organization's strategic plan and moves through various phases including analysis, design, implementation, testing, and maintenance. We'll focus our discussion of BCP on information technology and IT-related issues.

PHASE 1: ORGANIZATIONAL STRATEGIC PLAN

Business continuity planning starts with your organization's strategic plan, which informs you of the relative importance of resources, processes, systems, and other organizational assets. It's important to understand and develop a ranking of the importance of these assets because you cannot (and should not) develop a business continuity plan that enables you to recover every asset within minutes of some sort of disaster. That would be prohibitively expensive and unnecessary. Your organization can afford to live without some assets (i.e., systems and information) for several days or even weeks. Payroll software may be an example here. For other assets, such as customer ordering and supply chain applications, it may be critical that your organization gets those up and running

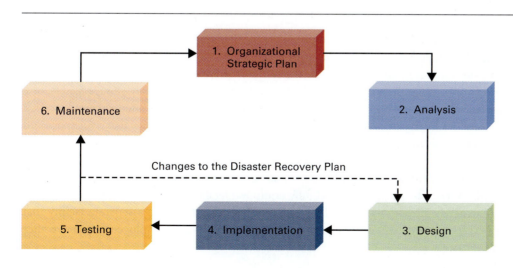

Figure 7.13

Business Continuity Planning (BCP)

with minimal interruption. Data centers are also typically identified as high priorities for most organizations. According to CPM Research, "improved business continuity" was cited 70 percent of the time by respondents as being a key data center issue.[9]

PHASE 2: ANALYSIS

In the BCP analysis phase, you perform impact analysis, threat analysis, and impact scenario analysis, and then build a requirement recovery document.

- (1) *Impact analysis*—Here you seek to truly differentiate between critical, core IT applications and information and those that are noncritical. Key factors supporting your analysis include: the financial impact to the organization for the loss of IT applications and information over time, implications for stakeholders (e.g., customer loss of power if you provide utilities), and cost estimates of recovery. Impact analysis is often called **risk assessment,** the process of evaluating IT assets, their importance of the organization, and their susceptibility to threats.

- (2) *Threat analysis*—In step 2 of BCP analysis, you document the possible threats to your organization and its assets. These can and often do include disease, earthquakes (depending on the geographical location of your organization), fire, flood, cyber attack, terrorism, and utility outages. An assessment of these helps you develop an understanding of the magnitude of threats and how you should choose to recover from them. Note that in the case of e-business activities threats can include greatly increased shopping traffic. For example, on the day after Thanksgiving in 2006 Wal-Mart's Web site went down because so many people visited its site in the hope of buying the hard-to-find T.M.X. Elmo.[10]

- (3) *Impact scenario analysis*—In step 3, you consider each threat (from step 2) and build a worst-case scenario for each (as opposed to smaller impact scenarios such as 10 percent of the workforce out due to a flu outbreak). An impact scenario analysis provides further definition and detail concerning the scope and magnitude of each possible disaster.

- (4) *Requirement recovery document*—Armed with the information from steps 1 through 3, you finally build a **requirement recovery document,** a detailed document which describes (a) the distinction between critical and noncritical IT systems and information, (b) each possible threat, and (c) the possible worst-case scenarios that can result from each disaster. This document becomes the basis for the design phase which follows.

PHASE 3: DESIGN

Using the requirement recovery document, in the design phase, you design a formal, technical, and detailed plan for recovering from a disaster—a **disaster recovery plan.** A good disaster recovery plan takes into consideration the location of the backup information. Many organizations choose to store backup information in an off-site storage facility, or a place that is located separate from the company and often owned by another company, such as a collocation facility. A **collocation facility** is available to a company that rents space and telecommunications equipment from another company. One such company is StorageTek, which specializes in providing off-site data storage and disaster recovery solutions.

A good disaster recovery plan also considers the actual facility where employees will work. A **hot site** is a separate and fully equipped facility where the company can move immediately after a disaster and resume business. A **cold site** is a separate facility that does not have any computer equipment but is a place where employees can move after the disaster.

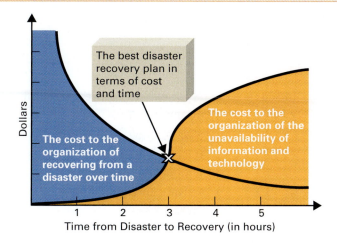

Figure 7.14

Deciding How Much
to Spend on Disaster
Recovery

A disaster recovery plan should be based on a *disaster recovery cost curve* (Figure 7.14). A ***disaster recovery cost curve*** charts (1) the cost to your organization of the unavailability of information and technology and (2) the cost to your organization of recovering from a disaster over time. Where the two curves intersect is the best recovery plan in terms of cost and time. Being able to restore information and IT systems quickly in the event of a disaster is obviously a crucial aspect of an IT infrastructure.

PHASE 4: IMPLEMENTATION

At this point, business continuity planning diverges somewhat from the SDLC. In the SDLC, you would develop and test the solution before implementing it. In business continuity planning, you must begin to implement your disaster recovery plan before testing it. That is, you need to engage any businesses that will be providing collocation facilities, hot sites, and/or cold sites, and implement the necessary procedures for recovering from a disaster. You train your employees concerning what to do in case of any of the disasters. You also evaluate each IT system and ensure that it is configured optimally for recovering from a disaster. You can now test the disaster recovery plan.

PHASE 5: TESTING

Testing in business continuity planning involves executing simulated scenarios of disasters and having employees execute on the disaster recovery plan to ensure that the solution satisfies your organization's recovery requirements. If noticeable deficiencies are identified, your organization should return to steps 3 and 4 (design and implementation) and reconfigure and reimplement the disaster recovery plan accordingly.

This sort of testing does not stop once you believe you have developed an optimal plan. The environment in which your organization operates changes almost daily. You should test your disaster recovery plan on at least an annual basis, and more realistically several times a year.

PHASE 6: MAINTENANCE

Finally, you need to continually assess new threats and reevaluate your IT systems and related assets to determine their changing importance to the organization. As with the SDLC, no "system" is ever complete; it needs constant monitoring, support, and maintenance.

ENTERGY SURVIVES KATRINA

Based in New Orleans, Entergy Corp. employs 14,500 people to provide electricity to 2.6 million utility consumers in Arkansas, Louisiana, Texas, and Mississippi. In late August 2005, Hurricane Katrina tested the resolve of all of Entergy's employees and the preparedness of its disaster recovery plan.

Employees rose to the occasion and the disaster recovery plan was executed well. Although returning all utilities to every customer in the region took several months (because of factors well beyond Entergy's control), it was Entergy's dedication to building a successful disaster recovery plan that paid dividends.

Located in the Gulf of Mexico in the heart of hurricane country in the southern part of the United States, the energy company had an effective disaster recovery plan well in place. Entergy tested its disaster recovery plan at least once a year. The previous year that test had come in the form of preparing for Hurricane Ivan, which ultimately made landfall to the east in Florida. Just five months before Hurricane Katrina hit, the company conducted a massive storm drill which simulated what everyone thought was the worst-case scenario—a major hurricane followed by extreme flooding.

Entergy's disaster recovery plan included several key elements, including:

- Start the execution of the disaster recovery plan at least 72 hours in advance of the predicted landfall of a hurricane.
- Activate Entergy's disaster recovery site in Little Rock, Arkansas.
- Activate Entergy's storm command center (also called *The Power House*) in Jackson, Mississippi.
- Still in advance of the predicted landfall of a hurricane, prepare the company's systems that would be most critical in restoring electricity to utility consumers.

According to everyone, the disaster recovery plan worked well, but Ray Johnson, CIO of Entergy, thought some changes needed to be made. As he explained it, "We never follow the plan to the letter. In the IT space, the plan is very solid in terms of what we have to do. But we're always working—our core IT staff in conjunction with representatives from the business areas—to see if we need to change priorities."[11]

Student Learning Outcomes Revisited

1. **Describe how a service-oriented architecture can be used as a philosophical approach to help the organization of the future meet all its IT-related needs.** A service-oriented architecture can be applied to help your organization respond to:

   - *Customers*—through multichannel service delivery and the provision of customizable products and services.
   - *End users*—through fully integrated ERP systems supporting interoperability and mobile computing.

   - *Software development*—as a framework for supporting development methodologies such as RAD, XP, and agile that lead to exciting new deployments such as Web 2.0.
   - *Information needs*—including access to all types of integrated information (and business intelligence and knowledge), standard information formats, integrity controls, and the elimination of redundant information.

- *Hardware requirements*—through the integration of different technologies, providing large storage capacities, and maintaining safe and secure telecommunications platforms.

2. **Define and describe the various hardware and software infrastructure considerations in an organization.** Hardware and software infrastructure considerations include:

- Enterprise resource planning (ERP) systems provide interoperability within an ERP vendor and among modules of different ERP vendors and also hide the underlying IT infrastructure of information and hardware from end users and customers.

- Network infrastructures include: *Decentralized*—little or no sharing of IT and other resources such as information; *Centralized*—sharing of information systems in one central area or one central mainframe; *Distributed*—distributing the information and processing power of IT systems via a network; *Client/server*—one or more computers that are servers which provide services to other computers, called clients; *Tiered (layer)*—the IT system is partitioned into tiers where each tier performs a specific type of functionality.

3. **Compare and contrast commonly used metrics for assessing the success of IT systems and IT-related initiatives.** Metrics are simply ways to measure something. Common IT metrics can be categorized as:

- *Infrastructure-centric metrics*—Measures of efficiency, speed, and/or capacity of technology, including *throughput, transaction speed, system availability, accuracy, response time,* and *scalability.*
- *Web-centric metrics*—Measures of the success of your Web and e-business initiatives, including *unique visitors, total hits, page exposures, conversion rate, click-through, cost-per-thousand (CPM), abandoned registrations,* and *abandoned shopping carts.*
- *Call center metrics*—Measures of the success of call center efforts, including *abandon rate, average speed to answer (ASA), time service factor (TSF),* and *first call resolution (FCR).*
- *Financial metrics*—Also called *capital analysis financial models,* including *payback*

method, cost-benefit ratio, return on investment (ROI), net present value (NPV), and *internal rate of return (IRR).*

4. **Describe business continuity planning (BCP) and its phases.** *Business continuity planning (BCP)* is a rigorous and well-informed organizational methodology for developing a *business continuity plan,* a step-by-step guideline defining how the organization will recover from a disaster or extended disruption of its business processes. The phases of business continuity planning include:

- *Phase 1: Organizational strategic plan*—it all starts here with understanding the relative importance of resources, systems, processes, and other organizational assets.
- *Phase 2: Analysis*—perform impact analysis, threat analysis, and impact scenario analysis and build a *requirement recovery document,* a detailed document that describes (1) the distinction between critical and noncritical IT systems and information, (2) each possible threat, and (3) the possible worst-case scenarios that can result from each disaster.
- *Phase 3: Design*—using the requirement recovery document, create a *disaster recovery plan,* which identifies collocation facilities, hot sites, and cold sites and illustrates a disaster recovery cost curve (the cost to your organization of the unavailability of information and technology as compared to the cost to your organization of recovering from a disaster over time).
- *Phase 4: Implementation*—engage businesses that will provide collocation facilities, hot sites, and cold sites; implement necessary procedures for recovering from a disaster; train employees; evaluate each IT system to ensure its configuration is optimal for recovering from a disaster.
- *Phase 5: Testing*—executing simulated scenarios of disasters and having employees execute on the disaster recovery plan.
- *Phase 6: Maintenance*—continually assess new threats and reevaluate your IT systems and related assets to determine their changing importance to the organization.

CLOSING CASE STUDY ONE

INTERNATIONAL TRUCK MAKES A HUGE BET ON A SERVICE-ORIENTED ARCHITECTURE

Service-oriented architectures (SoAs) do seem to be the future for integrated IT systems within an organization, bringing together both applications and information in a seamless fashion. But SoAs are still in their infancy, and some companies don't want to wait until they mature. They are willing to bet on a service-oriented architecture right now. One such company is International Truck and Engine Corporation.

International Truck's SoA resulted from needing more timely information so it could identify assembly-plant problems sooner. Its current IT systems, all legacy information systems, didn't share information easily, and that led to bottlenecks in production, excessive defects and returns, shortfalls in inventory, and a host of other problems that can spell doom for a manufacturing-intensive company like International Truck.

So, the company forged ahead in embracing an SoA, knowing that it would be able to buy many of the software components that it needed and that others would have to be written from scratch by in-house IT specialists. The first focus for International Truck was the Common Vehicle Tracking system, a system that tracks production according to a specific vehicle or vehicle type. International truck produces everything from RV motor homes to military transports.

The Common Vehicle Tracking system was a high-profile, high-payoff project with a tight deadline. The company expected the system to save it at least $3 million annually. The system, now complete and installed in one factory, tracks in near real time all information relating to works-in-progress and finished inventory. Prior to its implementation, Art Data, Vice President of Information Technology at International Truck, succinctly explained, "We weren't doing it very well." International Truck's legacy systems stored isolated data and information in applications such as computer-aided manufacturing, in-house developed order management, and even commercial ERP software.

The new system uses a combination of many different types of software, one of the primary goals of a service-oriented architecture. For example, it uses a data integration tool from SSA Global to extract information from International Truck's Baan ERP system. From there, in-house developed software bridges to the order management system.

International Truck is also working on an SoA extension to interface with the systems of its dealers. The company already has a centralized server that its 400 dealers use to access parts catalogs and sales tools. However, dealers can choose their own internal dealer management software systems. This makes communicating information in a common format problematic, at best. International Truck is currently working with automotive industry software vendors to create common services (i.e., software modules) that will communicate information in a standard format.

In the future, International Truck will even extend its SoA architecture perspective into the vehicles themselves. Using the vehicles' electronics system, GPS, and cellular technology, owners of the trucks will be able to track the location of their vehicles.[12]

Questions

1. With respect to its customers (dealers in this case), how is International Truck using a service-oriented architecture to meet their needs? How does using an SoA further help International Truck erect an entry barrier (from Chapter 1)?

2. With respect to information needs, what advantages and efficiencies is International Truck hoping to gain by using a service-oriented architecture? Why are these advantages and efficiencies not possible with its current legacy systems?

3. Recalling our discussion of software development methodologies in Chapter 6 that focus on component-based development (i.e., RAD, XP, and agile), how is International Truck able to integrate new software modules with existing ones?

4. What key infrastructure-centric metrics could International Truck use to justify its movement toward a service-oriented architecture? For each that you identify, provide a short description of why the metric is important.

5. How important is it for International Truck to have a good business continuity plan in place? What key IT systems and other IT resources do you believe would be at the top of the list for quick recovery? Why?

CLOSING CASE STUDY TWO

ROGER WILLIAMS MEDICAL CENTER BOOSTS ITS IT INFRASTRUCTURE

Roger Williams Medical Center is a 220-bed hospital located in Providence, Rhode Island. It has been widely recognized as a leading provider of health care, not only on the East coast but throughout the United States. Roger Williams faced a difficult challenge implementing several key new IT systems because of its aging IT infrastructure.

According to Kevin Frederick, Director of Technology, at Roger Williams, "Our legacy systems had reached the end of their life cycle, and we knew that we would need a big jump in processing power and storage capacity to support our new applications." Those new applications included MEDITECH, a new comprehensive patient-care system, and the Picture Archive Communication System (PACS). PACS stores and distributes electronic images from CAT scans, MRI, ultrasound and other image-based tests (totaling more than 19,000 annually), allowing health care providers to diagnose conditions and diseases using high-resolution monitors.

To achieve the scalability, availability, and performance required, Roger Williams contracted HP Services to design, develop, deliver, and support its needed IT infrastructure. That infrastructure includes a server farm of 41 servers connected to a storage area network with 4 terabytes of capacity to start.

Kevin made the following statements regarding working with HP Services and its IT infrastructure: "The BladeServer systems [server farm] enabled us to reduce the footprint of our racked servers by 50 percent, while giving us plenty of headroom for growth . . . The blades have a smart design—with power integrated into the chassis, they are easy to deploy and fast to swap. If a problem were to develop, we can easily deploy one of our 'cold spares' and minimize any disruption of service. HP Services spent the week assembling the SANS and educated us along the way. I couldn't have asked for it to go any better." Even users of the new system frequently comment on how much faster the new system performs.

The IT infrastructure certainly supports scalability and increased processing capacity. After the new system had been online for nine months, Roger Williams added 11 more servers as it expanded the user-facing applications within MEDITECH and PACS. Many of those user-facing applications are critical to Roger Williams' success. These include numerous clinical modules, Patient Tracker (for emergency room services), and Long Term Care (for nursing home support).

The future of Roger Williams and its IT infrastructure is to develop an intensive business continuity plan that will provide for redundant data servers.[13,14]

Questions

1. In this chapter, we noted that many effectiveness metrics depend on the application under scrutiny, such as supply chain management and customer relationship management. What sort of effectiveness metrics would the health care industry likely use to evaluate the success of IT systems?

Where possible, highlight the use of these effectiveness metrics by Roger Williams.

2. In the final part of this case study, Roger Williams was making plans to create a business continuity plan for its information. Why do you think the hospital had not already developed such a plan in the event of a disaster? How is HP's new IT infrastructure going to help Roger Williams build a robust business continuity plan?

3. According to the network infrastructures we discussed in this chapter, how would you characterize Roger Williams' new IT infrastructure? Justify your answer.

4. As a part of a business continuity plan, many businesses identify cold sites or hot sites to which they can move to carry on their business activities. What about a hospital like Roger Williams? What if it suffered a disaster such as a flood or hurricane? Where could it move to provide quality patient care?

5. What infrastructure-centric metrics can you find in this case study? Why are they so important to Roger Williams? What other infrastructure-centric metrics might be important to the hospital?

Key Terms and Concepts

1-tier infrastructure, 204
2-tier infrastructure, 206
3-tier infrastructure, 206
Abandon rate, 208
Abandoned registration, 208
Abandoned shopping cart, 208
Accuracy, 207
Application service provider (ASP), 210
Average speed to answer (ASA), 208
Benchmark, 206
Benchmarking, 206
Business continuity plan, 211
Business continuity planning (BCP), 211
Call center metric, 208
Centralized infrastructure, 202
Click-through, 208
Client/server infrastructure (client/server network), 203

Cold site, 212
Collocation facility, 212
Conversion rate, 208
Cost-per-thousand (CPM), 208
Decentralized infrastructure, 202
Disaster recovery cost curve, 213
Disaster recovery plan, 212
Distributed infrastructure, 203
Effectiveness, 206
Efficiency, 206
First call resolution (FCR), 208
Hot site, 212
Infrastructure, 197
Infrastructure-centric metric, 206
Interoperability, 200
n-tier infrastructure, 206
Page exposures, 208
Requirement recovery document, 212
Response time, 207

Risk assessment, 212
Scalability, 207
Service level agreement (SLA), 210
Service level objective (SLO), 210
Service level specification (SLS), 210
Service-oriented architecture (SoA or SOA), 194
System availability, 207
Throughput, 206
Tiered infrastructure (layer infrastructure), 204
Time service factor (TSF), 208
Total hits, 208
Transaction speed, 206
Unique visitors, 208
Web-centric metric, 208

Short-Answer Questions

1. How can a service-oriented architecture (SoA) be used to guide the organization of the future?

2. How have ERP systems evolved over the last 30 years?

3. Why is interoperability important?

4. What are the main differences between a decentralized infrastructure and a centralized infrastructure?

5. How does a client/server infrastructure work?

6. What are the four types of a tiered infrastructure?

7. How do efficiency and effectiveness metrics differ?

8. What are some commonly used infrastructure-centric metrics?

9. What are some commonly used Web-centric metrics?

10. Why are service level agreements important when contracting the services of an application service provider (ASP)?

11. What is a business continuity plan?

12. Why do organizations implement a disaster recovery plan before testing it?

Assignments and Exercises

1. **SECURITY METRICS** In this chapter, we focused on metrics for measuring the success of your IT systems including infrastructure-centric metrics, Web-centric metrics, call center metrics, and financial metrics. Another important area of metrics is security metrics, or how well you are doing at stopping viruses from coming in, protecting against identify theft, and the like. Do some research on the Web and develop a list of commonly used metrics in the area of security. Be sure to define each metric.

2. **CREATING A CAMPUS IT INFRASTRUCTURE** You have been assigned the role of student IT infrastructure manager. Your first assignment is to approve the designs for the new on-campus Internet infrastructure. You're having a meeting at 9:00 A.M. tomorrow morning to review the designs with the student IT employees. To prepare for the meeting, you must understand the student requirements and their current use of the Internet, along with future requirements. The following is a list of questions you must answer before attending the meeting. Provide an answer to each question.

   - Do you need to have a disaster recovery plan? If so what might it include?
   - Does the system require backup equipment?
   - When will the system need to be available to the students?
   - What types of access levels will the students need?
   - How will you ensure the system is reliable?
   - How will you build scalability into the system?
   - What are the minimum performance requirements for the system?
   - How will the system handle future growth?

3. **EFFICIENCY AND EFFECTIVENESS METRICS** Choose any of the Perspective boxes in this chapter or the opening case and identify and describe at least seven metrics that could be used to measure the success of the IT systems in your chosen example. For each metric, categorize it as either an efficiency or effectiveness metric. Justify your categorizations.

4. **APPLICATION SERVICE PROVIDERS** There are numerous application service providers that enable organizations to access and use Web-based application software. In the chapter we identified Salesforce.com as one such ASP. Search the Web and find at least five other ASPs. What are the names of the companies? What application software do they provide over the Web? What additional services do they provide, if any?

5. **PERSONAL BENCHMARKS AND BENCHMARKING** How do you use benchmarks and benchmarking in your personal life? Think about grades, making money, supporting charities, and the like. Choose one significant way in which you use benchmarks and benchmarking in your personal life and describe it. What are your benchmark values? How were you able to derive your benchmark values? Where did they come from?

Discussion Questions

1. On page 208, we listed and defined numerous Web-centric metrics. Which of those are efficiency metrics and which of those are effectiveness metrics? For each, provide justification for your answer and an illustration using a real-life or hypothetical Web business example.

2. IT infrastructures often mimic organizational hierarchies and the philosophical approach organizations take to the placement of the IT function (see Chapter 2). Describe which common network infrastructure (decentralized, centralized, distributed, client/server, or tiered) would best support the three structural placements of the IT function we listed on page 49.

3. What type of IT infrastructure does your school have? If it uses a client/server infrastructure how does your school's client/server network increase student productivity? What recommendations, based on the contents of this chapter, could you recommend to the IT people who manage the infrastructure?

4. How is the concept of interoperability an important aspect that you rely on in your daily life? Think about the many devices, appliances, modes of transportation, and so on that you use every day. Which of these support the concept of interoperability? How would your life change if they didn't support interoperability?

5. Many people say that efficiency and effectiveness metrics are interrelated and that you can't really have one without the other or that no organization can truly be successful without both. How are efficiency and effectiveness metrics interrelated? Must you succeed in one set before addressing the other? If so, which is first and why?

6. Consider an e-business like Amazon.com. Which Web-centric metrics on page 208 would be most important to it? Justify your answers. Now consider a content provider like CNN (www.cnn.com). Which Web-centric metrics would be most important to it? Justify your answers. Why would two e-businesses have such a different focus on Web-centric metrics?

CHAPTER PROJECTS

Group Projects

- Assessing the Value of Outsourcing Information Technology: Creating Forecasts (p. 372)
- Creating a Decision Support System: Buy versus Lease (p. 376)
- Developing an Enterprise Resource Planning System: Planning, Reporting, and Data Processing (p. 377)
- Evaluating the Next Generation: Dot-Com ASPs (p. 379)
- Evaluating the Security of Information: Wireless Network Vulnerability (p. 386)

e-Commerce Projects

- Best in computer statistics and resources (p. 388)
- Meta data (p. 389)
- Finding hosting services (p. 393)
- Searching for shareware and freeware (p. 398)

CHAPTER EIGHT OUTLINE

STUDENT LEARNING OUTCOMES

1. Define ethics and describe the two factors that affect how you make a decision concerning an ethical issue.

2. Define and describe intellectual property, copyright, Fair Use Doctrine, and pirated software.

3. Define privacy and describe ways in which it can be threatened.

4. Describe the ways in which information on your computer or network is vulnerable and list measures you can take to protect it.

PERSPECTIVES

WEB SUPPORT

www.mhhe.com/haag

- Exploring Google Earth
- Protecting your computer against viruses
- Searching for shareware and freeware
- Ethical computing guidelines
- Privacy laws and legislation

Protecting People and Information
Threats and Safeguards

There's a company in Little Rock, Arkansas, called Acxiom, that handles consumer information, mainly for marketing purposes. That is to say, Acxiom stores and analyzes information, both its own and its clients'. Acxiom gets the information it sells from many sources, including the three major credit bureaus (TransUnion, Equifax Inc., and Experian Inc.). Nine of the country's 10 largest credit-card issuers are clients along with many other high profile financial companies in the banking and insurance industries. Forty percent of Acxiom's revenue comes from banking alone.

The company's inventory includes 20 billion records on consumers that include names, addresses, Social Security numbers, and public-record information. In fact, Acxiom has a database with information on about 110 million Americans, or 96 percent of U.S. households. The company categorizes consumers into one of 70 lifestyle clusters that include such groups as "Rolling Stones," "Single City Struggles," and "Timeless Elders."

To help clients react quickly to changing market conditions, Acxiom offers hundreds of lists. One of these is a daily updated "pre-movers file" which lists people who are about to change residences. Another list is of people who use credit cards, and the list is sorted in order of frequency of use.

For example, Capital One Financial Corporation, a financial services company based in Virginia, sends out about 1 billion pieces of mail every year that largely consist of advertising intended to entice consumers to sign up for credit cards. Acxiom's information and analysis help Capital One send credit card solicitations only to those who are likely to want another credit card.

Another service that Acxiom provides is the merging of huge databases. The merger of Bank One and J. P. Morgan is a case in point. Both companies had huge, independent databases, and merging such mountains of information is Acxiom's specialty. First the information must be cleaned (called "data hygiene" in the industry), that is, duplicate records must be identified and combined. Acxiom also adds records from its own database to those of its clients, complementing and completing the clients' customer information.

Acxiom is only one of the many companies that collect and sell data on consumers.[1,2,3,4]

Questions

1. Do you feel comfortable about so many people collecting information about you and distributing it freely?

2. Is it an invasion of your privacy or just good business?

3. Should there be any laws regulating the collection and use of data by data brokers like Acxiom?

Introduction

As you know, the three components of an IT system are people, information, and information technology. Most of what you've seen in previous chapters has dealt with IT and how it stores and processes information. In this chapter we're going to concentrate on information—its use, ownership, and protection. The best environment for handling information is one that has stability without stagnation and change without chaos.

To handle information in a responsible way you must understand

- The importance of ethics in the ownership and use of information.
- The importance to people of personal privacy and the ways in which it can be compromised.
- Threats to information and how to protect against them (security).

The most important part of any IT system consists of the people who use it and are affected by it. How people treat each other has always been important, but in this information-based and digital age, with huge computing power at our fingertips, we can affect more people's lives in more ways than ever before. How we act toward each other, and this includes how we view and handle information, is largely determined by our ethics.

You don't have to look far to see examples of computer use that is questionable from an ethical viewpoint. For example,

- People copy, use, and distribute software they have no right to.
- Employees search organizational databases for information on celebrities and friends.
- Organizations collect, buy, and use information and don't check the validity or accuracy of that information.
- Misguided people create and spread viruses that cause trouble for those using and maintaining IT systems.
- Information system developers put systems on the market before they're completely tested. A few years ago, the developers of an incubator thermostat control program didn't test it fully, and two infants died as a result.[5]
- Unethical people break into computer systems and steal passwords, information, and proprietary information.
- Employees destroy or steal proprietary schematics, sketches, customer lists, and reports from their employers.
- People snoop on each other and read each other's e-mail and other private documents.

Ethics

LEARNING OUTCOME 1

Ethical people have integrity. They're people who are just as careful of the rights of others as they are of their own rights. They have a strong sense of what's fair and right and what isn't. But even the most ethical people sometimes face difficult choices.

Ethics are the principles and standards that guide our behavior toward other people. Acting ethically means behaving in a principled fashion and treating other people with respect and dignity. It's simple to say, but not so simple to do since some situations are complex or ambiguous. The important role of ethics in our lives has long been recognized. As far back as 44 B.C., Cicero said that ethics are indispensable to anyone who wants to have a good career. Having said that, Cicero, along with some of the greatest minds over the centuries, struggled with what the rules of ethics should be.

Our ethics are rooted in our history, culture, and religion, and may stay the same and yet also shift over time. In this electronic age there's a new dimension in the ethics debate—the amount of personal information that we can collect and store, and the speed with which we can access and process that information.

TWO FACTORS THAT DETERMINE HOW YOU DECIDE ETHICAL ISSUES

How you collect, store, access, and use information depends to a large extent on your sense of ethics—what you perceive as right and wrong. Two factors affect how you make your decision when you're faced with an ethical dilemma. The first is your basic ethical structure, which you developed as you grew up. The second is the set of practical circumstances inevitably involved in the decision that you're trying to make, that is, all the shades of gray in what are rarely black or white decisions.

Your ethical structure and the ethical challenges you'll face exist at several levels (see Figure 8.1).[6] At the outside level are things that most people wouldn't consider bad, such as taking a couple of paper clips or sending an occasional personal e-mail on company time. Do these things really matter? At the middle level are more significant ethical challenges. One example might be accessing personnel records for personal reasons. Could there ever be a personal reason so compelling that you would not feel ethical discomfort doing this? Reading someone else's e-mail might be another middle-level example. At the innermost ethical level are ethical violations that you'd surely consider very serious, such as embezzling funds or selling company records to a competitor. And yet, over time, your ethical structure can change so that even such acts as these could seem more or less acceptable. For example, if everyone around you is accessing confidential records for their own purposes, in time you might come to think such an act is no big deal. And this might spell big trouble for you.

It would be nice if every decision were crystal clear, such as in the innermost circle in Figure 8.1, but ethical decisions are seldom so easy. Ideally, your personal ethics should

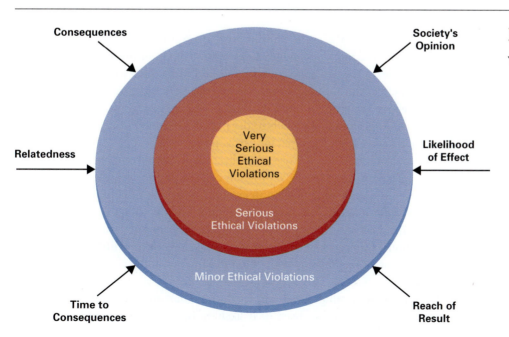

Figure 8.1

Your Ethical Structure

tell you what to do. But the practical circumstances of a decision inevitably also influence you in an ethical dilemma:[7]

1. *Consequences.* How much or how little benefit or harm will come from a particular decision?

2. *Society's opinion.* What is your perception of what society really thinks of your intended action?

3. *Likelihood of effect.* What is the probability of the harm or benefit that will occur if you take the action?

4. *Time to consequences.* How long will it take for the benefit or harm to take effect?

5. *Relatedness.* How much do you identify with the person or persons who will receive the benefit or suffer the harm?

6. *Reach of result.* How many people will be affected by your action?

No matter how strong your sense of ethics is, these practical aspects of the situation may affect you as you make your decision—perhaps unduly, perhaps quite justifiably. Thus, ethical dilemmas usually arise not out of simple situations but from a clash between competing goals, responsibilities, and loyalties. Ethical decisions are complex judgments that balance rewards for yourself and others against responsibilities to yourself and others. Inevitably, your decision process is influenced by uncertainty about the magnitude of the outcome, by your estimate of the importance of the situation, sometimes by your perception of conflicting "right reactions," and more than one socially acceptable "correct" decision.

LEARNING OUTCOME 2

INTELLECTUAL PROPERTY

An ethical issue you will almost certainly encounter is one related to the use or copying of proprietary software. Software is a type of intellectual property. ***Intellectual property*** is intangible creative work that is embodied in physical form.[8] Music, novels, paintings, and sculptures are all examples of intellectual property. So also are your company's product sketches and schematics and other proprietary documents. These documents along with music, novels, and so on are worth much more than the physical form in which they are delivered. For example, a single U2 song is worth far more than the CD on which it's purchased. The song is also an example of intellectual property that is covered by copyright law.

Copyright law protects the authorship of literary and dramatic works, musical and theatrical compositions, and works of art. ***Copyright*** is the legal protection afforded an expression of an idea, such as a song, video game, and some types of proprietary documents. Having a copyright means that no one can use your song or video game without your permission. As a form of intellectual property, software is usually protected by copyright law, although sometimes it falls under patent law, which protects an idea, such as the design of a sewing machine or an industrial pump valve.

Copyright law doesn't forbid the use of intellectual property completely. It has some notable exceptions. For example, a TV program could show a video game you created without your permission. This would be an example of the use of copyrighted material for the creation of new material, i.e., the TV program. And that's legal; it falls under the Fair Use Doctrine. The ***Fair Use Doctrine*** says that you may use copyrighted material in certain situations, for example, in the creation of new work or, within certain limits, for teaching purposes. One of those limits is on the amount of the copyrighted material you may use.

Generally, the determining factor in legal decisions on copyright disputes is whether the copyright holder has been or is likely to be denied income because of the infringement. Courts will consider factors such as how much of the work was used and how, and when and on what basis the decision was made to use it.

Remember that copyright infringement is *illegal.* That means it's against the law, outside of a fair use situation, to simply copy a copyrighted picture, text, or anything else without permission, whether the copyrighted material is on the Internet or not. In particular, it's illegal to copy copyrighted software. But there's one exception to that rule: In the United States, you may always make one copy of copyrighted software to keep for backup purposes. When you buy copyrighted software, what you're paying for is the right to use it—and that's all.

How many more copies you may make depends on the copyright agreement that comes with the software package. Some software companies state emphatically that you may not even put the software on a second computer, even if they're both yours and no one else uses either one. Other companies are less restrictive, and agree to let you put a copy of software on multiple machines—as long as only one person is using that software package at any given time. In this instance, the company considers software to be like a book in that you can have it in different places and you can loan it out, but only one person at a time may use it. Music companies often allow three copies of a CD or individual music track to be played on different platforms, like your computer, your stereo system, and your MP3 player.

If you copy copyrighted software and give it to another person or persons, you're pirating the software. ***Pirated software*** is the unauthorized use, duplication, distribution, or sale of copyrighted software.[9] Software piracy costs businesses an estimated $12 billion a year in lost revenue. Microsoft gets more than 25,000 reports of software piracy every year, and the company reportedly follows up on all of them. Countries that experience the greatest losses are (in rank order) the United States, Japan, the United Kingdom, Germany, China, France, Canada, Italy, Brazil, and the Netherlands. One in four business applications in the United States is thought to be pirated.[10] In some parts of the world, more than 90 percent of business software is pirated. The Software and Information Industry Association (SIIA) and the Business Software Alliance (BSA) say that pirated software means lost jobs, wages, and tax revenues, and is a potential barrier to success for software start-ups around the globe.

Privacy

LEARNING OUTCOME 3

Privacy is the right to be left alone when you want to be, to have control over your own personal possessions, and not to be observed without your consent. It's the right to be free of unwanted intrusion into your private life. Privacy has several dimensions. Psychologically, it's a need for personal space. All of us, to a greater or lesser extent, need to feel in control of our most personal possessions, and personal information belongs on that list. Legally, privacy is necessary for self-protection.[11] If you put the key to your house in a special hiding place in your yard, you want to keep that information private. This information could be abused and cause you grief. In this section, we'll examine some specific areas of privacy: individuals snooping on each other; employers' collection of information about employees; businesses' collection of information about consumers; government collection of personal information; and the issue of privacy in international trade.

PRIVACY AND OTHER INDIVIDUALS

Other individuals, like family members, associates, fellow employees, and hackers, could be electronically invading your privacy. Their motives might be simple curiosity, an attempt to get your password, or to access something they have no right to. Obviously, there are situations in which you're well within your rights, and would be well advised to see what's going on. Examples may be if you suspect that your child is in electronic contact with someone or something undesirable, or if you think that someone is using your computer without permission. Many Web sites are offering programs, collectively referred to as snoopware, to help people monitor what's happening on a computer.

For general snooping you can get key logger software and install it on the computer you want to monitor. **_Key logger,_** or **_key trapper, software,_** is a program that, when installed on a computer, records every keystroke and mouse click. It records all e-mail (whether you're using Eudora or Microsoft Outlook), instant messages, chat room exchanges, Web sites you visit, applications you run, and passwords you type in on that computer.

Also available for monitoring computer use are screen capture programs that periodically record what's on the screen. (They get the information straight from the video card.) These programs don't trap every single screen, just whatever is on the screen when the capturing program activates. But they still give whoever is doing the monitoring a pretty good idea of what the computer user is up to. Other tools for monitoring include packet sniffers (that examine the information passing by) on switches, hubs, or routers (the devices on networks that connect computers to each other), and log analysis tools that keep track of logons, deletions, and so forth.

As you're probably already aware, e-mail is completely insecure. E-mail content might as well be written on a postcard for all the privacy it has. Not only that, but each e-mail you send results in at least three or four copies being stored on different computers (see Figure 8.2). It's stored first in the computer you're using. Second, it's stored by the e-mail server, the computer through which it gets onto the Internet. Third, it's stored on the recipient's computer, and may also be archived on the recipient's e-mail server.

While you probably realize that your e-mail is not totally private, do you realize that other electronic output leaves its mark too? For example, if you use a color laser printer, your printouts have patterns of yellow dots on the back that are not visible unless you have a blue light and a microscope. These dots identify the model and serial number of your printer and the time the printout was made. Printer manufacturers introduced this feature at the request of the Secret Service, which is the agency responsible for investigating counterfeit currency.

Another example is those photos you take with your digital camera. With the right software you can load the photo and see a whole block of information like the date the photo was taken, the camera type and serial number, whether the owner of the camera signed up for a warranty, and various other details. Your CD burner leaves a distinct signature on the CDs you burn. That is, any CD that your computer burns can be traced back to your CD drive. Of course, it stands to reason that your cell phone, when it's on,

Figure 8.2

The E-Mail You Send
Is Stored on Many
Computers

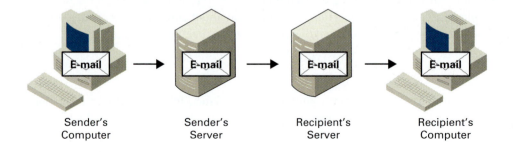

Sender's Computer   Sender's Server   Recipient's Server   Recipient's Computer

can tell people where you are by virtue of the fact that it registers itself with the towers it uses to send and receive calls.

EDRs or Event Data Recorders are now becoming a standard feature on new vehicles. The EDR is part of the airbag control module and was originally included to improve the performance of airbags. When the airbag is deployed, data for the five seconds prior to impact is transferred to a computer chip. About seven pages of information can be downloaded from the chip. This information includes the car's speed at the time of impact, the engine's RPMs, the percent throttle, whether the brakes were applied, and whether the driver's seat belt was buckled. The system is even designed to record a second impact which is frequently what happens in a collision. This is invaluable information to have about an accident and many reckless and inebriated drivers have been taken off the roads because of it.

IDENTITY THEFT

About 10 million adults in the United States were victims of identity theft in 2006, according to a survey released by the National Association of Certified Fraud Examiners. The Better Business Bureau estimates the average loss to be about $1,000 per person, not to mention the countless hours spent in cleaning up credit reports and filing for new identification documents, such as Social Security numbers and driver's licenses. The Federal Trade Commission says that the cost of identity theft to businesses and consumers is as much as $60 billion per year.

Identity theft is the forging of someone's identity for the purpose of fraud. The fraud is often for financial gain, and the stolen identity is used to apply for and use credit cards in the victim's name or to apply for a loan. But it can also be simply to disguise a real identity, particularly if the thief is hiding from law enforcement or is running some sort of scam. Figure 8.3 shows a breakdown of identity theft by age. The list of companies and organizations whose data on individuals has been breached is long. It includes DSW, MCI, Time Warner, the Department of Justice, CitiGroup, Boeing, Ford Motor Company, and the Marines, to name just a few. In 2006, 36 million people were at risk for compromised personal information from breaches in the computer systems of organizations by hackers, lax security, or theft of notebook computers. In 300 separate breaches,

Figure 8.3

Identity Theft Complaints (by Victim Age) Received by the FTC in 2006

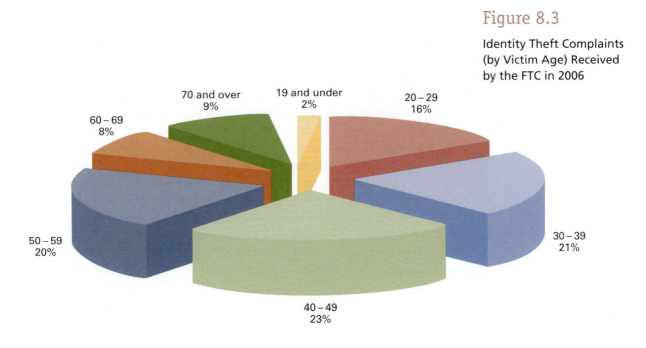

more than 97 million records were put at risk of identity theft.[12] Following are three examples of what happened when people became the victims of identity theft.

- An 82-year-old woman in Fort Worth, Texas, discovered that her identity had been stolen when the woman using her name was involved in a four-car collision. For 18 months, she kept getting notices of lawsuits and overdue medical bills that were really meant for someone else. It took seven years for her to get her financial good name restored after the identity thief charged over $100,000 on her 12 fraudulently acquired credit cards.

- A 42-year-old retired Army captain in Rocky Hill, Connecticut, found that an identity thief had spent $260,000 buying goods and services that included two trucks, a Harley-Davidson motorcycle, and a time-share vacation home in South Carolina. The victim discovered his problem only when his retirement pay was garnished to pay the outstanding bills.

- In New York, members of a pickpocket ring forged the driver's licenses of their victims within hours of snatching the women's purses. If you steal someone's cash only, your haul usually won't be more than $200, probably much less. On the other hand, if you steal the person's identity, you can net on average between $4,000 and $10,000.

A common way to steal identities online is called phishing. **Phishing** (also called **carding** or **brand spoofing**) is a technique to gain personal information for the purpose of identity theft, usually by means of fraudulent e-mail. One way this is done is to send out e-mail messages that look as though they came from legitimate businesses like AOL, MSN, eBay, PayPal, insurance companies, or online retailers like Amazon.com. The messages look genuine with official-looking formats and logos. These e-mails typically ask for verification of important information like passwords and account numbers. The reason given is often that this personal information is needed for accounting or auditing purposes. Since the e-mails look authentic, up to one in five recipients responds with the information, and subsequently becomes a victim of identity theft and other fraud.

Legitimate businesses don't send out such e-mails. If you get such an e-mail, DON'T provide any information without checking further. For example, you could call the company and ask about it. Another clue is bad grammar and misspellings. More than one typo in an official communication is a warning sign.

A second kind of phishing is to persuade people by e-mail to click on a Web site included in the message and provide personal information. Favorite targets of this type of scheme are eBay and PayPal. You get an e-mail that purports to come from eBay and tells you that your account has been compromised or one pretending to come from PayPal saying that your PayPal account is about to pay out on merchandise worth hundreds of dollars that you didn't order. The idea is to get you to go to a site that will steal information like your eBay or PayPal password and then ask for other information, like credit card numbers.

A more sophisticated variation on this is **pharming**, which is the rerouting of your request for a legitimate Web site. You may type in the correct address for your bank and be redirected to a fake site that collects information from you. You may even get to the legitimate site and then be linked to the fake site after you have put in identifying information. You don't notice this because the fake site address is very slightly different from the real one, perhaps just one letter off or different. Make sure to look for the padlock—in the browser, not the site—to let you know that you are at a secure site before entering data (see Chapter 5 on Web e-commerce security).

Pharming is accomplished by getting access to the giant databases that Internet providers use to route Web traffic. Once they have access, they can make little changes so that you are diverted to the fake site either before or after you access the real one. It works so well because it's very hard to spot the fake site.

One of the most worrying types of identity theft is medical record theft. Someone who steals your medical records to get medical care will most likely add to or change your records so that when you need care your records are not accurate. This could lead to your getting medication that you're allergic to or not getting a procedure that you need. According to the World Privacy Forum (WPF) almost 20,000 people filed complaints about theft of their medical records between January 1992 and April 2006. Again, according to the WPF, about $100 billion dollars of health care costs are the result of health care fraud. More than 600 health identity theft cases were tried in 2005 and 516 of those people were convicted. See Figure 8.4 for some advice from the Federal Trade Commission regarding identity theft.

PRIVACY AND EMPLOYEES

Companies need information about their employees and customers to be effective in the marketplace. But people often object to having so many details about their lives available to others. If you're applying for a job, you'll most likely fill out a job application, but that's not the only information a potential employer can get about you. For a small fee, employers, or anyone else, can find out about your credit standing, your telephone usage, your insurance coverage, and many other interesting things. An employer can also

Figure 8.4

Phishing Facts and What to Do If You're at Risk

Some Facts on Phishing . . .

- In January 2004 there were 198 phishing sites, but by February 2005 that number had risen to 2,625, according to the Anti-Phishing Working Group.

- The same group says that the number of unique phishing e-mails reached 13,141 in February of 2004.

- Symantec says that its Brightmail spam filters blocked an average of 33 million phishing attempts per week in December 2004, compared to an average of only 9 million during the previous July.

- The Phemon Institute says consumers lost $500 million to phishers in 2004.

- Also from the Phemon Institute: Of 1,335 people surveyed, about 70 percent visited a fake site, and as many as 15 percent said they had provided personal information to the fake site.

. . . And What to Do If You Suspect You're at Risk

The FTC says that if you believe your personal information may have been compromised, you should:

- Close your credit-card accounts (using an ID Theft Affidavit form) and change all your passwords.

- Place a fraud alert on your credit reports with one of the major credit bureaus (Equifax, Experian, and TransUnion).

- Ask government agencies like the Department of Motor Vehicles to flag your file so that no one can get documents in your name.

get information on what you said on the Internet from companies who collect and collate chat room exchanges. And an employer can ask a job applicant to take drug and psychological tests, the results of which are the property of the company.

After you're hired, your employer can monitor where you go, what you do, what you say, and what you write in e-mails—at least during working hours. The American Management Association says that as of March 2005, 60 percent of employers monitored employee e-mails, both incoming and outgoing. That figure is up from 47 percent in 2001.[13] One reason that companies monitor employees' e-mail is that they can be sued for what their employees send to each other and to people outside the company.

Chevron Corporation and Microsoft settled sexual harassment lawsuits for $2.2 million each because employees sent offensive e-mail to other employees and management didn't intervene. Other companies such as Dow Chemical Company, Xerox, the New York Times Company, and Edward Jones took preemptive action by firing people who sent or stored pornographic or violent e-mail messages.[14]

About 70 percent of Web traffic occurs during work hours, and this is reason enough for companies to monitor what, and for how long, employees are surfing the Web. The FBI reports that 78 percent of surveyed companies indicated that employees had abused Internet privileges by downloading pornography, pirating software, or some other activity that wasn't work related. Also, 60 percent of employees said that they visit Web sites or surf for personal use at work. Again, various software packages are available to keep track of people's Web surfing. Some software actually blocks access to certain sites.

Businesses have good reasons for seeking and storing personal information on employees. They

- Want to hire the best people possible and to avoid being sued for failing to adequately investigate the backgrounds of employees.

- Want to ensure that staff members are conducting themselves appropriately and not wasting or misusing company resources. Financial institutions are even required by law to monitor all communications including e-mail and telephone conversations.

- Can be held liable for the actions of employees.

MONITORING TECHNOLOGY   Numerous vendors sell software products that scan e-mail, both incoming and outgoing. The software can look for specific words or phrases in the subject lines or in the body of the text. An e-mail-scanning program can sneak into your computer in Trojan-horse software. That is, it can hide in an innocent-looking e-mail or some other file or software.

Some companies use an approach less invasive than actually reading employees' e-mail. Their e-mail inspection programs just check for a certain level of e-mail to and from the same address. When this indicates that there may be a problem, the employee is informed of the situation and asked to remedy it. No intrusive supervisory snooping is necessary.[15]

An employer can track your keyboard and mouse activity with the type of key logger software that you read about in the previous section. An alternative that's sometimes harder to detect is a hardware key logger. A ***hardware key logger*** is a hardware device that captures keystrokes on their journey from the keyboard to the motherboard. These devices can be in the form of a connector on the system-unit end of the cable between the keyboard and the system unit. There's another type of hardware key logger that you can install into the keyboard. Both have enough memory to store about a year's worth of typing. These devices can't capture anything that's not typed, but they do capture every keystroke, including backspace, delete, insert, and all the others. To defeat them you'd have to copy the password (or whatever you want kept secret) and paste it into its new

THE CASINO CHIPS ARE WATCHING YOU

Everyone knows that the casinos in Las Vegas have numerous cameras that track all activity on the floor. But the Hard Rock Hotel and Casino has gone one better by keeping track of individual betting tokens in its high-limit blackjack room where minimum bets are $100. Managers know where each high denomination token is at all times and can better guard against token theft and counterfeiting.

The way the casino does this is to fit the plastic tokens that are about the size of a half-dollar with RFID (radio frequency identification) chips like the ones that Wal-Mart uses to track its products all the way from the factory to the store shelves. It's also the same technology that's used to keep track of health care supplies, aerospace parts, and many other products.

Up until now, casinos have been able to track slot-machine players by means of "frequent player" cards that players insert into the machines. Table games, however, were more difficult since the only objective option was video cameras, and otherwise it was up to dealers and pit bosses to estimate how much money gamblers were wagering. The level of betting by customers determines the type and number of freebies and/or discounts customers are entitled to.

With RFID chips embedded into the gambling tokens, pit bosses can keep track of players, their average bets, the denomination of chips they're using, and a wealth of other information.

It works like this: The gambling chips with RFID are sold to a gambler, and when the chips hit the table, sensors below the surface of the table read the data and send it to the computer system. The pit boss then just has to watch the monitor to keep track of how the players are betting and how much they're winning or losing.[16]

---

location. The key logger keeps a record of the keystrokes you use, if any, in your copy-and-paste operation, but not what you copied and pasted.

There is little sympathy in the legal system for the estimated 27 million employees whom the American Management Association says are under surveillance. Employers have the legal right to monitor the use of their resources and that includes the time they're paying you for. In contrast to your home, you have no expectation of privacy when using the company's resources.

The most recent federal bill that addressed electronic monitoring of employees is the Electronic Communications Privacy Act of 1986. Although, in general, it forbids the interception of wired or electronic communications, it has exceptions for both prior consent and business use.

Some state laws have addressed the issue of how far employers can go and what they can do to monitor employees. Connecticut has a law that took effect in 1999 that requires employers in the private sector to notify employees in writing of electronic monitoring. And Pennsylvania, a year earlier, permitted telephone marketers to listen in on calls for quality control purposes as long as at least one of the parties is aware of the action.[17]

PRIVACY AND CONSUMERS

Businesses face a dilemma.

- Customers want businesses to know who they are, but, at the same time, they want them to leave them alone.
- Customers want businesses to provide what they want, but, at the same time, they don't want businesses knowing too much about their habits and preferences.
- Customers want businesses to tell them about products and services they might like to have, but they don't want to be inundated with ads.

Like it or not, massive amounts of personal information are available to businesses from various sources. A relatively large Web site may get about 100 million hits per day, which means that the site gets about 200 bytes of information for each hit. That's about 20 gigabytes of information per day.[18] This level of information load has helped to make customer relationship management (CRM) systems one of the fastest growing areas of software development. Part of managing customer relationships is personalization. Web sites that greet you by name and Amazon.com's famous recommendations that "People who bought this product also bought . . ." are examples of personalization, which is made possible by the Web site's knowledge about you.[19]

Apart from being able to collect its own information about you, a company can readily access consumer information elsewhere. Credit card companies sell information, as do the Census Bureau and mailing list companies. Web traffic tracking companies such as DoubleClick follow you (and other surfers) around the Web and then sell the information about where you went and for how long. DoubleClick can collect information about you over time and provide its customers with a highly refined profile on you. DoubleClick is also an intermediary for companies that want to advertise to Web surfers. When hired by a company wanting to sell something, DoubleClick identifies people who might be receptive and sends the ad to them as a banner or pop-up ad. Proponents of this practice claim that it's good for the surfers because they get targeted advertising and less unwanted advertising. You can judge for yourself how true this claim is. DoubleClick, at first, undertook to track consumers without attaching their identity to the information. Then, in 1999, DoubleClick changed its policy and announced that it would attach consumer names to personal information and e-mail addresses. However, in response to negative consumer reaction, DoubleClick withdrew its proposed change. Interestingly, DoubleClick didn't state it would never resume the abandoned policy, but agreed only to wait until standards for such activity are in place.[20]

COOKIES The basic tool of consumer Web monitoring is the cookie. A *cookie* is a small file that contains information about you and your Web activities, which a Web site you visit places on your computer. A cookie has many uses. For example, it's used to keep ID and password information so that you don't have to go through the whole verification process every time you log onto a Web site. It's also used to store the contents of electronic shopping carts, so that the next time you log on, the Web site will be able to see your wish list (which is stored on your computer in a cookie).

A cookie can also be used to track your Web activity. It can monitor and record what sites you visit, how long you stay there, what Web pages you visited, what site you came from and the next site you went to. This type of cookie is called a *unique cookie*. Some cookies are temporary and some stay on your computer indefinitely.

Third-party or *common cookies* are the ones that have many privacy advocates disturbed. These are different from the unique cookies that a Web site you visit puts onto your hard disk. A common cookie is one that started out as a unique cookie, but the original site sold access to it to a third party, like DoubleClick, that can then change the cookie so that the third party can track the surfer's activity across many sites. The third party collects information about surfers without names or other identifiable personal information. They usually collect an IP address, which they then link to a random identifying ID so that the surfer can be identified at other sites. Surveys have shown that the vast majority of people (91 percent) don't like the idea of unknown companies gathering information about them that they have provided to sites with whom they chose to interact.[21]

You have two options if you want to block cookies. First, you can set your browser to accept or reject all cookies. Or you can get it to warn you when a site wants to put a cookie on your computer. Second, you can get cookie management software with additional options that are not available on your browser. For example, CookieCop 2, from *PC Magazine*, will let you accept or reject cookies on a per-site basis. It also allows you to replace banner ads with the image of your choice and to block ads for sites you find offensive. With this or other cookie-stopper software, you can disable pop-up windows, and stipulate that certain cookies can stay on your hard drive for the duration of one session only.

SPAM   *Spam* is unsolicited e-mail (electronic junk mail) from businesses that advertise goods and services. Often spam mass mailings advertise pornography, get-rich-quick schemes, and miracle cures. If you haven't been inundated with spam, you're either very lucky or you don't use the Internet much. Spam has become a severe irritant to consumers and a costly matter for businesses, who must sort through hundreds of e-mail messages every day deleting spam and hoping that they don't delete e-mail messages that are actually legitimate customer orders.

You can get spam filters to block out spam, but spammers are clever about including nonprinting characters in their subject lines and addresses that fool the filters into letting them pass. For example, say a spammer wanted to send out a message about a new weight loss drug called *Off*. The spammer would alter the spelling of the word or add invisible HTML tags so that the subject line would be: O*F*F or O<i></i>F<u></u>F. The HTML tags <i> and <u> would normally italicize and underline text, respectively, and the </i> and </u> would undo the italicizing and bolding, but since there's no text in between the tags do nothing except evade the filter.

Experts estimate that up to 70 percent of e-mail traffic in 2004 was spam and in June and July of 2004 spam reached the staggering figure of over 85 percent.[22] And now it's at more than 86 percent with no end in sight, according to experts. In Europe, it's not quite as bad at 62 percent, which amounts to 16 billion messages per day. An individual spammer can send out 80 million or so spams per day. AOL and Microsoft say that their servers block a billion spam messages every day.[23] Many states have passed laws to regulate spam and the Federal Government passed an anti-spam law in 2003 called the CAN-Spam Act (see Figure 8.6 on page 240), which was widely criticized by anti-spam activists as legitimizing spam, since it set down rules for spamming rather than banning it altogether.

Most experts doubt that the CAN-Spam Act hurts the spammers who are the source of most of the spam. They say that it just costs legitimate businesses time and money since they have to maintain do-not-spam lists and follow the legal guidelines when sending out e-mails to customers. Since the bulk of spam comes from spammers who spoof (disguise) the origin of the e-mail, they can usually operate for a long time in defiance of the law. Irate spam trackers, some of whom have become cyber vigilantes, have gone so far as to "out" spammers and publicize information about them on the Web in an effort to stop them.

One trick that spammers use to collect addresses for spamming is to send out e-mail purporting to add you to a general do-not-spam list if you reply. In fact, what it does is add your e-mail address to the list of "live" ones.

ADWARE AND SPYWARE   If you've downloaded a game or other software from the Web for free, you may have noticed that it came with banner ads. These ads are collectively known as adware. *Adware* is software to generate ads that installs itself on your computer when you download some other (usually free) program from the Web (see Figure 8.5 on the next page). Adware is a type of *Trojan horse software,* meaning that it's software you don't want hidden inside software you do want. There's usually a disclaimer, buried somewhere in the multiple "I agree" screens, saying that the software

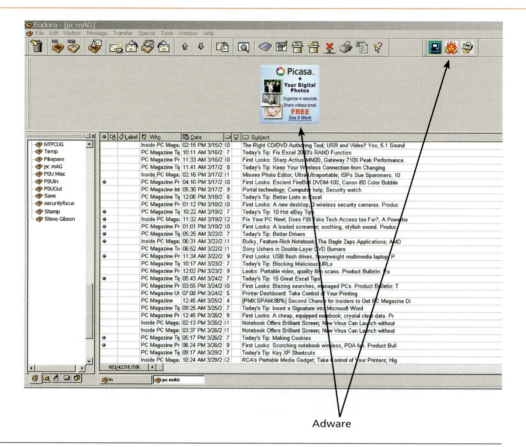

Figure 8.5

Adware in a Free
Version of Eudora, an
E-Mail Application from
Qualcomm

Adware

includes this adware. At the bottom of several small-print screens you're asked to agree to the terms. Very few people read the whole agreement, and advertisers count on that. This sort of product is sometimes called *click-wrap* because it's like commercial software that has an agreement that you agree to by breaking the shrink-wrap.

Most people don't get upset about pure adware, since they feel it's worth having to view ads to get software for free. However, there's a more insidious extra that's often bundled with free downloadable software called spyware. **Spyware** (also called **sneakware** or **stealthware**) is malicious software that collects information about you and your computer and reports it to someone without your permission. It usually comes hidden in downloadable software and tracks your online movements and/or mines the information stored on your computer. The first release of RealNetworks' RealJukebox sent information back to the company about what CDs the people who downloaded the software were playing on that computer. This information collection was going on when the customer wasn't even on the Web.[24]

Spyware is fast becoming the hidden cost of free software. Software such as Kazaa Media Desktop and Audiogalaxy, the successors to Napster for sharing music and other files online, includes spyware. If you download free software and it has banner ads, it's quite possible that it has spyware, too. There's usually something in the "I agree" screens telling you about spyware, but it can be hard to find. Spyware can stay on your computer long after you've uninstalled the original software.

You can detect various kinds of Trojan horse software with The Cleaner from www.moosoft.com. Also check out www.wilders.org for Trojan First Aid Kit (TFAK). The best-known spyware detection programs, also called stealthware blockers, are Ad-Aware (free from www.lavasoftUSA.com) and PestPatrol. The software scans your whole

IS YOUR MUSIC CD HIJACKING YOUR COMPUTER?

When you buy a shrink-wrapped CD at a reputable music store, you don't expect it to open up your computer to every hacker with evil in mind. That's exactly what happened to a lot of people in 2005 when Sony, as part of a copy protection scheme, embedded a rootkit in its music CDs. A *rootkit* is software that gives you administrator rights to a computer or network and its purpose is to allow you to conceal processes, files, or system data from the operating system.

Sony's rootkit was designed to transfer itself to your computer surreptitiously. The CD would play only from the player included on the CD. Other players didn't recognize it as an audio CD, and instead opened the CD as a data CD.

The original intent was twofold: first, to allow consumers to make up to three copies to play on different platforms, but to prevent P2P distribution and large-scale copying; second, to relay back to Sony what people were doing with Sony's CDs. What it also did was open up a backdoor for anyone who knew about it to get into your system and do whatever they wanted, like using it to send out millions of spam messages or to spread viruses.

The fallout from this scheme was a nightmare for Sony. The company lost millions of dollars when it had to pull 4.7 million copy-protected discs that represented 52 titles including Van Zant, Celine Dion, Neil Diamond, and Bette Midler. Lawsuits rained down on Sony. There were several class action suits and a large number of small claims court actions; states, including Texas filed lawsuits, as did Canada and various countries in Europe. A Sony spokesperson, questioned about the rootkit shortly after it was first discovered, said that since no one even knows what a rootkit is, he didn't think it would be a problem. Well, a lot more people know about it now!

---

computer, identifies spyware programs, and offers to delete them. If you want to check out free software for spyware before you download it, go online to www.spychecker.com, a site that will tell you if particular free software includes adware or spyware.

Even without spyware, a Web site can tell a lot about its Web visitors from its Web log. A **Web log** consists of one line of information for every visitor to a Web site and is usually stored on a Web server. At the very least, a Web log can provide a Web site company with a record of your clickstream.

A **clickstream** records information about you during a Web surfing session such as what Web sites you visited, how long you were there, what ads you looked at, and what you bought. If, as a consumer, you want to protect information about your surfing habits, you can use various software packages to do so. Apart from cookie management software you can avail yourself of **anonymous Web browsing (AWB)** services, which, in effect, hide your identity from the Web sites you visit. An example is Anonymizer at www.anonymizer.com. This site, and others like it, sends your Web browsing through its server and removes all identifying information. Some of the ABW services that are available include disabling pop-up promotions, defeating tracking programs, and erasing browsing history files. If you don't want to go through an outside server, you can download software to do the job. SurfSecret is a shareware antitracking package available from www.surfsecret.com.

As a final note on the subject, remember that even if a company promises, and fully intends, to keep its customer information protected, it may not be possible. When faced with a subpoena, the company will have to relinquish customer records. Furthermore, courts have ruled in bankruptcy cases that customer files are assets that may be sold to pay debts.

PRIVACY AND GOVERNMENT AGENCIES

Government agencies have about 2,000 databases containing personal information on individuals.[25] The various branches of government need information to administer entitlement programs, such as Social Security, welfare, student loans, law enforcement, and so on.

LAW ENFORCEMENT   You've often heard about someone being apprehended for a grievous crime after a routine traffic stop for something like a broken taillight. The arrest most likely ensued because the arresting officer ran a check on the license plate and driver's license. The officer probably checked the National Crime Information Center (NCIC) database and found the outstanding warrant there. Timothy McVeigh and others responsible for the bombing of the federal building in Oklahoma City were caught in this way.

The NCIC database contains information on the criminal records of more than 20 million people. It also stores information on outstanding warrants, missing children, gang members, juvenile delinquents, stolen guns and cars, and so on. The NCIC has links to other government and private databases, and guardians of the law all over the country can access NCIC information. Sometimes they do so in response to something suspicious, and other times it's just routine. For example, Americans returning from outside the country are routinely checked through the NCIC when they come through customs.

Given its wealth of information and accessibility, it's not surprising that NCIC system has been abused. Several police departments have found that a significant number of employees illegally snooped for criminal records on people they knew or wanted to know.

The Federal Bureau of Investigation (FBI) has caused a stir lately because of its electronic surveillance methods. First there was Carnivore, a rather unfortunate name, which has since been changed to DCS-1000. DCS-1000 connects hardware to an ISP to trap all e-mail sent to or received by the target of the investigation. It takes a court order to use DCS-1000, and, of course, the target is typically unaware of the surveillance. Intercepting communications is not new: The FBI put the first tap on a phone in 1885, just four years after the invention of the telephone.[26] DCS-1000, with a court order, traps all communications involving the individual named in the court order.

Because it can be hard to identify the data packets of one individual's e-mail amongst all the other Internet traffic, it's entirely possible that other people's e-mail might be scooped up in the net. And this is what happened in March 2000 when FBI agents were legally intercepting messages of a suspect, but someone else was caught in the trap. The information on the innocent party was obtained under the Freedom of Information Act. The FBI said the incident was an honest mistake and a result of miscommunication between it and the ISP.[27] But this is the sort of mistake that scares people. Most people want law enforcement to be able to watch the bad guys—that's necessary for our collective safety. But the prospect of information being collected on law-abiding citizens who are minding their own business worries a lot of people.

In 2001, the FBI acknowledged an enhancement to DCS-1000 called Magic Lantern, which is key logger software. The FBI installs it by sending the target an innocent-looking Trojan-horse e-mail, which contains the key logger software. The hidden software then sends information back to the FBI periodically.[28]

Another federal agency, the National Security Agency (NSA), uses a system called Echelon that uses a global network of satellites and surveillance stations to trap phone, e-mail, and fax transmissions. The system then screens all this information looking for certain keywords and phrases and analyzes the messages that fit the search criteria.

At the local level, the actions of the Tampa Police Department at the 2001 Super Bowl caused an outcry from privacy advocates. Police, with the agreement of the NFL, focused video cameras on the faces of tens of thousands of spectators as they entered the stadium. The images were sent to computers which, using facial recognition software, compared the images to a database of pictures of suspected criminals and terrorists. The police spokesperson said that the action was legal since it's permissible to take pictures of people in public places. That's true in so far as you have no expectation of privacy in a public place. Indeed surveillance of people has been going on for years without much protest in gambling casinos, Wal-Mart stores, and other businesses in the private sector. But the American Civil Liberties Union (ACLU) protested the surveillance of Super Bowl spectators on the grounds that it was surveillance by a government agency without court-ordered authorization. The fact that the state was involved made it unacceptable to the ACLU.

OTHER FEDERAL AGENCIES   The Internal Revenue Service (IRS) gets income information from taxpayers. But the agency has access to other databases, too. For example, the IRS keeps track of vehicle registration information so that it can check up on people buying expensive cars and boats to make sure they're reporting an income level that corresponds to their purchases. The IRS can go to outside government databases as well. Verizon says that it gets 22,000 requests for phone records from the IRS, FBI, and other government agencies per year. It seldom informs the customer of the request. America Online (AOL) has a special fax number reserved just for subpoenas.

The Census Bureau collects information on all the U.S. inhabitants it can find every 10 years. All citizens are requested to fill out a census form, and some people get a very long and detailed form requiring them to disclose a lot of personal information. The information that the Census Bureau collects is available to other government agencies and even to commercial enterprises. The bureau doesn't link the information to respondents' names but sells summarized information about geographic regions. Some of these regions are relatively small, however, consisting of fewer than 100 city blocks.

It's fairly safe to assume that anytime you have contact with any branch of government, information about you will be subsequently stored somewhere. For example, if you get a government-backed student loan, you provide personal information such as your name, address, income, parents' income, and so on. Some of the information nuggets attached to the loan would be the school you're attending, the bank dispersing the loan, your repayment schedule, and later, your repayment pattern.

LAWS ON PRIVACY

The United States doesn't have a comprehensive or consistent set of laws governing the use of information. However, some laws are in place. Recent legislation includes the Health Insurance Portability and Accountability Act (HIPAA) and the Financial Service Modernization Act. HIPAA, enacted in 1996, requires that the health care industry formulate and implement the first regulations to keep patient information confidential. The act seeks to

- Limit the release and use of your health information without your consent.
- Give you the right to access your medical records and find out who else has accessed them.
- Overhaul the circumstances under which researchers and others can review medical records.
- Release health information on a need-to-know basis only.
- Allow the disclosure of protected health information for business reasons as long as the recipient undertakes, in writing, to protect the information.

- **Identity Theft and Assumption Deterrence Act,** 1998, strengthened the criminal laws governing identity theft, making it a federal crime to use or transfer identification belonging to another. It also established a central federal service for victims.

- **USA Patriot Act,** 2001 and 2003, allows law enforcement to get access to almost any information, including library records, video rentals, bookstore purchases, and business records when investigating any act of terrorism or hostile intelligence activities. In 2003 Patriot II broadened the original law.

- **Homeland Security Act,** 2002, provided new authority to government agencies to mine data on individuals and groups including e-mails and Web site visits; put limits on the information available under the Freedom of Information Act; and gave new powers to government agencies to declare national heath emergencies.

- **Sarbanes-Oxley Act,** 2002, sought to protect investors by improving the accuracy and reliability of corporate disclosures and requires companies to (1) implement extensive and detailed policies to prevent illegal activity within the company and (2) respond in a timely manner to investigate illegal activity.

- **Fair and Accurate Credit Transactions Act,** 2003, included provisions for the prevention of identity theft including consumers' right to get a credit report free each year, requiring merchants to leave all but the last five digits of a credit card number off a receipt, and requiring lenders and credit agencies to take action even before a victim knows a crime has occurred when they notice any circumstances that might indicate identity theft.

- **CAN-Spam Act,** 2003, sought to regulate interstate commerce by imposing limitations and penalties on businesses sending unsolicited e-mail to consumers. The law forbids deceptive subject lines, headers, return addresses, etc., as well as harvesting e-mail addresses from Web sites. It requires businesses that send spam to maintain a do-not-spam list and to include a postal mailing address in the message.

Figure 8.6
Recent Information-
Related Laws

The Financial Services Modernization Act requires that financial institutions protect personal customer information and that they have customer permission before sharing such information with other businesses. However, the act contains a clause that allows the sharing of information for "legitimate business purposes." See Figure 8.6 for recent information-related laws.

LEARNING OUTCOME 4

Security

So, what can put your important information resource in jeopardy? Well, countless things. Hard disks can crash, computer parts can fail, hackers and crackers can gain access and do mischief, thieves engaged in industrial espionage can steal your information, and disgruntled employees or associates can cause damage. The FBI estimates that computer sabotage costs businesses somewhere close to $10 billion every year. Companies are increasing their spending on Internet security software, a fact that Symantec Corp. can attest to. Symantec is the largest exclusive developer of computer security software and has a market value of $19 billion, making it one of the most valuable software companies in the world.[29]

SECURITY AND EMPLOYEES

Most of the press reports are about outside attacks on computer systems, but actually, companies are in far more danger of losing money from employee misconduct than they are from outsiders. It's estimated that 75 percent of computer crime is perpetrated by insiders, although this is not a problem that's restricted to computer misuse. A 300-restaurant chain with 30 employees in each location loses, on average, $218 per employee.

But white-collar crime is where the big bucks are lost (see Figure 8.7). White-collar crime in general, from Fortune 100 firms to video stores to construction companies, accounts for about $400 billion in losses every year—$400 billion is $108 billion more than the whole federal defense budget—and information technology makes it much easier to accomplish and conceal the crime. Of all white-collar fraud, the biggest losses are those incurred by management misconduct. Manager theft of various kinds is about four times that of other employees. Take embezzlement, for example. The average cost of a nonmanagerial employee's theft is $60,000, while that for managerial employees is $250,000. The most astonishing aspect of this is that most insider fraud (up to two-thirds) is never reported to the legal authorities, according to the Association of Certified Fraud Examiners (ACFE).

Computer-aided fraud includes the old standby crimes like vendor fraud (sending payment to a nonexistent vendor or payment for goods not delivered), writing payroll checks to fictitious employees, claiming expense reimbursements for costs never incurred, and so on. In addition, there are newer crimes such as stealing security codes, credit card numbers, and proprietary files. Intellectual property is one of the favorite targets of theft by insiders. In fact, the companies that make surveillance software say that employers are buying and installing the software not so much to monitor employees as to track how intellectual property, like product design sketches, schematics, and so on, is moving around the network.

Fraud examiners have a rule of thumb that in any group of employees, about 10 percent are completely honest, 10 percent will steal, and, for the remaining 80 percent, it will depend on circumstances. Most theft is committed by people who are strapped for cash, have access to funds that are poorly protected, and perceive a low risk of getting caught.

SECURITY AND OUTSIDE THREATS

In 2006, companies spent, on average, $5 million each to recover corporate data that was lost or stolen. That's 30 percent more than in 2005. The losses are the result of many problems such as someone breaking into their systems, malicious insider activity,

	Who's Committing Fraud
61%	Fraud committed by men
39%	Fraud committed by women
$250,000	Median loss from fraud committed by men
$102,000	Median loss from fraud committed by women
41%	Fraud committed by managers
39.5%	Fraud committed by employees
19.3%	Fraud committed by owners/executives

Figure 8.7

Figures on Fraud

Source: 2006 ACFE Report to the Nation on Occupational Fraud and Abuse.

malware like spyware and viruses, and the theft of USB devices, notebook computers, and flash memory cards. The average cost per record that was compromised was $140.[30]

The threats from outside are many and varied. Competitors could try to get your customer lists or the prototype for your new project. Cyber vandals could be joyriding in cyberspace looking for something interesting to see, steal, or destroy. You could become the victim of a generalized attack from a virus or worm, or could suffer a targeted attack like a denial-of-service attack. If you have something worth stealing or manipulating on your system, there could be people after that, too. For example, the online gambling industry is plagued by attacks where hackers have illicitly gained access to the servers that control the gambling, corrupting games to win millions of dollars. Exploiting well-known system weaknesses accounts for a large part of hacker damage, while only 5 percent results from breaking into systems in new ways.[31]

The people who break into the computer systems of others are "hackers" (see Figure 8.8). *Hackers* are generally knowledgeable computer users who use their knowledge to invade other people's computers. They have varying motives. Some just do it for the fun of it. Others (called hacktivists) have a philosophical or political message they want to share, and still others (called crackers) are hired guns who illegally break in, usually to steal information, for a fee. The latter can be a very lucrative undertaking. Some highly skilled crackers charge up to $1 million per job. There are also "good guys," called white-hat hackers, who test the vulnerability of systems so that protective measures may be taken.

TYPES OF CYBER CRIME   Cyber crimes range from electronically breaking and entering to cyberstalking and murder. In October 1999, a 21-year-old woman was shot and killed outside the building where she worked. Her killer had been electronically stalking her for two years. He became obsessed with the young lady and had even posted a Web site dedicated to her on which he announced his intention to kill her. He got her Social Security number online, found out where she worked, tracked her down, and shot her, after which he shot himself.

Most cyber crimes are not as bad as murder, but they can be serious nonetheless. Computer viruses and denial-of-service attacks are the two most common types of cyber crime against which companies need to protect themselves.

A *computer virus* (or simply a *virus*) is software that is written with malicious intent to cause annoyance or damage. A virus can be benign or malicious. The benign ones

Figure 8.8

Hacker Types

- White-hat hackers find vulnerabilities in systems and plug the holes. They work at the request of the owners of the computer systems.

- Black-hat hackers break into other people's computer systems and may just look around, or they may steal credit card numbers or destroy information, or otherwise do damage.

- Hacktivists have philosophical and political reasons for breaking into systems. They often deface a Web site as a protest.

- Script kiddies, or script bunnies, find hacking code on the Internet and click-and-point their way into systems, to cause damage or spread viruses.

- Crackers are hackers for hire and are the hackers who engage in corporate espionage.

- Cyberterrorists are those who seek to cause harm to people or to destroy critical systems or information. They try to use the Internet as a weapon of mass destruction.

"You can ignore this e-mail and try to keep your site up, which will cost you tens of thousands of dollars in lost customers, or you can send us $10K bank wire to make sure that your site experiences no problems + we will give you our protection for a year."

Above is the message that the managers of Protx, an online-payment processing firm in London, received by e-mail. The incident was the third time the company had been attacked within the year, and it was the most savage attack. At one point, the Protx network was bombarded by a blitz of traffic, to the tune of 500 megabits per second (that's about five times more traffic per second than a large ISP would handle). This barrage came from thousands of computers whose power had been commandeered by the attackers in what's called a distributed denial-of-service attack, and it knocked the company offline.

As is often the case, the attacks were conducted with bot viruses. A bot virus is a program that attackers plant in someone else's computer that allows the perpetrator to use the resources—the CPU or hard disk, for example—for their own purposes.

In the case of Protx, computer security experts were called in to stop the attacks and prevent the same sort of thing from happening in the future. They found that as soon as they shut down one stream of attacks, another one would start from a different hijacked network. It cost Protx about $500,000 to secure its network against future attacks. Such costs are usually annual expenses and don't include the cost of shutting down the original attacks or the cost of the business lost by the victim company.[32]

just display a message on the screen or slow the computer down, but don't do any damage. The malicious kind targets a specific application or set of file types and corrupts or destroys them.

Today, worms are the most prevalent type of virus. Worms are viruses that spread themselves; they don't need your help, just your carelessness.

A *worm* is a type of virus that spreads itself, not just from file to file, but from computer to computer via e-mail and other Internet traffic. It finds your e-mail address book and helps itself to the addresses and sends itself to your contacts, using your e-mail address as the return address. The Love Bug worm was one of the early worms that did a lot of damage and got major press coverage. It's estimated that the Love Bug and its variants affected 300,000 Internet host computers and millions of individual PC users causing file damage, lost time, and high-cost emergency repairs costing about $8.7 billion.[33,34] Ford Motor Company, H. J. Heinz, Merrill Lynch, AT&T, Capitol Hill, and the British Parliament all fell victim to the Love Bug worm. Newer versions of worms include Klez, a very rapidly spreading worm, Nimda, and Sircam.

A *denial-of-service attack (DoS)* floods a server or network with so many requests for service that it slows down or crashes. The objective is to prevent legitimate customers from accessing the target site. E*Trade, Yahoo!, and Amazon.com have all been victims of this type of attack.

As well as knowing what viruses can do, you need to know what they can't do. Computer viruses can't

- Hurt your hardware, such as your monitor, or processor.
- Hurt any files they weren't designed to attack. A virus designed for Microsoft's Outlook, for example, generally doesn't infect Qualcomm's Eudora, or any other e-mail application.

SECURITY PRECAUTIONS

In Chapter 7, Enterprise Infrastructure, Metrics, and Business Continuity Planning, you learned about business contigency plans and in *Appendix B: Network Basics* you read about intrusion detection. These are both very important components of any company's computer system security. There are also standard precautions that a company, and any individual who wants protection from the computer-based attacks, should take.

The most basic protection is to have anti-virus software running on your computer. ***Anti-virus software*** detects and removes or quarantines computer viruses. New viruses are created every day and each new generation is more deadly (or potentially more deadly) than the previous one. You should update your anti-virus software regularly and make sure it's running all the time so that it kicks in when you download e-mail and other files.

Many of the anti-virus software packages on the market also protect you against other cyber evils, like spyware and adware. They will also block cookies, pop-up ads, and embedded objects and scripts you may get if you download a Flash file, for instance.

Spam protection is theoretically good to have, although it may let some spam through and may mark as spam something that isn't. You can usually choose to have the spam deleted, quarantined (in its own folder), or marked so that it stands out when you look in your Inbox. *Anti-phishing software* is also available to protect you from identity theft. The MyVault feature of ZoneAlarm, for example, will block data such as Social Security number, credit card numbers, and passwords from leaving your computer. Anti-phishing toolbars warn you when you arrive at a known phishing site. Symantec's anti-phishing software places a toolbar beneath the Address Bar which turns red if you land at a phishing site.

ZoneAlarm, which is a firewall program with additional features, will let you know if a program is trying to access the Internet for whatever reason, as spyware on your computer may be attempting to do. ZoneAlarm from www.zonealarm.com is a very popular software firewall. ZoneAlarm also offers protection from ads and cookies. A ***firewall*** is hardware and/or software that protects a computer or network from intruders. The firewall examines each message as it seeks entrance to the network, like a border guard checking passports. Unless the message has the "right" markings, the firewall will block it from entering. You can set your firewall so that it identifies certain programs that are always allowed to visit a Web site. Your e-mail program would be an example. Any competent network administrator will have at least one firewall on the network to keep out unwelcome guests. Protection is available against rootkits, for example, which we discussed in the Industry Perspective box, "Is Your Music CD Hijacking Your Computer?" on page 237.

There are other issues you might think about, *Rootkit finders* are available from Kaspersky's and F-Secure security software. There are also free programs available. Removing rootkits is a tricky task and different software packages meet with varying degrees of success.

There are also programs that will block certain sites, which is useful if you have under-age children. Some people suggest using FireFox or Opera as your default browser since Microsoft's Internet Explorer has long been a favorite target of hackers.

ACCESS AUTHENTICATION   While firewalls keep outsiders out, they don't necessarily keep insiders out. In other words, unauthorized employees may try to access computers or files. One of the ways that companies try to protect computer systems is with authentication systems that check who you are before they let you have access.

There are three basic ways of proving your access rights: (1) what you know, like a password; (2) what you have, like an ATM card; (3) what you look like (more specifically what your fingerprint or some other physical characteristic looks like).

PROTECTING PERSONAL RFID-STORED INFORMATION

Radio frequency ID chips are very small, almost paper-thin chips, in some instances, that store and wirelessly transmit and receive information. For example, Wal-Mart has for several years been implementing RFID for inventory control. The company will eventually require all its suppliers to implement RFID technology. The tags will be on crates and pallets so that they can be tracked through the supply chain. Other applications of RFID include:

- Embedding RFID chips in passports
- Monitoring the temperature of perishable items (DHL)
- Tagging consumer products with RFID instead of bar codes (many companies including Best Buy)
- Contactless credit cards (J.P. Morgan)

- Tagging overseas shipments of suppliers (Australian Department of Defense)
- Tracking cattle

The most controversial use of RFID technology is when people wear it or have it implanted into their bodies. These chips have information, often medical, that can be read in case the person becomes incapacitated. VeriChip makes such a chip and believes that over 40 million people in the United States will someday have them implanted under the skin.

The challenge then becomes one of protecting your personal RFID information. It can be read wirelessly, meaning that people can build reading devices and obtain your medical information by coming within three feet of you. You'll learn more about RFID in Chapter 9.[35,36,37,38]

Passwords are very popular and have been used since there were computers. You can password-protect the whole network, a single computer, a folder, or a file. But passwords are not by any means a perfect way to protect a computer system. People forget their passwords, so someone may have to get them new passwords or find the old one. Banks spend $15 per call to help customers who forget their passwords. Then if a hacker breaks into the system and steals a password list, everyone has to get a new password. One bank had to change 5,000 passwords in the course of a single month at a cost of $12.50 each.[39]

Which brings us to biometrics, or what you look like. **Biometrics** is the use of physiological characteristics—such as your fingerprint, the blood vessels in the iris of your eye, the sound of your voice, or perhaps even your breath—to provide identification. Roughly a dozen different types of biometric devices are available at the moment, with fingerprint readers being the most popular. About 44 percent of the biometric systems sold are fingerprint systems. They work just like the law enforcement system where your fingerprint is stored in the database, and when you come along, your finger is scanned, and the scan is compared to the entry in the database. If they match, you're in. See Chapter 9 for more information on biometrics.

ENCRYPTION   If you want to protect your messages and files and hide them from prying eyes, you can encrypt them. **Encryption** scrambles the contents of a file so that you can't read it without having the right decryption key. There are various ways of encrypting messages. You can switch the order of the characters, replace characters with other characters, or insert or remove characters. All of these methods alter the look of the message, but used alone, each one is fairly simple to figure out. So most encryption methods use a combination.

Companies that get sensitive information from customers, such as credit card numbers, need some way of allowing all their customers to use encryption to send the information. But they don't want everyone to be able to decrypt the message, so they might use public key encryption. *Public key encryption (PKE)* is an encryption system that uses two keys: a public key that everyone can have and a private key for only the recipient. So if you do online banking, the bank will give you the public key to encrypt the information you send them, but only the bank has the key to decrypt your information. It works rather like a wall safe, where anyone can lock it (just shut the door and twirl the knob), but only the person with the right combination can open it again.

Summary: Student Learning Outcomes Revisited

1. **Define ethics and describe the two factors that affect how you make a decision concerning an ethical issue.** *Ethics* are the principles and standards that guide our behavior toward other people. How you decide ethical issues must depend especially on your basic ethical structure but also for better or worse on the practical circumstances. Your basic ethics you probably acquired growing up. The practical circumstances that you might allow to affect you include

   - *Consequences.* How much or how little benefit or harm will come from a particular decision?
   - *Society's opinion.* What do you perceive society thinks of your intended action?
   - *Likelihood of effect.* What is the probability of the harm or benefit if you take the action?
   - *Time to consequences.* How long will it take for the benefit or harm to take effect?
   - *Relatedness.* How much do you identify with the person or persons who will receive the benefit or suffer the harm?
   - *Reach of result.* How many people will be affected by your action?

2. **Define and describe intellectual property, copyright, Fair Use Doctrine, and pirated software.** *Intellectual property* is intangible creative work that is embodied in physical form. *Copyright* is the legal protection afforded an expression of an idea, such as a song or a video game and some types of proprietary documents. The *Fair Use Doctrine* says that you may use copyrighted material in certain situations. *Pirated software* is the unauthorized use, duplication, distribution or sale of copyrighted software.

3. **Define privacy and describe ways in which it can be threatened.** *Privacy* is the right to be left alone when you want to be, to have control over your own personal possessions, and not to be observed without your consent. Your privacy can be compromised by other individuals snooping on you; by employers monitoring your actions; by businesses that collect information on your needs, preferences, and surfing practices; and by the various government agencies that collect information on citizens.

4. **Describe the ways in which information on your computer or network is vulnerable and list measures you can take to protect it.**

   - Employees can embezzle and perpetrate fraud of other types. Most of the financial losses due to computer fraud that is suffered by companies is caused by employees.
   - Hackers and crackers try to break into computers and steal, destroy, or compromise information.
   - Hackers can spread *computer viruses* or launch *denial-of-service attacks (DoS)* that can cost millions in prevention and cleanup.

   Measures you can take are to install

   - Anti-virus software to find and delete or quarantine viruses
   - Anti-spyware and anti-adware software
   - Spam protection software
   - Anti-phishing toolbar
   - Firewalls
   - Anti-rootkit software
   - Encryption
   - Biometrics

CLOSING CASE STUDY ONE

CAUTIONARY TALES OF INDISCREET E-MAIL

Wrongdoing at Computer Associates and at Enron, once giants in their respective industries, was brought to light by forgotten and/or deleted e-mails. The recovered e-mails brought down guilty individuals, but caused some innocents to suffer as well.

COMPUTER ASSOCIATES

In 2000, Charles Wang, chairman of Computer Associates (CA), a business software development giant, was number one on *Forbes*'s list of wealthiest people with earnings of $650 million, $649 million of which was performance-based. However, early in 2002, federal investigators began investigating Computer Associates for improperly booking more than $2 billion in revenue. It had apparently become common practice for executives to keep quarterly reports open so that later deals could be backdated, making the quarterlies look better. By the end of 2002, Wang had been retired to an honorary, uncompensated position, largely because of the accounting discrepancies being investigated.

Computer Associates' Board of Directors, hoping to avoid the sort of disaster that killed Arthur Andersen, hired experienced criminal lawyers to conduct an investigation to get to the truth. After searching hundreds of employee computers, the investigation turned up e-mails, deleted and saved, that provided evidence of fraud. These e-mails were not on the main system, but rather were stored on individual machines.

By April 2004, three former executives of the company had pled guilty to obstruction of justice charges and by September that number had risen to seven who had pled guilty or been indicted. The obstruction of justice charges came from the top executives' misleading the independent lawyers about the facts of their actions, knowing that the falsehoods would be passed on to federal investigators. Attorney–client privilege did not apply since the outside lawyers were hired to do an independent investigation and did not represent individual executives. By the time the main part of the investigation was over, most of the top-level executives of CA had been fired.

ENRON

When the Federal Energy Regulatory Commission (FERC), which was investigating Enron, unearthed and published confiscated e-mails, not only Enron's employees got a nasty shock when their old e-mails turned up on the Web. Everyone who had sent e-mails to Enron e-mail addresses found themselves caught in the federal net. So, people who were never accused of wrongdoing and didn't even work at Enron suddenly found their e-mail messages displayed for all the world to see, even if the message was as innocent as the confirmation of a golfing date.

FERC gathered a boatload of records, paper and electronic, during its investigation of Enron's alleged energy-market manipulations. In March 2003, FERC posted 1.6 million e-mail messages and other documents on the Web in a searchable database. The e-mails are from the period 2000–2003. So anyone can go to the Web site (www.ferc.gov/industries/electric/indus-act/wem/03-26-03-release.asp) and easily view the e-mails and calendars of 176 current and former Enron employees. The e-mails appear in full—including sender and receiver names.

Among the e-mail messages are lots of personal communications like executives discussing employees and vice versa; romantic messages; discussions of break-ups (liaisons and marriages); in-law problems; personal photos, and so on.

FERC said that, since Enron owned the messages, it was incumbent on the company to identify personal communications and request their exclusion.

A couple of days after the e-mail database appeared on the Web, FERC agreed to take off the most sensitive documents, like a document that listed the Social Security number of every employee. In early April, on the order of a U.S. Court of Appeals, the database was shut down for 10 days to allow Enron to examine all the documents and make up a list of documents it wanted removed.

About 100 Enron volunteers spent 350 hours going through hundreds of thousands of e-mails looking for specific terms like "Social Security Number," "credit card number," "kids," and "divorce." FERC removed about 8 percent of the database, which amounted to about 141,000 documents.[40,41]

Questions

1. If you were to give advice to someone who had just started using e-mail, or even someone who's been using e-mail for a while, what would

you tell that person should be the one guiding principle in all their e-mail communications? Put your advice into one sentence.

2. Now expand on your one guiding principle in question 1, and offer 10 rules for writing e-mails. What should those 10 rules be?

3. Imagine you're a manager in a lawn care business and you have an office staff of five people. Your lawyer suggests that you issue guidelines or rules to your staff about

storing e-mail on the company's server and on the computers they use in their work for you. What should those guidelines be? What would the rules be? Be sure to explain your rationale.

4. Do you think there should be federal guidelines governing a business's e-mail traffic just as there are regarding a business's financial records? If so, what should they be? If not, why not?

CLOSING CASE STUDY TWO

THE PROBLEM OF INFORMATION PROTECTION

The theft of consumer information—particularly financial information—is causing huge headaches for financial and data companies. This case looks at three incidents that occurred recently at ChoicePoint, Bank of America, and Polo Ralph Lauren.

CHOICEPOINT

The opening case study in this chapter highlighted the Acxiom Corporation, a company that gathers, packages, and sells information about consumers. A direct competitor to Acxiom is ChoicePoint, a company that is a spin-off of Equifax, which is one of the three major credit bureaus.

ChoicePoint has more than 20 billion records that include information on almost every adult in the United States. ChoicePoint sells this information to customers, such as potential employers, for purposes of verification.

ChoicePoint found itself in the headlines when personal financial information on 145,000 customers was stolen in a very high-profile identity fraud theft. And this time there was no sophisticated electronic attack or break-in; rather the theft was accomplished through old-fashioned "social engineering." Social engineering is getting information that you have no right to by conning people who have access to it. What the identity thieves did was to pose as fake companies buying information on people in every state and the District of Columbia. So far, 750 confirmed cases of identity theft have surfaced from the ChoicePoint security breach.

The U.S. Attorney's Office in Los Angeles charged that ChoicePoint had been scammed previously in 2002 resulting in fraud to the tune of $1 million.

THE BANK OF AMERICA

The Bank of America was also the victim of information theft accomplished in an old-fashioned way. Personal information recorded on tapes belonging to 1.2 million federal employees, including members of Congress, was on a commercial jet en route to a safe backup facility when the tapes were stolen.

Both the Bank of America and ChoicePoint thefts occurred in February 2005 and were followed very quickly by the introduction of privacy legislation at both the state and federal levels.

POLO RALPH LAUREN

Another example of embarrassment and worse involved Polo Ralph Lauren. It seems that between June 2002 and December 2004, the company was storing credit card information on its point-of-sale system instead of deleting it immediately after transactions had been completed. The realization that this data had been compromised led HSBC North America—the issuer of some of the credit cards whose numbers had been stolen—to notify 180,000 consumers of the possibility of identity theft. MasterCard, Visa U.S.A. and Discover Financial Services customers have all been affected. American Express says it has not seen any activity that has looked suspicious.[42,43]

Questions

1. If you were the manager of a company where it was discovered that credit card information had been stolen, what responsibility would you have to the people whose personal information was compromised? What are the pros and cons of notifying and of not notifying possible victims?

2. E*Trade, a leader in online brokerage services, is the first company to go to a two-factor authentication system optionally available to its customers with accounts of $50,000 or more. The first factor is the ID and password that customers have always needed, and second, they use a security token or, as E*Trade calls it, a *Digital Security ID.* This is a little device that you can carry on your key chain that displays a new random six-digit number every minute. E*Trade's host system must, of course, synchronize with the device.

    When you log in, you have to type in this number after your ID and password. Since the number changes so often it's virtually impossible to hack an account with this two-pronged protection. From a consumer's point of view, do you think this is a good idea? What are the advantages and disadvantages of the system to businesses and customers? With which online transactions would you consider it worthwhile to enforce this level of security? Remember that you might have a lot of these tokens if you use a lot of online services.

3. In this case study you saw how personal information can be stolen from huge databases and data warehouses. What other ways are there that thieves can obtain personal information about you that would allow them to steal your identity and run up debts in your name? To what extent would you be liable for these debts? What would you have to do (what steps would you take) to reestablish your financial identity if you discovered your identity had been stolen?

4. In the case of the Bank of America, the data was being shipped on tapes to a safe location. This is very good backup policy to make sure that in the event of a major disaster like a fire or flood, data can be quickly restored enabling the company to be back in operation as soon as possible. However, this procedure leaves the company vulnerable to old-fashioned theft of the physical tapes containing personal information. What are two ways that this information that travels on trucks and planes could be protected?

Key Terms and Concepts

Adware, 235
Anonymous Web browsing (AWB), 237
Anti-virus software, 244
Biometrics, 245
Clickstream, 237
Computer virus (virus), 242
Cookie, 234
Copyright, 226
Denial-of-service attack (DoS), 243

Encryption, 245
Ethics, 224
Fair Use Doctrine, 226
Firewall, 244
Hacker, 242
Hardware key logger, 232
Identity theft, 229
Intellectual property, 226
Key logger software (key trapper software), 228
Pharming, 230

Phishing (carding or brand spoofing), 230
Pirated software, 227
Privacy, 227
Public key encryption (PKE), 246
Spam, 235
Spyware (sneakware or stealthware), 236
Trojan horse software, 235
Web log, 237
Worm, 243

Short-Answer Questions

1. What are ethics, and how do ethics apply to business?
2. What situation would qualify as an exception to the copyright law?
3. What is privacy?
4. What is pirated software?
5. What is identity theft?
6. What does a key logger do?
7. What is spyware?
8. What is a denial-of-service attack?
9. What is public key encryption?

Assignments and Exercises

1. **HELPING A FRIEND** Suppose you fully intend to spend the evening working on an Excel assignment that's due the next day. Then a friend calls. Your friend is stranded miles from home and desperately needs your help. It will take most of the evening to pick up your friend, bring him home, and return to your studying. Not only that, but you're very tired when you get home and just fall into bed. The next day your friend, who completed his assignment earlier, suggests you just make a copy, put your own name on the cover, and hand it in as your own work. Should you do it? Isn't it only fair that since you helped your friend, the friend should do something about making sure you don't lose points because of your generosity? What if your friend promises not to hand in his or her own work so that you can't be accused of copying? Your friend wrote the assignment and gave it to you, so there's no question of copyright infringement.

2. **FIND OUT WHAT HAPPENED** In December 2001, British Telecom (BT) filed a lawsuit against Prodigy in New York federal court, claiming it owns the hyperlinking process. If BT wins this lawsuit then the company will be able to collect licensing revenue from the 100 billion or so links on the Web. BT has a patent that it says amounts to ownership of the hyperlinking process. Prodigy (and everyone else in the world) stores Web pages with a displayed part, which the browser shows, and a hidden part that the viewer doesn't see, and which contains hidden information including the addresses that are used by the displayed portion. This, BT said, is the essence of its U.S. patent No. 4873662. In reference to this case, answer the following questions:
   A. Has a ruling been handed down on this matter yet? If so, what was the result?
   B. If any kind of hyperlinking is, in fact, the essence of the patent held by BT, what about library card catalogs; are they infringements, too? Why or why not? What else could be?

3. **INVESTIGATE MONITORING SYSTEMS** The text listed several monitoring systems, other systems that defeat them, and an e-mail encryption program. Find two more of the following:
   A. Programs that monitor keyboard activity
   B. Programs that find keyboard monitoring programs
   C. E-mail encryption programs

4. **CHECK OUT THE COMPUTER ETHICS INSTITUTE'S ADVICE** The Computer Ethics Institute's Web site at www.cspr.org/program/ethics.htm offers the "Ten Commandments of Computer Ethics" to guide you in ethical computer use. The first two are
   - *Thou shalt not use a computer to harm other people.* This one is the bedrock for all the others.
   - *Thou shalt not interfere with other people's computer work.* This one stems from the first and includes small sins like sending frivolous e-mail and crimes like spreading viruses and electronic stalking.

   Look up the other eight and give at least two examples of acts that would be in violation of these guidelines.

Discussion Questions

1. When selling antiques, you can usually obtain a higher price for those that have a *provenance*, which is information detailing the origin and history of the object. For example, property owned by Jacqueline Kennedy Onassis and Princess Diana sold for much more than face value. What kinds of products have value over and above a comparable product because of such information? What kind of information makes products valuable? Consider both tangible (resale value) and intangible value (sentimental appeal).

2. Personal checks that you use to buy merchandise have a standard format. Checks have very few different sizes, and almost no variation in format. Consider what would happen if everyone could create his or her own size, shape, and layout of personal check. What would the costs and benefits be to business and the consumer in terms of buying checks, exchanging them for merchandise, and bank check processing?

3. Consider society as a business that takes steps to protect itself from the harm of illegal acts. Discuss the mechanisms and costs that are involved. Examine ways in which our society would be different if no one ever broke a law. Are there ever benefits to our society when people break the law, for example, when they claim that the law itself is unethical or unjust?

4. Can you access all the IT systems at your college or university? What about payroll or grade information on yourself or others? What kinds of controls has your college or university implemented to prevent the misuse of information?

5. You know that you generally can't use a PC to access the information stored on a Macintosh-formatted disk. What other instances of difficulty in accessing information have you experienced personally or heard of? For example, have you used different versions of MS PowerPoint or MS Access that won't work on all the PCs that you have access to?

6. Have you, or someone you know, experienced computer problems caused by a virus? What did the virus do? Where do you think you got it? How did you fix the problem? What was the cost to you in time, trouble, and stress?

7. What laws do you think the United States should pass to protect personal information? Or none? Why? Should some personal information be more protected than other information? Why or why not?

8. The issue of pirated software is one that the software industry fights on a daily basis. The major centers of software piracy are in places like Russia and China where salaries and disposable income are comparatively low. Given that people in developing and economically depressed countries will fall behind the industrialized world technologically if they can't afford access to new generations of software, is it reasonable to blame someone for using pirated software when it costs two months' salary to buy a legal copy of MS Office? If you answered no, specify at what income level it's okay to make or buy illegal copies of software. What approach could software companies use to combat the problem apart from punitive measures, like pressuring the government to impose sanctions on transgressors?

CHAPTER PROJECTS

Group Projects

- Assessing the Value of Outsourcing Information Technology: Creating Forecasts (p. 372)
- Making the Case with Presentation Software: Information Technology Ethics (p. 374)
- Assessing a Wireless Future: Emerging Trends and Technology (p. 378)
- Evaluating the Next Generation: Dot-Com ASPs (p. 379)
- Evaluating the Security of Information: Wireless Network Vulnerability (p. 386)

e-Commerce Projects

- Exploring Google Earth (p. 392)
- Protecting Your Computer (p. 395)
- Searching for Shareware and Freeware (p. 398)
- Ethical Computing Guidelines (p. 392)
- Privacy Laws and Legislation (p. 395)

CHAPTER NINE OUTLINE

STUDENT LEARNING OUTCOMES

1. Describe the emerging trends and technologies that will have an impact on the changing Internet.

2. Define the various types of technologies that are emerging as we move toward physiological interaction with technology.

3. Describe the emerging trends of Near Field Communication, Bluetooth, WiFi, cell phones, and RFID, as they relate to the wireless environment.

4. Define and describe emerging technologies that, while purely technology, can and will impact the future.

PERSPECTIVES

WEB SUPPORT

www.mhhe.com/haag

- Searching job databases
- Interviewing and negotiating tips
- Financial aid resources
- Searching for MBA programs
- Free and rentable storage space
- Global statistics and resources

CHAPTER NINE

Emerging Trends and Technologies
Business, People, and Technology Tomorrow

OPENING CASE STUDY:
CAN AN E-SOCIETY REPLACE
OUR REAL SOCIETY?

If you step back and view our world and society, you'll notice some very interesting changes and trends. People are spending more and more time online. On the average, people now spend more time online than watching TV. The average child under the age of 12 spends only 45 minutes outdoors per week in unstructured activities, with much of the rest of the time spent in structured outdoor activities (mainly sport leagues) or indoors in front of a computer. We are definitely moving in the direction of becoming an e-society, supported and enabled by the many technological advances of today and the promises of the capabilities of technology tomorrow.

Second Life (http://secondlife.com) is a form of an e-society on the Internet. There, you can create an avatar of yourself, becoming whoever you want to be. You can buy land on which to build a home or business. Of course, you need to carefully pick the location of your virtual business, based on the location of competitors around you and the amount of traffic that moves through the virtual neighborhood in which you plan to open your business.

Like many social networking sites (Second Life is definitely a form of one of these), you can connect with people with common interests. You can form groups focusing on such topics as movies, music, and hobbies. At all times of the day and night, you can meet people at nightclubs, fashion shows, and art gallery openings.

Second Life supports a fully running economy. You can take risks and be entrepreneurial. If no one likes what you are doing, you'll go out of business and be forced to sell off assets to pay your debts. If people do like what you're doing, you can become a millionaire in Second Life. And while the money on Second Life is in the currency of Linden Dollars (named after Second Life's creator) you can exchange your Linden Dollars for real U.S. dollars and have them transferred to your bank account. Likewise, you can transfer real dollars from your bank account and buy Linden Dollars in Second Life, enabling you to expand your business, buy more property, and so on.

A basic account to start your virtual life in Second Life is free. You get avatar capabilities but you can't do certain things like own land. If you want those types of privileges, you have to pay a membership fee, $72 for an annual membership.

Second Life boasts of a population over 6 million worldwide. Do you have a virtual life on Second Life?[1,2]

Questions

1. How many social networking sites do you belong to? How much time per week, on the average, would you say that you spend on those social networking sites?

2. Beyond social networking sites, how much time in total do you spend online per week? What are the major activities you perform online?

3. Although we are reaching more people online, are we becoming a society that is disassociated with the real environment around us? Is being online so much (often in fantasy environments) good or bad?

Introduction

Technology is changing every day. But even more important than simply staying up with the changes in technology, you need to think about how those changes will affect your life. It's fun to read and learn about "leading- and bleeding-edge" technologies. It is something we encourage you to do. The consequences of those technology changes, however, may have an impact on all our lives more far reaching than you can imagine.

In this final chapter, we will take a look at several leading- and bleeding-edge technologies, including speech recognition, biometrics, implant chips, and chipless RFID, among others. These new technologies can and will impact your personal and business life. Technology for the sake of technology (though fun) is never necessarily a good thing, and can even be counterproductive. Using technology appropriately to enhance your personal life and to move your organization toward its strategic initiatives, on the other hand, is always a good thing.

This has been both an exciting and a challenging chapter for us to write. The excitement is in the opportunity to talk with you about some emerging technological innovations. The challenge has been to not spotlight the technologies themselves overmuch, so as to help you focus on how those technologies will affect your life.

So, as you read this chapter, have fun but don't get caught up exclusively in the technology advances themselves that are on the horizon. Try to envision how those new technologies will change the things that you do and the way you do them, both from a personal and organizational perspective. As throughout this book, we remind you always to consider how to make new technology relevant and productive for you.

To introduce you to just a few of the many new technologies on the horizon, we've chosen those that we believe will have the greatest impact. We present those emerging technologies within the context of four important trends (see Figure 9.1).

Figure 9.1

Emerging Trends and Technologies

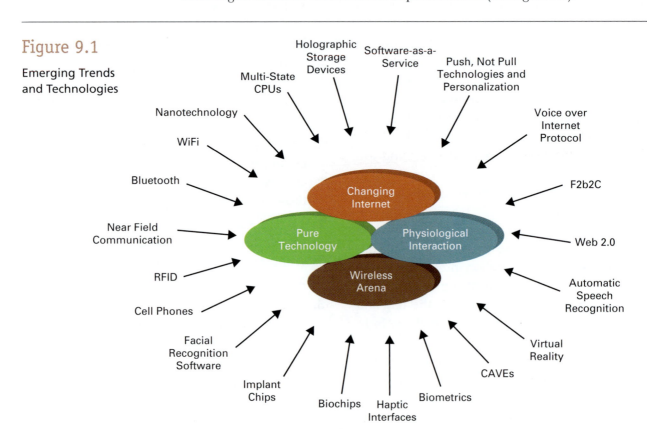

The Changing Internet

Few technologies have grown to widespread use and changed as fast as the Internet. Over the next several years, you will witness many new Internet-based trends and technologies. Among those will be software-as-a-service; push (not pull) technologies and personalization; F2b2C (which also enables personalization); Internet telephony (i.e., Voice over Internet Protocol, VoIP); and Web 2.0. All of these trends and technologies are fostering the concept of an e-society.

SOFTWARE-AS-A-SERVICE

Software-as-a-service (SaaS) is a delivery model for software in which you pay for software on a pay-per-use basis instead of buying the software outright. As more technology choices become available to you (smart phones, PDAs, tablet PCs) and your need to be mobile using them also increases, these devices may not have the capacity necessary to store all your software needs. For that matter, you may need a given piece of software—photo and video editing software, for instance—perhaps only a couple of times a year. It makes sense then that renting software would be a good alternative. That is what the SaaS model aims to deliver.

In the SaaS model you pay for software on a pay-per-use basis using a personal application service provider. An *application service provider (ASP)* supplies software applications (and often related services such as maintenance, technical support, information storage, and the like) over the Internet that would otherwise reside on customers' computers. We discussed ASPs in Chapter 7 and how the business world is already using them.

Let's focus for a moment on your personal use of an ASP (see Figure 9.2). In the future, ASPs will provide personal productivity software for you to use (for a pay-per-use

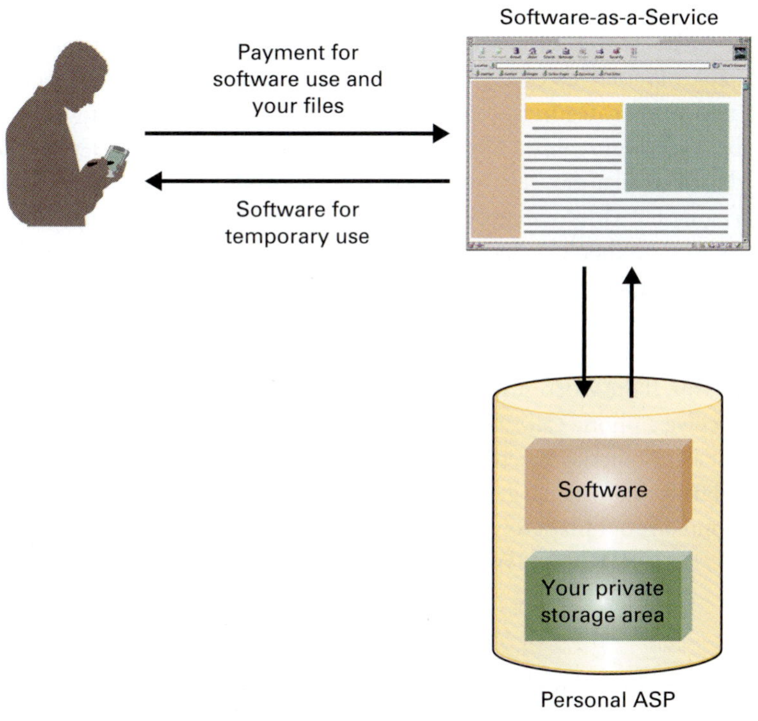

Software-as-a-Service

Payment for software use and your files

Software for temporary use

Software

Your private storage area

Personal ASP

Figure 9.2

The Software-as-a-Service Model and a Personal Application Service Provider (ASP)

fee or monthly subscription fee using the SaaS model) and storage so you can store your files on their Web servers as opposed to on your own personal devices.

For example, you might be in an airport and need to build a workbook with your PDA, which might not have a complete version of Excel. So, you would use your PDA to connect to the Internet and a personal ASP. With your PDA, you would use the personal ASP's Excel software to create your workbook and save it on the ASP's Web server. When you finally got back to the office, you would use your computer there, connect to the same ASP, and retrieve your workbook and save it on your computer.

There are many issues you'll have to consider when determining whether or not to use a personal ASP, with privacy and reliability definitely being important ones. If all your information is on a Web-based server, it will be easier for someone to gain access to it (for the wrong reasons) than if you stored all your information on your home or office computer. When considering reliability, you need to think about what happens if the personal ASP's Web site goes down. How will you perform your work? These are important facets of your personal service level agreement into which you would enter with your personal ASP. In spite of potential drawbacks, we believe personal ASPs and the SaaS model will become a part of your everyday life in the future.

PUSH, NOT PULL, TECHNOLOGIES AND PERSONALIZATION

We live in a *pull* technology environment. That is, you look for, request, and find what you want. On the Internet, for example, you visit a specific site and request information, services, and products. So, you're literally "pulling" what you want. Future emphasis will be on *push* technologies. In a ***push technology*** environment, businesses and organizations come to you via technology with information, services, and product offerings based on your profile. This isn't spam or mass e-mailings. We briefly discussed the concept of push technology in Chapter 5 within the concepts of mobile computing and m-commerce.

For example, in some parts of the country you can subscribe to a cell service that pushes information to you in the form of video rental information. Whenever you pass near a video store, your cell phone (which is GPS-enabled) triggers a computer within the video store that evaluates your rental history to see if any new videos have arrived that you might be interested in viewing. In this case, the system generates a personal data warehouse of rental history—including dimensions for the day of the week, the time of the day, and video categories—concerning you and then evaluates information in the smaller cubes (see Figure 9.3). The evaluation seeks to affirm that (1) you usually rent videos on that particular day, (2) you usually rent videos during that time of that day, and (3) there is a distinct video category from which you rent videos during that time of the day. If so, the system then checks to see if there are any movies in that category that you haven't rented and that it hasn't previously contacted you about.

If so, the video store computer will call your cell phone with a message concerning a new release. It will also give you street-by-street directions to the video store and hold the video for you. If the video store doesn't have any new releases that might interest you, you won't receive a phone call.

You might also someday receive a personalized pizza delivery message on your television as you start to watch a ball game. The message might say, "We'll deliver your favorite sausage and mushroom pizza to your doorstep before the game begins. On your remote control, press the ORDER NOW button."

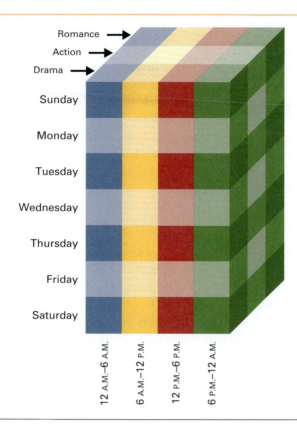

Figure 9.3

Tracking What You Want and When You Want It with a Data Warehouse

Of course, situations such as these rely on IT's ability to store vast amounts of information about you. Technologies such as databases and data warehouses will definitely play an important role in the development of push technologies that do more than just push spam and mass e-mail. In the instance of the pizza delivery message on your television, a local pizza store would have determined that you like sausage and mushroom pizza and that you order it most often while watching a ball game.

F2B2C: A NEW E-COMMERCE BUSINESS MODEL

In the e-commerce world, business models are identified by the players such as B2B (Business-to-Business) and G2C (Government-to-Consumer). We now have the notion of introducing a third player to create an entirely new e-commerce business model. The first of these new business models to surface is *F2b2C (Factory-to-business-to-Consumer),* an e-commerce business model in which a consumer communicates through a business on the Internet and directly provides product specifications to a factory that makes the customized and personalized product to the consumer's specifications and then ships it directly to the consumer.[3]

You should notice in F2b2C that the "F" and "C" are capitalized while the "b" (for business) is not. In this model, the business is simply an Internet intermediary that provides a communication conduit between the factory and the consumer. When this happens, a form of disintermediation occurs. Broadly defined, *disintermediation* is the use of the Internet as a delivery vehicle, whereby intermediate players in a distribution channel can be bypassed. The travel agent industry is a good example of where disintermediation has occurred. Now, you can connect directly to an airline and purchase tickets, often receiving bonus mileage if you do. The Internet has disintermediated travel agents, since you need them less.

Think about connecting to a site on the Internet and custom-ordering something like a pair of pants. You would specify your exact size, inseam, waist, hip, and thigh measurements, and so on, and other information such as color, style of pockets, how many belt loops (if any) . . . the list could grow quite long. The Web site would immediately pass along your information to a factory that would create a customized and personalized pair of pants for you and ship them to your door. Is this possible? Well, it already exists to some extent. Later in the chapter, you'll read about how companies are using biometrics to create custom-fitting clothing and shoes.

VOICE OVER INTERNET PROTOCOL (VOIP)

VoIP, or *Voice over Internet Protocol,* allows you to send voice communications over the Internet and avoid the toll charges that you would normally receive from your long distance carrier. Simply put, VoIP allows you to use your Internet connection (which must be broadband such as DSL or cable) to make phone calls. This is different from today's DSL model which splits your phone line so that you can make phone calls and surf the Web at the same time. In today's model, your telephone calls are still routed through your traditional telephone service provider to whom you must pay charges for long distance phone calls. Using VoIP, your telephone calls are routed through a VoIP provider (which may be your ISP) and you pay only a flat monthly fee—usually in the neighborhood of $20 to $25 per month—to make unlimited long distance calls.

For home use, you can already use the VoIP services offered by the likes of Vonage, Lingo, Quintum, and AT&T. You can keep your existing phone number and you do have access to a number of value-added features such as call-waiting, caller ID, and so on. Most VoIP providers offer you free unlimited long distance calling only within your country; international long distance calls may still incur an additional fee.

This certainly speaks to the growing importance of the Internet. Most of you probably cannot imagine life without the Internet already. That will be even more true once the Internet becomes the technological infrastructure that also supports all your phone calls. You can read more about VoIP in *Appendix B.*

WEB 2.0

The *Web 2.0* is the so-called second generation of the Web and focuses on online collaboration, users as both creators and modifiers of content, dynamic and customized information feeds, and many other engaging Web-based services. To be sure, "2.0" has caught on as a hot buzz term, for example, the Family 2.0 (family members living on and communicating through the Internet), Company 2.0 (the complete Web-enabled company), and TV 2.0 (TV-type broadcast shows delivered via the Web). Some of the exciting applications of Web 2.0 include:

- *Wiki*—a Web site that allows you—as a visitor—to create, edit, change, and often eliminate content. Wikipedia (www.wikipedia.org) is the most popular. Wikis are actually an interesting implementation of sourcing, called *crowdsourcing,* when businesses provide enabling technologies that allow people (i.e., crowds)—instead of a designated paid employee—to create, modify, and oversee the development of a product or service. In the case of a Wiki, that product is information.
- *Social networking site*—a site on which you post information about yourself, create a network of friends, share content such as photos and videos, and

OFFSHORE OUTSOURCING TUTORING

In Chapter 6 we introduced you to the three major geopolitical forms of outsourcing—onshore, nearshore, and offshore. Each brings with it some distinct advantages and disadvantages when outsourcing the development of IT systems.

But what about education? Many college students go overseas to study—perhaps for a quarter or semester and sometimes for a full four years to get a degree. That's a form of nearshore or offshore outsourcing. Even earlier in the education process, many K-12 students are turning to offshore outsourcing for tutoring support.

One company providing this is Educomp (www.educomp.com), which provides one-on-one tutoring via the Internet in the areas of math and science. Using Educomp would be considered offshore outsourcing tutoring because it is based in New Delhi, India. Armed with only a personal computer and a webcam, students here in the United States can get private, real-time tutoring from an Educomp employee.

Most Indian tutoring companies charge in the neighborhood of $100 per month for unlimited, interactive tutoring over the Internet. Compare that to typical tutoring services in the United States which usually charge around $100 per hour for face-to-face tutoring.

Moreover, most Indian tutoring service companies guarantee that their tutors have—at a minimum—an undergraduate degree in the discipline they teach. Again, compare that to the United States, where almost 30 percent of high school math teachers do not have either a major or minor in the discipline of math.[4]

---

communicate with other people. We've discussed several social networking sites throughout the text including Myspace, Facebook, Facebox, orkut, and Cyworld (and Second Life in this chapter's opening case study).

- *Blog*—a Web site in the form of a journal in which you post entries in chronological order and often includes the capabilities for other viewers to add comments to your journal entries.
- *RSS feed*—a technology that provides frequently published and updated digital content on the Web.
- *Podcasting*—generally refers to your ability at any time to download audio and video files for viewing and listening using portable listening devices and personal computers.

Many of these technologies, and the Web 2.0 in general, will forever change how you live your personal life and how you conduct business.

E-SOCIETY

The general and strong trend today in society is toward becoming an e-society. Although we provide no formal definition for an e-society, you can quickly grasp that it is all about living life in, on, and through technology, with the Internet being at the epicenter. People are finding life-long soul mates on Match.com and numerous other dating-related sites; others (especially young people) are flocking to, spending a great deal of time on, and developing friendships on sites such as Myspace, Facebook, and YouTube; people are building very successful home-based e-businesses on eBay; children are receiving tutoring via the Web (see the nearby Global Perspective); just as we wrote this section, PokerStars.net was dealing hand number 9,738,225,821—90 minutes later it dealt hand number 9,739,309,711, meaning that online poker enthusiasts had played over 1 million hands in 90 minutes (roughly 11,000 hands per minute); also at the time we wrote this section, eBay was posting its 60 billionth lot for auction (yes, that is 60,000,000,000).

The simple fact of the matter is that we live in a digital world, with technology not just for the sake of doing business but pervading our personal lives so much so that many people cannot imagine a world without technology. That technology-based world is enabling the growth of an e-society.

Physiological Interaction

LEARNING OUTCOME 2

Right now, your primary physical interfaces to your computer include a keyboard, mouse, monitor, and printer (basically, your input and output devices). These are physical devices, not physiological. Physiological interfaces capture and utilize your real body characteristics, such as your breath, your voice, your height and weight, and even the iris in your eye. Physiological innovations include automatic speech recognition, virtual reality, cave automatic virtual environments, haptic interfaces, and biometrics, along with many others.

AUTOMATIC SPEECH RECOGNITION

An *automatic speech recognition (ASR)* system not only captures spoken words but also distinguishes word groupings to form sentences. To perform this, an ASR system follows three steps.

1. *Feature analysis*—The system captures your words as you speak into a microphone, eliminates any background noise, and converts the digital signals of your speech into phonemes (syllables).

2. *Pattern classification*—The system matches your spoken phonemes to a phoneme sequence stored in an acoustic model database. For example, if your phoneme was "dü," the system would match it to the words do and due.

3. *Language processing*—The system attempts to make sense of what you're saying by comparing the word phonemes generated in step 2 with a language model database. For example, if you were asking a question and started with the phoneme "dü," the system would determine that the appropriate word is do and not due.

ASR is certainly now taking its place in computing environments. The important point is that ASR allows you to speak in a normal voice; thus it supports physiological interaction.

VIRTUAL REALITY

On the horizon (and in some instances here today) is a new technology that will virtually place you in any experience you desire. That new technology is *virtual reality,* a three-dimensional computer simulation in which you actively and physically participate. In a virtual reality system, you make use of special input and output devices that capture your physiological movements and send physiological responses back to you. These devices include:

- *Glove*—An input device that captures and records the shape and movement of your hand and fingers and the strength of your hand and finger movements.
- *Headset (head-mounted display)*—A combined input and output device that (1) captures and records the movement of your head and (2) contains a screen that covers your entire field of vision and displays various views of an environment based on your movements.
- *Walker*—An input device that captures and records the movement of your feet as you walk or turn in different directions.

APPLICATIONS OF VIRTUAL REALITY   Virtual reality applications are popping up everywhere, sometimes in odd places. The most common applications are found in the entertainment industry. There are a number of virtual reality games on the market, including downhill Olympic skiing, race-car driving, golf, air combat, and marksmanship. Other applications include

- Matsushita Electric Works—You design your kitchen in virtual reality and then choose the appliances you want and even request color changes.
- Volvo—For demonstrating the safety features of its cars.
- Airlines—To train pilots how to handle adverse weather conditions.
- Motorola—To train assembly-line workers in the steps of manufacturing a new product.[5]
- Health care—To train doctors how to perform surgery using virtual cadavers.[6]

Let's consider the potential ramifications of virtual reality and how you might someday interact with your computer. New virtual reality systems include aroma-producing devices and devices that secrete fluid through a mouthpiece that you have in your mouth. So, you could virtually experience a Hawaiian luau. The aroma-producing device would generate various smells and the mouthpiece would secrete a fluid that tastes like pineapple or roasted pig. If you were using virtual reality to surf big waves, the mouthpiece would secrete a fluid that tastes like salt water.

CAVE AUTOMATIC VIRTUAL ENVIRONMENTS

A **CAVE (cave automatic virtual environment)** is a special 3-D virtual reality room that can display images of other people and objects located in other CAVEs all over the world. CAVEs are **holographic devices,** that create, capture, and/or display images in true three-dimensional form. If you watch any of the *Star Trek* movies, you'll see an example of a holographic device called the holodeck.

In working form, you would enter a CAVE room. At the same time, someone else would enter another CAVE room in another location (see Figure 9.4). Numerous digital video cameras would capture the likenesses of both participants and re-create and send those images to the other CAVEs. Then, you and the other person could see and carry on a normal conversation with each other, and you would feel as if that other person were in the same room with you.

Current CAVE research is also working on the challenges of having other physical objects in the room. For example, if you sat on a couch in your CAVE, the couch would

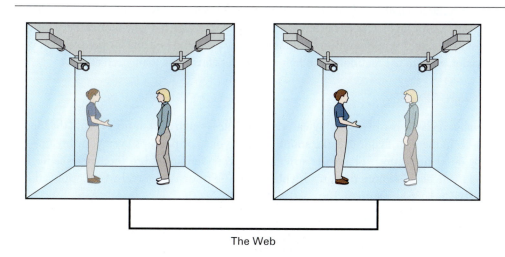

The Web

Figure 9.4

CAVEs (Cave Automatic Virtual Environments)

capture the indentation you made in it and pass it to the couch in the other CAVE. That couch would respond by constricting a mesh of rubber inside it so that your indentation would also appear there. And what about playing catch? Which person would have the virtual ball and which person would have the real ball? The answer is that both would have a virtual ball. When throwing it, the CAVE would capture your arm movement to determine the speed, arc, and direction of the ball. That information would be transmitted to the other CAVE, and it would use that information to make the virtual ball fly through the air accordingly.

Unlike virtual reality, in some CAVEs you don't need any special gear. Let your imagination run wild and think about the potential applications of CAVEs. An unhappy customer could call a business to complain. Within seconds, a customer service representative would not answer the phone but rather appear in the room with the unhappy customer. That would be an example of great customer service. Your teacher might never attend your class. Instead the teacher would enter a CAVE and have his or her image broadcast into the classroom. You might not really be in class either but rather a holographic likeness of you. Are CAVEs a realistic possibility? The answer is definitely yes. We believe that CAVEs are the successor to virtual reality. So, virtual reality may not be a long-term technological innovation but rather a stepping-stone to the more advanced CAVE. Whatever the case, CAVEs will not only significantly alter how you interact with your computer (can you imagine the thrill of video games in a CAVE?), they will even more significantly alter how you interact with other people. With CAVE technologies, you can visit your friends and relatives on a daily basis no matter where they live. You may even have television shows and movies piped into your home CAVE.

HAPTIC INTERFACES

A *haptic interface* uses technology to add the sense of touch to an environment that previously only had visual and textual elements. Applications of virtual reality we discussed previously that incorporate the use of gloves and walkers use implementations of haptic interfaces.

Many arcade games include haptic interfaces. For example, when you get on a stationary jet ski and control its movement (on screen) by adjusting your weight side-to-side and leaning backward and forward, you are interfacing with the arcade game via a haptic interface. Many joysticks and game controllers provide feedback to the user through vibrations, which is another form of a haptic interface.

Interacting with an arcade game via a haptic interface is a "fun" application of the technology and one that is making companies a lot of money. But consider this: With a haptic interface, sight-challenged people can feel and read text with their fingers while interacting with a computer. The fact is anyone can use technology to make money. Perhaps the most exciting thing about new technologies is the potential benefits for people. Can you envision ways to use technology to help people less fortunate than yourself?

BIOMETRICS

Biometrics is the use of physiological characteristics—such as your fingerprint, the blood vessels in the iris of your eye, the sound of your voice, or perhaps even your breath—to provide identification. That's the strict and narrow definition, but biometrics is beginning to encompass more than just identification. Consider these real-world applications in place today (see Figure 9.5):

- *Custom shoes*—Several shoe stores, especially those that offer fine Italian leather shoes, no longer carry any inventory. When you select a shoe style you like, you

Figure 9.5

Custom-Fit Clothes through Biometrics

place your bare feet into a box that scans the shape of your feet. That information is then used to make a custom pair of shoes for you. It works extremely well if your feet are slightly different from each other in size or shape (as is the case with most people). To see this, visit www.digitoe.com.

- *Custom wedding gowns*—Following the custom-fit shoe idea, many bridal boutiques now do the same thing for wedding dresses. Once the bride chooses the style she likes, she steps into a small room that scans her entire body. That information is used to create a wedding dress that fits perfectly. Both custom shoes and custom wedding dresses are examples of the future implementation of F2b2C.

- *Custom bathrobes*—Some high-end spa resorts now actually have patrons walk through a body-scanning device upon check-in. The scanning device measures the patron's body characteristics and then sends that information to a sewing and fabricating facility that automatically creates a custom-fit bathrobe.

BIOMETRIC SECURITY   The best form of security for personal identification encompasses three aspects:

1. What you know
2. What you have
3. Who you are

The first—*what you know*—is something like a password, something that everyone can create and has. The second—*what you have*—is something like a card such as an ATM card you use at an ATM (in conjunction with your password, what you know). Unfortunately, most personal identification security systems stop there. That is, they do not include *who you are,* which is some form of a biometric.

It's no wonder crimes like identity theft are spiraling out of control. Without much effort, a thief can steal your password (often through social engineering) and steal what you have. For the latter, the thief doesn't actually have to steal your physical card; he or she simply has to copy the information on it. However, stealing a biometric—such as your fingerprint or iris scan—is much more difficult.

Many banks are currently converting ATMs to the use of biometrics, specifically an iris scan, as the third level of personal identification security. When you open an account and request ATM use, the bank will issue you an ATM card (you pick the password). The bank will also scan your iris and create a unique 512-byte representation of the scan. To use an ATM, you must insert your card, type in your password, and allow the machine to scan your iris. The ATM uses all three forms of identification to match you to your account. You can then perform whatever transaction you wish.

Some private schools for young children now require parents and guardians to submit to iris scans. Once the scan is captured and the person is verified as a parent or guardian, the information is entered into a security database. Then, when the parent or guardian comes to the school to pick up a child, his or her iris scan is compared to the one stored in the database. Parents and guardians cannot, under any circumstances, take a child from the school without first going through verification via an iris scan.

INTEGRATING BIOMETRIC PROCESSING AND TRANSACTION PROCESSING

Once society accepts the use of biometrics for security and identification purposes, organizations of all types will be able to add another dimension of business intelligence to their data warehouses—that dimension will capture and record changes in physiological characteristics (see Figure 9.6).

Consider, as a hypothetical example, a woman using an ATM—equipped with iris scanning capabilities—to withdraw cash. Current research suggests that it might be possible to use an iris scan to determine not only that a woman is pregnant but also the sex of the unborn child. (That is a very true statement.) When the woman has her iris scanned, the bank might be able to tell that she is pregnant and expecting a boy. When the woman receives her cash and receipt, the receipt would have a coupon printed on the back for 10 percent off any purchase at Babies "Я" Us. Furthermore, the ATM would generate another receipt that says "buy blue."

The key here is for you to consider that transaction processing systems (TPSs) of the future will be integrated with biometric processing systems (BPSs). The TPS will capture and process the "events" of the transaction—when, by whom, where, and so on. The BPS will capture and process the physiological characteristics of the person performing the transaction. Those physiological characteristics may include the presence of alcohol or illegal drugs, hair loss, weight gain, low blood sugar, vitamin deficiencies, cataracts, and yes—even pregnancy.

When businesses start to gather this type of intelligence, you can leave it to your imagination to envision what will happen. For example, because of the noted pregnancy in our previous example of the woman using an ATM, the bank might offer financing for a mini-van, evaluate the size of the family's home and perhaps offer special financing for

Figure 9.6

Integrating Biometric and Transaction Processing to Create Business Intelligence

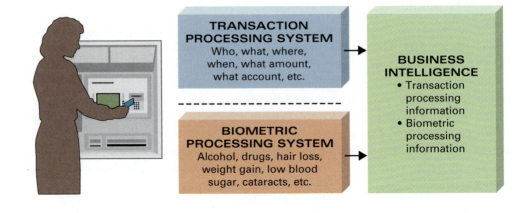

WII—REVOLUTIONIZING VIDEO GAMES THROUGH HAPTIC INTERFACES

Just a few short months after its debut, Nintendo's Wii outsold Microsoft's Xbox 360 and Sony's PlayStation 3, its primary competitors. Wii isn't a game but rather a video game console that allows you to play many different video games. Some of the games include *The Legend of Zelda: Twilight Princess, WarioWare: Smooth Moves,* and *Super Paper Mario.*

What is so revolutionary about Wii is that it incorporates *haptic interfaces.* Using a wireless controller, you can point at objects on the screen and the game console can also detect your motions and rotations in three dimensions.

When you bowl, for example (a very simple example at that), you see the bowling lane on the screen. You hold the wireless controller in your hand, press a button and hold it, and then go through the actual motion of bowling, releasing the button when you want to release the virtual bowling ball. You see the result of your actions on screen as the ball rolls down the lane and knocks down the pins.

Other video game publishers have since worked feverishly to add haptic interfaces to their games, including Electronic Arts (*The Godfather*) and Ubisoft (*Princess of Persia: Two Thrones*). As you read this text, you can probably name many more, as we suspect that haptic interface–based video games are here to stay and quickly becoming the mainstay.[7]

a second mortgage so another room can be added, or establish a tuition account for the child and place $25 in it. These possibilities will further intensify competition in almost all industries.

OTHER BIOMETRICS AND BIOMETRIC DEVICES   Biometrics is a "hot topic" in research circles right now. Although we haven't the space to discuss them all, you might want to watch for these:

- *Biochip*—a technology chip that can perform a variety of physiological functions when inserted into the human body. Biochips have been proven in some cases to block pain for people who suffer severe spinal injuries, help paralyzed people regain some portion of their motor skills, and help partially blind people see better.
- *Implant chip*—a technology-enabled microchip implanted into the human body that stores important information about you (such as your identification and medical history) and that may be GPS-enabled to offer a method of tracking.
- *Facial recognition software*—software that provides identification by evaluating facial characteristics.

Whatever becomes a reality in the field of biometrics promises to forever change your life and how you interact with technology.

The Wireless Arena

LEARNING OUTCOME 3

Throughout this text, we've discussed the technologies that make wireless communications possible and applications of wireless technologies in which companies have gained a significant competitive advantage. We've discussed such wireless technologies as Bluetooth and WiFi—both of which were designed to activate wireless communication via technology devices such as cell phones, printers, network hubs, and of course computers.

- *Bluetooth* is a standard for transmitting information in the form of short-range radio waves over distances of up to 30 feet.
- *WiFi (wireless fidelity)* is a standard for transmitting information in the form of radio waves over distances up to about several miles.

Bluetooth has become very popular for the wireless headsets (actually more like ear pieces) for cell phones. You may own one of these for your cell phone, and you've undoubtedly seen people using them. WiFi is usually the type of wireless communication used in a network environment. Verizon, for example, offers the BroadbandAccess PC Card, which you can use to wirelessly connect your computer or laptop to Verizon's wireless broadband network. Many businesses have private, firewalled wireless networks that use WiFi for their employees.

Let's now turn our attention to (1) cell phones and (2) RFID (radio frequency identification). Cell phones are a significant "disruptive technology" now and will be more so in the future. RFID, while still emerging as a technology, will definitely be around for many years and dramatically change your personal life and the way the business world works.

THE NEXT GENERATION OF CELL PHONE TECHNOLOGY

For most people, a cell phone is a necessary part of life. Even today's most basic cell phones support phone calls (that's obvious) and also real-time text messaging, photos (taking, sending, and receiving), games, and many other features. Tomorrow's cell phones may very well become the only technology you need.

Among the many innovations you'll see in cell phones over the next couple of years will be storage (in the form of a hard disk), processor capability, music enhancements, and video support. Already, new cell phones are being demonstrated that have 2 gigabytes of storage and processor speeds up to 500 Mhz. As these capacities and speeds increase, you may be able to wirelessly connect a keyboard, monitor, mouse, and printer to your cell phone. Your cell phone will essentially become your notebook computer.

Tomorrow's cell phones may spell the end for dedicated MP3 players like Apple's iPod. With enough battery life and storage capacity, many people will opt to use their cell phones for music and eliminate the other piece of equipment they have to carry around to listen to music. Video on demand will also become a reality through your cell phone. Apple's iPhone, for example, combines three technologies: (1) cell phone, (2) iPod, and (3) wireless Internet communication.

But there is a downside. Cell phones are the next great and uncharted space for hackers and viruses. The even worse news is that the development of antivirus cell phone software is very much in its infancy, far behind the capabilities of the people wanting to hack into your cell phone and unleash deadly cell phone viruses. Think about your ISP. It has antivirus software (and many more types of "anti" software such as spam blocker software and anti-spyware software) on its servers to stop a lot of malware from making it to your computer via e-mail. But that doesn't stop all malware from getting to you. You still need all types of "anti" software loaded onto and running on your computer at all times.

When was the last time your cell phone service provider contacted you about new types of "anti" software you can download onto your cell phone for added protection? That has probably never happened, and it should raise a red flag for you. Do you download ring tones from the Internet? If so, your cell phone is susceptible to getting a virus. Some cell phone viruses, created in a laboratory environment, can make international calls and run your battery dead and your bill into the thousands of dollars.

As your cell phone becomes increasingly more important to you—and it will—and becomes increasingly more supportive of complex computer tasks, your challenge will continue to be: Be protected.

RFID (RADIO FREQUENCY IDENTIFICATION)

RFID (radio frequency identification) uses a microchip (chip) in a tag or label to store information, and information is transmitted from, or written to, the tag or label when the microchip is exposed to the correct frequency of radio waves. You're probably already familiar with some implementations of RFID. For example, toll roads have lanes through which drivers can move if they have an RFID device that automatically charges to an account as they drive down the road. Exxon/Mobil provides an RFID-enabled key ring (called Speedpass) to its customers. The Speedpass key ring contains customer account information. A customer, when making a purchase, simply waves the key ring at a reader (as opposed to swiping a credit card). The reader communicates with the RFID chip on the key ring, reads the customer's account information, and proceeds with the account charge.

The most common implementation of RFID is the passive RFID chip (see Figure 9.7). A passive RFID chip has no power source itself and sits idle until passed near a reader that emits radio waves. The antenna surrounding the RFID chip picks up the radio waves and the RFID chip stores those waves as a form of energy until it has enough to literally "jolt" itself to life. The RFID chip then sends its information to the reader, which is connected to some sort of computer system containing account information and the like. After sending its information, the RFID chip goes back into passive mode. This is exactly how Exxon/Mobil's Speedpass RFID key ring works.

RFID IN USE TODAY The current applications of RFID technologies are many, including:

- **Anti-theft car keys**—inside the casing of the car key is an RFID chip. When you insert the key into the ignition, the RFID chip must communicate with the reader in your ignition system (and pass the equivalent of a password) for the car to start. So, it does criminals no good to make a copy of your car key. Of course, if you lose your car keys, it often costs in excess of $300 to get them replaced.

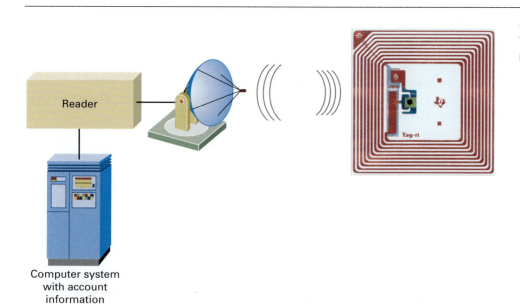

Reader

Computer system with account information

Figure 9.7

How Passive RFID Works

WHEN RFID GETS "INKED" AND GOES CHIPLESS

If you look carefully at Figure 9.7 and the RFID chip on the right, you can see the actual "chip" as a very small black rectangle surrounded by numerous red lines. (The red lines are the antenna structure.) Somark Innovation's latest innovation aims to eliminate the chip itself, creating a *chipless RFID chip.*

It is doing so with a biocompatible chipless RFID ink "tattoo." The ink is injected into the skin of animals. The chipless RFID, then, can be read as any other traditional RFID chip, that is, while not being in line of sight. According to Ramos Mays, chief scientist at Somark Innovations, "This is a true proof-of-principle [similar to a proof-of-concept prototype we discussed in Chapter 6] and mitigates most of the technological risk. This proves the ability to create a synthetic biometric or *fake fingerprint* with Biocompatible Chipless RFID Ink and read it through hair."

Somark plans to use this first in the livestock industry to help identify and track cattle. This will certainly help in the case of an outbreak of BSE (Mad Cow Disease). But don't let your mind stop with chipless RFID ink for animals. What about tattoos for people?

If you get a tattoo using the chipless RFID ink, you could be tracked unknowingly by literally anyone with an RFID reader. How does that make you feel? Do you still want to get a tattoo?[8]

- **Library book tracking**—instead of a bar code on which the ISBN is stored, the RFID chip contains that information. Books are much easier to check in and check out. Even the Vatican library now uses RFID chips in its books. The old inventory process took over 30 days. Using wireless handheld RFID readers, the new inventory process takes only a day.

- **Livestock tracking**—livestock of all kinds is now tagged with RFID chips upon entering the country. The system can then track where the livestock has been on its journey throughout the United States. In the case of a biological outbreak, the system can easily identify which livestock were at the location where the outbreak is believed to have occurred.

- **Supply chain**—almost every major participant in the supply chain process is now mandating that the other participants tag merchandise, trays of merchandise, boxes and skids of merchandise, and so on with RFID chips. These major participants include Wal-Mart, the Department of Defense (DOD), the Food and Drug Administration (FDA), Target, Albertson's, TESCO (United Kingdom retailer), and Carrefour (France retailer).

- **Passports**—implemented in the United States in 2007, all newly issued U.S. passports now contain an RFID chip in the cover of the passport. The RFID chip contains all your passport information.

The above list is just a few of the thousands of implementations of RFID in the business world.

THE FUTURE OF RFID   Today, almost every product is identified uniquely by a UPC (universal product code). However, every like product has the same UPC. So, two cans of diet Coke with lime, for example, have identical UPCs. This makes them indistinguishable. With RFID technologies, each individual piece of merchandise will have a unique EPC (electronic product code). The EPC will include the UPC designation but then also provide a unique number for each different can of diet Coke with lime that can be tied to expiration dates, supply chain movements, and just about anything else you can imagine.

Once again, use your imagination here. If every product in a grocery store can wirelessly communicate with the checkout system, there will be no need to go through that process. While you shop, you'll bag your items when placing them in your cart. When you walk out the front door, an RFID system will wirelessly communicate with your credit card in your wallet, wirelessly communicate with every product in your grocery cart, tally up your bill, and charge your credit card account appropriately.

And think about washing clothes. Suppose you load your washer full of "whites" like socks and towels. Accidentally, you throw in a red shirt but don't see it. Fortunately, each piece of clothing will have an RFID chip that will include washing instructions. Your washing machine will wirelessly communicate with each piece of clothing and determine that one piece does not belong. The washing machine will not work and will notify you that you are mixing clothes.

Are these all realities destined for the future? We believe so. What the future holds for RFID is limited only by your imagination.

Pure Technology

LEARNING OUTCOME 4

Let's close our look at emerging technologies with a few that have broad applicability in numerous ways. These include nanotechnology, multistate CPUs, and holographic storage devices.

NANOTECHNOLOGY

One of the single greatest drawbacks to technological advances is size. The best chip manufacturers can do is to make circuit elements with a width of 130 nanometers. A nanometer is one-hundred-thousandth the width of a human hair. That may seem very, very small, but current manufacturing technologies are beginning to limit the size of computer chips, and thus their speed and capacity.

Nanotechnologies aim to change all that. As a greatly simplified definition, we would say that **nanotechnology** is a discipline that seeks to control matter at the atomic and sub-atomic levels for the purpose of building devices on the same small scale. So, nanotechnology is the exact opposite of traditional manufacturing. In the latter, for example, you would cut down a tree and whittle it down until it becomes a toothpick. That is, traditional manufacturing starts with something large and continually compresses and slices it until it becomes the desired small size. In nanotechnology, you start with the smallest unit and build up. That is, you start working with atoms and build what you want.

In nanotechnology, everything is simply atoms. Nanotechnology researchers are attempting to move atoms and encourage them to "self-assemble" into new forms. Nanotechnology is a bleeding-edge technology worth watching. The changes it will bring about will be unbelievable. Consider these:

Change the molecular structure of the materials used to make computer chips, for instance, and electronics could become as cheap and plentiful as bar codes on packaging. Lightweight vests enmeshed with sensors could measure a person's vital signs. Analysis of a patient's DNA could be done so quickly and precisely that designer drugs would be fabricated on the fly. A computer the size of your library card could store everything you ever saw or read.[9,10]

MULTI-STATE CPUS

Right now, CPUs are binary-state, capable of working only with information represented by a 1 or a 0. That greatly slows processing. What we really need to increase speed are

CPUs that are multi-state. *Multi-state CPUs* work with information represented in more than just two states, probably 10 states with each state representing a digit between 0 and 9. When multi-state CPUs do become a reality, your computer will no longer have to go through many of the processes associated with translating characters into binary and then reversing the translation process later. (We cover this process in *Appendix A*.) This will make them much faster. Of course, the true goal is to create multi-state CPUs that can also handle letters and special characters without converting them to their binary equivalents.

HOLOGRAPHIC STORAGE DEVICES

Again, right now, storage devices store information on a two-dimensional surface, but research in the holographic realm will change that, creating *holographic storage devices* with many sides or faces (see Figure 9.8). This is similar in concept to small cards that you may have seen which change the picture or image as you view the cards from different angles.

Figure 9.8

3-D Crystal-Like Objects in a Holographic Storage Device

If and when holographic storage devices do become a reality, you may be able to store an entire set of encyclopedias on a single crystal that may have as many as several hundred faces. Think how small technology will become then.

Most Important Considerations

Throughout this chapter, we've discussed some key emerging trends and technologies. They certainly are exciting and promise that the future will be different and dynamic, to say the least. We have suggested that you anticipate these changes and how they will affect you personally and in your career.

As we close this chapter (and perhaps your studies in this course), let's take a close look at five key topics. Each is a culmination in some way of the material you've learned in this course. Each is inescapable in that it will happen and you must deal with it. Finally, each is vitally important and reaches far beyond the technologies that either necessitate or support it. For you, these last few pages are a chance to reflect on what you've learned and to place that knowledge within the bigger picture.

THE NECESSITY OF TECHNOLOGY

Like it or not, technology is a necessity today. It's hard to imagine a world without it. Just as we need electricity to function on an everyday basis, we need technology as well.

Of course, that doesn't mean you should adopt technology just for the sake of the technology or only because it sounds fun. Rather, you need to carefully evaluate each technology and determine if it will make you more productive, enhance your personal life, enrich your learning, or move your organization in the direction of its strategic goals and initiatives.

Technology is not a panacea. If you throw technology at a business process that doesn't work correctly, the result will be that you'll perform that process incorrectly millions of times faster per second. At the same time, you can ill afford to ignore technology when it really will help you and your organization become more efficient, effective, and innovative.

CLOSING THE GREAT DIGITAL DIVIDE

We must, as a human race, completely eliminate the great digital divide. The *great digital divide* refers to the fact that the world is becoming one marked by "have's" and "have not's" with respect to technology. That is, the traditional notion of a third world economy is now being defined by the extent to which a country has only limited access to and use of technology.

The power of technology needs to be realized on a worldwide scale. We cannot afford to have any technology-challenged nation or culture (within reason). The great digital divide only adds to global instability. If you live and work in a technology-rich country, don't keep it to yourself. When possible, take technology to other countries by creating international business partnerships and strategic alliances. Join in a nonprofit program to spread computer literacy and access in a third world country, or in this country. This may afford you great satisfaction, and the world will benefit greatly from your efforts.

TECHNOLOGY FOR THE BETTERMENT OF SOCIETY

Life isn't just about making money. As you approach the development and use of technological innovations (or even standard technologies), think in terms of the betterment of people and society in general. (Making money and helping people often go hand in hand, in fact.)

Medical research is performing marvelous work in the use of technology to treat ailments and cure diseases. But if these efforts are purely profit-driven, we may never wholly realize the fruits of them. For example, therapists are using virtual reality to teach autistic people to cope with increasingly complex situations. We know for a fact that this use of technology isn't making anyone a lot of money. But it isn't always about making money. It's about helping people who face daily challenges far greater than ours. You're fortunate to be in an environment of learning. Give back when you have the chance.

EXCHANGING PRIVACY FOR CONVENIENCE

On a personal level, you need to consider how much of your personal privacy you're giving up in exchange for convenience. The extreme example is GPS-enabled implant chips. The convenience is knowing where you are and being able to get directions to your destination. But you're obviously giving up some privacy. Is this okay? Convenience takes on many forms. When you use a discount card at a grocery store to take advantage of sales, that grocery store then tracks your purchasing history in great detail. You can bet that the grocery store will use that information to sell you more tailored products.

It really is a trade-off. In today's technology-based world, you give up privacy when you register for sweepstakes on certain Web sites. You give up privacy just surfing the Web because tracking software monitors your activities. Even when you click on a banner ad, the Web site you go to knows where you came from. Although such trade-offs may seem insignificant, small trade-offs can add up to a big trade-off over time.

Because you are very much a part of this trend, it's often hard to see the big picture and understand that every day you're giving up just a little more privacy in exchange for a little more convenience. Don't ever think that organizations won't use the information they're capturing about you. They're capturing it so they can use it. Of course, much of it will be used to better serve you as a customer, but some of it may not.

ETHICS, ETHICS, ETHICS

As our final note to you, we cannot stress enough again the importance of ethics as they guide your behavior toward other people in your career. We realize that business is business and that businesses need to make money to survive. But the recent scandals involving Enron and others in the corporate world should be a reminder of how important your personal ethical compass is to you. Success shouldn't come to the detriment of other people. It's quite possible to be very ethical and very successful. That's our challenge to you.

Summary: Student Learning Outcomes Revisited

1. **Describe the emerging trends and technologies that will have an impact on the changing Internet.**
Emerging trends and technologies that will have an impact on the changing Internet include:

- *Software-as-a-service (Saas)*—delivery model for software in which you pay for software on a pay-per-use basis instead of buying the software outright.

- *Push*—technology environment in which businesses and organizations come to you via technology with information, services, and product offerings based on your profile.
- *F2b2C (Factory-to-business-to-Consumer)*—an e-commerce business model in which a consumer communicates through a business on the Internet and directly provides product specifications to a factory that makes the customized and personalized product to the consumer's specifications and then ships it directly to the consumer.
- *VoIP (Voice over Internet Protocol)*—allows you to send voice communications over the Internet and avoid the toll charges that you would normally receive from your long distance carrier.
- *Web 2.0*—second generation of the Web focusing on online collaboration, users as both creators and modifiers of content, dynamic and customized information feeds, and many other services.

2. **Define the various types of technologies that are emerging as we move toward physiological interaction with technology.** Emerging technologies in the area of physiological interaction include:

- *Automatic speech recognition (ASR)*—a system that not only captures spoken words but also distinguishes word groupings to form sentences.
- *Virtual reality*—three-dimensional computer simulation in which you actively and physically participate.
- *CAVE (cave automatic virtual environment)*—special 3-D virtual reality room that can display images of other people and objects located in other CAVEs all over the world.
- *Haptic interface*—uses technology to add the sense of touch to an environment that previously only had visual and textual elements.
- *Biometrics*—use of physiological characteristics—such as your fingerprint, the

blood vessels in the iris of your eye, the sound of your voice, or perhaps even your breath—to provide identification.

3. **Describe the emerging trends of Near Field Communication, Bluetooth, WiFi, cell phones, and RFID, as they relate to the wireless environment.** Emerging trends related to the wireless environment include:

- *Near Field Communication (NFC)*—short-range wireless technology developed mainly for use in mobile phones.
- *Bluetooth*—standard for transmitting information in the form of short-range radio waves over distances of up to 30 feet.
- *Wifi*—standard for transmitting information in the form of radio waves over distances up to about several miles.
- Cell phones—advances in storage capacity, processor capability, music enhancements, and video support—and threats such as viruses and hackers.
- *RFID (radio frequency identification)*—the use of a chip or label to store information, by which information is transmitted from, or written to, the tag or label when the chip is exposed to the correct frequency of radio waves.

4. **Define and describe emerging technologies that, while purely technology, can and will impact the future.** These technologies include:

- *Nanotechnology*—a discipline that seeks to control matter at the atomic and sub-atomic levels for the purpose of building devices on the same small scale.
- *Multi-state CPU*—works with information represented in more than just two states, probably 10 states with each state representing a digit between 0 and 9.
- *Holographic storage device*—a device that stores information on a storage medium that is composed of 3-D crystal-like objects with many sides or faces.

CLOSING CASE STUDY ONE

THE NBA GOES NFC

You might hold a future technological innovation in your hand right now if you attended an Atlanta Hawks basketball game during the 2006–2007 season. The Atlanta hawks distributed some 250 Nokia 3220 phones to season tickets holders who also have Chase Visa cards and are Cingular Wireless subscribers.

The phones are NFC-enabled. **NFC,** or **Near Field Communication,** is a wireless transmission technology being developed primarily for cell phones to support mobile commerce (m-commerce) and other cell phone activities. NFC—unlike other wireless technologies such as Bluetooth and Wifi which use radio waves for communication—works on magnetic field induction.

Atlanta Hawk season ticket holders lucky enough to be given one of these phones could use them for many purposes including:

- Buying food, drinks, merchandise, and other concessions
- Downloading player animations, ring tones, and wallpaper (of the Atlanta Hawks team, of course)

For buying merchandise, the phones contained electronic wallet (e-wallet) software that acted as an intermediary between the concession reader device that contained the total for the purchase amount and the user's Chase Visa card. Without fumbling around to find cash or a credit card, the user simply waved his or her phone within four centimeters of the reader device. The person's Chase Visa account was then automatically charged the appropriate amount. This is quite similar to how RFID works, which we covered in this chapter. However, unlike many RFID implementations, which require you to carry a special RFID-enabled card or other device, NFC technology is embedded into your cell phone, something that most people carry around with them all the time.

For downloading content to the cell phone, the Atlanta Hawks created 60 smart posters. These smart posters—although seemingly just paper posters on the wall—contained electronic content such as ring tones and images. Using the phone, a season ticket holder could select the content he or she wanted, and then—again—wave the phone within four centimeters of the poster. The selected content was then downloaded to the cell phone. Player animations were free, but other content such as ring tones cost about $2 to $3 each, with the billing being handled by Cingular.

Near Field Communication is a technology that has been endorsed by just about every mobile network operator. Further, most payment service providers (i.e., banks, credit card issuers, debit card issuers, and pre-paid card issuers) have also endorsed NFC as the short-range communications media of the future for mobile phones. Big companies like Motorola and MasterCard are among the many endorsing the use of NFC.

The goal is to allow you to keep your account and card information on your cell phone. Most people now have cell phones and carry them with them wherever they go. In the case of bank and credit card accounts, the e-wallet software interacts with very little private financial information stored on the cell phone. The cell phone typically contains only an account number. The e-wallet software uses that account number to connect to the issuer's infrastructure via the cell phone network. On the back end on the issuer's side, account information is accessed and updated. The only communication back to the e-wallet software on the cell phone is that the transaction was either successful or denied.

When fully implemented, NFC-enabled financial transactions via your cell phone will enable you to buy a variety of goods and services. Some of these purchases can be extremely small (called micropayments), even less than $1. These types of purchases will be extremely fast, enabling retailers to move people more quickly through lines.

You will probably even be able to buy some types of merchandise, store it on your cell phone, and save it for later "consumption" or use. For example, at a movie theater you could buy tickets early in the day for an evening show time and save them on your cell phone. When you get to the movie theater in the evening, you walk directly through the line where tickets are taken, stopping only long enough for a reader device to determine that your cell phone has the appropriate tickets.[12,13]

Questions

1. Do a little research on the Web. To what extent has Near Field Communication and these types of contactless payments become a reality? What cell phone service providers offer electronic wallet capabilities?

2. How might NFC-enabled financial transactions support the software-as-a-service model? How might NFC-enabled financial transactions support the push technology concept?

3. What about security? If someone steals your NFC-enabled phone, they may have access to your accounts. What are providers doing in the area of security?

4. How are NFC-enabled financial transactions further evidence that we are moving toward an e-society? Can you foresee a time when physical cards (credit, debit, and the like) will no longer be needed? What other cards do you carry in your wallet that could become a part of your e-wallet in your phone?

5. How can NFC-enabled financial transactions be used to support the notion of the *Long Tail* we discussed in Chapter 5?

CLOSING CASE STUDY TWO

TRACKING YOUR CHILDREN

You may not have children yet, but chances are that you someday will. Given the number of predators looking for children, parents today are more concerned for the safety of their children than ever before.

CELL PHONES FOR THE PARENTS OF CHILDREN

Most adults have cell phones, including those who also have children. And now children are quickly becoming the largest group of purchasers of cell phones and cell phone services. According to M:Metrics (a wireless research company), Sprint alone has 2.4 million subscribers ages 13 to 17 in the United States. And that doesn't include children who have cell phone services with AT&T, Cricket, and the many other cell phone service providers.

Even children as young as four years old are getting cell phones. For these young children, many cell phone manufacturers provide cell phones with only four (very large) buttons. The parents of these youngsters program the cell phone by providing a different phone number for each large button. That way children don't even have to remember a phone number, just which button to push.

Moreover, new cell phone services are available that allow parents to track the location of a child using global positioning system (GPS) technology. Such a ser-

vice, called *Family Locator,* is offered by Sprint. The service is for families with multiple phones on the same service plan. When signing up, parents can specify which of the individual phones they would like to track via GPS technology.

Then, using the Locator function, a parent can view on-screen (or at a secure Web site) the location of a particular phone, and thus the location of the child using the phone. If GPS capability isn't available at the location of the child, the system can still determine location based on the nearest cell phone tower.

Parents can also program a child's phone to immediately send a text message upon safe arrival to school, a day care center, or any other location. The child doesn't have to take any action to send the text message. Using GPS technology, when the location of the cell phone matches the preassigned text messaging location, the phone automatically sends the message.

TRACKING YOUR CHILD DRIVING A CAR

Horizon Technologies recently released a GPS tracking-based technology that many parents are installing in the cars of their children. Called *Millennium Plus,* the system allows an administrator (a parent, in this case) to access a secure Web site and view tremendous detail of the car on which the device is installed. This information can include speed, direction, and real-time maps showing the car in motion. Further, the *Millennium Plus* allows parents to disable the starter and lock and unlock doors remotely.[14,15]

Questions

1. After reading this case study, you may immediately think of yourself and your parents' ability to track you. But think about parents with a 10-year-old child. Is it an invasion of that child's privacy? Why or why not? Up to what age do you believe parents should be able to track the location of a child? Justify your answer.

2. With a service like *Family Locator,* you may never again lose your cell phone. You could, when signing up for cell phone service, specify that you would like to track yourself. If you ever lose your phone, you could log on to a Web site and determine its location. Is this a service you would be interested in? How much would you be willing to pay each month for this service?

3. When a parent does a location search on a child (based on the location of the child's cell phone), should the child's cell phone notify him/her that a parent is looking for him/her? Should parents disclose when they are tracking their children or is this a parental right? Justify your answer.

4. Think broadly for a moment concerning other applications of these sorts of tracking technology. What if a parent didn't want a child to go into a certain store? Could this sort of tracking technology be used such that the parent would receive a text message if the child entered that store or parked near that store? Has this taken tracking capabilities too far? Why or why not?

5. Think about your partner (girlfriend, boyfriend, whatever). Would the two of you be willing to establish reciprocal service that allowed each of you to track the other? Why or why not?

Key Terms And Concepts

Application service provider (ASP), 255
Automatic speech recognition (ASR), 260
Biochip, 265
Biometrics, 262
Blog, 259
Bluetooth, 266
Cave automatic virtual environment (CAVE), 261
Crowdsourcing, 258
Disintermediation, 257
Facial recognition software, 265
Factory-to-business-to-Consumer (F2b2C), 257

Feature analysis, 260
Glove, 260
Haptic interface, 262
Headset (head-mounted display), 260
Holographic device, 261
Holographic storage device, 270
Implant chip, 265
Language processing, 260
Multi-state CPU, 270
Nanotechnology, 269
Near Field Communication (NFC), 274
Pattern classification, 260
Podcasting, 259

Push technology, 256
Radio frequency identification (RFID), 267
RSS feed, 259
Social networking site, 258
Software-as-a-service (Saas), 255
Virtual reality, 260
Voice over Internet Protocol (VoIP), 258
Walker, 260
Web 2.0, 258
WiFI (wireless fidelity), 266
Wiki, 258

Short-Answer Questions

1. How will software-as-a-service (Saas) make use of a personal application service provider?

2. How does push technology differ from spam?

3. What is disintermediation? How does the F2b2C e-commerce model support disintermediation?

4. What exciting applications are associated with the Web 2.0?

5. How does automatic speech recognition work?

6. What are the devices commonly associated with virtual reality?

7. What role do haptic interfaces play?

8. What is the best form of personal identification?

9. How can you expect cell phones to change in the future?

10. What is RFID?

11. How does nanotechnology differ from traditional manufacturing?

Assignments and Exercises

1. **SELLING THE IDEA OF IMPLANT CHIPS AT YOUR SCHOOL** Let's assume for a moment that your team is in favor of using implant chips that contain vitally important information such as identification and medical information. Your task is to put together a sales presentation to your school that would require all students to obtain implant chips. In your presentation, include the following:

   A. The school-related information that each implant chip would contain
   B. The nonschool-related information that each implant chip would contain
   C. The processes within your school that would use the information on the implant chips
   D. The benefits your school would realize by requiring implant chips
   E. The benefits students would realize by having implant chips

   Your presentation should be no more than five minutes, so it must be a powerful selling presentation.

2. **FINDING A GOOD AUTOMATIC SPEECH RECOGNITION SYSTEM** Research the Web for automatic speech recognition (ASR) systems. Make a list of the ones you find. What are the prices of each? Are they speaker-independent or speaker-dependent? Do they support continuous speech recognition or discrete speech recognition? What sort of add-on vocabularies can you purchase? How comfortable would you feel speaking the contents of a term paper as opposed to typing it? Would you have to be more or less organized to use speech recognition as opposed to typing? Why?

3. **UNDERSTANDING THE RELATIONSHIPS BETWEEN TRENDS AND TECHNOLOGICAL INNOVATIONS** In this chapter, we presented you with numerous key technologies and how they relate to four important trends. (See Figure 9.1 on page 254 for the list of technologies and trends.) For each trend, identify all the technologies presented in this chapter that can have an impact. For each technology that you do identify, provide a short discussion of how it might have an impact.

4. **RESEARCHING APPLICATIONS OF RFID** Visit the Web and perform a search on RFID for applications that we didn't discuss in this chapter. Prepare a short PowerPoint presentation highlighting each. Also, search the Web for the leading providers of RFID technologies. What companies did you find? Does one seem to stand out above the rest? If so, which is it?

5. **RESEARCHING INTELLIGENT HOME APPLIANCES** Visit a local appliance store in your area and find three home appliances that contain some sort of intelligence (i.e., an embedded computer chip that takes over some of the functionality and decision making). For each appliance, prepare a short report that includes the following information:

   - A description and price for the intelligent home appliance
   - The "intelligent" features of the appliance
   - How those features make the appliance better than the nonintelligent version

Discussion Questions

1. There is currently much legislation pending in many states that would make it illegal for people to use a cell phone while driving a car. The reason is that society has already noticed a significant increase in the number of traffic accidents in which one of the drivers involved in the accident was using a cell phone. Think beyond that for a moment and include wearable computers. As this new technology becomes more widely available, isn't it possible for someone to be driving a car while using a computer? Should the government enact legislation to prevent it? Why or why not?

2. In a push technology environment, businesses and organizations will come to you with information, services, and product offerings based on your profile. How is a push technology environment different from mass mailings and spam? Is it an invasion of your privacy to have organizations calling you on your cell phone every time you come near a store? Why or why not? Should you be able to "opt in" or "opt out" of these offerings? Is this really any different from someone leaving a flyer at your house or on your car while it's parked in a parking lot?

3. There are three steps in automatic speech recognition (ASR): feature analysis, pattern classification, and language processing. Which of those three steps is the most challenging for a computer to perform? Why? Which of those three steps is the least challenging for a computer to perform? Why? If ASR systems are to become automatic speech understanding systems, which step must

undergo the greatest improvement in its capabilities? Why?

4. Much debate surrounds the use of biometrics. Many people like it because biometrics can provide identification and increase security. Other people see it as a tremendous invasion of your privacy. Just as you read in this chapter, a bank—by using biometric identification—may be able to tell if a woman is pregnant. So, the greatest challenge to overcome is not technological but rather societal. What do you think needs to happen for society to accept the use of biometrics? How long do you think it will be before society accepts the use of biometrics? In what year do you believe the U.S. federal government will begin requiring a biometric of every newborn child?

5. What are the ethical dilemmas associated with using facial recognition software? Is the use of this type of software really any different from a store asking to see your driver's license when you use your credit card? Why or why not? Should the government be able to place digital video cameras on every street corner and use facial recognition software to monitor your movements? Why or why not?

6. When (and if) CAVEs become a common reality, you'll be able to visit your family and friends anytime you want no matter where they live. What sort of impact will this have on the travel industry? If you can see your relatives in a CAVE as often as you want, will you be more or less inclined to buy a plane ticket and visit them in person? Why or why not?

CHAPTER PROJECTS

Group Projects

- Assessing the Value of Outsourcing Information Technology: Creating Forecasts (p. 372)
- Making the Case with Presentation Software: Information Technology Ethics (p. 374)
- Developing an Enterprise Resource Planning System: Planning, Reporting, and Data Processing (p. 377)
- Assessing a Wireless Future: Emerging Trends and Technology (p. 378)
- Evaluating the Next Generation: Dot-Com ASPs (p. 379)
- Evaluating the Security of Information: Wireless Network Vulnerability (p. 386)

e-Commerce Projects

- Interviewing and Negotiating Tips (p. 389)
- Free and Rentable Storage Space (p. 391)
- Financial Aid Resources (p. 393)
- Global Statistics and Resources (p. 394)
- Searching for MBA Programs (p. 399)
- Searching Job Databases (p. 399)

APPENDIX A

COMPUTER HARDWARE AND SOFTWARE

Student Learning Outcomes

1. DEFINE INFORMATION TECHNOLOGY (IT) AND ITS TWO BASIC CATEGORIES: HARDWARE AND SOFTWARE.

2. DESCRIBE THE CATEGORIES OF COMPUTERS BASED ON SIZE.

3. COMPARE THE ROLES OF PERSONAL PRODUCTIVITY, VERTICAL MARKET, AND HORIZONTAL MARKET SOFTWARE.

4. DESCRIBE THE ROLES OF OPERATING SYSTEM AND UTILITY SOFTWARE AS COMPONENTS OF SYSTEM SOFTWARE.

5. DEFINE THE PURPOSE OF EACH OF THE SIX MAJOR CATEGORIES OF HARDWARE.

A Quick Tour of Technology

Information technology (IT) is any computer-based tool that people use to work with information and support the information and information-processing needs of an organization. IT includes the Internet, spreadsheet software, a satellite, a gamepad for playing video games . . . the list of the technology you can find in your immediate life is almost endless (see Figure A.1). There are two basic categories of information technology: hardware and software. ***Hardware*** consists of the physical devices that make up a computer, for instance, keyboard, mouse, modem, flash memory drive (also called a

Figure A.1

Information Technology (IT) Includes Many Tools

thumb drive), printer. **Software** is the set of instructions your hardware executes to carry out a specific task for you such as creating a graph (spreadsheet software, for example) and surfing the Web (Internet Explorer, for example). Combined, hardware and software in aggregate are what people refer to as a *computer,* and even that term is becoming more blurred each day with digital media players, cell phones, and the like.

All hardware falls into one or another of six categories. Here's a quick summary.

1. Input: **Input devices** are tools you use to enter information and commands.
2. Output: **Output devices** are tools you use to see, hear, or otherwise recognize the results of your information-processing requests.
3. Storage: **Storage devices** are tools you use to store information for use at a later time.
4. Processing: The **central processing unit (CPU)** is the actual hardware that interprets and executes the software instructions and coordinates the operation of all other hardware. **RAM,** or **random access memory,** is a temporary holding area for the information you're working with, as well as the system and application software instructions that the CPU currently needs.
5. Telecommunications: A **telecommunications device** is a tool you use to send information to and receive it from another person or computer in a network. Telecommunications, as a field, and its associated devices is so broad that we've devoted an entire module to the topic. Please read Appendix B to learn about cable and DSL modems, home networks, fiber optics, and much more.
6. Connecting: *Connecting devices* include such things as USB ports into which you would connect a printer and connector cords to connect your printer to the port.

The two main types of software are application and system software. **Application software** is the software that enables you to solve specific problems or perform specific tasks. Microsoft PowerPoint, for example, can help you create slides for a presentation, so it's application software. Adobe Dreamweaver is an example of application software because it helps you create and publish a Web page or Web site. A business would use payroll software, collaborative software such as videoconferencing, and inventory management software.

System software handles tasks specific to technology management and coordinates the interaction of all technology devices. System software includes both operating system software and utility software. **Operating system software** is system software that controls your application software and manages how your hardware devices work together. Popular personal operating system software includes Microsoft Windows, Mac OS (for Apple computers), and Linux (an open-source operating system). There are also operating systems for networks (Microsoft Windows Server is an example), operating systems for personal digital assistants (Windows Mobile is an example), and operating systems for just about every other type of technology configuration, even for refrigerators.

Utility software is software that provides additional functionality to your operating system software. Utility software includes anti-virus software, screen savers, spam blocker software, uninstaller software (for properly removing unwanted software), and a host of other types. Some types of utility software are nice to have, like screen savers, while others are essential. For example, anti-virus software protects you from computer viruses that can be deadly for your computer. You definitely need anti-virus software.

This ends our quick tour of technology. In the remainder of this appendix we'll explore categories of computers by size, software in more detail, and hardware in more detail.

Categories of Computers by Size

Computers come in different shapes, sizes, and colors. Some are small enough that you can carry them around with you, while others are the size of a family refrigerator. Size is usually related to power and speed, and thus price.

PERSONAL DIGITAL ASSISTANTS (PDAS)

A *personal digital assistant (PDA)* is a small handheld computer that helps you surf the Web and perform simple tasks such as note taking, calendaring, appointment scheduling, and maintaining an address book. Most PDA screens are touch sensitive, allowing you to write directly on the screen, with the screen capturing what you're writing. PDAs offer a variety of operating system software; some use Windows CE (which stands for Compact Edition) or Palm OS (specifically for Palm devices). PDAs today cost between $100 and $500, depending on capabilities and features.

TABLET PCS

A *tablet PC* is a pen-based computer that provides the screen capabilities of a PDA with the functional capabilities of a notebook or desktop computer. Similar to PDAs, tablet PCs allow you to use a writing pen or stylus to write notes on the screen and touch the screen to perform functions such as clicking on a link while visiting a Web site. Tablet PCs come in two designs—convertibles and slates. Convertible tablet PCs look like notebook computers, including a screen that you lift up and set in position with a full keyboard and touch pad underneath. Using a convertible PC, you can swivel the screen and lay it flat on the keyboard, converting it into a notebook with no top that closes.

Figure A.2

PDAs, Tablet PCs, and Notebooks

Slate tablet PCs come with no integrated physical keyboard, making the tablet the entire computer. You can buy a docking station for a slate tablet PC, giving you the ability to connect a keyboard and mouse.

NOTEBOOK COMPUTERS

A *notebook computer* is a small, portable, fully functional, battery-powered computer. Notebooks come equipped with all the technology you need to meet your personal needs and weigh as little as 3 pounds. If you need a fully functional computer in a variety of places—home, work, school, and/or on the road—then a notebook computer may be just the answer. Notebook computers range in price from about $600 to several thousand dollars depending on the selected configuration.

DESKTOP COMPUTERS

A *desktop computer* is the most popular choice for personal computing needs. You can choose a desktop computer with a horizontal system box (the box is where the CPU, RAM, and storage devices are held) or choose a desktop computer with a vertical system box (called a tower) that you usually place on the floor near your work area. Desktop computers range in price from a little less than $500 to several thousand dollars. Dollar for dollar with comparable characteristics, a desktop computer is faster and more powerful than a notebook computer. Some desktops are built especially for gaming (see Figure A.3).

Figure A.3

Desktop for Gaming

Which one you need—PDA, tablet PC, notebook, or desktop computer—is a function of your unique individual needs. PDAs offer great portability and allow you to keep a calendar, send and receive e-mail, take short notes, and even access the Web. But they're not designed to help you write a term paper, build a Web site, or create a complex graph with statistical software. For these and more complex tasks, you would need a notebook, tablet PC, or a desktop computer.

So, the next question is, should you buy a notebook or a tablet PC? Most likely, you need a computer that supports full word processing, spreadsheet, presentation, Web site development, and some other capabilities. You need to decide where you'll need your computer. If you need to use your computer both at home and at school (or perhaps at work), then you should buy one of these because they are, in fact, portable. So, if you'd like to be able to surf the Web and get e-mail in your hotel room while on a business or vacation trip, a notebook computer or a tablet PC may be what you need.

In the future, we believe the capabilities of PDAs will improve so that you can in fact perform "complex" tasks such as creating an elaborate spreadsheet or graph and even integrating speech recognition. To learn more about some of today's best PDAs, connect to the Web site that supports this text at www.mhhe.com/haag.

MINICOMPUTERS, MAINFRAME COMPUTERS, AND SUPERCOMPUTERS

PDAs, notebooks, and desktop computers are designed to meet your personal information-processing needs. In business, however, many people often need to access and use the same computer simultaneously. In this case, businesses need computing technologies that multiple people (perhaps hundreds or even thousands) can access and use at the same time. Computers of this type include minicomputers, mainframe computers, and supercomputers (see Figure A.4).

A *minicomputer* (sometimes called a *mid-range computer*) is designed to meet the computing needs of several people simultaneously in a small to medium-size business

Figure A.4

Minicomputers,
Mainframes, and
Supercomputers

environment. Minicomputers are more powerful than desktop computers but also cost more, ranging in price from $5,000 to several hundred thousand dollars. Businesses often use minicomputers as servers, either for hosting a Web site or as an internal computer on which shared information and software is placed. For this reason, minicomputers are well suited for business environments in which people need to share common information, processing power, and/or certain peripheral devices such as high-quality, fast laser printers.

A *mainframe computer* (sometimes just called a *mainframe*) is a computer designed to meet the computing needs of hundreds of people in a large business environment. So mainframe computers are a step up in size, power, capability, and cost from minicomputers. Mainframes can easily cost in excess of $1 million. With processing speeds greater than 1 trillion instructions per second (compared to a typical desktop that can process approximately three billion instructions per second), mainframes can easily handle the processing requests of hundreds (or thousands) of people simultaneously.

A *supercomputer* is the fastest, most powerful, and most expensive type of computer. Organizations such as NASA and the National Weather Service that are heavily involved in research and "number crunching" employ supercomputers because of the speed with which they can process information. Very large, customer-oriented businesses such as General Motors and AT&T also employ supercomputers just to handle customer information and transaction processing. Their business needs require the high level of support and the powerful processing power provided by supercomputers.

How much do you really need to know about the technical specifics (CPU speed, storage disk capacity, and so on), prices, and capabilities of minicomputers, mainframe computers, and supercomputers? Probably not much, unless you plan to major in information technology. What you should concentrate on is the technical specifics, prices, and capabilities of

PDAs, tablet PCs, notebooks, and desktop computers. These tools will be your companions for your entire business career. Learn about them and know them well—on an ongoing basis.

Software: Your Intellectual Interface

LEARNING OUTCOME 3

The most important tool in your technology tool set is software. Software contains the instructions that your hardware executes to perform an information-processing task for you. So, software is really your *intellectual interface*, designed to automate processing tasks. Without software, your computer is little more than a very expensive doorstop. As we've stated, there are two categories of software: application software and system software.

APPLICATION SOFTWARE

Application software is the software you use to meet your specific information-processing needs, including payroll, customer relationship management, project management, training, word processing, and many, many others. Application software can be categorized as either personal productivity software or vertical and horizontal market software.

PERSONAL PRODUCTIVITY SOFTWARE   *Personal productivity software* helps you perform personal tasks—such as writing a memo, creating a graph, and creating a slide presentation—that you can usually do even if you don't own a computer. You're probably already familiar with some personal productivity software tools including Microsoft Word, Microsoft Excel, Netscape Communicator, Mozilla Firefox, and Quicken (personal finance software).

Figure A.5 describes the 10 major categories of personal productivity software and some of the more popular packages within each category.

VERTICAL AND HORIZONTAL MARKET SOFTWARE   While performing organizational processes in your career, you'll also frequently use two other categories of application software: vertical market software and horizontal market software.

Vertical market software is application software that is unique to a particular industry. For example, the health care industry has a variety of application software unique to that market segment, including radiology software, patient-scheduling software, nursing allocation software, and pharmaceutical software. Vertical market software is written specifically for an industry. Health care industry patient-scheduling software wouldn't work well for scheduling hair styling and manicure appointments in a beauty salon.

Horizontal market software, on the other hand, is application software that is general enough to be suitable for use in a variety of industries. Examples of horizontal market software include

- Inventory management
- Payroll
- Accounts receivable
- Billing
- Invoice processing
- Human resource management

Category	Examples*
Word processing—Helps you create papers, letters, memos, and other basic documents	• Microsoft Word • Corel WordPerfect
Spreadsheet—Helps you work primarily with numbers, including performing calculations and creating graphs	• Microsoft Excel • Corel Quattro Pro
Presentation—Helps you create and edit information that will appear in electronic slides	• Microsoft PowerPoint • Corel Presentations
Desktop publishing—Extends word processing software by including design and formatting techniques to enhance the layout and appearance of a document	• Microsoft Publisher • Quark QuarkXPress
Personal information management (PIM)—Helps you create and maintain (1) to-do lists, (2) appointments and calendars, and (3) points of contact	• Microsoft Outlook • Corel Central
Personal finance—Helps you maintain your checkbook, prepare a budget, track investments, monitor your credit card balances, and pay bills electronically	• Quicken Quicken • Microsoft Money
Web authoring—Helps you design and develop Web sites and pages that you publish on the Web	• Adobe Flash • Adobe Dreamweaver
Graphics—Helps you create and edit photos and art	• Microsoft PhotoDraw • Adobe PhotoShop
Communications—Helps you communicate with other people	• Microsoft Outlook • Internet Explorer
Database management system (DBMS)—Helps you specify the logical organization for a database and access and use the information within a database	• Microsoft Access • FileMaker FileMaker Pro

* Publisher name given first.

Figure A.5
Categories of Personal Productivity Software

The preceding functions (and many others) are very similar, if not identical, across many different industries, enabling software publishers to develop one particular piece of software (e.g., accounts receivable) that can be used by many different industries.

Personal productivity software is actually a type of horizontal market software in that it is general enough to be suitable for use in a variety of industries. No matter what industry you work in, you need basic word processing software for creating memos, business plans, and other basic documents.

There are, however, some key differences between personal productivity software and horizontal (and vertical) market software. First is the issue of price. You can buy a full suite of personal productivity software for less than $400. In contrast, some individual horizontal and vertical market software packages may cost $500,000 or more. Second is the issue of customizability. When you purchase personal productivity software, you cannot change the way it works. That is, you're buying the right to use it but not to change how it operates. With horizontal and vertical market software you may be able to purchase the right to change the way the software works. So, if you find a payroll software package that fits most of your organizational needs, you can buy the software and the right to change the operation of the software so that it meets your needs precisely. This is a very common business practice when purchasing and using horizontal and vertical market software.

In Chapter 6 (Systems Development), we discuss how organizations go about the process of developing software for their particular needs, including how organizations can and do purchase vertical and horizontal market software and then customize that software.

LEARNING OUTCOME 4

SYSTEM SOFTWARE

System software supports your application software. System software controls how your various technology tools work together as you use your application software to perform specific information-processing tasks. System software includes two basic categories: operating system software and utility software.

OPERATING SYSTEM SOFTWARE *Operating system software* is system software that controls your application software and manages how your hardware devices work together. For example, using Excel to create a graph, if you choose to print the graph, your operating system software takes over, ensures that you have a printer attached and that the printer has paper (and tells you if it doesn't), and sends your graph to the printer along with instructions on how to print it.

Your operating system software supports a variety of useful features, one of which is multitasking. *Multitasking* allows you to work with more than one piece of software at a time. Suppose you wanted to create a graph in Excel and insert it into a word processing document. With multitasking, you can have both pieces of application software open at the same time, and even see both on the screen. So, when you complete the creation of your graph, you can easily copy and paste it into your word processing document without having to exit the spreadsheet software and then start your word processing software.

There are different types of operating system software for personal environments and for organizational environments that support many users simultaneously. The latter, called *network operating systems* or *NOSs,* we explore in *Appendix B: Network Basics.* Popular *personal* operating systems include

- *Microsoft Windows Vista*—Microsoft's latest personal computer operating system in a wide range of editions including Vista Home Basic, Vista Home Premium, Vista Business, and Vista Ultimate.
- *Microsoft Windows XP Home*—Microsoft's predecessor to the Vista personal computer operating system designed specifically for home users.
- *Microsoft Windows XP Professional (Windows XP Pro)*—Microsoft's predecessor to the Vista personal computer operating system with enhanced features to support home users and business users.
- *Mac OS*—Apple's operating system.
- *Linux*—An open-source operating system that provides a rich operating environment for high-end workstations and network servers.

Open-source software is software for which the source code (how the software was actually written) is publicly available and free of charge. Unlike commercial software, open-source software is created and maintained by a distributed network of engineers, software developers, and users, each making contributions to the open-source software.

The advantages of open-source software are numerous. Because the source code is available, users of the software may modify the software to suit their needs and take comfort in the fact that changes they wish to make to the software are fully under their control. You can compare this with commercial, or closed-source, software, for which the customer must go to the vendor and pay for changes to be made and wait until the vendor has made those changes.

There are many examples of open-source software, including

- The Apache Web server
- Linux operating system
- MySQL, an open-source DBMS with commercial support

If you're considering purchasing a notebook computer that you'll use extensively at school connected to a network there, we recommend that you contact your school's technology support department to determine which operating system is best for you.

UTILITY SOFTWARE *Utility software* adds functionality to your operating system software. Sometimes it is crucial. A simple example is screen saver software (which is probably also a part of your operating system). The most important utility software is anti-virus software. *Anti-virus software* is utility software that detects and removes or quarantines computer viruses. Viruses are everywhere today, with 200 to 300 new ones surfacing each month. Some viruses are benign: They do something annoying like causing your screen to go blank but do not corrupt your information. Other viruses are deadly, perhaps reformatting your hard disk or altering the contents of your files. You definitely need anti-virus software to protect your computer. We talk much more about this vitally important topic and guarding against possible attacks that can be launched against your computer from cyberspace in Chapter 8.

Other types of utility software include

- *Crash-proof software*—Utility software that helps you save information if your system crashes and you're forced to turn it off and then back on again.
- *Uninstaller software*—Utility software that you can use to remove software from your hard disk that you no longer want.
- *Disk optimization software*—Utility software that organizes your information on your hard disk in the most efficient way.
- *Spam blocker software*—Utility software that filters unwanted e-mail from your inbox. Spam is roughly equivalent to unsolicited telephone marketing calls. The term *spam* is said to derive from a famous Monty Python sketch ("Well, we have Spam, tomato and Spam, egg and Spam, egg, bacon and Spam . . .") that was current when spam first began arriving on the Internet.
- *Anti-spyware software*—Utility software that detects and removes spyware and other unwanted software that can track every electronic move you make.

You definitely need utility software. Don't think of utility software as "optional" software just because it "adds" functionality to your computer. The above examples are just a few of the many types of utility software you'll find in a utility software suite. If you think about the above examples of utility software and what it does for you, especially anti-virus software, you can see how varied and helpful it is.

Hardware: Your Physical Interface

To properly understand the significant role of your hardware (the physical components of your computer), it helps to know something about how your computer works. You work with information in the form of characters (A–Z, a–z, and special ones such as an asterisk, a question mark, etc.) and numbers (0–9). Computers, on the other hand, work only with 1s and 0s in terms of what we call bits and bytes. Computers, that is, use electricity to function, and electrical pulses have two states: on and off, which are assigned the values of 1 and 0, respectively.

What are bits and bytes? A ***binary digit (bit)*** is the smallest unit of information that your computer can process. A bit can either be a 1 (on) or a 0 (off). The technical challenge is to be able to represent all our natural language characters, special symbols, and numbers in binary form. ASCII is one agreed-upon standard to do this. ***ASCII (American Standard Code for Information Interchange)*** is the coding system that most personal computers use to represent, process, and store information. In ASCII, a group of eight bits represents one natural language character and is called a ***byte.***

For example, if you were to type the word *cool* on the keyboard, your keyboard (a hardware device) would change it into four bytes—one byte for each character—that would look like the following to be used by your computer (see Figure A.6):

01100011   01001111   01001111   01001100
   c   o   o   l

This grouping of 1s and 0s would be used for "cool" as it moves around or is stored on your computer—as it travels from one device to another, is stored on a storage device, and is processed by your CPU.

There are three important conclusions that you should draw from this discussion so far. First, your hardware works with information in a different form (although with the same meaning) than you do. You work with characters, special symbols, and the numbers 0–9. Your computer, on the other hand, represents all these in a binary form, a unique collection of 1s and 0s. Second, the term *byte* is the bridge between people and a computer. A computer can store one character, special symbol, or number in a byte.

Third, the primary role of your input and output devices is to convert information from one form to another. Input devices convert information from human-readable form into bits and bytes, while output devices convert the 1s and 0s to something people can recognize. All other hardware works with bits and bytes.

Figure A.6

Information as It Moves from You through Your Computer

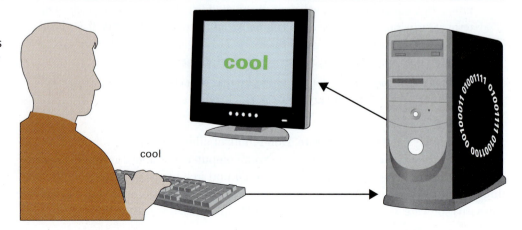

COMMON INPUT DEVICES

An *input device* is a tool you use to enter information and commands. You can use a keyboard to type in information, for example, and use a mouse to point and click on buttons and icons. As you saw in the previous section, input devices are responsible for converting information in human-readable form to the binary code that computers use. Below are the principal types of input devices being used today (see Figures A.7 and A.8).

- *Keyboards* are the most often used input devices for desktop and notebook computers, while styluses are the most frequently used input devices for PDAs and tablet PCs. A *stylus* is a penlike device used to write or draw on a PDA or tablet PC. Keyboards and styluses allow you to input both information and commands and both are used in business and personal settings.
- *Pointing devices* are devices that are used to navigate and select objects on a display screen.
- *Mouse*—a pointing device that you use to click on icons or buttons. The three types are mechanical (using a ball), optical (using red light), and wireless (using waves).
- *Trackball*—is similar to a mechanical mouse, but it has the ball on the top.
- *Touchpad*—is the little dark rectangle that you use to move the cursor with your finger, often found on notebook computers.
- *Pointing stick*—is a little rod (like a pencil-top eraser) used almost exclusively on notebook computers.

Figure A.7

Categories of Input Devices

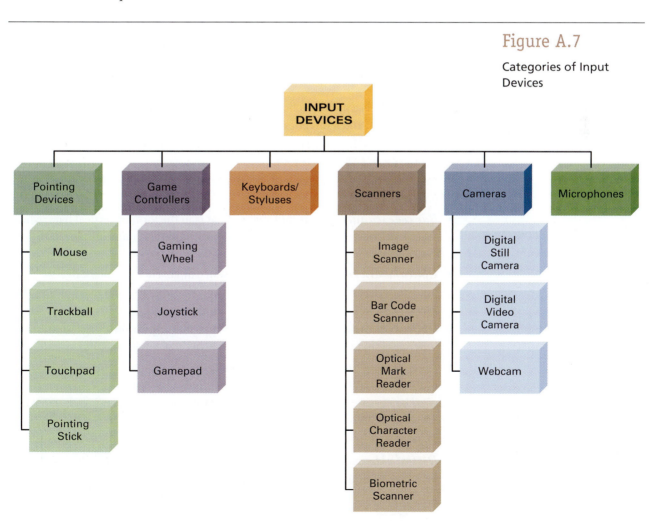

Figure A.8

Common Input Devices

- *Game controllers* are used for gaming to better control screen action.
  - *Gaming wheel*—is a steering wheel and foot pedals for virtual driving.
  - *Joystick*—is a vertical handle with programmable buttons that control action.
  - *Gamepad*—is a multifunctional input device with programmable buttons, thumb sticks, and a directional pad.
- *Scanners* are used to convert information that exists in visible form into electronic form.
  - *Image scanner*—captures images, photos, text, and artwork that already exist on paper.
  - *Bar code scanner*—reads information that is in the form of vertical bars, where their width and spacing represent digits (often used in point-of-sale [POS] systems in retail environments).
  - *Optical mark reader*—detects the presence or absence of a mark in a predetermined spot on the page (often used for true/false and multiple choice exam answers).
  - *Optical character reader*—reads characters that appear on a page or sales tag (often used in point-of-sale [POS] systems in retail environments).
  - *Biometric scanner*—scans some human physical attribute like your fingerprint or iris for security purposes.
- *Digital cameras* capture still images or video as a series of 1s and 0s. Some will capture only stills, others do both.
  - *Digital still camera*—digitally captures still images in varying resolutions.
  - *Digital video camera*—captures video digitally.
  - *Webcam*—captures digital video to upload to the Web.
  - *Microphones*—capture audio for conversion into electronic form.

COMMON OUTPUT DEVICES

An *output device* is a tool you use to see, hear, or otherwise recognize the results of your information-processing requests. The most common output devices for both business and personal computing environments are monitors and printers, but speakers and plotters (printers that generate drawings) are also output devices (see Figure A.9). Any device that converts the digital form of information in a computer to something that you can see, read, or hear is an output device.

MONITORS   Monitors come in two varieties: CRT or flat-panel displays (see Figure A.10). *CRTs* are the monitors that look like traditional television sets, while *flat-panel displays* are thin, lightweight monitors that take up much less space than CRTs. Flat-panel displays are either liquid crystal display or gas plasma display. *Liquid crystal display (LCD) monitors* make the screen image by sending electricity through crystallized liquid trapped between two layers of glass or plastic. *Gas plasma displays* send electricity through gas trapped between two layers of glass or plastic to create a screen image.

When selecting a monitor, the important features to consider, besides its price and physical size, are the monitor's (1) viewable image size, (2) resolution, and (3) dot pitch.

1. The *viewable image size (VIS)* is the size of the image. The quoted size (17", 19", etc.) is measured diagonally from corner to corner. In a flat-panel display, this size is the same as the distance from corner to opposite corner of the monitor's frame, while in a CRT it's slightly less since the image doesn't completely fill the screen area on a CRT. The physical size of a CRT, for a comparable image size, is usually larger since it's much deeper than the flat-panel displays.

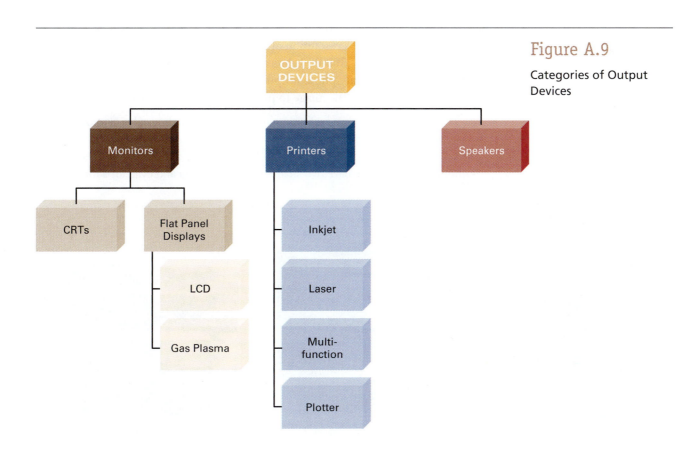

Figure A.9

Categories of Output Devices

Figure A.10

Monitors Are Common
Output Devices

2. The ***resolution of a screen*** is the number of pixels it has. ***Pixels (picture elements)*** are the dots that make up the image on your screen. For example, a monitor with a resolution of 1,280 × 1,024 has 1,280 pixels across and 1,024 pixels down the screen. The higher the resolution the better the image.

3. ***Dot pitch*** is the distance between the centers of a pair of like-colored pixels. So, a monitor with .24 mm dot pitch is better than one with .28 mm dot pitch because the dots are smaller and closer together, giving you a better quality image.

PRINTERS   Printers are another common type of output device (see Figure A.11). The sharpness and clarity of a printer's output depend on the printer's resolution. The ***resolution of a printer*** is the number of dots per inch (dpi) it produces. This is the same principle as the resolution in monitors. As is the case with monitors, the more dots per inch, the better the image, and consequently, the more costly the printer. High-end personal printers usually have a resolution of 1,600 × 1,600 or better. Multiplying these numbers together gives you 2,560,000 dots per square inch. Some printers, especially those that advertise high-quality photo output, achieve resolutions of 9,600 × 2,400 by making multiple passes across the image to produce the clarity needed.

- ***Inkjet printers*** make images by forcing ink droplets through nozzles. Standard inkjet printers use four colors: black, cyan (blue), magenta (purplish pink), and yellow. Some inkjet printers produce high-quality images and are often advertised as photo printers. These have two shades each of magenta and cyan for a total of six colors.

Figure A.11

Printers Are Also
Common Output Devices

- **Laser printers** form images using the same sort of electrostatic process that photocopiers use. Laser printers are usually more expensive than inkjets, but they have become dramatically cheaper lately. They usually provide better quality images than inkjets. They come in black and white and in color versions.

- **Multifunction printers** scan, copy, and fax, as well as print. These devices are very popular in homes and small offices since they offer so many features all in one unit. Multifunction printers can be either inkjet or laser.

- **Plotters** form their output by moving a pen across the surface of a piece of paper. Plotters were the first type of printer that could print with color and render graphics and full-size engineering drawings. As a rule, plotters are much more expensive than printers. They are most frequently used for CAE (computer-aided engineering) applications, such as CAD (computer-aided design) and CAM (computer-aided manufacturing).

COMMON STORAGE DEVICES

As opposed to RAM, which is temporary memory, storage media don't lose their contents when you turn off your computer. The main issues to consider when choosing a storage medium are (1) whether you want portability, (2) how much storage space you need, and (3) whether you need to change the information on the medium.

Some storage devices, such as hard disks, offer you easy update capabilities and high storage capacity, but may not be portable. Others, like flash memory devices, while they are portable and updateable, have less storage space. Still others like DVD-ROMs are portable with high capacity, but the information that comes on them can't be changed (see Figure A.12).

Capacities of storage media are measured in megabytes, gigabytes, and terabytes. A **megabyte (MB** or **M** or **Meg)** is roughly 1 million bytes; a **gigabyte (GB** or **Gig)** is roughly 1 billion bytes; and a **terabyte (TB)** is roughly 1 trillion bytes. A consumer hard disk would have a capacity of between 1 and 250 gigabytes while a hard disk for a large organization (also called a **hard disk pack**) can hold in excess of 100 TB of information. Common storage devices include

- Magnetic storage media:
  - **Hard disk**—magnetic storage device with one or more thin metal platters or disks that store information sealed inside the disk drive. You usually get one installed in your system unit (the computer box) when you buy a computer. If you need more hard disk space or want portability, you can get an external unit that you can plug into the USB ports. (We'll discuss USB ports in a later section.) A hard disk offers ease of updating and large storage capacity.

- **Optical storage media** are plastic discs on which information is stored, deleted, and/or changed using laser light and include CDs and DVDs, of which there are several types:
  - **CD-ROM (compact disc—read-only memory)**—an optical or laser disc whose information cannot be changed. A CD stores up to 800 Meg of information.
  - **CD-R (compact disc—recordable)**—an optical or laser disc that you can write to one time only.
  - **CD-RW (compact disc—rewritable)**—an optical or laser disc on which you can save, change, and delete files as often as you like.

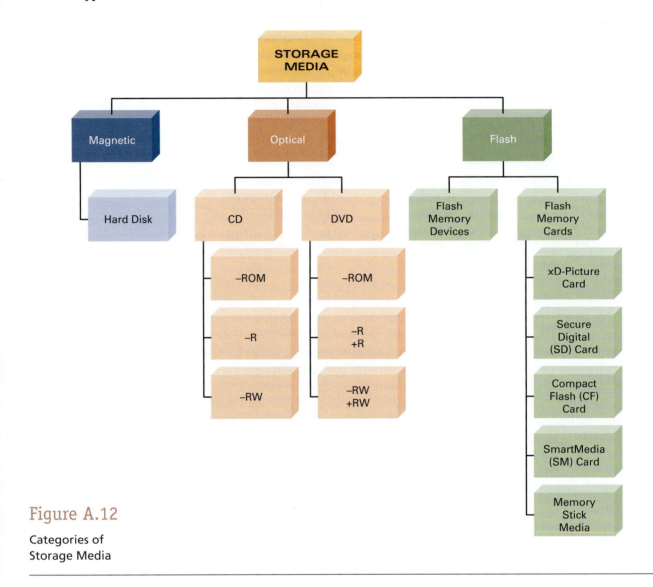

Figure A.12

Categories of
Storage Media

- ***DVD-ROM***—a high-capacity optical or laser disc whose information cannot be changed. The capacity of a DVD, unlike that of a CD, varies according to type.
- ***DVD-R*** or ***DVD+R (DVD—recordable)***—a high-capacity optical or laser disc to which you can write one time only.
- ***DVD-RW*** or ***DVD+RW*** (depending on the manufacturer)—a high-capacity optical or laser disc on which you can save, change, and delete files.
- Flash memory comes in two varieties: flash memory device and flash memory cards (see Figure A.13). A ***flash memory device*** (also called a jump drive or thumb drive) is a flash memory storage device that is small enough to fit on a key ring and plugs directly into the USB port on your computer. A flash memory card, on the other hand, has to be inserted into a reader, which in turn plugs into the USB port. ***Flash memory cards*** have

Figure A.13

Common Types of Flash Memory

high-capacity storage units laminated inside a small piece of plastic. There are several different types.

- ***xD-Picture (xD) cards***—flash memory card that looks like a rectangular piece of plastic smaller than a penny and about as thick, with one edge slightly curved. xD cards have capacities ranging from 32 to 512 megabytes.
- ***Secure Digital (SD) cards*** and ***MultiMediaCards (MMC)***—flash memory cards that look identical to each other (but SD cards have copy protection built-in), are a little larger than a quarter, and are slightly thicker than a credit card.
- ***CompactFlash (CF) cards***—flash memory cards slightly larger than a half-dollar, with capacities up to 6 gigabyte.
- ***SmartMedia (SM) cards***—flash memory cards that are a little longer than a CF card and about as thick as a credit card with capacities of up to 512 megabytes.
- ***Memory Stick Media cards***—elongated flash memory cards about the width of a penny developed by Sony with capacities up to 1 gigabyte.

CPU AND RAM

Together, your CPU and RAM make up the real brains of your computer (see Figure A.14). Your CPU largely determines the power (and also the price) of your computer. The ***central processing unit (CPU)*** is the hardware that interprets and executes the system and application software instructions and coordinates the operation of all other hardware. ***Random access memory (RAM)*** is a temporary holding area for the information you're working with as well as the system and application software instructions that the CPU currently needs.

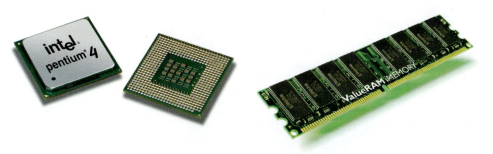

Figure A.14

CPU and RAM

You'll often hear the CPU referred to as a microprocessor or a CPU chip. The dominant manufacturers of CPUs include Intel (with its Celeron, Pentium, and Xeon series for personal computers) and AMD (with its Athlon and Opteron series). As a consumer, you'll probably find the most useful information about CPUs is their relative speeds.

Today's CPU speed is usually quoted in gigahertz. ***Gigahertz (GHz)*** is the number of billions of CPU cycles per second that the CPU can handle. The more cycles per second, the faster the processing and the more powerful the computer. Gigahertz refers to how fast the CPU can carry out the steps it takes to execute software instructions—a process sometimes called the CPU cycle or machine cycle. A ***CPU cycle (machine cycle)*** consists of retrieving, decoding, and executing the instruction, then returning the result to RAM, if necessary (see Figure A.15). When you load (or open) a program, you're telling your computer to send a copy of the program from the storage device (hard disk or CD) into RAM. In carrying out the software instructions, the CPU repeatedly performs machine cycles as follows:

1. *Retrieve an instruction:* The ***control unit,*** which is the component of the CPU that directs what happens in your computer, sends to RAM for instructions and the information it needs. If the instruction says to add 4 and 6, for example, the two numbers travel as information with the *add* instruction. The instruction travels from RAM on the system bus. The ***system bus*** consists of electrical pathways that move information between basic components of the motherboard, including between RAM and the CPU. When the instruction reaches the CPU it waits temporarily in ***CPU cache,*** which is a type of memory on the CPU where instructions called up by the CPU wait until the CPU is ready to use them. It takes much less time to get the instruction from CPU cache to the control unit than from RAM, so CPU cache speeds up processing.

2. *Decode the instruction:* The CPU gets the instruction out of cache and examines it to see what needs to be done, in this case, add 4 and 6.

3. *Execute the instruction:* The CPU then does what the instruction says to do. In our example, it sends the two numbers to the arithmetic logic unit to be added.

Figure A.15

Your CPU and RAM
at Work

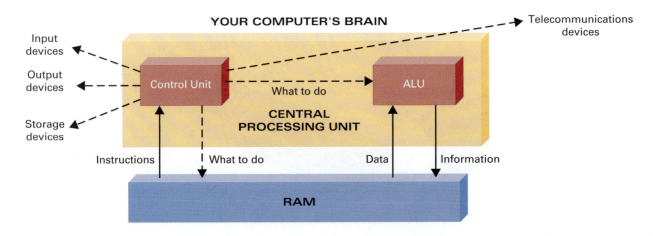

The ***arithmetic logic unit (ALU)*** is a component of the CPU that performs arithmetic, as well as comparison and logic operations.

4. *Store the result in RAM:* The CPU then sends the result of the addition, 10, to RAM. There's not always a result to send back to RAM. Sometimes the CPU does intermediate calculations that don't get saved.

You'll sometimes hear the CPU speed referred to as the "clock speed." This refers to the CPU clock. Every CPU has its own ***CPU clock,*** which is simply a sliver of quartz that beats at regular intervals in response to an electrical charge. The beat of the CPU clock is like the drummer in a marching band. Just as the drummer keeps everyone marching in time, the CPU clock keeps all your computer's operations synchronized. Each beat or tick of the CPU clock is called a clock cycle and is equivalent to a CPU cycle (machine cycle). The CPU uses the CPU clock to keep instructions and information marching through your CPU at a fixed rate.

RAM is a sort of whiteboard that your CPU uses while it processes information and software instructions. When you turn off your computer, everything in RAM disappears—that's why we call it "temporary." When you first start your computer, system instructions that are necessary to keep your computer running get written into RAM. Then, as you open applications, like Microsoft Word or Excel, the instructions to make those programs run join the operating system in RAM. As you type in your document or enter information into your workbook, that too is stored in RAM. When you've finished your work and save it, a copy is transferred from RAM to your disk or CD.

The most important thing you need to know about RAM is its capacity for storing instructions and information. RAM capacity is expressed in megabytes or gigabytes. You'll remember that a megabyte is roughly 1 million bytes. A byte is equivalent to a character. So RAM with a capacity of 256 megabytes can hold 256 million characters—that includes operating system instructions as well as the applications and information that you're currently using.

NOTEBOOK COMPUTER CPUS AND RAM   A notebook computer is to a desktop computer as a recreational vehicle is to a traditional home—everything is smaller, and power to run devices is limited since you have to carry the power sources with you. A ***mobile CPU*** is a special type of CPU for a notebook computer that changes speed, and therefore power consumption, in response to fluctuation in use. A desktop CPU, running at 1 GHz, uses between 75 and 1,090 watts of power whereas a mobile CPU might run at a much smaller 34 watts. RAM modules for notebook computers are smaller than those for desktop computers.

CONNECTING THE HARDWARE OUTSIDE TO THE HARDWARE INSIDE

Since the CPU controls all computer hardware, all hardware devices must be connected to the CPU, just as your limbs are connected to your brain through your spinal cord.

The CPU, along with RAM, is located on the large circuit board (called the *motherboard*) inside your system unit. The connector (or plug) on the end of the cable coming out of your printer connects it to the motherboard which then carries information between the CPU and the printer.

WIRED CONNECTIONS   All devices that are not wireless have connectors on the ends of cables that plug into ports on the computer. A ***port*** is the place on your system unit, monitor, or keyboard through which information and instructions flow to and from your computer system. For wired connections it's the opening or socket where you insert the connector, and for wireless devices a port is where the wave information goes in and out.

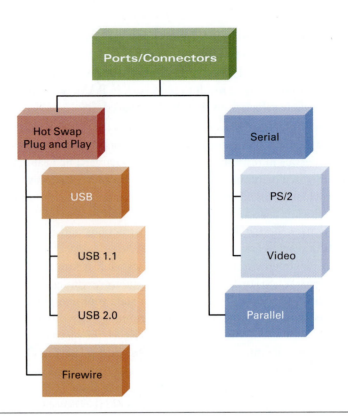

Figure A.16

Categories of Connectors
and Ports

The ports are accessible on the outside of the system unit and that means that you don't have to open up the system unit to plug in your scanner. There are various types of connectors/ports (see Figure A.16) including:

- *USB (universal serial bus) port*—fit small flat plug-and-play, hot-swap USB connectors, and, using USB hubs, you can connect up to 127 devices to a single USB port on your computer. *Hot swap* is an operating system feature that allows you—while your computer is running—to unplug a device and plug in a new one (without first shutting down your computer). *Plug and play* is an operating feature that finds and installs the device driver for a device that you plug into your computer. USB connectors/ports come in two speeds: USB 1.1 and USB 2.0 (which is faster), and in two physical shapes called Type A and Type B, respectively. Type A USB connectors/ports are all the same size and shape, but Type B USB connectors are smaller, squarer, and come in several different sizes. Type B connectors are usually on the end of the cable that plugs into the device (like a digital camera).
- *Firewire ports*—(also called *IEEE 1394* or *I-Link*) fit hot-swap, plug-and-play Firewire connectors, and you can connect up to 63 Firewire devices to a single Firewire port by daisy-chaining the devices together.
- *PS/2 ports*—fit PS/2 connectors, which you often find on keyboards and mice. PS/2 is a special type of serial connector/port. Serial connectors/ports are gradually being replaced by USB and Firewire.
- *Parallel ports*—fit parallel connectors, which are large flat connectors found almost exclusively on printer cables, but which are losing popularity in favor of USB.

Figure A.17 on the next page provides photo illustration of many of the ports and connectors we've just described.

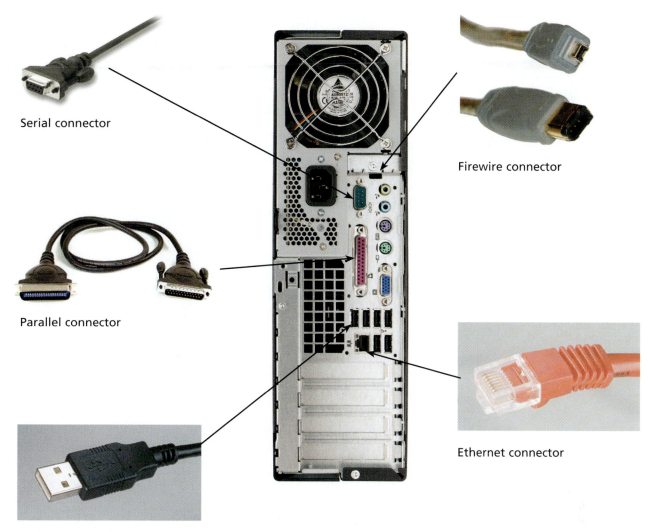

Serial connector

Firewire connector

Parallel connector

Ethernet connector

USB connector

Figure A.17

Ports and Connectors to Connect Devices to the CPU on the Motherboard

WIRELESS CONNECTIONS   Wireless devices transfer and receive information in the form of waves, either infrared or radio waves. Different types of waves have different frequencies. The three types most frequently used in personal and business computer environments are infrared, Bluetooth, and WiFi.

- *Infrared*—also called *IR* or *IrDA (infrared data association)* uses red light to send and receive information. Infrared light has a frequency that's below what the eye can see. It's used for TV remotes and other devices that operate over short distances (the effective distance is about one mile) that are free of obstacles.

- *Bluetooth*—is a standard for transmitting information in the form of short-range radio waves over distances of up to 30 feet and is used for purposes such as wirelessly connecting a cell phone or a PDA to a computer.

- *WiFi (wireless fidelity)*—is a standard for transmitting information in the form of radio waves over distances up to about several miles. WiFi has several forms. For example, WiFi is also called *IEEE 802.11a, b, g* or *n*, each of which is a unique type. WiFi is usually the type of wireless communication used in a network environment.

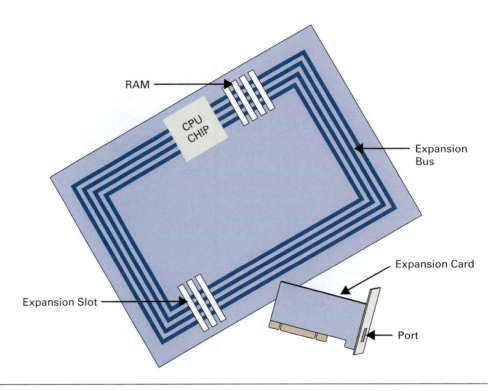

Figure A.18

The Expansion Bus, Expansion Slots, and Expansion Cards

EXPANSION CARDS AND SLOTS   Whether wired or wireless, ports are sometimes directly on the motherboard and sometimes on expansion cards. An *expansion card* (or *board*) is a circuit board that you insert into the expansion slot on the motherboard and to which you connect a peripheral device. An *expansion slot* is a long skinny socket on the motherboard into which you insert an expansion card. Information coming from and going to expansion slots and ports moves along wires (called a "bus") to the CPU. The *expansion bus* is the set of pathways along which information moves between devices outside the motherboard and the CPU (see Figure A.18). We have already discussed the system bus that moves information between basic motherboard components, including RAM and the CPU.

Figure A.19

PC Cards Connect External Devices to Your Notebook Computer

   To add devices to your notebook computer, you slide a PC Card into the PC Card slot on the notebook, and connect the device to the PC Card. A *PC Card* (which is an updated version of the traditional PCMCIA card) is the expansion card you use to add devices to your notebook computer. PC Cards look like thick credit cards. *PC Card slots* are the openings, one on top of the other, on the side or front of a notebook, where you connect external devices with a PC Card (see Figure A.19). For example, if you wanted to add a CD-ROM drive, you'd slide a PC Card into the slot and then connect the CD-ROM drive to the connector on the PC Card. One of the great things about PC Cards is that you can hot-swap devices.

Summary: Student Learning Outcomes Revisited

1. **Define information technology (IT) and its two basic categories: hardware and software.** *Information technology (IT)* is any computer-based tool that people use to work with information and support the information and information-processing needs of an organization. For example, IT includes cell phones, PDAs, software such as spreadsheet software, and output devices such as printers. *Hardware* consists of the physical devices that make up a computer (often referred to as a computer system). *Software* is the set of instructions that your hardware executes to carry out a specific task for you.

2. **Describe the categories of computers based on size.** Categories of computers by size include personal digital assistants, tablet PCs, notebook computers, desktop computers, minicomputers, mainframe computers, and supercomputers. A *personal digital assistant (PDA)* is a small handheld computer that helps you surf the Web and perform simple tasks such as note taking, calendaring, appointment scheduling, and maintaining an address book. A *tablet PC* is a pen-based computer that provides the screen capabilities of a PDA with the functional capabilities of a notebook or desktop computer. A *notebook computer* is a small, portable, fully functional battery-powered computer designed for you to carry around with you. A *desktop computer* is the most popular choice for personal computing needs. These four are all computers designed for use by one person. A *minicomputer (mid-range computer)* is designed to meet the computing needs of several people simultaneously in a small to medium-size business environment. A *mainframe computer (mainframe)* is a computer designed to meet the computing needs of hundreds of people in a large business environment. A *supercomputer* is the fastest, most powerful, and most expensive type of computer. In the order given, PDAs are the smallest, least powerful, and least expensive while supercomputers are the largest, most powerful, and most expensive.

3. **Compare the roles of personal productivity, vertical market, and horizontal market software.** *Application software* executes your specific programs and tasks. *Personal productivity software* helps you perform personal tasks—such as writing a memo, creating a graph, and creating a slide presentation—that you can usually do even if you don't own a computer. *Vertical market software* is application software that is unique to a particular industry. *Horizontal market software* is application software that is general enough to be suitable for use in a variety of industries. Personal productivity software is very inexpensive when compared to both vertical market and horizontal market software. With personal productivity software, you do not obtain the right to change the way the software works. If you buy vertical market or horizontal market software, you can often buy the right to change the way the software works.

4. **Describe the roles of operating system software and utility software as components of system software.** *System software* handles technology management tasks and coordinates the interaction of all your technology devices. *Operating system software* controls your application software and manages how your hardware devices work together. So, operating system software really enables you to run application software. *Utility software* adds additional functionality to your operating system, including such utilities as anti-virus software, screen savers, crash-proof software, uninstaller software, disk optimization, spam blocking, and anti-spyware software. Although these "add" functionality, you definitely need utility software, especially anti-virus software.

5. **Define the purpose of each of the six major categories of hardware.** The six major categories of hardware are

   - *Input devices*—Convert information and commands from a form that you understand into a form your computer can understand.

   - *Output devices*—Help you see, hear, or otherwise accept the results of your information-processing requests, that is, convert information from a form your computer understands into a form you can understand.

   - *CPU and RAM*—The real brains of your computer that execute software instructions

(CPU) and hold the information, application software, and operating system software you're working with (RAM).

- **Storage devices**—Store information for use at a later time.

- **Telecommunications devices**—Send information to and from persons and locations.
- Connecting devices—Connect all your hardware devices to each other.

Key Terms and Concepts

Anti-spyware software, 289
Anti-virus software, 289
Application software, 282
Arithmetic logic unit (ALU), 299
ASCII (American Standard Code for Information Interchange), 290
Bar code scanner, 292
Binary digit (bit), 290
Biometric scanner, 292
Bluetooth, 301
Byte, 290
CD-R (compact disc—recordable), 295
CD-ROM (compact disc—read-only memory), 295
CD-RW (compact disc—rewritable), 295
Central processing unit (CPU), 282, 297
Communications software, 287
CompactFlash (CF) card, 297
Control unit, 298
CPU cache, 298
CPU clock, 299
CPU (machine) cycle, 298
Crash-proof software, 289
CRT, 293
Database management system (DBMS), 287
Desktop computer, 284
Desktop publishing software, 287
Digital camera, 292
Digital still camera, 292
Digital video camera, 292
Disk optimization software, 289
Dot pitch, 294
DVD-R or DVD+R (DVD—recordable), 296
DVD-ROM, 296
DVD-RW or DVD+RW, 296
Expansion bus, 302
Expansion card (board), 302
Expansion slot, 302

Firewire port (IEEE 1394 or I-Link), 300
Flash memory card, 296
Flash memory device, 296
Flat-panel display, 293
Game controller, 292
Gamepad, 292
Gaming wheel, 292
Gas plasma display, 293
Gigabyte (GB or Gig), 295
Gigahertz (GHz), 298
Graphics software, 287
Hard disk, 295
Hardware, 281
Horizontal market software, 286
Hot swap, 300
Image scanner, 292
Information technology (IT), 281
Infrared, IR, or IrDA (infrared data association), 301
Inkjet printer, 294
Input device, 282, 291
Joystick, 292
Keyboard, 291
Laser printer, 295
Linux, 288
Liquid crystal display (LCD) monitor, 293
Mac OS, 288
Mainframe computer (mainframe), 285
Megabyte (MB or M or Meg), 295
Memory Stick Media card, 297
Microphone, 292
Microsoft Windows XP Home, 288
Microsoft Windows XP Professional (Windows XP Pro), 288
Microsoft Windows Vista, 288
Minicomputer (mid-range computer), 284
Mobile CPU, 299

Mouse, 291
Multifunction printer, 295
MultiMediaCard (MMC), 297
Multitasking, 289
Notebook computer, 284
Open-source software, 288
Operating system software, 282
Optical character reader, 292
Optical mark reader, 292
Optical storage media, 295
Output device, 282, 293
Parallel port, 300
PC Card, 302
PC Card slot, 302
Personal digital assistant (PDA), 283
Personal finance software, 287
Personal information management software (PIM), 287
Personal productivity software, 286
Pixels (picture elements), 294
Plotter, 295
Plug and play, 300
Pointing device, 291
Pointing stick, 291
Port, 299
Presentation software, 287
PS/2 port, 300
Random access memory (RAM), 282, 297
Resolution of a printer, 294
Resolution of a screen, 294
Scanner, 292
Secure Digital (SD) card, 297
SmartMedia (SM) card, 297
Software, 282
Spam blocker software, 289
Spreadsheet software, 287
Storage device, 282
Stylus, 291
Supercomputer, 285

Short-Answer Questions

1. What are the two categories of information technology (IT)?
2. What are the six categories of hardware?
3. What is the difference between application software and system software?
4. Dollar for dollar with comparable characteristics, which is faster and more powerful—a desktop computer or a notebook computer?
5. What is the difference between vertical and horizontal market software?
6. What do the terms *bit* and *byte* mean?

7. What is a gaming wheel and how does it differ from a gamepad?
8. What is the difference between a CRT and a flat-panel display?
9. How would you measure the size of a screen?
10. How is the resolution of a printer comparable to the resolution of a screen?
11. How does a CD differ from a floppy disk?
12. What are three types of flash memory cards?
13. What is a mobile CPU?
14. Which wireless standard is used by networks?

Assignments and Exercises

1. **COMPARING DIFFERENT TYPES OF COMPUTER SYSTEMS** Computers come in varying sizes and levels of power and performance. Use the Web to find out about computer system configurations. Do some comparison shopping for three types of computers: desktops, notebooks, and tablet PCs. Choose three Web sites that sell computer systems. From each of these sites, choose the most expensive and least expensive computer systems you can find for each of the three types of computers. Create a table for each of the three types of computers and compare them based on the following criteria:
   - Type and speed of CPU
   - Type and speed of RAM
   - Amount of CPU cache
   - System bus speed
   - Hard disk capacity and speed (revolutions per minute or rpm)
   - Number and type of ports

2. **CUSTOMIZING A COMPUTER PURCHASE** One of the great things about the Web is the number of e-tailers that are now online offering you a variety of products and services. One such e-tailer is Dell, which allows you to customize and buy a computer. Connect to Dell's site at www.dell.com. Go to the portion of Dell's site that allows you to customize either a notebook or desktop computer. First, choose an already-prepared system and note its price and capability in terms of CPU speed, RAM size, monitor quality, and storage capacity. Now, customize that system to increase CPU speed, add more RAM, increase monitor size and quality, and add more storage capacity. What's the difference in price between the two? Which system is more in your price range? Which system has the speed and capacity you need?

3. **UNDERSTANDING THE COMPLEXITY OF SOFTWARE** Software instructions on how to open Microsoft Word or send information to a printer must be provided to a computer in great detail

and with excruciating accuracy. Writing code to make the computer execute these instructions properly and in the right order is not a simple task. To understand how detailed you must be, pick a partner for this project and envision that you are standing in a kitchen. The task for one of you is to write down all the instructions that are necessary to make a peanut butter and jelly sandwich. When the instructions are complete, have the other person follow those instructions exactly. How successful was the second person in making the sandwich? Did your instructions include every single step? What did you leave out?

4. **ADDING MEDIA TO A PRESENTATION** We certainly live in a "multimedia" society, in which it's often easy to present and receive information using a variety (multi) of media. Presentation tools such as Microsoft's PowerPoint can help you easily build presentations that include audio, animation, and video. And this may help you get a better grade in school. Using your preferred presentation software, document the steps necessary to add a short audio or video clip to a presentation. How does the representation of the clip appear on a slide? How can you initiate it? Does your presentation software include any clips that you can insert or do you have to record your own? Now, try recording a short audio clip. What steps must you perform?

5. **OPERATING SYSTEM SOFTWARE FOR PDAS** The personal digital assistant (PDA) market is a ferocious, dynamic, and uncertain one. One of the uncertainties is what operating system for PDAs will become the dominant one. For notebooks and desktops right now, you're pretty well limited to the Microsoft family unless you buy an Apple computer (in which case your operating system is Mac OS) or want to venture into using Linux (which we wouldn't recommend for most people). Do some research on the more popular PDAs available today. What are the different operating systems? What different functionality do they offer? Are they compatible with each other? Take a guess—which one will come out on top?

APPENDIX B

NETWORK BASICS

Student Learning Outcomes

1. IDENTIFY AND DESCRIBE THE FOUR BASIC CONCEPTS ON WHICH NETWORKS ARE BUILT AND DESCRIBE WHAT IS NEEDED TO SET UP A SMALL PEER-TO-PEER NETWORK AT HOME.

2. DESCRIBE THE COMPONENTS USED TO BUILD LARGE BUSINESS NETWORKS AND DEFINE AND COMPARE LOCAL AREA NETWORKS (LANS), WIDE AREA NETWORKS (WANS), AND METROPOLITAN AREA NETWORKS (MANS).

3. COMPARE AND CONTRAST THE VARIOUS INTERNET CONNECTION POSSIBILITIES.

4. COMPARE AND CONTRAST THE TYPES OF COMMUNICATIONS MEDIA.

5. STATE THE FOUR PRINCIPLES OF COMPUTER SECURITY AND DESCRIBE HOW DIFFERENT NETWORK SECURITY DEVICES REFLECT THOSE PRINCIPLES.

6. DESCRIBE CLIENT/SERVER BUSINESS NETWORKS FROM A BUSINESS AND PHYSICAL POINT OF VIEW.

Introduction

When you're surfing the Web, accessing software on your school's server, sending e-mail, or letting your roommate use his or her computer to access the files on your computer, your computer is part of a network. A ***computer network*** (which we simply refer to as a network) is two or more computers connected so that they can communicate with each other and share information, software, peripheral devices, and/or processing power. Many networks have dozens, hundreds, or even thousands of computers.

BASIC PRINCIPLES OF NETWORKS

LEARNING OUTCOME 1

Networks come in all sizes, from two computers connected to share a printer, to the Internet, which is the largest network on the planet, joining millions of computers of all kinds all over the world. In between are business networks, which vary in size from a dozen or fewer computers to many thousands.

Some basic principles apply to all networks, large or small.

1. Each computer on a network must have a network interface (either as an expansion card or integrated into the motherboard, or even through software for a modem) that provides the entrance or doorway in that computer for information traffic to and from other computers.

2. A network usually has at least one connecting device (like a hub, switch, or home/broadband router) that ties the computers on the network together and acts as a switchboard for passing information.

3. There must be communications media like cables or radio waves connecting network hardware devices. The communications media transport information around the network between computers and the connecting device(s).

4. Each computer must have software that supports the movement of information in and out of the computer. This could be modem software and/or a network operating system.

First, we'll examine the smallest networks—a few computers connected in a home or dorm room—and then move on to larger business networks. We'll discuss network devices, LANs, WANs, and MANs, and communications media. Finally, we'll describe network security and illustrate the client/server software model.

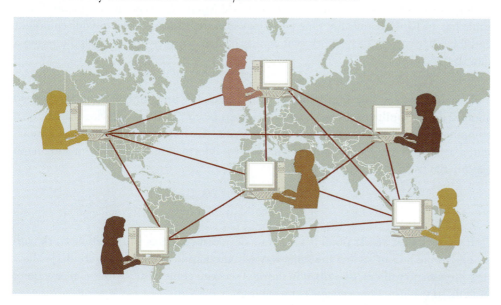

Home Networks

If you have a computer at home with cable or DSL Internet access, you may already be familiar with several network components. A typical home setup has

- An Ethernet network card in each computer, and/or a wireless Ethernet card in each laptop computer.
- Network cables to transmit signals, or no cables if you're using wireless.
- A DSL or cable line from your ISP, and a broadband or home router to pass messages and files back and forth.

NETWORK CARDS IN EACH COMPUTER

First, each computer needs a network interface. A **network interface card (NIC)** is an expansion card for a desktop computer or a PC card for a notebook computer that connects your computer to a network and provides the doorway for information to flow in and out. The network interface card has a jack (or port) for a network cable that connects your computer to a network. Some computers have network interfaces built into their motherboards, referred to as integrated network interfaces.

An **Ethernet card** is the most common type of network interface card. It has a jack, usually an RJ-45 that looks like a telephone jack, only a little larger. You run a network cable from your Ethernet card to a hub or switch, or you can use a cable with different wiring called a *crossover cable* to plug straight into another computer or printer if you have only two devices to connect.

WIRED AND WIRELESS TRANSMISSION MEDIA

The most common transmission medium for a home network is Cat 5 cable, which is similar to phone cable (ordinary twisted-pair cable). **Cat 5,** or **Category 5,** cable is a better-constructed version of the phone twisted-pair cable. Each end of the Cat 5 cable has an RJ-45 connector. One end plugs into the Ethernet card in your computer and the other end into a network switch or broadband router (which we'll discuss in a moment).

If you'd like to access your home network wirelessly with your computer, you'll need another device on the network. A **wireless access point (WAP)** is a device that allows a computer to use radio waves to access a network. A wireless access point has a transmitter and a receiver for the bidirectional flow of information. It also has an antenna to capture the radio waves out of the air.

If your wireless access point is a separate device, it connects to a wired network with a cable to the hub or switch the same way wired computers do (see Figure B.1). Many new broadband routers (described in the next section) come with a wireless access point built in, so you may not need any extra cables.

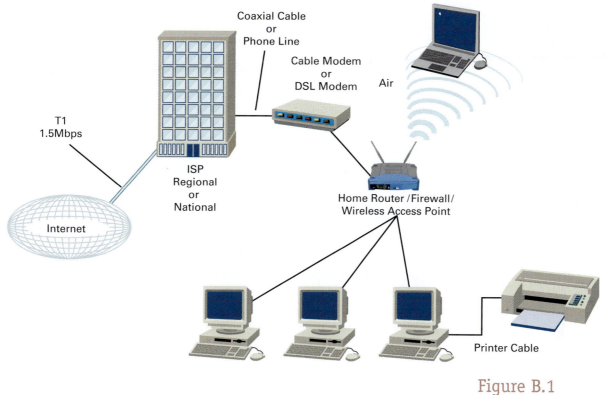

Figure B.1

Typical Home Network

Your notebook and any other device that accesses the network wirelessly must have a wireless adapter. Wireless adapters are available as PC Cards for notebook computers, or sometimes come built into notebooks. The wireless adapter incorporates a transmitter, receiver, and antenna, just like the wireless access point. If all your devices have wireless adapters, you can create a completely wireless network, in which the only cable used is the one connecting to the cable or DSL service.

HOME INTERNET SERVICE AND BROADBAND ROUTERS

A home network with no outside connections can still be used to share files and printers. But in order to access any services or sites outside your home, you need Internet service and equipment to connect it to your home network. Two common types of home Internet service are DSL, available through your telephone company, and cable Internet connection, available from your cable company.

A DSL or cable modem connection is designed to support only one computer, so if you want to connect more computers, you need another device, commonly called a broadband router or home router. A **broadband router** or **home router** is a device to connect several computers together to share a DSL or cable Internet connection in a home or small office. It has one port to plug in your Internet connection, and usually has several ports to plug in home computers or printers.

Broadband routers are a rapidly changing part of the home network marketplace. Early models required an external DSL or cable modem, but some newer models include that built in. Early models had only one port for a computer and required a separate device to interconnect multiple computers. Many broadband routers today even include a built-in wireless access point.

NETWORK SOFTWARE

As always, when you have hardware you need software to make it work. For a small network, Windows will do fine (use version Windows 98 SE or newer) and must be installed on each network computer. To make the files on your computer available to the other computers on the network, you have to turn on the file-sharing option in Windows and indicate which drives, directories, or files to share. When you do this, the files on one computer will appear as additional folders on the other computer.

LEARNING OUTCOME 2

Network Components

Large networks are built in much the same way as small networks, using the same types of components. One difference is that home network devices often perform several different functions that are separated onto separate devices in large networks. Let's take a closer look at these different network components, and also look at how they're used in larger networks at corporations and universities.

HUBS

A **hub** is a device that connects computers together and passes messages by repeating all network transmissions to all the other computers. Because of this, only one computer on a hub can transmit at a time. A network built on a hub is also called a *shared* network, because all the computers share the entire network and have to take turns using it.

Imagine a building that has several offices, a manufacturing floor, and no telephones—only a public-address system. When the ordering clerk needs to check inventory, he or she pushes the button on the microphone, and the PA system broadcasts his or her voice over all the speakers in the building. Someone on the shop floor counts the supplies, goes to his or her microphone, and his or her voice is transmitted over every speaker in the building.

This is how hubs work, and you can see several problems with this approach. Only one computer can transmit at a time, because every message is sent to every computer, tying up every communications line. For the same reason, information transmitted over hubs isn't private—you wouldn't want your boss discussing your raise request with the Human Resources department over a set of loudspeakers that are heard throughout the entire building.

Hubs are also inefficient for the computers on the network to use, because every time a message comes across, they have to interrupt what they're doing to determine whether the message pertains to them (see Figure B.2). And finally, hubs can have *collisions* when two computers decide to start sending at the same time. This garbles both of their messages, and they would have to stop sending and try again later. In fact, the more computers connected to a hub, the more frequently collisions happen, sometimes to the point that very little actual data gets transmitted.

Historically, hubs were very inexpensive compared to other types of network devices. They've been largely replaced by switches, but in spite of their shortcomings, they're still used in some home and small offices and in older business networks.

SWITCHES

A **switch** is a network device that connects computers and passes messages by repeating each computer's transmissions only to the intended recipient, not to all the computers

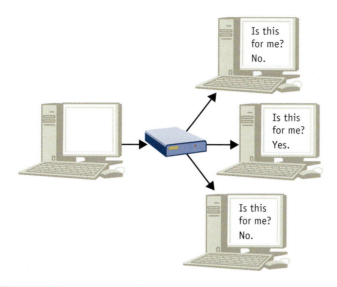

Figure B.2

Hub

connected. Several computers can have different conversations at the same time through a switch, and such a network is called a *switched* network.

A switch works like a small business telephone system. When the marketing director needs to check on the status of a brochure, she calls the graphic artist to ask about it. At the same time, the shop supervisor can be giving a delivery date to the shipping manager. And the telephones all have speakers, so the operator can still get everyone's attention all at once if necessary.

You can see several advantages over hubs. Many data transmissions can happen at the same time, so a switch gives better support to a busy network (see Figure B.3). Information transmitted over switches is generally private, unless it's specifically meant to be broadcast to all the computers on the network. Likewise, computers on switches are more efficient than computers on hubs, because they only have to process messages actually meant for them, plus occasional broadcasts. And finally, switches don't have collisions, because different transmissions don't interfere with each other.

The advantages of switches are so great that switches have almost completely replaced hubs in new installations. Switches are the most commonly used components in networks today, and range in size from four- and eight-port models (connecting four or eight computers or printers) in home networks, to 24- and 48-port models (connecting 24 or 48 devices) common in business networks, to very large switches with hundreds of ports used to connect large call centers or run entire floors of office buildings.

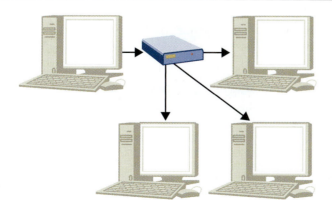

Figure B.3

Switch

ROUTERS

Routers connect together separate networks of computers, unlike hubs and switches that connect individual computers. A **router** is a device that passes network traffic between smaller *subnetworks* (or *subnets*) of a larger network.

Think of a large business with a warehouse in one building, management offices in another, and manufacturing in yet another. Long ago, each building had its own telephone system with its own extensions—the warehouse has numbers 100–199; management has extensions 200–299; and manufacturing has numbers 400–699.

At first, the telephone systems weren't connected, and the telephones would call only within the same building. But then the business ran telephone cables from each building to a central phone system to tie them all together. Now the warehouse phone system "knows" that if it gets a call for any extension other than 100–199, it routes the call to the central system to direct to the proper building. And the central system knows to route any call starting with 1 to the warehouse phone system, any call starting with 2 to management, and any call starting with 4, 5, or 6 to manufacturing.

Routers work the same way. When a computer wants to send a message to another computer on a different subnet (like in a different building), it actually sends the message to the router on its subnet. The router then looks at the message's destination address—where the message is going—and figures out how to get it there. Medium-sized networks may have only one router at the center, in which case it can always deliver messages directly. Larger networks may have many routers connected together, in which case messages may pass through several routers on their way from one computer to another (see Figure B.4).

It's important to understand that even though you have a router, you still need a hub or a switch to plug the computers into. Because large routers are expensive, it's not practical to build them with enough ports to directly support all the computers on a network. Home routers that run your Internet connection usually have both a router and a hub or switch built into the same box. But even though they may be labeled routers, remember that switching and routing are really two separate functions.

Hubs and switches can often be taken out of the box, hooked up to computers, and used without any configuration. But routers need to be programmed with information about which computer addresses are on which subnets, so installing a router generally

Figure B.4

Routers

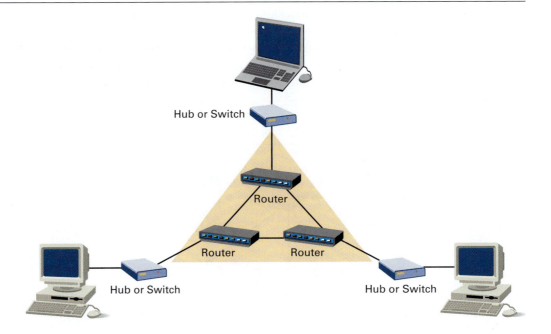

requires someone with knowledge of network administration. Adding to or reconfiguring the network generally requires reconfiguring the router.

Classifying Networks by Distance

We've discussed the different devices used to build networks, and next we'll talk about ways networks are connected together. One way of describing large networks is in terms of the geographic area they cover. The size of a network can also impact whether an organization owns the communications lines or leases them from an independent provider.

LANs, WANs, AND MANs

A *local area network (LAN)* is a network that covers a building or buildings in close proximity, such as one campus of a university or corporation. The defining characteristic of a LAN isn't the actual size, but rather that the geographic area it serves is continuous. So the large network on a two-square mile campus of an aircraft manufacturer would be considered all one LAN, but the small networks of a daycare center with two buildings a city block apart would be considered separate LANs.

A *wide area network (WAN),* then, is a set of connected networks serving areas or buildings not in immediate proximity to each other. Another way to think of a WAN is as a network of networks. WANs generally use routers to connect LANs together, just as LANs can use routers to connect different subnets together.

Imagine a business that's large enough to have a production plant near a railroad and trucking depot, and separate corporate headquarters in a downtown office park. It has separate telephone systems on each site—in fact, the production plant has separate telephone systems in the warehouse, the manufacturing building, and the packing and shipping plant. But they also have telephone lines connecting the production plant and the headquarters, and the telephone systems know how to send calls from one to the other. In fact, except for using a different type of telephone line, sending calls from one site to the other is set up exactly the same as sending calls from one building to another.

WANs work the same way to connect networks (LANs) on different sites. WANs may connect networks at different locations around a city, or in different cities across a state, a country, or even the entire world.

Because WANs connect areas that are some distance apart, organizations don't usually own the communications lines that WANs run over. Instead, the lines are usually leased, often from a telephone or cable television company, or other commercial communications provider. Some types of WAN circuits are 56 kilobits per second (56 Kbps) leased lines; T1, running at 1.544 megabits per second (1.544 Mbps); and DS3, running at 44.736 Mbps. (T1 and DS3 are described in more detail in this module under Internet Connection Types.)

A metropolitan area network is a relatively recent term for a specific type of WAN. A *metropolitan area network* or *municipal area network (MAN)* is a set of connected networks all within the same city or metropolitan area, but not in immediate proximity to each other.

Internet

An internet, with a lowercase *i*, comes from the word internetworking, and is a network of networks, connecting networks managed by different organizations. The largest internet of all is the ***Internet*** (with a capital *I*) which is a vast network of computers that connects millions of people all over the world.

To understand how computers send network communications across the Internet, consider the business described earlier that has telephone systems in separate buildings and on separate sites. When employees place calls to other buildings, each building's phone system directs the calls through a central system that knows how to route the calls to their destinations.

Besides the connections to the different buildings, the company also has connections to the public telephone system, so employees can make phone calls to place materials orders, and receive calls to accept orders for products. The company's outside telephone lines don't run directly to each building, but rather to the central system that knows how to route calls among all the buildings.

When employees at this company want to make outside calls, they dial a code starting with 9 (a digit different from the first digit of any of their local extensions), and the central system knows to route their calls over the outside lines to the public telephone system. And when customers call, they dial one of the company's telephone numbers, and the public telephone system sends the calls over the company's outside phone lines to the central system, which routes the calls to the correct departments. If customers don't know the right phone numbers to call, they can look up the company's name in a telephone directory and find the numbers they need.

This is much the way the Internet works. When a computer needs to send a message to another computer somewhere else on the Internet, it sends the message to its local router. If the router doesn't recognize the recipient as being attached to one of its LAN, MAN, or WAN connections, it sends the message over the connection to its Internet Service Provider (ISP). The ISP has bigger routers that learn paths to get to even more networks. Even if they're not connected directly to the receiving network, the ISP's routers send the message to another router, which may send the message to still *another,* and so forth, until the message finally gets to the receiving network. There, the receiving router will at last deliver the message to the computer at the ultimate destination.

Computers and routers refer to each other using network addresses, commonly Internet Protocol (IP) addresses, like *192.168.1.1.* This is similar to the way telephone systems use telephone numbers, like *+1 (414) 555-1212,* to route calls. You probably remember the phone numbers of some of your friends and family, but no one knows all the different phone numbers in the world.

Similarly, you don't have to remember the low-level network address of every computer you send network messages to. Instead, you can use names for computers, like www.mhhe.com, and your computer looks up the receiving computer's address for you in a directory called the Domain Name System, or DNS. Without DNS, the Internet would be virtually impossible to use.

BANDWIDTH

The most common measurement used when comparing different types of communications media is bandwidth, which refers to capacity. ***Bandwidth,*** or capacity of the communications medium, is the amount of information that a communications medium can transfer in a given amount of time. You can think of bandwidth as the width of a drinking straw: the wider the straw, the more quickly you can move the liquid from the cup into your mouth. In fact, in the communications industry, bandwidth is sometimes referenced informally as what size "pipe" you have between two locations.

Bandwidth is described as a quantity of data transferred in an amount of time, most commonly as a number of bits per second. A *bit* is the smallest possible amount of data, representing a single 1 or 0, and is abbreviated as the letter *b.* A *byte* is eight bits, and is used to store one letter or symbol of text, so the number of bits divided by eight gives you the approximate number of text characters. (See *Appendix A* for more information about bits, bytes, and characters.)

Bandwidth is sometimes represented in bits per second, abbreviated *bps*. Because a single bit is such a small quantity, and communications media speeds are constantly increasing, the bandwidth of different media is more likely to be represented in thousands of bits per second (kilobits per second—Kbps or kbps), millions of bits per second (megabits per second—Mbps), or billions of bits per second (gigabits per second—Gbps).

For example, if a particular communications medium has a bandwidth of 16 Mbps, then 16 millions bits can be transferred in a single second. This module has about 70,000 characters in it, which is approximately 560,000 bits, so it could be transferred in less than half a second across a 16 Mbps channel.

INTERNET CONNECTION TYPES

Like the circuits used to make wide-area connections, Internet circuits aren't usually owned by individual companies. Instead, the circuits are supplied by an Internet Service Provider. Types of Internet circuits include:

- Dial-up circuits, using an ordinary telephone line and a modem.
- Digital Subscriber Line (DSL), which runs a high-speed connection over a telephone line without interfering with the voice telephone service.
- Cable modem, which runs a high-speed connection over a cable television line without interfering with television reception.
- Satellite modem, which runs a high-speed connection through your cable TV satellite without interfering with television reception.
- Dedicated high-speed lines such as T1 and DS3, which run on separate circuits and are generally used for business connections.

DSL, cable modem, and dedicated lines are classified as broadband connections. A **broadband** connection is a high-bandwidth (high-capacity) telecommunications line capable of providing high-speed Internet service. The Federal Communications Commission defines broadband as a capacity of 200 kbps (200 kilobits, or thousands of bits, per second) both upstream (to the Internet) and downstream (from the Internet). Other industry experts feel that broadband implies a speed of at least 750 kbps.

DIAL-UP CONNECTIONS   To make a telephone or dial-up connection, you need a computer, a phone line, a modem, and, of course, an Internet service provider. Just as people use telephones to talk over telephone lines, a **telephone modem (modem)** is a device that connects a computer to your phone line so that you can access another computer or network. And as it is with people and telephones, the computer at the other end needs a modem too.

A modem converts the digital signals from your computer into an analog form (by modulating the signal) that can be transmitted over a phone line, and then converts the analog signal back to digital signals (by demodulating the signal) for the computer at the receiving end of the transmission (see Figures B.5 and B.6). The word modem is a contraction of the modem's function of **mo**dulating outgoing and **dem**odulating incoming transmissions.

Modems are sometimes integrated into the motherboards of new computers, particularly laptops and notebook. If your computer doesn't have a built-in modem, you can buy a card to plug into an expansion slot of your desktop, or a PC card for your notebook. A modem is the slowest type of

Figure B.5

Digital and Analog Signals

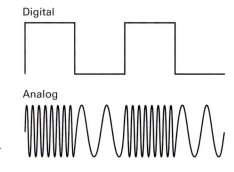

Digital

Analog

Digital	Digital-to-Analog Conversion	Analog	Analog-to-Digital Conversion	Digital
Digital uses discrete electronic pulses to represent information		Analog uses a continuous electronic stream to represent information		

Telephone Line

Figure B.6

The Role of a
Telephone Modem

Internet connection you can get. The fastest possible transmission speed using a modem over a normal telephone line is 56 kbps, or about 56,000 bits per second.

DIGITAL SUBSCRIBER LINE   A *Digital Subscriber Line (DSL)* is a high-speed Internet connection using phone lines, which allows you to use your telephone for voice communication at the same time. There are different kinds of DSL systems, including ADSL or asymmetric DSL, SDSL or symmetric DSL, and HDSL or high-bit-rate DSL, that offer different combinations of speeds from the Internet provider to the customer and from the customer to the provider.

DSL works similarly to a traditional modem, modulating and demodulating the computer's digital signal into an analog form for transmission over the telephone line. However, unlike traditional modems which modulate into audible sounds (the screech you hear if you pick up a telephone while your computer is connected to the Internet through its modem), DSL modems use frequencies too high for you to hear; this is how they can allow telephone conversations to happen at the same time. Even so, DSL modems sometimes cause clicks, pops, or buzzing on telephone lines, so most DSL connections use a splitter or filter to make sure that only voice calls go to the telephone and only DSL signals go to the DSL modem (see Figure B.7).

Figure B.7

DSL Internet Access

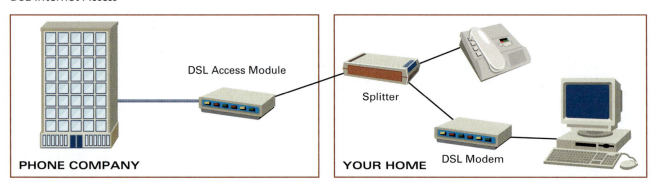

DSL Access Module

Splitter

PHONE COMPANY

YOUR HOME   DSL Modem

Because the high frequencies used by DSL are outside the range that telephone lines were originally designed to carry, only telephone lines that meet certain criteria can deliver DSL service. You need to live within about three miles of the phone company. (In larger cities, phone companies have branch offices that can connect you throughout the metropolitan area.) The phone company may have restrictions about the type of equipment it uses to provide your phone line—a relatively recent central system, and a direct line to your house without any signal processing devices along the way. And the speed of your connection may depend on the distance to the phone company and the quality of your line. Speeds may vary from 144 kbps to 1.5 Mbps, or even up to 6 Mbps for a business-class DSL connection.

DSL circuits—the physical cabling to your house—are always provided by the phone company. The phone company usually provides the Internet service that you use over the DSL connection, too. However, in some areas, you may be able to buy your Internet service from an independent service provider instead. To connect to a DSL circuit, you need the filter or splitter provided by the phone company (to keep noise out of your telephone conversations) and the DSL modem. The cable from the DSL modem connects to your computer in one of two ways: either to an Ethernet card, or to a USB port.

DSL service has three big advantages over dialup connections:

1. DSL is much faster—up to 30 times faster than a traditional modem.

2. You can use the line for voice calls at the same time.

3. DSL can be an always-on connection—because it doesn't interfere with voice calls, you can leave it connected all the time, instead of having to wait for your modem to connect each time you want to use the Internet.

CABLE MODEM   If you have wired cable television, you know it comes into your home on a coaxial cable that connects to your television set. This same cable can connect you to the Internet, too. Both cable TV signals and your Internet connection travel from the cable company on one wire.

A splitter at your home splits the signals on the incoming cable, sending one part to the TV and the other to your cable modem. A *cable modem* is a device that uses your TV cable to deliver an Internet connection (see Figure B.8). The cable from the cable modem attaches to either an Ethernet card (an expansion card that connects your

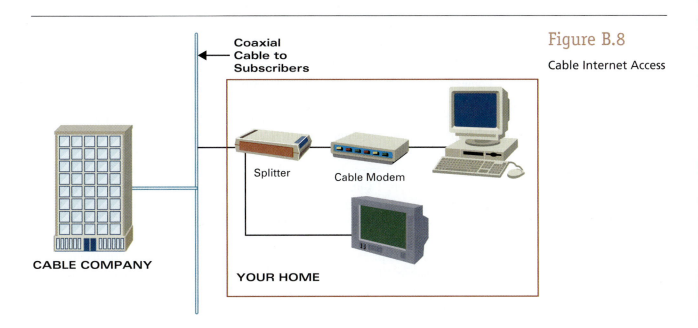

Coaxial
Cable to
Subscribers

Splitter   Cable Modem

CABLE COMPANY

YOUR HOME

Figure B.8

Cable Internet Access

computer to a network) or to a USB port in your computer. Like DSL, cable modems provide an always-on connection. However, unlike DSL, cable modems don't use a phone line at all.

The speed of transmission with a cable modem is much faster than a phone modem, running at about 10 Mbps (10 million bits per second). While the speed of a DSL connection is guaranteed, though, the speed of a cable Internet connection depends on how many users are online, because the connection to the cable company is shared throughout a neighborhood. If all your neighbors are surfing the Web with a cable connection at the same time you are, you may notice a reduction in your access speed.

SATELLITE MODEM   If you have wireless cable television, that is, if you receive your cable programming via a satellite, you can often also obtain your Internet service through the same provider of your satellite cable. A *satellite modem* allows you to get Internet access from your satellite dish. In certain instances, you may not be receiving your cable programming via satellite, but you may be able to receive your Internet service via a dedicated satellite dish. It really all depends on where you live and what types of services are offered for cable programming and Internet service.

The concept and implementation of receiving your Internet service from your satellite cable programming provider are the same as for using a cable modem. You would have a splitter with wiring for your cable programming going to your television and wiring for your Internet service going to your computer or a connecting device such as a hub or router.

T1, DS3, FRAME RELAY, AND ATM   A *T1* is a high-speed circuit typically used for business connections, running at speeds up to 1.544 Mbps (1.544 million bits per second), and a *DS3* is a high-speed business network circuit running at 44.736 Mbps. T1s were originally designed to carry 24 telephone conversations on phone companies' long-distance lines between cities. Later, equipment was developed to connect computer networks over T1 and DS3 lines. A T1's speed of 1.544 Mbps is about 24 times the speed of an analog telephone modem. A DS3 line is equivalent to 28 T1 lines bundled together, and its total speed of 44.736 Mbps is about 672 times the speed of an analog modem.

With some providers, a portion of the price of T1 and DS3 lines depends on the distance they run. Because of this distance-based pricing and their overall higher cost than some other connection types, T1 and DS3 lines are most commonly used for metropolitan area network connections—between two branches of a business within the same city. One advantage of T1 lines is that, because of their origin in voice telephony, it's possible to split their 24 channels between voice and computer communications, using the same T1 circuit to connect both telephone systems and computer networks at two offices.

Frame Relay and Asynchronous Transfer Mode (ATM) are services that the phone company or other telecommunications providers can set up over high-speed lines like T1s and DS3s to create "virtual circuits" connecting multiple offices. These virtual circuits can provide network connections from each office to every other one without having to run physical lines directly between each pair.

For example, if a business had four offices that all needed to be connected to each other, it would take six T1 lines to hook them all up (see Figure B.9). With Frame Relay or ATM, each office has a single T1 line going to the communications provider (for a total of four), and the provider makes it work the same as it would if the six direct lines actually existed.

Remember that the price of T1 and DS3 lines can depend on the distance they run. With Frame Relay or ATM, the T1 or DS3 lines actually run from each office to the telecommunications provider, rather than from office to office, so the distance and price can both be lower than when T1 lines are run directly from office to office.

T1 Lines without Frame Relay/ATM

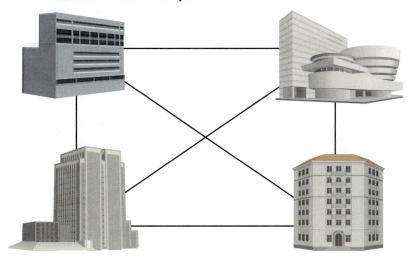

T1 Lines for Frame Relay/ATM

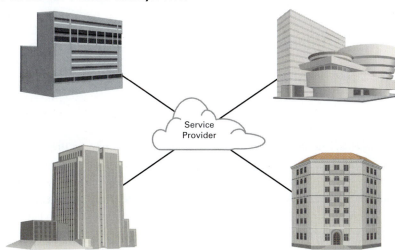

Virtual Circuits

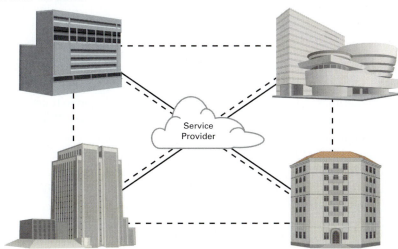

Figure B.9

Frame Relay/ATM Virtual Circuits

Branch Office Connections without Frame Relay/ATM

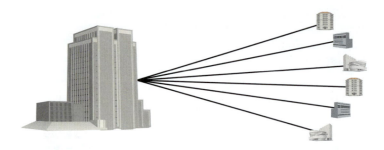

Branch Office Connections Using Frame Relay/ATM

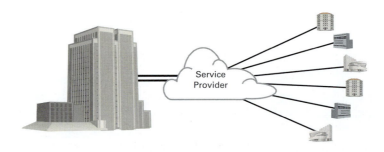

Figure B.10

Frame Relay/ATM Circuit
Aggregation

Because of this, Frame Relay and ATM are also used to connect many branch offices to a single main office. If a business had six branch offices, it would take six T1 lines to connect all the branches back to the headquarters (see Figure B.10)—each potentially running a great distance. With Frame Relay or ATM, the business can instead install a DS3 from its headquarters to the communications provider and a T1 to each branch office. The provider makes it work as it would if the headquarters had a direct connection to each branch office, and the business potentially spends less money than if it ran all of the T1 lines directly between offices. And the company has a single DS3 connection at its headquarters instead of six separate T1 connections, simplifying circuit management and potentially increasing reliability.

VOICE OVER IP

We've just talked about different types of communications lines that can carry network information, but now it's time to turn that inside out. Several types of communications lines—telephone lines, T1s, and DS3s—were originally developed to transmit voice telephone calls, and later adapted to carry computer data. Voice over IP (VoIP) does the opposite—it's a means of transmitting a voice telephone call over a computer data network. *Voice over IP (VoIP)* allows you to send voice communications over the Internet and avoid the toll charges that you would normally receive from your long-distance carrier.

Why go to the trouble of sending voice calls over a computer network when they can already be sent directly through existing telephone systems and services? The answer has everything to do with overhead and with metered billing, meaning you pay an additional amount for each call and/or for each minute of the call.

Offices in most businesses and universities today have at least two different cables run to them—one that goes back to a telephone system, and one that goes back to a network hub or switch. On many telephone systems, the telephone extension number is assigned to a particular port on the central equipment. So when an employee moves from one office to another, making his or her telephone extension work in the new office involves either changing wiring or reprogramming the phone system.

In contrast, network addresses are assigned directly to the computer or other device, regardless of which switch or hub port it's connected to. So moving a VoIP extension from one office to another is as easy as unplugging the network phone from one location, carrying it to another, and plugging it back in. This reduction of maintenance effort can dramatically reduce the overhead of telephone system operation during office expansions and moves. Additionally, office technicians no longer have to maintain two sets of wiring to two different systems, which can also reduce overhead.

Both network companies like Cisco Systems and telephone companies like Nortel are producing VoIP telephones that look like any other business phone, except they plug into a network jack instead of a telephone jack. Many even have an extra network jack on them for your PC, so your phone and computer can share a single connection back to the building's hub or switch.

Voice over IP is also starting to gain popularity with home users across the Internet. In most parts of the world, traditional telephone calls made from one local dialing area to another have metered billing, and some large U.S. cities even have metered billing for local calls.

Network access is often unmetered, though, particularly for broadband home access (cable modem and DSL). If you already have an Internet connection, you can use a network telephone or network phone software for your PC to make calls to other VoIP users anywhere in the world at no additional cost per call or per minute—for the moment, anyway. Most telephone billing rates in the United States are set by federal and state governments by regulations called tariffs, and it remains to be seen how long it will be before Voice over IP becomes tariffed as well.

Network Communications Media

LEARNING OUTCOME 4

The objective of networks and telecommunications is to move information from one place to another. This may be as simple as sending information to the office next door, or as far-reaching as sending a message to the other side of the world. Whatever the case, information must travel over some path from its source to its destination. *Communications media* are the paths, or physical channels, in a network over which information travels.

All communications are either wired or wireless. *Wired communications media* transmit information over a closed, connected path. *Wireless communications media* transmit information through the air. Forms of wired and wireless communications media include:

Wired
- Twisted-Pair Cable
- Coaxial Cable
- Optical Fiber

Wireless
- Infrared
- Microwave
- Satellite

WIRED COMMUNICATIONS MEDIA

Wired communications media are those which tie devices together using cables of some kind. Twisted-pair, coaxial cable, and optical fiber are the types of cabling you'd find in computer networks.

TWISTED-PAIR   *Twisted-pair cable* is a bundle of copper wires used for transmitting voice or data communications and comes in several varieties. The Cat 5 that you already read about in connection with home networks earlier in this appendix is one type. Most of the world's phone system is twisted-pair and since it's already in place, it's an obvious choice for networks.

The simplest type of twisted-pair phone cabling (Cat 1) provides a slow, fairly reliable path for information at up to 64 kilobits per second (Kbps), while a better type (Cat 3) provides up to 10 megabits per second (Mbps). However, distance, noise on the line, and interference tend to limit reliability for most types of twisted-pair cabling. For example, a crackle that changes a credit card number from 5244 0811 2643 741 to 5244 0810 2643 741 is more than a nuisance; in business it means retransmitting the information or applying a charge to the wrong person's credit card.

Cat 5 or Category 5 provides a much higher bandwidth than ordinary phone cable, meaning it carries more information in a given time period, at least for distances up to 100 meters. It's commonly used for connections at 100 megabits per second (Mbps), and an enhanced version called Category 5e is capable of carrying 1 gigabit per second (Gbps). Cat 5 is relatively inexpensive and is fairly easy to install and maintain. Because of these advantages, it's the most widely used cabling for data transfer in today's LANs. Note, however, that twisted-pair of any kind is relatively easy to tap into and so it's not very secure. It's even possible to access the information by simply detecting the signals that "leak" out.

COAXIAL CABLE   An alternative to twisted-pair cable is *coaxial cable (coax),* which is one central wire surrounded by insulation, a metallic shield, and a final case of insulating material. (Coax is the kind of cable that delivers cable television transmissions and also carries satellite TV from the dish to your house.) While coaxial cable was once the cable of choice for internal LAN wiring, it has been almost completely replaced by twisted-pair cable. Coaxial cable is capable of carrying at least 500 Mbps, or the equivalent of 15,000 voice calls, simultaneously. Because of its shielded construction, coaxial cable is much less susceptible to outside interference and information damage than twisted-pair cable. However, coaxial cable is generally more expensive than twisted-pair and is more difficult to install and maintain. Security is about the same with coaxial cable as with twisted-pair, except that the radiation, or leaking, of information is much less. Coax is commonly used for leased line private networks.

OPTICAL FIBER   The fastest and most efficient medium for wired communication is *optical fiber,* which uses a very thin and flexible glass or plastic fiber through which pulses of light travel. Information transmission through optical fiber works rather like flashing code with a light through a hollow tube.

Optical fiber's advantages are size (one fiber has the diameter of a human hair); capacity (easily hundreds of gigabits per second, and getting faster every year); much greater security; no leakage of information. It's very hard to "tap" into optical fiber. Attempts are pretty easy to detect since installing a tap disrupts service on the line—and that's noticeable. Optical fiber is also used for nearly all connections between different buildings, as it doesn't conduct electricity and so is immune to damage from lightning strikes. Optical fiber is more expensive than twisted-pair cable, however, and requires highly skilled technicians to install and maintain.

WIRELESS COMMUNICATIONS MEDIA

For many networks, wired communications media are simply not feasible, especially for telecommunication across rugged terrain, great distances, or when one or more parties may be in motion. For whatever reason, if wired communications media don't fit your needs, wireless may be the answer. Wireless communications radiate information into the air, either very narrowly beamed or in many directions like ripples from a pebble tossed into a pond. Since they radiate through the air, they don't require direct cable connections of any kind. Obviously, security is a big problem since the information is available to anyone in the radiation's path. However, wireless encryption methods are good, and getting better.

INFRARED AND BLUETOOTH FOR VERY SHORT DISTANCES   Infrared is the oldest type of wireless communication. *Infrared* uses red light to send and receive information. The light is invisible to humans, but snakes and some other animals can see it. Your TV remote control uses infrared. You can use infrared to connect handheld devices, such as pocket PCs, to peripheral devices such as printers. Wireless keyboards and mice usually connect to your PC with an infrared link. Infrared communication is totally line-of-sight, meaning that you can't have anything blocking the path of the signal, or it won't work. Infrared transmission has very limited bandwidth (typically 1 Mbps).

A relatively new and competing wireless technology is called Bluetooth. Named for a Viking king, *Bluetooth* is a standard for transmitting information in the form of short-range radio waves over distances of up to 30 feet and is used for purposes such as wirelessly connecting a cell phone or PDA to a computer. Virtually all digital devices, like keyboards, joysticks, printers, and so on, can be part of a Bluetooth system. Bluetooth is also adaptable for home appliances like refrigerators and microwave ovens.

OMNIDIRECTIONAL MICROWAVE (WIFI) FOR SHORT DISTANCES   Another method of short-distance wireless communications is omnidirectional (all directions) microwave transmission. *Microwave transmission* is a type of radio transmission. Microwaves occupy a portion of the electromagnetic spectrum between television signals and visible light. Microwave ovens use high-powered microwaves to heat food and can interfere with some types of microwave wireless transmissions.

The most common types of wireless networking used today—802.11b and 802.11g (known to most people as WiFi)—use microwave transmissions. *WiFi (wireless fidelity)* is a standard for transmitting information in the form of radio waves over distances up to about several miles. WiFi is actually a wireless industry alliance that provides testing and certification that 802.11 devices communicate with each other properly. *IEEE 802.11b and 802.11g* are two versions that run at 11 Mbps and 54 Mbps, respectively.

DIRECTIONAL MICROWAVE FOR MEDIUM DISTANCES   Microwaves may be transmitted very directionally with a parabolic dish antenna or can be radiated in a wide curved path for broader use. Microwave transmission is a line-of-sight medium. That is, the microwave signal cannot follow the curved surface of the earth. So to send the information over a distance of more than about 20 miles you'd have to use repeaters (see Figure B.11). A *repeater* is a device that receives a radio signal, strengthens it, and sends it on. (You've probably seen microwave towers—they're the tall towers with lots of little dishes on them that stand near industrial complexes.) Microwave signals have difficulty getting through walls or trees or other solid objects, so there must be a clear path from sender to receiver.

Figure B.11

Microwave

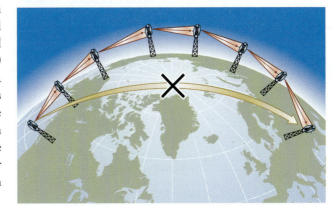

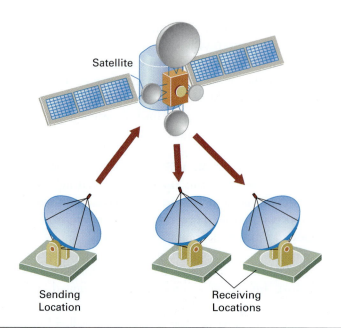

Figure B.12

Satellite

SATELLITES FOR LONG DISTANCES *Communications satellites* are microwave repeaters in space. They solve the problem of line-of-sight since the transmission shoots up into the sky in a straight line, bounces off, and shoots back down to earth again (see Figure B.12). Since satellites are so high, an array of them can cover essentially the whole earth (as the two dozen or so GPS satellites do). As with land-based repeaters, satellites receive information from one location and relay it to another. You'd usually use satellite communications to connect land-based networks in far-flung locations or to connect moving vehicles to each other or to the organizational network.

Satellite communications are cost effective for moving large amounts of information, especially given a large number of receiving sites. For example, K-Mart and other retailers place very small aperture terminal (VSAT) satellite dishes on the roofs of their stores. The VSATs allow individual stores to transmit information to the home office, and the home office, in turn, can transmit information to all the stores simultaneously. Satellite radio is another example of far-flung satellite transmission. If you have satellite radio in your car, you'll never be completely out of range of your favorite satellite radio station.

LEARNING OUTCOME 5

Network Security

Thinking about network security may call to mind images from movies of computer rooms criss-crossed by laser beams, voice and handprint recognition, security cameras, and CDs or DVDs full of top-secret blueprints. Or it may make you think of jumpsuit-wearing technicians clipping wires onto someone else's connection, greasy-haired teenagers illuminated only by the green glow of their computer monitors, or an investigator frantically trying to guess the criminal's password as the footsteps in the hallway get ever closer.

These images, although dramatic, don't give you much of an idea of the real threats to computer and network security and how to guard against them. In reality, connecting computers together can make it easier to take advantage of existing security weaknesses—attacks can be performed from any distance away instead of only from within the same room—and introduces some new weaknesses.

PRINCIPLES OF COMPUTER SECURITY

The best way to understand network security is to look at the components of computer security, evaluate different threats in terms of these components, and then figure out how to reduce the effectiveness or damage of those threats. The basic principles of computer and network security are confidentiality, authenticity, integrity, and availability. Within the context of computer and network security

- *Confidentiality* means that information can be obtained only by those authorized to access it. In even simpler terms, it means keeping secrets secret. Confidential information includes things like bank statements, business plans, credit card reports, and employee evaluations. Threats to confidentiality include network transmissions that can be captured or monitored by unauthorized individuals, passwords that are easily guessed, and even printouts left lying out in plain sight. In the world outside of computers, confidentiality is protected by sealing envelopes and locking doors and file cabinets.

- *Authenticity* means that information really comes from the source it claims to come from. It's important to be sure of the authenticity of things like military orders, medical diagnoses, and buy/sell directions to your stockbroker. Threats to authenticity include fraudulent e-mail messages claiming to be from your bank (probably spoofing), Web sites registered at names that are common misspellings of popular sites, and Web browsers that can be manipulated into making it look as though you're at a different site than you really are. Nonelectronic authenticity is provided by signatures (although they can be forged), or by trusting only people you know personally.

- *Integrity* means that information has not been altered. This is closely related to authenticity. You would be concerned about the integrity of your bank balance, contents of your corporate Web site, medical prescriptions, and credit card charges. Threats to integrity include network transmissions that can be forged or taken over by unauthorized individuals and Web servers with flaws that allow their content to be replaced. Integrity is hard to guarantee in the physical world—how can you *really* be sure that no one has changed even a single word of your mortgage contract?—and is generally dependent on a certain degree of trust that's much harder to apply to electronic communications.

- *Availability* means simply that a service or resource is available when it's supposed to be. If a mail-order Web site is unavailable during the Christmas season, a retailer could lose millions of dollars in sales. If a corporate e-mail server is frequently unavailable, the company may lose some of the trust of its business partners. Threats to availability include unintentional network failures, poorly written server software that stops working when presented with unusual inputs, and deliberate attempts to send so much traffic to a company's network that legitimate communications are unable to get through. Noncomputer-related availability is provided by designing buildings with multiple exits in case one is blocked by fire, making photocopies of important documents, and installing electrical generators in hospitals to keep life-critical equipment operating if the city power fails.

FIREWALLS AND INTRUSION DETECTION SYSTEMS

Networks are designed to connect computers together and move information between them. But what if attackers are trying to break into your computers through your network connection? Just as a company may install card readers or hire a guard to admit only staff wearing employee badges, a **_firewall_** is software and/or hardware that protects a computer or network from intruders (see Figure B.13). As hardware, a firewall is a device that permits or denies network traffic based on security policy. Firewalls provide protection against threats to _confidentiality, authenticity,_ and _integrity_ by blocking traffic that doesn't look like legitimate access to networked computers.

Some firewalls make their policy decisions based entirely on network addresses. For example, if you have caller ID on your telephone, you may choose to answer calls only if they come from your friends or family. Likewise, a simple firewall can examine network traffic and permit only the traffic coming from a known source.

Other firewalls may permit traffic from an unknown source if it appears to be a response to a request that was made by a computer on the protected network. For example, if you call a friend at the office but she's in a meeting, you might leave a message for her to call you back. When she does, you may recognize the phone number of her office as a number you just called and answer the call, even though the office number isn't on the list of phone numbers you'd normally answer.

Even more advanced firewalls make decisions based on the content of the network traffic. Thinking back to the company with a security guard in the lobby, the guard

Figure B.13

Firewall, Intrusion Detection System, and Virtual Private Network

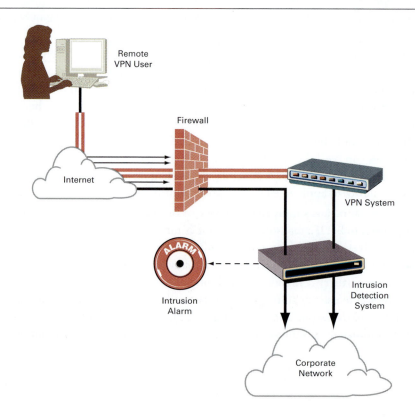

may allow a delivery person to enter the building if he's carrying envelopes or pizza, but not if he's carrying dynamite or bottles of acid. Of course, acid may be a regular delivery item in a chemical plant; not every company will want the same firewall policies.

While a firewall typically has a predefined policy about the network traffic it will allow, an ***intrusion detection system (IDS)*** is a device that watches network traffic for intrusion attempts and reports them. An ***intrusion prevention system (IPS)*** is a type of IDS that also takes action against intrusion attempts, for example, by creating new policies in a firewall to block the source of the attack. Intrusion detection and prevention systems work by having information about many different types of network attacks and matching the current network traffic against their lists of attack characteristics. When they sense an attack in progress, they can e-mail or page network administrators about the attack, so they can take appropriate action.

Denial-of-service attacks simply interfere with network *availability*. A ***denial-of-service (DoS)*** **attack** floods a server or network with so many requests for service that it slows down or crashes. Imagine if someone called every pizza delivery service in town and ordered 20 pizzas delivered to your office. Eventually you'd manage to sort out the confusion and you wouldn't have to pay for the pizzas, but meanwhile you'd be too busy dealing with the situation to get any work done.

Firewalls and intrusion detection and prevention systems can protect *availability* by preventing or reducing the effect of denial-of-service attacks. Some denial-of-service attacks use network capabilities that are technically permissible, but are almost never seen in legitimate network traffic; these attacks are easy to foil by denying those types of traffic. Other denial-of-service attacks send completely legitimate but useless traffic. Blocking those attacks involves recognizing an increase in network traffic beyond normal levels, determining the source or sources, and then blocking even legitimate-appearing traffic from those locations.

Most home broadband devices—for DSL and cable modem Internet connections—include a simple firewall. Home networking manufacturers have been packing more and more capabilities into their products, and even though the devices may be marketed as routers or firewalls, they generally contain a router, a firewall, and a switch or hub to connect multiple home computers. Some even include the DSL or cable modem, and some have a wireless access point, all in a device not much larger than a paperback book.

ENCRYPTED COMMUNICATIONS: SSL AND VIRTUAL PRIVATE NETWORKS

Earlier, we talked about types of network devices on which communications can be overheard—hubs and wireless access points. This is a threat to *confidentiality*—unauthorized individuals could be watching your communications. So if you're using wireless access, or are in a location where you don't know whether you're connected to a hub or a switch—or simply somewhere that you don't know who has access to the communications lines and equipment between you and your network destination—what can you do to protect the privacy of your communications?

The solution is encrypted communication. ***Encryption*** scrambles the contents of a file so that you can't read it without having the right decryption key. It means scrambling your communication in such a way that only the intended recipient can unscramble it. If you wanted to send the message, "Reschedule the grand opening for April 10," the encrypted version might look like

V'9:P)9@A1,||>[D:J_sepnvIf.Xj2FAs_[Dhud+'.

One way of using encryption to protect network transmissions is called Secure Sockets Layer (SSL), or somewhat less commonly, by the name of its successor, *Transfer Layer Security (TLS)*. SSL is a security technology that encrypts each network conversation—between one network client and one server—individually. Web traffic using SSL is called **https,** instead of just **http.** When you browse to a secure Web site and see the padlock icon, it's telling you that your browser is using SSL/TLS to encrypt your communications with the Web server. We cover more on SSL and other types of security technologies with respect to electronic commerce in Chapter 5.

In contrast, a *virtual private network (VPN)* uses encryption to protect the confidentiality of *all* network transmissions between two endpoints. Typically, one endpoint is a large office or headquarters, and the other endpoint may be a single computer, or it may be another office. All network communications between the two locations are routed through the VPN to be encrypted. This makes it look as though they have a dedicated network connection between them, even though they may really be communicating over public network links, hence the name, *virtual private network.*

OTHER SECURITY THREATS: MALWARE

You've probably heard of computer worms, viruses, and spyware, collectively known as malware. *Malware* is a contraction of **mal**icious sof**tware,** and refers to software designed to harm your computer or computer security. Malware existed even before most computers were connected to networks, but increased connectivity between computers has made it dramatically easier for malware to transfer to new victims.

A *virus* is software that is written with malicious intent to cause annoyance or damage. The virus software is activated unintentionally by the computer user. A *worm* is a type of virus that replicates and spreads itself, not just from file to file, but from computer to computer via e-mail and other Internet traffic. Viruses spread by tricking users into running them, for instance, by pretending to be an interesting program or e-mail message; worms spread by taking advantage of errors or weaknesses in computer programs. Viruses and worms most commonly threaten *availability,* by damaging or removing files, or by tying up a computer doing so much unauthorized work that it can't get its real job done.

Viruses and worms can be countered by running anti-virus software. Anti-virus software works very similarly to the intrusion detection systems described earlier. It has a long list of characteristics of known worms and viruses, and when it sees files being transferred or software running on the computer that has those characteristics, it alerts the user and often "quarantines" the file to part of the hard drive where it can't do any harm. Some anti-virus software can even remove the malicious instructions from computer files so that they are still useful once they're disinfected.

Anti-virus software can be run at different places in the network. Some viruses are transferred from computer to computer in e-mail messages, and anti-virus software on the e-mail server will help protect against them. It's very important to run anti-virus software on every PC, to protect against worms and viruses trying to attack the computer directly. And some companies have servers where customers can upload purchase orders or problem reports; they may run anti-virus software on those servers to screen all incoming files.

Spyware is a more recent type of malware than viruses and worms. *Spyware* (also called *sneakware* or *stealthware*) is malicious software that collects information about you and your computer and reports it to someone else without your permission. Therefore, spyware is a threat to *confidentiality.* Spyware most often gets installed on your computer secretly along with a piece of software you knew you were getting; for example, some peer-to-peer file sharing programs are notorious for including spyware.

The best defense against spyware is to install software only from trustworthy sources, but that can be hard to determine. Anti-spyware software is available that works just like antivirus software, recognizing patterns of known spyware and removing them from your computer. Two popular anti-spyware programs are Ad-Aware (www.lavasoftusa.com) and Spybot Search & Destroy (www.safer-networking.org).

Another category of malware is servers and bots. Sometimes after breaking into a computer, attackers will set up *unauthorized servers.* These servers are often used to distribute illegal copies of movies, music, and software, or may even be used to distribute kits for breaking into other computers.

In the context of malware, *bots* are programs designed to be controlled by an attacker to perform unauthorized work over a period of time. Some bots are used to send spam, making it look like it's coming from the victim's computer instead of from the attacker's. Other bots try to break into computers or perform denial-of-service (DoS) attacks against other networks or systems.

Bots and unauthorized servers can sometimes be detected by anti-virus or anti-spyware software—but they may be indistinguishable from legitimate servers. They can also sometimes be discovered by network intrusion detection systems. Sometimes they're even discovered by network administrators, noticing an unusual amount of network traffic coming from a single computer.

The Client/Server Software Model

LEARNING OUTCOME 6

So far, we've talked about how computers are connected together on networks without discussing the roles of the computers themselves. In the peer-to-peer home networks described at the beginning of the chapter, the computers were all equal. Each one had its own files and devices, which it could share with the other computers. But unless you're a business with very few computers, you'd probably use a client/server network instead of a peer-to-peer network.

A *client/server network* is a network in which one or more computers are servers and provide services to the other computers, which are called clients. The server or servers have hardware, software, and/or information that the client computers can access. Servers are usually powerful computers with large storage systems. Depending on the network, the server could be a high-end PC or a minicomputer and large companies often have several servers, each of which may provide services to different parts of the company. It's usually cheaper and more efficient to have software on a server where everyone can access it:

- A network license allowing a fixed number of people or everyone on the network to use a software package is usually cheaper than buying separate copies of software for each computer.

- It's easier to update one server copy of software than to update hundreds or even thousands of separate copies.

- Control and security of software and information are easier if they're on the server.

The parts of the network that connect the servers are usually built with stricter specifications than the parts that connect the clients. The servers' network equipment may have

- Higher-bandwidth connections, to carry the traffic from many clients across the company accessing the servers simultaneously.

- Higher-powered network processors, to route the greater traffic loads.

- Duplicate connections to the rest of the network, to provide continued service if one connection is accidentally or maliciously cut.
- Uninterruptible power supplies, which use batteries to keep the network running even when the power fails.

CLIENT/SERVER—A BUSINESS VIEW

The term client/server network can mean a network structure, that is, one or more computers providing services to other computers. However, client/server is a term that also describes a business model. As a business model, client/server describes distributed processing. That is, it describes where processing takes place. Different companies have different processing needs. For example, if your school has an online system on which you can check your grades, you'll probably find that you can't change grades at your end—access to that kind of processing is severely restricted. On the other hand, a bank employee would need to be able to process a loan at his or her computer.

You can use one of five basic client/server implementation models. Which one you use depends on your business environment and where you want processing implemented. Client/server networks differ according to three factors:

1. Where the processing for the presentation of information occurs, that is, where the information that you see on the screen or printout is formatted, and the editing of information as you enter it.
2. Where the processing of logic or business rules occurs. *Logic* deals with the processing that the software implements. For example, in a payroll application, the logic would dictate how to handle overtime, sick leave, and vacation time.
3. Where the data management component (DBMS) and information (database) are located. Or, put another way, how the information in the database is stored and retrieved.

Here's an example of the concept. Say you have a data warehouse with information on sales over the past five years. Your client workstation gets its information from your company's OLTP (online transaction processing) server or servers. Software on the servers extracts the information you need and transfers it to your client workstation. Your client workstation then builds the data warehouse according to your requirements and you can use your data warehouse for the OLAP (online analytical processing) you need.

In this example, you see a separation of duties to suit particular business needs. The servers process companywide OLTP software on transaction information and copy to your workstation the information you want to have. Your client computer has, and processes, only the information that you need. This is called a distributed data management model where the server's only duty is to help with data management; the client does everything else (see Figure B.14). This is one way of assigning the processing, logic, and data management. In the set of models that you'll see next, this is Model 5.

Each of the five business client/server models that follow has a different way of parceling out the three tasks of presentation processing, logic processing, and data management.

CLIENT/SERVER MODEL 1: DISTRIBUTED PRESENTATION In this first model, the server handles almost all functions, including a major portion of the presentation. The only processing that the client does is to help with formatting the information you see on the screen or printout.

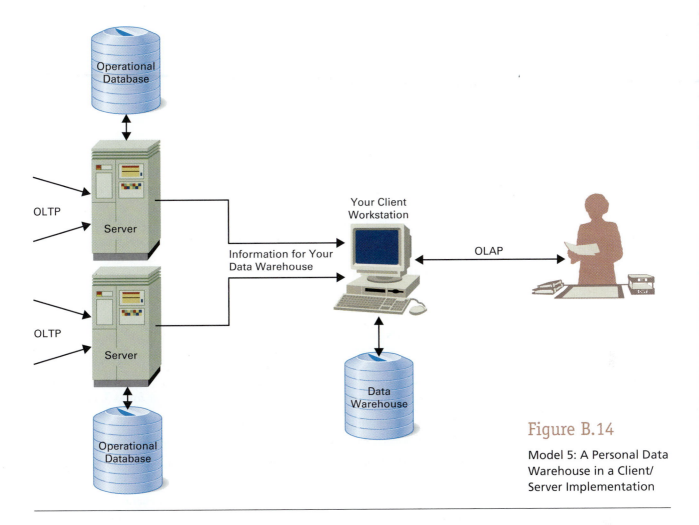

Figure B.14

Model 5: A Personal Data Warehouse in a Client/Server Implementation

CLIENT/SERVER MODEL 2: REMOTE PRESENTATION In the second model, the client handles all presentation functions. The processing of business rules happens on the server as does data management.

CLIENT/SERVER MODEL 3: DISTRIBUTED LOGIC In this model, the server handles all data management and the client handles all presentation formatting, but the logic processing is shared between the server and the client.

CLIENT/SERVER MODEL 4: REMOTE DATA MANAGEMENT In the fourth model, duties are fully separated again. The server handles data management only, and the client processes business rules and formats the presentation of results.

CLIENT/SERVER MODEL 5: DISTRIBUTED DATA MANAGEMENT In this final model, the client handles all presentation formatting and business rule processing, and both the server and client share data management duties.

Which model you choose depends on the organization of your business and where you want processing to occur. We have already looked at Model 5, so now let's examine a more complicated case—Model 3, distributed logic.

CLIENT/SERVER IMPLEMENTATION: MODEL 3 In model 3 (distributed logic) the server handles the entire data management function, the client handles the entire presentation function, and server and client share in the processing or application of business rules (see Figure B.15).

Suppose you're the manager of the manufacturing division of an organization and need to give pay raises to each of your employees. You use the following divisional and organizational rules for determining pay raises.

Divisional Rules

1. Each manufacturing employee begins with a base raise of $2,500.
2. No manufacturing employee can receive less than a $2,000 raise.
3. If loss of time because of injury is longer than three days, then deduct $500 from the pay raise.
4. If the employee worked less than five days of overtime, then deduct $500 from the pay raise.

Organizational Rules

1. No employee with less than five years of experience can receive a pay raise that exceeds $2,500.
2. Each employee's pay raise must be within 20 percent of last year's raise.
3. Each employee who has taken three or more business-related trips in the last year gets an extra $500 raise.

The following process would then determine the exact pay raise for each employee.

1. You would request information for the employee.
2. Your client workstation would send that request to the server.
3. The server would retrieve the employee information from the employee database.
4. The server would return the employee information to your client workstation.
5. Your client workstation would execute the divisional manufacturing business rules (or logic) that apply to pay raises for manufacturing employees.
6. Your client workstation would format and present the information pertaining to the employee and the appropriate pay raise.
7. You would submit the proposed pay raise for processing.
8. Your client workstation would send that information to the server.
9. The server would execute the organizational business rules or logic relating to pay raises for all employees.
10. The server would return the employee's pay raise (modified according to the organizational business rules) to your work station.
11. Your client workstation would format and present the modified pay raise.
12. You would submit the finalized pay raise for final processing.
13. Your client workstation would send that information to the server.
14. The server would update the employee database to reflect the employee's pay raise.

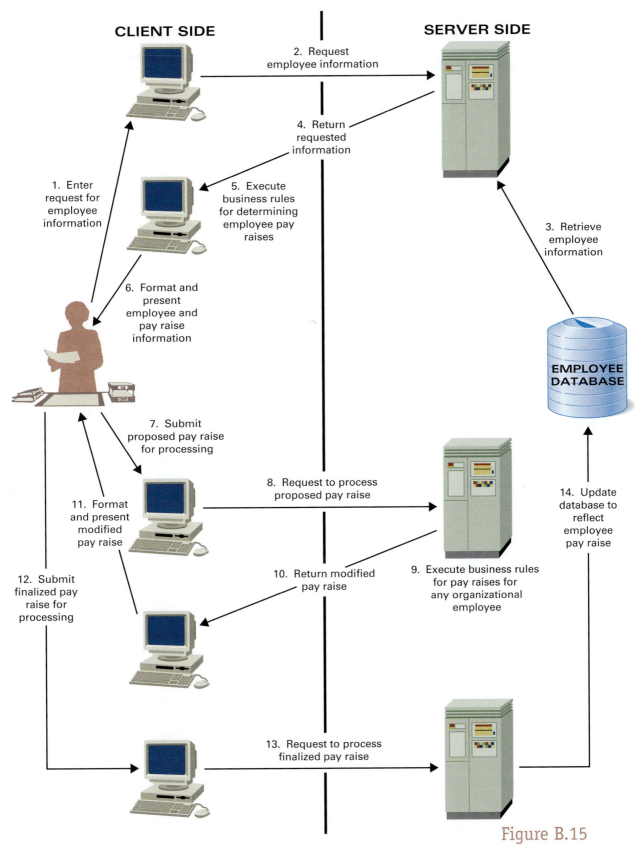

CLIENT SIDE

SERVER SIDE

2. Request employee information

4. Return requested information

1. Enter request for employee information

5. Execute business rules for determining employee pay raises

3. Retrieve employee information

6. Format and present employee and pay raise information

EMPLOYEE DATABASE

7. Submit proposed pay raise for processing

8. Request to process proposed pay raise

14. Update database to reflect employee pay raise

11. Format and present modified pay raise

10. Return modified pay raise

9. Execute business rules for pay raises for any organizational employee

12. Submit finalized pay raise for processing

13. Request to process finalized pay raise

Figure B.15

Model 3: Client/Server Implementation for Employee Pay Raises

In this example the server was responsible for data management (retrieving and updating employee information) and executing the business rules or logic that apply to all employees for pay raises. Your client workstation is responsible for editing your entry of information, formatting the presentation of information to you, and executing the business rules or logic that apply to pay raises for manufacturing employees.

When you take the process of distributed logic apart as we did in this example, it seems very complex and tedious. And if you're writing the software to do it, it is. However, as a knowledge worker, the process is completely transparent, meaning that you don't know (or care) how data management, logic, and presentation are handled.

From a management point of view, client/server is a very tidy, organized, and flexible way to make information that all managers need available to them, while keeping information and processing that individual departments need local to the appropriate office.

Summary: Student Learning Outcomes Revisited

1. **Identify and describe the four basic concepts on which networks are built and describe what is needed to set up a small peer-to-peer network at home.** There are four basic concepts on which almost all networks are built. They are

   - *Network interface cards (NICs)* in each computer
   - A connecting device like a *hub, switch,* or *home/broadband router*
   - At least one communications medium
   - Network operating system software

   To set up a peer-to-peer network at home, you'd need

   - *Ethernet cards* (as the NICs) in each computer
   - A home/broadband router
   - *Cat 5* cables
   - A network operating system, like Windows

2. **Describe the components used to build large business networks and define and compare local area networks (LANs), wide area networks (WANs), and metropolitan area networks (MANs).** Large business networks are built using

   - Network interfaces in each computer
   - *Hubs* or *switches,* to connect the computers together into subnetworks
   - *Routers,* to connect the subnetworks together

   A *local area network (LAN)* covers a geographically contiguous area. A *wide area network (WAN)* is a set of connected networks serving areas not in immediate proximity. A *metropolitan area network (MAN)* is a set of connected networks all within the same city or metropolitan area, but not geographically continuous.

3. **Compare and contrast the various Internet connection possibilities.** There are five ways described in this book to connect a computer or network to the Internet. They are

   - Phone line and *modem,* which uses a phone line and prevents your using the same line for voice communication at the same time. It's the slowest type of connection.
   - Phone line and *Digital Subscriber Line (DSL),* which, although it uses the phone line, does not prevent simultaneous voice communication. A DSL connection is a *broadband* connection.
   - Cable TV line and *cable modem,* which brings Internet access in with your cable modem and doesn't use the phone line at all. It's also broadband.
   - Cable programming via a satellite and *satellite modem,* which supports both cable television programming and Internet access.
   - *T1,* a high-speed business circuit running at 1.544Mbps, or *DS3,* a very-high-speed business circuit running at 44.736Mbps.

4. **Compare and contrast the types of communications media.** *Communications*

media are the paths, or physical channels, over which information travels in a network. There are two options: wired and wireless. Wired communications media include **twisted-pair cable, coaxial cable,** and **optical fiber.** Of these, optical fiber is the fastest and the most secure. Wireless communications media include **infrared, Bluetooth, WiFi, microwave,** and satellite. Infrared and Bluetooth are for very short distances only, Wi-Fi is for short distances, microwave has short and medium distance versions, and satellite is for long distance.

5. **State the four principles of computer security and describe how different network security devices reflect those principles.** The four principles of computer security are

- **Confidentiality,** meaning that information can only be obtained by those authorized to access it
- **Authenticity,** meaning that information really comes from the source it claims to come from
- **Integrity,** meaning that information hasn't been altered
- **Availability,** meaning that a service or resource is available when it's supposed to be

    Firewalls protect confidentiality, authenticity, and integrity by blocking traffic that doesn't look like legitimate access to networked computers. **Intrusion detection systems (IDSs)** protect all types of computer security by watching for network intrusion attempts and reporting them; intrusion prevention systems (IPSs) take action to block them. **Encryption methods,** including SSL and **virtual private networks (VPNs),** protect confidentiality by scrambling your communication in such a way that only the intended recipient can unscramble it.

6. **Describe client/server business networks from a business and physical point of view.** A **client/server network** is a network in which one or more computers are servers and provide services to the other computers, which are called clients.

    Business View: There are five different configurations based on three factors:

- Where the processing for the presentation of information occurs
- Where the processing of logic or business rules occurs
- Where the data management component (DBMS) and information (database) are located.

    Physical View: The concepts on which larger networks are based are the same as those on which small networks are built. However, the network equipment for the servers may have higher-bandwidth connections and more powerful processors, duplicate connections to the rest of the network, and uninterruptible power supplies to keep the servers available during power failures.

Key Terms and Concepts

Bandwidth, 316
Bluetooth, 325
Broadband, 317
Broadband router (home
    router), 311
Cable modem, 319
Cat 5 (Category 5), 310
Client/server network, 331
Coaxial cable (coax), 324
Communications media, 323
Communications satellite, 326
Computer network, 309
Denial-of-service (DoS) attack, 329
Digital Subscriber Line (DSL), 318
DS3, 320
Encryption, 329
Ethernet card, 310

Firewall, 328
Hub, 312
Infrared, 325
Internet, 316
Intrusion detection system
    (IDS), 329
Intrusion prevention system
    (IPS), 329
Local area network (LAN), 315
Malware, 330
Metropolitan area network
    (municipal area network,
    MAN), 315
Microwave transmission, 325
Network interface card (NIC), 310
Optical fiber, 324
Repeater, 325

Router, 314
Satellite modem, 320
Spyware, 330
Switch, 312
T1, 320
Telephone modem, 317
Twisted-pair cable, 324
Virtual private network (VPN), 330
Virus, 330
Voice over IP (VoIP), 322
Wide area network (WAN), 315
WiFi (wireless fidelity), 325
Wired communications media, 323
Wireless access point (WAP), 310
Wireless communications
    media, 323
Worm, 330

Short-Answer Questions

1. How is a peer-to-peer network different from a client/server network?
2. What is an Ethernet card?
3. What does a network switch do?
4. What is bandwidth?
5. What do you need to have a dial-up connection to the Internet?
6. How is a DSL Internet connection different from a telephone modem connection?
7. What impact does Frame Relay have on a metropolitan area network?
8. What is Cat 5 cable used for?
9. What is Bluetooth?
10. What does WiFi do?
11. How does a VPN protect confidentiality?
12. How is client/server model 1 different from client/server model 2?

Assignments and Exercises

1. **WHAT ARE THE INTERNET ACCESS OPTIONS IN YOUR AREA?** Write a report on what sort of Internet connections are available close to you. How many ISPs offer telephone modem access? Is DSL available to you? Is it available to anyone in your area? Does your cable company offer a cable modem? If your school has residence halls, does it offer network connections? Compare each available service on price, connection speed, and extras like a help line, list of supported computers and operating systems, and people who will come out to your home and help you if you're having difficulties. What type of Internet connection do you currently use? Do you plan to upgrade in the future? If so, to what type of connection? If not, why not?

2. **INVESTIGATE BUILDING YOUR OWN HOME NETWORK** Build your own home network on paper. Assume you have the computers already and just need to link them together. Find prices for switches and routers on the Web. Also research Ethernet cards and cables. If you were to get a high-speed Internet connection

like DSL or cable modem, how much would it cost? Can you buy your own, or would you have to rent the modem from the phone or cable company?

3. **DEMONSTRATE THE IMPACT OF WIRELESS TECHNOLOGY** How many devices do you own or use that transmit signals (not just computer data) wirelessly? Think of as many as you can, and make a list showing the different types of signaling used by each device. Don't forget that some devices use multiple wireless technologies, like cell phones with both cellular signals for voice transmissions and Bluetooth for syncing their address books. Hint: Don't forget cordless phones, TV and stereo remotes, radios, and portable computers and PDAs with infrared capability (look for a small, glossy black window somewhere on the edge of the case). Can any of your devices communicate with each other?

4. **INVESTIGATE SATELLITE RADIO** At the time of writing, there were two satellite radio services: Sirius and XM. Do a little surfing on the Web and find out if there are any others now. Also find out what you have to buy to install each type, how much the antenna costs, how the system would work in your car, and how much the monthly subscription is.

5. **CONSIDER THE IMPORTANCE OF NETWORK SECURITY** Write a report about the importance of computer and network security in your daily life, in terms of the four principles of computer security. If you have a job in addition to being a student, write about computer security in your workplace. If you don't work outside the classroom, write about how computer security affects you at school and in your personal life. You may be surprised at how many things you do depend on some aspect of secure computer records and communications, like banking, grades, e-mail, timesheets, library and movie rental records, and many more.

6. **FIND OUT ABOUT FIREWALLS** Go to the Web and find out about software and hardware that protect your computer and home network, respectively.

   If you have only one computer connected to the Internet, then a software firewall like Zone Alarm will most likely be enough protection from intruders. Find three different firewall software packages on the Web. A good place to start looking would be the sites that sell anti-virus software. Compare the firewall software on price and features. Some sites to try are

   - Symantec at www.symantec.com
   - Trend Micro at www.trendmicro.com
   - McAfee at www.mcafee.com
   - The Virus List (a virus encyclopedia) at www.viruslist.com

   If you have a home network, look into hardware firewall options. How many different hardware firewalls can you find on the Web site of your favorite electronics retailer? (Hint: Look in the feature lists of home routers and broadband routers, even if they don't have the word firewall in their name.)

APPENDIX C
CAREERS IN BUSINESS

Student Learning Outcomes

1. IDENTIFY THE CAREER FIELD AND BUSINESS SPECIALIZATION IN WHICH YOU ARE INTERESTED.

2. PROVIDE TYPICAL JOB TITLES AND DESCRIPTIONS FOR YOUR CAREER FIELD.

3. LIST AND DESCRIBE THE IT SKILLS YOU NEED TO GAIN WHILE IN SCHOOL.

Introduction

In the business world, you need to be "a jack of all trades and a master of one." That means that you need to excel in a particular business functional area (or specialization), such as finance, accounting, marketing, or any of the other many business specializations. It also means that, while your expertise lies within one functional area, you need to be competent in all the other functional areas.

Think about majoring in marketing, for example. You need expertise in consumer behavior, marketing strategies, branding techniques, and many other marketing-oriented concepts. But as a marketing analyst, you need other skills to be successful. You need knowledge of accounting and finance so you can put together a budget and monitor expenses. You need team and employee management skills so you can work effectively in a group and manage other people. You need knowledge of production and operations management so you can understand works-in-progress information and transportation optimization algorithms.

No matter what your career choice, you need knowledge of information technology tools that will allow you to perform your tasks more efficiently and effectively. This textbook isn't about trying to get you to major in information technology or choose MIS as a career. It's about informing you of the role of information technology and MIS in an organization and enabling you to select and use the right IT tools to carry out your tasks.

In this appendix, we want to explore with you many of the career specializations in business, including:

- Accounting
- Finance
- Hospitality and tourism management
- Information technology
- Management
- Marketing
- Production and operations management
- Real estate and construction management

At your school, there are probably departments devoted to providing degrees in these specializations. While titles and nomenclatures may differ (e.g., production and operations management is often called management science, operations research, statistics and operations technology, or some other variation), those specializations represent the major functional areas in a typical business.

After providing you with a brief introduction to each specialization, we include the following information:

- List of typical job titles and their descriptions
- IT tools you should focus on learning while in school
- Statistics concerning the job market

It is our hope that, after reading this appendix, you will come to understand that IT and MIS are important no matter what your career choice. You may be taking this class because it's a required part of the business curriculum. It's required because, no matter what career you choose, you need knowledge of IT and MIS. It's similar to taking a human resource management class. While you may not be majoring in human resource management, you will at some time in your career have to manage people. Knowing how to manage them effectively is a career opportunity for you.

We believe that being able to identify the right technology tools and use them effectively is also a career opportunity for you. We encourage you to take some time to critically evaluate the many specializations in business, select the one you're most interested in, and then identify what information technology tools you need to learn in school to make your business career a success.

Accounting

Accounting is the language of business. All businesses, for-profit and not-for-profit, need accountants to communicate financial information. Accountants must understand all aspects of business in order to properly communicate the financial information.

There are five broad areas of accounting—public practice, industry, government, nonprofit, and education. The first three are the most common. In public accounting, the accountant serves as an outside advisor to business organizations. The primary areas of responsibility are auditing, which involves examining the financial statements of a company to assure compliance with generally accepted accounting practices; and tax advisory services, which involve helping businesses plan the most beneficial structure and practices for applying tax rules and regulations, as well as preparing the actual tax returns.

Industry accounting is working within a company to manage investor relations, banking relations, daily financial affairs, and plan new products or services. Since almost all activities in a company involve either cash inflow or outflow, the accounting function is involved in almost every business decision of an organization.

Government accounting can range from working at the city level to working at the federal level. Typical positions are auditors, revenue managers, and budget analysts. There are also many government agent positions with organizations such as the FBI, ATF, and IRS. These positions involve enforcement of federal laws and regulations. Any accounting position requires knowledge of broad business concepts, government regulations, and the financial implications of both.

TYPICAL JOB TITLES AND DESCRIPTIONS

The typical job titles found in accounting and their descriptions are listed below.

Chief Financial Officer—Corporate officer primarily responsible for managing the financial risks of the business or agency. This officer is also responsible for financial planning and record keeping, as well as financial reporting to higher management. Additional duties involve investor relations, banking relations, and long-term financial planning.

Management Accountant—Also called cost, managerial, industrial, corporate, or private accountant—records and analyzes the financial information of the companies for which they work. Other responsibilities are budgeting, performance evaluation, cost management, and asset management. Management accountants usually are part of executive teams involved in strategic planning or new product development. They analyze and interpret financial information needed by corporate executives in order to make sound business decisions. They also prepare financial reports for other groups, including stockholders, creditors, regulatory agencies, and tax authorities. Within accounting departments, management accountants may work in various areas, including financial analysis, planning and budgeting, and cost accounting.

Environmental Accountant—Helps businesses understand their environmental costs and factor these costs into their financial and other decision-making processes. Helps businesses find ways to save money through environmental protection measures. Using special environmental cost assessment systems, environmental accountants help companies improve their decisions regarding product mixing, manufacturing, waste management options, and other areas.

Government Accountants and Auditors—Work in the public sector, maintaining and examining the records of government agencies and auditing private businesses and individuals whose activities are subject to government regulations or taxation. Accountants employed by federal, state, and local governments guarantee that revenues are received and expenditures are made in accordance with laws and regulations. Those employed by the federal government may work as Internal Revenue Service agents or in financial management, financial institution examination, or budget analysis and administration.

Internal Auditor—Verifies the accuracy of the organization's internal records and checks for mismanagement, waste, or fraud. Internal auditors examine and evaluate their firms' financial and information systems, management procedures, and internal controls to ensure that records are accurate and controls are adequate to protect against fraud and waste. They also review company operations, evaluating their efficiency, effectiveness, and compliance with corporate policies and procedures, laws, and government regulations. Internal auditors also may recommend controls for their organization's computer system, to ensure the reliability of the system and the integrity of the data.

Public Accountant—Performs a broad range of accounting, auditing, tax, and consulting activities for clients, which may be corporations, governments, nonprofit organizations, or individuals. Some public accountants concentrate on tax matters, such as advising companies about the tax advantages and disadvantages of certain business decisions and preparing individual income tax returns. Others offer advice in areas such as compensation or employee health care benefits, the design of accounting and data-processing systems, and the selection of controls to safeguard assets. Still others audit clients' financial statements and inform investors and authorities that the statements have been correctly prepared and reported. Public accountants, many of whom are Certified Public Accountants (CPAs), generally have their own businesses or work for public accounting firms.

Tax Accountant—Responsible for tax planning and tax return preparation. Requires an understanding of tax laws and other regulations for individuals, estates, trusts, and businesses (both large and small). Is frequently consulted for the legal/tax structuring of new business ventures to ensure the most beneficial application of tax regulations.

INFORMATION TECHNOLOGY SKILLS YOU SHOULD PURSUE

To be effective in accounting, we recommend that you gain knowledge in the IT tools and concepts listed below and on the next page.

Accounting Information Systems—Almost all accounting systems are computerized. The accountant must know how to operate the software and be able to quickly learn new software as the technology changes.

Database Management—Many accounting systems require ad hoc reports and structural changes to keep up with changes to the company. The accountant is responsible for keeping the accounting system current. This requires knowledge of database management systems as accounting information is stored in a database.

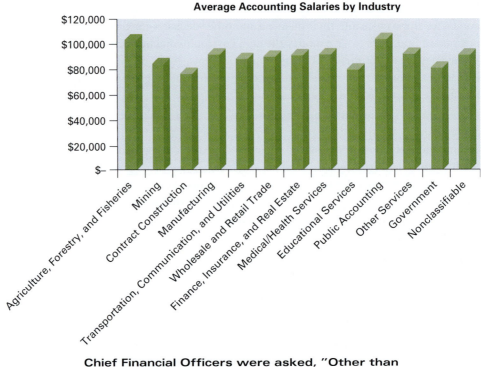

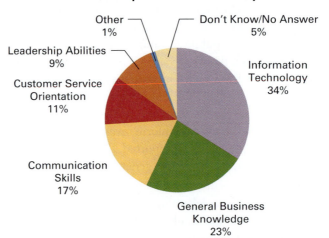

Figure C.1

Employment and Other Information in Accounting[1,2]

Database Design—To properly audit an accounting system, the accountant must understand the design of the database and be able to follow transactions through the system.

Web Research—Accountants must frequently consult rules and regulations which are available on the Internet. The ability to rapidly search and apply information is a necessity for any accounting position.

Spreadsheet Modeling—Financial projections and analyses require extensive use of electronic spreadsheets. Accountants must be expert at these skills to be productive.

Network Security—The accountant is responsible for the security of the assets of a company. Knowledge of the computer systems and networks is required to assure the security of the company's information.

Finance

Finance plays an integral part in the decision-making process at most companies. There are several distinct areas of study in finance that lead to very different professional job tracks. These tracks, broadly described, are corporate finance, banking, and investments. However, a common thread to each of these tracks is the basic tools that you use to aid in decision making. In addition, finance professionals need to have strong interpersonal skills to aid others in making the correct decisions for their companies or their personal finances.

The study of finance draws heavily from three different academic disciplines: accounting, economics (especially microeconomics), and statistics. These disciplines provide the informational and analytical frameworks with which a decision maker works on a day-to-day basis. Thus, a finance professional must have a background in each of these areas of study. The finance professional can work at a company, aiding in the allocation of resources; or in the banking industry, providing funds for businesses and individuals; or in the investments industry, aiding individuals or institutions with the investment of their resources. In all of these roles, the decision maker must rely on information technology to support the analysis and decisions being made, and in many situations the IT function in a company will be integral to the implementation of the decisions made. Of growing importance is the maintenance of large databases containing information regarding clients, customers, projects, and other areas that are a focus of research by the finance professional. These databases can be either provided by third-party vendors, or created by the finance professional.

TYPICAL JOB TITLES AND DESCRIPTIONS

The typical job titles found in finance and their descriptions are listed below.

Corporate Treasurer—Responsible for controlling the cash needs of the corporation. The cash-budgeting process will identify whether the corporation has a cash surplus or deficit. Any surplus will be invested in short-term, safe investment securities. Any deficit will need to be provided for with bank loans or issues of commercial paper.

Corporate Financial Analyst—Aids in the investment of corporate resources. Prepares project reports for the capital budgeting process and helps the various operating units control spending and manage their investment in both short-term and long-term assets. Includes management of inventory investment, accounts receivable investment, and cash management.

Bank Loan Officer—Works with individuals, small businesses, and large corporations to provide funds for their spending needs. This can range from the purchase of a car to the financing of a fleet of airplanes. Strong analytical skills as well as interpersonal skills are a requirement in this field.

Trust Officer—Works at a commercial bank primarily with two very different groups. First are individuals who establish trusts for estate planning and other reasons. Second are business and municipal issuers of bonds. In this second role, the trust officer serves to ensure that the interests of the investors are met by the issuer.

Security Analyst—Works in the markets to provide investment information and sometimes advice to individual and institutional investors. Can work either for a brokerage firm or for an institutional investment company.

Portfolio Manager—Typically works for institutions such as mutual funds or insurance companies. Directs the investment decisions for these institutions, choosing which stocks, bonds, and other investments are appropriate. Directs the efforts of several security analysts in this process.

Stock Broker—Works primarily with individuals to aid in investment in stocks and bonds. Purchases and sells stocks at the direction of the client. In some circumstances is also responsible for providing information and even an investment strategy for the client.

INFORMATION TECHNOLOGY SKILLS YOU SHOULD PURSUE

To be effective in finance, we recommend that you gain knowledge in the IT tools and concepts listed below.

Spreadsheet Modeling—An advanced knowledge of spreadsheet modeling is essential to most careers in finance. Forecasting future cash flows and evaluating changes in assumptions will aid the decision maker.

Statistical Packages—Statistical analysis helps the decision maker identify and measure the risk inherent in a project. The advanced statistical packages available support this analysis.

Database Management—The ability to create, maintain, and manipulate databases is essential to the decision-making tools in finance. Information such as returns, credit risk measures, and so on are used by investors.

Figure C.2

Employment and Other Information in Finance [3,4]

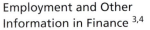

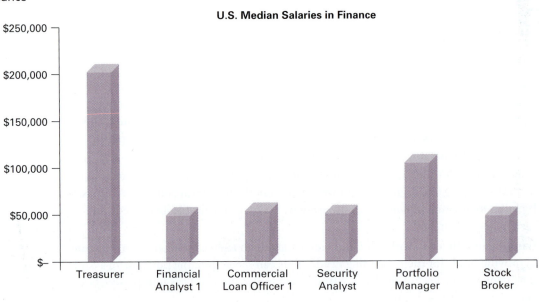

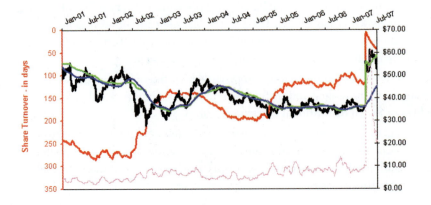

Internet and Web Portals—Corporations use Web sites to provide investors with information regarding the company. Automated bill payment is a means of controlling accounts receivable and accounts payable, both for individuals and businesses.

Search Engines—Information is the lifeblood of decision making. Being able to accurately and efficiently gather information is a critical skill.

Technology Strategy and Innovation—Banks are innovating new ways to efficiently process customer deposits/withdrawals. Businesses are creating new payment systems via intranets. An understanding of how this innovation affects the company is critical to the finance professional.

Hospitality and Tourism Management

If you dream about exotic vacations, traveling to alluring destinations, and having fun, a career in hospitality and tourism management (HTM) might be for you. HTM is one of the world's largest, most diverse, and exciting industries. According to the World Travel and Tourism Council (www.wttc.org), by the end of 2007, the industry is expected to generate $7.1 trillion in economic activity (or 10.4 percent of the world's total Gross Domestic Product) and account for 8.3 percent of the world's total employment. That is in excess of 231 million jobs—or one out of every 12 jobs. With a projected 4.3 percent per annum real growth rate for the next 10 years, the industry outlook is extremely favorable. By 2017, the industry is expected to reach $13.2 trillion and employ nearly 263 million people. Careers can range from hotel general managers and controllers to restaurant operators and event planners to technology developers and electronic commerce specialists. In fact, you can find positions associated with every academic business discipline somewhere in the hospitality and tourism field.

Hospitality and tourism businesses make money by serving guests and creating for their guests unique, personable, and memorable experiences. These businesses are especially challenging to operate because of the intangible nature of what consumers purchase and the perishability of the services or products sold (for example, revenue from rooms not sold today or cruise ships that sail away not filled can never be recouped). Adding to the challenge are the heterogeneity of the customers (each customer has different needs and expectations), the simultaneous production and consumption of the services, the dependence on labor, and the ease with which products and services can be copied.

TYPICAL JOB TITLES AND DESCRIPTIONS

A sampling of typical job titles found in hospitality and tourism management and their descriptions are listed below. Increasingly, to be effective in any hospitality business role, one must have a solid grounding in concepts related to information technology (IT) because of its pervasiveness throughout and impact on every aspect of the business. It is not enough to understand only one business discipline (e.g., marketing, finance, accounting, human resources, etc.) but rather at least one, if not more, business disciplines and the roles technology plays to enable (or sometimes constrain) activities, service, customer loyalty, business strategies, etc. IT has become an indispensable tool for any business and such an integral part of the business that practically every business decision affects IT, and every IT decision impacts the business. And this is especially so in hospitality and tourism. IT can help organizations drive revenues and cut costs (thereby improving profitability), enhance guest service and experiences (thereby improving loyalty), improve managerial controls (thereby reducing loss or theft), and enhance communications and reporting (thereby improving information flows so that people are empowered to make informed decisions and perform their jobs to help the organization operate effectively and efficiently and to help staff "wow" guests and create outstanding and memorable experiences).

General Manager—Responsible for overseeing an entire operation (e.g., hotel, restaurant, casino, theme park, etc.). Typically works his/her way through the various departments of the operation to understand it from the ground up. Sets strategy, oversees the financial aspects of the business, interfaces with the community, helps market the operation, manages people, and is accountable to the owner of the operation. Relies on operational systems and reports to manage, control, and direct the business. Uses technology to track and communicate with customers, suppliers, and employees.

Controller—Responsible for the accounting and financial aspects of the operation. Establishes and manages budgets, maintains the books, prepares financial reports, acquires funding for capital projects, and controls against theft and waste. Typically a heavy spreadsheet user and maintains the back-office accounting systems.

Director of Sales and Marketing—Oversees the sales and marketing activities of the operation and is typically responsible for group business (i.e., corporate accounts, meetings, and conventions). In charge of all the operation's marketing collateral, promotions, and electronic commerce initiatives. Also responsible for the sales and catering system, lead tracking system, and sales force automation.

Director of Human Resources—Responsible for all aspects of staffing and team building. Responsibilities include hiring and termination decisions, benefits administration, payroll, policy compliance, training, promotions, special programs, and succession planning. Uses time and attendance systems, payroll systems, and human resource information systems.

Director of Room Operations—Responsible for all guest service functions in a hotel. These include front desk, bell staff, housekeeping, concierge, and reservations. Responsible in part for managing several key systems, including the property management system, the reservation system, the telephone and call accounting systems, the guest lock system, and in-room guest amenities (e.g., movies, high-speed Internet access, mini bars, etc.).

Revenue Manager—Responsible for setting rates, restrictions, and selling strategies for hotel rooms and managing room inventory allocated to the various distribution channels used by the hotel. Relies on the hotel's revenue (yield) management system, reservation system, and property management system to perform his/her daily tasks.

Food and Beverage Director—Oversees all food and beverage operations. Manages day-to-day operations, purchasing, and inventory management. Key systems maintained and used include point-of-sale, inventory management, and purchasing and receiving systems. Culinary expertise is helpful to complement strong business acumen.

IT Manager—Oversees, maintains, and secures the various computer systems used throughout the organization, provides support to end users, and assists with the selection, procurement, and implementation of computer applications and hardware.

INFORMATION TECHNOLOGY SKILLS YOU SHOULD PURSUE

To be effective in hospitality and tourism management, we recommend that you gain knowledge in the IT tools and concepts listed below.

Personal Computer (PC) Applications—Proficiencies in Microsoft Office applications, electronic mail, and the Internet are essential to every professional position in the hospitality and tourism industry.

Hospitality-Specific Applications—There are numerous systems required to run a hospitality and tourism operation. Some of the core systems include the hotel property management system (to manage hotel room inventory and check in/out guests), the central reservations system (for hotel bookings), the point-of-sale system (for food, beverage, and gift shop sales), the revenue (yield) management system (for managing hotel rates, restrictions, and selling strategies), the accounting system (for maintaining the books), and the guest history/loyalty system (for guest preferences, past purchases, frequent travel program management, and CRM).

Database Management—The underlying technology behind most hospitality applications is a database management system. This allows information to be collected, stored, managed, and reported.

Project Management—Hospitality businesses are complex entities with many variables that must be carefully managed, especially when technology applications are involved. Important responsibilities of any manager (not just an IT manager) are to be able to simultaneously manage many activities (tasks or projects) and multiple personnel, budget for and allocate resources, and deliver results by holding people accountable and managing scope. To do this, strong project management skills are an absolute must.

Business Analysis—Because the impacts of technology are far-reaching within the organization and impact job skills/duties, business processes, and information flows, it is important to have a strong analytical mind to understand how and where to use technology, the potential implications (both good and bad), and the resource needs. A large part of any business person's role is to be able to see problems and opportunities and to match technology where appropriate to solve problems and capitalize on opportunities.

Decision Support Systems/Executive Information Systems—Hospitality and tourism operations are fast paced and information intensive. Managers must be able to use software applications to analyze and interpret information, model the business under different scenarios, and make informed and timely decisions.

Computer/Network Security—Given our dependence upon technology, both as individuals and as business organizations, and the many potential threats that come with using technology and conducting business digitally (e.g., exposure to viruses and worms, hacking, computer outages, etc.), managers must be well versed (at least from a macro level) about these vulnerabilities, educate their employees, and be prepared to take preemptive action, that is, develop and implement strategies, practices, and policies to protect the organization so that systems, data, identities, and assets are not compromised.

Electronic Commerce—Electronic commerce goes beyond hotel and restaurant bookings and merchandise or gift certificate purchases, etc. Hospitality and tourism professionals must know how to use the Internet to effectively and cost-efficiently reach consumers, serve them, and gain their loyalty. It is important to understand Web site design principles, interactive or electronic marketing, Web positioning strategies, and search engine optimization. Increasingly important is tapping into Travel 2.0, a term coined to reflect the next generation of Internet developments occurring in the travel space. Adapted from the concept of Web 2.0, Travel 2.0 reflects the growing interactive, multimedia experience of the Web and increased consumer empowerment as a result of the democratization of information, consumer-generated content, social networking, comparison-shopping tools, mashups (the combining of content from multiple Web sites into a single display), and more.

Distribution Channel Management—One of the most complex aspects of the hospitality and tourism business today is distribution channel management. Having the

Position	Nationwide	150–350 Rooms	>800 Rooms
Banquet Director	$42,436	$35,019	$65,740
Catering Sales Manager	37,795	35,824	48,225
Controller	68,541	59,707	95,532
Director of HR	59,717	53,073	82,202
Director of MIS	54,636	53,045	60,972
Director of Sales	68,269	N/A	99,495
Director of Rooms	63,688	59,685	73,607
Executive Chef	67,505	61,665	95,532
General Manager	85,616	102,625	165,970
Restaurant Manager	37,151	37,131	42,436

Figure C.3

Median Salaries for Hotel Positions (by Hotel Size)[5]

ability to build and manage channel relationships, synchronize channel information, track channel productivity, integrate the various technologies, and maintain the technology infrastructure required to support the many available distribution channels is a competitive necessity.

Revenue Management—One of the greatest career growth areas is revenue management, which involves analyzing and forecasting supply and demand patterns and trends and setting appropriate room rates, sell strategies, and room inventory allotments to maximize hotel revenues. This area brings together statistics, marketing, and finance.

Customer Relationship Management (CRM)—At the heart of any hospitality and tourism firm is the guest, the primary reason for being in business. Taking a guest-centric view of the business to provide unique and personalized experiences is fundamental to building guest loyalty and maintaining a competitive edge.

IT Strategy—It is important for business executives to understand how to align IT with the business strategy and allocate resources appropriately to achieve business goals and create competitive advantage. One must be able to assess risk factors, evaluate costs versus benefits, and build convincing business cases to win the necessary approval, support, and resources to launch IT project initiatives.

Information Technology

Information technology (IT) tools and management information systems (MIS) are now so pervasive in business environments and every aspect of your life that it's hard to imagine how the world would operate without them.

As this book is about IT and MIS, we have often discussed the varied careers in this specialization. Careers in this field range from the very managerial—such as the chief information officer (CIO) who oversees the use of information as an important organizational resource—to the very technical such as network security specialists who develop security and encryption algorithms and fight the never-ending battle protecting network resources from viruses and worms. Regardless, all IT people need to possess a solid understanding of the business environment and need to possess people-oriented and communications skills. IT specialists work daily with business colleagues in other functional areas to develop IT systems that meet business needs. IT people must, therefore, be able to communicate clearly and articulately and understand how the IT system serves the greater good of the organization.

TYPICAL JOB TITLES AND DESCRIPTIONS

The typical job titles found in information technology and their descriptions are listed below.

Programmer—Responsible for taking technical design documents concerning a new IT system and writing the software. Requires tremendous expertise in any of the many popular software programming languages such as Java, ASP, and C++. May also require expertise in development tools such as Rational Rose.

Business Analyst—Responsible for working with end users to determine the logical requirements for a new IT system and then building the technical design documents that a programmer will use to write the software. Requires tremendous people skills for soliciting and understanding end user requirements. May also require expertise in development tools which can create a repository of design documents for an IT system.

Database Designer/Developer—Responsible for working with end users to determine information requirements for a new IT system and then designing and implementing a database solution. Requires expertise in data modeling (such as E-R diagramming) and the use of popular DBMS tools such as Oracle and DB/2.

Web Services Expert—Facilitates the development of network-based IT systems that support e-commerce activities for an organization. Requires expertise in a number of IT tools and concepts including databases, security, and Web Services programming languages and tools such as ASP, XML, ASP.Net, XML.Net, C#, and Visual Studio.Net.

Network Engineer—Responsible for a wide range of activities associated with the design, development, implementation, and maintenance of IT networks. May include expertise in security and encryption methodologies. Usually requires expertise in the development of methodologies to stop, eliminate, and/or quarantine viruses and worms.

Data Warehouse Analyst/Developer—Responsible for working with end users to determine information requirements for new IT systems and then designing and implementing a data warehouse solution. Requires expertise in both database modeling and data warehouse information modeling. Requires expertise in the use of popular data warehousing platforms such as Cognos and Informatica.

INFORMATION TECHNOLOGY SKILLS YOU SHOULD PURSUE

To be effective in information technology, we recommend that you gain knowledge in the IT tools and concepts listed below.

Programming Languages—Programming languages are special-purpose languages that programmers use to write the actual software code. While you may not be a programmer, you must understand both basic and advanced programming constructs to understand what a proposed system can and cannot do.

Development Platforms—Development platforms are support software tools for logical and technical modeling and writing software. Not only do they provide a repository of project information, they also often support the automated translation of logical requirements into technical requirements and/or technical requirements into various platforms of implementation.

Job Type	Average Low	Average High
CIO	$50,000	$240,000
Director of IS	48,000	150,000
MIS Manager	60,000	85,000
Project Manager	33,000	85,000
Senior Software Engineer	40,000	130,000
Software Engineer	45,000	90,000
Web Developer	37,000	90,000
Applications Manager	52,500	100,000

Search Term	Hits on Monster.com
Programmer	5000+
Visual Basic	5000+
Chief Information Officer	1615
Database (Administrator)	5000+
Network (numerous terms included)	4089
Web Services	5000+
Data Warehouse (and variations)	5000+

Figure C.4

Employment and Other Information in Information Technology[6]

Databases—Databases are central to the information management activities of any organization. Databases support the design and implementation of logically related information. Database-stored information can then be used, manipulated, and massaged according to the needs of the end user without regard to the physical storage characteristics of information.

Data Warehouses—These support the management and assimilation of information for decision making and important business analysis activities. Data warehouses summarize and aggregate information in multiple dimensions or perspectives, giving end users the ability to "slice and dice" their way through the information to see patterns, identify problems, and identify competitive advantage opportunities.

Networks and Security—These include a vast array of technologies including communications protocols, telecommunications hardware such as routers, and architectures such as 2-tier and 3-tier (i.e., client/server networks).

Multimedia Tools—This tool set includes a variety of hardware and software associated with the capturing, creating, and manipulating of information in forms other than text and numbers. Such information includes audio, video, still photos, art, and so on.

Management

Managers play a critical role in shaping the future of U.S. businesses. Managers must be well-educated, creative, and effective. Managers hold over 3 million jobs in the United States and are in every industry. Managers plan, organize, direct, control, and coordinate the operations of organizations and major departments or programs. Organizations today operate in an increasingly complex and fast-changing environment, and managers depend increasingly on the use of technology to carry out their responsibilities. Successful managers possess a broad range of interpersonal and analytical skills.

The management major is one of the most eclectic disciplines in all of academia. *Administrative services managers* perform a broad range of duties in virtually every sector of the economy. They coordinate and direct support services to organizations as diverse as insurance companies, computer manufacturers, and government offices. *Marketing managers* develop the firm's detailed marketing strategy. Along with *product development managers* and *market research managers,* they determine the demand for products and services offered by the firm and its competitors. *Public relations managers* direct publicity programs to targeted audiences. They sometimes specialize in a specific area, such as crisis management—or in a specific industry, such as health care. *Sales managers* direct the firm's sales program. They assign sales territories, set goals, and establish training programs for the sales representatives. As computers are increasingly used to record and organize data, *financial managers* are spending more time developing strategies and implementing the long-term goals of their organization. *Human resources managers* handle all aspects of human resources work, including employment, compensation, benefits, and employee relations. *Management analysts,* or *management consultants,* analyze and propose ways to improve an organization's structure, efficiency, or profits.

TYPICAL JOB TITLES AND DESCRIPTIONS

The typical job titles found in management and their descriptions are listed below.

Business Development Manager—Is a team leader. The team is responsible for developing meaningful and profitable relationships with business partners. The manager recruits, trains, and enables subordinates to identify and exploit revenue opportunities with business partners. The manager coordinates and updates all ongoing relationships using the company's information technology system.

Entrepreneur—Entrepreneurs begin businesses and become their own boss. They usually start by creating and operating a small business. Sometimes, they purchase a franchise as a way to start. Increasingly, entrepreneurs are starting their first business on the Internet using e-commerce applications. Successful entrepreneurs face many options, including selling their business for large profits or equity in larger corporations, for example, the owners of Ben & Jerry's Ice Cream.

Human Resources Manager—Human resources (HR) managers serve as a link between management and employees. The HR manager provides specialized services to members of the organization. The manager's goal is to foster positive relationships, increase job satisfaction, and make sure all customers' or clients' needs are met. The HR manager's responsibilities include: administration, recruitment, compensation and benefits, training and development, health and safety, and employee relations.

Management Analyst—Management analysts define the nature and extent of problems and develop solutions. The individual analyzes relevant data including annual revenues, employment, and expenditures. They interview managers and employees while observing their operations. In recent years, information technology and e-commerce have provided new opportunities for management analysts. Companies hire management analysts to develop strategies for entering and remaining competitive in the new electronic marketplace.

Project Manager—The project manager has direct accountability for all aspects of assigned projects including development of strategy and tactical plans. The individual creates timelines for implementation; identifies resources required for the project; and oversees actual execution through to the final analysis. This position typically requires a master's degree; however, a bachelor's degree in business, with certification, is often sufficient.

Retail Manager—Retail managers are responsible for day-to-day management of a department or store. A major responsibility is to make sure that sales targets are met by ensuring that products and services are available and finding the best ways for selling them quickly and profitably. Primary goals of retail managers are to improve the economic performance of the company; increase customer satisfaction; and provide for continued growth.

Supply Chain Manager—The supply chain manager is responsible for managing and improving the supply chain of products and information flow. The individual builds relationships and linkages with customers and integrates them throughout the organization. The manager also assesses financial feasibility and impacts on businesses processes. The supply chain manager develops metrics for assessing supply chain value and links them with corporate revenue management. Managers use relevant feedback to improve the supply chain processes.

INFORMATION TECHNOLOGY SKILLS YOU SHOULD PURSUE

To be effective in management, we recommend that you gain knowledge in the IT tools and concepts listed below.

Database Management and Integration—Project managers use IT to develop various requirements, budgets, and schedules for projects. They schedule and coordinate projects using IT. Project managers develop projects that upgrade the firm's information security and other resources.

Internet and Web Portals—IT tools are invaluable resources for managers. They are able to access information critical to organizational success. HR managers use the Internet to link with employees, recruiters, and other organizations.

Spreadsheets—Spreadsheets help managers to organize work; calculate value; develop bar graphs or pie charts to display financial and other data; and determine the comparative cost of employee benefit programs and selected projects under consideration.

Enterprise Resource Planning (ERP)—In many corporations, managers recognize the need for a corporatewide system for communicating and sharing information. ERP provides an IT-based approach for creating and managing such a system.

Database Management—Managers create a centralized database relating to customers and the nature of contacts. The database includes client information, concerns, and resolutions. The database is available to relevant organization members.

Geographical Information Systems (GIS)—Managers that depend on natural resources such as fisheries for their business use GIS to identify, protect, and manage these resources. GIS is used to determine the habitats and migration patterns of various species, for instance.

Electronic Commerce (E-Commerce)—Business-to-Business and Business-to-Customer transactions via the Internet have accelerated the need for business

Median Salaries for Selected Positions in Management*

Human Resources Manager	$89,950
Marketing Manager	92,680
Retail Store Manager	42,160
Sales Manager	98,510
Restaurant Manager	42,120
Purchasing Manager	81,440
Food Service Manager	44,930
Administrative Services Manager	69,540
Public Relations Manager	85,820
Industrial Production Manager	81,960

Source: http://www.bls.gov/oes/current/oes_alph.htm.

*These are base median salaries for a select few positions. The salaries do not include other benefits usually reflected in total compensation.

Median Salary by State for Retail Store Managers

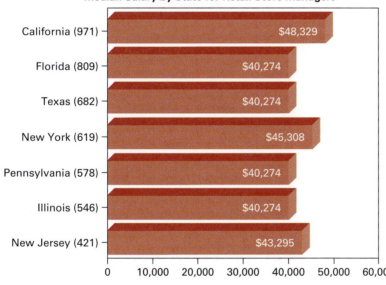

California (971) — $48,329
Florida (809) — $40,274
Texas (682) — $40,274
New York (619) — $45,308
Pennsylvania (578) — $40,274
Illinois (546) — $40,274
New Jersey (421) — $43,295

Figure C.5

Employment and Other Information in Management

managers to understand the potential of IT. Managers need the skills required for success in e-commerce.

Marketing

Marketing as a career field and business specialization encompasses a broad range of activities including marketing, product development, advertising, public relations, promotions, and sales. Combined, these activities are undertaken to market and sell a company's products and services in a profitable way and give the company a competitive advantage in the marketplace.

Marketing programs in a business school often have the largest number of student majors because of the vast array of marketing positions and because of the perceived glamour of the field. While the field may be glamorous, it is also highly competitive, requiring a unique blend of people skills and technical skills. Marketing professionals work extensively with technology in many ways. They use statistical and data-mining tools to better understand consumer buying behaviors and make decisions regarding target marketing. They often interface with supply chain management (SCM) and customer relationship management (CRM) systems to enable the company to integrate and capitalize on its vast chain of suppliers and customers. Many marketing professionals use sophisticated personal computer applications to develop marketing and promotional material such as flyers and other forms of advertisements. Marketing is most often the primary interface to the company's customers as marketing includes sales, promotions, advertising, and even customer service.

TYPICAL JOB TITLES AND DESCRIPTIONS

The typical job titles found in marketing and their descriptions are listed below.

Creative Marketing Specialist—Designs creative marketing solutions for all forms of advertising including print, Web-based, radio, and television. Possesses a tremendous knowledge of how people perceive and react to different types of advertising and promotional campaigns.

Marketing Coordinator—Manages and directs all marketing and advertising campaigns. Works closely with brand managers to uniquely identify and describe each "brand" within a company.

Account Manager—Develops, coordinates, and executes marketing strategies aimed at a select number of customers, with some account managers being responsible for only one customer. Develops very personal one-to-one relationships with key executives within the account.

Market Research Analyst—Designs, implements, and analyzes the information gathered from market research surveys and other instruments. Analyzes a variety of customer and consumer demographic information to determine competitive advantages in new marketing and advertising campaigns and new product development.

Market Development Manager—Contributes to the definition and development of new market opportunities for the company. May focus on products, geographical regions, and/or customer segments. Responsible for determining how best for the company to launch into a new area.

Brand Manager—Drives branding strategies and ensures that all external communications convey the message of the brand. Works closely with marketing communications and market development professionals to help the company achieve a competitive advantage through its branding efforts.

Product Development Manager—Responsible for acquiring insight into customer wants and needs and translating that insight into product specifications and quality. Works extensively in the field with focus groups of customers and often with product engineers in product design.

Product Manager—Charged with a product line and its contribution to the total sales of the company. Works to increase the profitability of existing products and to develop new products. Manages the entire product line life cycle from strategic planning to tactical and implementation activities.

Title	Average Salary
Advertising Manager	$ 53,602
Marketing Manager	53,602
Marketing Vice President	90,500–125,000
Public Relations Vice President	90,000
Public Relations Manager	55,000

Salary Information for Public Relations Managers		
Area	Average Base Pay	Average Incentive
Northeast	$78,400	$8,600
Southeast	74,500	8,500
North Central	70,400	7,500
South Central	71,200	6,900
West Coast	78,700	8,800

Figure C.6

Employment and Other Information in Marketing[7,8]

INFORMATION TECHNOLOGY SKILLS YOU SHOULD PURSUE

To be effective in marketing, we recommend that you gain knowledge in the IT tools and concepts listed below.

Customer Relationship Management (CRM) Systems—Marketing professionals are the primary interface to a company's customers. Knowledge of CRM software is essential for managing the relationships established with customers.

Budget Analysis/Impact Software—Marketing professionals spend much of their time evaluating the financial feasibility of new products and services, advertising campaigns, promotional strategies, and the like. Budget analysis/impact software allows marketing professionals to explore a variety of "what if" scenarios for a given situation or campaign.

Database Management—Marketing professionals work with vast amounts of information stored in the form of a database. Knowledge of the logical organization of a database and how the information can be accessed is essential.

Data Warehouses and Data-Mining Tools—These tools offer marketing professionals a way of summarizing large amounts of information and viewing it from different perspectives. This is often the first step in understanding the relationships inherent (but often hidden) in large amounts of information. Although marketing professionals usually do not design and build the actual data warehouse, they must understand the process and must also be well versed in using the data-mining tools for extracting information from a data warehouse.

Communications Support Software—This may include simple e-mail software but also extends to contact management software that enables marketing professionals to track their contacts with customers.

Desktop Publishing Software—Many marketing professionals are responsible for the development of "copy" material that will eventually become some form of paper-based advertisement such as a flyer or an insert in a newspaper. These documents must be developed using desktop publishing software to yield the highest quality.

Production and Operations Management

In general terms, production and operations management is a specialization that deals with the production, manufacturing, warehousing, and transportation of physical products and also the operations of some business environments such as how to schedule nurses in a hospital. So, production and operations management encompasses such aspects as inventory management, production design and control, logistics and transportation, raw materials acquisition and storage, employee scheduling, and so on. Along with finance and accounting, production and operations management is one of the most analytical and technical specializations in business.

Production and operations management touches on many major business initiatives. For example, to determine the right levels of inventory and timing of shipments, people in production and operations management must understand the needs and desires of customers, so customer relationship management is very much a part of production and operations management. People in production and operations management are often in charge of creating a tight supply chain with suppliers and customers, as well, so supply chain management is essential to effective production and operations management. Statistical and data-mining tools are also very important to a person in production and operations management. Many initiatives in this specialization focus on the "bottom line," that is, increasing bottom-line net profits by reducing costs. For this reason, people in production and operations management use highly sophisticated statistical and data-mining tools to explore every opportunity to drive costs out of the production, manufacturing, warehousing, and transportation functions.

TYPICAL JOB TITLES AND DESCRIPTIONS

The typical job titles found in production and operations management and their descriptions are listed below.

Production Scheduler—Usually found in a manufacturing environment focusing on preparing production schedules. Generates late-order reports, prioritizes operations and materials flow, and determines human resource allocations within a manufacturing environment. A knowledge of ERP (enterprise resource planning) systems is usually required.

Inventory Manager—Facilitates the planning for and procurement of inventory items including indirect materials and direct materials. Maintains accurate inventory counts and determines the optimal inventory levels to keep. Monitors inventory for potential stock-outs, oversupplies, and inventory obsolescence. Often helps to determine master schedule for production and manufacturing processes.

Quality Assurance Analyst—Works with all departments to ensure that QA/QC (quality assurance/quality control) guidelines are followed and metrics are met. Manages and oversees quality specifications for raw materials, processing, and packaging. Performs quality audits periodically to help the organization maintain its desired quality levels.

Purchasing Manager—Works directly with suppliers to develop programs that result in the low-cost acquisition of high-quality materials. Negotiates terms of contracts with suppliers.

Operations Analyst—Analyzes a variety of business operation segments including marketing, sales, purchasing, distribution, and warehousing. Makes recommendations concerning how to optimize business operations by reducing costs. Often works with sales and marketing groups to make recommendations on product performance, price adjustments, and product eliminations.

Search Term	Hits on Monster.com
Production Scheduler	249
Inventory Manager	5,000+
Quality Assurance	5,000+
Purchasing Manager	2,668
Operations Analyst	4,063
Statistics/Research Analyst	4,718
Logistics	5,000+

	Years of Experience		
	1–3 Years	4–7 Years	7+ Years
Product Fulfillment Manager	$46,200 to 52,100	$50,300 to 57,600	$55,700 to 64,300
Warehouse Manager	49,200 to 53,200	51,600 to 60,200	59,100 to 65,200
Operations Director	75,300 to 83,200	81,600 to 90,400	91,400 to 110,400

Figure C.7

Employment and Other Information in Production and Operations Management[9]

Statistical/Research Analyst—Analyzes a variety of business operation segments using sophisticated statistical and data-mining tools to determine how best to improve a company's operations. May include determining market segments for new or existing products, setting prices, and a variety of other business issues that require significant statistical analysis.

Logistics Analyst—Focuses on the development of optimal solutions for logistical issues including cargo weight solutions, locations for distribution centers, and routing schedules for transportation modes such as trains and fleet trucks. Works extensively with supply chain management (SCM) systems to integrate logistics solutions within the company's supply chain activities.

INFORMATION TECHNOLOGY SKILLS YOU SHOULD PURSUE

To be effective in production and operations management, we recommend that you gain knowledge in the IT tools and concepts listed below.

Statistical Tools—For most careers in production and operations management, a detailed knowledge of statistics is essential, including the use of popular statistical software tools such as SAS and STATISTA.

Advanced Decision Support Spreadsheet Functions—Spreadsheet decision-support functions such as goal seeking, optimization, and statistical tools provide support for the many careers in production and operations management.

Supply Chain Management (SCM) Systems—A knowledge of supply chain management (SCM) systems allows a person in this specialization to work with every department in a company, integrating solutions to maximize customer value.

Production and Inventory Control Software—There are many types of vertical market software relating to production and inventory control. These are essential for this career as most jobs require the use of such tools.

Material Requirements Planning Software—This is often called enterprise resource planning (ERP) software and allows a production and operations manager to understand the operations of a business from beginning to end and to optimally model those operations.

Data-Mining Tools—As data warehouses are becoming more widespread, production and operations managers can use data-mining tools to find new relationships in data warehouse information and employ a variety of statistical techniques to explore data warehouse information.

Scheduling Software—Scheduling software facilitates the optimal scheduling of a variety of resources within a business environment including people, plant equipment, transportation modes, and manufacturing operations.

Real Estate and Construction Management

Often when people think of the real estate industry, they think only of residential real estate agents selling homes. In fact, real estate is an approximately $3 trillion per year industry encompassing residential, office, retail, industrial, and many other property types. People in the real estate industry are developers, brokers, investors, Wall Street analysts, pension fund advisors, and many others.

The field of real estate and construction management (RECM) is inherently interdisciplinary. Feasibility and development analysts must understand urban economics, consumer behavior, and finance and regulatory issues. Appraisers estimate the value of property using systematic procedures, judgment, and statistics and may also be called on to provide expert testimony in legal proceedings. Construction lenders need to understand money and credit, to be sure, but they must also understand construction project scheduling, estimating, and contracts. A corporate real estate professional must understand the corporation's core business and how real estate assets can contribute to both the "top line" and "bottom line." Real estate developers epitomize this interdisciplinary approach. The real estate developer coordinates and directs the activities of many professionals and consultants, from the time the development project is simply a concept, through construction, occupancy, and the eventual disposition of the property.

TYPICAL JOB TITLES AND DESCRIPTIONS

The typical job titles found in real estate and construction management and their descriptions are listed below.

Commercial Real Estate Loan Officer—Responsible for soliciting and servicing a variety of commercial real estate loans, including large and complex transactions for real estate investments, development, and construction. Requires familiarity with financial analysis and modeling as well as other concepts, practices, and procedures in the field.

Commercial Real Estate Appraiser—Examines and evaluates commercial property to estimate a fair market value for loan collateral. Analyzes local and national market trends and investment valuation using a variety of techniques. Prepares very complex and detailed reports and is called upon to testify in court proceedings and act as a consultant.

Property Manager—Responsible for the financial and physical maintenance of commercial, industrial, or residential properties including oversight of leasing of properties in the portfolio. Responsible for analyzing information on operating costs as well as preparation of the annual budget for the properties.

Real Estate Development Manager—Directs the activities of firms that acquire real property for development or redevelopment. Leads the company in these endeavors as the head of the development team.

Real Estate Development Representative—May acquire land for new development or older properties for redevelopment. Assists the company in these endeavors as a part of the development team.

Construction Manager—Responsible for the overall management of construction projects and may oversee multiple projects. Ensures construction projects are completed on time, within budget, and to the client's satisfaction. Performs a variety of tasks and leads and directs the work of others.

Construction Field Superintendent—Oversees the daily construction activities at the work site, including project scheduling, delivery of equipment and materials, and progress of the project. Resolves contract disputes and arranges any necessary order changes. Requires a familiarity with a variety of construction management concepts, practices, and procedures.

Real Estate Financial Analyst—Responsible for building and maintaining complex financial models. Prepares look-back analyses of acquisitions and developments, draws conclusions, and makes recommendations. Analyzes capital markets alternatives, derivatives, and their impact on the company's financial position and earnings outlook. Examines capital investments and their impact on the company's financial position and earnings outlook as well as key expenses for potential cost savings.

INFORMATION TECHNOLOGY SKILLS YOU SHOULD PURSUE

To be effective in real estate and construction management, we recommend that you gain knowledge in the IT tools and concepts listed below.

The Internet and Web Portals—The use of Web portals, or virtual project sites, allows professionals to store and share project documents, schedules, and other information 24×7 in a real-time environment.

Geographic Information Systems (GIS)—GIS aids in site selection, feasibility analysis, and investment strategy by combining spatial and tabular information allowing the real estate professional to use maps that are alive and relevant.

Database Management and Integration—Supports the varied needs of accounting, lease administration, finance, and property management, allowing the entire project team to share information and support the client's needs.

Spreadsheet Modeling—Allows the real estate analyst to efficiently perform discounted cash flow analysis, ratio analysis, and underwriting analysis, and to measure the sensitivity of various assumptions.

Computer Aided Design (CAD)—CAD provides for digital imaging of architectural designs allowing users to test the results of changes in layout and design on the functionality and efficiency of the building.

Project Scheduling—Construction project scheduling involves estimates of timing, precedence, and critical path essential to the completion and success of development projects.

Automated Valuation—An Automated Valuation System (AVS) uses statistical and other analyses to automate the loan underwriting process, loan origination, collateral scoring, and appraisal.

Customer Relationship Management (CRM) Systems—Combines contact management, calendars, schedules, and client information into a database providing a centralized repository of contacts in which all team members share one contact record and subsequent relationship activity.

Specialty Software—ARGUS is the industry standard commercial real estate cash flow projection, transaction analysis, and asset valuation solution. CircleDeveloper™ is real estate development pro forma software in use by thousands of owners, developers, brokers, advisers, and financial institutions involved in property development. DYNA is a versatile forecasting and portfolio management solution used by many asset managers, REITs and other institutional investors around the globe.

Figure C.8

Employment Information in Real Estate
and Construction Management

Executive Positions ($100,000 plus)	Move Up Positions ($80,000–$100,000)
Chief Commercial Real Estate Executive	Senior Construction Manager
Chief Construction Executive	Commercial Real Estate Appraiser
Level V Construction Cost Engineer	Leasing Administration Manager
Chief Mortgage Executive	Construction Project Manager
Chief Property Acquisition Officer	Commercial Real Estate Loan Officer
Commercial Real Estate Manager	Mortgage Credit Supervisor
Director of Construction Management	Loss Prevention and Construction Safety Manager
Facilities Maintenance Manager	Manager
Mortgage Loan Area Manager	Mortgage Loan Processing Supervisor
Mortgage Operations Manager	Property Manager
Real Estate and Relocation Director	Retail Real Estate Representative
Real Estate Attorney	
Retail Real Estate Manager	
Trust Director—Real Estate	

Move Up Positions ($50,000–$80,000)	Starting Positions ($30,000–$50,000)
Chief Mortgage Credit Manager	Leasing Manager
Lead Construction Representative	Community Development Representative
Estimating Manager	Construction Inspection Services Manager
Facilities Planner	Mortgage Collector
Development Manager	Mortgage Credit Analyst
Level II Commercial Real Estate Loan Officer	Construction Estimator 1
Mortgage Collections Manager	Mortgage Loan Processor
Construction Field Superintendent	Apprentice Real Estate Appraiser
Mortgage Credit Manager	Associate Real Estate Sales Agent
Real Estate Appraisal Manager	Assistant Construction Supervisor
Facilities Maintenance Supervisor	
Real Estate Property Acquisition Associate	
Regional Property Operations Manager	
Trust Manager—Real Estate	

Assignments and Exercises

There is only one assignment and exercise for this module, and it's all about you. What you've just read is a summary and broad overview of the many career opportunities in the business world. It's now your turn to think seriously about your future career and perform some research.

Business Specialization	Job Title

Classes Offered by Your School	IT Skills You Need to Acquire

Locations You Would Consider	Companies You Would Consider

Jobs on Monster.com		
Job Title	**Location**	**Salary**

Group Projects

CASE 1:
ASSESSING THE VALUE OF CUSTOMER RELATIONSHIP MANAGEMENT

TREVOR TOY AUTO MECHANICS

Trevor Toy Auto Mechanics is an automobile repair shop in Phoenix, Arizona. Over the past few years, Trevor has seen his business grow from a two-bay car repair shop with only one other employee to a 15-bay car repair shop with 21 employees.

Trevor wants to improve service and add a level of personalization to his customers. However, Trevor has no idea who his best customers are, the work that is being performed, or which mechanic is responsible for the repairs. Trevor is asking for your help. He has provided you with a spreadsheet file, **TREVOR.xls,** that contains a list of all the repairs his shop has completed over the past year including each client's name along with a unique identifier. The spreadsheet file contains the fields provided in the table below.

Column	Name	Description
A	CUSTOMER #	A unique number assigned to each customer.
B	CUSTOMER NAME	The name of the customer.
C	MECHANIC #	A unique number assigned to the mechanic who completed the work.
D	CAR TYPE	The type of car on which the work was completed.
E	WORK COMPLETED	What type of repair was performed on the car.
F	NUM HOURS	How long in hours it took to complete the work.
G	COST OF PARTS	The cost of the parts associated with completing the repair.
H	TOTAL CHARGE	The amount charged to the customer for the repair.

Your analysis should include (1) Trevor's best customers (top 10 in terms of volume and revenue); (2) Trevor's worst customers (bottom 10 in terms of lowest volume and lost revenue); and (3) the mechanics that perform the repairs for each customer.

SOME PARTICULARS YOU SHOULD KNOW

1. As you consider the information provided to you, think in terms of what information is important. You might need to use the existing information to create new information.

2. In your analysis, provide examples of the types of marketing campaigns Trevor should offer his most valuable customers.

3. Upon completing your analysis, please provide concise yet detailed and thorough documentation (in narrative, numeric, and graphic forms) that justifies your recommendations.

4. File: **TREVOR.xls** (Excel file).

CASE 2:
ANALYZING THE VALUE OF INFORMATION

AFFORDABLE HOMES REAL ESTATE

In late 1995, a national study announced that Eau Claire, Wisconsin, was the safest place to live. Since then, housing development projects have been springing up all around Eau Claire. Six housing development projects are currently dominating the Eau Claire market: Woodland Hills, Granite Mound, Creek Side Huntington, East River Community, Forest Green, and Eau Claire South. These six projects each started with 100 homes, have sold all of them, and are currently developing phase 2.

As one of the three partners and real estate agents of Affordable Homes Real Estate, it is your responsibility to analyze the information concerning the past 600 home sales and choose which development project to focus on for selling homes in phase 2. Because your real estate firm is so small, you and your partners have decided that the firm should focus on selling homes in only one of the development projects.

From the Wisconsin Real Estate Association you have obtained a spreadsheet file that contains information concerning each of the sales for the first 600 homes. It contains the following fields:

Column	Name	Description
A	LOT #	The number assigned to a specific home within each project
B	PROJECT #	A unique number assigned to each of the six housing development projects (see table to follow)
C	ASK PRICE	The initial posted asking price for the home
D	SELL PRICE	The actual price for which the home was sold
E	LIST DATE	The date the home was listed for sale
F	SALE DATE	The date on which the final contract closed and the home was sold
G	SQ. FT.	The total square footage for the home
H	# BATH.	The number of bathrooms in the home
I	# BDRMS	The number of bedrooms in the home

The following numbers have been assigned to each of the housing development projects:

Project Number	Project Name
23	Woodland Hills
47	Granite Mound
61	Creek Side Huntington
78	East River Community
92	Forest Green
97	Eau Claire South

It is your responsibility to analyze the sales list and prepare a report that details which housing development project your real estate firm should focus on. Your analysis should cover as many angles as possible.

SOME PARTICULARS YOU SHOULD KNOW

1. You don't know how many other real estate firms will also be competing for sales in each of the housing development projects.

2. Phase 2 for each housing development project will develop homes similar in style, price, and square footage to their respective first phases.

3. As you consider the information provided to you, think in terms of what information is important and what information is not important. Be prepared to justify how you approach your analysis.

4. Upon completing your analysis, please provide concise, yet detailed and thorough, documentation (in narrative, numeric, and graphic forms) that justifies your decision.

5. File: **REALEST.xls** (Excel file).

CASE 3:
EXECUTIVE INFORMATION SYSTEM REPORTING

POLITICAL CAMPAIGN FINANCE

When it comes to campaign finance, Americans want a system that minimizes the influence of "fat cats" and organized money, that keeps campaign spending at sensible levels, that fosters healthy electoral competition, that doesn't take advantage of wealthy candidates, and that doesn't require candidates to spend all of their waking hours raising money.

Indeed, the much maligned congressional campaign finance system we have now is itself a product of well-intended reform efforts, passed by Congress in 1974 to achieve these ideals. Dozens of new reform plans have emerged during the 1990s that also reach for these goals. Yet, no reform scheme, however well intended, is likely to produce a perfect congressional campaign finance system.

The city of Highlands Ranch, Colorado, wishes to organize its campaign contributions records in a more strategic format. The city council is considering various executive information system packages that can show them overall views of the contribution information as well as give them the ability to access more detailed information. You have been hired to make recommendations about what reports should be available through the soon-to-be-purchased executive information system.

The table below is a list of the information that will be the foundation for the reports in the proposed executive information system. To help you develop realistic reports, the city has provided you with a spreadsheet file that contains specific contributions over the last six months.

Column	Name	Description
A	DATE	The actual date that the contribution was made
B	CONTRIBUTOR	The name of the person or organization that made the contribution
C	DISTRICT	The district number that the councilperson belongs to
D	AMOUNT	The amount of the contribution
E	TYPE	The description type of where the contribution amount was given
F	COUNCILPERSON	The councilperson's name
G	PARTY	The councilperson's political party

What the city council is most interested in is viewing several overall reports and then being able to request more detailed reports. So, as a consultant, your goal is to develop different sets of reports that illustrate the concept of drilling down through the information provided. For example, you should develop a report that shows overall campaign contributions by district (each of the eight different districts) and then also develop more detailed reports that show contribution by political party and contribution by type.

SOME PARTICULARS YOU SHOULD KNOW

1. The council would much rather see information graphically than numerically. So, as you develop your reports, do so in terms of graphs that illustrate the desired relationships.

2. As you consider the information provided to you, think in terms of overall views first and then detailed views second. This will help you develop a logical series of reports.

3. If you wish, you can explore a variety of software tools or functions to help you create the reports. Then prepare your presentation using a presentation graphics package that lets you create a really great presentation of your recommendations.

4. Again, your goal is not to create reports that point toward a particular problem or opportunity. Rather, you are to design a series of logical reports that illustrate the concept of drilling down.

5. File: **CONTRIBUTE.xls** (Excel file).

CASE 4:
BUILDING VALUE CHAINS

HELPING CUSTOMERS DEFINE VALUE

StarLight is a Denver-based retailer of high-quality apparel, shoes, and accessories. In 1915, with money earned in the Colorado gold mines, Anne Logan invested in a small downtown Denver shoe store. A few years later, Anne expanded her business by adding fine apparel. Today, StarLight has 97 retail stores and discount outlets throughout the United States. Since the beginning, StarLight's business philosophy has reflected its founder's beliefs in exceptional service, value, selection, and quality. To maintain the level of service StarLight's customers have come to expect, the company empowers its employees to meet any customer demand, no matter how unreasonable it may seem. With so many stores, it's difficult for Cody Sherrod, StarLight's vice president for Business Information and Planning, to know the level of service customers receive, what customers value, and what they don't. These are important questions for a retailer striving to provide the finest customer experience and products while keeping costs to a minimum.

Cody decided a value chain analysis would be helpful in answering these questions. So, customer surveys were designed, distributed, completed, collected, and compiled into a database. Customers were asked to value their experience with various processes in the StarLight value chain. Specifically, for each value chain process, customers were asked whether this area added value to their experience or reduced the value of their experience. Customers were asked to quantify how much each process added or reduced the value of the services they received. Using a total of 100 points for the value chain, each customer distributed those points among StarLight's processes. The survey results in the database consist of the fields shown in the table on the next page.

Field Name	Description
Survey ID	An ID number uniquely identifying the survey
VA/VR	A field that identifies whether the current row of information reflects a value-added response or a value-reducing response
Date	Survey response date
Mgmt/Acctg/Finance/Legal	Customer value experience, if any, with management, accounting, finance, and the legal departments
HR Mgmt	Customer value of the attitude and general personnel environment
R&D/Tech Dev	Customer perceived value of the quality of research and technology support
Purchasing	Customer value placed on the quality and range of product selection
Receive and Greet Customers	Customer value placed on initial contact with employees
Provide Direction/Advice/Info	Customer value placed on initial information provided by employees
Store Location/Channel Availability & Convenience	Customer value placed on location, availability, and convenience
Product Display/Site or Catalog Layout	Customer value placed on aesthetic appeal of merchandise display and layout
Sales Service	Customer value placed on quality of service provided by sales associates
Marketing	Customer value placed on the effectiveness of marketing material
Customer Follow-up	Customer value placed on postsales service and follow-up

Cody has asked you to gather the raw survey material into two value chains, the value-added chain and the value-reducing chain. You'll create chains that summarize the survey information and size the process areas proportionately as described in Chapter 2. Specifically, your job is to perform the following:

1. Create queries or reports in the provided database to summarize the value-added amounts and the value-reducing amounts for each process.

2. Draw two value chains using that summary information to size the depicted area for each process. Use the value chains in Chapter 2 as reference.

3. Compare the value-added and value-reducing process percentages. Do they correlate in any way? If so, why do you think that is? If not, why not?

4. In the table description provided, a dashed line is drawn between the "purchasing" process and the "receive and greet customers" process. Processes above the line are considered support processes, while processes below are considered primary processes. Create a database query to compare how customers value the total of support processes versus primary processes. Do this for both value-added and value-reducing processes. Do the results make sense or are they surprising? Explain your answer.

SOME PARTICULARS YOU SHOULD KNOW

1. Remember that the total value-added/value-reducing amount for each process must equal 100 percent.
2. The survey values in the database are not percentages although the sum of all responses for a given survey equals 100.
3. File: **STARLIGHT.mdb** (Access file).

CASE 5:
USING RELATIONAL TECHNOLOGY TO TRACK PROJECTS

FOOTHILLS CONSTRUCTION

Foothills Construction Company is a Denver-based construction company that specializes in subcontracting the development of single family homes. In business since 1993, Foothills Construction Company has maintained a talented pool of certified staff and independent consultants allowing the flexibility and combined experience required to meet the needs of its nearly 300 completed projects in the Denver metropolitan area. The field of operation methods that Foothills Construction is responsible for as it relates to building include structural development, heating and cooling, plumbing, and electricity.

The company charges its clients by billing the hours spent on each contract. The hourly billing rate is dependent on the employee's position according to the field of operations (as noted below).

Figure GP.1 shows a basic report that Foothills Construction managers would like to see every week concerning what projects are being assigned as well as a summary of assignment hours and changes. Foothills Construction organizes its internal structure in four different operations: Structure (500), Plumbing (501), Electrical (502), and Heating and Ventilation (503). Each of these operational departments can and should have many subcontractors who specialize in that area.

Figure GP.1

Foothills Construction Project Detail

FOOTHILLS CONSTRUCTION PROJECT DETAIL

PROJECT NAME	ASSIGN DATE	EMP LAST NAME	EMP FIRST NAME	JOB DESCRIPTION	ASSIGN HOUR	CHARGE/HOUR
Chatfield						
	Thursday, February 10, 2005	Jones	Anne	Heating and Ventalation	3.4	$84.50
	Thursday, February 10, 2005	Sullivan	David	Electrical	1.8	$105.00
	Friday, February 11, 2005	Frommer	Matt	Plumbing	4.1	$96.75
	Saturday, February 12, 2005	Newman	John	Electrical	1.7	$105.00
	Saturday, February 12, 2005	Bawangi	Terry	Plumbing	4.1	$96.75
Summary of Assignment Hours and Charges					15.10	$1,448.15
Evergreen						
	Thursday, February 10, 2005	Smithfield	William	Structure	3.0	$35.75
	Thursday, February 10, 2005	Newman	John	Electrical	2.3	$105.00
	Thursday, February 10, 2005	Nenior	David	Plumbing	3.3	$96.75
	Friday, February 11, 2005	Marbough	Mike	Heating and Ventalation	2.6	$84.50
	Saturday, February 12, 2005	Johnson	Peter	Electrical	2.0	$105.00
	Saturday, February 12, 2005	Newman	John	Electrical	3.6	$105.00
	Saturday, February 12, 2005	Olenkoski	Glenn	Structure	1.9	$35.75
Summary of Assignment Hours and Charges					18.70	$1,543.65
Roxborough						

Page: 1

Because of the boom in home sales over the last several years, Foothills Construction has decided to implement a relational database model to track project details according to project name, hours assigned, and charges per hour for each job description. Originally, Foothills Construction decided to let one of its employees handle the construction of the database. However, that employee has not had the time to completely implement the project. Foothills Construction has asked you to take over and complete the development of the database.

The entity classes and primary keys for the database have been identified as the following:

Entity	Primary Key
Project	Project Number
Employee	Employee Number
Job	Job Number
Assign	Assign Number

The following business rules have also been identified:

1. A job can have many employees assigned but must have at least one.
2. An employee must be assigned to one and only one job number.
3. An employee can be assigned to work on one or more projects.
4. A project can be assigned to only one employee but need not be assigned to any employee.

Your job is to be completed in the following phases:

1. Develop and describe the entity-relationship diagram.
2. Use normalization to assure the correctness of the tables (relations).
3. Create the database using a personal DBMS package (preferably Microsoft Access).
4. Use the DBMS package to create the basic report in Figure GP.1.

SOME PARTICULARS YOU SHOULD KNOW

1. You may not be able to develop a report that looks exactly like the one in Figure GP.1. However, your report should include the same information.
2. Complete personnel information is tracked by another database. For this application, include only the minimum employee number, last name, and first name.
3. Information concerning all projects, employees, and jobs is not readily available. You should, however, create information for several fictitious systems to include in your database.
4. File: Not applicable.

CASE 6:
BUILDING A DECISION SUPPORT SYSTEM

CREATING AN INVESTMENT PORTFOLIO

Most experts recommend that if you're devising a long-term investment strategy you should make the stock market part of your plan. You can use a DSS to help you decide what stocks to put into your portfolio. You can use a spreadsheet to do the job. The information you need on 10 stocks is contained in a Word file called **STOCKS.doc.** This information consists of

1. Two years of weekly price data on 10 different stocks.
2. Stock market indices from
   - The Dow Jones Industrial Average
   - NASDAQ Composite
3. Dividends and cash flow per share over the last 10 years (Source: Yahoo Finance).

Using this information, build a DSS to perform stock analysis consisting of the following tasks:

1. Examine Diversification Benefits
   A. Calculate the average return and standard deviation(s) of each of the 10 stocks.
   B. Form six different portfolios: two with two stocks each; two with three stocks each; two with five stocks each.

   Answer the following questions using your DSS:

   - How does the standard deviation of each portfolio compare to the (average) standard deviation of each stock in the portfolio?
   - How does the average return of the portfolio compare to the average return of each stock in the portfolio?
   - Do the benefits of diversification seem to increase or diminish as the number of stocks in the portfolio gets larger?
   - In the two-stock and five-stock portfolios what happens if you group your stocks toward similar industries?

2. Value Each of the Stocks
   A. Estimate the dividend growth rate based on past dividends.
   B. Estimate next year's dividend using this year's dividend and the estimated growth rate.
   C. Generate two graphs, one for past dividends and one for estimated dividends for the next five years.

SOME PARTICULARS YOU SHOULD KNOW

1. When performing your calculations, use the weekly returns. That is, use the change in the price each week rather than the prices themselves. This gives you a better basis for calculation because the prices themselves don't usually change very much.
2. File: **STOCKS.doc** (Word file).

CASE 7:
ADVERTISING WITH BANNER ADS

HIGHWAYSANDBYWAYS.COM

Business is booming at HighwaysAndByways, a dot-com firm focusing on selling accessories for car enthusiasts (e.g., floor mats, grill guards, air fresheners, stereos, and so on). Throughout the past year, HighwaysAndByways has had Web site management software tracking what customers buy, the Web sites from which customers came, and the Web sites customers went to after visiting HighwaysAndByways. That information is stored in a spreadsheet file and contains the fields in the accompanying table. Each record in the spreadsheet file represents an individual visit by a customer that resulted in a purchase.

HighwaysAndByways is interested in determining three items and has employed you as a consultant to help. First, HighwaysAndByways wants to know on which Web sites it should purchase banner ad space. Second, HighwaysAndByways wants to know which Web sites it should contact to determine if those Web sites would like to purchase banner ad space on the

Column	Name	Description
A	CUSTOMER ID	A unique identifier for a customer who made a purchase
B	TOTAL PURCHASE	The total amount of a purchase
C	PREVIOUS WEB SITE	The Web site from which the customer came to visit HighwaysAndByways
D	NEXT WEB SITE	The Web site the customer went to after making a purchase at HighwaysAndByways
E	TIME SPENT	The amount of time that the customer spent at the site

HighwaysAndByways Web site. Finally, HighwaysAndByways would like to know which Web sites it should develop reciprocal banner ad relationships with; that is, HighwaysAndByways would like a list of Web sites on which it would obtain banner ad space while providing banner ad space on its Web site for those Web sites.

SOME PARTICULARS YOU SHOULD KNOW

1. As you consider the information provided to you, think about the levels of information literacy. In other words, don't jump to conclusions before carefully evaluating the provided information.

2. You don't know if your customers made purchases at the Web site they visited upon leaving HighwaysAndByways.

3. Upon completing your analysis, please provide concise yet detailed and thorough documentation (in narrative, numeric, and graphic forms) that justifies your recommendations.

4. File: **CLICKSTREAMS.xls** (Excel file).

CASE 8:
ASSESSING THE VALUE OF OUTSOURCING INFORMATION TECHNOLOGY

CREATING FORECASTS

Founded in 1992, Innovative Software provides search software, Web site accessibility testing/repair software, and usability testing/repair software. All serve as part of its desktop and enterprise content management solutions for government, corporate, educational, and consumer markets. The company's solutions are used by Web site publishers, digital media publishers, content managers, document managers, business users, consumers, software companies, and consulting services companies. Innovative Software solutions help organizations develop long-term strategies to achieve Web content accessibility, enhance usability, and comply with U.S. and international accessibility and search standards.

Innovative Software has a 10-year history of approximately 1 percent in turnover a year and its focus has always been on customer service. With the informal motto of "Grow big, but stay small," it takes pride in 100 percent callbacks in customer care, knowing that its personal service has been one thing that makes it outstanding.

Innovative Software has experienced rapid growth to six times its original customer-base size and is forced to deal with difficult questions for the first time, such as, "How do we serve this many customers? How do we keep our soul—that part of us that honestly cares very much about our customers? How will we know that someone else will care as much and do as good a job as we have done?" In addition, you have just received an e-mail from the company CIO, Sue Downs, that the number of phone calls from customers having problems with one of your newer applications is on the increase.

As customer service manager for Innovative Software, your overriding goal is to maintain the company's reputation for excellent customer service, and outsourcing may offer an efficient means of keeping up with expanding call volume. Innovative Software is reviewing a similar scenario, that of e-BANK, which outsourced its customer service in order to handle a large projected number of customers through several customer interaction channels. Although e-BANK had excellent people, it felt that its competencies were primarily in finance, rather than in customer service and that it needed to have the expertise that a customer-service-focused company could offer. e-BANK also discovered that it was cost effective to outsource its customer service center.

Additionally, the outsourcing approach was relatively hassle-free, since e-BANK did not have to set up its own call center.

SOME PARTICULARS YOU SHOULD KNOW

1. Create a weekly analysis from the data provided in **FORECAST.xls.**
2. The price of the products, the actual product type, and any warranty information is irrelevant.
3. Develop a growth, trend, and forecast analysis. You should use a three-day moving average: a shorter moving average might not display the trend well and a much longer moving average would shorten the trend too much.
4. Upon completing your analysis, please provide concise yet detailed and thorough documentation (in narrative, numeric, and graphic forms) that justifies your recommendations.
5. File: **FORECAST.xls** (Excel file)

CASE 9:
DEMONSTRATING HOW TO BUILD WEB SITES

WITH HTML

Building a good Web site is simple in some respects and difficult in others. It's relatively easy to learn to write HTML code. Building an effective and eye-catching Web site is a horse of a different color. That is to say, there is a stretch between just using the technology and using the technology to your best advantage.

Your task in this project is to build a presentation (using presentation graphics software such as Microsoft PowerPoint) that achieves two goals. First, your presentation should show your audience how to write simple HTML code to create a Web site. Your presentation should include the HTML code for

- Text formatting (bold, italic, and the like)
- Font families and sizing
- Font colors
- Background colors and images
- Links
- Images
- Numbered and bulleted lists

Next, your presentation should provide the audience with a list of guidelines for creating an *effective* Web site. For this, you should definitely embed links into your presentation that go to Web sites that illustrate good Web site design, displaying examples of both effective and ineffective designs.

SOME PARTICULARS YOU SHOULD KNOW

1. In a file called **HTML.doc,** we've provided many links to Web sites that teach you how to write HTML code.
2. In a file called **DESIGN.doc,** we've provided many links to Web sites that teach you how to design Web sites effectively.
3. Files: **HTML.doc** and **DESIGN.doc** (Word files).

CASE 10:
MAKING THE CASE WITH PRESENTATION SOFTWARE

INFORMATION TECHNOLOGY ETHICS

Management at your company is concerned about the high cost of computer crime, from lawsuits over e-mail received to denial-of-service attacks and hackers breaking into the corporate network to steal information. You've been asked to make a presentation to inform your colleagues of these issues. Develop a presentation using a presentation package such as Microsoft's PowerPoint.

You can choose your presentation's emphasis from the following topics:

- Ethics as it relates to IT systems
- Types of crime aimed at IT systems (such as viruses)
- Types of crime that use IT systems as weapons (such as electronic theft of funds from one account to another)
- Security measures, how good they are, what they cost, how expensive they are to implement
- Electronic monitoring of employees (from employer and employee standpoints)
- Collection and use of personal information on consumers

SOURCES OF INFORMATION

- In the file **ETHICS.doc,** you'll find sources for the topics listed above.
- The Web is a great place to find lots of information.
- Most business publications, such as *Business Week, Information Week, Fortune,* and *The Wall Street Journal,* frequently have good articles on ethics, cybercrime, and security. You can get some of these articles on the Web.
- General news publications such as *Newsweek* and *USA Today* print articles on these topics.

Your task is to weave the information you find into a coherent presentation using graphs and art where appropriate.

SOME PARTICULARS YOU SHOULD KNOW

1. Content Principles

   - Each slide should have a headline
   - Each slide should express one idea
   - Ideas should follow logically

2. Design Principles

- Follow the "Rule of 7," which is no more than 7 lines per slide and 7 words per line
- Keep it simple
- Keep it organized
- Create a path for the eye
- Divide space in an interesting way
- Use at least 30-point type
- Use color and graphics carefully, consistently, and for a specific purpose
- Use high-contrast colors (black/white, deep blue/white, etc.)

3. File: **ETHICS.doc** (Word file)

CASE 11:
BUILDING A WEB DATABASE SYSTEM

WEB-BASED CLASSIFIED SYSTEM

With the emergence of the Internet as a worldwide standard for communicating information, *Gabby's Gazetteer*, a medium-size community newspaper in central Colorado, is looking to enter the electronic commerce market.

In the listing of classified ads, advertisers place a small ad that lists items they wish to sell and provide a means (e.g., telephone number) by which prospective buyers can contact them.

The nature of a sale via a newspaper classified system goes as follows:

- During the course of the sale, the information flows in different directions at different stages.
- First, there is a downstream flow of information (from seller to buyer)—the listing in print on the newspaper. (Thus, the classified ad listing is just a way of bringing a buyer and seller together.)
- When a potential purchaser's interest has been raised, then that interest must be relayed upstream, usually by telephone or in person.
- Finally, a meeting should result that uses face-to-face negotiation to finalize the sale—if the sale can be agreed upon.

By placing the entire system on the Internet, the upstream and downstream communications are accomplished using a Web browser. The sale becomes more of an auction, because many potential buyers, all with equal status, can bid for the same item.

Any user who is trying to buy an item can

- View items for sale
- Bid on an item they wish to purchase

Any user who is trying to sell an item can

- Place a new item for sale
- Browse a list of the items that he or she is trying to sell, and examine the bids that have been made on each of those items
- Accept a bid on an item that he or she is selling

This system should also allow users to do some very basic administrative tasks, such as

- Browse the listings to see what is for sale
- Register with the system (users can browse without registering; but they must register if they want to sell an item or bid for an item)

Figure GP.2

Gabby's Gazetteer Classified Registration System

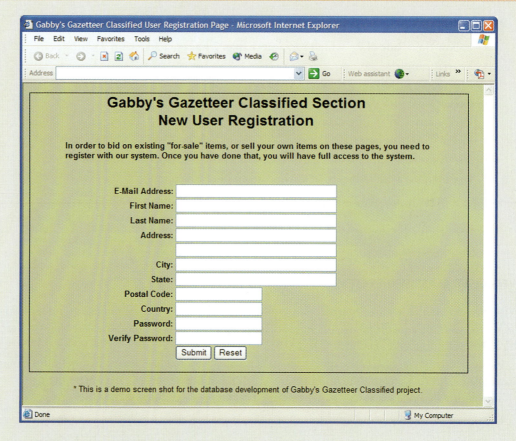

- Log on to the system
- Change their registration details

Your job will be to complete the following:

1. Develop and describe the entity-relationship diagram for the database that will support the above activities.
2. Use normalization to ensure the correctness of the tables.
3. Create the database using a personal DBMS package.

SOME PARTICULARS YOU SHOULD KNOW

1. Use Figure GP.2 as a baseline for your database design.
2. File: Not applicable.

CASE 12:
CREATING A DECISION SUPPORT SYSTEM

BUY VERSUS LEASE

A leading supplier of grapes to the wine-producing industry in California, On the Vine Grapes, wants to expand its delivery services and expand its reach to market by increasing its current fleet of delivery trucks. Some of the older vehicles were acquired through closed-end leases with required down payments, mileage restrictions, and hefty early termination penalties. Other vehicles were purchased using traditional purchase-to-own loans, which often resulted in high depreciation costs and large maintenance fees. All vehicles were acquired one at a time through local dealers.

On the Vine Grapes has asked you to assist in developing a lease/buy cost analysis worksheet in order to make the most cost-effective decision. Currently the director of operations, Bill Smith, has identified a 2008 Ford F-550 4x2 SD Super Cab 161.8 in. WB DRW HD XLT as the truck of choice for the business. This vehicle has a retail price of $34,997.00 or a lease price of $600/month through Ford Motor Credit Company.

Here are some basic fees and costs that you need to factor in:

1. **Lease Costs**

Refundable security deposit	$500
First month's payment at inception	$500
Other initial costs	$125
Monthly lease payment for remaining term	$600
Last month payment in advance	No
Allowable annual mileage	15,000
Estimated annual miles to be driven	20,000
Per mile charge for excess miles	0.10

2. **Purchase Costs**

Retail price including sales taxes, title	$34,997
Down payment	$4,000
Loan interest rate	8.75%
Will interest be deductible business or home equity interest?	Yes
Is the gross loaded weight of the vehicle over 6,000 lbs?	Yes

3. **Common Costs and Assumptions**

Total lease/loan term	36
Discount percent	8.75
Tax bracket—combined federal and state	33%
Business use percentage	100%

SOME PARTICULARS YOU SHOULD KNOW

1. In the file **BUYORLEASE.xls** is a template you can use to enter the information. There is also a sheet that has been developed to assist you with the annual depreciation for an automobile.
2. Create a detailed summary sheet of the lease/buy option for On the Vine Grapes.
3. File: **BUYORLEASE.xls** (Excel file).

CASE 13:
DEVELOPING AN ENTERPRISE RESOURCE PLANNING SYSTEM

PLANNING, REPORTING, AND DATA PROCESSING

The State Annual Report on Enterprise Resource Planning and Management was developed to provide a comprehensive view of the management and use of technology by the Higher Educational System of Colorado. This report shows the statewide issues surrounding information technology, priorities for the ensuing two years, initiatives and projects, performance management, and the information technology resources utilized to support the business processes of Higher Education during fiscal year 2004–2005. A comparison report is also generated to produce a percentage change in funds from fiscal year 2003–2004 to fiscal year 2004–2005.

Chief information officer (CIO) for the Department of Higher Education, David Paul, was required to report the estimated expenditures for technology across five appropriation categories: Employee Salaries/Benefits, Other Personal Services (OPS—noncareer service employees with no permanent status), Expenses (all hardware purchases under $1,000, travel, training, and general office expenses), Operating Capital Outlay (OCO), and Data Processing Services. Most of these performance management initiatives have been measured using manual processes. Several reporting units documented the need for automated measurement tools in the future to take advantage of the full opportunities for improvement. David Paul has asked you to assist him in organizing this information and calculating some of the requirements established by the State Board of Education. Along with the appropriation categories mentioned above, each institution is categorized according to status (2 Year, 4 Year Public, or 4 Year Private). This will aid in the overall analysis for current and future resource planning.

SOME PARTICULARS YOU SHOULD KNOW

1. You need to create a detailed report for:
   a. Summary of overall change from 2003–2004 fiscal year (FY) to 2004–2005 FY
   b. Percentage of budget allocated to data processing services
   c. Percentage of 2 year, 4 year public, and 4 year private institutions allocating resources to data processing services
2. Develop a graphical representation of the percentage of 2 year, 4 year public, and 4 year private institutions allocating resources to data processing services
3. File: **COLORADOHIGHERED.xls** (Excel file)

CASE 14:
ASSESSING A WIRELESS FUTURE

EMERGING TRENDS AND TECHNOLOGY

"Intelligent wireless handheld devices are going to explode, absolutely explode over the next several years."—Steve Ballmer, CEO, Microsoft.

Wireless, mobility, small form factor, pervasive computing, the anytime network—whatever name you choose—it's here. The price of easy-to-handle devices which provide access to a variety of applications and information is rapidly falling while the efficiencies of such devices are increasing. More and more, the business user is looking to use mobile devices to perform tasks that previously could be handled only by the desktop PC. End-user adoption is skyrocketing. The next 18 months will demonstrate a true growing period for mobile computing as the world changes to one characterized by the mobile user.

As this market sector grows, software and information companies are evolving their products and services. Wireless mobility and associated functionality provide new market opportunities for both established companies and new entrants to increase efficiency and take advantage of new revenue possibilities. The services to Internet-enabled mobile devices create a vast array of new business opportunities for companies as they develop products and services that utilize location, time, and immediate access to information in new and innovative ways.

Some of the lower profile topics that are currently being developed at this time include:

- Hard drives for wireless devices
- Global-roaming movement
- Mobile power supplies that run on next-generation fuel cells

All three could bring about significant changes in the wireless space.

You have been asked to prepare a presentation using a presentation package such as Microsoft's PowerPoint. Using the list of wireless solution providers and manufacturers provided in WIRELESS.htm, select at least two developers and create a presentation that will emphasize the following topics:

1. What are the current products or services under development?
2. What is the target market for that product or service?
3. What are the key features that product or service will bring to the wireless industry?
4. Which provider/manufacturer/developer seems to be the first to market with their product?
5. How is the wireless product or service content being delivered?
6. Are the products or services able to deploy interactive multimedia applications to any digital wireless device, on any carrier, or across any type of network?
7. Are there any new privacy concerns that are being discussed in relation to the new products or services? (These can include concerns from being able to track users' preferences, purchasing history or browsing preferences, or the capability to track a user's physical location while using a wireless device.)
8. How does this product or solution affect the global marketplace?
9. What is the current retail price for the wireless products or solutions?
10. Is current bandwidth available to the wireless industry a concern?

Your task is to weave the information you find into a coherent presentation using graphs and art where appropriate.

SOME PARTICULARS YOU SHOULD KNOW

1. Content Principles

   - Each slide should have a headline
   - Each slide should express one idea
   - Ideas should follow logically

2. Design Principles

   - Follow the "Rule of 7"—no more than 7 lines per slide and 7 words per line
   - Keep it simple
   - Keep it organized
   - Create a path for the eye
   - Divide space in an interesting way
   - Use at least 30-point type
   - Use color and graphics carefully, consistently, and for a specific purpose
   - Use high-contrast colors (black/white, deep blue/white, etc.)

3. File: **WIRELESS.htm** (html file)

CASE 15:
EVALUATING THE NEXT GENERATION

DOT-COM ASPS

E-business is creating a new set of challenges not only for dot-com start-ups but also for well-established brick-and-mortar companies. Driven by the need to capture increasing shares of business online, IT managers take the first step by deciding on a commerce application. Then they face the most important decision: whether to assign implementation, deployment, and application hosting to internal IT resources or to contract for these services with an ASP.

A few years ago, no one had even heard the term *application service provider (ASP)*. Now the ASP market is a certified phenomenon. In the short space of two years, the concept of leasing applications to businesses has grown to an interesting but unproven proposition in an ever-expanding industry.

You have been hired by Front Range Car Rental, a major car rental company in Colorado, to research ways to use technology to leverage more business. The company needs a Web service written which transacts reservations on its back-end mainframe system. This Web service will need to be made available to airline partners to integrate the travel booking process. When consumers book a flight, they are also given the option to reserve a car from the airline site. The rental details will need to be captured and transported to the car rental company's Web service, which processes the reservation. This new capability will help the car rental company to drive more bookings and achieve a competitive advantage in a highly commoditized market.

The major task that Front Range Car Rental needs you to research is what the cost benefits would be for in-house implementation and an ASP deployment. You have been given an analysis spreadsheet, **DOTCOMASP.xls,** with all the detailed information; however, you will need to use the Internet in order to find current price information. Another file, **DOTCOMASP_SEARCH. htm,** has been developed for you with a list of search engines that will provide you with a focal point for your research.

SOME PARTICULARS YOU SHOULD KNOW

1. All ASPs are not created equal. Here are some questions to help you identify their strengths, weaknesses, capabilities, and core competencies.

   - Does the ASP offer full life-cycle services, including proof-of-concept, installation, operations, training, support, and proactive evolution services?
   - What is the ASP's depth and breadth of technical expertise? What are the company's specialties?
   - Where and how did key technical staff obtain their expertise?
   - Does the ASP have actual customers online and if so, what results have they achieved?
   - Does the ASP offer service-level agreements and what are the penalties for SLA violations?
   - Specifically, how does the ASP's infrastructure deliver:
     High availability (uptime)?
     Assured data integrity?
     Scalability?
     Reliability?
     High performance?
     Security and access control?
   - Does the ASP offer 24 × 7 technical support to end users? Escalation procedures? High-priority problem resolution? Dedicated account managers?
   - Can the ASP provide development expertise to customize the applications?
   - How does the ASP handle updates? Adding product modules?
   - Is the ASP capable of assisting with add-on projects such as bringing a new factory online or adding a new supplier?
   - Can the ASP provide a comprehensive suite of integrated applications (versus a single application)?

2. File: **DOTCOMASP.xls** (Excel File) and **DOTCOMASP_SEARCH.htm** (html file)

CASE 16:
ANALYZING STRATEGIC AND COMPETITIVE ADVANTAGE

DETERMINING OPERATING LEVERAGE

Pony Espresso is a small business that sells specialty coffee drinks at office buildings. Each morning and afternoon, trucks arrive at offices' front entrances, and the office employees purchase various beverages with names such as Java du Jour and Café de Colombia. The business is profitable. But Pony Espresso offices are located to the north of town, where lease rates are less expensive, and the principal sales area is south of town. This means that the trucks must drive cross-town four times each day.

The cost of transportation to and from the sales area, plus the power demands of the trucks' coffee brewing equipment, is a significant portion of the variable costs. Pony Espresso could reduce the amount of driving—and, therefore, the variable costs—if it moves the offices much closer to the sales area.

Pony Espresso presently has fixed costs of $10,000 per month. The lease of a new office, closer to the sales area, would cost an additional $2,200 per month. This would increase the fixed costs to $12,200 per month.

Although the lease of new offices would increase the fixed costs, a careful estimate of the potential savings in gasoline and vehicle maintenance indicates that Pony Espresso could reduce the variable costs from $0.60 per unit to $0.35 per unit. Total sales are unlikely to increase as a result of the move, but the savings in variable costs should increase the annual profit.

You have been hired by Pony Espresso to assist in the cost analysis and new lease options to determine a growth in profit margin. You will also need to calculate a degree of operating leverage to better understand the company's profitability. Degree of operating leverage (DOL) will give the CEO of Pony Espresso, Darian Presley, a great deal of information for setting operating targets and planning profitability.

SOME PARTICULARS YOU SHOULD KNOW

1. Consider the information provided—especially look at the change in the variability of the profit from month to month. From November through January, when it is much more difficult to lure office workers out into the cold to purchase coffee, Pony Espresso barely breaks even. In fact, in December of 2005, the business lost money.

2. First, develop the cost analysis on the existing lease information using the monthly sales figures provided to you in the file **PONYESPRESSO.xls.** Second, develop the cost analysis from the new lease information provided above.

3. You need to calculate the variability that is reflected in the month-to-month standard deviation of earnings for the current cost structure and the projected cost structure.

4. Do not consider any association with downsizing such as overhead; simply focus on the information provided to you.

5. You will need to calculate the EBIT—earnings before interest and taxes.

6. Would the DOL and business risk increase or decrease if Pony Espresso moved its office? *Note:* Variability in profit levels, whether measured as EBIT, operating income, or net income, does not necessarily increase the level of business risk as the DOL increases.

7. File: **PONYESPRESSO.xls** (Excel file).

CASE 17:
BUILDING A DECISION SUPPORT SYSTEM

BREAK-EVEN ANALYSIS

Ski-YA! is a Colorado-based company that sells high-performance ski equipment. When it comes to the serious business of sliding downhill, the Ski-YA! dudes of Colorado don't trouble themselves with petty categories; to them, all alpine snow equipment is summed up in one word, AWESOME!

This season's offerings at Ski-YA! are no exception. Skis continue to grow wider for better flotation beyond the groomers, and the sidecuts, the stick's hourglass shape designed to help a skier turn, now reflect the needs of terrain skiers. Even bindings have been rejiggered: forget the drill and screwdriver; the latest fittings snap or slide into place, extending ski life and improving energy transfer.

The Ski-YA! company wants to begin selling a new pair of skis, labeled the Downhill Demons, in the upcoming ski season. It wants to know how many skis it will have to sell in order to break even on its investment in materials and equipment. The chief financial officer has provided the following information:

Fixed Costs

Metal molding machine:	$200,000
Milling machine:	$150,000
Sander and grinder:	$10,000
Presses:	$25,000
Silkscreen machine:	$50,000

Variable Costs (per Unit)

Packaging material	$5.00
Raw material	$100.00
Shipping	$20.00

The marketing department estimates that it can sell the new skis for $400.00 per unit. Further projections estimate that an average of 200 units will be sold per month. The goal is that the skis will break even and start to earn a profit within the first year. Ski-YA!'s target profit level for the end of the first fiscal year is $100,000.

SOME PARTICULARS YOU SHOULD KNOW

1. First, create a break-even analysis where your goal is to determine how many units you must sell to recover all of your fixed costs.

2. Then create a target profit analysis where your goal is to determine how many units you must sell to reach a predefined profit level. The difference between the two is that at breakeven your target profit is zero, whereas when you specify a target profit that is greater than zero, you are setting your goal above the break-even point.

3. You will want to create a table sheet that contains the data used to generate the break-even/target profit chart. This includes 10 data points on either side of the break-even/target profit point.

4. Finally create a chart where you can visually measure your break-even or target profit level along with total fixed and variable costs. If you choose to calculate the number of months before you reach a break-even or target profit, those numbers will be reported here.

5. File: **SkiYA.xls** (Excel file).

CASE 18:
CREATING A FINANCIAL ANALYSIS

QUALIFICATION AND AMORTIZATION WORKSHEETS

The Foothills Savings Bank (FSB) is a federally insured stock savings bank which was organized in 1982 as a privately insured savings and loan association in Denver, Colorado. It received federal insurance in 1985 and a federal savings bank charter in 1986. FSB is a member of the Federal Home Loan Bank (FHLB) system and its deposits are insured by the Federal Deposit Insurance Corporation (FDIC) to the maximum amount provided by law.

The Foothills Savings Bank offers loans for owner-occupied properties, second homes, and investment homes. FSB offers first trust residential conventional fixed rate and ARM (adjustable rate mortgage) loans. Conventional financing is any mortgage that is not insured or guaranteed by federal, state, or local governments. FSB is now offering an online prequalification worksheet for its customers or prospective customers to use. FSB requires a minimum of 10 percent down, which is generally required for conventional financing.

It is your responsibility to complete a mortgage qualification worksheet and then create a mortgage amortization analysis worksheet from the data in the mortgage qualification worksheet.

SOME PARTICULARS YOU SHOULD KNOW

1. A template for the mortgage qualification worksheet has been created; however, you need to complete the formulas.

2. The Qualifying Section:
   - The first qualifying number needs to calculate the maximum monthly payment, assuming there are no long-term debts. It is computed by multiplying the total income by the housing cost ratio and dividing the result by 12.
   - The second qualifying number takes into account the monthly debt payments, applying the total debt service ratio. It is calculated by multiplying the total debt by the debt service ratio and dividing the result by 12.
   - Mortgage companies usually qualify people for monthly payments that are no higher than the lesser of the two results.
   - By default, your worksheet should assume a housing cost ratio of 0.28 and a total debt service ratio of 0.36, which are standards often used for conventional mortgages.

3. The Loan Amount Section:

   The table created below the qualifying section calculates the amount of a loan you might qualify for with the monthly payment. Depending on the circumstances, some or all of the following will be true:
   - In all cases, the monthly payment will include principal and interest payments.
   - In most cases, it will include a monthly escrow deposit to cover taxes and mortgage insurance, if any. In some cases, homeowner's insurance is also included in this calculation. Use your best guess estimates for these figures.
   - If the customer is buying a condominium or co-op unit, the monthly payment figure may also include the homeowner's dues and/or maintenance fees. You will need to estimate these monthly costs and type them into the appropriate cells.

4. Creating an amortization analysis worksheet:
   - Use the data from the mortgage qualification worksheet to create an amortization table. You will need to calculate beginning balance, principal paid, interest paid, total principal, total interest, and ending balance per payment period for the life of the loan.

5. File: **Mortgage.xls** (Excel file).

CASE 19:
BUILDING A SCHEDULING DECISION SUPPORT SYSTEM

AIRLINE CREW SCHEDULING

Rockies Airline is a new airline company that maintains a schedule of two daily flights between Salt Lake City, Denver, and Chicago. Rockies Airline took to the air on February 11, 2004, with the inauguration of service between Denver International Airport and Salt Lake City. Every Rockies Airline aircraft is outfitted with roomy all-leather seats, each equipped with 24 channels of DIRECTV programming.

Rockies Airline must strategically position itself as a low-cost provider in a very volatile industry. Therefore, it must work toward finding a minimum cost assignment of flight crews to a given flight schedule while satisfying restrictions dictated by the Federal Aviation Administration. Rockies Airline needs to solve the crew scheduling problem that is an involved and time-consuming process.

To begin, you will want to figure out all the possible crew rotations. You will want to find an approximate expected cost of each combination and then solve the traditional crew scheduling problem by using these costs. Second, you will want to calculate the crew constraints in order to determine the decision variables, constraints, and objectives.

You have been given Rockies Airline flight schedule as follows:

From	To	Departure	Arrival	Departure	Arrival
Salt Lake City	Denver	9:00 AM	12:00 PM	2:00 PM	5:00 PM
Salt Lake City	Chicago	10:00 AM	2:00 PM	3:00 PM	7:00 PM
Denver	Salt Lake City	8:00 AM	11:00 PM	2:00 PM	5:00 PM
Denver	Chicago	9:00 AM	11:00 PM	3:00 PM	5:00 PM
Chicago	Salt Lake City	8:00 AM	12:00 PM	2:00 PM	6:00 PM
Chicago	Denver	10:00 AM	12:00 PM	4:00 PM	6:00 PM

SOME PARTICULARS YOU SHOULD KNOW

1. A crew that leaves a city in the morning has to return there at night.
2. The crew can be brought back on another airline. This would always be on an 8 PM flight. There are 6 airplanes in use.
3. When a crew is flying, the cost is $200 per hour.
4. When a crew is waiting or being flown back, the cost is $75 per hour.
5. How should the company schedule its crews to minimize cost?
6. *Hint:* You will want to install the Solver Add-in to assist with this.
7. File: **CREWSCHEDULING.xls** (Excel file).

CASE 20:
CREATING A DATABASE MANAGEMENT SYSTEM

MOUNTAIN BIKE RENTALS

Vail Resort in Vail, Colorado, is internationally known as one of the best places in North America for mountain biking. Since 1973, Slopeside Bike Rentals has been a tradition in the area. At Slopeside Bike Rentals customers will find the largest selection of bikes, parts, accessories, books, maps, clothing, shocks, helmets, eyewear, shoes, car racks, and touring gear in the area with everything you need for on and off the road. Its state-of-the-art demo and rental program has everything from premium dual suspension to kids' bikes and trailers.

You have been employed for the past three summers by Slopeside Bike Rentals. Recently, there has been a surge in business and the owners need a more accurate way to manage the rental business. You have decided to create a database to help the owners keep track of the bike rentals, who the customers are, amount paid, and any damage to the bikes when they are rented. Currently Slopeside Bike Rentals owns 13 mountain bikes in its fleet of rentals. The bikes vary in type, size, and parts. When customers rent bikes, they are required to leave their driver's license number and to give you a home address, phone number, and credit card number.

You have designed the entity classes and primary keys for the database as the following:

Entity	Primary Key
Bike	Bike_ID
Customer	Customer_ID
Rental	Rental_ID

You have also identified the following business rules:

1. Rentals can have many customers assigned but must have at least one.
2. A bike must be assigned to one and only one rental type.
3. A customer can rent one or more bikes at one time.
4. A bike can be assigned to only one customer but need not be assigned to any customer.

Your job is to be completed in the following phases:

1. Develop and describe the entity-relationship diagram.
2. Use normalization to assure the correctness of the tables (relations).
3. Create the database using a personal DBMS package (preferably Microsoft Access).
4. Slopeside Bike Rentals has the following fee structures for its 13 bike rentals:

Description	Cost per Hour
Specialized Rockhopper	$12
Specialized Rockhopper	12
Trek Fuel 70	12
Trek Fuel 80	15
Trek Fuel 80	15
Trek Fuel 90	16
Marin Downhill FRS	16
Marin Downhill FRS	16
Marin Downhill FRS	16
Specialized Stumpjumper FSR	18
Specialized Stumpjumper FSR	18
Specialized Stumpjumper FSR	18
Specialized Stumpjumper Hardtail	20

5. Use the DBMS package to create the basic report in Figure GP.3.

Figure GP.3

Slopeside Bike
Rental Report

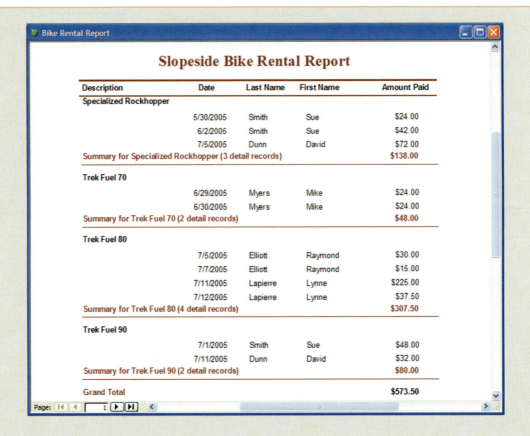

SOME PARTICULARS YOU SHOULD KNOW

1. You may not be able to develop a report that looks exactly like the one in Figure GP.3. However, your report should include the same information.
2. One of your tables will need a composite primary key.
3. File: Not applicable.

CASE 21:
EVALUATING THE SECURITY OF INFORMATION

WIRELESS NETWORK VULNERABILITY

Empty cans of Pringles could be helping malicious hackers spot wireless networks that are open to attack. Security companies have demonstrated that a directional antenna made with a Pringles can most often significantly improves the chances of finding wirelessly networked computers. An informal survey carried out by i-sec (an Internet security research company) using the homemade antenna found that over two-thirds of the networks surveyed were doing nothing to protect themselves. Known as the "PringlesCantenna," these are rapidly becoming popular because they are cheap (under $10) and easy to set up.

Not surprisingly, wireless network security, particularly regarding wireless local area networks (WLANs), is the number one concern of network managers, and an entire industry has grown to serve the ever-changing demands of wireless-network-based information integrity. As companies and home users have gradually adopted wireless technology, special security precautions are required to deal with the unique nature of wireless communications. After all, wireless purposely puts information out on the airwaves, and anyone within range and equipped with an appropriate receiver (e.g., PringlesCantenna) would be able to grab this information and put it to all kinds of questionable use. Since this is the case, many wireless networks implement inherent authentication and encryption mechanisms to provide basic assurance to wireless users that their information will at least be difficult to decrypt and their networks at least challenging to crack.

SOME PARTICULARS YOU SHOULD KNOW

1. Create an analysis report based on a thorough Internet search that discusses the tips, techniques, and best practices to protect against this type of amateur hacking.

2. Include a summary of the types of detection and prevention technology available, specifically the use of firewalls and intrusion detection software.

3. In your analysis report, include the current statistics on identity theft, the number of times networks are hacked, and the total annual cost of online security breaches to corporations.

4. During your research, you might also consider finding statistics on the percentage of companies that have yet to implement adequate security measures and the percentage of companies that spend 5 percent or less of their IT budgets on security for their networks.

5. File: Not applicable.

CASE 22:
ASSESSING THE VALUE OF SUPPLY CHAIN MANAGEMENT

OPTIMIZING SHIPMENTS

One of the main products of the Fairway Woods Company is custom-made golf clubs. The clubs are manufactured at three plants (Denver, Colorado; Phoenix, Arizona; and Dallas, Texas) and are then shipped by truck to five distribution warehouses in Sacramento, California; Salt Lake City, Utah; Albuquerque, New Mexico; Chicago, Illinois; and New York City, New York. Because shipping costs are a major expense, management is investigating a way to reduce them. For the upcoming golf season, an estimate has been created as to the total output needed from each manufacturing plant and how much each warehouse will require to satisfy its customers. The CIO from Fairway Woods Company has created a spreadsheet for you, **FAIRWAYS.xls,** of the shipping costs from each manufacturing plant to each warehouse as a baseline analysis.

SOME PARTICULARS YOU SHOULD KNOW

1. The problem presented involves the shipment of goods from three plants to five regional warehouses.

2. Goods can be shipped from any plant to any warehouse, but it costs more to ship goods over long distances than over short distances.

3. The challenge presented is to determine the amounts to ship from each plant to each warehouse at a minimum total shipping cost in order to meet the regional demand, while not exceeding the plant supplies.

4. Specifically you need to focus on:

   a. Minimizing the total shipping cost.

   b. Total shipped must be less than or equal to supply at plant.

   c. Totals shipped to warehouses must be greater than or equal to demand at warehouses.

   d. Number to ship must be greater than or equal to 0.

5. File: **FAIRWAYS.xls** (Excel file).

Electronic Commerce Projects

BEST IN COMPUTER STATISTICS AND RESOURCES

For both personal and professional reasons, you'll find it necessary to stay up with technology and technology changes throughout your life. Right now, knowing about technology—the latest trends, new innovations, processor speeds, wireless communications capabilities, and the like—can help you support technology infrastructure recommendations for a company in one of your term papers. That same kind of information can help you determine which personal technologies you need to buy and use.

As you progress through your career, you'll make numerous business presentations and recommendations, most of which will contain some sort of discussion of the best uses of technology from an organizational point of view. Indeed, if you plan to move up the corporate ladder to the C-level (CEO, CFO, CIO, etc.), a knowledge of the organizational uses of technology is essential. Connect to several Web sites that offer computer statistics and resources and answer the following questions for each.

- **A.** What categories of personal technologies are covered?
- **B.** What categories of organizational uses of technology are covered?
- **C.** To what extent is time-based (e.g., year-by-year) numerical data provided?
- **D.** Who supports the site? Is the site for-profit or not-for-profit?
- **E.** Are the various types of research reports free or do you have to pay a fee?
- **F.** How helpful is the site from a personal point of view?
- **G.** How helpful is the site from an organizational point of view?

CONSUMER INFORMATION

Many consumer organizations provide databases of information on the Internet. At those sites you can read the latest product reviews, search for new pharmaceuticals that cure diseases (or alleviate symptoms of them), and access safety information for products such as automobiles and children's toys.

These types of sites are invaluable to you for a number of reasons. First, they can help you be better informed and make more intelligent decisions when making product and service purchases. Second, you'll also find these sites a good resource when writing term and research papers. Sites such as Better Business Bureau (www.bbb.org), Consumer Reports (www.consumerreports.org), Consumer World (www.consumerworld.org), and Consumer Information Publications (www.pueblo.gsa.gov) post a wealth of information you can use in your personal and academic life.

Pick a product you're interested in purchasing, do some looking around on the Internet at consumer information sites, and answer the following questions.

- **A.** What sites did you review? Which were helpful and why?
- **B.** Is the information opinion only, completely factual, or a combination of the two?
- **C.** Who supports the sites you reviewed? The government? Not-for-profit organizations? For-profit organizations?
- **D.** How important will this type of consumer information become as electronic commerce becomes more widespread on the Internet?

INTERVIEWING AND NEGOTIATING TIPS

During your job search process, the Internet can offer you very valuable specific information. In the area of interviewing and negotiating, for example, the Internet contains more than 5,000 sites devoted to interviewing skills, negotiating tips, and the like.

Interviewing and negotiating are just as important as searching for a job. Once you line up that first important interview, you may still not land the job if you're not properly prepared. If you do receive a job offer, you may be surprised to know that you can negotiate such things as moving expenses, signing bonuses, and allowances for technology in your home.

We've provided Web sites for you that address the interviewing and negotiating skills you need in today's marketplace. Review some of these sites (and any others that you may find). Then, develop a list of do's and don'ts for the interviewing process. Next, develop a list of tips that seem helpful to you that will increase your effectiveness during the negotiation process. Once you've developed these two lists, prepare a short class presentation. In your presentation, be sure to include the names of the Web sites you visited as well as their addresses. Distribute this presentation electronically to everyone in your class.

META DATA

Meta data means "data about the data." In the context of Web pages, it refers to the notations in the header (**<head>**) part of the Web page. Here's an example:

<html>
<head>
<title>Management Information Systems for the Information Age</title>
<META name = "description" content = "Everything you wanted to know about computer systems in business">
<Meta name = "keyword" content = "MIS, business IT, database, artificial intelligence, security, electronic commerce">
</head>

Although the **<title>** part of the header is not, strictly speaking, meta data, it is strongly related. That's the wording that describes the page when you add it to your Favorites list. It's also very important for search engines because it determines the placement of your Web site within the list of possible answers to a search term.

The wording within the **<META…>** tags is used by some search engines to classify your Web page. However, you can't depend on that since many do not. Find three of these sites and answer the following questions:

A. Does Google use the **<METAdata…>** tag to classify your Web page?

B. How can you ensure that a search engine will classify your Web site as being about the topic you intend? (Say, for instance, you have a site about robots.)

C. There are internationally recognized standards for meta data tags. What is the name of one of these?

D. Find a software package that generates meta data tags. What is it called and how much does it cost?

E. What was the best piece of advice you found on creating meta data on a Web page?

BUREAU OF LABOR STATISTICS

The Bureau of Labor Statistics (BLS, at www.bls.gov) of the U.S. Federal government states that its role is as the "principal fact-finding agency for the Federal Government in the broad field of labor economics and statistics." As you might well guess then, the BLS provides a wealth of information concerning employment and the economy. Connect to the BLS's Web site and answer the following questions.

    A. What type of information is contained on the *Kid's Page*? Did you find any of the information also suitable to you?

    B. What sort of information concerning workplace safety and illness is available? How is this information categorized? How would this type of information be helpful to a business manager?

    C. What type of demographic information is available? What "demographics" make up the key categories by which demographic information is provided?

    D. What is contained in the *Occupational Outlook Handbook*? How often is it updated? What parts of the handbook are particularly relevant to you as you prepare to enter the job market? Why?

    E. Within Inflation & Consumer Spending, the BLS provides a lot of information concerning consumer price indexes and producer price indexes. What is the consumer price index and what does it mean? What is the producer price index and what does it mean?

    F. What interesting statistics do you find when reviewing employment by state information? How is your state faring as compared to other states?

DEMOGRAPHICS

For organizations focusing on meeting wants or desires of end consumers, the demographic makeup of the target audience is key. The more you know about your target audience, the better equipped you are to develop and market products. Demographics is a broad general term that can include any characteristic such as zip code, annual income, gender, age, marital status, hobbies, and so on.

    And you can find all sorts of demographic information on the Internet. Connect to a couple of different demographic-related Web sites and see what they have to offer. As you do, answer the following questions for each.

    A. Who is the target audience of the site?

    B. Who is the provider of the site?

    C. Is the provider a private (for-profit) organization or a not-for-profit organization?

    D. How often is the demographic information updated?

    E. Does the site require that you pay a subscription fee to access its demographic information?

    F. How helpful would the information be if you wanted to start a new business or sell various types of products?

FREE AND RENTABLE STORAGE SPACE

Information is an essential resource in the information age. You must ensure its integrity, know that it's useful, and always know that you have a backup of your information just in case your primary storage is damaged or stolen. To help, you can use the services of a file hosting service on the Web. These sites offer you storage of your information that can be accessed from anywhere in the world. You can use the services of these sites to back up your information and also create an environment in which you can share your information with other people.

A few of these file hosting services include My Docs Online (www.mydocsonline.com), Box (www.box.net), and Yahoo! Briefcase (http://briefcase.yahoo.com). Visit any of these sites and a few others that you find through searches and answer the following questions for each.

A. Does the site provide free storage? If so, what is the limit?

B. What type of information can you store (video, text, photos, etc.)?

C. Can you establish multiple users with different passwords who can access your storage area?

D. Must you sign a contract for a certain duration (annual, etc.)?

E. Are there different levels of services provided such as personal, enterprise, workgroup, and so on?

F. To you, is using a file hosting service on the Web better than backing up your information to writable CDs or DVDs? Why or why not?

GATHERING COMPETITIVE INTELLIGENCE

When considering new business opportunities, you need knowledge about the competition. One of the things many new business owners fail to do is to see how many competitors there are and what differentiates them before launching their business. You may find there are too many and that they would be tough competition for you. Or, you may find that there are few competitors and the ones who are out there aren't doing a terrific job.

Generate a new business idea you could launch on the Internet. (Perform this task in less than 15 minutes focusing on the products or services you will sell.) Now, seek out and look at some of the Web sites of businesses in the competitive space you're thinking of entering. As you do, answer the following questions.

A. How many sites did you find that are offering the same products or services you're planning to offer?

B. How did you find those sites?

C. How many are in your country and how many are in other countries?

D. Did you come across a site from another country that has a unique approach that you did not see on any of the sites in your own country?

E. In general, has competition intensified because of the Internet and the Web? Justify your answer.

ETHICAL COMPUTING GUIDELINES

Ethical computing encompasses many topics: privacy, intellectual property, abuse of resources, character defamation, to name just a few. Unethical behavior can be as mild as rudeness in an e-mail or as lethal as stalking and death threats. Some unethical behavior is illegal, but not all of it is.

The Computer Ethics Institute Web site at www.brook.edu/its/cei/cei_hp.htm has a list of 10 commandments to guide the use of information technology and the Association for Computer Machinery (ACM) specifies a code of ethical behavior as do many other organizations.

Find answers to the following questions on the Web:

A. Find a code of ethics from an organization of your choosing. What do you think are the best five guiding principles from all the tips that you found?

B. Are chain letters good or bad? Are they illegal? Summarize the opposing arguments you find.

C. How does anonymous e-mail work and why would you use it?

D. What are five ways that e-mail use can be unethical?

E. Why is the deliberate spreading of viruses unethical? Name at least five reasons.

EXPLORING GOOGLE EARTH

Google Earth is a free virtual globe program that uses satellite and aerial images combined with a geographic information system. It allows you to pick a place on the globe and zoom in to see all sorts of features like the locations of schools, sports venues, coffee shops, shopping malls, movie/DVD rental stores, etc. The list is very long.

You can even layer multiple searches and save your results. The site also hosts a large Google Earth Community that shares information and annotations.

The image resolution varies across regions, but most large cities around the world are depicted in high-resolution detail showing buildings and streets and trees and other features.

Download the Google Earth application from http://earth.google.com and answer the following questions:

A. In the area where you live, how is the resolution compared to the resolution for Washington, D.C.?

B. Can you see your own street? How about individual houses?

C. Zoom in to your home county and mark elementary schools. How many are there? Less than 10? More than 10? More than 50?

D. Choose a university location and zoom in. How clearly can you see the buildings? How about the cars in the parking lots?

E. Can you find the Eiffel Tower in Paris, France; the Brandenburg Gate (Brandenburger Tor) in Berlin, Germany; and Buckingham Palace in London, England?

FINANCIAL AID RESOURCES

On the Internet, you can find valuable databases that give you access to financial aid resources as you attend school. These resources can be in the form of scholarships—money you don't have to pay back—and standard student loans. And there are a variety of financial aid lenders, ranging from traditional banks, to the government, to private parties wanting to give something back to society. Find at least three Web sites that provide financial aid databases and answer the following questions for each.

A. Do you have to register as a user to access information?

B. Do you have to pay a fee to access information?

C. Can you build a profile of yourself and use it as you search?

D. Can you apply for aid while at the site or must you request paper applications that you need to complete and return by mail?

E. By what sort of categories of aid can you search?

F. What about your school? What sort of searchable database of financial aid does it offer? How does it compare to the other sites you visited? Does your school's financial aid site provide any links to other sources of information? If so, what are those sources?

FINDING HOSTING SERVICES

There are many options for hosting services for e-commerce Web sites. You can decide to acquire the necessary computer and communications hardware and software to manage your own technical infrastructure, or you can let a specialist firm do it for you. Unless you're really into the technical side of things, it's probably better to work with a firm that specializes in it. They are called *Web hosting services* and there are plenty of them around. Cost, reliability, security, and customer service are some of the criteria you might use in selecting a hosting service. If you're planning to have your business located in a country with poor telecommunications services, don't forget that you can choose a hosting service located in a country with a more reliable telecommunications infrastructure, anywhere in the world.

Some companies provide directories that make it easy for you to find and compare prices and features of Web hosting companies, sort of like shopping malls for Web hosting services. An example of such a company is FindYourHosting.com (www.findyourhosting.com). Take a look at its site to see some of the options available. As you consider Web hosting services, answer the following questions.

A. Compare the costs of the various hosting services. Were you able to find one that seems to be within a reasonable budget?

B. How can you evaluate the reliability of various Web hosting services?

C. How can you evaluate the quality of a Web hosting company's customer service? What do you have a right to expect in the way of customer service and also security?

GLOBAL STATISTICS AND RESOURCES

Thomas Friedman said it best: The world is flat. Simply put, we are one big group of people, no longer constrained by geographic borders, time zones, language, or even culture. To be successful in the business world, you must be willing to have international suppliers, international customers, and international business partners.

Therefore, knowing about specific regions and countries around the world is vitally important. Right now, regions such as the Pacific Rim are emerging as world economic powers. In 5 to 10 years that may be Central and South America or perhaps Russia. Beyond that, Africa may emerge. Within each of those regions, some countries are emerging more quickly than others.

Pick a country that interests you and also that you know little about. Connect to some of the global statistics and resources Web sites we've provided on the Web site for this book as well as any other sites you can find and answer the following questions for the country you chose.

A. What is the current population?

B. What are the primary industries and exports?

C. What is the primary language?

D. What are the country's natural resources?

E. What population demographics were you able to find (e.g., gender ratio, birth and death rates, education, income distribution, etc.)?

F. What is the country's government type?

GOLD, SILVER, INTEREST RATES, AND MONEY

Gold and silver have traditionally been kept as hedges against inflation and an uncertain future. Many people consider a rise in the price of gold and/or silver to be an early indicator of a slowing economy, perhaps leading to recession or even a depression.

During the first half of 2006, for the first time since 1981, when mortgage rates were 15 percent or more, the price of gold went above $600 per ounce. The reason is said to be the falling price of the dollar compared to other world currencies. The mounting national debt and uncertainty about U.S. foreign policy were also contributing to a sense of insecurity about the future.

Analysts were concerned that for the above reasons, inflation would start creeping up, although the Federal Reserve was working to try and keep inflation low, since high inflation rates damage the economy in many ways. Find answers to the following questions on the Web:

A. What is the current price of gold and silver? How does it compare to the price on January 1, 2006?

B. What is the Federal Reserve's current interest rate compared to the rate on January 1, 2006?

C. What is the current rate of inflation compared to what it was on January 1, 2006?

D. What is the current exchange rate for the dollar compared to the British pound (£), the Euro (€), and the Yen (¥) today? How do these compare to the rates on January 1, 2006?

E. What were all of the above values in the year that you were born?

PRIVACY LAWS AND LEGISLATION

Privacy laws in the United States tend to be aimed at specific industries, such as the video rental industry, or agencies of the federal government. There are also specific privacy laws that are passed on a state-by-state basis. For example, California has a law that requires companies that discover their databases have been breached to inform people whose personal information was included in that database. This law was passed to try to address the rising rate of identity theft.

Other industrialized countries have different approaches to privacy legislation. The European Union has issued a directive that all member nations enact laws to guarantee citizens specific privacy rights, but New Zealand has, perhaps, the most restrictive set of privacy laws.

Search the Web and find answers to the following questions:

A. How did Choice Point, the Bank of America, LexisNexis, and DSW Shoe Stores contribute to the heightened interest of legislators in privacy laws?

B. What are the major provisions of the European directive on the protection of personal information gathered by businesses?

C. What are the pro and con arguments on the topic of the U.S. Homeland Security Act as it applies to personal privacy? List at least three points on each side.

D. What are the main stipulations of the Family Educational Rights and Privacy Act (FERPA)?

E. What is the main stipulation of the Freedom of Information Act?

PROTECTING YOUR COMPUTER

As you've no doubt already learned, anti-virus software finds, and may eliminate, viruses that find their way onto your computer or are trying to get into your computer system.

One method that anti-virus software uses is to examine the files on your computer looking for virus signatures, that is, content embedded in the files that matches a virus definition in its virus dictionary. Another method is to recognize when your computer is "acting funny" in a way that might indicate the presence of a virus.

The key to successful virus detection is in keeping the virus dictionary and the definition of "acting funny" current so that new viruses can be detected. To do this you must update your anti-virus software regularly. Most anti-virus software lets you set it up so that it goes to the Internet and updates itself on a regular basis. Find three sites that offer anti-virus software and answer the following questions:

A. What does the software at each site cost?

B. Does the site have information on current and past viruses?

C. Does the site sell any other type of computer protection like a firewall or spyware protection? If so, list what's available.

D. Does the site sell different software for a network than it does for an individual user? What's the difference?

E. Does the software allow you to schedule automatic updating?

LEARNING ABOUT INVESTING

Investing can be as simple as finding a company that performs well financially and buying some of their stock. Or, if you want to spread your investment over a number of stocks and you don't want to select each stock personally, you can invest in a mutual fund. Of course, there are thousands of mutual funds with all types of investment objectives. So, any way you go you must pick your investment wisely. You can find many helpful Web sites on the Internet to get you up to speed quickly.

Choose three Web sites and answer the following questions:

A. Is the site designed for first-time investors or those that are more experienced? Who sponsors the site?

B. Can you search for a specific topic?

C. Are specific stocks or mutual funds reviewed or evaluated?

D. Does the site provide direct links to brokerage or stock quoting sites?

E. Is a forum for submitting questions available? If so, are frequently asked questions (FAQs) posted?

LOCATING INTERNSHIPS

Have you ever noticed that a large number of jobs require expertise or experience? That being the case, how does someone gain relevant experience through a job when job experience is required to get the job? As it turns out, that has always been a perplexing dilemma for many college students, and one way to solve it is by obtaining an internship. Internships provide you with valuable knowledge about your field, pay you for your work, and offer you that valuable experience you need to move up in your career.

On the Web site for this text (www.mhhe.com/haag), we have provided you with a number of Web sites that offer internship possibilities—visit a few of them. For each site you visit, answer the following questions.

A. Who owns and maintains the site? Is it a for-profit or not-for-profit organization?

B. Do you find any internships in line with your career?

C. What about pay? Do you find both paying and nonpaying internships?

D. How do these internship sites compare to the more traditional job database sites such as Monster.com?

E. What sort of internship resources does your school provide?

F. How does your school's internship site compare to the other sites you visited on the Web?

SMALL BUSINESS ADMINISTRATION

The Small Business Administration (SBA, at www.sba.gov) of the U.S. Federal government has a goal of assisting almost 1.2 million prospective and existing small businesses in the year 2008, an approximate 22 percent increase over the 980,000 small businesses it helped in 2002. You can be among those 1.2 million small businesses, if you have the entrepreneurial spirit, an innovative idea, and solid business skills.

For existing small businesses, the SBA provides consultative services and loans for business growth. For start-up businesses, the SBA aids in finding capital, refining business ideas, developing a pro forma income statement, and a host of other activities. Visit the SBA's Web site and answer the following questions.

A. What elements does the SBA require to appear in a business plan? What support does the SBA provide while you create your business plan?

B. What tools does the SBA provide to help you in estimating your costs and revenues?

C. While applying for a loan, what information does the SBA require that you provide?

D. What educational services does the SBA provide so you can learn the basics of incomes statements and balance sheets?

E. In what ways does the SBA support the creation of small businesses that are diversity-owned?

STOCK QUOTES

When you buy stock in a company, you're betting on its success. Although it's no guarantee of how the stock price will do in the future, most people look at the price of stock and how it has fared over previous months and years to get an indication of whether it's a strong buy or not.

Both stocks and mutual funds are offered by the share and you can buy as much or as little of the stock or mutual fund as you like. However, some stocks are priced at hundreds of thousands of dollars, and the price alone may take them off your list for consideration.

Choose three stock quoting services, examine what it takes to retrieve a stock or mutual fund quote and answer the following questions:

A. Are the quotes provided free of charge or for a fee?

B. Does the site require a ticker symbol (the abbreviation used by experienced investors) or can you type in a company name?

C. Are the quotes in real time or are they delayed (15 to 20 minutes old)? Can you get price charts?

D. Are prices charts available? How about historic prices?

E. Can you create and save a personal portfolio of stocks?

RESEARCHING STOREFRONT SOFTWARE

If you decide to sell products on the Internet, there is software that you can use to make it easy to create a Web site. This type of software is called *storefront software.* There are many software products for you to choose from. Some will cost you a lot of money, but others are free. FreeMerchant.com for example, has a Basic Store for $9.95 per month, a Bronze Package for $24.95 per month, a Silver Package for $49.95 per month, and a Gold Package for $99.95 per month. What you get in each of these packages is listed in detail on the FreeMerchant.com Web site (www.freemerchant.com).

Since there are many options to choose from, it would be worth your while to do a little research to see if you can find an article that compares current versions of storefront software. A site like ZDNet.com (www.zdnet.com) would be a good place to start your search. Build up a list of features that you will need for your e-commerce site, and then compare your needs with the features offered by the various software packages. They all sound good when you read about them on the vendor's Web sites so be sure you take a "test drive" of the software before you sign up.

Another possibility would be to sign up for a shopping mall. Find your way to Amazon.com's zShops or Yahoo!Store and see that you think of these alternatives. Finally, you'll need a way for your customers to pay you for what they buy. This involves getting a merchant account which permits you to accept credit cards. Most of the storefront sites will explain how merchant accounts work and will help you get a merchant account.

A. What features have you decided your storefront software must provide?

B. How have you evaluated the pros and cons of using a storefront software package versus the options offered by the likes of Amazon.com and Yahoo!?

C. See if you can track down users of software options you are considering. Send them an e-mail and ask them what they like and dislike. You may be surprised at their answers.

SEARCHING FOR SHAREWARE AND FREEWARE

Perhaps the notion of shareware/freeware appeals to you. You'd like to be able to try the software before you buy it. If you want software such as a screen saver or anti-virus software, you're in luck. But what if you want some shareware to help you compose music or keep track of your soccer team's schedule? Well, then you'll have to go searching for that software. You could use a general-purpose search engine such as Yahoo! and type in shareware and music or soccer. But suppose those few titles don't meet your needs.

Finding shareware/freeware titles can be daunting for two reasons. First, currently there are over 1 million shareware and freeware titles available to you. Second, most shareware/freeware developers don't have their own Web sites. As many don't develop their software as a business, they can't justify the cost of supporting their own Web sites. To address both of these challenges, Web sites have been created that maintain databases of thousands of shareware/freeware software titles. Find such a site and answer the following questions.

A. How does the site group the software?

B. Can you search by operating system or platform?

C. Does the site provide descriptions of the software?

D. Can you search by file size?

E. Are screen captures from the software provided?

F. Are reviews and/or ratings of the software provided?

G. When was the last update for the site?

SEARCHING JOB DATABASES

There are, quite literally, thousands of sites that provide you with databases of job postings. Some are better than others. Some focus on specific industries, others offer postings for only executive managers.

Think for a moment about the job you want. What would be its title? In which industry do you want to work? In what part of the country do you want to work? What exceptional skills can you offer an employer? Connect to a couple of different job search database sites, search for your job, and answer the following questions for each site.

A. What is the date of last update?

B. Are career opportunities abroad listed as a separate category or are they integrated with domestic jobs?

C. Can you search for a specific organization?

D. Can you search by geographic location? If so, how? By city? By zip code?

E. Can you apply for a position online? If so, how do you submit your résumé?

F. Do you have to register to build an online résumé (e-résumé)?

G. Once a potential employer performs a search that matches your résumé, how can that employer contact you?

H. Once you build your résumé, can you use it to perform a job search?

I. Are there valuable tips available for building a good résumé?

SEARCHING FOR MBA PROGRAMS

Many of you will undoubtedly choose to continue your education by obtaining an MBA. And you probably should. The market for the best business positions is extremely competitive, with hiring organizations seeking individuals who can speak more than one language, have job experience, and have extended their educational endeavors beyond just getting an undergraduate degree. Not too long ago, the key competitive advantage was in having that undergraduate degree, a true distinction over those with just a high school education. Now, the competitive advantage lies in having an MBA.

Each year, *U.S. News and World Report* ranks the top business schools in the nation. On the Web site that supports this text, you'll find a list of the Web sites for some of the top 50 business schools in the nation.

Choose a couple of different business schools from the list of 50, visit their Web sites, and answer the following questions for each.

A. What business school did you choose?

B. Does that school offer a graduate program in your area of interest?

C. Can you apply online?

D. Does the site list tuition and fee costs?

E. Does the site contain a list of the graduate courses offered in your area of interest?

F. Does the school offer some distance learning formats for some of the courses? Are you interested in taking courses via distance learning?

GLOSSARY

1-tier infrastructure the most basic setup because it involves a single tier on a single machine.

2-tier infrastructure the basic client/server relationship.

3-tier infrastructure the most common approach used for Web applications today.

A

Abandoned registrations number of visitors who start the process of completing a registration page and then abandon the activity.

Abandoned shopping carts the number of visitors who create a shopping cart and start shopping and then abandon the activity before paying for the merchandise.

Abandon rate the percentage of callers who hang up while waiting for their call to be answered.

Accuracy usually measured inversely as *error rate,* or the number of errors per thousand (or million) that a system generates.

Ad hoc (nonrecurring) decision decision you make infrequently (perhaps only once) and for which you may even have different criteria for determining the best solution for each time.

Ad-supported derives revenue by selling advertising space, much like the concept of an affiliate program.

Adware software to generate ads that installs itself on your computer when you download some other (usually free) program from the Web.

Affiliate program an arrangement made between two e-commerce sites that directs viewers from one site to the other.

Agent-based modeling way of simulating human organizations using multiple intelligent agents, each of which follows a set of simple rules and can adapt to changing conditions.

Agile methodology a form of extreme programming that aims for customer satisfaction through early and continuous delivery of useful software components.

Analysis phase of the systems development life cycle involves end users and IT specialists working together to gather, understand, and document the business requirements for the proposed system.

Anonymous Web browsing (AWB) service hides your identity from the Web sites you visit.

Anti-spyware software utility software that detects and removes spyware and other unwanted software that can track every electronic move you make.

Antivirus software detects and removes or quarantines computer viruses.

Application generation subsystem of a DBMS contains facilities to help you develop transaction-intensive applications.

Application service provider (ASP) supplies software applications (and often related services such as maintenance, technical support, and the like) over the Internet that would otherwise reside on its customers' in-house computers.

Application software the software that enables you to solve specific problems or perform specific tasks.

Arithmetic logic unit (ALU) a component of the CPU that performs arithmetic, as well as comparison and logic operations.

Artificial intelligence (AI) the science of making machines imitate human thinking and behavior.

ASCII (American Standard Code for Information Interchange) the coding system that most personal computers use to represent, process, and store information.

Automatic speech recognition (ASR) a system that not only captures spoken words but also distinguishes word groupings to form sentences.

Average speed to answer (ASA) the average time, usually in seconds, that it takes for a call to be answered by an actual person.

B

Back office system used to fulfill and support customer orders.

Backup the process of making a copy of the information stored on a computer.

Bandwidth capacity of the communications medium, refers to the amount of information that a communications medium can transfer in a given amount of time.

Bar code scanner reads information that is in the form of vertical bars, where their width and spacing represent digits (often used in point-of-sale [POS] systems in retail environments).

Benchmarking a process of continuously measuring system results, comparing those results to optimal system performance (benchmark values), and identifying steps and procedures to improve system performance.

Benchmarks baseline values a system seeks to attain.

Binary digit (bit) the smallest unit of information that your computer can process.

Biochip a technology chip that can perform a variety of physiological functions when inserted into the human body.

Biometrics the use of physiological characteristics—such as your fingerprint, the blood vessels in the iris of your eye, the sound of your voice, or perhaps even your breath—to provide identification.

Biometric scanner scans some human physical attribute, like your fingerprint or iris, for security purposes.

Biomimicry learning from ecosystems and adapting their characteristics to human and organizational situations.

Blog a Web site in the form of a journal in which you post entries in chronological order and often includes the capabilities for other viewers to add comments to your journal entries.

Bluetooth a standard for transmitting information in the form of short-range radio waves over distances of up to 30 feet, used for purposes such as wirelessly connecting a cell phone or a PDA to a computer.

Bot computer program that runs automatically.

Botnet network of malware-bot infected computers.

Broadband connection that is a high-bandwidth (high-capacity) telecommunications line capable of providing high-speed Internet service.

Broadband (home) router   a device to connect several computers together to share a DSL or cable Internet connection in a home or small office.

Business continuity plan   a step-by-step guideline defining how the organization will recover from a disaster or extended disruption of its business processes.

Business intelligence (BI)   collective information about your customers, your competitors, your business partners, your competitive environment, and your own internal operations that gives you the ability to make effective, important, and often strategic business decisions.

Business process   standardized set of activities that accomplishes a specific task, such as processing a customer's order.

Business requirement   a detailed set of knowledge worker requests that the system must meet to be successful.

Business to Business (B2B) e-commerce   when a business sells products and services to customers who are primarily other businesses.

Business to Consumer (B2C) e-commerce   when a business sells products and services to customers who are primarily individuals.

Business to Government (B2G) e-commerce   occurs when a business sells products and services to a government entity.

Buyer agent or shopping bot   an intelligent agent on a Web site that helps you, the customer, find the products and services you want.

Buyer power   in Porter's Forces Model it is high when buyers have many choices from whom to buy, and low when their choices are few.

Byte   a group of eight bits that represents one natural language character.

C

Cable modem   a device that uses your TV cable to deliver an Internet connection.

Call center metrics   measure the success of call center efforts.

Capacity planning   determines your projected future IT infrastructure requirements for new equipment and additional network capacity.

Cat 5 (Category 5) cable   a better-constructed version of twisted-pair phone cable.

CAVE (cave automatic virtual environment)   a special 3-D virtual reality room that can display images of other people and objects located in other CAVEs all over the world.

CD-R (compact disc—recordable)   an optical or laser disc that you can write to one time only.

CD-ROM (compact disc—read-only memory)   an optical or laser disc whose information cannot be changed. A CD stores up to 800 Meg of information.

CD-RW (compact disc—rewritable)   an optical or laser disc on which you can save, change, and delete files as often as you like.

Centralized infrastructure   involves sharing of information systems in one central area or one central mainframe.

Central processing unit (CPU)   the hardware that interprets and executes the system and application software instructions and coordinates the operation of all the hardware.

Chief information officer (CIO)   responsible for overseeing every aspect of an organization's information resource.

Chief privacy officer (CPO)   responsible for ensuring that information is used in an ethical way and that only the right people have access to certain types of information such as financial records and payroll.

Chief security officer (CSO)   responsible for the technical aspects of ensuring the security of information such as the development and use of firewalls, intranets, extranets, and anti-virus software.

Chief technology officer (CTO)   responsible for overseeing both the underlying IT infrastructure within an organization and the user-facing technologies (such as CRM systems).

Choice   the third step in the decision-making process where you decide on a plan to address the problem or opportunity.

Click-and-mortar   refers to those organizations that have a presence in the physical world such as a building you can visit and also a presence in the virtual world of the Internet.

Click-and-order (pure play)   an organization that has a presence in the virtual world but no presence in the physical world.

Clickstream   a stored record about your Web surfing session, such as which Web sites you visited, how long you were there, what ads you looked at, and what you bought.

Click-through   a count of the number of people who visit one site, click on an ad, and are taken to the site of the advertiser.

Client/server infrastructure (client/server network)   a network in which one or more computers are servers and provide services to the other computers, called clients.

Coaxial cable (coax)   one central wire surrounded by insulation, a metallic shield, and a final case of insulating material.

Cold site   a separate facility that does not have any computer equipment but is a place where the knowledge workers can move after the disaster.

Collocation facility   available to a company that rents space and telecommunications equipment from another company.

Communications medium   the path, or physical channel, in a network over which information travels.

Communications protocol (protocol)   a set of rules that every computer follows to transfer information.

Communications satellite   microwave repeater in space.

Communications software   helps you communicate with other people.

CompactFlash (CF) card   a flash memory card that is slightly larger than a half-dollar, with a capacity of up to 6 gigabytes.

Competitive advantage   providing a product or service in a way that customers value more than what the competition is able to do.

Competitive intelligence (CI)   business intelligence focused on the external competitive environment.

Component-based development (CBD)   a general approach to systems development that focuses on building small self-contained blocks of code (components) that can be reused across a variety of applications within an organization.

Computer network (network)   two or more computers connected so that they can communicate with each other and share information, software, peripheral devices, and/or processing power.

Computer virus (virus)   software that is written with malicious intent to cause annoyance or damage.

Consumer to Business (C2B) e-commerce   when an individual sells products and services to a business.

Consumer to Consumer (C2C) e-commerce   when an individual sells products and services to other individuals.

Consumer to Government (C2G) e-commerce   when an individual sells products and services to a government entity.

Control unit   the component of the CPU that directs what happens in your computer, sends to RAM for instructions and the information it needs.

Conversion rate   the percentage of potential customers who visit your site who actually buy something.

Cookie   a small record deposited on your hard disk by a Web site containing information about you.

Copyright   the legal protection afforded an expression of an idea, such as a song, video game, and some types of proprietary documents.

Cost-per-thousand (CPM)   sales dollars generated per dollar of advertising, commonly used to make the case for spending money to appear on a search engine.

CPU cache   a type of memory on the CPU where instructions called up by the CPU wait until the CPU is ready to use them.

CPU clock   a sliver of quartz that beats at regular intervals in response to an electrical charge.

CPU (machine) cycle   consists of retrieving, decoding, and executing the instruction, then returning the result to RAM, if necessary.

Crash-proof software   utility software that helps you save information if your system crashes and you're forced to turn it off and then back on again.

Critical success factor (CSF)   a factor simply critical to your organization's success.

Crossover   the process within a genetic algorithm where portions of good outcomes are combined in the hope of creating an even better outcome.

Crowdsourcing   when businesses provide technologies that enable people (i.e., crowds)—instead of a designated paid employee—to create, modify, and oversee the development of a product or service.

CRT   a monitor that looks like a traditional television set.

Customer relationship management (CRM) system   uses information about customers to gain insights into their needs, wants, and behaviors in order to serve them better.

Customer self-service system   an extension of a TPS that places technology in the hands of an organization's customers and allows them to process their own transactions.

D

Data   raw facts that describe a particular phenomenon.

Data administration   the function in an organization that plans for, oversees the development of, and monitors the information resource.

Data administration subsystem   of a DBMS helps you manage the overall database environment by providing facilities for backup and recovery, security management, query optimization, concurrency control, and change management.

Database   a collection of information that you organize and access according to the logical structure of that information.

Database administration   the function in an organization that is responsible for the more technical and operational aspects of managing the information contained in organizational information repositories (databases, data warehouses, and data marts).

Database management system (DBMS)   helps you specify the logical organization for a database and access and use the information within a database.

Data definition subsystem   of a DBMS helps you create and maintain the data dictionary and define the structure of the files in a database.

Data dictionary   contains the logical structure for the information in a database.

Data management   component of a DSS that performs the function of storing and maintaining the information that you want your DSS to use.

Data manipulation subsystem   of a DBMS helps you add, change, and delete information in a database and query it for valuable information.

Data mart   a subset of a data warehouse in which only a focused portion of the data warehouse information is kept.

Data-mining agent   an intelligent agent that operates in a data warehouse discovering information.

Data-mining tool   a software tool you use to query information in a data warehouse.

Data warehouse   a logical collection of information—gathered from many different operational databases—used to create business intelligence that supports business analysis activities and decision-making tasks.

DBMS engine   accepts logical requests from the various other DBMS subsystems, converts them into their physical equivalent, and actually accesses the database and data dictionary as they exist on a storage device.

Decentralized infrastructure   involves little or no sharing of information systems.

Decision support system (DSS)   a highly flexible and interactive IT system that is designed to support decision making when the problem is not structured.

Demand aggregation   the combining of purchase requests from multiple buyers into a single larger order, which justifies a discount from the business.

Denial-of-service (DoS) attack   floods a server or network with so many requests for service that it slows down or crashes.

Design   the second step in the decision-making process, where you consider possible ways of solving the problem, filling the need, or taking advantage of the opportunity.

Design phase   of the systems development life cycle builds a technical blueprint of how the proposed system will work.

Desktop computer the type of computer that is the most popular choice for personal computing needs.

Desktop publishing software extends word processing software by including design and formatting techniques to enhance the layout and appearance of a document.

Development phase of the systems development life cycle takes all your detailed design documents from the design phase and transforms them into an actual system.

Differentiation (in Porter's three generic strategies) offering a product or service that is perceived as being "unique" in the marketplace.

Digital camera captures still images or video as a series of 1s and 0s.

Digital dashboard displays key information gathered from several sources on a computer screen in a format tailored to the needs and wants of an individual knowledge worker.

Digital immigrants people who were born and raised in a time prior to the digital society in which we now live.

Digital natives generation of people ushered into this world in the midst of the digital revolution.

Digital still camera digitally captures still images in varying resolutions.

Digital Subscriber Line (DSL) a high-speed Internet connection using phone lines, which allows you to use your phone for voice communications at the same time.

Digital video camera captures video digitally.

Digital wallet both software and information—the software provides security for the transaction and the information includes payment information (for example, the credit card number and expiration date) and delivery information.

Direct materials materials that are used in production in a manufacturing company or are placed on the shelf for sale in a retail environment.

Disaster recovery cost curve charts (1) the cost to your organization of the unavailability of information and technology and (2) the cost to your organization of recovering from a disaster over time.

Disaster recovery plan a detailed process for recovering information or an IT system in the event of a catastrophic disaster such as a fire or flood.

Disintermediation use of the Internet as a delivery vehicle, whereby intermediate players in a distribution channel can be bypassed.

Disk optimization software utility software that organizes your information on your hard disk in the most efficient way.

Distributed infrastructure involves distributing the information and processing power of IT systems via a network.

Distribution chain the path followed from the originator of a product or service to the end consumer.

Document management system manages a document through all the stages of its processing—similar to a workflow system except that the focus is more on document storage and retrieval.

Dot pitch the distance between the centers of a pair of like-colored pixels.

Drone bot-infected computer.

DS3 a high-speed business network circuit running at 44.736 Mbps.

DVD-R or DVD+R (DVD—recordable) a high-capacity optical or laser disc to which you can write one time only.

DVD-ROM a high-capacity optical or laser disc whose information cannot be changed.

DVD-RW or DVD+RW (depending on the manufacturer) a high-capacity optical or laser disc on which you can save, change, and delete files.

E

E-collaboration the use of technology to support work activities with integrated collaboration environments, knowledge management with knowledge management systems, social networking with social networking systems, learning with e-learning tools, and informal collaboration to support open-source information.

Effectiveness refers to doing the right thing.

Efficiency doing something right (e.g., in the least time, at the lowest cost, with the fewest errors, etc.).

Electronic Bill Presentment and Payment (EBPP) a system that sends bills (usually to end consumers) over the Internet and provides an easy-to-use mechanism (such as clicking on a button) to pay them if the amount looks correct.

Electronic check a mechanism for sending money from your checking or savings account to another person or organization.

Electronic commerce (e-commerce) commerce, but it is commerce accelerated and enhanced by IT, in particular the Internet.

Electronic data interchange (EDI) the direct computer-to-computer transfer of transaction information contained in standard business documents, such as invoices and purchase orders, in a standard format.

Electronic government (e-government) the use of digital technologies to transform government operations in order to improve efficiency, effectiveness, and service delivery.

Electronic marketplace (e-marketplace) an interactive business providing a central space where multiple buyers and sellers can engage in e-commerce and/or other e-commerce business activities.

Electronic portfolio (e-portfolio) collection of Web documents used to support a stated purpose such as demonstrating writing, photography, or job skills.

Encryption scrambles the contents of a file so that you can't read it without having the right decryption key.

Enterprise resource planning (ERP) system software system for business management, supporting areas such as planning, manufacturing, sales, marketing, distribution, accounting, finance, human resource management, project management, inventory management, service and maintenance, transportation, and e-business.

Entry barrier a product or service feature that customers have come to expect from organizations in a particular industry and that must be offered by an entering organization to compete and survive.

Ethernet card the most common type of network interface card.

Ethics   the principles and standards that guide our behavior toward other people.

Expansion bus   the set of pathways along which information moves between devices outside the motherboard and the CPU.

Expansion card (board)   a circuit board that you insert into the expansion slot on the motherboard and to which you connect a peripheral device.

Expansion slot   a long skinny socket on the motherboard into which you insert an expansion card.

Expert system (knowledge-based system)   an artificial intelligence system that applies reasoning capabilities to reach a conclusion.

External information   describes the environment surrounding the organization.

Extranet   an intranet that is restricted to an organization and certain outsiders, such as customers and suppliers.

Extreme programming (XP) methodology   breaks a project into tiny phases and developers cannot continue on to the next phase until the first phase is complete.

F

F2b2C (Factory to business to Consumer)   e-commerce business model in which a consumer communicates through a business on the Internet that directly provides product specifications to a factory that makes the customized and personalized product to the consumer's specifications and then ships it directly to the consumer.

Facial recognition software   software that provides identification by evaluating facial characteristics.

Fair Use Doctrine   allows you to use copyrighted material in certain situations.

Feature analysis   captures your words as you speak into a microphone, eliminates any background noise, and converts the digital signals of your speech into phonemes (syllables).

Feature creep   occurs when developers add extra features that were not part of the initial requirements.

Filter function   filters a list and allows you to hide all the rows in a list except those that match criteria you specify.

Financial cybermediary   an Internet-based company that makes it easy for one person to pay another person or organization over the Internet.

Financial EDI (financial electronic data interchange)   an electronic process used primarily within the Business to Business e-commerce model for the payment of purchases.

Firewall   software and/or hardware that protects a computer or network from intruders.

Firewire (IEEE 1394 or I-Link) port   fits hot-swap, plug-and-play Firewire connectors and you can connect up to 63 Firewire devices to a single Firewire port by daisy-chaining the devices together.

First call resolution (FCR)   the percentage of calls that can be resolved without having to call back.

First-mover advantage   being the first to market with a competitive advantage and thus having a significant impact on gaining market share.

Five Forces Model   helps business people understand the relative attractiveness of an industry and the industry's competitive pressures.

Flash memory card   has high-capacity storage units laminated inside a small piece of plastic.

Flash memory device (jump drive, thumb drive)   a flash memory storage device that is small enough to fit on a key ring and plugs directly into the USB port on your computer.

Flat-panel display   thin, lightweight monitor that takes up much less space than a CRT.

Focus   (in Porter's three generic strategies) focusing on offering products and services (1) to a particular market segment or buyer group, (2) within a segment of a product line, and/or (3) to a specific geographic market.

Foreign key   a primary key of one file (relation) that appears in another file (relation).

Forensic image copy   an exact copy or snapshot of the contents of an electronic medium.

Front office system   the primary interface to customers and sales channels.

Fuzzy logic   mathematical method of handling imprecise or subjective information.

G

Game controller   used for gaming to better control screen action.

Gamepad   a multifunctional input device with programmable buttons, thumb sticks, and a directional pad.

Gaming wheel   a steering wheel and foot pedals for virtual driving.

Garbage-in garbage-out (GIGO)   if the information coming into your decision-making process is in bad form (i.e., garbage-in), you'll more than likely make a poor decision (garbage-out).

Gas plasma display   sends electricity through gas trapped between two layers of glass or plastic to create a screen image.

Genetic algorithm   an artificial intelligence system that mimics the evolutionary, survival-of-the-fittest process to generate increasingly better solutions to a problem.

Geographic information system (GIS)   a decision support system designed specifically to analyze spatial information.

Gigabyte (GB or Gig)   roughly 1 billion bytes.

Gigahertz (GHz)   the number of billions of CPU cycles per second that the CPU can handle.

Glove   an input device that captures and records the shape and movement of your hand and fingers and the strength of your hand and finger movements.

Government to Business (G2B) e-commerce   when a government entity sells products and services to businesses.

Government to Consumer (G2C) e-commerce   the electronic commerce activities performed between a government and its citizens or consumers including paying taxes, registering vehicles, and providing information and services.

Government to Government (G2G) e-commerce   either (1) the electronic commerce activities performed within a single nation's government or (2) the electronic commerce activities performed between two or more nations' governments including providing foreign aid.

Graphics software   helps you create and edit photos and art.

H

Hacker   a knowledgeable computer user who uses his or her knowledge to invade other people's computers.

Haptic interface   uses technology to add the sense of touch to an environment that previously had only visual and auditory elements.

Hard disk   magnetic storage device with one or more thin metal platters or disks that store information sealed inside the disk drive.

Hardware   the physical devices that make up a computer (often referred to as a computer system).

Hardware key logger   a hardware device that captures keystrokes on their journey from the keyboard to the motherboard.

Headset (head-mounted display)   a combined input and output device that (1) captures and records the movement of your head, and (2) contains a screen that covers your entire field of vision.

Help desk   a group of people who respond to knowledge workers' questions.

Holographic device   a device that creates, captures, and/or displays images in true three-dimensional form.

Holographic storage device   stores information on a storage medium that is composed of 3-D crystal-like objects with many sides or faces.

Horizontal e-marketplace   an electronic marketplace that connects buyers and sellers across many industries, primarily for MRO materials commerce.

Horizontal government integration   the electronic integration of agencies, activities, and processes across a specific level of government.

Horizontal market software   application software that is general enough to be suitable for use in a variety of industries.

Hot site   a separate and fully equipped facility where the company can move immediately after the disaster and resume business.

Hot swap   an operating system feature that allows you—while your computer is running—to unplug a device and plug in a new one without first shutting down your computer.

Hub   a device that connects computers together and passes messages by repeating all network transmissions to all the other computers.

I

Identity theft   the forging of someone's identity for the purpose of fraud.

Image scanner   captures images, photos, text, and artwork that already exist on paper.

Implant chip   a technology-enabled microchip implanted into the human body that stores important information about you (such as your identification and medical history) and that may be GPS-enabled to offer a method of tracking.

Implementation   the final step in the decision-making process where you put your plan into action.

Implementation phase   of the systems development life cycle distributes the system to all the knowledge workers and they begin using the system to perform their everyday jobs.

Information   data that have a particular meaning within a specific context.

Information agent   intelligent agent that searches for information of some kind and brings it back.

Information granularity   the extent of detail within the information.

Information-literate knowledge worker   can define what information they need, know how and where to obtain that information, understand the information once they receive it, and can act appropriately based on the information to help the organization achieve the greatest advantage.

Information partnership   two or more companies cooperating by integrating their IT systems, thereby providing customers with the best of what each can offer.

Information technology (IT)   any computer-based tool that people use to work with information and support the information and information-processing needs of an organization.

Infrared, IR, or IrDA (infrared data association)   uses red light to send and receive information.

Infrastructure   a relative term meaning "the structure beneath a structure."

Infrastructure-centric metric   is typically a measure of the efficiency, speed, and/or capacity of technology.

Inkjet printer   makes images by forcing ink droplets through nozzles.

Input device   tool you use to enter information and commands.

Insourcing   using IT specialists within your organization to develop the system.

Integrated collaboration environment (ICE)   the environment in which virtual teams do their work.

Integration testing   verifies that separate systems can work together.

Integrity constraint   rule that helps ensure the quality of the information.

Intellectual property   intangible creative work that is embodied in physical form.

Intelligence   the first step in the decision-making process where you find or recognize a problem, need, or opportunity (also called the diagnostic phase of decision making).

Intelligent agent   software that assists you, or acts on your behalf, in performing repetitive computer-related tasks.

Inter-modal transportation   the use of multiple channels of transportation—railway, truck, boat, and so on—to move products from origin to destination.

Internal information   describes specific operational aspects of an organization.

Internet   a vast network of computers that connects millions of people all over the world.

Internet service provider (ISP)   a company that provides individuals, organizations, and businesses access to the Internet.

Interoperability   the capability of two or more computing components to share information and other resources, even if they are made by different manufacturers.

Intranet   an internal organizational Internet that is guarded against outside access by a special security feature called a firewall (which can be software, hardware, or a combination of the two).

Intrusion-detection software   looks for people on the network who shouldn't be there or who are acting suspiciously.

Intrusion detection system (IDS)   a device that watches network traffic for intrusion attempts and reports them.

Intrusion prevention system (IPS)   type of intrusion detection system (IDS) that also takes action against intrusion attempts, for example, by creating new policies in a firewall to block the source of the attack.

Invisible backlog   the list of all systems that an organization needs to develop but—because of the prioritization of systems development needs—never get funded because of the lack of organizational resources.

IT culture   affects the placement structurally of the IT function within an organization and manifests the philosophical approach to the development, deployment, and use of IT within an organization.

J

Joint application development (JAD)   occurs when knowledge workers and IT specialists meet, sometimes for several days, to define and review the business requirements for the system.

Joystick   vertical handle with programmable buttons that controls action.

Just-in-time (JIT)   an approach that produces or delivers a product or service just at the time the customer wants it.

K

Keyboard   the most often used input device for desktop and notebook computers.

Key logger (key trapper) software   a program that, when installed on a computer, records every keystroke and mouse click.

Knowledge   (1) provides contextual explanation for business intelligence; (2) points toward actions to take to affect business intelligence; (3) includes intellectual assets such as patents and trademarks; and (4) includes organizational know-how for things such as best practices.

Knowledge-based system (expert system)   an artificial intelligence system that applies reasoning capabilities to reach a conclusion.

Knowledge management (KM) system   an IT system that supports the capturing, organization, and dissemination of knowledge (i.e., know-how) throughout an organization.

L

Language processing   attempts to make sense of what you're saying by comparing the word phonemes generated in step 2 with a language model database.

Laser printer   forms images using the same sort of electrostatic process that photocopiers use.

Legacy information system (LIS)   represents a massive, long-term business investment; such systems are often brittle, slow, and nonextensible.

Linux   an open-source operating system that provides a rich operating environment for high-end workstations and network servers.

Liquid crystal display (LCD)   makes the screen image by sending electricity through crystallized liquid trapped between two layers of glass or plastic.

Local area network (LAN)   a network that covers a building or buildings in close proximity, such as one campus of a university or corporation.

Location mashup   a geographic information system (GIS) that displays a particular geographic area and then overlays content according to the user's desires.

Logical view   focuses on how you as a knowledge worker need to arrange and access information to meet your particular business needs.

Long Tail   refers to the tail of a sales curve—first offered by Chris Anderson, editor-in-chief of *Wired Magazine,* as a way of explaining e-commerce profitability.

Loss leader   product sold at or below cost to entice customers into a store in the hope that they will also buy more profitable products.

Loyalty program   rewards customers based on the amount of business they do with a particular organization.

M

Mac OS   Apple's operating system.

Mainframe computer (mainframe)   a computer designed to meet the computing needs of hundreds of people in a large business environment.

Maintenance phase   of the systems development life cycle monitors and supports the new system to ensure it continues to meet the business requirements.

Maintenance, repair, and operations (MRO) materials (indirect materials)   materials that are necessary for running a modern corporation, but do not relate to the company's primary business activities.

Malware   software designed to harm your computer or computer security.

Malware bot   bot that is used for fraud, sabotage, DoS attacks, or some other malicious purpose.

Management information systems (MIS)   deals with the planning for, development, management, and use of information technology tools to help people perform all tasks related to information processing and management.

Marketing mix   the set of marketing tools that your organization will use to pursue its marketing objectives in reaching and attracting potential customers.

Mashup   a combination of content from more than one source.

Mass customization   the ability of an organization to give its customers the opportunity to tailor its product or service to the customers' specifications.

M-commerce   the term used to describe electronic commerce conducted over a wireless device such as a cell phone, PDA, or notebook.

Megabyte (MB or M or Meg)   roughly 1 million bytes.

Memory Stick Media card   elongated flash memory card about the width of a penny developed by Sony with capacities up to 512 megabytes.

Metropolitan (municipal) area network (MAN)   a set of connected networks all within the same city or metropolitan area, but not in immediate proximity to each other.

Microphone   captures audio for conversion into electronic form.

Microsoft Windows Vista   Microsoft's latest personal computer operating system in a wide range of editions including Vista Home Basic, Vista Home Premium, Vista Business, and Vista Ultimate.

Microsoft Windows XP Home   Microsoft's predecessor to Vista designed specifically for home users.

Microsoft Windows XP Professional (Windows XP Pro) Microsoft's predecessor to Vista with enhanced features to support home users and business users.

Microwave transmission   a type of radio transmission.

Minicomputer (mid-range computer)   a computer designed to meet the computing needs of several people simultaneously in a small to medium-size business environment.

Mobile computing   broad general term describing your ability to use technology to wirelessly connect to and use centrally located information and/or application software.

Mobile CPU   a special type of CPU for a notebook computer that changes speed, and therefore power consumption, in response to fluctuation in use.

Mobisode   short one-minute video clips of TV shows designed for viewing on a small cell phone screen.

Model management   component of a DSS that consists of both the DSS models and the DSS model management system.

Monitoring-and-surveillance agent (predictive agent) intelligent agent that constantly observes and reports on some entity of interest, that could, for example, be a network or manufacturing equipment.

Mouse   a pointing device that you use to click on icons or buttons.

Multi-agent system   system in which groups of intelligent agents have the ability to work independently and interact with each other.

Multi-channel service delivery   the term that describes a company's offering of multiple ways in which customers can interact with it.

Multidimensional analysis (MDA) tool   slice-and-dice technique that allows you to view multidimensional information from different perspectives.

Multifunction printer   a printer that can scan, copy, and fax, as well as print.

MultiMediaCard (MMC)   flash memory card that looks identical to an SD card (but SD cards have copy protection built-in), is a little larger than a quarter, and is slightly thicker than a credit card.

Multimedia (HTML) résumé   a multimedia format displayed on the Web for employers to explore at their convenience.

Multi-state CPU   works with information represented in more than just two states, probably 10 states with each state representing a digit between 0 and 9.

Multitasking   allows you to work with more than one piece of software at a time.

Mutation   the process within a genetic algorithm of randomly trying combinations and evaluating the success (or failure) of the outcomes.

N

Nanotechnology   a discipline that seeks to control matter at the atomic and sub-atomic levels for the purpose of building devices on the same small scale.

Near Field Communication (NFC)   a wireless transmission technology being developed primarily for cell phones to support mobile commerce (m-commerce) and other cell phone activities.

Nearshore outsourcing   contracting an outsourcing arrangement with a company in a nearby country.

Network hub   a device that connects multiple computers into a network.

Network interface card (NIC)   an expansion card for a desktop computer or a PC card for a notebook computer that connects your computer to a network and provides the doorway for information to flow in and out.

Neural network (artificial neural network or ANN)   an artificial intelligence system that is capable of finding and differentiating patterns.

Nonrecurring (ad hoc) decision   one that you make infrequently (perhaps only once) and you may even have different criteria for determining the best solution each time.

Nonstructured decision   a decision for which there may be several "right" answers and there is no precise way to get a right answer.

Normalization   process of assuring that a relational database structure can be implemented as a series of two-dimensional tables.

Notebook computer   a small, portable, fully functional, battery-operated computer.

N-tier infrastructure   balances the work of the network over several different servers.

O

Objective information   quantifiably describes something that is known.

Offshore outsourcing   contracting with a company that is geographically far away.

Online ad (banner ad)   small advertisement that appears on other sites.

Online analytical processing (OLAP)   the manipulation of information to support decision making.

Online training   runs over the Internet or off a CD or DVD.

Online transaction processing (OLTP)   the gathering of input information, processing that information, and updating existing information to reflect the gathered and processed information.

Onshore outsourcing   the process of engaging another company in the same country for services.

Open-source information   content that is publicly available (in a broad sense), free of charge, and most often updateable by anyone.

Open-source software   software for which the source code (how the software was actually written) is publicly available and free of charge.

Operating system software   system software that controls your application software and manages how your hardware devices work together.

Operational database   a database that supports OLTP.

Optical character reader   reads characters that appear on a page or sales tag (often used in point-of-sale [POS] systems in retail environments).

Optical fiber   uses a very thin and flexible glass or plastic fiber through which pulses of light travel.

Optical mark reader   detects the presence or absence of a mark in a predetermined spot on the page (often used for true/false and multiple choice exams answers).

Optical storage media   plastic discs on which information is stored, deleted, and/or changed using laser light.

Output device   a tool you use to see, hear, or otherwise recognize the results of your information-processing requests.

Outsourcing   the delegation of specific work to a third party for a specified length of time, at a specified cost, and at a specified level of service.

Overall cost leadership   (in Porter's three generic strategies) offering the same or better quality product or service at a price that is less than what any of the competition is able to do.

P

Page exposures   average number of page exposures to an individual visitor.

Parallel implementation   using both the old and new system until you're sure that the new system performs correctly.

Parallel port   fits parallel connectors, which are large flat connectors found almost exclusively on printer cables.

Path-to-profitability (P2P)   a formal business plan that outlines key business issues such as customer targets (by demographic, industry, etc.), marketing strategies, operations strategies (e.g., production, transportation, and logistics), and projected targets for income-statement and balance-sheet items.

Pattern classification   matches your spoken phonemes to a phoneme sequence stored in an acoustic model database.

PC Card   the expansion card you use to add devices to your notebook computer.

PC Card slot   the opening on the side or front of a notebook, where you connect an external device with a PC Card.

Peer-to-peer collaboration software   permits users to communicate in real time and share files without going through a central server.

Personal digital assistant (PDA)   a small handheld computer that helps you surf the Web and perform simple tasks such as note taking, calendaring, appointment scheduling, and maintaining an address book.

Personal finance software   helps you maintain your checkbook, prepare a budget, track investments, monitor your credit card balances, and pay bills electronically.

Personal information management software (PIM)   helps you create and maintain (1) to-do lists, (2) appointments and calendars, and (3) points of contact.

Personal productivity software   helps you perform personal tasks—such as writing a memo, creating a graph, and creating a slide presentation—that you can usually do even if you don't own a computer.

Pharming   the rerouting of your request for a legitimate Web site, that is, you type in the correct address for your bank and are redirected to a fake site that collects information from you.

Phased implementation   implementing the new system in phases (e.g., accounts receivables, then accounts payable) until you're sure it works correctly and then implementing the remaining phases of the new system.

Phishing (carding or brand spoofing)   technique to gain personal information for the purpose of identity theft, usually by means of fraudulent e-mail.

Physical view   deals with how information is physically arranged, stored, and accessed on some type of storage device such as a hard disk.

Pilot implementation   having only a small group of people use the new system until you know it works correctly and then adding the remaining people to the system.

Pirated software   the unauthorized use, duplication, distribution or sale of copyrighted software.

Pixels (picture elements)   the dots that make up the image on your screen.

Planning phase   of the systems development life cycle, in which you create a solid plan for developing your information system.

Plotter   form output by moving a pen across the surface of a piece of paper.

Plug and play   an operating feature that finds and installs the device driver for a device that you plug into your computer.

Plunge implementation   discarding the old system completely and immediately using the new system.

Podcasting   your ability at any time to download audio and video files for viewing and listening using portable listening devices and personal computers.

Pointing device   a device that is used to navigate and select objects on a display screen.

Pointing stick   a little rod (like a pencil-top eraser) used almost exclusively on notebook computers.

Pop-under ad   a form of a pop-up ad that you do not see until you close your current browser window.

Pop-up ad   small Web page containing an advertisement that appears on your screen outside the current Web site loaded into your browser.

Port   a place on your system unit, monitor, or keyboard through which information and instructions flow to and from your computer system.

Predictive analytics   uses a variety of decision tools and techniques—such as neural networks, data mining, decision trees, and Bayesian networks—to analyze current and historical data and make predictions about the likelihood of the occurrence of future events.

Presentation software   helps you create and edit information that will appear in electronic slides.

Primary key   a field (or group of fields in some cases) that uniquely describes each record.

Primary value processes   (in value-chain analysis) the chain of processes that takes in the raw materials and makes, delivers, markets, sells, and services your organization's products or services.

Privacy   the right to be left alone when you want to be, to have control over your own personal possessions, and not to be observed without your consent.

Project manager   an individual who is an expert in project planning and management, defines and develops the project plan, and tracks the plan to ensure all key project milestones are completed on time.

Project milestone   represents a key date by which you need a certain group of activities performed.

Project plan   defines the what, when, and who questions of systems development including all activities to be performed, the individuals, or resources, who will perform the activities, and the time required to complete each activity.

Project scope document   a written definition of the project scope, usually no longer than a paragraph.

Proof-of-concept prototype   a prototype you use to prove the technical feasibility of a proposed system.

Prototype   a smaller-scale representation or working model of the user's requirements or a proposed design for an information system.

Prototyping   the process of building a model that demonstrates the features of a proposed product, service, or system.

PS/2 port   fits PS/2 connectors, which you often find on keyboards and mice.

Public key encryption (PKE)   an encryption system that uses two keys: a public key that everyone can have and a private key for only the recipient.

Push technology   an environment in which businesses and organizations come to you via technology with information, services, and product offerings based on your profile.

Q

Query-and-reporting tool   similar to a QBE tool, SQL, and a report generator in the typical database environment.

Query-by-example (QBE) tool   helps you graphically design the answer to a question.

R

Random access memory (RAM)   a temporary holding area for the information you're working with as well as the system and application software instructions that the CPU currently needs.

Rapid application development methodology (RAD, rapid prototyping)   emphasizes extensive user involvement in the rapid and evolutionary construction of working prototypes of a system to accelerate the systems development process.

Recovery   the process of reinstalling the backup information in the event the information was lost.

Recurring decision   a decision that you have to make repeatedly and often periodically, whether weekly, monthly, quarterly, or yearly.

Relation   describes each two-dimensional table or file in the relational model (hence its name relational database model).

Relational database   uses a series of logically related two-dimensional tables or files to store information in the form of a database.

Repeater   a device that receives a radio signal, strengthens it, and sends it on.

Report generator   helps you quickly define formats of reports and what information you want to see in a report.

Request for proposal (RFP)   a formal document that describes in detail your logical requirements for a proposed system and invites outsourcing organizations (or "vendors") to submit bids for its development.

Requirement recovery document   a detailed document which describes (1) the distinction between critical and noncritical IT systems and information, (2) each possible threat, and (3) the possible worst-case scenarios that can result from each disaster.

Requirements definition document   defines all the business requirements and prioritizes them in order of business importance.

Resolution of a printer   the number of dots per inch (dpi) it produces.

Resolution of a screen   the number of pixels it has.

Response time   average time to respond to a user-generated event, such as a request for a report, a mouse click, and so on.

Reverse auction   the process in which a buyer posts its interest in buying a certain quantity of items with notations concerning quality, specification, and delivery timing, and sellers compete for the business by submitting successively lower bids until there is only one seller left.

RFID (radio frequency identification)   uses a microchip (chip) in a tag or label to store information, and information is transmitted from, or written to, the tag or label when the microchip is exposed to the correct frequency of radio waves.

Risk assessment   the process of evaluating IT assets, their importance to the organization, and their susceptibility to threats to measure the risk exposure of these assets.

Rivalry among existing competitors   in the Five Forces Model is high when competition is fierce in a market, and low when competition is more complacent.

Router   a device that passes network traffic between smaller subnetworks (or subnets) of a larger network.

RSS feed   a technology that provides frequently published and updated digital content on the Web.

Run-grow-transform (RGT) framework   an approach in which you allocate in terms of percentages how you will spend your IT dollars on various types of business strategies.

S

Sales force automation (SFA) system   automatically tracks all of the steps in the sales process.

Satellite modem   modem that allows you to get Internet access from your satellite dish.

Satisficing   the process of making a choice that meets your needs and is satisfactory, without necessarily being the best possible choice available.

Scalability   refers to how well your system can adapt to increased demands.

Scanner   used to convert information that exists in visible form into electronic form.

Scope creep   occurs when the scope of the project increases beyond its original intentions.

Screenagers   the term applied to the current generation of young people because they spend so much time in front of a screen.

Secure Digital (SD) card   flash memory card that looks identical to an MMC card (but SD cards have copy protection built-in), is a little larger than a quarter, and is slightly thicker than a credit card.

Secure Electronic Transaction (SET)   a transmission security method that ensures transactions are legitimate as well as secure.

Secure Sockets Layer (SSL)   creates a secure and private connection between a Web client computer and a Web server computer, encrypts the information, and then sends the information over the Internet.

Selection   the process within a genetic algorithm that gives preference to better outcomes.

Selfsourcing (also called end-user development)   the development and support of IT systems by end users (knowledge workers) with little or no help from IT specialists.

Selling prototype   a prototype you use to convince people of the worth of a proposed system.

Service level agreement (SLA)   a formal contractually obligated agreement between two parties; within different environments, an SLA takes on different meanings.

Service level specification (SLS) or service level objective (SLO)   supporting document to a service level agreement that clearly defines key metrics for success regarding the SLA.

Service-oriented architecture (SOA or SoA)   a software architecture perspective that focuses on the development, use, and reuse of small self-contained blocks of code (called *services*) to meet all the application software needs of an organization.

Sign-off   the knowledge workers' actual signatures indicating they approve all the business requirements.

Smart card   a plastic card the size of a credit card that contains an embedded chip on which digital information can be stored and updated.

SmartMedia (SM) card   flash memory card that's a little longer than a CF card and about as thick as a credit card with capacities of up to 512 megabytes.

Social engineering   conning your way into acquiring information that you have no right to.

Social networking site   a site on which you post information about yourself, create a network of friends, share content such as photos and videos, and communicate with other people.

Social network system   an IT system that links you to people you know and, from there, to people your contacts know.

Software   the set of instructions that your hardware executes to carry out a specific task for you.

Software-as-a-service (SaaS)   delivery model for software in which you would pay for software on a pay-per-use basis instead of buying the software outright.

Software suite   bundled software that comes from the same publisher and costs less than buying all the software pieces individually.

Spam   unsolicited e-mail (electronic junk mail) from businesses that advertises goods and services.

Spam blocker software   utility software that filters unwanted e-mail from your inbox.

Spoofing   the forging of the return address on an e-mail so that the e-mail message appears to come from someone other than the actual sender.

Spreadsheet software   helps you work primarily with numbers, including performing calculations and creating graphs.

Spyware (sneakware, stealthware)   malicious software that collects information about you and your computer and reports it to someone else without your permission.

Steganography   the hiding of information inside other information.

Storage device   a tool you use to store information for use at a later time.

Structured decision   a decision where processing a certain kind of information in a specified way will always get you the right answer.

Structured query language (SQL)   a standardized fourth-generation query language found in most DBMSs.

Stylus   penlike device used to write or draw on a PDA or tablet PC.

Subjective information   attempts to describe something that is unknown.

Supercomputer   the fastest, most powerful, and most expensive type of computer.

Supplier power   in the Five Forces Model is high when buyers have few choices from whom to buy, and low when their choices are many.

Supply chain management (SCM)   tracks inventory and information among business processes and across companies.

Supply chain management (SCM) system   an IT system that supports supply chain management activities by automating the tracking of inventory and information among business processes and across companies.

Support value processes   (in value-chain analysis) including infrastructure, human resource management, technology development, and procurement that ensure the smooth operations of the primary value processes.

Swarm (collective) intelligence   collective behavior of groups of simple agents that are capable of devising solutions to problems as they arise, eventually leading to coherent global patterns.

Switch   a network device that connects computers and passes messages by repeating each computer's transmissions only to the intended recipient, not to all the computers connected.

Switching cost   a cost that makes customers reluctant to switch to another product or service supplier.

System availability   usually measured inversely as *downtime,* or the average amount of time a system is down and unavailable to end users and customers.

System bus   electrical pathways that move information between basic components of the motherboard, including between RAM and the CPU.

Systems development life cycle (SDLC)   a structured step-by-step approach for developing information systems.

System software   handles tasks specific to technology management and coordinates the interaction of all technology devices.

System testing verifies that the units or pieces of code written for a system function correctly when integrated into the total system.

T

T1 a high-speed business network circuit typically used for business connections, running at speeds up to 1.544 Mbps (1.544 million bits per second).

Tablet PC a pen-based computer that provides the screen capabilities of a PDA with the functional capabilities of a notebook or desktop computer.

Technical architecture defines the hardware, software, and telecommunications equipment required to run the system.

Technology innovation failure a reward system for trying new technologies even if they prove to be unsuccessful.

Technology-literate knowledge worker person who knows how and when to apply technology.

Telecommunications device tool you use to send information to and receive it from another person or computer in a network.

Telephone modem (modem) a device that connects your computer to your phone line so that you can access another computer or network.

Terabyte (TB) roughly 1 trillion bytes.

Test conditions the detailed steps the system must perform along with the expected results of each step.

Testing phase of the systems development life cycle verifies that the system works and meets all the business requirements defined in the analysis phase.

Threat of new entrants in the Five Forces Model is high when it is easy for new competitors to enter a market, and low when there are significant entry barriers to entering a market.

Threat of substitute products or services in the Five Forces Model is high when there are many alternatives to a product or service, and low when there are few alternatives from which to choose.

Throughput the amount of information that can pass through a system in a given amount of time.

Tiered infrastructure (layer infrastructure) the IT system is partitioned into tiers (or layers) where each tier (or layer) performs a specific type of functionality.

Time service factor (TSF) the percentage of calls answered within a specific time frame, such as 30 or 90 seconds.

Total hits number of visits to your Web site, many of which may be by the same visitor.

Touchpad the little dark rectangle that you use to move the cursor with your finger, often found on notebook computers.

Trackball similar to a mechanical mouse, but it has a ball on the top.

Transaction processing system (TPS) a system that processes transactions within an organization.

Transaction speed the speed at which a system can process a transaction.

Trojan horse software software you don't want hidden inside software you do want.

Trojan horse virus hides inside other software, usually an attachment or download.

Twisted-pair cable a bundle of copper wires used for transmitting voice or data communications; it comes in several varieties.

U

U3 Smart drive looks like and is a USB flash drive, but it stores and can launch and run software on any computer.

Ubiquitous computing computing and technology support anytime, anywhere with access to all needed information and access to all business partners, both internal and external to the organization.

Unallocated space the set of clusters that have been set aside to store information, but have not yet received a file, or still contain some or all of a file marked as deleted.

Uninstaller software utility software that you can use to remove software from your hard disk that you no longer want.

Unique visitors the number of unique visitors to your sites in a given time.

Unit testing tests individual units or pieces of code for a system.

USB (universal serial bus) port fits small flat plug-and-play, hot-swap USB connectors, and, using USB hubs, you can connect up to 127 devices to a single USB port on your computer.

User acceptance testing (UAT) determines if the system satisfies the business requirements and enables knowledge workers to perform their jobs correctly.

User agent (personal agent) an intelligent agent that takes action on your behalf.

User documentation highlights how to use the system.

User interface management component of a DSS that allows you to communicate with the DSS.

Utility software software that provides additional functionality to your operating system software.

V

Value chain the chain or series of business processes, each of which adds value to your organization's products or services for customers.

Value-chain analysis a systematic approach to assessing and improving the value of business processes within your organization to further increase its competitive strengths.

Vertical e-marketplace an electronic marketplace that connects buyers and sellers in a given industry (e.g., oil and gas, textiles, and retail).

Vertical government integration electronic integration of agencies, activities, and processes up and down federal, state, and local government levels.

Vertical market software application software that is unique to a particular industry.

View allows you to see the contents of a database file, make whatever changes you want, perform simple sorting, and query to find the location of specific information.

Viewable image size (VIS) the size of the image on a monitor.

Viral marketing encourages users of a product or service supplied by a B2C e-commerce business to encourage friends to join in as well.

Virtual private network (VPN)   uses encryption to protect the confidentiality of *all* network transmissions between two endpoints.

Virtual reality   a three-dimensional computer simulation in which you actively and physically participate.

Virtual team   a team whose members are located in varied geographic locations and whose work is supported by specialized ICE software or by more basic collaboration systems.

Virus (computer virus)   software that is written with malicious intent to cause annoyance or damage.

VoIP (Voice over Internet Protocol)   allows you to send voice communications over the Internet and avoid the toll charges that you would normally receive from your long distance carrier.

W

Walker   an input device that captures and records the movement of your feet as you walk or turn in different directions.

Waterfall methodology   a sequential, activity-based process in which one phase in the SDLC is followed by another from planning through implementation.

Web 2.0   so-called second generation of the Web, which focuses on online collaboration, users as both creators and modifiers of content, dynamic and customized information feeds, and many other engaging Web-based services.

Web authoring software   helps you design and develop Web sites and pages that you publish on the Web.

Web browser software   enables you to surf the Web.

Webcam   captures digital video to upload to the Web.

Web-centric metric   a measure of the success of your Web and e-business initiatives.

Web log   consists of one line of information for every visitor to a Web site and is usually stored on a Web server.

Web page   a specific portion of a Web site that deals with a certain topic.

Web portal   a site that provides a wide range of services, including search engines, free e-mail, chat rooms, discussion boards, and links to hundreds of different sites.

Wide area network (WAN)   a set of connected networks serving areas or buildings not in immediate proximity to each other.

WiFi (wireless fidelity or IEEE 802.11a, b, g, or n)   a standard for transmitting information in the form of radio waves over distances up to about 300 feet.

Wiki   a Web site that allows you—as a visitor—to create, edit, change, and often eliminate content.

Wired communications media   transmit information over a closed, connected path.

Wireless access point (WAP)   a device that allows a computer to use radio waves to access a network.

Wireless communications media   transmit information through the air.

Word processing software   helps you create papers, letters, memos, and other basic documents.

Workflow   defines all of the steps or business rules, from beginning to end, required for a business process.

Workflow system   facilitates the automation and management of business processes.

Workshop training   held in a classroom environment and is led by an instructor.

Worm   a type of virus that replicates and spreads itself, not just from file to file, but from computer to computer via e-mail and other Internet traffic.

X

xD-Picture (xD) card   flash memory card that looks like a rectangular piece of plastic smaller than a penny and about as thick, with one edge slightly curved.

NOTES

CHAPTER 1

1. Greenemeier, Larry, and Nicholas Hoover, "The Hacker Economy," *InformationWeek*, February 12, 2007, pp. 32–39.

2. "Sexcerpts," *Rocky Mountain News*, March 25, 2006, p. 2E.

3. "America's Largest Corporations, Fortune 2006 500," *Fortune*, April 17, 2006.

4. www.systransoft.com

5. Kallman, Ernest, and John Grillo, *Ethical Decision Making and Information Technology* (San Francisco: McGraw-Hill, 1993).

6. Kontzer, Tony, "Brink's Gets Smarter about Learning," *InformationWeek*, December 15, 2003, www.informationweek.com/story/showArticle.jhtml?articleID=16700281, accessed December 20, 2003.

7. Porter, Michael, "How Competitive Forces Shape Strategy," *Harvard Business Review*, March/April 1979.

8. "Accenture: Customer Satisfaction Driving Egovernment," from www.nua.com/surveys/index.cgi?f=VS&art_id=905358759&rel=true, accessed December 2, 2003.

9. Greenspan, Robyn, "U.S. Web Usage and Traffic, August 2004," ClickZ Network, Jupitermedia Corporation, September 21, 2004, www.clickz.com/stats/sectors/traffic_patterns/print.php/3410151, accessed February 26, 2005.

10. "Benchmarking E-Government: A Global Perspective," United Nations Division for Public Economics and Public Administration, released May 2002, www.unpan.org

11. Malykhina, Elena, "Order-Management Software Brings Automation to Online Florist," *InformationWeek*, February 23, 2005, www.informationweek.com/shared/printableArticleSrc.jhtml?articleID=60402303, accessed February 28, 2005.

12. Edwards, Own, "Bow Tech: ASAP Case Study," *Forbes ASAP*, June 3, 1996, pp. 54–58.

13. Rodgers, Zachary, "What MySpace Means for Marketers," ClickZ Network, May 6, 2005, Jupitermedia Corporation, www.clickz.com/features/article.php/3565776, accessed March 28, 2006.

14. MySpace.com, www.myspace.com, accessed March 28, 2006.

15. McGee, Marianne, "The Useless Hunt for Data," *InformationWeek*, January 1/8, 2007, p. 19.

CHAPTER 2

1. Claburn, Thomas, "Let's Make a Deal Online," *InformationWeek*, March 5, 2007, p. 52.

2. "Configuring 9 500 Percent ROI for Dell," i2 White Paper, www.i2.com/customer/hightech_consumer.cfm, accessed May 5, 2004.

3. Malykhina, Elena, "Retailers Take Stock," *InformationWeek*, February 7, 2005, www.informationweek.com/shared/printableArticleSrc.jhtml?ArticleID=59301319, accessed March 3, 2005.

4. "Websmart," *BusinessWeek*, November 24, 2003, p. 96.

5. Koudal, Peter, et al., "General Motors: Building a Digital Loyal Network through Demand and Supply Chain Integration," Stanford Graduate School of Business, Case GS-29, March 17, 2003.

6. McGee, Marianne Kolbasuk, "APC Wants to Know You a Whole Lot Better," *InformationWeek*, September 11, 2006, pp. 55–57.

7. American Power Conversion Corporation, www.apc.com; *APC—Corporate Profile*, www.apc.com/corporate/profile.cfm, accessed April 21, 2007.

8. Surmacz, Jon, "Collaborate and Save: Collaboration Technology Can Save Big Money for the Oil and Gas Industry," *CIO Magazine*, November 5, 2003, www2.cio.com/metrics/2003/metric625.html, accessed June 19, 2004.

9. Davenport, Thomas, and Laurence Prusak, *What's the Big Idea? Creating and Capitalizing on the Best Management Thinking* (Boston: Harvard Business School Press, 2003).

10. McGee, Marianne Kolbusak, "Let's Talk: Constellation Gets Collaborative," *InformationWeek*, September 11, 2006, pp. 98–102.

11. Rashid, Mohammad, et al., "The Evolution of ERP Systems: A Historical Perspective," www.ideagroup.com, accessed May 11, 2004.

12. Babcock, Charles, "FedEx Integration Wins Customers for Keeps," *InformationWeek*, September 11, 2006, pp. 112–14.

13. Whiting, Rick, "Sun Raises the Bar on Build to Order," *InformationWeek*, September 11, 2006, pp. 106–8.

14. Ricadela, Aaron, "100,000 Small Pieces," *InformationWeek*, September 11, 2006, pp. 43–48.

CHAPTER 3

1. McGee, Marianne Kolbasuk, "High Cost of Data Loss," *InformationWeek*, March 20, 2006, pp. 34–46.

2. Lemos, Robert, "TJX Theft Tops 45.6 Million Card Numbers," SecurityFocus, March 30, 2007, http://www.securityfocus.com/news/11455, accessed April 20, 2007.

3. Watterson, Karen, "A Data Miner's Tools," *BYTE*, October 1995, pp. 170–72.

4. "Britannia Airways—Keeping the Crews Flying High," Customer Success Stories from Open Text Corp., www.opentext.com/customers/success-stories.html (Britannia Airways), accessed May 5, 2005.

5. Cash, James, "Gaining Customer Loyalty," *InformationWeek*, April 10, 1995, p. 88.

6. Marlin, Steven, "County in Washington State Expands GIS Capabilities," *InformationWeek*, May 2, 2005, www.informationweek.comstory/showArticle.jhtml?articleID=162100493, accessed May 19, 2005.

7. Maselli, Jennifer, "Insurers Look to CRM for Profits," *InformationWeek*,

May 6, 2002, www.informationweek
.com/story/IWK20022050250007,
accessed March 1, 2005.

8. "Laurentian Bank Creates Online
   Scoring Models for Dealer
   Financing," Customer Success
   Story from SAS Corporation, www
   .sas.com/success/laurentian.html,
   accessed April 21, 2005.

9. Kling, Julia, "OLAP Gains Fans
   among Data-Hungry Firms,"
   Computerworld, January 8, 1996,
   pp. 43, 48.

10. Hutheesing, Nikhil, "Surfing with
    Sega," *Forbes,* November 4, 1996,
    pp. 350–51.

11. LaPlante, Alice, "Big Things
    Come in Smaller Packages,"
    Computerworld, June 24, 1996,
    pp. DW/6–7.

12. Weier, Mary Hayes, "QUERY: What's
    Next in BI?" *InformationWeek,*
    March 5, 2007, pp. 27–29.

13. Dragoon, Alice, "Business Intelli-
    gence Gets Smart(er)," *CIO Maga-
    zine,* September 15, 2003, www
    .cio.com/archive/091503/smart.html,
    accessed June 10, 2004.

14. Gray, Paul, "Business Intelligence: A
    New Name or the Future of DSS?"
    in T. Bui, H. Sroka, S. Stanek, and
    J. Goluchowski (eds.), *DSS in the
    Uncertainty of the Internet Age*
    (Katowice, Poland: University of
    Economics in Katowice, 2003).

15. Willen, Claudia, "Airborne Opportu-
    nities," *Intelligent Enterprise* 5,
    no. 2 (January 14, 2002).

16. Bosavage, Jennifer, "BI Helps
    H&B Hit Business Targets,"
    InformationWeek Business
    Intelligence Pipeline, February 22,
    2005, www.bizintelligencepipeline
    .com/showArticle.jhtml?articleID=
    60402524, accessed March 1, 2005.

17. Hoover, J. Nicholas, "Get Well
    Soon," *InformationWeek,*
    December 4, 2006, pp. 26–28.

18. Schlosser, Julie, "Tech@Work,"
    Fortune, March 3, 2003, www
    .fortune.com/fortune/subs/
    print/0,15935, 427294,00.html?
    cookie=11073974157, accessed
    January 10, 2004.

19. Whiting, Rick, "Analysis Gap,"
    Informationweek, April 22, 2002,

www.informationweek.com/story/
IWK20020418S0007, accessed
April 24, 2004.

20. "Bigelow Teas," Customer Spotlight
    from Business Objects, at
    www.businessobjects.com/company/
    customers/spotlight/bigelow.asp,
    accessed May 17, 2005.

21. "Red Robin International," com-
    pany success story from Cognos at
    www.cognos.com/company/success/
    ss_entertainment.html, accessed
    January 13, 2004.

22. "Mining the Data of Dining,"
    Nation's Restaurant News, May 22,
    2000, pp. S22–S24.

23. Brown, Erika, "Analyze This,"
    Forbes, April 1, 2002, pp. 96–98.

24. Levinson, Meredith, "The Brain Behind
    the Big, Bad Burger and Other
    Tales of Business Intelligence, *CIO
    Magazine,* March 15, 2005, at www
    .cio.com/archive/031505/intelligence
    .html, accessed May 1, 2005.

CHAPTER 4

1. Brewin, Bob, "IT Goes on a Mis-
   sion: GPS/GIS Effort Helps Pinpoint
   Shuttle Debris," *Computerworld,*
   February 10, 2003, pp. 1, 6.

2. Ursery, Stephen, "Chattanooga,
   Tenn., Builds Tree Inventory," *American City & County,* July 2003, p. 18.

3. "Transit Agency Builds GIS to Plan
   Bus Routes," *American City &
   County,* April 2003, pp. 14–16.

4. Sharp, Charles, "Fire Screen," *Best's
   Review,* October 2004, pp. 120–22.

5. Gambon, Jill, "A Database That
   'Ads' Up," *InformationWeek,*
   August 7, 1995, pp. 68–69.

6. Simon, Herbert, *The New Science
   of Management Decisions,* rev. ed.
   (Englewood Cliffs, NJ: Prentice Hall,
   1977).

7. Kauderer, Steven, and Amy Kuehl,
   "Adding Value with Technology,"
   Best's Review, October 2001, p. 130.

8. "M/W Planning: It's All in the
   Data," *Railway Age,* January 2001,
   pp. 60–61.

9. Marlin, Steven, Cristina McEachern,
   and Anthony O'Donnell, "Cross
   Selling Starts with CRM System,"

Wall Street & Technology, December
2001, pp. A8–A10.

10. "Software Integration from Down
    on the Farm," *Fleet Equipment,*
    April 2004, pp. 8–10.

11. "Chicago Tracks Fleet Vehicles on
    Web-Based Maps," *American City &
    County,* June 2003, p. 56.

12. Stewart, Mary Ann, "Tracking Cattle
    in the Heartland," *Geospatial Solu-
    tions,* September 2005, pp. 20–25.

13. Malykhina, Elena, "Maps Meet
    Mashups," *InformationWeek,*
    March 17, 2007, http://www
    .informationweek.com/showArticle
    .jhtml;jsessionid=F4CSRST1GWTH0Q
    SNDLPSKHSCJUNN2JVN?articleID=
    198001255&queryText=
    %22geographic+information%22,
    accessed April 27, 2007.

14. Kay, Alexx, "Artificial Neural
    Networks," *Computerworld,*
    February 12, 2001, p. 60.

15. Ibid.

16. Perry, William, "What Is Neural
    Network Software?" *Journal of
    Systems Management,* September
    1994, pp. 12–15.

17. Port, Otis, "Diagnoses That Cast a
    Wider Net," *BusinessWeek,* May 22,
    1995, p. 130.

18. Baxt, William G., and Joyce Skora,
    "Prospective Validation of Arti-
    ficial Neural Network Trained to
    Identify Acute Myocardial Infarc-
    tion," *The Lancet,* January 6, 1997,
    pp. 12–15.

19. McCartney, Laton, "Technology for
    a Better Bottom Line," *Information-
    Week,* February 26, 1996, p. 40.

20. Whiting, Rick, "Companies Boost
    Sales Efforts with Predictive Analy-
    sis," *InformationWeek,* February 25,
    2002.

21. Ibid.

22. Punch, Linda, "Battling Credit Card
    Fraud," *Bank Management,* March
    1993, pp. 18–22.

23. "Cigna, IBM Tech Tool Targets
    Health Care Fraud," *National Under-
    writer Property & Casualty—Risk &
    Benefits,* October 1994, p. 5.

24. Anthes, Gary H., "Picking Winners
    and Losers," *Computerworld,*
    February 18, 2002, p. 34.

25. "Weblining," *BusinessWeek Online,* April 3, 2000, www.businessweek.com, accessed May 29, 2005.

26. Llewellyn, Mike, "Check One, Two," *Dealerscope,* March 2005, p. 82.

27. Johnson, Colin, "Breeding Programs," *Financial Management,* February 2001, pp. 18–20.

28. Ruggiero, Murray, "Enhancing Trading with Technology," *Futures,* June 2000, pp. 56–59.

29. Patrick, C., L. Hui, S. F. Frency, Keith Ng, and C. C. Chan, "A Study of the Roll Planning of Fabric Spreading Using Genetic Algorithms," *International Journal of Clothing Science & Technology,* 2000, pp. 50–62.

30. Begley, S., "Software au Naturel," *Newsweek,* May 8, 1995, pp. 70–71.

31. Goldbert, David E., "Genetic and Evolutionary Algorithms Come of Age," *Communications of the ACM,* March 1994, pp. n113–119.

32. Hill, Alice, "Google Inside Out," *Maximum PC,* April 2004, pp. 44–48.

33. Thibodeau, Patrick, "Agents of Change," *Computerworld,* September 6, 2004, p. 24.

34. Dobbs, Sarah Boehle Kevin, Donna Gordon Goldwasser, and Jack Stamps, "The Return of Artificial Intelligence," *Training,* November 2000, p. 26.

35. Totty, Patrick, "Pinpoint Members with New Data-Mining Tools," *Credit Union Magazine,* April 2002, pp. 32–34.

36. Wolinsky, Howard, "Advisa Helps Companies Get More from Their Data: Helps Managers to Understand Market," *Chicago Sun-Times,* December 20, 2000, p. 81.

37. Anthes, Gary H., "Agents of Change," *Computerworld,* January 27, 2003, pp. 26–27.

38. Bonabeau, Eric, "Swarm Intelligence," *O'Reilly Emerging Technology Conference,* April 22–25, 2003, Santa Clara, CA.

39. Bonabeau, Eric, and Christopher Meyer, "Swarm Intelligence: A Whole New Way to Think about Business," *Harvard Business Review,* May 2001, pp. 107–14.

40. Bonabeau, "Swarm Intelligence."

41. Whiting, Rick, "Businesses Mine Data to Predict What Happens Next," *InformationWeek,* May 29, 2006, www.informationweek.com/shared/printableArticleSrc.jhtml?articleID=188500520, accessed April 27, 2007.

42. McGee, Marianne Kolbasuk, "Mayo Builds toward Customized Medicine," *InformationWeek,* August 9, 2004, www.informationweek.com/shared/printableArticleSrc.jhtml?articleID=26806448, accessed April 25, 2007.

43. McGee, Marianne Kolbasuk, "Mayo and IBM Search for Personalized Medicine," *InformationWeek,* August 4, 2004, www.informationweek.com/shared/printable/ArticleSrc.jhtml?articleID=26805830, accessed April 25, 2007.

44. McGee, Marianne Kolbasuk, "IBM Partners with Cleveland Clinic for Better Medical Data Access," *InformationWeek,* September 30, 2004, www.informationweek.com/shared/printableArticle.Src.jhtml?articleID=48800505, accessed April 25, 2007.

CHAPTER 5

1. Malykhina, Elena, "Online Sales Get Boost When Buyers Return to Work," *InformationWeek,* November 28, 2005, p. 34.

2. "After Black Friday Comes Cyber Monday," CNNMoney.com, November 28, 2005, http://money.cnn.com/2005/11/21/news/economy/cyber monday/, accessed January 6, 2006.

3. "Pourquoi Paypal est promu a un bel avenir? The C2B Revolution: Consumer Empowerment," August 27, 2005, http://c2b.typepad.com/, accessed April 22, 2007.

4. The Lockheed Martin Corporation, About Us, http://www.lockheedmartin.com/wms/findPage.do?dsp=fec&ci=4&sc=400, accessed April 22, 2007.

5. "The President's Management Agenda," Executive Office of the President, Office of Management and Budget, Summer 2001, www.whitehouse.gov/omb/budget/fy2002/mgmt.pdf, accessed May 30, 2005.

6. "Global exchange Services and ChinaECNet Establish B2B Exchange for China's $80 Billion Electronics Industry," Global exchange Services, Inc., www.gxs.com.gxs/press/release/press20040318, accessed April 4, 2004.

7. "Introduction to China eHub System," ChinaECNet Organization, www.chinaecnet.com/eng/eHub/int.asp, accessed May 30, 2005.

8. "eBags.com Celebrates Five Years of Helping Customers Find the Perfect Bag Online," eBags.com, www.ebags.com/info/aboutebags/index.cfm?Fuseaction=pressitem&release_ID=102, accessed April 6, 2004.

9. "Awards," eBags.com, www.ebags.com/info/aboutebags/index.cfm?Fuseaction=awards, accessed May 30, 2005.

10. Perez, Juan Carlos, "Update: AOL Launches New Bill-Paying Tool," *The Standard,* March 16, 2004, www.thestandard.com/article.php?story=20040316172813723, accessed April 7, 2004.

11. "AOL Bill Pay Help," America Online, Inc., http://billpay.aol.com/bpweb/help/index.html, accessed May 29, 2005.

12. Lenhart, Amanda, and Amry Madden, "Teens, Privacy, and Online Social Networks," Pew Internet and American life Project, April 18, 2007, http://www.pewinternet.org/pdfs/PIP_Teens_Privacy_SNS_Report_Final.pdf, accessed April 20, 2007.

13. Burns, Enid, "Wi-Fi Increases Time Spent Online," Incisive Inter active Marketing LLC, February 26, 2007, http://www.clickz.com/showPage.html?page=clickz_print&id=3625105, accessed April 23, 2007.

14. Burns, Enid, "Mobile Internet Population Grows," Incisive Interactive Marketing LLC, August 14, 2006, http://www.clickz.com/showPage.html?page=clickz_print&id=3623146, accessed April 23, 2007.

15. "Mobile-Gaming Boom May Force Changes in Mobile Payments," Digital Transactions, February 11, 2005,

http://www.digitaltransactions
.net/newsstory.cfm?newsID=503,
accessed April 23, 2007.

16. Anderson, Chris, "The Long Tail,"
Wired Magazine, October 2004,
http://www.wired.com/wired/
archive/12.10/tail.html, accessed
April 24, 2007.

17. Anderson, Chris, *The Long Tail* (New
York: Hyperion, 2006).

18. Barr, Meghan, "Webkinz's Plush
Creatures Take on E-Lives," *Denver
Post,* April 8, 2007, p. 6L.

19. Hoffman, Martin, "VW Revs Its B2B
Engine," *Optimize,* March 2004,
pp. 22–30.

20. Hansen, Meike-Uta, "Volkswagen
Drives Supply-Chain Innovation,"
Optimize, April 2005, www
.optimizemag.com/showArticle
.jhtml;jesssionid=AWFT0BGTAWLIQ
QSNDBCSKHSCJUMEKJVN?
articleID=159904448, accessed
May 29, 2005.

21. Burns, Enid, "Mobile Content Usage
Is Higher in Developing Countries,"
Interactive Marketing LLC, March 2,
2007, http://www.clickz
.com/showPage.html?page=clickz_
print&id=3625143, accessed
April 23, 2007.

22. Heilemann, John, "Unlocking the
Middle Kingdom," *Business 2.0,*
April 2006, pp. 44–46.

23. Schonfeld, Erick, "Cyworld Attacks,"
Business 2.0, April 2006, pp. 84– 89.

CHAPTER 6

1. Mitchell, Robert, "This Integration
Project Could Be a Lifesaver,"
Computerworld, January 22, 2007,
http://www.computerworld
.com/action/article.do?command=
viewArticleBasic&taxonomyName=
web_services&articleId=278040&
taxonomyId=61&intsrc=kc_feat,
accessed April 24, 2007.

2. Krill, Paul, "FedEx Seeks Improved
Software Testing," *Computerworld,*
December 20, 2006, http://www
.computerworld.com/action/article
.do?command=viewArticleBasic&
articleId=9006342, accessed
April 24, 2007.

3. Roth, Sabine, "Profile of CAS Software AG," March 29, 2005,
www.cas.de/English/Home.asp,
accessed June 9, 2005.

4. Barnes, Cecily, "More Programmers
Going 'Extreme,' " April 9, 2001,
www.news.com, accessed June 1,
2005.

5. "Who We Are," www.agilealliance
.org, accessed June 2, 2005.

6. Gilhooly, Kym, "Visualization Tools
for Requirements Definition,"
Computerworld, November 6, 2006,
http://www.computerworld.com/
action/article.do?command=view
ArticleBasic&taxonomyId=1&articleId
=269197&intsrc=hm_topic, accessed
April 24, 2007.

7. "Industry Associations," connex-
tions.net/IndustryAssoc.asp, accessed
June 1, 2005.

8. "Outsourcing's Next Wave," *Fortune,* July 15, 2004, www.fortune
.com, accessed June 2, 2005.

9. Cohen, Peter, "Twelve Technical
and Business Trends Shaping the
Year Ahead," May 6, 2004,
www.babsoninsight.com, accessed
June 2, 2005.

10. McDougall, Paul, "Big Surge
Expected in Offshore Outsourcing
by Banks, Study Says," *Information-
Week,* March 1, 2007, http://www
.informationweek.com/showArticle.
jhtml;jsessionid=KSBBY442RAYGCQ
SNDLOSKHSCJUNN2JVN?articleID=
197700448&queryText=outsourcing,
accessed April 24, 2007.

11. "Statistics Related to Offshore Outsourcing," May 2005, www.rttsweb
.com, accessed June 1, 2005.

12. Babcock, Charles, "In-Stock Parts
Lead to Loyalty," *InformationWeek,*
March 27, 2006, pp. 60–62.

13. "Count to 10 and Be Secure," *InformationWeek,* December 4, 2006,
pp. 53–55.

14. Greenemeier, Larry, "A Not-So-
Desperate Measure," *Information-
Week,* December 18/25, 2006,
pp. 57–58.

CHAPTER 7

1. Thibodeau, Patrick, "IRS Flood Spurs
Telecommuting," *Computerworld,*
June 30, 2006, http://www.computer
world.com/action/article.do?
command=viewArticleBasic&article
Id=9001560, accessed April 30, 2007.

2. "President Bush's Proposed FY06
Budget Represents Growth in IT
Spending for Federal Government,"
February 8, 2005, www.bitpipe.com,
accessed May 19, 2005.

3. "ERP Outsourcing Picks Up and
Takes Off," www.outsourcing.com,
accessed May 19, 2005.

4. "Company Profile," www.delmonte
.com, accessed May 16, 2005.

5. "Industry Implementations,"
www.dmreview.com, accessed
May 16, 2005.

6. Weier, Mary Hayes, "Coca-Cola
Launches Ambitious Technology
Project with Bottlers," *Information-
Week,* April 23, 2007, www
.informationweek.com/shared/
printableArticleSrc.jhtml?articleID=
199200834, accessed April 30, 2007.

7. "London Stock Exchange," Case
study at Microsoft.com, www
.microsoft.com/casestudies/casestudy
.aspx?casestudyid=51828, accessed
April 30, 2007.

8. Bettendorf, Michael, "London Stock
Exchange Chooses Windows over
Linux for Reliability," *Information-
Week,* December 18/25, 2006, p. 7.

9. "The State of the Data Center,"
InformationWeek, December 18/25,
2006, p. 9.

10. Murphy, Chris, and Antone Gon-
salves, "Elmo's at It Again,"
InformationWeek, December 18/25,
2006, p. 21.

11. Overby, Stephanie, "It Pays to Have
a Disaster Recovery Plan in Place,"
CIO Magazine, September 16, 2005,
www.cio.com/article/print/11931,
accessed April 30, 2007.

12. Murphy, Chris, "SOA Isn't Perfect,
but It Solves a Problem," *InformationWeek,* September 11, 2006,
pp. 60–61.

13. McGee, Marianne Kolbasuk,
"Aggressive Treatment," *InformationWeek,* May 2, 2005, www
.informationweek.com/shared/
printableArticleSrc.jhtml?articleID=
162100352, accessed April 30, 2007.

14. "Prescription for Change," *InformationWeek,* December 18/25, 2006,
pp. 44–45.

CHAPTER 8

1. Behar, Richard, "Never Heard of Acxiom? Chances Are It's Heard of You," *Fortune,* February 23, 2004, pp. 140–48.

2. Herman, Josh, "Marketing News: Albany, N.Y., Reflects True Test Market," *Marketing News,* February 1, 2004.

3. "American Banker: TransUnion Teams with Acxiom on Anti-Fraud Tool," *American Banker,* February 23, 2004, www.acxiom.com, accessed May 27, 2005.

4. Bleed, Jake, "Acxiom Thrives on Sorting Bank Megamergers," *Arkansas Democrat-Gazette,* February 8, 2004, www.acxiom.com, accessed May 27, 2005.

5. Pliagas, Linda, "Learning IT Right from Wrong," *InfoWorld,* October 2, 2000, pp. 39–40.

6. Fogliasso, Christine, and Donald Baack, "The Personal Impact of Ethical Decisions: A Social Penetration Theory Model," Second Annual Conference on Business Ethics Sponsored by the Vincentian Universities in the United States, New York, 1995.

7. Jones, T. M., "Ethical Decision-Making by Individuals in Organizations: An Issue-Contingent Model," *Academy of Management Review,* 1991, pp. 366–95.

8. Baase, Sara, *The Gift of Fire: Social, Legal and Ethical Issues in Computing* (Upper Saddle River, NJ: Prentice Hall, 1997).

9. Moores, Trevor, "Software Piracy: A View from Hong Kong," *Communications of the ACM,* December 2000, pp. 88–93.

10. Software and Information Industry of America, www.siaa.net/shared-content/press/.2000/5-24-00.html, accessed May 31, 2005.

11. Rittenhouse, David, "Privacy and Security on Your PC," *ExtremeTech,* May 28, 2002, www.extremetech.com, accessed May 31, 2005.

12. Vanbokkelen, James, "2006: The Year of the Breach," *Federal Computer Week,* December 18, 2006. p. 1.

13. Tam, Pui-Wang, Erin White, Nick Wingfield, and Kris Maker, "Snooping E-Mail by Software Is Now a Workplace Norm," *The Wall Street Journal,* March 9, 2005, pp. B1, B3.

14. Corbin, Dana, "Keeping a Virtual Eye on Employees," *Occupational Health & Safety,* November 2000, pp. 24–28.

15. Pliagas, "Learning IT Right from Wrong."

16. Sanders, Peter, "Casinos Bet on Radio-ID Gambling Chips," *The Wall Street Journal,* May 13, 2005, pp. B1, B7.

17. Vaught, Bobby, Raymond Taylor, and Steven Vaught, "The Attitudes of Managers Regarding the Electronic Monitoring of Employee Behavior: Procedural and Ethical Considerations," *American Business Review,* January 2000, pp. 107–14.

18. Parker, Laura, "Medical-Privacy Law Creates Wide Confusion," *USA Today,* October 17–19, 2003, pp. 1A, 2A.

19. Medford, Cassimir, "Know Who I Am," *PC Magazine,* February 7, 2000, pp. 58–64.

20. Charters, Darren, "Electronic Monitoring and Privacy Issues in Business-Marketing: The Ethics of the DoubleClick Experience," *Journal of Business Ethics,* February 2002, pp. 243–54.

21. Naples, Mark, "Privacy and Cookies," *Target Marketing,* April 2002, pp. 28–30.

22. Forelle, Charles, "IBM Embraces Bold Method to Trap Spam," *The Wall Street Journal,* March 22, 2005, pp. B1, B2.

23. Angwin, Julia, "Elusive Spammer Sends Web Service on a Long Chase," *The Wall Street Journal,* May 7, 2003, pp. A1, A10.

24. Graven, Matthew P., "Leave Me Alone," *PC Magazine,* January 16, 2001, pp. 151–52.

25. Baase, *The Gift of Fire.*

26. Rittenhouse, "Privacy and Security on Your PC."

27. Soat, John, "IT Confidential," *InformationWeek,* June 3, 2002, p. 98.

28. Salkever, Alex, "A Dark Side to the FBI's Magic Lantern," *BusinessWeek Online,* November 27, 2001, www.businessweek.com, accessed May 14, 2005.

29. Bank, David, "Keeping Information Safe," *The Wall Street Journal,* November 11, 2004, pp. B1, B2.

30. Fontana, John, "Average Data Breach Costs Companies $5 Million," *Network World,* November 6, 2006, p. 20.

31. "Europe Plans to Jail Hackers," zdnet.com/2100-11105-889332.html, April 23, 2002, accessed May 31, 2005.

32. "Tech-Savvy Blackmailers Hone a New Form of Extortion," *The Wall Street Journal,* May 5, 2005, pp. B1, B3.

33. Meyer, Lisa, "Security You Can Live With," *Fortune,* Winter 2002, pp. 94–99.

34. "Fast Times," *Fortune,* Summer 2000, pp. 35–36.

35. "Chase Brings 'blink' Technology to Tiger," http://www.LSUsports.net, accessed May 2, 2007.

36. "Australia Sends First Active RFID Tag System to Middle East," *Defense Daily International,* April 20, 2007.

37. Roybal, Joe, "All Tagged Up," *Beef,* April 2007, p. 34.

38. Graafstra, Amal, "How Radio-Frequencey Identification and I Got Personal," *IEEE Spectrum,* March 2007, pp.18–23.

39. Radcliff, Deborah, "Beyond Passwords," *Computerworld,* January 21, 2002, pp. 52–53.

40. Eyres, Patricia, "Legal Traps for Unwary Managers during Corporate Criminal Investigations," *Business Credit,* February 2005, pp. 62–63.

41. Berman, Dennis, "Online Laundry: Government Posts Enron's E-Mail," *The Wall Street Journal,* October 6, 2003, pp. A1, A12.

42. Jaikumar, Vijayan, "Breach of Credit Data May Have Broad Scope," *ComputerWorld,* April 18, 2005, p. 6.

43. "Data Security Breaches Lead to Calls for Legislation," *ABA Bank Compliance,* March 2005, p. 7.

CHAPTER 9

1. Hof, Robert, "My Virtual Life," *BusinessWeek,* May 1, 2006, http://www.businessweek.com/magazine/content/06_18/b3982001.htm, accessed May 4, 2007.

2. "What Is Second Life," Linden Research, Inc., http://secondlife.com/whatis/, accessed May 4, 2007.

3. Lu, Stephen C-Y, "Process Planning as Negotiation—A Step toward F2B2C Ecommerce," STC/O CAPP Working Group, January 24, 2001, www.3s.hmg.inpg.fr/ci/GAMA/01Lu.pdf, accessed June 6, 2005.

4. Overdorf, Jason, "Tutors Get Outsourced," *Business 2.0,* August 2006, p. 32.

5. Adams, Nina, "Lessons from the Virtual World," *Training,* June 1995, pp. 45–47.

6. Flynn, Laurie, "VR and Virtual Spaces Find a Niche in Real Medicine," *New York Times,* June 5, 1995, p. C3.

7. Kesten, Lou, " 'Paper Mario' Leads the Latest Wii Wave," *Kansas City Star,* May 3, 2007, www.kansascity.com/211/v-print/story/91776.html, accessed May 5, 2007.

8. "Somark Innovations Announces Successful Live Animal Testing of Biocompatible Chipless RFID Ink in Cattle and Laboratory Rats," Somark Innovations, January 9, 2007, http://www.somarkinnovations.com/Files/SomarkBiocompatibleChipless-RFIDInk.pdf, accessed May 5, 2007.

9. Corcoran, Elizabeth, "The Next Small Thing," *Forbes,* July 23, 2001, pp. 96–106.

10. Center to Integrate Nanotechnologies, United States Department of Energy, http://cint.lanl.gov, accessed June 1, 2005.

11. Wasserman, Todd, "An Eyeball Test for Better Ads," *Business 2.0,* March 2007, p. 34.

12. "Atlanta NFC Pilot, and Others, Will Lead to Late '06 Commercialization," Digital Transactions, December 14, 2005, www.digitaltransactions.net/newsstory.cfm?newsID=800, accessed May 6, 2007.

13. "Motorola Looks to Start Commercial M-Wallet Service by Summer," Digital Transactions, February 9, 2006, www.digitaltransactions.net/newsstory.cfm?newsID=852, accessed May 6, 2007.

14. "Peace of Mind Is Only a Click Away," *Denver Home,* May/June 2007, p. 57.

15. Duryee, Tricia, "Cellphone Can Keep Kids on Radar Screen," *Denver Post,* April 14, 2006, pp. 1a, 13a.

PHOTO CREDITS

CHAPTER 9

Page 263: (left): © Euan Myles / Getty Images.

Page 263 (middle): Andersen Ross / PhotoDisc / Getty Images.

Page 263 (right): © Stockbyte / Getty Images.

Page 267: Courtesy Texas Instruments.

APPENDIX A

Page 281 (top left): Creative Technology Ltd.

Page 281 (top middle): Courtesy of Fossil.

Page 281 (middle left): Gateway, Inc.

Page 281 (middle right): ©2005 SANYO North America Corporation. All Rights Reserved.

Page 281 (bottom left): Photo Courtesy of Kensington Technology Group (www.kensington.com).

Page 281 (bottom middle): Used with permission of Eastman Kodak Company.

Page 281 (bottom right): Photo by Apple via Getty Images.

Page 282 (top): Courtesy of Microsoft Hardware.

Page 282 (bottom): Courtesy of NVIDIA.

Page 283: Treo 650 smartphone by palmOne.

Page 283 (top right): Courtesy of Dell Inc.

Page 283 (bottom right): Image reprinted with permission from ViewSonic Corporation.

Page 284: Photo courtesy of Overdrive PC.

Page 285: (top left): Hewlett-Packard Company.

Page 285 (bottom left): Photo Courtesy of Cray Inc.

Page 285 (right): Courtesy of International Business Machines Corporation. Unauthorized use not permitted.

Page 292 (top left): Hewlett-Packard Company.

Page 292 (bottom left): Courtesy of Microsoft Hardware.

Page 292 (right): Photo used with permission from Plantronics, Inc.

Page 294 (top left): Image reprinted with permission from ViewSonic Corporation.

Page 294 (top middle): © 2007 AOC Monitors. All rights reserved.

Page 294 (top right): Copyright © 2007 Apple Inc. All rights reserved.

Page 294 (bottom left): Courtesy of Epson America, Inc.

Page 294 (bottom middle): Hewlett-Packard Company.

Page 294 (bottom right): Courtesy of Epson America, Inc.

Page 297: (top left): Courtesy of SanDisk Corporation.

Page 297 (top right): Image courtesy of Kingston Technology.

Page 297 (bottom left): Photo Courtesy of Intel Corporation.

Page 297 (bottom right): Image courtesy of Kingston Technology.

Page 301(top left): Courtesy of Belkin International, Inc.

Page 301 (middle left): Courtesy of Belkin International, Inc.

Page 301 (bottom left): © Crutchfield Corporation.

Page 301 (center): Hewlett-Packard Company.

Page 301 (top right): Photo by R.D. Cummings, Pittsburg State University.

Page 301 (bottom right): © Crutchfield Corporation.

Page 302: FirewireDirect.com / www.firewiredirect.com.

APPENDIX B

Page 310 (top): Courtesy of NETGEAR Inc.

Page 310: Photo courtesy of 3com Corporation.

Page 310: Photo by R.D. Cummings, Pittsburg State University.

Page 310 (bottom): Courtesy of Linksys.

Page 311 (top): Proxim Corporation.

Page 311 (bottom): Courtesy of Linksys.

Page 312: Microsoft product box shot reprinted with permission from Microsoft Corporation.

Page 324 (top): © Spencer Grant / Photo Edit.

Page 324 (middle): © Mark Antman / The Image Works.

Page 324 (bottom): PhotoDisc / Getty Images.